the law of
Unfair Dismissal

University of
Chester

Library

the law of
Unfair Dismissal

Third Edition

Steven D Anderman BA, LLB, MSC

Birkett Westhorp and Long Professor of Law, University of Essex

Butterworths
LexisNexis™

Members of the LexisNexis Group worldwide

United Kingdom	Butterworths Tolley, a Division of Reed Elsevier (UK) Ltd, Halsbury House, 35 Chancery Lane, LONDON, WC2A 1EL, and 4 Hill Street, EDINBURGH EH2 3JZ
Argentina	Abeledo Perrot, Jurisprudencia Argentina and Depalma, BUENOS AIRES
Australia	Butterworths, a Division of Reed International Books Australia Pty Ltd, CHATSWOOD, New South Wales
Austria	ARD Betriebsdienst and Verlag Orac, VIENNA
Canada	Butterworths Canada Ltd, MARKHAM, Ontario
Chile	Publitecsa and Conosur Ltda, SANTIAGO DE CHILE
Czech Republic	Orac sro, PRAGUE
France	Editions du Juris-Classeur SA, PARIS
Hong Kong	Butterworths Asia (Hong Kong), HONG KONG
Hungary	Hvg Orac, BUDAPEST
India	Butterworths India, NEW DELHI
Ireland	Butterworths (Ireland) Ltd, DUBLIN
Italy	Giuffré, MILAN
Malaysia	Malayan Law Journal Sdn Bhd, KUALA LUMPUR
New Zealand	Butterworths of New Zealand, WELLINGTON
Poland	Wydawnictwa Prawnicze PWN, WARSAW
Singapore	Butterworths Asia, SINGAPORE
South Africa	Butterworths Publishers (Pty) Ltd, DURBAN
Switzerland	Stämpfli Verlag AG, BERNE
USA	LexisNexis, DAYTON, Ohio

© Reed Elsevier (UK) Ltd 2001

A CIP Catalogue record for this book is available from the British Library.

ISBN 0 406 92181 4

Printed and bound in Great Britain by William Clowes Limited, Beccles and London

Visit Butterworths LexisNexis *direct* at www.butterworths.com

Preface

For more than 30 years unfair dismissal legislation has been a firmly-established element of statutory employment protection. The right to complain of unfair dismissal is the statutory employment right most frequently litigated. It is also one of the few individual employment rights that purports to place limits on managerial discretion to decide who to dismiss and for what reasons. It therefore provides a study of the potential cutting edge of labour legislation into management prerogatives.

The third edition of this book has been undertaken to provide an analysis that takes stock of the current state of the law so as to serve as a framework for understanding and following new developments in the law. The framework will be useful for the preparation of cases for employment tribunals and for the consideration and preparation of appeals from particular tribunal decisions.

Yet this third edition also provides far more clearly than the first a case study of a statutory employment right being weakened by judicial interpretation. It makes the point that in so far as statutory employment protections are drafted in such a way as to contain a major element creating a wide discretion for the judiciary, there is little guarantee that the results will resemble the intentions of Parliament. It also raises the issue of whether the design of employment protection legislation should more carefully anticipate the tendency of the judiciary to limit the protection provided by such legislation so that it does not too drastically create inroads into managerial discretion.

I should like to thank all those who helped me in the preparation of this book, in particular Michael Rubenstein, Editor of Industrial Relations Law Reports; my colleagues at Essex University Law Department, Bob Watt

and Sheldon Leader; Hugh Collins, author of *Justice in Dismissal*; Simon
Deakin and Gill Morris, co-authors of *Labour Law*; Gareth Thomas and
Ian Wood, who produce Smith and Wood's *Industrial Law*; Paul Davies
and Mark Freedland for their conversations and their publications.

My heartfelt thanks go to my wife Gunilla and son Ben for putting up
with me generally and while this book was written.

Steven D Anderman
November 2001

Contents

Chapter 6.   Capability or qualifications: ill-health   209

Chapter 7.   Capability or qualifications: unsatisfactory work performance   225

Chapter 8.   Unfair redundancy   235

Appendix III.   The exclusion of approved voluntary procedures   433

Appendix IV.   Compensation for loss of pension rights   439

Abbreviations

CS	Court of Session
EAT	Employment Appeals Tribunal
ECJ	European Court of Justice
EPCA	Employment Protection (Consolidation) Act 1978
ERA 1996	Employment Rights Act 1996
ERA 1999	Employment Relations Act 1999
ETO	Economic, technical or organisational [reason]
ILO	International Labour Organisation
IT	Industrial tribunal
MPL	Maternity and Parental Leave [Regulations 1999]
NICA	Northern Ireland Court of Appeal
NIRC	National Industrial Relations Court
SOSR	Some other substantial reason
TULRCA	Trade Union and Labour Relations (Consolidation) Act 1992
TUPE	Transfer of Undertakings (Protection of Employment) Regulations 1981
TURERA	Trade Union Reform and Employment Rights Act 1993

Table of statutes

Table of cases

D

G

H

I

J

L

S

Z

Decisions of the European Court of Justice are listed below numerically.
These decisions are also included in the preceding alphabetical list.

Introduction

Since its introduction in 1971, legislation providing a right to dismissed employees to complain of unfair dismissal has become a firmly established element of statutory employment protection. This legislation has moreover become the major source of litigation in employment questions, constituting more than 50% of the workload of employment tribunals. The statute has had a considerable influence upon managerial practice as well as collective labour relations, with voluntary disciplinary procedures proliferating in response to the law. Even in periods characterised by widely divergent approaches to collective labour law it has been accepted by Conservative as well as Labour governments.

The consensus prior to 1980 was partly caused by the acceptance of both Labour and Conservative governments of the need for domestic British legislation to respond to the development of international standards, in particular the ILO Recommendation 119. Yet another reason for the continued existence of the legislation was the growing realisation that such legislation did not simply provide a protection for the worker against management, it also acted as a spur to management practice to create a greater formality to disciplinary arrangements.

During the 1980–97 period, the consensus over such legislation was called into question. Large groups of workers were excluded from the protection of the legislation by the Conservative government raising the minimum service requirement for complaints of unfair dismissal to two years for all employees. In retrospect, the apparent consensus concerning the need for the continued existence of unfair dismissals legislation in some form, never extended to the precise form it was to be given. The fluctuations that have characterised labour law generally during the period have had a certain degree of influence upon the law of unfair dismissal. This is clearly true of the legislation itself. Thus, the Trade Union and Labour Relations Act 1974 modified the corresponding provisions of the 1971 Industrial Relations Act. The Employment Protection Act 1975 and the Trade Union and Labour Relations Amendment Act 1976 in turn modified the 1974 Act. The Employment Protection Consolidation Act consolidated these changes into one Act but the Employment Acts 1980 and 1982[1] introduced significant amendments to change the nature of the coverage of the enactment, standards of proof of reasonableness and the nature and type of remedies. Finally the Employment Relations Act 1999 greatly strengthened the law of unfair dismissals by introducing a new maximum limit to the compensation award of £50,000 (now £51,700), expanding the use of the remedy of interim relief and greatly increasing the types of automatically unfair dismissals or dismissals for a prohibited reason. The relevant provisions governing the law of unfair dismissals today are to be found in Part X of the Employment Rights Act 1996 and ss 152-167 and 237-239 of the Trade Union Labour Relations (Consolidation) Act 1992 (see Appendix I).

The reception given to the legislation by the judiciary has also varied over time. The appeals body sitting astride the tribunal system has had its nature and composition altered three times. The NIRC from 1971 to 1974 was replaced by the High Court Queen's Bench Division in 1974, which in turn was replaced by the Employment Appeal Tribunal in 1976, which has had five Presidents in its 25 years.

The significance of these changes should not be underestimated. The interpretation given to the statutory language by tribunals and judiciary can in many ways be as important as the design of the statute. The proposition that judges do not make law but only apply it must be looked at in the context of the discretion allowed for judicial interpretation by the particular enactment and the uses to which that discretion is put by the particular judges. In the case of unfair dismissals legislation the statutory language allows for varying interpretations and the three different appeal bodies have not been conspicuously uniform in the way they have chosen to interpret that language. Nor has the EAT itself been entirely consistent during more than 25 years of its tenure. Moreover, and even more

---

1   Together with the Unfair Dismissal (Variation of Qualifying Period) Orders (SI 1979/959) and (SI 1985/782).

importantly, the Court of Appeal has varied in its approach to the issues of the respective roles of tribunal and appeal tribunal and the scope of appeal from tribunal decisions on questions of 'law'.

In the face of these developments the first purpose of this book is to take stock of the current law of unfair dismissal – to examine the existing statutory provisions and describe and summarise how the Employment Appeal Tribunal, as well as courts of higher instance, have imposed their particular interpretations upon the statutory language. One use to which this examination may be put is to provide a framework with which to analyse and prepare dismissal cases, either directly for employment tribunal hearings or to assess the likely results should such cases reach that stage. This examination should also allow the reader to consider possible grounds for appeal from tribunal decisions. The risks of giving a misleading picture can be minimised if readers will accept that the review of the case law upon which this framework is based is subject to correction, particularly by EAT and higher court decisions appearing after 1 July 2001. Nevertheless, it is hoped that the framework will continue to be useful in following subsequent developments.

A second use for this book is to give readers an opportunity to consider more closely the process of judicial interpretation of employment legislation. Given that the statutory language allows a range of 'reasonable' judicial responses, where within this range have the predominant judicial views been positioned? To what extent have the judges attempted to effectuate the purposes of the legislation? To what extent have they interpreted the statute according to another set of priorities? A detailed examination of the case law offers a fruitful field for such a study.

Moreover, given the widespread development of formal disciplinary procedures in industry a further level of understanding of the legislation and its interpretation may be obtained by looking more closely at what might be called its 'normative' effects upon organisation at the workplace. Clearly the statute does not operate solely through litigation; it also affects managerial practice and collective labour relations and particularly the operation of disciplinary procedures. It is legitimate to ask to what extent and in what way judicial interpretations of the statute have taken into account this normative function.

From the point of view of individual employment law, the primary purpose of the unfair dismissal law was to provide to individual employees a form of protection against arbitrary termination by employers of their employment relationship. The Act was prompted by the need to improve the employee's vulnerable position at common law.

Before the Industrial Relations Act 1971, the legal safeguards for ordinary employees against unreasonable and arbitrary dismissal at common law were minimal.[2] The common law viewed employer and employee as free and equal contracting parties, ignoring the obvious discrepancy in their bargaining power and the fact that the employment relationship provided income to a family unit for one party and constituted a cost of production or service for the other. Hence, as long as proper contractual notice of termination was given,[3] the employer was free to dismiss an employee for whatever reason he wished, with no obligation to reveal his reason for dismissal to the employee, much less to justify it.

If an employer dismissed an employee summarily, ie without notice, or with inadequate contractual notice, the employee could bring an action for 'wrongful dismissal', or breach of contract. The remedy for wrongful dismissal consisted essentially of monetary compensation[4] and this was limited to the pay employees should have received during the contractual period of notice, with a reduction for any pay they earned or should have been able to earn during the notice period, because of their common law obligation to mitigate the damage. In assessing damages for breach of the employment contract, no account was taken of the employee's difficulties in obtaining future employment after the notice period, since the employer in any case was legally entitled to dismiss the employee with proper notice. Moreover, if the manner of the dismissal was such as to humiliate the employee or make it more difficult to obtain other employment because of

2   A select group of people, eg registered dock workers, office holders such as police officers, hospital officials and university teachers, enjoy a higher measure of job security owing to the courts' recognition of their rights to lengthy periods of notice and their willingness through the declaration remedy to tell the employer that these employees in effect should be reinstated. As well, employees on long fixed-term contracts enjoy a substantial measure of protection at common law. See the discussion of this by Hepple and O'Higgins, *Employment Law* (4th edn, Sweet & Maxwell, 1980); Freedland, *The Contract of Employment* (OUP, 1976).

3   The appropriate length of notice was determined either by the express terms of the contract, by implication, eg from custom, or fixed by the minimum standards laid down in the Contracts of Employment Act 1963 (now ERA 1996, s 86).

4   With one rather unusual exception (*Hill v C A Parsons & Co Ltd* [1972] Ch 305, [1971] 3 All ER 1345, CA) the Court refused to order specific performance (ie reinstatement) of an employment contract. But see now the 'employee injunctions' in *Irani v Southampton and South-west Hampshire Health Authority* [1985] IRLR 203; *Powell v Brent London Borough Council* [1987] IRLR 466, CA; *Anderson v Pringle of Scotland Ltd* [1998] IRLR 64, CS. See relevant chapters in Deakin and Morris *Labour Law* (3rd edn, Butterworths, 2001); Smith and Woods *Labour Law* (7th edn, Butterworths, 2000); Anderman *Labour Law* (4th edn, Butterworths, 2001).

an implication of dishonesty, there was no additional compensation recoverable in the wrongful dismissal action.[5] Consequently, the unfair dismissals provisions were designed to create an important general protection against arbitrary dismissal, an essential plank in the so-called statutory 'floor' of employment protection for employees in their contractual relationship with their employer, a series of statutes which includes the Truck Acts, the Health and Safety at Work etc Act 1974, the Contracts of Employment Act 1972, the Redundancy Payments Act 1965, and the Employment Protection Act 1975.

Yet the enactment of the unfair dismissal law was not prompted entirely by considerations of individual employment law. The provisions were produced in part to reduce the number of strikes over dismissals, by the provision of a statutory procedure to resolve workshop disputes over dismissals. As was stated in the Industrial Relations Bill Consultative Document, para 52:[6]

'Britain is one of the few countries where dismissals are a frequent cause of strike action. It seems reasonable to link this with the fact that in this country, unlike most others, the law provides no redress for the employee who suffers unfair or arbitrary dismissal, if the employer has met the terms of the contract, eg on giving notice. Thus if an employee is dismissed without reasonable cause, and though this may severely prejudice his future livelihood, the law gives him no right of appeal against his dismissal. Both on grounds of principle and as a means of removing a significant cause of industrial disputes, the Government proposes to include provisions in the Industrial Relations Bill to give statutory safeguards against unfair dismissal.'

The unfair dismissals provisions were also intended to provide a stimulus to managers to develop and improve their own procedures to deal with disciplinary and dismissal disputes. The provision of a possibility of obtaining exclusion from the statutory procedure for employers and trade unions with approved voluntary dismissal procedures[7] was one, albeit mistaken, element in the stimulus to the establishment of new, and the improvement of existing, procedures. The Code of Practice was another.[8]

---

5   But cf *Cox v Phillips Industries Ltd* [1976] 3 All ER 161, [1976] ICR 138, [1975] IRLR 344, QB. See now *Johnson v Unisys Ltd* [2001] IRLR 279, HL, noted [2001] ILJ 305.
6   5 October 1970.
7   See Appendix III.
8   See Appendix II.

In the event, the statute has produced an enormous increase in the number of formal disciplinary procedures. Estimates range from 84% to 99% of the larger firms in industry now have such procedures.[9] Prudent employers have introduced such procedures to minimise the number of cases that result in dismissal claims, as well as to be prepared to present a plausible case should cases reach industrial tribunals.

These procedures also operate with a close eye upon the stream of judicial decisions. As Daniels and Milward[10] wrote 'the form and operation of voluntarily agreed norms and procedure have been effectively modified and guided by an awareness of the legal provisions and their operation'. Moreover, Dickens, Jones, Weekes and Hart described the way in which unfair dismissals stimulated 'the development, formulation and modification of procedure for handling discipline/dismissal issues, incorporating notions of due process and natural justice and encouraging the quasi-judicial managerial review of decisions'.[11]

One major question raised by this study of the case law is to what extent the interpretations of the EAT and the Court of Appeals have taken into account the legislative purpose of improving managerial efficiency by the establishment and maintenance of effective formal procedures in industry.

A FRAMEWORK FOR ANALYSING UNFAIR DISMISSAL CASES

The law of unfair dismissal may usefully be divided into three parts, each a stage in the proceedings and each consisting of a set of requirements that must be met either by the employee presenting the complaint or by the employer defending it.

Stage One

The first stage consists of the preliminary requirements which must be met before an employment tribunal may look at the merits of the unfair dismissals claim. This stage determines the scope of the Act by deciding who is entitled to make a claim and under what circumstances a claim will

---

9   L Dickens, M Jones, B Weekes and M Hart, *Dismissed: A Study of Unfair Dismissal and the Industrial Tribunal System* (Blackwell, 1985).

10   W W Daniels and Neil Milward *Workforce Industrial Relations in Britain* DE/PSI/SSRC Survey, London, at p 126.

11   *Dismissed* (n 9, above), p 252.

proceed to the second stage. The specific requirements imposed include certain technical qualifications and exclusions, such as (i) whether the individual is an 'employee' as defined by the Act; (ii) if an employee, whether he or she is qualified to make a complaint in the sense of not being in an employment expressly excluded by the Act; and (iii) whether the application has been presented in time (see Chapter 1). At this stage the employee must also show that he or she has been 'dismissed' in terms of the statutory definition, and if so on what date. Chapter 2 considers the date of dismissal, or more precisely the effective date of termination. The way in which the case law has interpreted the requirement that the employee must be 'dismissed' is discussed in Chapter 3.

Stage Two

If an employee is able successfully to move through the minefield of the preliminary requirements in the first stage, the tribunal will consider whether the dismissal is fair or unfair. The statutory provisions setting out the test of fairness are lengthy and complicated but the case law has interpreted them to operate in two stages. In the first, employers must clearly demonstrate their real reason for dismissal and that it is an acceptable reason under the statute. This is discussed in Chapter 4. Once the employer's reason is clarified and defined, in most situations the employment tribunals will go on to ask whether it was reasonable in the circumstances to dismiss the employee on that ground. The general test applied under ERA 1996, s 98(4) is discussed in Chapter 5, using Dismissals for Conduct to exemplify the general test as well as to consider that issue in its own right. Thereafter the specific tests of fairness – whether a variation of the 'reasonableness' test or an 'automatic unfairness' test – are considered in separate chapters (see Chapters 6–15).

Stage Three

The third stage consists of the remedies available to an employee once his or her dismissal is found to be unfair. In what circumstances is he or she entitled to an order of reinstatement or re-engagement (Chapter 16)? What is an unfairly dismissed employee's entitlement to compensation in its various forms (Chapter 17)? Under what circumstances may an employee be entitled to the special remedy of interim relief (Chapter 18)?

Chapter 1.
Qualifications and exclusions

Although s 94(1) of the Employment Rights Act 1996 asserts that every employee shall have the right not to be unfairly dismissed by his employer, it also warns that this right is subject to certain qualifications. Section 94(2) states that this section applies to every employment *except* in so far as its application is excluded by or under any provision of this Part, in particular ss 108-110, and by any of the provisions of TULR(C)A 1992, in particular ss 237-239.

At the start of every unfair dismissal case, therefore, it is necessary to ascertain whether in fact the individual making the complaint is qualified, that is to say

(1) that he or she is an 'employee' as defined by the Act,
(2) that he or she is not in an employment expressly excluded by the Act, and
(3) that he or she has presented a complaint in time.

A failure in any of these three respects, whether successfully raised as a defence by an employer or found directly by the industrial tribunal, could preclude an individual from proceeding with a claim for unfair dismissal.

1. IS THE INDIVIDUAL MAKING THE COMPLAINT AN 'EMPLOYEE'?

The individual making the complaint of unfair dismissal must be an 'employee' as defined by section 230(1) ERA 1996; that is, an individual 'who has entered into or works under (or who has worked under) a contract of employment ...'.[1] A contract of employment means a contract of service or apprenticeship, whether express or implied and (if it is express) whether it is oral or in writing. The statutory definition extends to contracts of employment for all grades of employment – clerical, manual and managerial. It includes the contracts of working directors,[2] or directors who are subject to the control of the company as a corporate legal entity.[3] It can extend to home workers in certain circumstances.[4] It also includes civil servants even though they may not otherwise be regarded as working under a contract of employment.[5]

By implication, however, the statutory definition of employee does not extend to 'office holders'.[6] Nor does it extend to self-employed workers, independent contractors, or labour only sub-contractors. These individuals generally contract to work on the basis of a contract for services rather than a contract of employment.

In determining for the purposes of ERA, s 230(11) whether an individual is self-employed under a contract for services or an employee under a

1   This presupposes that the contract of employment is not an illegal contract. See
     eg *Tomlinson v Dick Evans U Drive Ltd* [1978] ICR 639, [1978] IRLR 77, EAT;
     but see *Coral Leisure Group Ltd v Barnett* [1981] ICR 503, [1981] IRLR 204,
     EAT; *Hewcastle Catering Ltd v Ahmed and Elkamah* [1991] IRLR 473, CA
     (limits to the illegality doctrine); *Davidson v Pillay* [1979] IRLR 275, EAT. See
     too *Newland v Simons & Willer (Hairdressers) Ltd* [1981] ICR 521, [1981] IRLR
     359, EAT (the employee must know of the illegality). *Corby v Morrison* [1980]
     ICR 564, [1980] IRLR 218, EAT; *Willis v L A Michaels Ltd* (1984) EAT 825/83;
     McConnell v Bolik [1979] IRLR 422, EAT. *Royal Court Hotel Ltd v Cowan*
     (1984) EAT 41/84 (a term of the contract itself must provide for the illegality;
     it is not enough that the contract could lead to an illegality owing to a failure by
     the employee to declare tax). See discussion in C Mogridge, 'Illegal Employment
     Contracts: Loss of Statutory Protection' [1981] ILJ 23.
2   *Secretary of State for Trade and Industry v Bottrill* [1999] IRLR 326, CA; see
     also *Parsons v Albert J Parsons & Sons Ltd* [1979] ICR 271, [1979] IRLR 117,
     CA.
3   See eg *Wyatt and Weeks v Benfield & Loxley Ltd* (1976) EAT 1371/76.
4   *Nethermere (St Neots) Ltd v Taverna and Gardiner* [1984] ICR 612, [1984]
     IRLR 240, CA; *Airfix Footwear v Cope* [1978] ICR 1210, [1978] IRLR 396,
     EAT.
5   See eg *R v Lord Chancellor's Department, ex p Nangle* [1991] IRLR 343.
6   *Davies v Presbyterian Church of Wales* [1986] IRLR 194, CA; *Diocese of
     Southwark v Coker* [1998] ICR 140; *Barthorpe v Exeter Diocesan Board of
     Finance* [1979] ICR 900, 123 Sol Jo 585, EAT. See also eg *102 Social Club and
     Institute Ltd v Bickerton* [1977] ICR 911, 12 ITR 442, EAT. *Miles v Wakefield
     Metropolitan District Council* [1985] 1 All ER 905, [1985] IRLR 108, CA.

contract of employment, employment tribunals have considerable discretion in at least three respects:

(a) first, as the Court of Appeal has recently made plain, the question of employment or self-employment itself is not one of pure law. It is often one of fact and degree. Hence, employment tribunals have the discretion to weigh the factors that must be taken into account under the test that they choose to apply;

(b) secondly, employment tribunals are not bound to apply one particular legal test to determine whether the contract is one of employment or not. They may choose from among several relevant tests laid down by different lines of authority, depending on the circumstances;

(c) thirdly, they are not bound by the parties' own contractual description of their relationship. They may decide on the basis of the facts as found what was the real nature of the relationship.

Let us consider each in turn.

i) The question of employment or self-employment as a question of fact

Whether an individual is self-employed under a contract for services or is an employee working under a contract of employment is a question of fact for tribunals to decide. In *O'Kelly v Trusthouse Forte plc*[7] and *Nethermere (St Neots) Ltd v Taverna and Gardiner*[8] the Court of Appeal made it clear that it accepted the principle that the question was essentially one of fact for employment tribunals to determine, subject to the possibility of an appeal on the ground that the tribunal misdirected itself in law or that its decision was one which no tribunal properly directing itself on the relevant facts could have reached.

In *O'Kelly*'s case, a case concerning 'casual workers' in the hotel trade, the employment tribunal had directed itself on the question whether or not the complainants were 'employees' of the company under ERA 1996, s 230(1) under the following test.

'What we derive from the authorities is that the Tribunal should consider all aspects of the relationship, no single feature being in itself decisive and each of which may vary in weight and direction, and having given such balance to the factors as seems appropriate

---

7   [1984] QB 90, [1983] ICR 728, [1983] IRLR 369, CA.
8   [1984] ICR 612, [1984] IRLR 240, CA.

to determine whether the person was carrying on business on his own account.'

The tribunal then divided the facts of the case into three categories. They found nine factors to be consistent with the regular casuals being employed under a contract of employment as opposed to a contract for services, four factors to be not inconsistent with a contract of employment and five factors which were inconsistent with a relationship being that of employer and employee.

The majority of the tribunal then went on to say that whilst the relationship did have many of the characteristics of a contract of employment, there was one important ingredient missing – mutuality of obligation. Rejecting the argument put forward on the claimant's behalf that there was an implied obligation on the company to offer work to the regulars and for them to do the work when offered, the tribunal decided that the fact that preference was given to the regular casuals who in turn did the work as rostered was attributable not to any legal obligation but to economic forces, ie the economic strength of the company on the one hand and the desire of the regular casuals to remain on the list on the other.

The tribunal also found that 'all parties were fully aware of the custom and practice of the industry that casual workers were not considered to be employees working under a contract of employment' and went on to conclude that 'when the parties embarked upon their engagement pursuant to the known custom and practice of the industry, it was indicative of their intention not to create an employment relationship'. Taking account of all these factors, the tribunal held that the claimants 'were in business on their own account as independent contractors supplying services and are not qualified for interim relief because they were not employees who worked under a contract of employment'.

On appeal, the EAT relied on the judgment of Stephenson LJ in *Young & Woods Ltd v West*,[9] and held that the question of whether a particular relationship was one under a contract of employment or under a contract for services was a question of law upon which the appeal tribunal must make up its own mind on the basis of the facts found by the employment tribunal. The view taken by the EAT was that given a particular set of circumstances, there could be only one correct answer to whether there was a contract of employment and that in effect it was a pure question of law.

---

9   [1980] IRLR 201, CA.

The Court of Appeal, however, reversed the EAT and restored the employment tribunal. The Court's view was that the question of whether an individual was an employee under s 230(1) could not be a matter of pure law since the precise quality and weight to be attributed to the various facts is so much a matter of degree that it was unrealistic to regard the issue as attracting a clear legal answer. The majority of the Court of Appeal held that the question of the relative weight to be given to the various factors was one of fact for the employment tribunal to determine and that the appeal tribunal was not entitled to interfere with the employment tribunal's decision unless the employment tribunal had misdirected itself in law or had come to a perverse decision.[10]

More recently in *Carmichael v National Power plc*[11] the House of Lords emphasised this point by holding that the Court of Appeal could not use its own evaluation of letters exchanged between the parties or the device of implied terms to overrule a decision by the employment tribunal where the latter had ample evidence for its finding of fact.

ii) The tests to determine whether the contract is one of employment or not

To avoid being overturned on appeal an employment tribunal must properly direct itself on the test whether an individual is self-employed or works under a contract of service. Yet, employment tribunals have not been limited to any one particular test.[12] Historically, the courts chose to apply a 'control' test which defined employment by stipulating inter alia that tribunals should ask whether or not the employer controlled or had the right to control the job that the employee did and the way that it was done.[13]

10   *O'Kelly v Trusthouse Forte plc* [1984] QB 90, [1983] ICR 728, [1983] IRLR 369, CA; see too *Nethermere (St Neots) Ltd v Taverna and Gardiner* [1984] ICR 612, [1984] IRLR 240, CA.

11   [2000] IRLR 43, HL.

12   Lord Denning suggested a test of whether the work was an 'integral part of the business' (*Stevenson Jordan and Harrison Ltd v MacDonald and Evans* [1952] 1 TLR 101 at 111) or 'part and parcel of the business' (*Bank Voor Handel en Scheepvaart NV v Slatford* [1953] 1 QB 248, [1951] 2 All ER 779). This was later dismissed as 'raising more questions than it answered' (see remarks of MacKenna J in *Ready Mixed Concrete (South East) Ltd v Minister of Pensions and National Insurance* [1968] 2 QB 497, [1968] 1 All ER 433) and is rarely ever used.

13   *Mersey Docks and Harbour Board v Coggins and Griffiths (Liverpool) Ltd* [1947] AC 1, [1946] 2 All ER 345, HL. For a recent example of an application of the control test see *Wickens v Champion Employment Ltd* [1984] ICR 365, EAT.

In *Ready Mixed Concrete (South East) Ltd v Minister of Pensions and National Insurance*, MacKenna J suggested that a multi-factor test was a more appropriate test:[14]

'A contract of service exists if these three conditions are fulfilled. (i) The servant agrees that, in consideration of a wage or other remuneration, he will provide his own work and skill in the performance of some service for his master. (ii) He agrees, expressly or implied, that in the performance of that service he will be subject to the other's control in a sufficient degree to make that other master. (iii) The other provisions of the contract are consistent with its being a contract of service.'[15]

Condition (i) embodies a test of mutuality of obligation. As MacKenna J remarked later in the same case (at 51):

'There must be a wage or other remuneration. Otherwise there will be no consideration, and without consideration no contract of any kind. The servant must be obliged to provide his own work and skill.'

As we shall see, the test of mutuality of obligation has developed into one of the most important tests of employment. Yet, in the appropriate circumstances, another approach that has occasionally been used in unfair dismissal cases is to define what is a contract for services rather than a contract of employment and ask whether or not there was an entrepreneurial element in the relationship. This test was summarised by Cooke J in *Market Investigations Ltd v Minister of Social Security*[16] in the following terms:

'Is the person who has engaged himself to perform these services performing them as a person in business on his own account? If the answer to that question is "yes", then the contract is a contract for services. If the answer is "no", then the contract is a contract of service. No exhaustive list has been compiled and perhaps no exhaustive list can be compiled of the considerations which are relevant in determining that question nor can strict rules be laid down as to the relative weight which the various considerations should carry in particular cases. The most that can be said is that control will no doubt always have to be considered, although it can no longer be regarded as the sole determining factor; and that factors which

14   [1968] 2 QB 497, [1968] 1 All ER 433.
15   Ibid at 515.
16   [1969] 2 QB 173, [1968] 3 All ER 732.

may be of importance are such matters as whether the man performing the services provides his own equipment, whether he hires his own helpers, what degree of financial risk he takes, what degree of responsibility for investment and management he has, and whether and how far he has an opportunity of profiting from sound management in the performance of his task. The application of the general test may be easier in a case where the person who engages himself to perform the services does so in the course of an already established business of his own; but this factor is not decisive. ...'.[17]

Both the 'multi-factor' test as set out in *Ready Mixed Concrete* and the 'business on his own account' test in *Market Investigations* have to be considered in the context of the facts of the particular case. The 'business on his own account' test is useful as a litmus test of self employment.[18] However it should not be seen, when negated, as providing a positive test of employment.[19]

The courts have increasingly been concerned to ensure that the employment tribunals should make an assessment of the issue of 'mutuality of obligation'. Further in *Carmichael v National Power plc* the House of Lords chose to view the test of mutuality of obligation as the irreducible minimum condition for the existence of a contract of employment in the case of 'casual, as required' power station guides.[20] In *O'Kelly v Trusthouse Forte plc*[1] the Court noted that the employment tribunal, whilst directing itself in terms of determining 'whether the person was carrying on business on his own account', also was careful to give due weight to the issue of whether or not there was 'mutuality of obligation'. In *Nethermere (St Neots) Ltd v Taverna and Gardiner*,[2] a majority of the Court of Appeal was willing to find the tribunal's application of the 'business on her own account test' correct only when there was evidence that the tribunal had also made a finding that there was an irreducible

17 [1969] 2 QB 173 at 184. See too *Lee v Chung* [1990] ICR 409, [1990] IRLR 236, PC.

18 *Ferguson v John Dawson & Partners (Contractors) Ltd* [1976] 3 All ER 817, [1976] IRLR 346, CA.

19 Cf LJ Stephenson's remarks in *Nethermere (St Neots) Ltd v Taverna and Gardiner* [1984] IRLR 240 at 243, CA.

20 [2000] IRLR 43, HL. See too *Montgomery v Johnson Underwood Ltd* [2001] EWCA Civ 318, [2001] IRLR 269 (agency workers; test is mutuality and control); see *McMeechan v Secretary of State for Employment* [1997] IRLR 353, CA; *Motorola Ltd v Davidson* [2001] IRLR 4, EAT.

1 [1983] IRLR 369, CA.

2 [1984] IRLR 240, CA.

minimum of obligation on each side, the employer to provide work and remuneration and the employee to do the work provided under the employer's control.

Nevertheless, it would appear to remain open to employment tribunals to apply a common sense test. Thus in *Thames Television Ltd v Wallis*[3] the EAT suggested that it was a correct approach for tribunals to consider in the light of their industrial experience whether the contract was such an ordinary person looking at it could say that it was a contract of service. Moreover in *Withers v Flackwell Heath Football Supporters' Club*[4] the EAT suggested that the tribunal could ask the employee simply 'are you your own boss?' In that case however, the EAT said that the ultimate question for the tribunal 'is he on his own business rather than the business of the party for whom the work is being done?'

iii) The intention of the parties

The EAT and employment tribunals have also been left in no doubt that the way the parties choose to label their relationship will not be conclusive, if the evidence suggests that the legal nature of their relationship differs from the label the parties have attached to it. It is true that the parties' intention can be important in certain situations. Thus, as Lord Denning MR said in *Massey v Crown Life Insurance Co*,[5]

> 'it seems to me on the authorities that, when it is a situation which is in doubt or which is ambiguous, so that it can be brought under one relationship or the other, it is open to the parties by agreement to stipulate what the legal situation shall be. That was said in the *Ready Mixed Concrete* case in 1968 by Mr Justice MacKenna. He said (at 513) that "if we were doubtful what rights and duties the parties wished to provide for, a declaration of this kind might help in resolving the doubt and fixing them in the sense required to give effect to that intention". So the way in which they draw up their agreement and express it may be a very important factor in defining what the true relation was between them. If they declare that he is self-employed, that may be decisive'.

3   [1979] IRLR 136, EAT. See too *Cassidy v Ministry of Health* [1951] 2 KB 343; 1 All ER 574, CA.

4   [1981] IRLR 307, EAT.

5   [1978] IRLR 31 at 33. See too *BSM (1257) Ltd v Secretary of State for Social Service* [1978] ICR 894, EAT.

Yet, as MacNeil J pointed out in *Warner Holidays Ltd v Secretary of State for Social Services,*[6] whilst the parties' intention may be an important factor in such circumstances, it is not conclusive. Thus in *Young & Woods Ltd v West*[7] an employee chose to be paid as self-employed when he was offered different methods of payment when he was 'hired'. No deductions were made from his pay for tax, he was responsible for his own National Insurance contributions and he did not receive any holiday pay or sickness benefit from the company. Moreover, the agreement was made with the knowledge of the Inland Revenue who treated him for tax purposes as self-employed. Nevertheless when the employee's services were terminated by the company and he complained of unfair dismissal, a tribunal held that he was an employee as defined by the statute and entitled to bring a claim of unfair dismissal. The Court of Appeal upheld the industrial tribunal's decision stating per Lord Justice Ackner:

> 'It is by now well settled law that the label which the parties chose to use to describe their relationship cannot alter or decide their true relationship, but in deciding what that relationship is, the expression by them of their true intention is relevant but not conclusive'.[8]

2. WAS THE EMPLOYEE CONTINUOUSLY EMPLOYED FOR THE PERIOD REQUIRED BY THE ACT?

Under ERA 1996, s 108(1), an employee must normally have been continuously employed for a period of one calendar year ending with the effective date of termination[9] in order to be qualified to present a complaint of unfair dismissal. There are, however, a number of specific exceptions to the minimum requirement of continuous service, many consisting of cases of automatically unfair dismissal.[10]

The main exceptions to the requirement of continuous service are as follows:

6   [1983] ICR 440 at 454.
7   [1980] IRLR 201, CA; see also *Ferguson v John Dawson & Partners (Contractors) Ltd* [1976] 3 All ER 817, [1976] IRLR 346, CA.
8   [1980] IRLR 201 at 208. See also *Ferguson v John Dawson & Partners (Contractors) Ltd* [1976] 3 All ER 817, [1976] IRLR 346, CA; *Winfield v London Philharmonic Orchestra Ltd* [1979] ICR 726, EAT; *Thames Television Ltd v Wallis* [1979] IRLR 136, EAT.
9   ERA 1996, s 108(1).
10 ERA 1996, s 108(3).

(i)   dismissals (or selection for redundancy) for trade union reasons, ie reasons related to the employee's membership or non-membership in an independent trade union, or participation in the activities of such a union at the appropriate time;[11]

(ii)   reasons related to pregnancy, maternity or parental leave;[12]

(iii)   where the employee has asserted certain statutory rights against the employer;[13]

(iv)   reasons connected with health and safety at work;[14]

(v)   certain retail employees who refuse to work on Sundays;[15]

(vi)   employee trustees of an occupational pension scheme;[16]

(vii)   employee representatives or candidates for such posts;[17]

(viii) employees dismissed for redundancy;[18]

(ix)   employees dismissed for a spent conviction under the Rehabilitation of Offenders Act 1974;[19]

(x)   employees dismissed for 'blowing the whistle', ie making a protected disclosure within the terms of the legislation;[20]

(xi)   certain dismissals in connection with a transfer of undertaking;[1]

(xii)   certain dismissals for attempts to enforce rights under the National Minimum Wage Act,[2] Working Time Regulations[3] or Tax Credits Act 1999;[4]

(xiii) dismissals under paragraph (1) of the Part-Time Workers (Prevention of Less Favourable Treatment) Regulations 2000;[5]

(xiv)   dismissals under paragraph (3) or (6) of the Transnational Information and Consultation of Employees Regulations 1999.[6]

---

11   TULRCA 1992, ss 152(1), 153. See Chapter 10.

12   ERA 1996, s 108(3)(b). See Chapter 13.

13   ERA 1996, s 108(3)(g).

14   ERA 1996, s 108(3)(c).

15   ERA 1996, s 108(3)(d).

16   ERA 1996, s 108(3)(e).

17   ERA 1996, s 108(3)(f).

18   ERA 1996, s 108(3)(h).

19   Rehabilitation of Offenders Act 1974, s 4(3)(b): *Property Guards Ltd v Taylor* [1982] IRLR 175, EAT.

20   ERA 1996, s 108(3)(ff); Public Interest Disclosure Act 1998 ERA 1996, ss 103A, 105(6A) inserted by Public Interest Disclosure Act 1998 ss 5 and 6.

1   TUPE 1981, regulation 8.

2   ERA 1996, s 108(3)(gg).

3   ERA 1996, s 108(3)(dd).

4   ERA 1996, s 108(3)(gh).

5   ERA 1996, s 108(3)(i).

6   ERA 1996, s 108(3)(hh).

Finally employees dismissed on grounds of racial discrimination as defined by the Race Relations Act 1976 or sex discrimination as defined by the Sex Discrimination Act 1975 or disability discrimination under the Disability Discrimination Act 1995. In such cases, the employee will have a complaint under any of those Acts without having to meet a continuous service requirement. In the event, however, the employee's remedies will be restricted to those provided by the relevant Act because the requirement of one year's continuous service still must be met to qualify to prevent a claim under ERA 1996.

Computation of periods of continuous employment required by the act

Normally however, in order to be qualified to present a complaint of unfair dismissal, an employee must have been continuously employed by *an employer* under a contract of employment for a minimum of one year at the effective date of dismissal.[7] To ascertain whether an employee meets this qualification it is useful if not necessary to proceed in four separate steps, each of which is not without certain difficulties of statutory interpretation.

(a) The date when the employee 'starts work' with an employer must first be ascertained

As ERA 1996, s 211(1)(a) now reads:

'An employee's period of continuous employment for the purposes of any provisions of this Act ... begins with the day on which he *starts work* ...'.[8]

The phrase 'starts work' in s 211(1) has been held to refer to the beginning of an individual's employment under his contract of employment rather than *the date at which he actually started to be at work*. Thus in *General of the Salvation Army v Dewsbury*[9] a teacher whose full-time contract began on 1 May 1982 and ended on 31 April 1983 was held to

7   ERA 1996, s 108(1).
8   This is subject to s 211(2) which applies to a period of employment before the employee's eighteenth birthday.
9   [1984] ICR 498, [1984] IRLR 222, EAT.

have a year of continuous employment, notwithstanding that she actually took up full-time teaching duties only on 4 May 1982.

Moreover, the time at which the beginning of the period of continuous employment is to be calculated can be deemed to be postponed by the number of days the employee is away from work which by virtue of ss 215, 216 or 217 do not count towards continuous employment but do not break continuity. Thus ERA 1996, s 211(3) provides that:

> 'If an employee's period of continuous employment includes one or more [such] periods ... the beginning of the period (of continuous employment) shall be treated as postponed by the number of such days falling within that intervening period, or the aggregate number of days falling within those periods, calculated in accordance with the section in question.'

Finally, s 211(2) provides that where employees start work before their eighteenth birthday, their period of continuous employment *shall be treated as* beginning on their eighteenth birthday.

(b) The second step is to determine the employee's effective date of termination

ERA 1996, s 211(1)(b) states that an employee's period of continuous employment 'ends with the day by reference to which the length of his period of employment is to be ascertained for the purposes of the provision in question.' ERA 1996, s 108(1) states that s 94 does not apply to the dismissal of an employee unless he has been continuously employed for a period of not less than one year ending with the effective date of termination.

The complexities of determining the effective date of termination are discussed in detail in Chapter 2. It is worth pointing out here however that in ascertaining the effective date of termination, the period of notice to which an employee is entitled under ERA 1996, s 86 must be treated as part of an employee's period of continuous employment whether or not an employee actually receives this notice.[10]

---

10   ERA 1996, s 97(2); *Fox Maintenance Ltd v Jackson* [1978] ICR 110, [1977] IRLR 306, EAT; see further discussion Chapter 2.

(c) The third step is to determine whether the difference between the two dates amounts to at least a calendar year.

ERA 1996, s 210(2) makes it plain that any reference to a period of continuous employment of one year is a reference to a year of twelve calendar months. Section 210(3) adds quite explicitly that the computation of the period of continuous service shall be determined week by week; but where it is necessary to compute the length of an employee's period of employment, it shall be computed in months and years of twelve months in accordance with s 211.

(d) Assuming that the condition in the third step is met, the fourth step is to determine whether an employee's period of employment between those dates has been continuous or unbroken within the meaning of ERA 1996, ss 210–215

Sections 210–212 provide a method, using the week as a unit of account, to ascertain whether the employment has been 'continuous' in the sense of 'unbroken', as well as helping to determine which week shall count towards a period of continuous employment. Where a week does not count under ss 210–212, it also breaks the continuity of the period of employment unless it falls into one of the exceptions provided by ss 215–217.[11]
This is true even though s 210(5) creates a presumption of continuity. It states that a person's employment during any period shall, unless the contrary be shown, be presumed to have been continuous. This in cases of doubt places the burden of proof on the employer to prove that continuity was broken.[12]

WEEKS THAT COUNT.
(i) *a week during which the employee is working under a contract of employment.* Under s 212(1) any week during the whole or part of which the employee's relations are governed by a *contract of employment* counts in computing an employee's period of employment.

---

11   See discussion below.
12   See eg *Nicoll v Niccorode Ltd* [1981] IRLR 163, EAT; but see *Secretary of State for Employment v Cohen* [1987] IRLR 169 in which the EAT held that under ERA 1996, s 218 the presumption of continuity does not apply to a transfer of an undertaking, trade or business.

This provision makes continuous service a creature of statute even though it uses the contract of employment as a building block. It is not an invitation to a purely contractual interpretation of the statutory provisions. It is not possible for the parties to waive continuous service by agreement because that agreement would be void under ERA 1996, s 203.

The provisions of s 212(1) are mandatory and apply if and only if the statutory requirements are satisfied. Thus, as long as an employee works under a contract of employment even if the terms of that contract are changed, any week in which the employee worked part of that week under that contract will count.[13] Thus even if the employee resigns at the end of one week and is re-engaged during the following week both weeks count[14] provided that the employee is re-employed under the same contract.[15]

Similarly, even if the reason for the ending of the first employment is a frustration of the contract, if employment is resumed in the next week, the weeks still count.[16] If the statutory requirements for computing periods of continuous service are met, the precise reason why the first employment ceased is of no significance.

Thus, even where an employee leaves the employer, obtains alternative employment with a second employer and then returns to employment with the first employer, as long as the gap did not prevent the employee working part of each consecutive week on the same contract, both weeks shall count.[17]

Conversely, if the employer succeeds in separating periods of employment by at least two full weeks then under the terms of s 212(1), continuity is broken.[18] If the terms of the separation fit within the provisions of s 212(3) in respect of incapability or temporary cessation of work or an arrangement under s 212(3)(c) continuity may be maintained. Otherwise however, the statutory requirement of s 212(1) is not met. This offers employers a way to avoid the statutory rules regulating continuous service, but is not currently viewed as an agreement excluding or limiting 'the operation of any provisions of this Act' under ERA 1996, s 203.

Finally, s 212(1) presupposes that terms and conditions of employment are governed by the *same* contract of employment in order for weeks to

13   See eg *Wood v York City Council* [1978] IRLR 228, CA.
14   See eg *Carrington v Harwich Dock Co Ltd* [1998] IRLR 567, EAT.
15   See eg *Sweeney v J & S Henderson (Concessions) Ltd* [1999] IRLR 306, EAT.
16   *Tipper v Roofdec Ltd* [1989] IRLR 419, EAT.
17   *Sweeney v J & S Henderson (Concessions) Ltd* [1999] IRLR 306, EAT disapproving *Roach v CSB (Moulds) Ltd* [1991] IRLR 200, EAT. See Anderman (2000) ILJ 223 at 236.
18   See *Booth v United States of America* [1999] IRLR 16, EAT.

count. An interval between separate contracts will not be counted under s 212(1).[19]

(ii) *a week during which the employee's continuity of employment is preserved by statutory provision even if no contract existed between employer and employee.* Section 212(3) provides that even where employees are away from work and no longer have a contract their service may nevertheless be deemed to be continuous should they eventually return to work and the time away from work shall be credited towards their total period of service. Section 212(3) provides three types of cases in which in any week or part of a week an employee is away from work, although technically no longer under a contract of employment, the week nevertheless counts as a period of employment thus preserving continuity and being credited towards the employee's total period of service should he or she eventually return to work.

Section 212(3)(a) provides that for any week in which an employee is absent owing to sickness or injury, up to a maximum of 26 weeks,[20] that week will neither break continuity of service nor be excluded from the reckoning of total service.

There are four preconditions for s 212(3)(a) to apply; (1) there must be an original contract of employment; and (2) a termination of that contract; (3) a period when no contract of employment existed; and then (4) a later contract of employment with the same employer.[1] If the contract of employment has not been terminated, the weeks of incapability or illness would count under s 212(1).

The tribunal must ascertain that the period of absence has been both preceded and succeeded by a week in which there was a contract of employment with the employer and also whether the employee's absence in each week was due to incapability owing to illness or injury to perform the job under the original contract.

If the employee works for *another employer* during the period on a less demanding job or light work that does not necessarily preclude a finding that the employee was incapable to do the job with *the original employer*, particularly if the employee resumes work with the original employer within the twenty-six week period.[2] On the other hand, it has been held that a gap of 10 days after an employee retired from his original job on medical grounds

19   *Lewis v Surrey County Council* [1987] IRLR 509, HL.
20   See s 212(4).
1   *Pearson v Kent County Council* [1992] IRLR 110, EAT.
2   *Donnelly v Kelvin International Services* [1992] IRLR 496, EAT.

before he was re-employed by the same employer on a less demanding job did not qualify under s 212(3) since this 'incapacity' related only to the original job and not the new position.[3]

Section 212(3)(b) provides that where an employee is absent from work on account of a temporary cessation of work that week shall count in computing the employee's period of employment.[4]

Section 212(3)(b) refers first of all to a period of time during which there has been a cessation of the employee's work owing to a lack of work provided by the employer because it ceased to exist.[5] As the House of Lords stated in *Ford v Warwickshire County Council*,[6] it refers to the interval between (a) the date on which the employee who would otherwise be continuing to work under an existing contract of employment is dismissed *because for the time being his employer had no work for him to do*; and (b) the date on which work for him to do having become available again, he is re-engaged under a fresh *successor* contract of employment.[7] So in that case a school teacher, employed on consecutive fixed-term contracts of ten months (September to June) for eight years in succession, was held able to count summer vacation intervals as periods which counted towards employment continuity under s 212(3)(b). The fact of fixed-term contracts or the predictability of the periods of cessation were not relevant factors; what counted was the employer's *reason* for the cessation.

Section 212(3)(b) also refers to a *temporary* or *transient* cessation of work, one that lasts for a *relatively* short period of time. This has been held to be a question of fact for tribunals to decide but the case law provides that more than one approach may be taken by tribunals when engaged in this task. On the one hand it has been held that tribunals should take a 'broad' approach, ie look at all the relevant circumstances[8] and in particular

3   *Pearson v Kent County Council* [1993] IRLR 165, CA.
4   [1983] 2 AC 71, [1983] ICR 273, HL; see too *University of Aston, Birmingham v Malik* [1984] ICR 492; *Todd v Sun Ventilating Co Ltd* [1975] IRLR 4; *Thompson v Bristol Channel Ship Repairers and Engineers Ltd* (1970) 5 ITR 85; *Hunter v Smith's Docks Co Ltd* [1968] 2 All ER 81, [1968] 1 WLR 1865.
5   See eg *Byrne v City of Birmingham District Council* [1987] IRLR 191, CA.
6   [1983] IRLR 126, HL. See too *University of Aston, Birmingham v Malik* [1984] ICR 492; *Todd v Sun Ventilating Co Ltd* [1975] IRLR 4; *Thompson v Bristol Channel Ship Repairers and Engineers Ltd* (1970) 5 ITR 85; *Hunter v Smith's Docks Co Ltd* [1968] 2 All ER 81, [1968] 1 WLR 1865.
7   In *Lewis v Surrey County Council* [1987] IRLR 509, HL the House of Lords stated that an interval between *separate* contracts would not fit within s 212(3)(b) which was meant to apply to successor and predecessor contracts.
8   *Fitzgerald v Hall Russell & Co* [1970] AC 984, [1969] 3 All ER 1140.

the length of the period of employment as a whole,[9] as the way the parties viewed the position at the time the cessation began, what happened during the break and what happened on re-engagement.[10]

Yet it has also been accepted that a rare 'mathematical' approach may be taken by tribunals to the issue of a *relatively* short period of time. The obiter statement of Lord Diplock in *Ford*, which suggested that the length of the interval of cessation should be compared with the combined duration of the two periods of employment it bridged, has been approved as a test which tribunals may apply.[11]

Thus in *Sillars v Charrington Fuels Ltd*,[12] a case concerning a seasonal employee who over a period of 15 years had spent almost half of each year not in the company's employment, it was open to the tribunal to take a mathematical approach and decide that the periods out of employment were not short enough in relation to the periods in work to be viewed as temporary or transient.

It remains to be seen whether the EAT's suggestion in *Sillars v Charrington Fuels Ltd*[13] that the 'mathematical' test of Lord Diplock should be applied to cases of regular intervals of cessation whereas the 'broad' approach test was more apposite to irregular gaps, will be applied by employment tribunals.

The test is sufficiently wide to make it difficult for employers to avoid the application of the unfair dismissals law by arranging a series of short term contracts to deal with periods *when work is not available* but where the employer arranges a series of short term contracts with two week gaps between each contract and the *work is still available*, it is more difficult to fit within s 212(3)(b).[14]

Section 212(3)(c) provides that where an employee is absent from work in circumstances such that, by arrangement or custom, he is regarded as continuing in the employment of the employer for any purpose that week shall count as a period of employment.

The wording of s 212(3)(c) indicates that the arrangement must be in place when employees begin their period of absence.[15] For s 212(3)(c) to

9   *Flack v Kodak Ltd* [1986] IRLR 255, CA.
10   *Bentley Engineering Co Ltd v Crown and Miller* [1976] ICR 225, [1976] IRLR 146, HL.
11   *Sillars v Charrington Fuels Ltd* [1989] IRLR 152, CA.
12   Ibid.
13   [1988] IRLR 180, EAT. See Smith and Wood *Industrial Law* (7th edn, 2000) at p 154.
14   See *Booth v United States of America* [1999] IRLR 16, EAT.
15   *Morris v Walsh Western UK Ltd* [1997] IRLR 562, EAT.

apply it must be in the minds both of the employer and the employee that he is regarded as still being in employment and that the employment relationship is continuing.[16] An arrangement to preserve continuity made after a period during which the employee left, apparently permanently, cannot be changed retrospectively into a period within the meaning of s 212(3)(c).[17] Nor could a statement made by the employer upon re-employment that the previous period of absence would be treated retrospectively as unpaid leave.[18]

Finally, there are two further intervals in which weeks can count: the interval between the actual dismissal and the date where the employee would have been dismissed had he received proper statutory notice where the employee has been dismissed without adequate notice,[19] and an interval where the employee has obtained an order for reinstatement or re-engagement.[20]

Normally when an employment relationship between an employee and a particular employer is terminated either by resignation or by dismissal this has the effect of breaking the 'continuity' of service of the employee.[1] If the employee is re-employed by the same employer, however, continuity may be preserved under certain conditions.[2] Moreover under ERA 1996, s 218(6) where an employee is dismissed and obtains employment with another employer who was an associated employer[3] of the first employer at the time when the employee entered his employment or another employer

16   Ibid. See too *Booth v United States of America* [1999] IRLR 16, EAT.
17   *Murphy v A Birrell & Sons Ltd* [1978] IRLR 458, EAT.
18   *Morris v Walsh Western UK Ltd* op cit above, disapproving *Ingram v Foxon* [1985] IRLR 5, EAT.
19   ERA 1996, s 97(2); see Chapter 2.
20   ERA 1996, ss 113–116.
1   This may also be true if there has been an interval between separate contracts with the same employer. See eg *Lewis v Surrey County Council* [1987] IRLR 509, HL.
2   See eg *Jennings v Salford Community Service Agency* [1981] ICR 399, [1981] IRLR 76, EAT, EPCA; *Wood v York City Council* [1978] IRLR 228, CA; *Carrington v Harwick Dock Co Ltd* [1998] IRLR 567, EAT; *Sweeney v J & S Henderson Ltd* [1999] IRLR 306, EAT; see too *Roach v CSB (Moulds) Ltd* [1991] IRLR 200, EAT (disapproved in *Sweeney*); criticised in *Anerman* [2000] ILJ 223 at 236.
3   For definition of associated employer see ERA 1996, s 231. See eg *Gardiner v London Borough of Merton* [1980] IRLR 472, CA; *Hancill v Marcon Engineering Ltd* [1990] IRLR 51, EAT; *Southwest Launderettes Ltd v Laidler* [1986] IRLR 305, CA; *Pinkney v Sandpiper Drilling Ltd* [1989] IRLR 425, EAT; *Strudwick v IBL* [1988] IRLR 457, EAT; *Payne v Secretary of State for Employment* [1989] IRLR 352, CA.

who had purchased the business as a going concern[4] or in special circumstances upon the death of an employer[5] or a change in partnership[6] or if both employers are health service employers[7] or governors of schools maintained by a local education authority,[8] or bodies corporate.[9] A change in employer may not break continuity of employment. Furthermore where a transfer of undertaking takes place in accordance with the Transfer of Undertaking (Protection of Employment) Regulations 1982, an employee will retain continuity under the new employer.[10] Finally under s 215(1) it has been held that an employee may count a period wholly or mainly outside Great Britain for the purpose of determining whether that employee meets the service qualification.[11]

(iii) *Weeks which do not count but do not break continuous service.* Whilst as a general rule where a week is not credited to the employee as a week of employment it also destroys continuity.[12] ERA 1996, ss 215–217 provide that certain weeks during which an employee is away from work will not destroy 'continuity' even if they do not count towards total service. This

---

4   ERA 1996, s 218(2); *Macer v Aberfast Ltd* [1990] IRLR 137, EAT; *Dabell v Vale Industrial Services* [1988] IRLR 439, CA; but see *Justfern v D'Ingerthorpe* [1994] IRLR 164, EAT (assumes no complete closedown of business by original employer); *Secretary of State for Employment v (1) Cohen and (2) Beaupress* [1987] IRLR 169, EAT; *A & G Tuck Ltd v Bartlett and A & G Tuck (Slough) Ltd* [1994] IRLR 162, EAT (the employee does not have to enter the employment of the transferee at the moment of the transfer); *Lord Advocate v De Rosa and John Barrie (Contractor) Ltd* [1974] IRLR 215, HL; *Zarb v British and Brazilian Produce Co (Sales) Ltd* [1978] IRLR 78; *Melon v Hector Powe Ltd* [1981] 1 All ER 313, [1981] ICR 43, HL; *Woodhouse v Peter Brotherhood Ltd* [1972] 2 QB 520, [1972] 3 All ER 91; *Lloyd v Brassey* [1969] 2 QB 98, [1969] 1 All ER 382; *Evenden v Guildford City Association Football Club Ltd* [1975] QB 917, [1975] ICR 367; *Dhami v Top Spot Night Club* [1977] IRLR 231; *Crompton v Truly Fair (International) Ltd* [1975] ICR 359, [1975] IRLR 250; *Allen & Son v Coventry St* [1980] ICR 9, [1979] IRLR 399, EAT. *SI (Systems and Instruments) Ltd v Grist and Riley* [1983] ICR 788, [1983] IRLR 391, EAT.
5   ERA 1996, s 218(4).
6   ERA 1996, s 218(5); *Jeetle v Elster* [1985] IRLR 227, EAT: *Dowell v Nisbet* (1968) 3 ITR 403, IT.
7   ERA 1996, s 218(8)–(10).
8   ERA 1996, s 218(7). *Modiwear Ltd v Wallis Fashion Group* (1980) EAT 535/80.
9   ERA 1996, s 218(3). See eg *Gale v Northern General Hospital NHS Trust* [1994] IRLR 292, CA.
10   See discussion Chapter 14.
11   See *Weston v Vega Space Systems Engineering Ltd* [1989] IRLR 429, EAT.
12   ERA 1996, s 210(4).

is true of any week during any part of which an employee took part in a strike[13] or has been locked out.[14]

Finally, under ERA 1996, ss 216(2) and 211(3), the method to be used in calculating the period or periods under s 216(2) which do not count in computing the length of continuous service, is to take into account on aggregate the number of days between the last working day before the strike or lock-out and the day on which work was resumed in each of the periods and reduce the total period of continuous service by postponing the beginning of the period of service by that number of days.[15]

In other words rather than deducting a whole week for employees taking part in a strike or absent owing to a lock-out for only part of a week, the method adopted by ERA 1996, s 211(3) is to limit the period not counted to the actual days which are lost.

3. EXCLUDED CATEGORIES OF EMPLOYMENT

The following categories of employment are excluded from the provisions of ERA 1996 in respect of unfair dismissals:

(i)   An employee who on or before the effective date of termination reached the 'normal retiring age' for an employee holding his or her position in his firm or if there was no normal retiring age then in any other case, the age of 65 (ERA 1996, s 109(1)).

(ii)   A person who has agreed to a settlement of his complaint under s 18 of the Employment Tribunals Act 1996 where a conciliation officer has taken action in accordance with s 203(2)(e) or (f) of ERA 1996 or a qualifying compromise agreement under the Act has been made.

(iii)   A share fisherman as defined (ERA 1996, s 199).

(iv)   An employee who is excluded by virtue of a designated dismissal procedures agreement (ERA 1996, s 110).

(v)   A person employed under a contract of employment in police service (ERA1996, s 200).[16]

---

13   ERA 1996, s 216(1). See *Hanson v Fashions Industries (Hartlepool) Ltd* [1981] ICR 35, [1980] IRLR 393, EAT; *Bloomfield v Springfield Hosiery Finishing Co Ltd* [1972] 1 All ER 609, [1972] 1 WLR 386; *Clarke Chapman–John Thompson v Walters* [1972] 1 All ER 614, [1972] 1 WLR 378; *McGorry v Earls Court Stand Fitting Co Ltd* [1973] ICR 100, 8 ITR 109, NIRC.

14   ERA 1996, s 216(3).

15   ERA 1996, s 211(3).

16   See eg *Home Office v (1) Robinson and (2) Prison Officers' Association* [1981] IRLR 524, EAT.

(vi) A person excluded for reasons of national security (Employment Tribunals Act 1996, s 10. See too ERA 1996, s 193).[17]
      ...[18]

(vii) A person who has been dismissed for involvement in 'unprotected'[19] industrial action at the time of dismissal where the dismissal is not for automatically unfair reasons.[20]

i) Did the employee reach retiring age as defined by the act?

Under ERA 1996, s 109(1) the protection of unfair dismissal is withdrawn from those who on or before the effective date of termination[1] have attained[2] the normal retirement age in that undertaking for an employee holding the position which they held[3] or if there is no such 'normal retiring age' in the undertaking then the age of 65 (s 109(1)(b)).

The question of what is normal retiring age has been a somewhat vexing issue for the judiciary. On the one hand there are authorities asserting that the issue is to be ascertained by reference to the contractual retirement date. This was the view put forward by the Court of Appeal in *Nothman v Barnet London Borough Council*[4] which held that the normal retiring age was the age when employees holding the same position must or should retire in accordance with their contract. On the other hand, in *Post Office v Wallser*[5] the Court of Appeal held that the normal retiring age was a matter

---

17 *Council of Civil Service Unions v Minister for the Civil Service* [1984] 3 All ER 935, [1985] ICR 14, [1985] IRLR 28, HL, in which the Foreign Secretary issued certificates under EPA 1975, s 121 and EPCA 1978, s 138.

18 Note that the following exclusions have been repealed: the exclusion for part time employees, employees working abroad, employees on fixed term contracts with a waiver, and employees of an employer with 20 employees or less.

19 Eg 'unofficial industrial action' see Chapter 11.

20 Eg for certain actions in relation to health and safety, for 'whistle blowing'; for acting as an employee representative; and for family reasons. (TULRCA s 237(1)(a)). See Chapter 11.

1 See discussion in Chapter 2.

2 *Dixon v London Production Tools Ltd* [1980] IRLR 385, EAT.

3 A 'normal retiring age' in the meaning of ERA 1996, s 109(1)(a) must be the same whether the employee was a man or woman.

4 [1978] ICR 336, [1977] IRLR 489, CA; see also *Howard v Department of National Savings* [1981] ICR 208, [1981] IRLR 40, CA.

5 [1981] 1 All ER 668, [1981] IRLR 37, CA; see also *Duke v Reliance Systems Ltd* [1982] ICR 449, [1982] IRLR 347, EAT.

of evidence and did not depend exclusively on the relevant contract of employment.

In *Waite v Government Communications Headquarters*[6] the House of Lords effectively laid this controversy to rest. Lord Fraser of Tullybelton, speaking for the entire court, said the following:

> 'I therefore reject the view that the contractual retiring age conclusively fixes the normal retiring age. I accept that where there is a contractual retiring age, applicable to all, or nearly all, the employees holding the position which the appellant employee held, there is a presumption that the contractual retiring age is the normal retiring age for the group. But it is a presumption which, in my opinion, can be rebutted by evidence that there is in practice some higher age at which employees holding the position are regularly retired, and which they have reasonably come to regard as their normal retiring age. Having regard to the social policy which seems to underlie the Act – namely the policy of securing fair treatment, as regards compulsory retirement, as between different employees holding the same position – the expression "normal retiring age" conveys the idea of an age at which employees in the group can reasonably expect to be compelled to retire, unless there is some special reason in a particular case for a different age to apply. "Normal" in this context is not a mere synonym for "usual". The word "usual" suggests a pure statistical approach by ascertaining the age at which the majority of employees actually retire, without regard to whether some of them may have been retained in office until a higher age for special reasons – such as a temporary shortage of employees with a particular skill, or a temporary glut of work, or personal consideration for an employee who has not sufficient reckonable service to qualify for a full pension.'

Lord Fraser went on to suggest that

> '... The proper test is in my view not merely statistical. It is to ascertain what would be the reasonable expectation or understanding of the employees holding that position at the relevant time. The contractual retiring age will prima facie be the normal, but it may be displaced by evidence that it is regularly departed from in practice. The evidence may show that the contractual retirement age has been superseded by some definite higher age, and, if so, that will have

6   [1983] 2 AC 714, [1983] ICR 653, [1983] IRLR 341, HL.

become the normal retiring age. Or the evidence may show merely that the contractual retiring age has been abandoned and that employees retire at a variety of higher ages. In that case there will be no normal retiring age and the statutory alternatives of 65 for a man and 60 for a woman will apply.'

In *Hughes v Department of Health and Social Security, Department of Health and Social Security v Coy*,[7] Lord Justice Slade at the Court of Appeal stage derived the following principles from that passage in *Waite*:

'(1) Where there is a contractual retiring age applicable to all, or nearly all, the employees holding the same "position" as the claimant employee, there is a rebuttable presumption that the contractual retiring age is the "normal retiring age" for the group.

(2) The presumption, however, can be rebutted by evidence that there is in practice some higher age at which employees holding that "position" are regularly retired and which they would have reasonably come to regard as their normal retiring age.

(3) The proper test is to ascertain what would be the reasonable expectation or understanding of the employees holding that "position" at the relevant time.

(4) If the evidence merely shows that at the relevant time employees holding such "position" retire at a variety of ages, and that the contractual retiring age has been abandoned as the normal retiring age, s [109(1)] will not operate so as to preclude a man from making his application at any age lower than 65.'

The Court held that for the purpose of ascertaining the reasonable expectations of the group of similarly placed employees the relevant time was the effective date of termination.

Yet the Court also indicated that the application of the principles of *Waite*'s case could raise two further issues. First, how does one determine the relevant group of employees who constitutes the group of employees holding that 'position at the relevant time'? Secondly, what is the effect of employers changing their policy on the age of compulsory retirement on the normal retiring age?

7   [1984] IRLR 360, CA; see too *Barber v Thames Television plc* [1992] IRLR 410, CA; *Brooks v British Telecommunications plc* [1992] IRLR 66, CA; *Whittle v Manpower Services Commission* [1987] IRLR 441, EAT; *Highlands and Islands Development Board v MacGillivray* [1986] IRLR 210, Ct of Sess; *Barclays Bank plc v O'Brien* [1994] IRLR 580, CA.

The first question was raised by the fact in *Hughes'* and *Coy's* cases in which two employees with a normal retiring age of 65, according to the test in *Waite*, were told in a DHSS circular that after June 1981 their retiring age would be reduced in two stages to 60. The EAT, looking at all employees covered by the circular as the relevant group of employees in the position of Hughes and Coy held that the normal retiring age had been changed to 60.

The Court of Appeal, by a majority, with Lord Justice Donaldson dissenting, reversed and remitted the decision because the EAT had failed to consider whether the two employees by virtue of their earlier history as transferees from local authorities could be regarded as a special group with the wider category of employees covered by the circular. Both Slade LJ and Parker LJ were persuaded that there was an important issue that the ex-local authority employees who joined the Civil Service in 1948, could not be assumed to have their normal retiring age determined by the mere issuance of the DHSS circular, even though this did have such an effect upon the wider group of employees.

Given that, prior to 1981, for Hughes and Coy, practice had effectively displaced the contractual retiring age so that they could reasonably have regarded 65 rather than 60 as the normal retiring age, the correct task for the tribunal was to decide what effect the DHSS Circular of 1981 had had upon the reasonable expectations or understanding of the Hughes and Coy group as of the relevant time, ie the effective date of termination. As Lord Justice Slade put it, the reference in s 109(1) to 'an employee holding the position held by the employee, coupled with the special definition of "position" in s 235 necessitates [that] the relevant group, whose reasonable expectation and understanding at the relevant time has to be ascertained in the infinitely more limited Hughes group in the one case and Coy group in the other ...'.

On appeal, the House of Lords[8] held that while the employees' initial expectation may have been to work until 65, at the date of their dismissal that expectation must have changed because the employer had publicised the change in departmental policy and this was effective to change the 'normal retirement age' under s 109. Consequently, it is possible for an employee to have a 'normal retirement age' which is later than his or her contractual age if the employer's practice or policy creates a later retirement age.[9] However, it is open to the employer to change its policy provided

8   [1985] IRLR 263, HL.
9   See too *Brooks v British Telecommunications plc* [1992] IRLR 66, CA.

that this change is adequately communicated to employees.[10] The test, a
matter of fact for tribunals to decide,[11] is an objective test;

> 'what, at the effective date of termination of the claimant's
> employment and on the basis of the facts then known, was the age
> which employees of all age groups in the claimant's position could
> *reasonably* regard as the normal age of retirement applicable to the
> group'.[12]

(italics mine).

The designation of the relevant group within which employees in the
claimant's 'position' is determined by the statutory criteria in ERA 1996,
s 235:

> 'the following matters taken as a whole—
> (a)   his status as an employee
> (b)   the nature of his work and
> (c)   his terms and conditions of employment.'

ii) Agreements precluding complaints

Under s 18 of the Employment Tribunals Act 1996 it is possible to reach an
agreement between employer and employee which will preclude a complaint
to an employment tribunal for unfair dismissal. Such an agreement will not
be void under s 203(2) of the Employment Rights Act 1996 in two sets of
circumstances. The first is where an agreement to refrain from instituting a
continuing proceedings has resulted from an ACAS conciliation officer
taking action under s 18 of the Employment Tribunals Act 1996. Such an
agreement is usually recorded on form COT3.

The case law has given considerable discretion to conciliation officers.
If an agreement has been reached through the intermediary of an ACAS
conciliation officer, it may consist of an oral settlement,[13] it may be based

10   Ibid.
11   *Secretary of State for Education and Science v Birchall* [1994] IRLR 630, EAT.
12   *Brooks v British Telecommunications plc* [1992] IRLR 66, CA; see too *Barclays*
     Bank plc v O'Brien [1994] IRLR 580, CA (is there a norm for the group despite
     some differences in retiring age); cf *Secretary of State for Scotland v Meikle*
     [1986] IRLR 208, EAT; *Bratkco v Beloit Walmsley Ltd* [1995] IRLR 629, EAT.
13   *Gilbert v Kembridge Fibres Ltd* [1984] IRLR 52, EAT. See further *Sutherland*
     v Network Appliances Ltd [2001] IRLR 12, EAT; *Gloystarne & Co Ltd v Martin*
     [2001] IRLR 15, EAT.

on an implied claim of the employee which can be inferred from the employee's overt acts and attitudes.[14] Moreover, it is difficult to reopen such an agreement to question the conciliation officer's investigation of the underlying fairness of the agreement,[15] the possibility of exhausting a grievance procedure,[16] the extent of the information given by the officer to the employee,[17] or the possibility of economic duress.[18]

The second type of agreement that can preclude a complaint is one which is a legally binding compromise agreement without the involvement of ACAS which meets the tests of s 203(3) ie it must be

(a)   in writing;

(b)   relate to the particular proceedings;[19]

(c)   the employee must have received independent advice as to the terms of the agreement and its effects on his ability to pursue the employee's rights before an employment tribunal;

(d)   the independent adviser was professionally insured;

(e)   the agreement identifies the adviser; and

(f)   the agreement states that the conditions regulating compromise agreements under the Act are satisfied.

The definition of independent adviser for the purposes of the compromise agreement has been extended to include

(a)   qualified lawyers;

(b)   competent trade union officers, officials and employees authorised on behalf of the trade union to give advice;

---

14   *Moore v Duport Furniture Products Ltd* [1982] IRLR 31, HL; see too *Hennessy v Craigmyle & Co Ltd and ACAS* [1986] IRLR 300, CA.

15   Ibid.

16   *Hennessy v Craigmyle & Co Ltd and ACAS* [1985] IRLR 446, EAT.

17   Ibid [1986] IRLR 300, CA; see too *Slack v Greenham (Plant Hire) Ltd* [1983] IRLR 271, EAT.

18   There are limits to 'blanket' agreements: *Lunt v Merseyside TEC Ltd* [1999] IRLR 458, EAT. A qualifying agreement can relate to the terms of termination of employment. *Rock-It Cargo Ltd v Green* [1997] IRLR 581, EAT; see too *Thompson v Walon Car Delivery* [1997] IRLR 343, EAT (limits to benefit for transferee of a post transfer agreement between employee and transferor employer).

19   There are limits to 'blanket' agreements: *Lunt v Merseyside TEC Ltd* [1999] IRLR 458, EAT. A qualifying agreement can relate to the terms of termination of employment. *Rock-It Cargo Ltd v Green* [1997] IRLR 581, EAT; see too *Thompson v Walon Car Delivery* [1997] IRLR 343, EAT (limits to benefit for transferee of a post transfer agreement between employee and transferor employer).

(c) an advice centre worker (employee or volunteer) who has been certified in writing by the centre as competent to give advice; and

(d) if he is a person specified by order of the Secretary of State. This is intended to increase the use of compromise agreements under the Employment Rights (Dispute Resolution) Act 1998.[20]

iii) Presenting a valid complaint in time

Under s 111(2)(a) of the ERA 1996, a complaint of unfair dismissal must normally be presented to the employment tribunal within three months of the effective date of termination.[1] This time limit is a jurisdictional provision which the parties cannot waiver.[2] However s 112(2)(b) confers a residual discretion upon employment tribunals to allow a claim to be presented within a reasonable period afterwards when it considers that it was not reasonably practicable for the complaint to be presented during the prescribed period.

(a) Presenting a valid complaint within the three month period

The three month period is to be calculated by first finding the correct effective date of termination, then taking the date before it and then going forward three months. If the date before the effective date of termination is the last day of the month the three-month deadline expires on the last day of the third month even if it is a different number.[3]

The complaint must be presented before midnight of the last day of the period.[4] It is presented only when it is received.[5] If it is posted before the

20 See Earnshaw and Hardy 'Assessing an Arbitral Route for Unfair Dismissal' [2001] ILJ 289; Smith and Woods *Industrial Law* (7th edn, 2000) p 434.

1   Section 111(3) also allows presentation of a claim after notice of termination but prior to the effective date of termination under certain conditions. See *Presley v Llanelli Borough Council* [1979] ICR 419, [1979] IRLR 381, EAT; *Throsby v Imperial College of Science and Technology* [1978] QB 438, [1978] ICR 357, EAT. See too *Patel v Nagesan* [1995] IRLR 370, CA (employment tribunal jurisdiction under s 111(3) not affected by subsequent summary dismissal during the notice period).

2   *Rogers v Bodfari (Transport) Ltd* [1973] IRLR 172, NIRC.

3   *Pruden v Cunard Ellerman Ltd* [1993] IRLR 317, EAT.

4   *Hetton Victory Club Ltd v Swainston* [1983] ICR 341, [1983] IRLR 164, CA; *Post Office v Moore* [1981] ICR 623, EAT.

5   *Hammond v Haigh Castle Ltd* [1973] IRLR 91, NIRC.

end of the three month period but arrives after the period has expired, the issue for the tribunal is whether the claimant could reasonably have expected the application to be delivered in time in the ordinary course of post.[6]

The complaint to be valid must contain sufficient information to identify who is making it, against whom it is made[7] and what sort of complaint it is.[8] It must specify the grounds, with particulars thereof, on which relief is sought.[9]

(b) Not reasonably practicable to present a complaint within the three month period

As mentioned, ERA 1996, s 111(2)(b) confers upon tribunals a discretion to allow a claim to be presented within a reasonable period outside the prescribed period of three months where it considers that it was not reasonably practicable for the complaint to be presented within the prescribed period. When interpreting this provision the employment tribunal is involved essentially in determining an issue of fact.

As Shaw LJ put it in *Wall's Meat Co Ltd v Khan*:[10]

'It seems to me axiomatic that what is or is not reasonably practicable is in essence a question of fact. The question falls to be resolved by finding what the facts are and forming an opinion as to their effect having regard to the ordinary experience of human affairs. The test is empirical and involves no legal concept. Practical common sense is the keynote and legalistic footnotes may have no better result than to introduce a lawyer's complications into what should be a layman's pristine province. These considerations prompt me to express the emphatic view that the proper forum to decide such questions is the industrial tribunal, and that their decision should prevail unless it is plainly perverse or oppressive.'[11]

---

6   *St Basil's Centre v McCressan* [1991] IRLR 455, EAT.
7   If a new respondent is later added to a timeous complaint an application can be made to amend the complaint. See *Gillick v BP Chemicals Ltd* [1993] IRLR 437, EAT; *Drinkwater Sabey Ltd v Burnett* [1995] IRLR 238, EAT.
8   *Dodd v British Telecommunications plc* [1988] IRLR 16, EAT.
9   *Alex Munro (Butchers) Ltd v Nicol* [1988] IRLR 49, EAT.
10   [1979] ICR 52, [1978] IRLR 499, CA, *Biggs v Somerset County Council* [1996] IRLR 203, CA; *Schultz v Esso Petroleum Co Ltd* [1999] IRLR 488, CA.
11   [1979] ICR 52 at 587c, CA.

In other words, since an appeal to the EAT can only be on questions of law, it will not be open to the EAT to reverse an employment tribunal decision on the issue simply because it considers that the tribunal's decision on the facts found by it was or was not incorrect. The EAT's jurisdiction on appeal will be limited to the issues of perversity or misdirection.[12] Moreover, the Court of Appeal has also indicated that 'appeals on such questions involving as they so often do the dressing up of questions of fact so as to have the appearance of questions of law are in general undesirable and to be discouraged'.[13]

In directing itself upon the guidelines to the interpretation of s 111(2) an employment tribunal is likely to start with the principles suggested by the Court of Appeal in *Dedman v British Building and Engineering Appliances Ltd*.[14] In *Dedman*'s case Lord Denning suggested the following:

'If in the circumstances, the man knew or was put on inquiry as to his rights, and as to the time limit, then it was "practicable" for him to have presented his complaint within the time limit, and he ought to have done so, but if he did not know, and there was nothing to put him on inquiry, then it was not practicable and he should be excused'.[15]

Yet most importantly, Lord Denning also indicated that the knowledge of the employee is only the starting point for employment tribunals applying the test of practicability. They must go on to ascertain whether the delay could be said to be attributable to the individual's fault or some other case. As Lord Denning put it, in *Dedman*'s case:[16]

'Summing up, I would suggest that in every case the tribunal should inquire into the circumstances and ask themselves whether the man or his advisers were at fault in allowing the [time limit] to pass by without presenting the complaint. If he was not at fault, nor his

---

12   *Wall's Meat Co Ltd v Khan* (above); *Palmer and Saunders v Southend-on-Sea Borough Council* (above).
13   See remarks of Brandon LJ in *Wall's Meat Co Ltd v Khan* (above). See too remarks by M Dunn LJ in *Palmer and Saunders* case (above).
14   [1974] 1 All ER 520, [1974] ICR 53, CA. See eg *Times Newspapers Ltd v O'Regan* [1977] IRLR 101, 11 ITR 259, EAT; *Porter v Bandridge Ltd* [1978] 1 WLR 1145, [1978] ICR 943, CA; *Wall's Meat Co Ltd v Khan* [1979] ICR 52, [1978] IRLR 499, CA.
15   At p 61. See also *Churchill v Yeates & Sons Ltd* [1983] ICR 380, [1983] IRLR 187, EAT.
16   [1974] 1 All ER 520, [1973] IRLR 379, CA.

advisers – so that he had just cause or excuse for not presenting his complaint within the [time limit] – then it was "not practicable" for him to present it within that time.'

And in *Wall's Meat Co Ltd v Khan*[17] the Court of Appeal reiterated that the test of the majority in *Dedman*'s case was still applicable, albeit in the form of a 'just cause' test.

'I would venture to take the simplest test given by the majority in *Dedman*'s case [1974] ICR 53, 61. It is simply to ask this question: Had the man just cause or excuse for not presenting his complaint within the prescribed time? Ignorance of his rights – or ignorance of the time limit – is not just cause or excuse, unless it appears that he or his advisers could not reasonably be expected to have been aware of them. If he or his advisers could reasonably have been so expected, it was his or their fault, and he must take the consequences.'

Common to both authorities is the idea that the first task of the tribunal is to ascertain whether employees knew or *should have known* that they had a claim under the statute. As Lord Denning put it in *Dedman*'s case, the task for the tribunal was to ascertain:

'If in the circumstances the man knew or was put on inquiry as to his rights'.

If there are crucial facts which are not known to the employee which prevent him or her realising that they had a claim, that might be the basis of a finding that it was not reasonably practicable to bring a claim within the three month period.[18] But there must be proof that it was *reasonable* for the employee not to have known about the factual basis for a claim.[19]

And in *Wall's Meat Co Ltd v Khan*[20] it was stressed again by Lord Denning, speaking for the majority of the Court of Appeal that ignorance of his rights is not just cause or excuse, unless it appears that he or his advisers could not reasonably be expected to be aware of them. Thus whilst the employee's ignorance of his rights could make it not reasonably

---

17   [1979] ICR 52, [1978] IRLR 499, CA.
18   *Churchill v A Yeates & Sons Ltd* [1983] IRLR 187, EAT; *Machine Tool Industry Research Association v Simpson* [1988] IRLR 212, CA; *London Underground Ltd v Noel* [1999] IRLR 621, CA.
19   Ibid.
20   [1978] IRLR 499, CA.

practicable to lodge a complaint in the prescribed period, he must be able to show that his ignorance is reasonable.[1]

Moreover, if a complainant consults a skilled adviser, the adviser's actual knowledge, or the knowledge the adviser ought to have had, may well be imputed to the employee. This too is a question of fact. If an employee distrusts the advice given by one solicitor and immediately seeks advice from another source that factor may be influential in the practicality tests.[2] Moreover, if the bad advice comes from a tribunal official that may provide an acceptable excuse.[3]

Often, however if an employee goes to skilled advisers and they make a mistake, '... he must abide by their mistake. ... His remedy is against them.'[4]

In *Riley v Tesco Stores Ltd*[5] Lord Stephenson added:

'Whether you go to skilled advisers, or go to advisers, consult skilled advisers, or consult advisers, engaged skilled advisers, or engage advisers, does not seem to me to be material to the question of reasonable practicability. What matters is that the employee cannot of necessity prove reasonable impracticability by saying, "I took advice": and a third party, skilled or unskilled, only comes to be considered a possible excuse for the employee's delay if he gives advice or is authorised to act in time and fails to act or advise acting in time'.

Once an employment tribunal has ascertained that the employee knew of the existence of the claim it will be more difficult to show that it was not practicable to present a complaint within the prescribed period.[6] For example if the employee has been incapacitated by illness the assessment must include whether the illness was in the earlier or the far more critical weeks at the end of the period.[7]

---

1   Cf *Biggs v Somerset County Council* [1996] IRLR 203, CA.
2   *London International College v Sen* [1993] IRLR 333, CA.
3   See eg *Rybak v Jean Sorelle Ltd* [1991] ICR 127, [1991] IRLR 153, EAT; see too *London Underground Ltd v Noel*, above.
4   *Dedman* see note 14 above. See too *Siraj-Eldin v Campbell Middleton Burness & Dickson* [1989] IRLR 208, Ct of Sess.
5   [1980] ICR 323 at 330, [1980] IRLR 103, CA.
6   See eg *Wall's Meat Co Ltd v Khan* [1979] ICR 52 at 60F–61F; *Porter v Bandridge Ltd* [1978] ICR 943 at 954.
7   *Schultz v Esso Petroleum Co Ltd* [1999] IRLR 488, CA.

If the complaint was lost in the post, there is still a question whether reasonable steps were taken to confirm that the application had been received.[8]

To argue ignorance about the time limit will be more difficult because the employee will have to show why he did not make inquiries.[9] To argue mistake about the time limit would require the employee to show that the mistake was excusable or reasonable.[10]

For example, in *Riley v Tesco Stores Ltd*[11] an employee dismissed for theft had consulted the CAB who told her they could not consider her claim until after the hearing of the criminal proceedings. When she was acquitted three months later she presented her complaint. The tribunal dismissed her complaint for want of jurisdiction. It found that it was reasonably practicable for her to present her complaint on time even though she did not know of the time limit because she had engaged skilled advisers and their mistake was attributable to her.

On the other hand, in *Wall's Meat Co Ltd v Khan*,[12] an employment tribunal was prepared to find that an employee's mistaken view that his unfair dismissal claim was proceeding before the same tribunal as the one dealing with his claim for unemployment benefit was reasonable and the EAT and Court of Appeal upheld that exercise of the tribunal's discretion although expressing some concern about its 'benevolence'.

Yet employees can get into difficulty if they delay a complaint because of the mistaken view that they have to wait for the outcome of a pending proceeding.[13]

For example where the employee delays a complaint for unfair dismissal because of a pending criminal proceeding, it is not altogether clear how employment tribunals will treat the understandable tendency of the employee to wish to await the outcome of the criminal proceeding until bringing a claim. On the one hand in *Union Cartage Co Ltd v Blunden*[14]

---

8   *Capital Foods Retail Ltd v Corrigan* [1993] IRLR 430, EAT; *Camden and Islington Community Services NHS Trust v Kennedy* [1996] IRLR 381, EAT.
9   Ibid. See eg *Churchill v Yeates & Son Ltd* [1983] ICR 380, [1983] IRLR 187, EAT.
10   Ibid.
11   [1980] ICR 323, [1980] IRLR 103, CA.
12   [1979] ICR 52 at 56.
13   Cf *Slack v Greenham (Plant Hire) Ltd* [1983] ICR 617, [1983] IRLR 271, EAT (effect of conciliation process leading to an agreement under s 140(2)(d)).
14   [1977] ICR 420, [1977] IRLR 139, EAT. See support for this view by Ormrod LJ in his dissenting opinion in *Porter v Bandridge Ltd* [1978] ICR 943 at 953, CA.

the EAT suggested that the reluctance of the employee to proceed until the prosecution had come to an end could be a good ground for contending that it was not reasonably practicable for him to present a complaint on time. Yet the facts in that case were a bit unusual. An employee had consulted both a trade union and a solicitor concerning a theft charge which resulted in dismissal. He knew he had a right to make a claim for unfair dismissal but he did not know about the time limit. Because the employee had consulted the trade union and the solicitor only in respect of a defence in the criminal proceedings, the knowledge of the solicitor and trade union in respect of the time limit for a claim of unfair dismissal was not imputed to him. And because the employee himself was not on inquiry in respect of the time limit, the EAT would not reverse the tribunal's decision to allow a claim for unfair dismissal that was 24 days out of time.

On the other hand, Lord Denning in *Wall's Meat Co Ltd*[15] indicated that he would, along with the majority of *Porter v Bandridge Ltd*, be against the view taken by the EAT in the *Union Cartage Co* case.

'It seems to me that the reaction of the ordinary man who is charged with theft would be: "It's no good my claiming for unfair dismissal whilst this charge is still outstanding against me. I will wait and see what happens to it before making a claim". If that be his state of mind, then he is time barred as soon as the 3 months have elapsed without his presenting a claim. It was reasonably practicable for him to present his complaint of unfair dismissal within 3 months. His only reason for not doing so was because of the outstanding charge. That is not an acceptable reason for saying that it was not "reasonably practicable" to present his claim within 3 months.'

A similar difficulty arises when an employee is awaiting the results of an internal appeals procedure and the procedure does not provide for the employee's termination to be suspended pending the appeal. The task for the tribunal is to determine whether the employee was justified in delaying his claim until the results of the appeal are known because of an understandable desire not to appear to be undermining the voluntary procedure.

Speaking obiter in the judgment of the Employment Appeal Tribunal in *Crown Agents v Lawal*,[16] Kilner Brown J said:

15 [1979] ICR 52 at 55–56. See also support for Lord Denning's view in *Riley v Tesco Stores Ltd* [1980] ICR 323, [1980] IRLR 103, CA; *Norgett v Luton Industrial Co-operative Society Ltd* [1976] ICR 442, [1976] IRLR 306, EAT.
16 [1978] IRLR 542, EAT.

'Merely as a statement of general principle, it would seem to us that in cases where a person is going through a conciliation process, or is taking up a domestic appeal procedure, whether it be on discipline, or whether it be for medical reasons, that common sense would indicate that while he is going through something which involves him and his employer directly, he should be able to say, "It is not reasonably practicable for me to lodge my application within the three months." This is the view not only of this particular division of the appeal tribunal but we have taken steps to canvass the views of other members, including other judicial members. The view of the appeal tribunal as a whole is that normally, though by no means always, it would be open to say in the case of a person who is going through an appeal process and loses, that not only does the date go back to the original date of dismissal but that the applicant so caught by the effluxion of time should be able to satisfy an industrial tribunal that he is entitled to the benefit of what is usually called the "escape" clause.'

However in another EAT decision, *Bodha v Hampshire Area Health Authority*[17] Browne-Wilkinson J disagreed in these terms:

'Despite the reference to there having been consultation with other members of this appeal tribunal, the fact that both the argument and the judgment were concluded on the same date shows that such consultation was obviously not very widespread. For the reasons we have given, we do not think we should follow that dictum having had the matter fully argued before us. There may be cases where the special facts (additional to the bare fact that there is an internal appeal pending) may persuade an industrial tribunal, as a question of fact, that it was not reasonably practicable to complain to the industrial tribunal within the time limit. But we do not think that the mere fact of a pending internal appeal, by itself, is sufficient to justify a finding of fact that it was not "reasonably practicable" to present a complaint to the industrial tribunal.'

In *Palmer and Saunders v Southend-on-Sea Borough Council*, the Court of Appeal expressed a preference for the views in *Bodha*'s case over those in *Crown Agents*.[18] Yet it also expressed some concern that the words

---

17   [1982] ICR 200, EAT.
18   [1984] IRLR 119 at 125. See too *London Underground Ltd v Noel* [2000] ICR 109, [1999] IRLR 621, CA.

of the statute should not be interpreted to mean that which is reasonably capable physically of being done.[19]

'In the end, most of the decided cases have been decisions on their own particular facts and must be regarded as such. However we think that one can say that to construe the words "reasonably practicable" as the equivalent of "reasonable" is to take a view too favourable to the employee. On the other hand "reasonably practicable" means more than merely what is reasonably capable physically of being done – different, for instance, from its construction in the context of the legislation relating to factories: compare *Marshall v Gotham Co Ltd* [1954] AC 360. In the context in which the words are used in the 1978 Consolidation Act, however ineptly as we think, they mean something between these two. Perhaps to read the word "practicable" as the equivalent of "feasible" as Sir John Brightman did in *Singh*'s case and to ask colloquially and untrammelled by too much legal logic – "was it reasonably feasible to present the complaint to the Employment Tribunal within the relevant three months?" – is the best approach to the correct application of the relevant subsection'.

19   Ibid.

Chapter 2.
The effective date of termination

The effective date of termination, as defined by s 97(1) of the Employment Rights Act 1996 is an essential element in an employee's rights in a claim of unfair dismissal. That date defines the end of the employee's length of continuous service, and hence the qualifying period of service for a complaint[1] and the period for calculation of a basic award of compensation.[2] The date is important to establish the time when an employee is entitled to a written statement of the reasons for dismissal,[3] an employee's age at the time of dismissal for the purpose of the upper age limit,[4] the relevant law that applies at the time of the dismissal, and whether an employee's claim has been presented within the three month time limit for presenting complaints.[5]

In spite of its importance, however, the effective date of termination has not been clearly defined by legislation in all cases, nor has it been defined in the same way for all purposes.

There are three basic cases in which the effective date of termination is clearly defined for all purposes by legislation. The first is the case of dismissal with proper notice where the employee works out the notice. The date of dismissal is the date when the notice period expires.[6] The second

1   ERA, s 108(1).
2   ERA, s 119(1).
3   ERA, s 92.
4   ERA, s 109(1).
5   ERA, s 111(2).
6   ERA, s 97(1)(a). This however presupposes that in fact the notice was 'causative of the termination'. *TBA Industrial Products Ltd v Morland* [1982] ICR 686, [1982] IRLR 331, CA.

is the case of dismissal by the expiry of a fixed term without renewal under the same contract. The date of dismissal is the date of expiry of the contract.[7] The third case is the case of a valid dismissal without notice on a clearly indicated date. The effective date of termination is the date on which that dismissal takes effect, ie when it is communicated to the employee.[8]

There are three other cases in which the position is more complicated. The first complication occurs when an employee is dismissed without the notice to which he is entitled, either under s 86 of the ERA or under the provision of his contract, whether or not the employee has been paid wages in lieu of notice. The second occurs where the employee is given notice and then chooses to leave during the notice period. The third occurs where the employee is constructively dismissed. Let us consider each in turn.

I. DISMISSAL WITHOUT THE MINIMUM STATUTORY NOTICE

In cases where the employee is dismissed without due notice whether with or without wages in lieu of notice, the effective date of termination is a creature of statute in two important respects;

First, ERA, s 97(2) provides that where an employee is entitled to a statutory minimum period of notice from the employer under ERA, s 86, the date at which *the notice would have expired if duly given* will for certain purposes be treated as the effective date of dismissal, rather than the date the employee actually left his employment. The statutory extension of the date of effective termination under s 97(2) applies whether the dismissal was without adequate notice, without any notice at all or with pay in lieu of notice. The statutory extension has been held to apply even where the employee has under s 86(3) waived his or her entitlement to notice under s 86(1) since such a waiver relates only to the employee's contractual rights. It is not relevant to the determination of the statutory effective date of termination for the purpose of unfair dismissal[9] which is a creature of statute and not to be subject to modification by contractual waiver. Presumably there could be an argument under ERA s 203(1) that this amounts to contracting out of the provisions of the Act.[10]

---

7   ERA, s 97(1)(c).
8   ERA, s 97(1)(b).
9   *Secretary of State for Employment v Staffordshire County Council* [1989] IRLR 117, CA.
10   But see *Lambert v Croydon College* [1999] IRLR 346, EAT; see too Anderman, 'Interpreting Employment Protections and the Contract of Employment' (2000) ILJ 191.

This provision however must be treated with some caution. It has two important limitations:

(i) The notice period which the provision requires to be taken into account in ascertaining the 'effective date of termination' is the *statutory minimum* period of notice required to be given to the employee under the ERA, s 86, and not any longer period of notice to which the employee may be entitled under his or her contract of employment.[11]

(ii) The provision does not deem the end of the statutory notice period to be the effective date of termination for all conceivable purposes. It states that the date on expiry of proper notice shall be treated as the effective date of termination only for the purposes of ERA, s 108(1) (period of continuous service), ERA, s 119(1) (calculation of the basic award of compensation), and ERA, s 227(3) (amount of a week's pay). Consequently, the effective date of termination for any other purposes, such as the calculation of the three month period for a complaint of unfair dismissal to be presented to a tribunal, must be defined by reference to the case law.[12]

In examining the case law, however, the effective date of termination remains a creature of statute in yet another respect. Even though at common law it is now fairly well established that in most cases of repudiation, an acceptance is required to convert the repudiation into a termination[13] s 97(1) presupposes a unilateral rather than an 'acceptance' view of the repudiation in determining the timing of the effective date of termination. As the EAT put it in *Robert Cort & Son Ltd v Charman*[14]

'[s 97(1)] seems to have been drafted on the footing that the unilateral view is correct, ie dismissal even without the contractually required notice terminates the contract ...

Thus, in s [97(1)(a)] (dealing with the case of termination by notice) it is the date of the expiry of the notice served which is the effective date of termination: nothing in the subsection suggests that this is

11 *Fox Maintenance Ltd v Jackson* [1978] ICR 110, [1977] IRLR 306, EAT. If the employer justifiably dismisses the employee without notice for 'gross misconduct', under s 86(6) the period of notice would not be 'required by s 86' and hence the statutory prolongation would not apply. However, it is necessary for the tribunal to enquire into the merits to determine whether there was in fact conduct by the employee which would enable the employer to terminate without notice: see eg *Lanton Leisure Ltd v White and Gibson* [1987] IRLR 119, EAT.

12 See eg *Crank v HM Stationery Office* [1985] ICR 1, EAT.

13 *Photo Production Ltd v Securicor Transport Ltd* [1980] AC 827, [1980] 1 All ER 556, HL; *London Transport Executive v Clarke* [1981] ICR 355, [1981] IRLR 166, CA.

14 [1981] ICR 816, [1981] IRLR 437, EAT.

so only where the length of notice served complies with the contractual obligation. [S 97(2)] provides that where either no notice or notice shorter than that required by [s 86] is given, the effective date of termination is the date on which the notice required by [s 86] would have expired. Such provision would have been unnecessary if the draftsman had considered that the contract would not otherwise have been terminated by an unlawful notice.

Moreover, s [97(1)(b)] defines the effective date of termination as being the date on which "the termination takes effect". The word "termination" plainly refers back to the termination of the contract. But the draftsman of the section does not refer simply to the date of the termination of the contract, but to the date on which the termination "takes effect". As we have pointed out, even on the acceptance view the status of employer and employee comes to an end at the moment of dismissal, even if the contract may for some purposes thereafter continue. When dismissed without the appropriate contractual notice, the employee cannot insist on being further employed: as from the moment of dismissal, his sole right is a right to damages and he is bound to mitigate his damages by looking for other employment. We therefore consider it to be a legitimate use of words to say, in the context of s [97], that the termination of the contract of employment "takes effect" at the date of dismissal, since on that date the employee's rights under the contract are transformed from the right to be employed into a right to damages.

…This indicates that the date of the final termination of the contract is not necessarily "the effective date of termination" or "the relevant date": if, as in the case of repudiation, further *full* performance becomes impossible, that will be the relevant date.

Finally we consider it a matter of the greatest importance that there should be no doubt or uncertainty as to the date which is the "effective date of termination". An employee's rights to complain of unfair dismissal dependant upon his taking proceedings within three months of the effective date of termination (or in the case of redundancy payments "the relevant date"). These time limits are rigorously enforced. If the identification of the effective date of termination depends upon the subtle legalities of the law of repudiation and acceptance of repudiation, the ordinary employee will be unable to understand the position. The *Dedman* rule fixed the effective date of termination at what most employees would understand to be the date of termination, ie the date on which he ceases to attend his place of employment.

For these reasons we hold that, where an employer dismisses an employee summarily and without giving the period of notice required by the contract, for the purposes of s [97(1)] the effective date of termination is the date of summary dismissal whether or not the employer makes a payment in lieu of notice'.

Consequently, if an employer *clearly*[15] notifies employees that their employment will terminate immediately[16] or on a specific date,[17] the date that the notification is actually received[18] or whatever later date is stated will normally be regarded as the date of dismissal even if the employer's action in prematurely terminating the contract was wrongful. The timing of the dismissal is unaffected by the wrongfulness of the dismissal or by the fact that the employee can recover damages for breach of contract.[19] Nor assuming that the employer's letter is *unambiguous* does the fact that the employer offers to pay wages in lieu of notice affect the timing of the dismissal since the pay in lieu of notice is viewed as a matter of law as damages for breach of contract.[20] For example, in *Dedman's* case, the employer handed a letter to the employee on 5 May 1972 stating that there was 'no alternative but to terminate your employment immediately'. The employee left the premises that day, handing over his car and other company property. Yet, he was paid for the full month of May and given one month's pay in lieu of notice. The Court of Appeal held that the dismissal occurred on the date the letter was received because to find otherwise would be inconsistent with the terms of the letter. Thus, for purposes other than those specified in ERA, s 97(2), such as the three month period for presenting a complaint, the effective date of dismissal for an employee would be the date when the employer terminated the contract whether or not the termination was wrongful.

There may be an exception, however, where an employer asks the employee to leave work prematurely with full pay in lieu. In such a case the

---

15   See discussion below.

16   *Dedman v British Building and Engineering Appliances Ltd* [1974] 1 All ER 520, [1974] ICR 53; *Adams v GKN Sankey Ltd* [1980] IRLR 416, EAT.

17   *Dixon v Stenor Ltd* [1973] ICR 157, [1973] IRLR 28.

18   Where the dismissal is communicated in a letter, the effective date of communication is the date when the employee has actually read the letter or the date when he has a reasonable opportunity of reading it. *McMaster v Manchester Airport plc* [1998] IRLR 112, EAT; *Brown v Southall and Knight* [1980] ICR 617, [1980] IRLR 130, EAT.

19   *Stapp v Shaftesbury Society* [1982] IRLR 326, CA; *Octavius Atkinson & Sons Ltd v Morris* [1989] IRLR 158, CA; *Batchelor v British Railways Board* [1987] IRLR 136, CA.

20   *Adams v GKN Sankey Ltd* [1980] IRLR 416, EAT. See discussion below.

date of dismissal may be viewed as the last day of the full contractual period of notice if the arrangement is regarded as a form of 'paid leave'. The test of whether in a particular case a dismissal letter falls into the category of paid leave or termination depends upon the construction of the letter itself. As the EAT remarked in *Chapman v Letheby & Christopher Ltd*,[1]

> 'The construction to be put on the letter should not be a technical one, but should reflect what an ordinary, reasonable employee would understand by the words used. It should be construed in the light of facts known to the employee on the date he received the letter. Moreover, where an employer relies on a notice served by him as having a particular meaning, he should be required to demonstrate that it unambiguously has that meaning. If an employer can rely on ambiguities being resolved in his favour, the employee may be left in doubt as to where he stands and may lose his statutory rights.'

Thus in *Chapman*'s case, the employer sent a letter with two irreconcilable statements. On the one hand, the letter first gave 10 weeks notice of termination ending on Saturday 10 May 1980 then it referred to payment of a 'retainer' payment 'in lieu of notice'. The EAT held that the doubt created by the latter statement could not be allowed to override the clear statement of the date of termination. Furthermore, in *Adams v GKN Sankey Ltd*[2] a letter of dismissal sent by the employer dated 2 November 1979 which said 'you are given 12 weeks notice of dismissal from this company with effect from 5 November 1979. You will not be expected to work out your notice but will receive money in lieu of notice ...' was interpreted to mean that the employee's employment did not come to an end until 12 weeks after the 5 November. The letter was construed to a notice of dismissal which was to run for 12 weeks from 5 November not a dismissal which was to operate from 5 November. Moreover the clause that the employee will receive money in lieu of notice meant that the employee would receive money in lieu of working out her notice.

If an employee's position is determined to be that of 'paid leave', the effective date of dismissal for all purposes will be the date when the

---

1   [1981] IRLR 440, EAT; see too *Leech v Preston Borough Council* [1985] IRLR 337, EAT; cf earlier cases of *Brindle v H W Smith (Cabinets) Ltd* [1973] 1 All ER 230, [1972] IRLR 125; *Lees v Arthur Greaves (Lees) Ltd* [1974] 2 All ER 393, [1974] IRLR 93.
2   [1980] IRLR 416, EAT.

employee's period of contractual notice expires. The case falls under ERA, s 97(1)(a) rather than s 97(1)(b).[3]

2. COUNTER-NOTICE AND THE DATE OF TERMINATION

Where the employee has received notice of termination from an employer he may serve a counter-notice to terminate the contract on an earlier date than that fixed by the employer and still be taken to be dismissed by the employer for the purposes of ERA, s 97(2) and for the reasons for which the employee's notice is given.[4] In the event the effective date of dismissal could be the date that the employer's original notice expires rather than the date the employee's counter-notice expires.[5] The employee's counter-notice must actually be served within a period of notice, whether statutory, contractual or otherwise[6] and not prematurely in response to a mere warning of impending dismissal.[7]

If during the notice period an employee makes an agreement with his employer to terminate the contract, there is a risk that this could result in finding that the termination was not 'by the employer' under ERA, s 97(1) ie it may be regarded as a resignation or a termination by agreement.[8] Where however an employer agrees to an employee's request for a premature termination during a notice period, the likelihood is that it will be viewed as a termination by the employer with an agreed foreshortening of the notice period. The Court of Appeal in *Dedman*'s case[9] approved the following comments of the NIRC in *McAlwane v Boughton Estates Ltd*:[10]

'It would be a very rare case indeed in which it could properly be found that the employer and the employee had got together and,

---

3   Cf *Abrahams v Performing Rights Society* [1995] IRLR 486; *Rex Steward Jeffries Parker Ginsburg Ltd v Parker* [1988] IRLR 483, CA; but see *Cerberus Software Ltd v Rowley* [2001] EWCA Civ 78, [2001] IRLR 160.
4   ERA, s 95(2).
5   Ibid. But see ERA, s 97(1)(a) which appears to leave the question open.
6   See eg *Ready Case Ltd v Jackson* [1981] IRLR 312, EAT.
7   *Read Case Ltd v Jackson* [1981] IRLR 312, EAT, see also discussion in Chapter 3.
8   See eg *Harvey v Yankee Traveller Restaurant* [1976] IRLR 35, EAT. See also discussion in Chapter 3.
9   See also *Lees v Arthur Greaves (Lees) Ltd* [1974] 2 All ER 393, [1974] IRLR 93, CA; see also *Glacier Metal Co Ltd v Dyer* [1974] 3 All ER 21, [1974] IRLR 189.
10 [1973] 2 All ER 299, [1973] ICR 470, NIRC; cf *Thames Television Ltd v Wallis* [1979] IRLR 136, EAT. See discussion in Chapter 3.

notwithstanding that there was a current notice of termination of the employment, agreed mutually to terminate the contract, particularly when one realised the financial consequences to the employee involved in such an agreement'.[11]

3. CONSTRUCTIVE DISMISSAL AND THE DATE OF TERMINATION

As far as constructive dismissal under ERA, s 95(1)(c) is concerned, the effective date of dismissal has not been defined clearly by statute or judicial authority. However, the Court of Appeal's comments in *Western Excavating (ECC) Ltd v Sharp*[12] suggest that under s 95(1)(c) the action by the employee in 'releasing himself from his contractual obligation' is the terminating event, rather than the employer's prior repudiation.

In other words the language of s 95(1)(c) as interpreted by the Court of Appeal lends weight to the view that the employee's response is the important determining factor, whether or not the previous position at common law happens to be governed by an 'elective' rather than an 'automatic' view of the effects of the employer's repudiation.[13] Hence ERA, s 97(2) which, in certain circumstances, extends the effective date of termination to include the notice period where the contract of employment is *terminated by the employer*, would not necessarily be applicable to cases of constructive dismissal under s 95(1)(c). Rather, the effective date of termination in cases of constructive dismissal is likely to vary, depending on whether the employee leaves with or without notice.[14]

If the employee leaves without notice, his or her date of departure is likely to constitute the effective date of termination.[15] If the employee leaves with notice the position would appear to be that the effective date of termination is the end of the notice period. Indeed, the employee may be estopped from arguing otherwise.

---

11 Ibid.
12 [1978] QB 761, [1978] IRLR 27, CA.
13 See eg *Martin v Glynwed Distribution Ltd* [1983] ICR 511, [1983] IRLR 198, CA; *Hogwood v Dudley Metropolitan Borough Council* (1983) EAT 354/83; see discussion in Chapter 3.
14 Cf *BMK Ltd v Logue* [1993] IRLR 477, EAT.
15 Ibid; see too *G W Stephens & Son v Fish* [1989] ICR 324, EAT.

4. INTERNAL APPEALS PROCEDURES AND THE EFFECTIVE DATE OF TERMINATION

Where the contract provides a procedure for an appeal from dismissal, the effective date of termination will vary depending upon the contents of contractual provisions. If the contract expressly provides that the employee is not dismissed until the appeal is heard and decided, then the effective date of termination coincides with the dismissal. If the contract provides for suspension with pay pending the results of the appeal that may also extend the effective date of termination to the date the appeal is decided[16] but the contract must also contain a provision saving the contract in a fuller sense.[17]

If, on the other hand, the contract provides for suspension without pay without saving the rest of the contract until the appeal is decided, and the appeal is not successful then the effective date of termination is the date of the original dismissal since only the term providing a right of appeal is regarded as surviving the termination of the contract.[18]

As the EAT put it in *J Sainsbury Ltd v Savage*,

'In our view, when a notice of immediate dismissal is given, the dismissal takes immediate effect. The provisions of this contract as to the appeal procedure continue to apply. If an appeal is entered, then the dismissed employee is to be treated as being "suspended" without pay during the determination of his appeal, in the sense that if the appeal is successful then he is reinstated and he will receive full back-pay for the period of the suspension. If the appeal is not successful and it is decided that the original decision of instant dismissal was right and is affirmed, then the dismissal takes effect on the original date. In our view, that is the date on which the termination takes effect for the purposes of the Act'.

Lord Justice Brightman in the Court of Appeal decision in *Savage*'s case said:

---

16   *High v British Railways Board* [1979] IRLR 52, EAT.
17   *National Heart and Chest Hospitals Board of Governors v Nambiar* [1981] ICR 441, [1981] IRLR 196, CA. See also *Cooke v Ministry of Defence* (1984) Times, 14 May, CA.
18   *J Sainsbury Ltd v Savage* [1981] ICR 1, [1980] IRLR 109, CA; see also *Ward v London Borough of Newham* (1984) EAT 745/83; *Cooke v Ministry of Defence* (1984), Times, 14 May, CA.

'I find it difficult to improve on the reasoning of the Employment Appeal Tribunal ... it seems to me clear that, to take an example, if an employee is dismissed on 1 January on the terms that he then ceases to have the right to work under the contract of employment, and that the employer ceases likewise to be under an obligation to pay the employee, the contract of employment is at an end. That must be the position in the present case unless para 4(5) ... can be read as saving the contract of employment in all the circumstances pending conclusion of the appeal. In my view, the contract of employment is saved if the appeal succeeds, because the employee is reinstated with full back-pay. But if the appeal fails, then the inevitable result is that the employee is not only deprived of his right to work as from 1 January, but also of his right to remuneration from that date. If he has had no right to work after 1 January and no right to be paid after 1 January, the contract of employment must have been determined as from 1 January'.[19]

In *Drage v Governors of Greenford High School*[20], the Court of Appeal reiterated that the critical distinction was whether under the contract 'during the period between the initial notification and the outcome of the appeal the employee stands (a) dismissed with the possibility of reinstatement or (b) suspended with the possibility of the proposed dismissal not being confirmed and the suspension thus being ended.' In the second case, as in the *Drage* case itself, the effective date of termination is postponed until the date the employee is notified of the results of the internal appeal.

If the appeal is successful then not only is continuity preserved in the interval between dismissal and reinstatement but also the weeks will count as continuous service for certain purposes.[1]

19   [1981] ICR 1, [1980] IRLR 109, CA.
20   [2000] IRLR 314, CA, para 28 at para 32.
1   See eg ERA 1996, s 212 *Howgate v Fane Acoustics Ltd* [1981] IRLR 161, EAT.

Chapter 3.
Has the employee been dismissed?

Before an employment tribunal will examine the fairness or unfairness of a dismissal, it must be satisfied by employees that they have been dismissed in accordance with s 95 of the Employment Rights Act 1996. Dismissal for the purposes of the Act is not synonymous with being sacked. According to the rather technical definition in s 95 an employee shall be treated for the purposes of the Act as dismissed by his employer *if, but only if,* any one of three events occur:

(a) the employer terminates the employee's contract, whether with or without notice (s 95(1)(a));

(b) the employer fails to renew a fixed term contract under which the employee is employed (s 95(1)(b)); or

(c) the employee terminates his contract in circumstances entitling him to terminate it without notice by reason of the employer's conduct (whether the employer does so with or without notice) (s 95(1)(c)).

These three types of dismissal constitute an exhaustive list; the onus of proof lies upon the employee to establish that he or she was 'dismissed' under at least one of these heads in order to give jurisdiction to the tribunal over the unfair dismissal claim.

Two features of these definitions are particularly noteworthy. First, they overlap in part with the type of dismissal entitling an employee to a claim for wrongful dismissal at common law. Thus where the employee has been dismissed either without any notice or without adequate notice under his contract of employment, he may have a claim at common law for 'wrongful dismissal', ie, breach of contract, as well as a claim for unfair dismissal under the new statute.[1] In the case of dismissal by proper contractual notice and dismissal in the form of a decision not to renew a fixed-term contract,[2] however, the employee may have a claim under the statute but none at common law.

The second feature of these definitions of dismissal under the statute is that they rest on essentially contractual foundations. The test of dismissal under ERA, s 95(1)(a) is whether the *contract* of employment is terminated by the employer. Thus in theory an *employment relationship* may continue, but an employee may be entitled to claim unfair dismissal because the *contract* was terminated. Moreover, under s 95(1)(c) the test of constructive dismissal is also contractual; it presupposes that the employer's conduct constitutes a repudiation of the contract.[3]

The creation of a contractual basis to the requirement of dismissal adds an excessively technical requirement to a law designed to be the basis of claims by individuals without legal representation. It has opened the way to attempts by employers to reach into the general law of contract for doctrines such as discharge by frustration, employee repudiation or self-dismissal or termination by agreement in order to show that the particular termination of the contract was not 'by the employer' and that as a consequence the tribunal has no jurisdiction to consider the fairness of the termination under s 98(4).

Nevertheless, s 95(1)(c) has also resulted in an extension of the statutory definition of dismissal to resignations by the employee in response to abusive conduct by the employer, such as unfavourable transfers, downgradings, suspensions without pay, and changes in the contractual nature of work, hours of work or place of work, as well as other types of unreasonable treatment, provided that they amount to a contractual repudiation by the employer.

1   In the case of wrongful dismissal an employee can bring an action in the ordinary courts for an injunction or damages. An employee may now also make a claim for damages to an employment tribunal subject to a limit of £25,000. See Industrial Tribunal Extension of Jurisdiction Order 1994, SI 1994/1643; in Scotland SI 1994/1624. See *Treganowan v Robert Knee & Co Ltd* [1975] ICR 405, [1975] IRLR 247; *Turner v London Transport Executive* [1977] ICR 952, [1977] IRLR 441, CA. Recent wrongful dismissal cases have breathed new life into this action. See eg *Gunton v Richmond-upon-Thames London Borough Council* [1981] Ch 448, [1980] ICR 755; *R v BBC, ex p Lavelle* [1983] 1 All ER 241, [1983] 1 WLR 23; cf *Thomas Marshall (Exports) Ltd v Guinle* [1979] Ch 227, [1978] IRLR 174. But see *Johnson v Unisys Ltd* [2001] UKHL 13, [2001] IRLR 279, for limits on compensation.
2   See discussion of termination of fixed-term contracts in Chapter 15.
3   *Western Excavating (ECC) Ltd v Sharp* [1978] QB 761, [1978] IRLR 27, CA.

Initially this was achieved by the courts 'stretching' the concept of repudiation to allow it to fit under s 95(1)(a).[4] With the addition of s 95(1)(c) in 1975, however, the statute explicitly provided a form of employee termination as one of the statutory heads of dismissal. This was a timely statutory addition because the doctrinal controversies both in contract law generally[5] and in employment contract law in particular[6] were being resolved in favour of the view that a repudiation cannot normally ripen into a termination unless 'accepted', ie treated as putting an end to the contract, by the injured party which would have made it difficult to use s 95(1)(a) for that purpose. However even under s 95(1)(c) employees face a task of considerable legal technicality to prove that they have been constructively dismissed. They must show that the resignation occurred in circumstances such that they were entitled to resign without notice and this requires a showing not only that the employer has repudiated the contract but also that the employee has behaved in such a way as to 'accept' the repudiation turning it into a termination rather than waiving the repudiation by 'affirming' the contract.

The full implication of the importation of the doctrines of the law of contract into the statutory definition of dismissal can best be appreciated by looking at the subject under two separate heads:[7]

(i)   termination by the employer;
(ii) justified termination by the employee: constructive dismissal.

I. WAS THE TERMINATION BY THE EMPLOYER?

To fit within s 95(1)(a) employees may show that their employer terminated the contract either with or without notice, but they must show that the contract was in fact terminated *by the employer*. Thus, if the employer succeeds in showing that the contract was terminated by the resignation of the employee or by the employee's repudiation or self dismissal, or by operation of the doctrine of frustration or by mutual agreement, or if the contract was not terminated at all but was simply consensually varied, the employee will not be treated as dismissed for the purpose of this provision.

4   See eg remarks by Lord Denning in *Western Excavating* (above).
5   *Photo Production Ltd v Securicor Transport Ltd* [1980] AC 827, [1980] 1 All ER 556, HL.
6   *Gunton v Richmond-upon-Thames London Borough Council* [1981] Ch 448, [1980] IRLR 321, CA; *London Transport Executive v Clarke* [1981] ICR 355, [1981] IRLR 166, CA.
7   Section 95(1)(b) will be discussed in context in Chapter 15.

i) Dismissal versus resignation

Under s 95(1)(a), there are cases in which the employer's actions in
terminating the contract have been completely unambiguous. The employer
has either told the employee directly or sent a letter saying 'you are
dismissed' either immediately or as of a certain date. Similarly there are
many cases where the employee has quite unambiguously resigned. Yet
the circumstances of some cases may raise a basic question as to who
really terminated the contract. One example is where an employee has
resigned but the language used is unclear or is made ambiguous because
of the surrounding circumstances. Another is where an employee resigns
in response to a threat of dismissal. In such cases the employment tribunal
has to decide as a question of fact whether the resignation was genuine or
whether the resignation was really a dismissal or indeed whether there was
a termination by mutual agreement.[8]

At one stage employment tribunals were told by the EAT that they could
be guided by certain principles in deciding such cases. Thus, in *Sheffield
v Oxford Controls Co Ltd*[9] the EAT presided over by Arnold J (as he then
was) set out a principle deduced from earlier cases.

'It is plain, we think, that there must exist a principle, exemplified by
the four cases to which we have referred, that where an employee
resigns and that resignation is determined upon by him because he
prefers to resign rather than to be dismissed (the alternative having
been expressed to him by the employer in the terms of the threat that
if he does not resign he will be dismissed), the mechanics of the
resignation do not cause that to be other than a dismissal. The cases
do not in terms go further than that. We find the principle to be one
of causation. In cases such as that which we have just hypothesised,
and those reported, the causation is the threat. It is the existence of
the threat which causes the employee to be willing to sign, and to
sign, a resignation letter or to be willing to give, and to give, the oral
resignation.

But where that willingness is brought about by other
considerations and the actual causation of the resignation is no
longer the threat which has been made but it is the state of mind of
the resigning employee, that he is willing and content to resign on

---

8   See eg *Martin v Glynwed Distribution Ltd* [1983] ICI 511, [1983] IRLR 198,
     CA; *Staffordshire County Council v Donovan* [1981] IRLR 108, EAT; *Hogwood
     v Dudley Metropolitan Borough Council* (1983) EAT 354/83.
9   *Sheffield v Oxford Controls Ltd* [1979] ICR 396, [1979] IRLR 133, EAT.

the terms which he has negotiated and which are satisfactory to him, then we think there is no room for the principle to be derived from the decided cases'.[10]

In *Martin v Glynwed Distribution Ltd*,[11] however, the Court of Appeal made it clear that the 'principle' that Arnold J had derived from the case law was no more than an illustration and could not be used to explain or qualify the parliamentary definition. Under s 95(1)(a) the issue was essentially one of fact for employment tribunals to decide weighing the circumstances of the case.

In *Martin's* case an employee who substantially damaged a company's mini van whilst driving under the influence of drink, was told by a director that if he went through a disciplinary inquiry he would probably be dismissed. He was invited to resign and did so by giving a month's notice but subsequently he complained that he was unfairly dismissed. The employment tribunal decided that Mr Martin had terminated his own employment because the dismissal was not certain and there were certain advantages in resigning rather than facing the inquiry. The EAT by a majority, allowed an appeal because it thought that the tribunal had erred in law in failing to consider the causation of the resignation and the intention of the director as opposed to the effect of his statements on Mr Martin. The Court of Appeal restored the employment tribunal's decision, reasoning that it was not open to the EAT to query the weight that employment tribunals placed on the various factors involved in determining whether on the evidence, 'the reality of the situation was that the employer terminated the employment or the employee did'. The Court said that as long as the tribunal properly directed itself on the relevant law the only basis for an appeal from its decision will be that the decision was such that no reasonable employment tribunal could reach it on the facts as found.

Lord Donaldson[12] urged that in such cases,

'It is very important and sometimes difficult to remember that where a right of appeal is confined to questions of law, the Appellate Tribunal must loyally accept the findings of fact with which it is presented and where it is convinced that it would have reached a different conclusion of facts, it must resist the strong temptation to treat what are in truth findings of fact as holdings of law or mixed findings of fact and law'.

10   *Sheffield v Oxford Controls Ltd* [1979] IRLR 133 at 136, EAT.
11   [1983] ICR 511, [1983] IRLR 198, CA.
12   [1983] IRLR 198 at 199.

Similarly, in looking at the language used by an employee or an employer, employment tribunals have a wide discretion on the issue of what weight to give the circumstances in which the words are uttered. It is true that in cases where the facts as found are so clear that only one conclusion can be reached then an employment tribunal may be found to have been perverse if it decides otherwise.

Thus, in *Sothern v Franks Charlesly & Co*[13] the Court of Appeal overturned a tribunal decision and decided that the announcement of an office manager at the end of a partnership meeting that she was resigning was, in the circumstance, unambiguous. As Stephenson LJ put it:

'If this deliberate statement of resignation made by a middle aged manager hours after a row with her employer's senior partners at the end of their meeting was not an unambiguous resignation, I doubt if any employee could ever resign'.

Where however a statement is ambiguous, because it has been made in the heat of the moment or where the statement is clear but the context makes it ambiguous, the effect of the statement is a question of fact and the tribunal will be entitled to conclude that there is no real resignation.[14] The test of how the other party understood the language must be objective, ie what the 'reasonable' employer or employee might have understood the words to mean. As the EAT remarked in *B G Gale Ltd v Gilbert*:[15]

'the undisclosed intention of a person using language whether orally or in writing as to its intended meaning is not properly to be taken into account in concluding what its true meaning is. That has to be decided from the language used and the circumstances in which it was used'.[16]

Moreover, where there is an attempted retraction after the statement the effect of the retraction is a question of fact for employment tribunals to decide using a common sense approach.[17] However, the retraction must

13   [1981] IRLR 278, CA.
14   *Sovereign House Security Services Ltd v Savage* [1989] IRLR 115, CA; *Kwik-Fit (GB) Ltd v Lineham* [1992] IRLR 156, EAT; *Barclay v City of Glasgow District Council* [1983] IRLR 313, EAT.
15   [1978] ICR 1149, [1978] IRLR 453, EAT. See also *J & J Stern v Simpson* [1983] IRLR 52, EAT; cases n 14 above.
16   [1978] IRLR 453 at 454.
17   See *Sovereign House Security Services Ltd v Savage* [1989] IRLR 115, CA; *Kwik-Fit (GB) Ltd v Lineham* [1992] IRLR 156, EAT.

not come to slate as to amount in law to an attempt unilaterally to withdraw a dismissal or resignation that has already occurred.

As Phillips J stated in *Tanner v D T Kean Ltd*:[18]

'A word of caution is necessary because in considering later events it is necessary to remember that a dismissal or resignation once it has taken effect cannot be unilaterally withdrawn. Accordingly, as it seems to us later events need to be scrutinised with some care in order to see whether they are genuinely explanatory of the acts alleged to constitute dismissal or whether they reflect a change of mind'.[19]

Subject to this, the question is essentially one of fact for employment tribunals. The surrounding circumstances both before and after the statement can be weighed by the tribunal to determine whether the statement had the effect of a dismissal as opposed to a resignation.[20]

Of course if an employment tribunal, through misdirection, *ignores* an important element in the facts that must be weighed, its decision can be reversed on appeal. For example, in *J & J Stern v Simpson*,[1] an employment tribunal incorrectly attempted to construe the effect of words 'Go, get out, get out' without taking into account the surrounding circumstances in which they were uttered or subsequent events. Similarly in *Barclay v City of Glasgow District Council*[2] an employment tribunal was found to have erred in law in finding that an employer was entitled to treat an employee's unequivocal words of resignation as notice of termination in circumstances in which the employer knew that the employee was mentally defective.

ii) Termination by mutual agreement

Where a contract of employment is terminated by agreement between the employer and employee the termination can fall outside the definition of s 95(1)(a). The definition of dismissal in s 95(1)(a) is directed only to a case where the contract of employment is terminated by the employer alone.[3]

---

18   [1978] IRLR 110, EAT. See also *Sothern v Franks Charlesly & Co* (above).
19   Ibid at 111.
20   *Martin v Yeoman Aggregates Ltd* [1983] IRLR 49 at 51. See too cases n 17 above.
1   [1983] IRLR 52, EAT.
2   [1983] IRLR 313, EAT.
3   *Birch and Humber v University of Liverpool* [1985] IRLR 165, CA.

This is expressly provided by the statute in the case of an expiry of a fixed term (or fixed-task) contract.[4] Moreover, a mutual agreement by employer and employee to settle a dispute which includes the question whether or not the termination is by the employer as well as whether or not it is unfair will if duly registered operate to extinguish a claim.[5] Furthermore, if an employment tribunal finds that an employee and employer have quite genuinely agreed mutually to terminate the contract either because they have agreed to enter upon a new contract with different terms,[6] or because the employer has accepted the offer of resignation of the employee[7] the contract could be regarded as terminated by mutual agreement and not by the employer for the purposes of s 95(1)(a). In either case this could be true despite the existence of ERA 1996, s 203, which provides:

> '… any provision in an agreement (whether a contract of employment or not) shall be void insofar as it purports (a) to exclude or limit the operation of any provision of this Act, or (b) to preclude any person from presenting a complaint to, or bringing any proceedings under this Act, before an industrial tribunal'.[8]

Yet what view should be taken of a clause which an employer insists upon including in a works rule or other document which stipulates that certain conduct by the employee 'automatically terminates the contract'?

In *British Leyland (UK) Ltd v Ashraf*[9] an employee wishing to visit his sick mother signed a document before he left on five weeks unpaid leave. The document read in part that 'you have agreed to return to work on 21 February 1977. If you fail to do this your contract of employment will terminate on that date'. When Mr Ashraf failed to return on the 21st owing to his own illness an employment tribunal held that he had not been dismissed: his contract of employment had come to an end in accordance

---

4   See Chapter 15. See also *Thames Television Ltd v Wallis* [1979] IRLR 136, EAT for a failed effort to contend that a supervening mutual agreement made the termination consensual rather than an expiry of a fixed term.

5   See EPCA, s 134(3); *Moore v Duport Furniture Products Ltd* [1982] ICR 84, [1982] IRLR 31, HL.

6   See eg *Marriott v Oxford and District Co-operative Society Ltd (No 2)* [1970] 1 QB 186, [1969] 3 All ER 1126, CA; *Hawker Siddeley Power Engineering Ltd v Rump* [1979] IRLR 425, EAT.

7   See eg *Hogwood v Dudley Metropolitan Borough Council* [1983] EAT 354/83.

8   See eg *Council of Engineering Institutions v Maddison* [1977] ICR 30, [1976] IRLR 389, EAT; *Naqvi v Stephens Jewellers Ltd* [1978] ICR 631, EAT.

9   [1978] ICR 979, [1978] IRLR 330, EAT. See too *Tracy v Zest Equipment Co Ltd* [1982] IRLR 268, EAT; *Smith v Avana Bakeries Ltd* [1979] IRLR 423, EAT.

with the agreement. The EAT, Phillips J presiding, approved the employment tribunal's decision because it was sufficiently concerned about the practical difficulties management encountered with employees failing to return on time from holidays and claiming that they were sick to countenance a method by which 'freedom of contract' could be used to avoid the statutory protection.

In *Midland Electric Manufacturing Co Ltd v Kanji*[10] however, the EAT with Talbot J presiding upheld the decision of an employment tribunal that *Ashraf* did not apply to a case where the employee leaving on a five week leave of absence signed a document stating 'you are warned that, if you fail to return to work on the due date for whatever reason, including sickness, the company will consider that you have terminated your employment'.

The EAT distinguished *Ashraf*'s case on the point stating that although she signed the document, it did not amount to mutual agreement. Then, in *Igbo v Johnson Matthey Chemicals Ltd*,[11] the Court of Appeal overturned *Ashraf* stating that such a provision for automatic termination was void under s 203 because it has the effect of limiting the statutory right not to be unfairly dismissed. This more robust approach means that even if the employee signs such an agreement to be eligible for another benefit, it will have no effect for the purposes of determining whether the employee was dismissed or left through mutual agreement. Section 203 is used correctly to minimise the scope for imposed 'mutual agreement' to terminate an employment contract. This breathes new life into the statement of Donaldson J (as he then was) in *McAlwane v Boughton Estates Ltd*[12]

'it would be a very rare case, indeed, in which it could properly be found that the employer and the employee had got together ... and agreed mutually to terminate the contract, particularly when one realises the financial consequences to the employee involved in such an agreement'.

iii) Employee repudiation and self-dismissal

In a number of cases employers have convinced employment tribunals that certain repudiatory actions by employees could be viewed as 'self-

10   [1980] IRLR 185, EAT.
11   [1986] IRLR 215, CA.
12   [1973] ICR 470 at 473, NIRC.

dismissal' or 'constructive resignations' and hence not as dismissals under
s 95(1)(a).

For example where employees took part in a picket line around a
machine,[13] or called a staff meeting during working hours despite express
legislation to the contrary,[14] or refused employment in a less senior position
after being caught sleeping whilst on duty[15] employment tribunals and
the EAT have been prepared to treat their repudiations as terminating the
contract of employment.

These cases however were all decided under the assumption that
contracts of employment were an exception to the general rule of contract
law, that a repudiation itself does not amount to a termination until it is
accepted as such by the injured party. In *Rasool v Hepworth Pipe Co Ltd*[16]
the EAT, with Waterhouse J as chairman, suggested that such an approach
was incorrect because it ignored the fact that even where the employer
has repudiated the contract, it was necessary for the employer to elect to
treat the repudiation as discharging him from further performance of the
contract and in such a case it could not be said that it was the employee
who was terminating the contract.

Waterhouse J reasoned that according to the Court of Appeal in
Western Excavating Ltd v Sharp since termination in s 95(1)(c) referred to
the election of the employee to treat the employer's repudiation as a
termination, it followed that an election by the employers to treat a
repudiation as a discharge of further performance amounted to a
termination under s 95(1)(a).

And in *London Transport Executive v Clarke*[17] a majority of the Court
of Appeal made it clear that a contract of employment could not be
'automatically' terminated by a repudiation by the employee. The event
that determines the employment contract after a repudiation, as in the case
of contracts generally, is the other party's acceptance of that repudiation.
The majority of the court agreed that there could be no general exception
to that rule for employment contracts. Hence it was the employer's
acceptance of the repudiation that terminated the contract whether it takes
the form of a formal written notice or a refusal to call the employee to resume

13   *Gannon v J C Firth Ltd* [1976] IRLR 415, EAT.
14   *Johns and Bloomfield v Trust Houses Forte* [1975] IRLR 36; cf *Trust Houses
       Forte Ltd v Murphy* [1977] IRLR 186, EAT.
15   *Kallinos v London Electric Wire* [1980] IRLR 11, EAT; see also *Smith v Avana
       Bakeries Ltd* [1979] IRLR 423, EAT; see also *Trust House Forte Ltd v Murphy*
       [1977] IRLR 186, EAT.
16   [1980] ICR 494, [1980] IRLR 88, EAT.
17   [1981] ICR 355, [1981] IRLR 166, CA (Lord Denning MR dissenting).

work. As Dunn LJ commented, the previous EAT decisions to the contrary were incorrectly decided and would not be regarded as good law.

Thus far the Court of Appeal were simply reiterating the view of the majority of the Court of Appeal in *Gunton v Richmond-upon-Thames London Borough Council*.[18] Yet Dunn LJ went on to suggest that there might be an exception to the now firmly established general rule that contracts must be terminated by acceptance of repudiation and not by the repudiation itself. As Dunn put it:

'But there may be cases in which there has been no repudiation by the employee, and the employer has given notice of dismissal either in accordance with the terms of the contract or in breach of them: see *Gunton v Richmond-upon-Thames London Borough Council.* Such cases where the employee has no option but to accept the notice I would regard as an exception to the general rule as stated in the *Boston Deep Sea Fishing* case. To hold otherwise might, in some circumstances, enable the employer to take advantage of his own wrong where the employer gives notice within the statutory period after which an employee can claim compensation for unfair dismissal, although notice under the contract would have enabled him to do so. But considerations of that kind do not arise in this case and need not be decided.'

In the event, while the majority in the *Clarke* case may be said to have firmly rejected the concept of self-dismissal as proffered by Lord Denning, in his dissent, they did not completely extinguish the possibility that the view of Shaw LJ's dissent in *Gunton*'s case might not receive support in some future cases.

iv) Frustration versus dismissal

At common law if a contract is discharged by the operation of the doctrine of frustration, then the contract is regarded as terminated by the frustrating event rather than the action of the other party.

As it was described in *Marshall v Harland & Wolff Ltd*[19]

'the contract ceases to bind the parties if through no fault of either of them, unprovided for circumstances arise in which a contractual

---

18   [1981] Ch 448, [1980] ICR 755, CA.
19   [1972] ICR 101, [1972] IRLR 90, NIRC.

obligation becomes impossible of performance or in which performance of the obligation would be rendered a thing radically different than that which was undertaken by the contract'.

This opens the way for an employer to take a decision to end the employment relationship and not be regarded as dismissing the employee under s 95(1)(a).

In the employment context the doctrine of frustration has been applied to cases of (i) prolonged 'ill health', (ii) imprisonment and (iii) suspension or ending of an employee's qualification to perform work. Yet in all three instances, the courts have set certain limits to the applicability of the doctrine of frustration to employment contracts.

(a) Prolonged ill-health or frustration

In cases of prolonged ill-health both the NIRC and the EAT have spelt out the factors that employment tribunals should take into account in deciding whether an employee's illness had the effect of frustrating the contract of employment.

In *Marshall v Harland & Wolff Ltd*,[20] the NIRC stated:

'In considering the answer to this question, the Tribunal should take account of:—
(a) *The terms of the contract, including the provisions as to sickness pay* The whole basis of weekly employment may be destroyed more quickly than that of monthly employment and that in turn more quickly than annual employment. When the contract provides for sick pay, it is plain that the contract cannot be frustrated so long as the employee returns to work, or appears likely to return to work, within the period during which such sick pay is payable. But the converse is not necessarily true, for the right to sick pay may expire before the incapacity has gone on, or appears likely to go on, for so long as to make a return to work impossible or radically different from the obligations undertaken under the contract of employment.
(b) *How long the employment was likely to last in the absence of sickness* The relationship is less likely to survive if the employment was inherently temporary in its nature or for the

duration of a particular job, than if it was expected to be long term or even life long.

(c) *The nature of the employment* Where the employee is one of many in the same category, the relationship is more likely to survive the period of incapacity than if he occupies a key post which must be filled and filled on a permanent basis if his absence is prolonged.

(d) *The nature of the illness or injury and how long it has already continued and the prospects of recovery* The greater the degree of incapacity and the longer the period over which it has persisted and is likely to persist, the more likely it is that the relationship has been destroyed.

(e) *The period of past employment* A relationship which is of long standing is not so easily destroyed as one which has but a short history. This is good sense and, we think, no less good law, even if it involves some implied and scarcely detectable change in the contract of employment year by year as the duration of the relationship lengthens. The legal basis is that over a long period of service the parties must be assumed to have contemplated a longer period or periods of sickness than over a shorter period.

These factors are inter-related and cumulative, but are not necessarily exhaustive of those which have to be taken in to account'.

The question is and remains: was the employee's incapacity, looked at before the purported dismissal, of such a nature, or did it appear likely to continue for such a period, that further performance of his obligations in the future would either be impossible or would be a thing radically different from that undertaken by him and agreed to be accepted by the employer under the agreed terms of his employment?

Any other factors which bear upon this issue must also be considered.[1] Further, in *Egg Stores (Stamford Hill) Ltd v Leibovici*[2] the EAT proved willing to apply the doctrine of frustration along similar lines.

The EAT stated:

'It is possible to divide into two kinds the events relied upon as bringing about the frustration of a short term periodic contract of employment. There may be an event (eg a crippling accident) so dramatic and shattering that everyone concerned will realise

1   See eg *Harrison v George Wimpey & Co Ltd* (1972) 7 ITR 188, NIRC.
2   [1977] ICR 260, [1976] IRLR 376, EAT.

immediately that to all intents and purposes the contract must be regarded as at an end. Or there may be an event, such as illness or accident, the course and outcome of which is uncertain. It may be a long process before one is able to say whether the event is such as to bring about the frustration of the contract. But there *will* have been frustration of the contract, even though at the time of the event the outcome was uncertain, if the time arrives when, looking back, one can say that at some point (even if it is not possible to say precisely when) matters had gone on so long, and the prospects for the future were so poor, that it was no longer practical to regard the contract as still subsisting. Among the matters to be taken into account in such a case in reaching a decision are these:

(1)   the length of the previous employment;
(2)   how long it had been expected that the employment would continue;
(3)   the nature of the job;
(4)   the nature, length and effect of the illness or disabling event;
(5)   the need of the employer for the work to be done, and the need for a replacement to do it;
(6)   the risk to the employer of acquiring obligations in respect of redundancy payments or compensation for unfair dismissal to the replacement employee;
(7)   whether wages have continued to be paid;
(8)   the acts and the statements of the employer in relation to the employment, including the dismissal of, or failure to dismiss, the employee, and
(9)   whether in all the circumstances a reasonable employer could be expected to wait any longer'.

Yet there was evidence that the EAT was becoming concerned about the way that the doctrine of frustration could be used as a device to deprive employment tribunals of jurisdiction.

Thus, in *Harman v Flexible Lamps Ltd*,[3] the EAT suggested that the doctrine of frustration may not be applicable in ill-health cases. In that case, the employee was off work due to illness for a total of 13 weeks in 1978, and for 5 weeks in 1979. She returned to work but was away for most of March and April. The company wrote to the employee paying a week's wages in lieu of notice and saying that they would assume that she had

3   [1980] IRLR 418, EAT; see also *Converform (Darwen) Ltd v Bell* [1981] IRLR 195, EAT.

left their employ. The EAT held that this was not a case of frustration, but went on to say

> 'This contract was in any case terminable at a week's notice, and once the employer decided that the ill health of Miss Harman made it necessary to replace her, nothing was easier than to give her notice determining her job and to employ and train a replacement. In the employment field the concept of discharge by operation of law, that is frustration, is normally only in play where the contract of employment is for a long term which cannot be determined by notice. Where the contract is terminable by notice, there is really no need to consider the question of frustration and if it were the law that, in circumstances such as are before us in this case, an employer was in a position to say "this contract has been frustrated", then that would be a very convenient way in which to avoid the provisions of the Employment Protection (Consolidation) Act. In our judgment, that is not the law in these sort of circumstances'.

Nevertheless, as long as the definition of dismissal under s 95(1)(a) is based on contractual criteria it is difficult to imagine that the EAT can entirely preclude the doctrine of frustration from applying to extreme cases of prolonged ill-health. Whilst an employer who dismisses an employee as in *Harman*'s case[4] may find it difficult to argue that the contract was terminated by the doctrine of frustration, when an employee is not allowed to return to work after illness because his place has been filled as in *Hart v A R Marshall & Sons (Bulwell) Ltd*,[5] an employment tribunal may find and the EAT may be compelled to accept that the contract has been frustrated.

(b) Imprisonment as a frustrating event

Whether and when the absence of an employee owing to a sentence of imprisonment can be a frustrating event has also been a contentious issue in the case law. On the one hand despite the element of fault by the employee there has been some support for the view that a prison sentence of substantial length could frustrate an employment contract at the date of

---

4   [1980] IRLR 418, EAT.
5   [1978] 2 All ER 413, [1977] ICR 539, EAT.

sentencing.[6] Yet in *Chakki v United Yeast Co Ltd*[7] the EAT made it plain that a sentence of imprisonment is not an automatically frustrating event. In that case, an employee was sentenced to 11 months' imprisonment but was released on bail after only one day in prison. He later succeeded on appeal on being placed on probation.

The employer had immediately hired another replacement despite the employee's day in prison coinciding with the first of fourteen days' annual holiday. The EAT overturned an employment tribunal decision that the prison sentence frustrated the employment contract because it was an error of law in these circumstances to hold that the contract was immediately frustrated.

As the EAT put it

'We have therefore come to the conclusion that in this case the question of frustration has to be decided by finding the answers to the following questions. (1) Looking at the matter from a practical commercial point of view, when was it necessary for the respondents to decide as to the appellant's future and as to whether a replacement driver would have to be engaged? (2) At the time when the decision had to be taken, what would a reasonable employer have considered to be the likely length of the appellant's absence over the next few months? (3) If in the light of the appellant's likely absence it appeared necessary to engage a replacement, was it reasonable to engage a permanent replacement rather than a temporary one?'

Chakki's case was remitted to the employment tribunal to decide the issue of frustration on the basis of those questions.

The applicability of the doctrine of frustration to contracts of employment was further limited by the decision of the House of Lords in *Tarnesby v Kensington and Chelsea and Westminster Area Health Authority*.[8] In that case a consultant found guilty of professional misconduct was initially struck from the medical register. That decision was later changed to suspension for 12 months. The House of Lords rejected the argument that the contract had been frustrated, reasoning that the inability of the employee to perform his contractual duties for 12 months was not sufficient to frustrate the contract at common law. Lord Lowry

---

6   See remarks by Lord Denning in *Hare v Murphy Bros Ltd* [1974] 3 All ER 940, [1974] ICR 603, CA; see also *Harrington v Kent County Council* [1980] IRLR 353, EAT.

7   [1982] 2 All ER 446, [1982] ICR 140.

8   [1981] ICR 615, [1981] IRLR 369, HL.

also suggested that 'suspension from the register was not an unforeseen or unprovided for event brought about by legislation or otherwise but ... was a contemplated misfortune, the effect of which was clearly preordained ...'.

Moreover the fact that imprisonment often occurs as a result of the fault of the individual has more recently been applied to limit the applicability of the doctrine of frustration. Thus in *Norris v Southampton City Council*[9] the EAT made it plain that following the decision of the Court of Appeal in *London Transport Executive v Clarke*,[10]

'that on the state of the law in the light of existing authorities, where a man by his own conduct made it impossible for him to perform the contract it is not frustration, it is not discharge, it is not a dismissal of himself by himself, but is repudiatory conduct which entitles the employer to treat it as a repudiation and to dismiss him. The distinction between frustration and dismissal for breach of contract is of critical importance because if it is a case of frustration there is no dismissal. In the context of inability to perform the contract of employment there are two types of cases which generally arise. One is where the employee is prevented by illness or accident from doing the work required of him .The other is where the contract cannot be performed as a result of the employee's own conduct, as for example by deliberately absenting himself or committing some offence which results in his imprisonment. In the first type of case it is not the fault of the employee which leads to inability; in the second type of case it is. Frustration can only arise where there is no fault by either party: see *Maritime National Fish Ltd v Ocean Trawlers* [1935] AC 524. Thus accident or illness is a case where frustration arises because there is no fault. Where, however, there is fault as in the case of deliberate conduct which leads to impossibility of performance, then it is not a case of frustration but of repudiatory conduct: see *Joseph Constantine Steamship Line Ltd v Imperial Smelting Corpn Ltd* [1942] AC 154. It is appropriate to observe that Lord Denning MR has never accepted this view of the law. Not only did he express disagreement in the case of *London Transport Executive v Clarke* (supra) but he did so also in *Hare v Murphy Bros* [1974] IRLR 342 where his final conclusion was that in cases where impossibility

---

9   [1982] ICR 177, [1982] IRLR 141, EAT. Cf *Kingston v British Railways Board* [1982] ICR 392, [1982] IRLR 274, EAT.

10   [1981] ICR 355, [1981] IRLR 166, CA.

results from fault it leads to frustration. He now says it is self-dismissal'.[11]

Yet if recent cases have somewhat limited the applicability of the doctrine of frustration to termination of employment contracts, they have not entirely eliminated it.

2. CONSTRUCTIVE DISMISSALS: JUSTIFIED TERMINATION BY THE EMPLOYEE

As mentioned, even before the 1974 Act introduced an explicit constructive dismissal test (now ERA, s 95(1)(c)) an employer could inadvertently dismiss an employee by contractually repudiatory conduct under the predecessor of ERA, s 95(1)(a). For where an employer's action was a breach of contract sufficiently serious to amount to a repudiation of the contract at common law, it was regarded as terminating the contract, despite the fact that at common law a repudiation amounted to a termination only where it was 'accepted' by the other party.

Under sub-section (a) there were in fact two well-established types of repudiatory conduct. First, there was a repudiation by the employer, consisting of a breach of his or her essential positive contractual obligations. Thus, in *Marriott v Oxford and District Co-operative Society Ltd (No 2)*[12] an employer wrote a letter to the employee informing him that he was to be downgraded from supervisor to lower status and that his wages were to be reduced by £1 a week. Lord Denning analysed the legal effect of the letter in the following way.

'Seeing that the letter was not an offer, the next question is: was it a termination of the contract of employment by the employer within the meaning of s 3(1)(a) of the Act? I think it was. This letter in effect told the man: "We are not going to perform our existing contract with you. We are going to reduce your grading to a foreman, and we are going to pay you £1 a week less, whether you like it or not." That statement was a breach of contract. If Mr Marriott had accepted the repudiation and said "I will not agree to this reduction in my wages" and left at the end of the week, the contract would clearly have been terminated by the employer.'

11   See also *R v Powys County Council, ex p Smith* (1982) 81 LGR 342.
12   [1970] 1 QB 186, [1969] 3 All ER 1126, CA.

Secondly, there was a repudiation when the employer unjustifiably insisted that the employee do something that he or she was not contractually bound to do. As Sir John Donaldson put it in *Sutcliffe v Hawker Siddeley Aviation Ltd*[13] where an employer places an employee in a position where, by virtue of unjustified insistence that he or she must perform non-contractual work, and the employee has no option but to tender notice, the reality is, and the finding of the court or tribunal ought to be, that the employee is dismissed.

Since the *Western Excavating* case, however, it has been convenient to ignore altogether the employer repudiation element in s 95(1)(a) and treat that sub-section as limited to cases where the employer has clearly terminated, usually by stating to the employee that he wishes the contract to be at an end. This lays to rest, at least as far as that sub-section is concerned,[14] the rather contentious point that the Court of Appeal for a while reviewed the repudiation as a terminating event despite the need under contract law to look for an acceptance by the other party to turn a repudiation into a termination. As Lord Denning remarked in the *Western Excavating* case,[15] 'Marriott was not really an (a) case'. The court had to 'stretch it a bit' to fit under that sub-section. Since the amendment to s 95, Lord Denning acknowledged 'it would have been more properly brought under (c)'.

Hence in all situations today where the employee leaves in response to the employer's allegedly repudiatory conduct he or she will rely on ERA, s 95(1)(c). That sub-section was introduced to avoid the possibility that employers might attempt to circumvent the statutory protection by pressurising an employee to resign. It has been interpreted, however, to limit the kind of pressure by the employer that entitles an employee to resign solely to conduct which is contractually repudiatory. ERA, s 95(1)(c) states that an employee's resignation must take place in circumstances in which he is entitled to resign without notice by reason of the employer's conduct. Whilst the resignation itself may be with or without notice, the circumstances must be such as to justify a resignation without notice. By its terms, therefore, it appears to presuppose contractually repudiatory conduct by the employer since at common law only a wrongful repudiation entitles an employee to resign without notice.

---

13   [1973] ICR 560, [1973] IRLR 304, NIRC.
14   The issue may still be alive when determining the effective date of termination (see Chapter 2) or whether the employee has repudiated the contract.
15   [1978] IRLR 27 at 29.

In the *Western Excavating* case, Lawton LJ stated that the words 'entitled' to terminate the contract of employment 'without notice' in the statute are 'the language of contract; language which has a significant meaning in law in that it confers a right on an employee to be released from his contract and extinguishes the right of the employer to hold the employee to it'.[16] Lord Denning added that, 'the words of subsection (c) express a legal concept that is well settled under the rubric. Discharge by Breach. If the employer is guilty of conduct which is a significant breach going to the root of the contract of employment or which shows that the employer no longer intends to be bound by one or more of the essential terms of the contract then the employee is entitled to treat himself as discharged from any further performance of the contract'.[17] The Court of Appeal in the *Western Excavating* case thus made it quite clear that s 95(1)(c) provides essentially a contractual test and not a 'reasonableness' test of constructive dismissal. It pointed out that the latter approach which had been suggested by the EAT at one stage,[18] was an incorrect reading of the statute.

What was somewhat less clear from the *Western Excavating* case, however, was the precise nature of the principles which were to be applied by employment tribunals to unreasonable conduct by the employer to determine whether or not it constituted a contractual repudiation. Lord Denning suggested two separate tests of conduct evincing an intention not to be bound by the contract. One test was whether the acts by the employer were in breach of a *particular implied fundamental term*, that is to say that the employer failed to perform one of the essential terms of the contract. The second test of repudiation was one where the employer was guilty of conduct which was 'a significant breach going to the root of the contract of employment'. This appeared to make reference to a doctrine in the general law of contract of *fundamental breach*; a breach which was defined as depriving the employee of the substantial benefit of the contract even though it did not constitute a breach of a particular fundamental term of the contract.[19]

16   Ibid at 30.
17   Ibid at 29.
18   See eg *Gilbert v I Goldstone Ltd* [1977] 1 All ER 423, [1976] IRLR 257, EAT, *Logabax Ltd v Titherley* [1977] ICR 369, [1977] IRLR 97, EAT.
19   *Hong Kong Fir Shipping Co Ltd v Kawasaki Kisen Kaisha Ltd* [1962] 2 QB 26, [1962] 1 All ER 474; *The Mihalis Angelos* [1971] 1 QB 164, [1970] 3 All ER 125; *Cehave NV v Bremer Handelsgesellschaft mbH, The Hansa Nord* [1976] QB 44, [1975] 3 All ER 739, CA.

Lawton LJ was unwilling to provide any specific legal test. He asserted that lay members of employment tribunals would have little difficulty in recognising the kind of employer of whom an employee is entitled without notice to rid himself. It was unclear whether this suggested a third category of repudiation, ie abusive treatment or intolerable conduct by the employer, which would make a continuation of the contract impossible for the employee, or was simply an indication that there was sufficient room in traditional contractual repudiation categories for abusive treatment or intolerable conduct by the employer. For example Lawton LJ's own example of 'the persistent and unwanted amorous advances by an employer to a female member of the staff' could be classified as either an extreme example of repudiatory breach because the employer's conduct made further performance by the employee impossible or a breach of an implied obligation of employers not to destroy or seriously damage the mutual trust and confidence between employer and employee.

In any case, of course, under sub-section (c) the circumstances which justify resignation must also include the circumstances of the response of the employee to the employer's conduct. As it was stated in *Garner v Grange Furnishing Ltd*[20] the general view of the EAT is that the conduct of both parties has to be looked at when assessing whether or not the employer's conduct was such that the employee was entitled to rely on s 95(1)(c). This applies to both the timing and the manner of the employee's departure. For example, an employee must be careful not to leave his employment prematurely, that is, before the employer has actually committed a repudiation. Moreover, the employee must not stay on in circumstances which may imply that he has agreed to an otherwise repudiatory change or that he was waived his right to end the contract. As Lord Denning stated in the *Western Excavating* case '... the employee must make up his mind soon after the conduct of which he complained. If he continues for any length of time without leaving, he will be regarded as having elected to *affirm* the contract and will lose the right to treat himself as discharged and say that he was forced to go'.[1]

Despite the considerable degree of legal technicality and complexity inherent in the concept of repudiation, the Court of Appeal has determined that employment tribunals are to decide whether or not the employer's conduct amounted to a repudiation as a question of fact rather than one of

---

20   [1977] IRLR 206, EAT.
1   [1978] IRLR 27 at 29, CA. See also *W E Cox Toner (International) Ltd v Crook* [1981] ICR 823, [1981] IRLR 443, EAT.

law. As Lord Denning expressed it in *Woods v W M Car Services (Peterborough) Ltd*:[2]

> 'The circumstances (of constructive dismissal) are so infinitely various that there can be and is no rule of law saying what circumstances justify and what do not. It is a question of fact for the tribunal of fact – in this case the Industrial Tribunal'.

Thus as long as employment tribunals do not misdirect themselves in law, the basis for appeal to the EAT will be limited to perversity.[3]

As Lord Denning stated in *Woods'* case:

> '... I think that the Employment Appeal Tribunal in these cases of constructive dismissal should only interfere with the decision of the Industrial Tribunal if it is shown that (i) the Industrial Tribunal misdirected itself in law, or (ii) the decision was such that no reasonable Industrial Tribunal could reach it. The Employment Appeal Tribunal ought not to interfere merely because it thinks that upon those facts, it would not or might not itself have reached the same conclusion, for to do that would be for the Appeal Tribunal to usurp what is the sole function of the tribunal of fact'.[4]

Yet whether the Court of Appeal chooses to label the issue one of fact or one of law, the fact to be found, ie repudiation, is undoubtedly far more an admixture of law and fact than would have been a reasonableness test. As Arnold J (as he then was) remarked in *Courtaulds Northern Textiles Ltd v Andrew*:[5]

> 'Now it is of course true, applying the Court of Appeal's test, that in order to decide that the conduct is sufficient repudiatory to justify a conclusion of constructive dismissal one has to consider whether the conduct complained of constitutes either a fundamental breach of the contract or a breach of a fundamental term of the contract: two somewhat elusive conceptions which figure in our modern contract law'.

Employment tribunals must not misdirect themselves in law upon the relevant principles of repudiation (in particular the difference between

---

2   [1982] ICR 693, [1982] IRLR 413, CA.
3   See eg *W E Cox Toner (International) Ltd v Crook* [1982] ICR 823, [1981] IRLR 443, EAT.
4   [1982] IRLR 413 at 415.
5   [1979] IRLR 84, EAT.

breach and repudiation) and the difference between 'acceptance' of the repudiation and affirmation of the contract by the employee.[6]

The Court of Appeal has rather optimistically viewed the wide discretion given to employment tribunals over the question of repudiation.

As Lawton LJ put it in the *Western Excavating* case:

> '... for the chairman of an Industrial Tribunal in such a case to discuss with his lay members whether there had been a repudiation or a breach of a fundamental term by the employer would be for most lay members a waste of legal learning. There may occasionally be border-line cases which would require a chairman to analyse the legal principles applicable for the benefit of the lay members; but when such cases do occur he should try to do so in the kind of language which 19th century judges used when directing juries about the law applicable to contracts of employment, rather than the language which nowadays would be understood and appreciated by academic lawyers. I appreciate that the principles of law applicable to the termination by an employee of a contract of employment because of his employer's conduct are difficult to put concisely in the language judges used in Court. Lay members of Industrial Tribunals however, do not spend all their time in Court and when out of Court they may use, and certainly will hear, short words and terse phrases which describe clearly the kind of employer of whom an employee is entitled without notice to rid himself. This is what [s 95(1)(c)] is all about; and what is required for the application of this provision is a large measure of common sense'.

Nevertheless, to understand the concept that must be applied by tribunals it is necessary to consider a fairly extensive body of case law in some detail. The case law can usefully be grouped under the following three heads.

(i)   contractual repudiation by the employer: the traditional categories;
(ii) intolerable and abusive treatment by the employer: the new implied terms of mutual trust and confidence;
(iii) the circumstances of the employee's response.

---

6   See eg *W E Cox Toner (International) Ltd v Crook* (above).

i) Contractual repudiation by the employer: traditional categories

As mentioned repudiatory conduct by an employer has traditionally included two well-established types of conduct:

(a) In the first place an employer may unilaterally break an essential positive obligation owed by him to his employee under the contract, whether the obligation was express or implied. For example, an employer may withdraw an existing contractual right such as free transport, or fail to meet a contractual obligation such as the payment of wages. The essence of this type of repudiation is that the employer has failed to perform a positive contractual obligation and the employee is presented with a fait accompli.

(b) Secondly, an employer may insist that the employee agree to a change in existing working arrangements or terms and conditions of employment, or insist that the employee perform an act which he is not contractually obliged to do. In either case the employer is in effect renouncing the contract and his unjustified insistence on the change or act could constitute a repudiation of the contract.

(a) A failure to perform a positive contractual obligation

In all employment contracts, given their general purpose, there is an implication that an employer has certain essential obligations, viz to pay the contractually agreed remuneration, to provide contractually agreed work, to provide a safe system of work, etc.[7] Some contracts, given their particular nature, may expressly or by implication have other vital terms. For example, the contract of employment of a supervisor may have an implied term that the employer will not act in such a way as to undermine the supervisor's authority with his subordinate,[8] or a contract of employment of an employee may contain a vital term to the effect that the employer must provide free transport.[9] Where employers fail to meet an essential contractual obligation, whether special or common, they commit

---

7   There are also other implied obligations which apply to all contracts of employment: the implied obligation of mutual trust and confidence. See discussion of these implied terms in part II.

8   *Associated Tyre Specialists (Eastern) Ltd v Waterhouse* [1976] IRLR 386, EAT, *Wetherall (Bond Street W1) Ltd v Lynn* [1977] IRLR 333, EAT.

9   *Durrant and Cheshire v Clariston Clothing Co Ltd* [1974] IRLR 360, IT.

a serious breach of contract entitling employees to treat themselves as having been dismissed. Let us consider three well-established categories of essential obligations for most, if not all, employment contracts:

[i] THE OBLIGATION TO PAY CONTRACTUALLY AGREED REMUNERATION.
An employer's duty to pay agreed remuneration is a fundamental obligation under the contract of employment. A failure to pay agreed wages, at the customary time[10] or at all for any substantial period, or a unilateral reduction in the basic rate of pay, could be a sufficiently serious breach to amount to repudiation.

For example, in *R F Hill Ltd v Mooney*[11] a salesman employed on a contract stipulating a salary plus 1% commission on sales was forced to accept a change in the system of commission whereby it would be paid only for sales over a target figure. The EAT upheld the employment tribunal's decision that there was a constructive dismissal because the employer had failed to perform his obligation to pay remuneration by fundamentally altering the formula whereby the wages were calculated. The failure by the employer must be of 'sufficient materiality'. A failure caused by temporary cash flow difficulties is not enough. There must be an intention no longer to honour the existing contractual obligation.[12]

The principles that apply to the employer's duty to pay agreed remuneration also extend to other elements of pay and fringe benefits as long as they are contractual obligations; for example, commission or bonuses,[13] overtime pay,[14] the pay rate as opposed to earnings,[15] the use of company cars,[16] free transport,[17] or holiday pay or sick pay,[18] and the

10   *Adams v Charles Zub Associates Ltd* [1978] IRLR 551, EAT.
11   [1981] IRLR 258, EAT.
12   See also *Gillies v Richard Daniels & Co Ltd* [1979] IRLR 457, EAT; *Adams v Charles Zub Associates Ltd* [1978] IRLR 551, EAT; *Reid v Camphill Engravers* [1990] IRLR 268, EAT.
13   See eg *Logabax Ltd v Titherley* [1977] ICR 369, [1977] IRLR 97, EAT.
14   *Stokes v Hampstead Wine Co Ltd* [1979] IRLR 298, EAT.
15   See eg *Scott v Formica Ltd* [1975] IRLR 104, IT where the transfer of an employee to a new shift with a 3½ pence reduction in the hourly pay rate was held to be a repudiatory breach even though the shift allowance compensated for the lower hourly rate.
16   *Ramage v Harper-Mackay Ltd* [1966] ITR 503, IT; see also *Wain v Henry Wigfall & Son plc* (1983) EAT 267/83.
17   *Durrant and Cheshire v Clariston Clothing Co Ltd* [1974] IRLR 360, IT; *Chapman v Goonvean and Rostowrack China Clay Co Ltd* [1973] 2 All ER 1063, [1973] 1 WLR 678, CA.
18   Whether a contract provides a right to payment during illness over and above

failure to meet any such obligation could amount to a repudiation entitling an employee to terminate their contract.

The employer's basic obligation to pay agreed remuneration, moreover, may be repudiated by personnel practices which may not commonly be regarded as having this legal effect. For example, in *D & J McKenzie Ltd v Smith*[19] an employee 'suspended' for 2 or 3 weeks without pay because of a reduction in work was held to have been 'dismissed' because there was no term in the contract giving the employer the power to suspend without pay.[20] Moreover, where an employer lays off an employee without pay and has no contractual authority to do so, this may amount to a repudiatory act.[1] Furthermore, closures of workplaces whether temporary[2] or permanent[3] have also been held to amount to contractual repudiations.

In all such cases, the failure to pay wages must be a failure to pay in circumstances in which wages are contractually required. If an employer is entitled under the contract to lay off or suspend without pay for disciplinary reasons, a failure to pay wages is not a breach of contract, let alone a repudiatory breach. For example, in *White v Reflecting Roadstuds Ltd*, an employee who resigned in response to a transfer to a lower-paid job

---

statutory sick pay is sometimes a difficult question to decide. In *Mears v Safecar Security Ltd* [1981] IRLR 99, EAT it was suggested that where the contract was silent on the issue, the implication of a term governing sick pay will depend upon such factors as the knowledge of the parties at the time the contract was made, whether the employment was daily, indefinite or for a fixed term of years, and on occasion what the parties actually did during the contractual period. This effectively overruled the suggestion in *Orman v Saville Sportswear Ltd* [1960] 3 All ER 105, [1960] 1 WLR 1055 of a presumption in favour of a continued obligation on the part of the employer to continue paying as long as the contract was not determined by proper notice. See, too, *Howman & Son v Blyth* [1983] ICR 416, [1983] IRLR 139, EAT, in which it was found that the normal practice of the industry was to provide sick pay for a limited period only. A term can be implied in fact by a notice on the company notice board. See eg *Petrie v MacFisheries Ltd* [1940] 1 KB 258, [1939] 4 All ER 281. The contents of the written statement issued by the employer under EPCA, s 1 would be evidence of the employer's obligation.

19   [1976] IRLR 345, Ct of Sess.

20   See too ibid. See also *Burroughs Machines Ltd v Timmoney* [1976] IRLR 343, 11 ITR 173, EAT upheld on this point by Court of Session [1977] IRLR 404, Ct of Sess.

1   See *Jewell v Neptune Concrete Ltd* [1975] IRLR 147, EAT; *Johnson v Cross* [1977] ICR 872, EAT. *Waine v R Oliver (Plant Hire) Ltd* [1977] IRLR 434, EAT. But see *Kenneth MacRae & Co Ltd v Dawson* [1984] IRLR 5, EAT.

2   *Sheather v South East Kent Health District* (1976) EAT 423/76.

3   *Sanders v Ernest A Neale Ltd* [1974] 3 All ER 327, [1974] IRLR 236, NIRC.

category which was permitted under contract was held to have no claim of constructive dismissal.[4] In *Jones v British Rail Hovercraft Ltd*,[5] an indefinite suspension without pay pending the results of a police investigation was permitted by the rule book and hence did not amount to a dismissal. And in *Theedom v British Railways Board*,[6] a demotion of an employee to a lower position with a reduction in earnings of £35 per week for a disciplinary offence did not amount to a repudiation because the right to demote for disciplinary offences was an implied term of the contract. Similarly a failure to include an employee in a salary review[7] or a failure to provide opportunities for overtime pay,[8] where neither obligations were contractually required, have not been considered to amount to repudiation.[9]

In all such cases, moreover the breach must be sufficiently serious to amount to a repudiation. Thus a failure to pay salary on the due date would have to be more than a mistake and amount to a showing that the employer does not intend thereafter to honour the contract.[10] Furthermore while a unilateral reduction in the basic rate of pay even for good reasons and to a relatively small extent can amount to a material breach of the contract of employment,[11] there is still a test of degree.[12]

[II]   THE EMPLOYER'S OBLIGATION TO PROVIDE WORK TO DO.

The employer's obligation to ensure that employees receive contractually agreed remuneration sometimes creates an ancillary obligation to provide work in order to ascertain the remuneration, as in cases of commission, piecework, etc.[13] To what extent, however, is an employer obliged to provide an employee with work even where he otherwise meets his duty to pay the contractually agreed remuneration?

4   [1991] ICR 733, [1991] IRLR 347, EAT.
5   [1974] IRLR 279, IT.
6   [1976] IRLR 137, IT.
7   *Spencer v Alistair McCowan & Associates* [1975] IRLR 34, IT. See too *Murco Petroleum Ltd v Forge* [1987] IRLR 50, EAT.
8   Eg *Byrne v Lakers (Sanitation and Heating) Ltd* (1968) 3 ITR 105.
9   Cf *G Priestner Ltd v Frederick* (1977) EAT 612/76, where a failure by an employer to live up to a promise to use every endeavour to avoid a fall in pay in a new job was not necessarily enough to justify resignation.
10   *Adams v Charles Zub Associates Ltd* [1978] IRLR 551, EAT.
11   *Industrial Rubber Products v Gillon* [1977] IRLR 389, 13 ITR 100, EAT; *Johnson v Cross* [1977] ICR 872, EAT.
12   *Gillies v Richard Daniels & Co Ltd* [1979] IRLR 457, EAT. See also *Spafax Ltd v Harrison* [1980] IRLR 442, CA.
13   See eg *Devonald v Rosser & Sons* [1906] 2 KB 728, CA.

At common law, the general rule was that the employer's duty was to pay wages and not to provide the employee with work to do as well. As was said by Asquith J in *Collier v Sunday Referee Publishing Co Ltd*,[14] the contract of employment does not necessarily, or perhaps normally, oblige the master to provide the servant with work. 'Provided I pay my cook her wages regularly, she cannot complain if I choose to take any or all of my meals out'.

Yet in certain exceptional cases where the nature of the employee's work requires actual work as well as wages to meet the employer's obligations and employee's interests it has been held that there is a positive duty to provide work. Thus, the need of entertainers for publicity,[15] the need of skilled workers to work so as to maintain their skills, the need to preserve contacts and reputation in a trade or profession[16] and the need of apprentices for work[17] have all given rise to a positive obligation to provide the employee with work.[18]

In *Langston v Amalgamated Union of Engineering Workers*,[19] Lord Denning MR suggested that the common law position outlined by Asquith J in the *Collier* case might be changing; 'That was said thirty-three years ago. Things have altered much since then. To my mind, it is arguable that in these days a man has, by reason of an implication in the contract, a right to work. That is he has a right to have the opportunity of doing his work when it is there to be done'.

In *Breach v Epsylon Industries Ltd*,[20] moreover, the EAT reversed an employment tribunal which had appeared to have regarded *Turner v Sawdon & Co*[1] as authority for a general principle of law that employers were under no obligation to provide their employees with work to do. The EAT's view was that it was necessary for the employment tribunal to look to the circumstances of the case to decide whether, owing to the nature of the employment, a term should be implied to the effect that there was an obligation on the employer to provide work suitable for the employee in

14   [1940] 2 KB 647.
15   See eg *Marbé v George Edwardes (Daly's Theatre) Ltd* [1928] 1 KB 269; *Herbert Clayton & Jack Waller Ltd v Oliver* [1930] AC 209.
16   Eg *Hall v British Essence Co Ltd* (1946) 62 TLR 542; *Collier v Sunday Referee Publishing Co Ltd* [1940] 2 KB 647.
17   *Titmus and Titmus v Rose and Watts* [1940] 1 All ER 599; see also *Dunk v George Waller & Son Ltd* [1970] 2 QB 163, [1970] 2 All ER 630, CA.
18   *William Hill Organisation v Tucker* [1998] IRLR 313, CA.
19   [1974] 1 All ER 980, [1974] IRLR 15, CA.
20   [1976] ICR 316, [1976] IRLR 180, EAT.
1   [1901] 2 KB 653.

the position he held. Thus, in *Bosworth v Angus Jowett & Co Ltd,*[2] an obligation to provide work was implied in a sales director's contract under the criterion in *Breach*'s case to entitle the employee to work during the remainder of his fixed-term contract. Yet such cases appear to be authority for the proposition that certain types of employment give rise to an obligation to provide work rather than more general support for Lord Denning's assertion in *Langston*'s case.

Furthermore, underemployment of an employee on certain duties contained within his job description may not necessarily amount to a repudiation,[3] particularly where there is no contractual entitlement to exercising particular duties at a particular time. Where however an important element of the job is completely destroyed by the employer's action this could properly be treated as a repudiation.[4]

[III]   THE EMPLOYER'S OBLIGATION TO PROVIDE SAFE WORK.

Under the contract of employment there is a general implied duty of employers to take reasonable care for the safety of their employees. This duty includes a positive duty to organize work into a safe system as well as to provide a working environment which is suitably safe for the performance of contractual duties. This duty includes an obligation not to place employees in a position of exposure of an excessive physical risk or risk of stress or injury to mental health owing to excessive hours or workload. Under certain circumstances a failure to perform this obligation may be repudiatory. In *Graham Oxley Tool Steels Ltd v Firth*[5] the fact that employers left an employee working for several months in intolerably cold conditions was a breach of their implied contractual obligation to provide a proper working environment. Moreover, in *Waltons & Morse v Dorrington*[6] a non-smoker was entitled to resign and claim constructive dismissal when the employer failed to deal adequately with her complaints about exposure to the cigarette smoke of fellow employees. Further, in *Walker v Northumberland County Council*[7] a social worker was successful in a claim of negligence against his employers for a nervous

2   [1977] IRLR 374, EAT.
3   See eg *Peter Carnie & Son Ltd v Paton* [1979] IRLR 260, EAT; *Hemmings v International Computers Ltd* [1976] IRLR 37, IT.
4   *Ford v Milthorn Toleman Ltd* [1980] IRLR 30, CA; *Marconi Radar Systems Ltd v Bennett* (1982) EAT 793/82.
5   [1980] IRLR 135, EAT.
6   [1997] IRLR 488, EAT.
7   [1995] 1 All ER 737, [1995] IRLR 35.

breakdown suffered owing to the steadily increased workload and the failure of the employer to bring in help which had been promised. Finally, in *Johnstone v Bloomsbury Health Authority*[8] a doctor whose contract required him to work 40 hours per week and remain on call for another 48 hours claimed that the employer was in breach of its contractual duty to take reasonable care for the health and safety of the employee. The majority of the Court of Appeal held that whatever the express obligation, the employer was under an overriding implied obligation to take reasonable care not to injure the employee's health and safety.

Furthermore as the EAT put it in *British Aircraft Corpn Ltd v Austin*,[9] as part and parcel of the employer's duty to take reasonable care for the safety of their employees, they are also under an obligation to act reasonably in dealing with matters of safety or complaints about lack of safety which *are drawn to their attention by employees*. For example in the *British Aircraft Corpn* case, an employer's failure to investigate an employee's complaint about the inadequacy of protective eyewear made available to her was conduct entitling the employee to resign without notice. Further, in *Pagano v HGS*[10] the employer's failure to maintain vehicles in a roadworthy state in spite of numerous complaints by the employee about the state of the vehicles amounted to a contractual repudiation.

Yet it was also stated in the *Graham Oxley Tool Steels* case that there was no principle that a breach of a statutory duty under the Factories Act or a breach of the common law duty to take reasonable care for the safety of his work people by providing them with a safe system of work and proper plant and materials *by itself* results in a fundamental breach of contract by the employer.[11] What is necessary is to look at the contractual obligation to decide whether these have been a breach and whether the breach indicates an intention no longer to be bound by that contractual obligation.

The test of whether the employer's care was 'reasonable' clearly requires weighing the magnitude of the risks of injury which are reasonably foreseeable, the seriousness of the consequences to employees and the cost and practicability of preventing the risk given the resources of the employer and purpose of the employer's activity.[12] In one case it has been suggested that a band of reasonable employer responses could be applied

8   [1991] ICR 269, [1991] IRLR 118, CA.
9   [1978] IRLR 332, EAT.
10   [1976] IRLR 9, EAT.
11   [1980] IRLR 135, EAT.
12   See eg *Walker v Northumberland County Council* above.

to the test of fundamental breach of duty of care.[13] However it seems difficult to justify importing a method of statutory interpretation into what is an essentially a contractual test.

(b) Unjustified insistence, express contractual authority and the implied term of mutual trust and confidence

A second type of repudiatory act by the employer consists of an unjustified insistence upon a change in the nature of the employee's contractual performance or obligations such as the kind of work he can be required to perform, the hours of work he can be required to do, and the place at which he can be required to do the work. Commonly, this type of repudiation consists of an unjustified demotion, downgrading or transfer either in connection with a company re-organisation or disciplinary action.

There are two main issues that must be considered to establish constructive dismissal.

(i)   Did the employer have contractual authority for his insistence on the change? If so, the employer may simply be giving the employee a lawful instruction to perform the contract and the alternative to non-performance is resignation, which does not amount to constructive dismissal.[14] Yet care must be taken in assessing contractual authority. There are cases where the employer's *express* contractual authority has been limited by the implied term of mutual trust and confidence.

(ii)   If the change lies outside the contractual authority of the employer, insistence to the point of forcing a resignation may well be repudiatory. Yet there are two further issues to consider. First, was the change insisted upon a serious enough change to warrant the conclusion that the employer's insistence was repudiatory? Second, at the time the employee resigned, had the employer in fact insisted on the change to the point where the employee had no option but to resign? Had the employee in effect been told 'perform this non-contractual act or resign'? or had the employee jumped the gun and resigned too early?[15]

[i]   DID THE EMPLOYER HAVE CONTRACTUAL AUTHORITY FOR THE CHANGE?
The starting point for an analysis of an alleged unjustified insistence upon a change in the nature of an employee's contractual performance is whether

13   *Dutton & Clark Ltd v Daly* [1985] IRLR 363, EAT.
14   See eg *Spafax Ltd v Harrison* [1980] IRLR 442, CA.
15   See discussion in part III, below.

the employer was contractually entitled to insist on the change. In so far as the contract stipulates, expressly or *by implication*, such terms as the type of work to be performed, the place of work and the hours of work, an employer is entitled to insist that an employee obey his instructions to do a particular type of work, at a particular place for a particular number of hours, always assuming that his instructions are not otherwise unlawful, or involve a clear risk of personal safety,[16] or are of unclear authority. However, if an employer instructs an employee to perform a particular type of work, at a particular place, or during particular hours which are not part of the employee's contractual obligations, the employer has exceeded his contractual authority, and his insistence upon the employee performing the act or agreeing to a change in the terms of the contract to the point of resignation may constitute a repudiation.

For example, in *Ellis v Brighton Co-operative Society Ltd*, the employers had re-organised the working arrangements for delivering milk and this entailed a change in working hours for Mr Ellis from 48 to 58 hours per week.When Mr Ellis refused to accept the change in hours he was warned by his employer that he might be dismissed for breach of contract. The Appeal Tribunal, per Phillips J, commented

> 'The employers were wrong in thinking that they could dismiss him for a breach by him of his contract. Rather the situation was that if they required him to work new hours, he was unwilling and they would not retain him, then they constructively, as it were, were dismissing him for that reason'.

In addition to an insistence upon a non-contractual change in hours of work an employer's insistence upon a disadvantageous change of the kind of work involved in the job can also constitute a contractual repudiation.

Thus where an employee is downgraded to lower status work than that specified in the contract an employment tribunal will be entitled to find that the contract was repudiated. For example in *Wadham Stringer Commercials (London) Ltd and Wadham Stringer Vehicles Ltd v Brown*[17] where an employee was demoted from fleet sales director to retail salesman, given no salary increase and moved to demeaning offices the EAT upheld an employment tribunal's decision that these actions by the employer amounted to constructive dismissal entitling Mr Brown to resign.

16   See part II, below.
17   [1983] IRLR 46, EAT. See also *Ford v Milthorn Toleman Ltd* [1980] IRLR 30, CA.

Clearly, if the downgrading is accompanied by a loss of other contractual benefits as in *Brown*'s case, or involved an outright reduction in pay as in *Marriott*'s case, the employer's actions will constitute a repudiation. Yet it is possible for a mere demotion in status without loss of pay to amount to a repudiation.

For example in *Millbrook Furnishing Industries Ltd v McIntosh*[18] three highly skilled sewing machinists transferred to less skilled work in the bedding department with an assurance that their pay would be the same even though the wage structures in the two departments were different. They decided to resign after being issued with an ultimatum from the employer. The employment tribunal's decision that they were constructively dismissed was upheld by the EAT. And in *Bumpus v Standard Life Assurance Co Ltd*,[19] owing to a reorganisation of regional offices, Bumpus was demoted from Local Secretary to Chief Inspector, a change involving mainly his job and responsibilities. His salary was unaffected apart from a loss of a responsibility allowance of £150 to £200 per annum but he had opportunities to make greater commissions on sales. The employer argued that there was no demotion but only a sideways movement and that the change in conditions was minimal. The tribunal held, however, that the employer's insistence on a demotion in status, though not large, was substantial enough to constitute a repudiation of the contract of employment. Moreover, even where the change insisted upon by the employer is only a temporary change in duties this can be a repudiatory act particularly where the change is substantial and the duration of the temporary period uncertain. Thus in *McNeil v Charles Crimm (Electrical Contractors) Ltd*[20] the EAT allowed an appeal from an employment tribunal's decision that a change in job duties was non-repudiatory because it was not permanent. The EAT's view was that the change of terms was substantial even if it was only temporary. And in *Millbrook Furnishing Industries Ltd v McIntosh*[1] the employers asserted that their action was non-repudiatory because the change was only temporary. The EAT however upheld the tribunal's finding of repudiation because there was no indication how long the change would last.

Furthermore, even if the contract specifies that the employee may do two jobs, if it clearly indicates which is the predominant job then an attempt to alter the contract so that the lesser job becomes the predominant part of

18   [1981] IRLR 309, EAT.
19   [1974] IRLR 232, IT.
20   [1984] IRLR 179, EAT.
1   [1981] IRLR 309, EAT.

the person's work could entitle a tribunal to decide that the employer has repudiated the contract. For example in *Pedersen v Camden London Borough Council*[2] an employee was hired as a bar steward/catering assistant and worked almost exclusively as a bar steward for 4 years. When circumstances entailed a shift in his work to a large proportion of catering duties, an employment tribunal found this to be a unilateral alteration in the contract of a fundamental kind entitling the employee to resign and claim constructive dismissal. The Court of Appeal upheld the tribunal's decision on this question of fact.

On the other hand if the lesser part of an employment is completely discontinued it may be regarded as 'supplementary' rather than 'basic' to the contract, particularly where the supplementary element was not contained within the original contract.[3]

Furthermore, where the employer requires the employee to change his place of work without having contractual authority for such an instruction, the insistence on the move may amount to constructive dismissal. For example in *Maher v Fram Gerrard Ltd*[4] the employer required the employee to move from Swinton to Adlington although he was not obliged to do so under the contract. The employee resigned and the court held that this was simply an acceptance of the employers' repudiation and hence a termination by the employers.[5] Moreover, in *Bass Leisure v Thomas*[6] a driver based in Coventry was asked to operate in Erdington, 20 miles away, under a clause reserving to the employer the right to transfer her to a suitable alternative place of work. However the employer's right to transfer was qualified by the clause 'provided that it remains reasonably accessible from your normal residence'. After a trial period made it clear that the commuting was not feasible, Mrs Thomas resigned in the face of the employer's continued insistence that she continue at Erdington. The employer's conduct was held to be repudiatory, entitling the employee to claim constructive dismissal.

2   [1981] ICR 674n, [1981] IRLR 173, CA.
3   See eg *Land v West Yorkshire County Council* [1981] ICR 334, [1981] IRLR 87, CA; *Bond v CAV Ltd* [1983] IRLR 360, QB.
4   [1974] 1 All ER 449, [1974] ICR 31.
5   See also *Robertson v Howden & Co Ltd* (3 March, 1973, unreported), NIRC. An employee transferred temporarily from Scotland Street to Kinning Park was told he would have to remain there permanently. The NIRC held that his subsequent resignation was a constructive dismissal since this was not the kind of sideways move that the employer could demand; it was a variation of the contract requiring consent. But see *Express Lift Co v Bowles* [1977] ICR 474, [1977] IRLR 99, EAT.
6   [1994] IRLR 104, EAT.

[II]   THE SCOPE OF CONTRACTUAL AUTHORITY.

Of course, not all forms of insistence by employers on changes in hours, types of work or place of work are contractual repudiations. Much depends upon the way the contract defines these conditions of employment and now, given the wide discretion enjoyed by employment tribunals, much also depends upon the way tribunals interpret the terms of the contract in the less obvious cases.

In interpreting the terms of the contract, certain principles will guide employment tribunals. Thus the place where a person is employed under his contract is not necessarily where that person in fact works. It is where, under the contract of employment, he or she can be required to work. Thus in *Rank Xerox Ltd v Churchill*[7] a mobility clause in the contract providing that 'the company may require you to transfer to another location' was to be applied literally and could not be limited to a reasonable daily travelling distance. In *Managers (Holborn) Ltd v Hohne*[8] an employee who was working at premises at Holborn and was asked to move to Regent Street was unable to show that her contract contained a term limiting her place of work to High Holborn as opposed to Central London. In *Wilkinson v A Reyrolle & Co Ltd*[9] a transfer from Barking to Croydon was found to be within an employee's contractual terms because his 'place of employment' was in 'the Southern area'.

Moreover, where the contract of employment is silent on the place of work, it may not stop employment tribunals from implying a term judged on the basis of what in all the circumstances the parties if reasonable would have agreed if they had directed their needs to the problem rather than simply taking the place where the employee is actually working as the contractual place of work. For example in *Jones v Associated Tunnelling Co Ltd*[10] the EAT upheld a tribunal which when unable to ascertain whether the employee's express contractual obligation to move, implied a term that he would work in the general area within reasonable commuting distance of his home. As Browne-Wilkinson LJ put it:

'the starting point must be that a contract of employment cannot simply be silent on the place of work ... the position must be

---

7   [1988] IRLR 280, EAT.
8   [1977] IRLR 230, EAT.
9   (1976) EAT 283/76.
10   [1981] IRLR 477, EAT; see also *Courtaulds Northern Spinning Ltd v Sibson* [1988] IRLR 305, CA (HGV driver job implied mobility to any place within reasonable travelling distance to his home); *Little v Charterhouse Magna Assurance Co Ltd* [1980] IRLR 19, EAT.

regulated by the express or implied agreement of the parties in each case. [If there is no express term,] in order to give the contract business efficacy, it is necessary to imply some term into each contract of employment.'

On the other hand, where an employee had a job at a particular place of work as a shop assistant in a chain of retail shops, it could be inappropriate to imply a mobility clause.[11] Finally if a tribunal finds an implied mobility clause, it may make it subject to an implied qualification that reasonable notice must be given.[12] The work that an employee does can sometimes be defined in the contract more widely than the work the employee is actually doing.

For example in *Woods v W M Car Services (Peterborough) Ltd*[13] an employee taken on as Chief Secretary/Accounts Clerk had to alter her work from primarily secretarial work to work consisting of spending more than 80% of her time keeping accounts. She resigned in protest and claimed that she had been constructively dismissed. An employment tribunal found that there was no repudiation of any express or implied term by the employer. The EAT thought that the tribunal was wrong but upheld its decision because of the limits of its own appellate jurisdiction. The Court of Appeal also upheld the tribunal's exercise of discretion on this issue indicating however that they thought that the employers were entitled under the contract to insist upon the change. As Lord Justice Watkins put it:

'Employers must not, in my opinion, be put in a position where, through the *wrongful* refusal of their employees to accept change, they are prevented from introducing improved business methods in furtherance of seeking success for their enterprise'.

Yet, the test of contractual authority is complicated by two factors: the precise width of the express or implied contractual authority; and the limits that may be placed on express contractual authority by the implied terms of the contract, in particular the implied term of mutual trust and confidence.

The scope of an employer's contractual authority can be widened by the introduction of express or implied 'flexibility' and 'mobility' clauses and these can have the effect of widening the hours of work and type of work which an employee can be required to perform as well as the place

11   See *Aparau v Iceland Frozen Foods plc* [1996] IRLR 119, EAT.
12   *Prestwick Circuits Ltd v McAndrew* [1990] IRLR 191, Ct of Sess.
13   [1981] ICR 666, [1981] IRLR 347; see also *Jones v Associated Tunnelling Co Ltd* [1981] IRLR 477, EAT.

where he can be required to work. For example, in *Bex v Securicor Transport Ltd*[14] a business manager at the company's Brixton branch was told he would be transferred to the position of customer liaison officer. The contract contained a clause reading 'should the interest of the company demand it, you may be required to serve at various offices of the company's headquarters in London and the particular nature of your job may be changed'. The tribunal held that the employer was entitled to require Mr Bex to serve in the capacity of a customer liaison officer and the latter's resignation was not one which qualified as a dismissal.[15]

Similarly in *Dowsett Engineering Construction Ltd v Fowler*[16] an employee's contract contained a term incorporated from the staff handbook that read 'If you are employed on site you may be required to work overtime on being given reasonable notice'. Although the employee had been working weekend overtime on a voluntary basis for some time, the EAT held that the clause 'required' the employee 'to work overtime if overtime was asked to be done', and hence required him to accept a new weekend rota scheme as part of his existing contractual duties. The wider contractual authority conferred upon the employer by the clause meant that the employee's resignation in the face of the employer's insistence upon a change was not a justified termination by the employee within the meaning of s 95(1)(c).

Moreover, in *Melville v William Freeman & Co Ltd*[17] a wide express flexibility clause reading

'The company reserves the right to alter or change the boundaries or territories'.

was held to be an acceptable exercise of express contractual authority by the employer.

The contract can also be used to widen management discretion in other ways. For example in *London v James Laidlaw & Sons*,[18] the collective

---

14   [1972] IRLR 68.
15   See also *United Kingdom Atomic Energy Authority v Claydon* [1974] ICR 128, [1974] IRLR 6, NIRC ('the Authority reserves the right to require any member of their staff to work at any of their establishments in Great Britain or in posts overseas') and *Sutcliffe v Hawker Siddeley Aviation Ltd* [1973] ICR 560, [1973] IRLR 304, NIRC ('anywhere in the United Kingdom' in which the place of work at which an employee could be required to work was as defined by the mobility clause).
16   (1977) EAT 425/76.
17   (1983) EAT 609/83.
18   [1974] IRLR 136, IT.

agreement gave management authority to decide at what stage conditions were too wet for work. This term ensured that management's insistence on work in wet weather was within the contract.

In other instances the scope of an employer's contractual authority has been widened by the contents of a collective agreement being incorporated into an employee's contract either by implication or by reference in the written particulars required under s 2(3) of the 1996 Act. For example in *Express Lifts Co Ltd v Bowles*[19] the following clause from a collective agreement was so incorporated as an implied term:

> 'It is recognised by both workers and management in the industry that workers in it are to be mobile and ordinarily willing to work *in any part of the United Kingdom*'.

In the event, the employee's resignation in the face of his employer's insistence that he work away from home was not a 'constructive dismissal'. The employer had contractual authority for his insistence.[20]

Where, however, such clauses originate in documents other than the written statement which purports to widen managerial contractual authority they must in fact have been incorporated in the employee's contract of employment. For example, in *Stewart v Swan Hunter Shipbuilders Ltd*[1] the employers alleged that they were entitled to transfer the employee from crane driving to scaffolding or painting work by virtue of an agreement with a union giving the employer 'complete flexibility and interchangeability within groupings'. Yet the company were unable to show that the agreement had been incorporated in the employee's contract of employment by references in a written statement of particulars or by custom and practice.

[III] VARIATION AND CONSENT.

Where an employer alleges that an employee's original contractual obligations established at the formation of the contract have been widened by agreement of the employee, he must make a showing that the employee consented to the change. This is not always accomplished by a showing that the employee acquiesced in the change over a period of time.[2] Indeed,

19   [1977] IRLR 99, EAT.
20   See also *McCaffrey v EE Jeavons & Co Ltd* (1967) 2 ITR 636.
1   [1975] IRLR 143.
2   See *Trevellion v Hospital of St John and St Elizabeth* [1973] IRLR 176; *Cooper v Paterson Candy International Ltd* [1972] IRLR 107; *Morrison v Marquess of Exeter* [1973] IRLR 74; *Waine v R Oliver (Plant Hire) Ltd* [1977] IRLR 434, EAT.

even where the employer can show that the employee accepted extra payment for the additional duties, it may not constitute a consensual variation of the contract, if the employee evinces an intention not to accept the extra duties as a permanent change in his contract.[3]

Furthermore, where an employer alleges that although a particular clause was not originally incorporated in the contract, the contract was subsequently varied by agreement with a trade union, there are other contractual hurdles that may be encountered in proving that the collective term applied to the individual concerned. For example, in *Hawker Siddeley Power Engineering Ltd v Rump* an employee given an oral promise that his work would be confined to Southern England could not be held bound by written particulars requiring country-wide mobility under a Working Rule agreement because there had been no valid variation of the original oral term.[4] Similarly in *Robertson v British Gas Corpn*[5] a letter from the Gas Board indicating that 'incentive bonus scheme conditions will apply' was held to supervene a subsequent statement of written particulars issued by the employer which applied the provision of a collective agreement – the NJC agreement – and relating bonuses to the scheme agreed by it. These and other cases seem to suggest that representations made in the formation stage of the contract may be honoured as representations which tended to induce the bargain.

Nevertheless, where the employers are sufficiently careful to distinguish between an initial exploratory stage and a formal offer and acceptance stage, the courts have been willing to honour their exercise of their drafting power. For example, in *Deeley v British Rail Engineering Ltd*[6] the Court of Appeal was prepared to disregard the fact that the original advertisement, the employee's letter of application and the employer's acknowledgment all specified 'Sales Engineer (Export)' in determining the scope of the employee's contractual duties where the employer could show that he had issued a formal offer of employment and terms and conditions of employment all headed 'Sales Engineer' which contained an express clause to the effect that 'the duties will be as required by the Managing Director of British Rail Engineering Ltd or as the Railway Board may from time to time determine', and the employee's acceptance of the offer was headed

---

3   *Seegobin v Cook & Perkins Ltd* (1977) EAT 540/76; *Horrigan v London Borough of Lewisham* [1978] ICR 15.
4   But see the discussion of 'some other substantial reason' in Chapter 9.
5   [1983] IRLR 302, CA.
6   [1980] IRLR 147, CA.

'Sales Engineer'. The case apparently was regarded as one of a written contract rather than written statement under ERA, s 1.

In *Scott v Formica Ltd*[7] an employer claimed authority under an oral agreement with the union to transfer employees with a reduction of one pay grade, although the written particulars of the employee provided only for interchangeability between departments and shift-work within the same pay grade. The tribunal held that the employer was in breach of contract in insisting on a reduction in rate of pay. The written particulars had not been amended and the evidence of the oral agreement was sketchy. The tribunal indicated that the change was sufficiently important to require it to be brought to the employee's attention in some way and suggested that an amending notice could be given in their wage packets or by a talk by employer or union representative to the workforce.[8]

In *Singh v British Steel Corpn*[9] a change in shift system had been agreed with the unions but Singh had resigned from the union before the agreement had been made. The EAT held that the employee was not bound by the change. And in *Ellis v Brighton Co-operative Society*[10] the reorganisation of hours of work did not apply to Mr Ellis who was not a member of the union.

[IV] LIMITS TO EXPRESS CONTRACTUAL AUTHORITY.

Finally, even where the employer has a wide express contractual authority, that authority may be judicially limited by either one of two devices: either the express contractual obligation may be subject to a test of strict construction; or the employer's exercise of discretion under the express term may be subject to the employer's implied obligation not to undermine the mutual trust and confidence in the employment relationship. If there is any vagueness or ambiguity in the contractual term, it may be interpreted to contain an implied limitation on its scope. In *Parry v Holst & Co Ltd*,[11] a Divisional Court examined the following clause of the Working Rule Agreement in Civil Engineering: 'that at the discretion of the employer, an operative may be transferred at any time during the period of his employment from one job to another'. The court commented:

> 'On the face, it would apply to enable the company to transfer an employee anywhere at any rate in the United Kingdom. Nevertheless

7   [1975] IRLR 104, IT.
8   Cf *Gascol Conversions Ltd v Mercer* [1974] ICR 420, [1974] IRLR 155, CA.
9   [1974] IRLR 131.
10   [1976] IRLR 419, EAT.
11   (1968) 3 ITR 317.

there may be grounds for limiting that application. Such limitation as it seems to me just result from some implied term and indeed it has been suggested ... that it should be limited to moving the applicant from job to job either within distance of his home so that he can get back at night or at any rate within South Wales'.[12]

And in *Briggs v Imperial Chemical Industries*[13] the appellant, a process worker, was issued with a booklet containing the works rules applicable to the Billingham Factory: rule 17, headed 'Change of Occupation', reads thus:

'You must accept the right of the management to transfer you to another job with higher or lower rate of pay, whether day work, night work, or shift work'.

The High Court, per Lord Parker CJ, interpreted this rule in the following way:

'Although that work rule is in quite general terms, it is to my mind quite clear in the circumstances of this case that it would only entitle the management to transfer a process worker to another job within the Billingham Factory, and further only to transfer a process worker from one job to another job where he would again be a process worker. It is quite idle, as it seems to me, to suggest that rule 17 would enable the management to transfer a man from Billingham to some other factory miles away, or, to take an absurd example, to transfer a carpenter to a plumber's job. Read in that way, rule 17 as it seems to me bears out entirely what the tribunal have found, namely, that this man was not employed as a process worker on a particular job on the cyanide job, but as a process worker generally so that he could be called upon to do process worker's work in any part of the Billingham Factory'.

More recently in *Cowen v Haden Ltd*[14] the Court of Appeal was prepared to place a limit upon an express contractual term that provided that

'The employee's job title will be regional surveyor – southern region. He will be required to undertake, at the discretion of the company, any and all duties which reasonably fall within the scope of his capabilities'.

12   See also *Roynane v Northern Strip Mining Ltd* [1975] IRLR 303.
13   (1968) 3 ITR 276.
14   [1983] ICR 1 at 13, CA.

In deciding what the scope of his work was under the contract for the purpose of determining whether the employee was redundant the Court of Appeal held that the effect of the flexibility clause

> 'was not to give the employers the right to transfer him from his job as regional surveyor to any job as a quantity surveyor in their organisation, but only to require him to perform any duties reasonably within the scope of his capabilities as regional surveyor'.

In decisions on questions of constructive dismissal, however, the courts have been reluctant to apply limits to the scope of that contractual authority using a test of reasonableness. Thus where an employer enjoys express contractual authority to insist on a move and an employee resigns because of the unreasonable width of the contractual obligation, the employee runs a considerable risk that he or she will be held to have resigned in circumstances which did not amount to a constructive dismissal. For example in *Rank Xerox Ltd v Churchill*[15] the EAT was unwilling to limit the scope of a mobility clause stating that 'the company may require you to transfer to another location' to places only within a reasonable travelling distance. In *Express Lift Co Ltd v Bowles*[16] the EAT found that the fact there was a term of the employee's contract that he could be transferred to another place of work precluded consideration of whether the employer's discretion was reasonably exercised. Plainly, had the employee simply refused to move and was dismissed then this issue would be tested under s 98(4). Thus s 95(1)(c) has been held to be a contractual test.[17] The technique of strict construction has tended to be limited to a contractual obligation which offers some ambiguity for the judges or tribunals to fasten upon. In recent years, however, the courts have been willing to examine the employer's exercise of discretion within the scope of their contractual authority and where it is found to be abusive, arbitrary or capricious, it may be a breach of an implied fundamental term of mutual trust and confidence.

ii) Abusive treatment as breach of a fundamental term

Although the Court of Appeal in *Western Excavating* rejected a non-contract reasonableness test for constructive dismissal, there have

---

15   [1988] IRLR 280, EAT.
16   [1977] ICR 474, [1977] IRLR 99, EAT; see too *Melville v William Freeman & Co Ltd* (1983) EAT 609/83.
17   *Western Excavating (ECC) Ltd v Sharp* [1978] QB 761, [1978] IRLR 27, CA.

nevertheless been a number of cases in which tribunals have successfully asserted or courts with appellate jurisdiction have urged when faced with unreasonable conduct by the employer that contracts of employment generally are subject to an implied term that the employer must not destroy or seriously damage the mutual trust and confidence between employer and employee.[18]

As courts and tribunals have attempted to accommodate the contractual categories of constructive dismissal to the factual examples of unreasonable and abusive conduct of employers that have appeared before them, they have increasingly resorted to the creation of new implied obligations or the creative application of old implied obligations in the employment contract.

On occasion there have been signs of the EAT or the Court of Appeal categorising abusive treatment in terms of repudiatory breach[19] or even in terms of the impossibility of continuing the contract,[20] but on the whole the dominant mode so far has been the use of the implied term.[1]

This case law has resulted in an expansion of the traditional *contractual* obligations of employers. Thus, while the EAT has made it plain that it would not accept the creation of a general implied term in employment contracts that the employer must 'treat the employee in a reasonable manner',[2] and has also indicated that there are cases where extreme unreasonableness may not fit into a contractual category,[3] it has nevertheless created a wide basis for finding unreasonable and abusive behaviour to be a breach of the implied obligation of mutual trust and confidence.

The obligation of the employer not to destroy or seriously damage the mutual trust and confidence between employer and employee has its origins in the common law including the law of wrongful dismissal. In a number of cases where an employer had dismissed an employee without notice, the employee had attempted to bring an action for wrongful dismissal at common law based on the alleged breach of contract involved in the employer's failure to provide notice. The employer's defence at common law was that the employee's conduct was repudiatory consisting of a

18   See eg *Courtaulds Northern Textiles Ltd v Andrew* [1979] IRLR 84, EAT; *Robinson v Crompton Parkinson Ltd* [1978] ICR 401, [1978] IRLR 61, EAT.
19   See eg *BBC v Beckett* [1983] IRLR 43, EAT; *Garner v Grange Furnishing Ltd* [1977] IRLR 206, EAT.
20   See eg *Isle of Wight Tourist Board v Coombes* [1976] IRLR 413, EAT.
1   *Woods v W M Car Services (Peterborough) Ltd* [1982] ICR 693, [1982] IRLR 413, CA.
2   *Post Office v Roberts* [1980] IRLR 347, EAT.
3   *Walker v Josiah Wedgwood & Sons Ltd* [1978] ICR 744, [1978] IRLR 105, EAT.

'deliberate flouting of the essential contractual conditions'.[4] If the employer could successfully show that the employee's conduct was repudiatory then he could treat the contract as discharged without any further obligation to provide notice. In other words the industrial notion of summary or instant dismissal was rooted in the common law notion of contractual repudiation by the employer. In the course of these cases the principles of law applying to the definition of repudiation by the employee evolved from a more specific test of whether the employee had broken an essential obligation of fidelity, care and obedience into a view that 'a contract of service imposes upon the parties a duty of mutual respect'.[5]

In *Robinson v Crompton Parkinson Ltd*,[6] Kilner Brown took up the suggestion that an obligation of trust and confidence might be mutual and applied it to the cases of constructive dismissals.

> 'In a contract of employment, and in conditions of employment there has to be mutual trust and confidence between master and servant. Although most of the reported cases deal with the master seeking remedy against a servant or former servant for acting in breach of confidence or breach of trust, that action can only be upon the basis that trust and confidence is mutual. Consequently, when a man says of his employer, "I claim that you have broken your contract because you have clearly shown that you have no confidence in me and you have behaved in way which is contrary to the mutual trust which ought to exist between master and servant", he is entitled in these circumstances, it seems to us, to say that there is conduct which amounts to a repudiation of contract'.[7]

Lord Denning in *Woods v W M Car Service (Peterborough) Ltd*[8] endorsed this view of a parallel between the law of wrongful dismissal and constructive dismissal.

> 'Now under modern legislation we have the converse case. It is the duty of the employer to be good and considerate to his servants. Sometimes it is formulated as an implied term not to do anything likely to destroy the relationship of confidence between them, see *Courtaulds Northern Textiles Ltd v Andrew* [1979] IRLR 84. But I

---

4   *Laws v London Chronicle (Indicator Newspapers) Ltd* [1959] 2 All ER 285, [1959] 1 WLR 698, CA.
5   *Wilson v Racher* [1974] ICR 428, [1974] IRLR 114, CA.
6   [1978] ICR 401, [1978] IRLR 61, EAT.
7   Ibid at 65.
8   [1982] ICR 693, [1982] IRLR 413, CA.

prefer to look at it in this way: the employer must be good and considerate to his servants. Just as a servant must be good and faithful, so an employer must be good and considerate. Just as in the old days an employee could be guilty of misconduct justifying his dismissal, so in modern times an employer can be guilty of misconduct justifying the employee in leaving at once without notice. In each case it depends on whether the misconduct amounted to a repudiatory breach as defined in *Western Excavating (ECC) Ltd v Sharp* [1978] QB 761, [1978] IRLR 27'.

There have been cases which have attempted to apply an implied obligation of co-operation[9] to the employment relationship in constructive dismissal but the more common implied obligation in use has been that of mutual trust and confidence.[10] As Arnold J said in *Courtaulds Northern Textiles Ltd v Andrew*[11]

'In our view it is clearly established that there is implied in a contract of employment a term that the employers will not, without reasonable and proper cause, conduct themselves in a manner calculated or likely to destroy or seriously damage the relationship of confidence and trust between employer and employee'.

He added that

'it does seem to us that any conduct which is likely to destroy or seriously to damage that relationship must be something which goes to the root of the contract, which is really fundamental in its effect upon the contractual relationship'.

In *Woods v W M Car Services (Peterborough) Ltd*[12] Browne-Wilkinson J, after citing with approval to this passage of Arnold J, went on to make the further point that:

'To constitute a breach of this implied term it is not necessary to show that the employer intended any repudiation of the contract: the tribunal's function is to look at the employer's conduct as a whole and to determine whether it is such that its effect, judged reasonably

---

9   See *Associated Tyre Specialists (Eastern) Ltd v Waterhouse* [1977] ICR 218, [1976] IRLR 386, EAT; cf *White v London Transport Executive* [1982] QB 489, [1981] IRLR 261, EAT.
10   See *Woods* (above); *Post Office v Roberts* [1980] IRLR 347, EAT.
11   [1979] IRLR 84, EAT.
12   [1981] IRLR 347, EAT.

) and sensibly is such that the employee cannot be expected to put
) up with it ...'

In *Malik v BCCI*[13] the House of Lords defined the obligation of mutual trust and confidence in the following terms. Lord Nicholls stated that this obligation requires the employer

'... not to engage in conduct likely to undermine the trust and confidence required if the employment relationship is to continue in the manner the employment contract implicitly envisages ... The conduct must, of course, impinge on the relationship in the sense that, looked at objectively, it is likely to destroy or seriously damage the degree of trust and confidence the employee is reasonably entitled to have in his employer.'[14]

Lord Steyn defined the obligation as

'... not without reasonable and proper cause to conduct oneself in a manner likely to destroy, or seriously damage, the relationship of trust and confidence between employer and employee.'[15]

This definition not only reminds that the employer's unjustified conduct need not be *intended* to end the relationship or no longer be bound by the contract; it also confirms that this implied obligation can be viewed as an umbrella category to be applied quite widely to find abusive or unreasonable treatment repudiatory conduct by the employers. In certain cases the employer's repudiatory conduct has involved a failure to perform specific positive obligations. Thus in *Post Office v Strange*[16] a failure by the employer to provide the employee with the right of appeal to an appropriate level with the disciplinary procedure was viewed as a clear failure to perform the contract and hence a repudiation entitling the employee to resign. More recently in *W A Goold (Pearmark) Ltd v McConnell*[17] an employee ignored by his employer when asking for an explanation about his payment was able to prove that the employer's non-response was a repudiatory breach of a fundamental implied term in the contract of employment that employees will be given a reasonable and prompt opportunity to redress their grievances.

13   [1997] IRLR 462, HL.
14   Ibid at p 464, paras 13 and 14.
15   Ibid at p 471, para 70.
16   [1981] IRLR 515, EAT.
17   [1995] IRLR 516, EAT; see also *Wetherall (Bond Street W1) Ltd v Lynn* [1978] ICR 205 (a breach of grievance procedure).

Similarly, failures by employers to provide adequate support to employees during busy periods[18] or to provide an appraisal to probationers during a trial period,[19] or to respond to an employee's complaints about the lack of adequate safety equipment[20] or to undermine a supervisor's authority by criticising him in front of other employees,[1] or to protect an employee against harassment[2] from other employees,[3] including sexual harassment[4] have all been characterised as breaches of the particular implied terms of mutual trust and confidence.

The effect of this implied legal obligation on unreasonable conduct which is not deliberately repudiatory has been to project the legal framework quite deeply into the practice of personnel and human resources management. For example in *Gogay v Hertfordshire County Council*[5] a local authority employer was held to have broken the implied term of mutual trust and confidence by suspending a social worker pending a disciplinary investigation without reasonable and proper cause. Moreover, in *BBC v Beckett* the exercise of a contractual power to downgrade for disciplinary reasons was viewed as so disproportionate to the misconduct itself that it amounted to a repudiation.[6] Further, in *French v Barclays Bank plc*[7] the introduction of less favourable terms for a bridging loan for an employee after the employee had relocated was held to be conduct by the employer likely to destroy mutual trust and confidence between employer and employee.

Another example of repudiatory conduct by the employer is offered by the cases where an employer erroneously accuses an employee of theft. In *Fyfe & McGrouther Ltd v Byrne*,[8] the EAT stated that where an employer

18   *Seligman & Latz Ltd v McHugh* [1979] IRLR 130, EAT.
19   *White v London Transport Executive* [1982] QB 489, [1981] IRLR 261, EAT.
20   *British Aircraft Corpn Ltd v Austin* [1978] IRLR 332, EAT.
1   *Associated Tyre Specialists (Eastern) Ltd v Waterhouse* [1977] ICR 218, [1976] IRLR 386, EAT.
2   *Moores v Bude-Stratton Town Council* [2000] IRLR 676 (protection of council employee from town councillor's conduct).
3   See eg *Wigan Borough Council v Davies* [1979] ICR 411, [1979] IRLR 127, EAT; *Adams v Southampton and South West Hampshire Health Authority* IT 1560/156 (24 July 1984, unreported), IT.
4   See eg *Bracebridge Engineering Ltd v Darby* [1990] IRLR 3, EAT; see too (1) *Reed* and (2) *Bull Information Systems Ltd v Stedman* [1999] IRLR 299, EAT.
5   [2000] IRLR 703, CA.
6   [1983] IRLR 43, EAT; see also *Cawley v South Wales Electricity Board* [1985] IRLR 89, EAT.
7   [1998] IRLR 646, CA.
8   [1977] IRLR 29, EAT; *Robinson v Crompton Parkinson Ltd* [1978] ICR 401, [1978] IRLR 61, EAT.

makes a false accusation to the police without having any evidence to back up his suspicion that could entitle an employee to resign and claim to be constructively dismissed, because in such a case 'by adopting this attitude in a situation for which (the employee) was not responsible (the employer) had destroyed any basis of confidence that could ever exist between them and him in the future'.

In some other cases certain critical remarks by the employer to the employee have been held to be sufficiently abusive in the circumstances to amount to a repudiation. As Lord Denning remarked in *Wood*'s case a certain amount of trenchant criticism can reasonably be regarded as part of the day to day exchange between employee and employer.[9] Yet there can come a point when the remarks in context can reach the point where they make continued employment intolerable for the employee and entitle him or her to resign and be constructively dismissed.

To take one rather extreme example, in *Isle of Wight Tourist Board v Coombes*[10] an employee of 15 years' standing resigned when the Director to whom she was personal secretary stated, within her hearing to another employee, 'she is an intolerable bitch on a Monday morning'. The EAT per Bristow J agreed that this was conduct entitling the employee to resign particularly without any attempt to make an apology because it shattered the relationship which in this particular case was one of 'complete confidence'. Moreover in *Courtaulds Northern Textiles Ltd v Andrew*[11] where a manager exclaimed to a managerial employee 'you can't do the bloody job anyway' and he used these words maliciously – with no belief in their truth – in order to get rid of him, then it might be sufficient to justify a resignation as constructive dismissal, because as Lord Denning later remarked in *Wood*'s case, it would evince an intention no longer to be bound by the contract.[12]

Similarly, whilst words may sometimes be exchanged between employer and employee in the heat of the moment and even a certain amount of foul language may be used without amounting to a repudiation of the contract by the employee,[13] there can come a point where the language in the context is so intolerable that an employee cannot be expected to stay and at that

---

9   [1982] IRLR 413, CA.
10   [1976] IRLR 413, EAT.
11   [1979] IRLR 84, EAT; *La Piaff of Knightsbridge Ltd v Ruben* (1984) EAT 619/ 83.
12   See [1982] IRLR 413, CA at para 17.
13   *Chesham Shipping Ltd v Rowe* [1977] IRLR 391, EAT.

point verbal abuse can amount to a repudiation of the contract.[14] Thus in *Palmanor Ltd v Cedron*[15] an employee who was a barman at a nightclub came in one evening to be greeted with an accusation that he was late. When he replied that he was not late and that it was a night that he was supposed to start late he was insulted and sworn at by the manager. When he protested that the employer had no right to talk to him that way, he was again sworn at and told 'If you don't like it you can go'. Later he was also told 'If you leave me now don't bother to collect your money, papers or anything else, I'll make sure that you don't get a job anywhere in London'. The EAT agreed that the tribunal was justified in reaching its decision because this was not simply a case of abusive language but foul language accompanied by words from the manager which suggested a right to continue to speak to the employee in that way, conduct such that an employee could not be expected to tolerate.

A further category of abusive conduct consists of cases where an employee has been subjected to a sustained pattern of harassment by his or her employer. For example in *Garner v Grange Furnishing Ltd*[16] an employee resigned after being treated badly for a sustained period by the employer in circumstances of some mutual friction. The EAT upheld the employment tribunal's finding of constructive dismissal commenting that a series of small incidents over a period of time can eventually amount to a repudiation. In such circumstances 'the employer is making it impossible for the employee to go on working for him'.[17] And in *Wadham Stringer Commercials (London) Ltd and Wadham Stringer Vehicles Ltd v Brown*[18] an employee was gradually demoted from fleet sales director to a retail salesman and moved to a very small office. He protested in writing about his treatment. He was given instructions relating to his continued work as salesman and warned that unless he accepted them it would be presumed that he wished to resign. He replied that he was not resigning. He was then moved again to a smaller office with no ventilation, initially no telephone or light and situated next to the gentlemen's lavatory. When he finally resigned in response to the employer's treatment, the EAT upheld the employment tribunal's finding that he had been constructively dismissed.

---

14 *Palmanor Ltd v Cedron* [1978] ICR 1008, [1978] IRLR 303, EAT; see also *Ruben's* case, above.
15 [1978] ICR 1008, [1978] IRLR 303, EAT.
16 [1977] IRLR 206, EAT.
17 Ibid.
18 [1983] IRLR 46, EAT.

Yet in *Woods v W M Car Services (Peterborough) Ltd*[19] there was a sharp reminder that the test of whether an employer's actions amounted to repudiatory conduct was largely a question of fact for employment tribunals to decide. In *Wood*'s case the employer was subjected to a series of pressures from her new employer after she had agreed to stay after a takeover on terms 'no less favourable than before'. She was then asked to take a pay cut, work longer hours, accept a new job title and a change in the nature of her work to include predominantly accounts work rather than mainly clerical work. She resigned and claimed that she was constructively dismissed.

The employment tribunal considered the question of whether any one of the company's actions taken in isolation amounted to a repudiatory breach. They then asked whether the events taken together amounted to a breach of an implied term in the contract that the employers did not without reasonable and proper cause conduct themselves in a manner calculated or likely to destroy or seriously damage the relationship of confidence and trust between employer and employee. They concluded that none of the individual actions constituted a repudiatory breach and the employers' actions cumulatively did not amount to a breach of that implied term.

The EAT was convinced that the tribunal's decision was wrong. Indeed Mr Justice Browne-Wilkinson said

> 'In our view, an employer who persistently attempts to vary an employee's conditions of service (whether contractual or not) with a view to getting rid of the employee or varying the employee's terms of service does act in a manner calculated or likely to destroy the relationship of confidence and trust between employer and employee. Such an employer has therefore breached the implied term. Any breach of that implied term is a fundamental breach amounting to a repudiation since it necessarily goes to the root of the contract'.[20]

Nevertheless it would not allow an appeal because the tribunal had not made a mistake of law through misdirection or perversity. This approach was later confirmed as the correct approach by the Court of Appeal.

Yet while *Wood*'s case confirms that tribunals enjoy a wide discretion to decide when and whether conduct by the employer amounts to a repudiation,[1] there are outer limits to tribunal discretion. Thus, where the

---

19   [1982] ICR 693, [1982] IRLR 413, CA.
20   [1981] IRLR 347, EAT.
1   See also *La Piaff of Knightsbridge Ltd v Ruben* (1984) EAT 619/83.

employment tribunal appears to be mistaken about the contractual status of an employer's decision, that could provide the basis for an appeal against its determination of the fact of repudiation. For example, in *F C Gardner Ltd v Beresford*,[2] the EAT remanded a case where an employee resigned because she had been refused a wage increase for two years although other employees had received pay increases during that period. The EAT stressed that the test was not whether the employers behaved in a way that was not expected, but whether there was breach of a term of the contract sufficient to justify an employee as treating himself as discharged. The EAT also drew a distinction between a 'grievance' by the employee about the employer's treatment and victimisation by the employer in which the employee was deliberately singled out for treatment inferior to that given to everyone else. In the latter case, if it were done arbitrarily, capriciously and inequitably it could allow an employment tribunal to decide that there was a repudiation.

Furthermore, in *Watson v Stakis Hotels & Inns Ltd*[3] the EAT overturned a tribunal finding of constructive dismissal because the combination of criticism, irregularities in the issue of a final written warning and a transfer to another less favourable hotel did not amount to a repudiation by the employer. Moreover in *British Leyland (UK) Ltd v McQuilken*[4] where an employer created uncertainty about the future of the employee without actually breaking a term of the contract, it was not open to the employment tribunal to find that there was a constructive dismissal.

3. EMPLOYER REPUDIATION AND THE EMPLOYEE'S RESPONSE

Whether an employee is entitled to resign under s 95(1)(c) does not depend solely upon the employer's conduct. It also depends upon the nature of the employee's response to that conduct and in particular the timing of the employee's resignation. The employee must be careful not to 'jump the gun' and leave prematurely. He must also ensure that he does not unduly delay his departure so that, when he leaves, he does so in circumstances that imply that he had elected to affirm the contract rather than accept the repudiation and end the contract.

---

2   [1978] IRLR 63, EAT.
3   (1984) EAT 942/83.
4   [1978] IRLR 245, EAT.

In the first place, where an employer asks an employee to perform an act which he is not contractually obliged to perform, the employer's act does not become repudiatory until he insists on the change to the point where the employee has no reasonable option but to resign.[5] Technically, an employer's communication to an employee about an impending change may be nothing more than an attempt to win the employee's consent to that change rather than an attempt to impose new terms on the employee. For example, where an employer merely explores the possibility of a change in contractual terms, this may amount to an offer to vary the contract rather than a repudiation.[6]

Moreover, where an employer makes a proposal to an employee for a reorganisation of work, the employee should wait until the change is actually to be implemented rather than anticipating a decision that has not yet been taken. For example in *Rich v Chappell Piano Co Ltd*[7] the employee, a piano tuner, was informed at two meetings that the company would like the piano tuners as a group to consider the possibility of organising their own company, to which the employer would then transfer the piano-tuning part of the business. The employer suggested a target date of 1 October. Mr Rich wanted to have no part in the new organisation. He began to look for work elsewhere and soon found a job with Harrods. On 20 September he wrote to his employer claiming that the meetings about the reorganisation amounted to verbal notice of termination on 29 September. The employer responded in a letter stating that the proposals for reorganisation were only tentative and had not progressed beyond that point. In fact, no new organisation was formed on 1 October. Nevertheless, Mr Rich started work with Harrods on 8 October. The EAT agreed with the tribunal's decision that Mr Rich's resignation had taken place in circumstances that did not amount to a repudiation by the employer, because Mr Rich did not wait for the ideas about the reorganisation 'to crystallise into any form of certainty'.

Similarly in cases of a warning of future redundancy,[8] or a statement that an employee's contract would eventually be terminated if he did not

---

5   *Sutcliffe v Hawker Siddeley Aviation Ltd* [1973] ICR 560, [1973] IRLR 304, NIRC, 'The members of the court fully accept that an employer can place his employee in a position in which the employee really has no option but to tender his notice'.

6   See eg the first letter sent by the employer in *Marriott v Oxford and District Co-operative Society (No 2)* [1970] 1 QB 186, [1969] 3 All ER 1126, CA.

7   (1976) EAT 367/76, see also *Cole v Reedhire Ltd* (1976) EAT 54/76, *Devon County Council v Cook* [1977] IRLR 188, 12 ITR 347, EAT; *Breach v Epsylon Industries Ltd* [1976] ICR 316, [1976] IRLR 180; *Clarke v Peter Black & Partners* (1976) EAT 257/76; *John Carr (Gloucester) Ltd v Barnett* (1977) EAT 617/76.

8   *Morton Sundour Fabrics Ltd v Shaw* (1966) 2 ITR 84.

find a job elsewhere,[9] there is a need to wait until the change proposed by the employer is actually to be implemented, rather than anticipating a decision that has not yet been taken.

Of course, it is possible under s 95(1)(c) for a resignation in response to an anticipatory repudiation by the employer to amount to constructive dismissal. But this presupposes that the employer has clearly renounced his future performance under the contract. For example, in *Maher v Fram Gerrard Ltd*[10] the employers had made it quite clear that at some time in the near future the employee would have to work at Adlington if he wished to remain in their employment. His resignation at that point was held to be justified by the court because the employer's action in imposing the transfer was a plain indication of his intention not to be bound by the contract *at the time of the resignation* and hence had already amounted to a repudiation of the employee's contract. Similarly in *Wellworthy Ltd v Ellis*[11] where an employer announced his intention of introducing new terms and conditions unilaterally despite the existence of an agreement with a trade union which had been incorporated into the employee's contract, Mr Ellis was held entitled to take the employer at his word and to resign and claim to be constructively dismissed. The words themselves were sufficient to establish the anticipatory breach. It was not necessary to prove that the breach was inevitable.

On the other hand, because such a breach is anticipatory in form, an employer may retract a proposed repudiation if the retraction occurs before the employee has unequivocally accepted it and ended the contract.[12]

Where there is a genuine dispute between the parties about the terms of a contract of employment, it will not necessarily be an anticipatory breach of the contract for the employer to do no more than give his opinion and argue his point of view with the employee. That was quite different from an employer saying that he is not under any circumstances at all going to be bound by it.[13] Moreover, this could be true even where the employer's insistence is based upon a genuine but mistaken belief about the terms of

---

9   *Haseltine Lake & Co v Dowler* [1981] ICR 222, [1981] IRLR 25, EAT; *International Computers Ltd v Kennedy* [1981] IRLR 28, EAT, see also *British Leyland (UK) Ltd v McQuilken* [1978] IRLR 245, EAT.

10   [1974] 1 All ER 449, [1974] ICR 31, NIRC. But cf p 89, note 8.

11   (1984) EAT 915/83.

12   *Norwest Holst Group Administration Ltd v Harrison* [1984] IRLR 419, EAT. See also *Universal Cargo Carriers Corpn v Citati* [1957] 2 QB 401, [1957] 2 All ER 70; *Hochester v De La Tour* (1853) 2 E & B 678.

13   See *Financial Techniques (Planning Services) Ltd v Hughes* [1981] IRLR 32, CA; see too *Brown v JBD Engineering Ltd* [1993] IRLR 568, EAT.

the contract.[14] Yet there are certain limits to the extent to which an employer's subjective view of the interpretation of the contents of the contract will provide a defence to the claim that its actions amount to a repudiation of the contract.[15] If the employer, even in good faith, acts in such a way that its conduct viewed objectively amounts to a repudiatory breach, its good faith may not be a defence.[16]

Thus, the case law requires an employee to be careful not to resign before an employer has actually committed a contractual repudiation. An employee must now be able to distinguish between, on the one hand, a repudiation which is an accomplished fact even if in the form of an anticipatory repudiation, and on the other, a mere warning or a statement of expectation or a proposal, which could be regarded as an offer to vary rather than a repudiation.

On the other hand once an employer has in fact committed a repudiatory act, employees must be careful that their response does not imply a willingness to agree to the change in the contract. If employees resign immediately in response to a repudiatory act, they thereby register their view that they consider that the employer's act has brought their contract to an end. According to general principles of contract law they are viewed as 'accepting' the employer's repudiation.

The process of 'acceptance', however, is not without certain contractual technicalities.[17] Thus, to be effective, the acceptance of the repudiation must be unequivocal. In *Norwest Holst Group Administration Ltd v Harrison*[18] an employee who was told that he would no longer be a director and a manager of the company's design office replied in a letter headed 'without prejudice' that in view of the loss of directorship and apparent loss of salary he considered that the company's letter to him constituted 'a determination of my employment'. Yet the EAT reversed an employment tribunal finding that this constituted an acceptance of the repudiation. The

---

14   Ibid, see also *Frank Wright & Co (Holdings) Ltd v Punch* [1980] IRLR 217, EAT; cf *Woodar Investment Development Ltd v Wimpey Construction (UK) Ltd* [1980] 1 All ER 571, [1980] 1 WLR 277, HL.

15   See Templeman LJ's suggestion in *Hughes'* case that *Frank Wright & Co (Holdings) Ltd v Punch*, supra, should be regarded with some misgivings. See also the EAT's rejection of the subjectivity exception in *Millbrook Furnishings Industries Ltd v McIntosh* [1981] IRLR 309.

16   See *BBC v Beckett* [1983] IRLR 43, EAT (express disciplinary power wrongly exercised in 'good faith' held to be a constructive dismissal).

17   See eg *L Liptons Ltd v Marlborough* [1979] IRLR 179, EAT.

18   [1984] IRLR 419, EAT; cf *Hunt v British Railways Board* [1979] IRLR 379, EAT.

EAT, by a majority, reasoned that the employee's letter headed 'without prejudice' was more in the nature of an offer of compromise than an unequivocal statement. Moreover while the employee had indicated that the employer's letter constituted a determination of the contract, nowhere did he 'clearly state that he accepts that position'.

It is true that the special nature of a contract of employment makes the question of affirmation a difficult one. Thus, as it was expressed in *W E Cox Toner (International) Ltd v Crook*[19]

> 'An employee faced with a repudiation by his employer is in a very difficult position. If he goes to work the next day, he will himself be doing an act which in one sense is only consistent with the continued existence of the contract, he might be said to be affirming the contract. Certainly, when he accepts his next pay packet the risk of being held to affirm the contract is very great'.[20]

Nevertheless, as Lord Denning himself pointed out in *Marriott*'s case, an employee who stays at work but actively protests against imposed terms will still be regarded as accepting the repudiation rather than affirming the contract. Thus, in *Marriott*'s case Lord Denning MR analysed the employee's response to a letter downgrading him from foreman to a lower status in the following way:

> 'If Marriott had accepted the repudiation and said "I will not agree to this reduction in my wages" and left at the end of the week, the contract would clearly have been terminated by the employer. There can be no doubt about it. Does he lose his redundancy payment simply because he stayed on for three or four weeks whilst he got another job? I think not. He never agreed to the dictated terms. He protested against them. He submitted to them because he did not want to be out of employment.'

A further complication of the contractual requirement of acceptance of a repudiation is the timing of the acceptance. If the employee resigns immediately in response to the repudiatory act whether with or without

---

19   [1981] ICR 823, [1981] IRLR 443.
20   See *Land and Wilson v West Yorkshire Metropolitan County Council* [1981] ICR 334, [1981] IRLR 87, CA; see too *Hunt v British Railways Board* [1979] IRLR 379, EAT, in which it was said that the law does not allow the employee 'to have his cake and eat it' by claiming repudiation and acting as if he were still employed. Cf *Bashir v Brillo Manufacturing Co* [1979] IRLR 295, EAT, where an employee accepted sick pay for 2½ months after employer's repudiation.

notice then there will be little doubt that the acceptance of the repudiation is timely.

Some difficulty may arise, however, if the employee's response is delayed and the delay implies that the employee desires to continue the contract in spite of the employer's act. The employee's response could be viewed as a waiver of the right to end the contract and an acquiescence in a change in the contract. As Lord Denning MR expressed it in *Western Excavating (ECC) Ltd v Sharp*:

> '... the employee must make up his mind soon after the conduct of which he complains. If he continues for any length of time without leaving, he will be regarded as having elected to affirm the contract and will lose the right to treat himself as discharged.'

Yet it is by no means clear that the mere continuance at work necessarily amounts to *affirmation*.[1] As Browne-Wilkinson stressed in *W E Cox Toner (International) Ltd v Crook*[2] this 'short summary of the law given by Lord Denning' was not 'intended to be a comprehensive statement of the whole law'.

And as Browne-Wilkinson pointed out in *Crook*'s case, in the *Western Excavating* case, Lord Denning explained that *Marriott*'s case would now be treated as one of constructive dismissal.

> 'This decision to our mind establishes that, provided the employee makes clear his objection to what is being done, he is not to be taken to have affirmed the contract by contriving to work and draw pay for a limited period of time, even if his purpose is merely to enable him to find another job.'[3]

In *Crook*'s case, the employee was presented with a letter of censure by his employers which was found to be repudiatory by the employment tribunal. Yet the employee's reaction was to attempt to repudiate the employer's allegations whilst continuing to work. It was only after six months that he wrote to the employer threatening to resign and claim constructive dismissal unless the allegations were withdrawn. And although the employer immediately replied that they would not withdraw

---

1   See eg *Bumpus v Standard Life Assurance Co Ltd* [1974] IRLR 232, IT; see also *Maher v Fram Gerrard Ltd* [1974] 1 All ER 449, [1974] ICR 31, NIRC.

2   [1981] ICR 823, [1981] IRLR 443.

3   See eg *Waltons & Morse v Dorrington* [1997] IRLR 488, EAT (employee who delayed a few weeks looking for another job before resigning held not to have affirmed the contract).

their allegations, Mr Crook waited almost a month before resigning. The EAT decided that whether or not the conduct of the innocent party amounts to affirmation is a mixed question of fact and law and if the employment tribunal has correctly directed itself in law they were not entitled to substitute their decision for the employment tribunal.[4]

Nevertheless the EAT took the view that the employment tribunal had erred in 'directing' themselves that the delay of one month after the employee's ultimatum had been rejected, during which the employee continued to work, amounted to an affirmation of the contract. As the EAT put it:

> 'to stay at work for a period of one month to look around starting from the initial breach of contract might have been fatal; but to work for a further month, six months having already elapsed, seems to us inconsistent with saying that he had not affirmed the contract.'[5]

Is it essential that the employee's protest be explicit? In *Sheet Metal Components Ltd v Plumridge*,[6] the NIRC suggested that an express protest may not be necessary if the circumstances suggest that the employee's continuation in the job did not imply genuine consent to the change introduced by the employer. In *Plumridge*'s case three employees agreed to a transfer to work at a different location at lower earnings on a trial basis. They remained in employment for one or two months after the change until they received other employment. The NIRC held that the acceptance by the employees of a change, in circumstances in which they had no real option but to accept the move at least for some period of time, raised a clear implication that the variation was non-consensual.

At the same time, however, there must be *some* indication that the employee intends to treat the employer's action as a basis for constructive dismissal. Thus, in *Wethersfield Ltd v Sargent* the Court of Appeal made the point that in order to establish a claim of constructive dismissal while there is no legal requirement that the employee must state that he is leaving

---

4   But see the decision of the Court of Appeal in *Woods v W M Car Services (Peterborough) Ltd* [1982] ICR 693, [1982] IRLR 413, CA, which describes the tribunal finding on repudiatory breach as a 'finding of fact'.

5   See also *Simister v Bryrob Hire Group* (1983) EAT 372/83.

6   [1974] ICR 373, [1974] IRLR 86, NIRC. See too *Luckhurst v Kent Litho Co Ltd* (1976) EAT 302/76; *Shields Furniture Ltd v Goff* [1973] 2 All ER 653, [1973] ICR 187, NIRC; *Heddon v James White (Shopfitters) Ltd* (1977) EAT 613/76, in which it was stressed that there was a need to find positive evidence of agreement to find that a variation had occurred. But see *Hunt v British Railways Board* [1979] IRLR 379, EAT.

because of the employer's repudiatory conduct, where no reason is communicated to the employer, a tribunal may readily conclude that as a matter of evidence and fact the repudiatory conduct was not the reason for the employee's resignation.[7] Moreover, in *Walker v Josiah Wedgwood & Sons Ltd*[8] the EAT indicated that, whilst it was not necessary to make a formal assertion of the contractual position, it was necessary to indicate that the reason why the contract would not be continued was the conduct of the employer which was regarded as unjustified by the employee.

As Arnold J put it:

'... it is at least requisite that the employee should leave because of the breach of the employer's relevant duty to him, and that this should demonstrably be the case. It is not sufficient, we think, if he merely leaves ... And secondly, we think it is not sufficient if he leaves in circumstances which indicate some ground for his leaving other than the breach of the employer's obligations to him.'

In *Walker*'s case the fact that the employee had resigned without giving any reason and then when interviewed had referred to the fact that he 'had got a better job', led the EAT to uphold a tribunal finding that the employer's repudiation had not been 'accepted' by the employee. And in *Norwest Holst Group Administration Ltd v Harrison*[9] the majority of the EAT thought that an alternative ground for finding there was no constructive dismissal was the fact that the evidence strongly suggested that the threat of the loss of directorship was not the effective cause of the resignation.

Yet the test of acceptance of repudiation is ultimately one of whether the resignation was effectively caused by the employer's repudiation. In *Jones v F Sirl & Son (Furnishers) Ltd*[10] the employee faced with worsened terms and conditions waited three-and-a-half weeks until she was approached by another firm and offered a job before she resigned claiming constructive dismissal. The employment tribunal's conclusion that the resignation was in response to the job offer and not the repudiation was overturned by the EAT which stated that the test was not what was the sole cause of the resignation but rather what in fact was the *effective* cause.

---

7   [1999] IRLR 94, CA.
8   [1978] ICR 744, EAT.
9   [1984] IRLR 419, EAT. See also *Logabax Ltd v Titherley* [1977] ICR 369, [1977] IRLR 97, EAT; *Devon County Council v Cook* [1977] IRLR 188, 12 ITR 347, EAT.
10   [1997] IRLR 493. See too *Waltons and Morse v Dorrington* [1997] IRLR 488, EAT.

In this case the main operative cause was the fundamental breach of her contract by her employers.

Finally, merely because an employee tolerates a series of breaches of contract or repudiations by the employer and continues to work does not prevent an employee arguing that these incidents, together with a subsequent breach by the employer, amounted to a repudiatory breach of the implied term of mutual trust and confidence and were the cause of the resignation.[11]

The retention of a requirement of contractual repudiation in the test of constructive dismissal creates considerable difficulties for employees faced with unjustified treatment by the employer. Although the adoption of the contractual test has led to a growth of implied contractual obligations by the employer to the employee, it nevertheless creates unjustifiable technical difficulties for employees. A correct diagnosis of the dividing line between repudiatory and non-repudiatory conduct and affirmation and acceptance by the employer is an unduly heavy burden to be placed on employees who are untrained in the intricacies of contract law. Equally importantly, the retention of a contractual test creates the possibility that employers might circumvent the statutory protection by creating a wide discretion for changes in hours, place or kind of work by express terms in the contract, and then subsequently changing the terms of employee's work in any of those respects, making working life sufficiently trying to prompt resignation. Perhaps the repudiation test can be stretched to cover this situation by applying the reasoning in *BBC v Beckett*[12] to place limits on the employer's exercise of his express contractual powers under s 95(1)(c).[13]

---

11   *Lewis v Motorworld Garages Ltd* [1986] ICR 157, [1985] IRLR 465, CA.
12   [1983] IRLR 43, EAT.
13   See Elias, 'Unravelling the Concept of Dismissal' (1978) 1 ILJ 16 and 100; Kerr, 'Contract Doesn't Live Here Any More' (1984) MLR 30.

Chapter 4.
The employer's reason for dismissal

Once employees succeed in meeting the preliminary requirements of an unfair dismissal claim, by proving that they are 'qualified' to make their complaint and demonstrating to the tribunal that they have been 'dismissed', the next issue which the tribunal must consider is whether in the circumstances that dismissal was fair or unfair. This issue is tested predominantly under ERA 1996, s 98 and in two stages. The first stage is concerned to identify the employer's reason for dismissal. The concept of unfair dismissal under the Act requires employers to isolate their reason for dismissal as a preliminary step in testing the fairness of that dismissal.[1]

 1   Under ERA 1996, s 92 there is a separate requirement that employers must, if requested, provide a written statement of particulars of the reasons for the dismissal within 14 days of the request. To qualify for this right an employee must have at least one year's continuous service as of the effective date of termination; cf *IPC Business Press Ltd v Gray* [1977] ICR 858, 12 ITR 148. If an employer fails to provide a written statement, or if the written particulars are inaccurate or untrue, the employee may present a complaint to an employment tribunal. *Harvard Securities plc v Younghusband* [1990] IRLR 17, EAT; *Rowan v Machinery Installations (South Wales) Ltd* [1981] ICR 386, [1981] IRLR 122, EAT.

    The test of reasonableness of the employer's failure is objective, see eg *Daynecourt Insurance Brokers Ltd v Iles* [1978] IRLR 335, EAT. Thus it may be reasonable to 'fail' to provide a statement where the employer on reasonable grounds believes that there was no dismissal *Broomsgrove v Eagle Alexander Ltd* [1981] IRLR 127, EAT; cf *Brown v Stuart Scott & Co* [1981] ICR 166, EAT, or in cases of constructive dismissal *Dean v Bowers* (14 September 1984, unreported) IT, 14/60/75. A delay by the employer in responding to a request may not amount to a failure; see eg *Charles Lang & Sons Ltd v Aubrey* [1978] ICR 168, [1977]

The second stage operates only after the employer's reason for dismissal has been identified and, where the reason is not automatically unfair, is designed to test the reasonableness of the employer's decision.

The first stage, the identification of the *reason for dismissal*, makes two major requirements of employers. First s 98(1)(a) places a burden of proof upon them to establish their reason for dismissal or if they had more than one reason their principal reason for dismissal.[2]

As Lord Donaldson put it in *Union of Construction, Allied Trades and Technicians v Brain*[3] employers have to show why *in fact* they dismissed

IRLR 354, EAT – three weeks delay. However, a stage may eventually be reached where inaction on the part of the employer amounts to a failure; see eg *Lowson v Percy Main and District Social Club and Institute Ltd* [1979] ICR 568, [1979] IRLR 277, EAT: *Keen v Dymo Ltd* [1977] IRLR 118; *Joines v B & S (Burknall) Ltd* [1977] IRLR 83, IT. The time limit for presenting a complaint to employment tribunals is the same as that for a complaint of unfair dismissal: ERA 1996, s 111(2). To assert a right to a written statement does not require presentation of a complaint of alleged unfair dismissal.

To meet the statutory test of adequacy, 'the document must be of a kind that the employee, or anyone to whom he may wish to show it, can know from reading the document itself why an employee was dismissed' (*Horsley Smith and Sherry Ltd v Dutton* [1977] ICR 594, [1977] IRLR 172, EAT). See too *Marchant v Earley Town Council* [1979] ICR 891, [1979] IRLR 311, EAT. For example, where an employer sends a letter making reference to a previous letter, that will be sufficient if the covering letter that refers unambiguously to the earlier letter is attached. See too *Gilham v Kent County Council* [1985] IRLR 16, CA. The employer's written statement, moreover, will presumably be required to go further than a mere classification of the dismissal under one of the statutory heads listed in ERA 1996, s 98. Yet the employer's statement of the main factual grounds for the dismissal need not contain 'elaborate particulars', *Bonimart Ltd v Delemore* (1980) EAT/272; *Earl v Valleythorn Ltd* (1981) EAT/376.

Where a tribunal decides than an employee's complaint concerning the inadequacy of the written statement is well founded, it may in its discretion make a declaration as to what the employer's reasons for the dismissal were as well as an award to the employee of a sum equal to the amount of 2 weeks' pay, subject to no maximum limit.

An award against the employer in respect of an inadequate written statement is addition to any compensation the employee might receive for unfair dismissal.

Whilst the immediate financial penalty for an inadequate written statement may be limited to the 2 weeks' pay, a poorly prepared written statement may have more serious financial implications since the statement is 'admissible in evidence', inter alia, in any unfair dismissal hearing. (ERA 1996, s 92(5).) See *McKenna v O'Donnell* [1983] 1 NIJB, CA.

2   See eg *Maund v Penwith District Council* [1984] ICR 143, [1984] IRLR 24, CA; *Adams v Derby City Council* [1986] IRLR 163, EAT; *Derby City Council v Marshall* [1979] ICR 731, [1979] IRLR 261, EAT.

3   [1981] ICR 542, [1981] IRLR 224, CA.

the employee. This places no great burden upon them since they will know why they dismissed the employee.[4]

The second requirement that has to be met by employers is s 98(1)(b); that their reason fits within one of the categories established as 'potentially valid' by the statute, notably:

(i)   that the reason related to capability or qualification, s 98(2)(a);

(ii)   that the reason related to the conduct of the employee, s 98(2)(b);

(iii)   that the employee was redundant, s 98(2)(c);

(iv)   that the employer was prohibited by statute from continuing to employ the individual in his job, s 98(2)(d); or

(v)   some other substantial reason justifying the employee's dismissal, s 98(1)(b).

If employers fail to show their reason for dismissal was a potentially valid reason then the dismissal will be unfair at this preliminary stage.

Alternatively, an employee can succeed in proving that the employer's reason for dismissal is a prohibited reason under ss 99–105 of the ERA 1996[5] or that their reason for dismissal was based on the employee's race[6] or sex,[7] or disability[8] or is an automatically unfair dismissal, under the Transfer of Undertakings Regulations 1981,[9] or some other unlawful ground,[10] then the dismissal will also be unfair at this preliminary stage.

In addition, the categories of prohibited reasons for dismissal which are automatically unfair have been considerably expanded in recent years. Under the ERA 1996 as amended they include the following:

s 99   Pregnancy and childbirth[11]

s 100   Health and safety cases[12]

4   Ibid. See too *Smith v City of Glasgow District Council* [1985] IRLR 79, Ct of Sess.

5   Such as for a health and safety reason (ERA 1996, s 100); for an assertion of statutory rights (ERA 1996, s 104); a selection for redundancy (under s 105, ERA); for a reason connected with a transfer of an undertaking or inadmissible reason (TULRCA 1992, s 152 or 153). See Chapter 10.

6   Race Relations Act 1976.

7   Sex Discrimination Act 1975.

8   Disability Discrimination Act 1995.

9   See Chapter 14.

10   Eg dismissal for a spent conviction or a failure to disclose a spent conviction in contravention of s 4(3) of the Rehabilitation of Offenders Act 1974, see Rehabilitation of Offenders Act 1974. See eg *Hendry v Scottish Liberal Club* [1977] IRLR 5.

11   See Chapter 13.

12   See *Goodwin v Cabletel UK Ltd* [1997] IRLR 665, EAT; *Harvest Press Ltd v McCaffrey* [1999] IRLR 778, EAT; *Masiak v City Restaurants (UK) Ltd* [1999] IRLR 780, EAT.

s 101	Shop workers and betting workers who refuse Sunday work
s 101A	Working Time cases
s 102	Trustees of occupational pension schemes
s 103	Employee representatives
s 103A	Protected disclosures[12a]
s 104	Assertion of a statutory right[13]
s 104A	The national minimum wage
s 104B	Tax credit
s 105	Redundancy[14]

The characteristic feature of all such cases is that if the employee is able to show that the employer's reason for its decision to dismiss fits within their scope, tribunals have no further discretion. They must find that the dismissal is unfair. Whatever balance is struck between employee protection and employer discretion has been strictly limited by the language of the particular statutory provision. To underscore that these reasons for dismissal are prioritised as public wrongs, the usual qualification of a period of continuous service (s 108) and upper age limit (s 109) is waived and special remedies apply.

The task required of an employer to show a potentially valid reason has been described in *Union of Construction, Allied Trades and Technicians v Brain*[15] by Lord Donaldson in the following terms:

'Next the employer has to show that this reason falls into one of the four categories of reasons set out in [s 98(2)] or that it was "some other substantial reason of a kind such as to justify the dismissal of an employee holding the position which that employee held". This is not an exercise in elaborate legal classification. All that is required is that the tribunal shall consider whether, looking at the matter broadly and giving the words their meaning, the reason for the dismissal falls within one of these five descriptions'.

At this stage, to meet the burden of proof employers need only show that their reason was one that could justify dismissal, not one that necessarily did justify it.[16] Nevertheless, the employment tribunal has the

---

12a *Miklaszewicz v Stolt Offshore Ltd* [2001] IRLR 656, EAT.
13   See *Mennell v Newell & Wright (Transport Contractors) Ltd* [1997] IRLR 519, CA.
14   See Chapter 8.
15   [1981] ICR 542, [1981] IRLR 224, CA.
16   See eg *Mercia Rubber Mouldings Ltd v Lingwood* [1974] IRLR 82, NIRC; *Trust House Forte Leisure Ltd v Aquilar* [1976] IRLR 251, EAT.

task of establishing the real reason for dismissal.[17] It must state the reason it has found for dismissal[18] and an incorrect characterisation of the reason can be a ground for appeal as an error of law.[19]

1. PROVING THE REASON FOR DISMISSAL

In showing their reason for the purposes of s 98(1) and (2), employers are engaged in proving a question of fact. Yet the fact to be proved is the employer's motivation for the dismissal. As Cairns LJ put it in *Abernethy v Mott, Hay and Anderson*:[20]

'A reason for the dismissal of an employee is a set of facts known to the employer, or it may be of beliefs held by him, which cause him to dismiss the employee.'

And as Lord Denning MR said in the same case 'the reason shown for dismissal must be the principal reason which operated on the employer's mind'.[1]

It follows from this that the reason shown for dismissal 'must be in existence at the time when (the employee) is given notice'.[2] Thus any matters which occur or are discovered subsequent to the dismissal will normally have no relevance in ascertaining the reason for dismissal, since they were not known to the employer and could not have provided a motivation for it. A tribunal must judge matters as they stand at the date of dismissal and upon information known to or available to the employer at the time. As Lord Donaldson MR in *Union of Construction, Allied Trades and Technicians v Brain* put it,[3] 'the Act does not concern itself with possible justifications which occur to the employer later or which did not move him at the time'.[4]

---

17   *Abernethy v Mott, Hay and Anderson* [1974] IRLR 213, CA; *McCrory v Magee* [1983] IRLR 414, NICA; cf *Ely v YKK Fasteners (UK) Ltd* [1993] IRLR 500, CA.

18   *British Railways Board v Jackson* [1994] IRLR 235, CA.

19   *Wilson v Post Office* [2000] IRLR 834, CA.

20   [1974] ICR 323, [1974] IRLR 213, CA.

1   Ibid.

2   See *W Devis & Sons Ltd v Atkins* [1977] AC 931, [1977] ICR 662, HL; *Parkinson v March Consulting Ltd* [1997] IRLR 308, CA.

3   *Union of Construction and Allied Trades and Technicians v Brain* [1981] ICR 542, [1981] IRLR 224, CA.

4   See *W Devis & Sons Ltd v Atkins* n 2, above.

Thus, if in the course of hearing an internal appeal by the employee after dismissal the employer obtains information which provides the basis of *another* reason for his dismissal, the employer cannot use it as a substitute for the reason which was in his mind at the time of the dismissal for the purpose of s 98(1) and (2).[5] Where the procedure throws up new evidence relating to the original ground for dismissal, the tribunal may be able to take it into account.[6] Where moreover, the appeal procedure saves the contract in all the circumstances pending the conclusion of the appeal, this might enable the employer to use information that emerged in the course of the appeal to state a new reason for dismissal.[7] For technically the date of dismissal will have been postponed by the contract until the end of the appeal.[8]

Secondly, since the fact which must be proved is the employer's reason, can the fact itself consist of the employee's subjective belief? Can an honest but mistaken view of the facts which is the real cause of the dismissal meet the test of s 98(1) that the employer must show his reason for dismissal? The answer appears to differ depending upon the alleged reason for dismissal. Thus, on the one hand, in cases of dismissal for conduct or capability, the employer's subjective belief or, in some cases, suspicion can be the reason for dismissal as long as it is the real cause of the dismissal, since the Act states only that the reason must be 'related to' either capability or conduct.[9]

For example, in *Trust Houses Forte Leisure Ltd v Aquilar*[10] an employer dismissed an employee for defrauding customers. The employee had argued that under s 98(1) and (2) it was necessary for the employer to prove that the employee was in fact guilty of the conduct alleged. The EAT rejected this contention, explaining that it was not necessary for the employer to prove actual guilt if he could show that his view of the employee's guilt was the reason for the dismissal. The EAT concluded:

---

5   *Monie v Coral Racing Ltd* [1981] ICR 109, [1980] IRLR 464, CA. There may, however, be circumstances where such evidence is admissible under s 98(4).

6   *National Heart and Chest Hospitals v Nambiar* [1981] IRLR 196, EAT; *Sillifant v Powell Duffryn Timber Ltd* [1983] IRLR 91, EAT.

7   *J Sainsbury Ltd v Savage* [1981] ICR 1, [1980] IRLR 109, CA. Cf *Cooke v Minister of Defence* (1984) Times, 14 May, CA.

8   See *Drage v Governors of Greenford High School* [2000] IRLR 314, CA. See further discussion of internal appeals and effective date of termination, Chapter 2.

9   See eg *Monie v Coral Racing Ltd* [1981] ICR 109, [1980] IRLR 464, CA.

10   [1976] IRLR 251, EAT.

'The reason for the dismissal was the misconduct of Mr Aquilar in the sense that it was the employer's belief in that misconduct which led them to dismiss him'.

In *Monie v Coral Racing Ltd*[11] the Court of Appeal suggested that requiring the employer to prove his belief for the purposes of s 98(2)(b) may be too high a standard where more than one employee was involved. In such a case where there was a reasonable suspicion that one of two or possibly both employees must have acted dishonestly this would be enough for the purposes of s 98(2)(b) and 98(1)(b).

Yet neither case provides authority for the proposition that employers are entitled to put forward their subjective view without any supporting evidence that that was their view. Both the belief and the suspicion must be 'reasonable'.[12]

On the other hand, the view that in conduct and capability dismissals, the employer may rely on a 'reasonable' but mistaken subjective belief as to the facts does not appear to extend to cases of dismissal for a purely subjective test of the employer's reason for dismissal may not be acceptable in cases of dismissals where continued employment would contravene a statutory enactment. For example in *Bouchaala v Trusthouses Forte Hotels Ltd*[13] the EAT stated quite emphatically that there was no justification for expanding the words of s 98(2)(d) to include a case where the employer genuinely but mistakenly believed that continued employment would be unlawful because of a statutory restriction. Yet in the same decision the EAT held by a majority that the same genuine but mistaken belief of the employer that an employee could not continue in employment without violating a statute could constitute a dismissal for some other substantial reason under s 98(1)(b). This decision rather controversially makes use of the back door of s 98(1)(b) where a case fails to meet a crucial requirement of s 98(2)(d). It also allows a genuine but mistaken belief be held on a point of law which could have been ascertained by legal advice. It is unclear to what extent this genuine belief test will be applied more widely to s 98(1)(b) cases.

In cases where a subjective belief by the employer is acceptable under s 98(1) and (2), that belief must be a genuine one. As the EAT stated in

---

11   [1981] ICR 109, [1980] IRLR 464, CA.
12   Ibid.
13   [1980] ICR 721, [1980] IRLR 382, EAT; but see *Harper v National Coal Board* [1980] IRLR 260, EAT.

Trust Houses Forte,[14] the employer's description of the reason for the dismissal is by no means conclusive. The tribunal must look at the matter and determine what was the reason. And as Lord Cairns said in *Abernethy v Mott Hay and Anderson*,[15]

> 'if at the time of the dismissal the employer gives a reason for it, that is no doubt evidence, at any rate against him as to the real reason, but it does not necessarily constitute the real reason'.

It is for the tribunal to determine on all the evidence whether the employer has shown them what was the real reason for dismissal.

Hence where an employer fails to come forward with any supporting evidence apart from a bare assertion of belief, a tribunal will be entitled to conclude that his stated reason was not his real reason for dismissal. The paucity of evidence may be such as to cast doubts upon the genuineness of the employer's asserted beliefs. For example, in *Pringle of Scotland Ltd v Nelson*[16] the EAT upheld an employment tribunal which found that the employer had not shown that his reason for dismissal was dissatisfaction with the employee's performance when the written record of such dissatisfaction was not 'substantial'. As the EAT put it:

> 'Evidence of dissatisfaction was not enough if it was unaccompanied by acceptable evidence that it was this dissatisfaction which was the reason for the dismissal.'[17]

In that sense it may be said that an employer must have reasonable grounds for the genuineness of his belief or suspicion even for the purposes of s 98(1) and (2).[18]

Thus, in cases of a dismissal of an employee for refusing to take part in a reorganisation short of redundancy there is some need to show a factual

14   [1976] IRLR 251. In *Trust Houses Forte*, for example, there was some positive evidence of misconduct proved by the customer's identification of the employee. Moreover, there may be cases where an employer's considered judgment may itself be regarded as some evidence. For example, in *Cook v Thomas Linnell & Sons Ltd* [1977] ICR 770, [1977] IRLR 132 the EAT stated 'when responsible employers have genuinely come to the conclusion over a reasonable period of time that a manager is incompetent, we think that is some evidence that he is incompetent'. Yet this in turn presupposes some evidence of responsible assessment and genuine conclusions.

15   [1974] ICR 323, [1974] IRLR 213, CA.

16   (1983) EAT 627/83.

17   See also *Castledine v Rothwell Engineering Ltd* [1973] IRLR 99, IT; *Yates v British Leyland (UK) Ltd* [1974] IRLR 367.

18   See eg *Monie v Coral Racing Ltd* (above).

basis. Thus in *Ladbroke Courage Holidays Ltd v Asten*,[19] the EAT indicated that where an employer sought to rely on business reorganisation or economic necessity as a reason for dismissal, he should have some evidence to show that there was a reorganisation or that there was some need for economy.

Further, where the evidence suggests an alternative motive which conflicts with the employer's alleged reason a tribunal will be entitled to doubt whether the employer's asserted reason is the real or principal reason for dismissal. Thus, in *Timex Corpn v Thomson*[20] where an employer had shown that there was a redundancy situation but had produced evidence of dissatisfaction with the employee's job performance, raising the possibility that redundancy was used only as a pretext for getting rid of the employee, it was open to the tribunal to hold that they had not been satisfied as to the reason or principal reason for the dismissal of that particular employee and hence that the dismissal was unfair.[1]

Similarly, in cases where the employee alleges that the employer's stated reason for dismissal is a pretext and that the real reason was the trade union activities of the employee that tribunal will have discretion to determine upon the evidence what they consider the real reason to be,[2] subject only to the limits of misdirection or perversity.[3]

Moreover, in *O'Brien v International Harvester Co of Great Britain*,[4] an employer alleged that the dismissal was for incapability and that the employee was medically unfit for the job. The tribunal found on the facts,

19   [1981] IRLR 59, EAT; see also *Orr v Vaughan* [1981] IRLR 63, EAT; but see *Hollister v National Farmers' Union* [1979] ICR 542, [1979] IRLR 238, CA; *Robinson v British Island Airways Ltd* [1978] ICR 304, [1977] IRLR 477, EAT which talked of a 'genuine reorganisation' as a condition. See discussion in Chapter 9.

20   [1981] IRLR 522, EAT. See also *Pringle of Scotland Ltd v Nelson*, above; *Lomax v Ladbroke Racing Ltd* [1975] IRLR 363, IT.

1   See eg *Luckham Ltd v Tranter* (1984) EAT 633/83.

2   *Maund v Penwith District Council* [1984] IRLR 24, CA; *Duncan v Stockwell Clothing Manufacturers Co Ltd* (1983) EAT 608/83; *Taylor v Butler Machine Tool Co Ltd* [1976] IRLR 113, IT.

3   See eg *Therm-A-Stor Ltd v Atkins* [1983] IRLR 78, CA; see also Chapter 10.

4   [1974] IRLR 374. See too obiter in *Carlin v St Cuthbert's Co-operative Association Ltd* [1974] IRLR 188, NIRC. 'If an employer gives two reasons for dismissing an employee and only one is established by the evidence led before the tribunal, and there is no evidence as to which reason was subordinate to the other, the employer's defence may fail upon the view that what was in fact the principal reason for dismissal has not been proved'. The requirement to identify the principal reason under s 98(1) does not bind the tribunal in respect of s 98(4). Cf *Smith v City of Glasgow District Council* [1985] IRLR 79, Ct of Sess.

however, that the real reason was the employer's belief that the employee was malingering or not doing his best to facilitate his recovery – a reason related to conduct rather than capability – and that the employer had not met the burden of proof showing what was the principal reason for dismissal.[5]

Furthermore, where the employer's own description of events suggests a motive contrary to his stated motive the possibility of convincing the tribunal that his stated motive is his real motive is greatly reduced. For example in *Castledine v Rothwell Engineering Ltd*[6] it emerged from the evidence that although the dismissal was for alleged incapability the employer had given the employee a very good reference when he was dismissed, stating among other things 'at all times he carried out his duties satisfactorily very often under difficult conditions'. Indeed, a good reference by the employer may well estop an employer from claiming capability as the reason for the dismissal.

Similarly, where the employer gives particulars of the reasons for the dismissal in a written statement requested by the employee under s 92 of ERA 1996, the information contained in the statement would be admissible in evidence and the employer may well be estopped from denying the accuracy of the particulars contained in the statement.[7]

Yet tribunal discretion, it would appear, can also run the other way. In *McCrory v Magee (Heatwell Heating Systems)*[8] the Northern Ireland Court of Appeal held that a tribunal had not erred in law in holding that the employer's reason for dismissal was his belief or suspicion of the employee's dishonesty, notwithstanding that the employer had denied that he had dismissed the employee for stealing and had stated that his reason for dismissal was that the employee did not carry out his duties. Following *Abernethy*'s case, provided that it is satisfied on adequate evidence that the reason it selects was the employer's reason at the time of dismissal a tribunal could decide that the employer's reason was other than the reason proffered by the employer. Where there is a change in the label by the

---

5   See eg *Patterson v Messrs Bracketts* [1977] IRLR 137, EAT and *Bates Farms and Dairy Ltd v Scott* [1976] IRLR 214, EAT.

6   [1973] IRLR 99, IT. See also *Pinzeland v Richardson* (1976) EAT 221/76.

7   *Lomax v Ladbroke Racing Ltd* [1975] IRLR 363; see *Haspell v Restron & Johnson Ltd* [1976] IRLR 50, EAT; *Gilham v Kent County Council* [1983] IRLR 353, EAT.

8   [1983] IRLR 414, NICA.

tribunal, care must be taken to ensure that the employee is not placed at a procedural or evidential disadvantage.[9]

2. PROVING THAT THE REASON WAS A DESIGNATED REASON

The second requirement placed upon employers is to prove that their reason was a *designated* reason under s 98(2) or 98(1)(b). If the evidence produced by the employer indicates that the ground relied on does not fit with the statutory category a tribunal can find that the employer fails at this stage. For example, in *Thomson v Alloa Motor Co Ltd*,[10] an employment tribunal which held that the employer had shown a reason for dismissal under s 98(2)(b) of the Act when he had shown that the employee was dismissed for causing damage to a petrol pump on leaving work was held to have erred in law because conduct within the meaning of s 98(2)(b) did not extend to conduct outside the course of employment unless it reflected in some way on the employer/employee relationship.

Moreover, if employees allege that the employee has been dismissed for redundancy under s 98(2)(c) but fail to prove that the dismissal fits under the definition of redundancy provided by ERA 1996, s 139(1), then they may fail on that issue.[11] Of course, where the employer incorrectly labels the facts at the time of dismissal and this involves a mistake of law, a tribunal will not be precluded from finding on the basis of facts established at the hearing that the real reason is different from the label given to the set of facts by the employer. For example, in *Abernethy v Mott Hay and Anderson*[12] an employer honestly, but wrongly, believed that the facts of the case constituted redundancy. The tribunal concluded, however, after looking at the facts, that the employer's reason related to the capabilities

---

9   *Hotson v Wisbech Conservative Club* [1984] IRLR 422, EAT; *Clarke v Trimoco Group* [1993] IRLR 148, EAT; cf *Ely v YKK Fasteners (UK) Ltd* [1993] IRLR 500, CA.
10 [1983] IRLR 403, EAT.
11 *Gorman v London Computer Training Centre Ltd* [1978] ICR 394, [1978] IRLR 22, EAT; cf *Cowen v Haden Ltd* [1983] ICR 1, [1982] IRLR 225, EAT; *Carry All Motors Ltd v Pennington* [1980] ICR 806, [1980] IRLR 455, EAT; *Robinson v British Island Airways Ltd* [1978] ICR 304, [1977] IRLR 477, EAT; *Elliott v University Computing Co (GB) Ltd* [1977] ICR 147, EAT; *Babar Indian Restaurant v Rawat* [1985] IRLR 57, EAT.
12 [1974] ICR 323, [1974] IRLR 213, CA. See too *Shawkat v Nottingham City Hospital NHS Trust (No 2)* [2001] EWCA Civ 954, [2001] IRLR 555.

of the employee to do the work he was employed to do. When the case reached the Court of Appeal, Lord Denning MR commented:

> 'I do not think that the reason has got to be correctly labelled *at the time of dismissal* (author's italics). It may be that the employer is wrong in law as labelling it as dismissal for redundancy. In that case the wrong label can be set aside'.

Cairns LJ added:

> 'If at the time of dismissal the employer gives a reason for it that is no doubt evidence, at any rate as against him, as to the real reason for the dismissal but it does not necessarily constitute the real reason. He may knowingly give a reason different from the real reason out of kindness or because he might have some difficulty in proving the facts that actually led him to dismiss; or he may describe his reasons wrongly through some mistake of language or law. In particular in these days, when the word "redundancy" has a specific statutory meaning, it is very easy for an employer to think that the facts which led him to dismiss constitute a redundancy situation whereas in law they do not; and in my opinion the Industrial Tribunal was entitled to take the view that that was what happened here: the employers honestly thought that the facts constituted redundancy, but in law they did not'.

In *Abernethy*'s case the employers had given as their reason for dismissal '(a) redundancy and/or (b) the incapability of the employee for performing work of the kind which he was employed by the employer to do'. In other words, the employer had pleaded in the alternative and the facts were sufficient to identify capability even though not redundancy.

The key point is that if the employment tribunal can find facts which were relied upon by the employer then it may be entitled to correct the employer's mislabelling. For example, in *Gorman v London Computer Training Centre Ltd*,[13] where a case was remitted to an employment tribunal to decide whether in fact the employer's reason was redundancy, it was open to the employment tribunal to allow the employer to amend his answer to plead in the alternative that if the dismissal for technical reasons did not constitute redundancy, it was for some other substantial reason. The EAT argued that the pleadings of the employment tribunals could not be equated

---

13   [1978] ICR 394, [1978] IRLR 22, EAT; *Hotson v Wisbech Conservative Club* [1984] ICR 859, [1984] IRLR 422, EAT.

with the more formal rules of pleadings in the High Court. Moreover, there had been mention of the other substantial reason at issue during the course of the case. Finally it stated that the Court of Appeals' concern that facts found in relation to s 98(4) should not be applied to an unpleaded defence under s 98(1)(b) would not be offended if facts which were advanced to support the proposition that the employer's reason for dismissal fell under s 98(2)(c) were considered to determine whether it fell under s 98(1)(b).

Yet, the employment tribunal may not impute from the facts a reason to an employer where the employer itself had not advanced such a reason.

Consequently, where the employer's *only* designated reason for dismissal in his defence before the employment tribunal is based on an incorrect legal conclusion upon the facts, the employer may well fail at the first stage. For example in *Nelson v BBC*[14] the employer claimed that the reason for dismissal was redundancy. This was based on the incorrect supposition that the scope of the employee's work was confined to 'the Caribbean Service'. The employee's contract made it quite clear, however, that the employee was not restricted solely to such work. The EAT found that the dismissal could not be for reasons of redundancy, as the tribunal had mistakenly concluded, but considered the incorrect labelling 'only a very technical point'. The respondent had suggested for the first time before the EAT that the dismissal might be for some other substantial reason under s 98(1)(b).

The Court of Appeal found that the EAT had erred in law. 'It was not a question of whether the designated reason under s 98(1) and (2) was inaccurately stated, there never was any reason designated under s 98(1) at all'. The point was not merely a technical one. As Roskill LJ commented:

'What the Employment Appeal Tribunal did here was to look at facts which had been found in an altogether different context, namely, the context of [s 98(4)] made after a finding of redundancy under [s 98(2)(c)] and then treat those findings as if they could properly be applied to an unpleaded defence by the Corporation, never raised before the Industrial Tribunal, with no findings of fact by that tribunal directed towards it, to support dismissal under [s 98(1)(b)]'.

He added:

'One cannot really apply facts found in relation to [s 98(4)] to a possible but unpleaded defence under [s 98(1)] and then treat them

14   [1977] ICR 649, [1977] IRLR 148, CA. See also *Babar Indian Restaurant v Rawat* [1985] IRLR 57, EAT.

as applicable to that latter subsection. It may be that if an application to amend the defence had been made before the [Employment] Tribunal different considerations would have arisen. Then their findings of fact would, one hopes, also have been directed to that amended defence'.

In *Murphy v Epsom College*[15] the Court of Appeal endorsed the decision of the EAT that an employment tribunal had erred in holding that the reason for dismissal after a reorganisation was alternatively redundancy or some other substantial reason despite the fact that the employer had never sought to justify the dismissal on the latter ground, and the point was never ventilated at all at the tribunal hearing. As the EAT put it, 'unless the matter is expressly ventilated in the [employment] tribunal the parties will not have a full and proper opportunity to deploy their case on that matter. Natural justice requires that a party should not have a case decided against him on a ground on which he has not had an opportunity to be heard'. The Court of Appeal expressly agreed with the view.[16]

Moreover, as the House of Lords has stated in *Smith v City of Glasgow* where the employer puts forward several reasons and one is found to be not proven, it may be an error of law for the employment tribunal

'to accept as a reasonably sufficient reason for dismissal, a reason which, at least, in respect of an important part was neither established in fact nor believed to be true on reasonable grounds'.[17]

This may be viewed as a limitation on the improper use of multiple reasons by employers. Furthermore, in *Adams v Derby City Council*[18] the EAT stated that it can be an error of law for an employment tribunal to proceed to the issue of reasonableness of dismissal before the employer has satisfied it as to the reason for dismissal.

Finally, where an employee succeeds in proving that he or she was constructively dismissed, there may be special rules about the requirements placed by s 98(1) and (2) upon the employer. In *Derby City Council v Marshall*[19] the EAT held that where the council had failed to show a reason for dismissal, the tribunal had no duty to consider for itself whether the

---

15   [1985] ICR 80, [1984] IRLR 271, CA.
16   *Murphy v Epsom College* [1985] ICR 80, [1984] IRLR 271, CA. See also *Hotson v Wisbech Conservative Club* [1984] ICR 859, [1984] IRLR 422, EAT.
17   [1987] ICR 796, [1987] IRLR 326, HL; see too *Carlin v St Cuthbert's Cooperative Association Ltd* [1974] IRLR 188, NIRC.
18   [1986] IRLR 163, EAT.
19   [1979] ICR 731, [1979] IRLR 261, EAT.

council had a reason for dismissing an employee and had not erred in finding a dismissal unfair on that ground.

Yet, in *Berriman v Delabole Slate Ltd*[20] the Court of Appeal per Lord Browne-Wilkinson stated that 'the only way in which the statutory requirements of [ERA 1996] can be made to fit in a case of constructive dismissal is to read [s 98(1)] as requiring the employer to *show the reasons for his conduct which entitled the employee to terminate the contract* thereby giving rise to a deemed dismissal by the employer'.

Moreover the *Abernethy* principle can also work in the employer's favour in constructive dismissal cases. For example in *Ely v YKK Fasteners (UK) Ltd*[1] an employer was led to believe by the employee that he was ready to resign. The employee changed his mind and when the employer treated the employment as terminated, the tribunal viewed the case as one of constructive dismissal. The employer was held to be entitled to argue that the dismissal was for some other substantial reason under s 98(1)(b) of the Act. Waite LJ stated that:

'If resort can be had to a state of facts known to and relied on by the employer at the time, for the purpose of substituting a valid reason for any invalid or misdescribed reason given by the employer through misapprehension or mistake, there seems to me to be every justification for extending that principle to enable resort to be had to a set of facts known to and relied on by the employer, for the purpose of supplying him with a reason for dismissal which, as a consequence of his misapprehension of the true nature of the circumstances, he was disabled from treating as such at the time.'

Finally, employment tribunals are required to determine the reason or principal reason for dismissal without taking account of any industrial pressure that may have been exercised upon the employer to dismiss the employee.[2]

At all events, even if the employer is able adequately to identify his reason for dismissal for the purposes of s 98(1) and (2) there is still the major question of whether the dismissal for that reason was reasonable in the circumstances.

---

20   [1985] ICR 546, [1985] IRLR 305, CA.
1   [1993] IRLR 500, CA.
2   See eg *Hazells Offset Ltd v Luckett* [1977] IRLR 430, EAT; *Ford Motor Co Ltd v Hudson* [1978] 3 All ER 23, [1978] ICR 482, EAT.

Chapter 5.
Did the employer act reasonably in dismissing the employee?

I. INTRODUCTION

If employers succeed in showing that their reason for dismissal was a potentially valid reason for dismissal in accordance with s 98(1), the next step for an employment tribunal is to test the reasonableness of the employer's decision to dismiss under s 98(4).

That subsection specifically requires tribunals to determine the question whether the dismissal was fair or unfair, 'having regard to the reason shown by the employer'. Their decision must depend on 'whether in the circumstances (including the size and administrative resources of their undertaking) the employer acted reasonably or unreasonably in treating their reason as a sufficient reason for dismissing the employee'. The provision adds that the question shall be determined in accordance with equity and the substantial merits of the case.

One notable element in the current form of s 98(4) is its apparently 'neutral' burden of proof. The tribunal must look at the evidence and weigh and decide without any guidelines as to what it should do if the evidence is evenly balanced.[1] Of course this does not remove a burden on the employers to come forward with evidence for any of their assertions, and in particular that they acted reasonably.[2] Moreover, the impact of the employer's burden of proving the reason for the dismissal will influence

---

1   See eg *Post Office (Counters) Ltd v Heavey* [1989] IRLR 513, EAT.
2   *Martin v Automobile Proprietory Ltd* [1979] IRLR 64, EAT; see also *Abbotts and Standley v Wesson-Glynwed Steels Ltd* [1982] IRLR 51, EAT.

the burden of coming forward with evidence about the fairness of the dismissal decision for that reason.[3]

In determining as a question of fact whether or not the employer's decision to dismiss was reasonable or unreasonable in the meaning of the subsection, employment tribunals enjoy considerable discretion. They are viewed at 'industrial juries' applying the accepted standards of industry operating at the relevant time and place.[4] Thus, even where the Employment Appeal Tribunal or a court of higher instance may disagree with an employment tribunal's decision on the facts, they have no right to substitute their views for those of the tribunal. As Lord Donaldson put it in *Union of Construction and Allied Trades and Technicians v Brain*[5]

> 'whether someone acted reasonably is always a pure question of fact, so long as the Tribunal deciding the issue correctly directs itself on matters which should and should not be taken into account. But where Parliament has directed a Tribunal to have regard to equity, which means common fairness, the Tribunal's duty is very plain. It has to look at the question in the round and without regard to lawyers technicalities. It has to look at it in an employment and industrial relations context. It should therefore be very rare for any decision of an [Employment] Tribunal under this section to give rise to any question of law, and where Parliament has given to the Tribunals so wide a discretion appellate courts should be very slow to find that the Tribunal has erred in law'.

Moreover, in *Eclipse Blinds Ltd v Wright*[6] the Court of Sessions reminded that the weight to be attached to any evidence, and the inferences to be drawn from facts, are matters for the tribunal determining the facts and not for an appellate tribunal. In a number of cases the Court of Appeal has warned that care must be taken to avoid dressing up points of fact as points of law[7] and searching around with a fine toothcomb for some point of law.[8]

3   See *Smith v City of Glasgow District Council* [1987] IRLR 326, HL.
4   See eg *Grundy (Teddington) Ltd v Willis* [1976] ICR 323, [1976] IRLR 118, EAT.
5   [1981] ICR 542, [1981] IRLR 224, CA.
6   [1992] IRLR 133, Ct of Sess.
7   See eg remarks of Lord Denning in *Hollister v National Farmers Union* [1979] ICR 542 at 553. *Thomas & Betts Manufacturing Ltd v Harding* [1980] IRLR 255, CA.
8   See eg Lord Russell's remarks in *Retarded Children's Aid Society Ltd v Day* [1978] ICR 437 at 444, [1978] IRLR 128, CA; *Martin v Glynwed Distribution Ltd* [1983] IRLR 198, CA; *Spook Erection v Thackray* [1984] IRLR 116, Ct of Sess; *Kent County Council v Gilham* [1985] IRLR 18, CA.

In the decision of the Court of Appeal in *Kearney & Trecker Marwin Ltd v Varndell*,[9] Eveleigh LJ said the following:

'There is today too great a tendency to seize upon words in a judgment and use them as though they were laying down some new rule of law. ... We must not strive to create a body of judge-made law supplementing the law as laid down in the ... Act .... The Act itself provides quite enough law in all conscience and it is no part of the judicial function to increase the potential area of appeal, which ... is only on a point of law, by increasing the numbers of points of law governing the determination of a case'.

In *Kearney*, furthermore, the Court of Appeal also took the occasion to remind that whilst tribunals are obliged to state the reasons for their decisions,[10] they are not obliged to provide an analysis of the facts and arguments on both sides with reasons for rejecting those they did reject and for accepting those relied upon in support of their conclusion. Such 'full reasons'[11] are not necessary as long as the appeal tribunal is provided with the materials which will enable it to know that the tribunal made no error of law in reaching its findings of fact.[12]

And in *Union of Construction, Allied Trades and Technicians v Brain*,[13] Lord Justice Donaldson, said

'[Employment] tribunals' reasons are not intended to include a complicated and detailed analysis of the case either in terms of fact or law ... their purpose remains what it has always been which is to tell the parties in broad terms why they lost or, as the case may be, won. I think that it would be a thousand pities if these reasons began to be subjected to a detailed analysis and appeals were to be brought

---

9   [1983] IRLR 335, CA.
10   Rule 10(3) of the Employment Tribunals (Constitution and Rules of Procedure) Regulations 1993 SI 1993/2687.
11   See *Cooper v British Steel Corpn* [1975] IRC 454, [1975] IRLR 308, EAT. Since 1985 tribunals are allowed to give their reasons in summary form only or where a party requests it either orally at the hearing or in writing within 21 days after the summary reasons have been sent to the parties. (See Rule 10 as amended.) Employment Tribunals (Constitution and Rules of Procedure) Regulations 1993, SI 1993/2687.
12   *Kearney & Trecker Marwin Ltd v Varndell* [1983] IRLR 335 at para 35, CA, see now *Levy v Marrable & Co Ltd* (1984) EAT 797/83, [1984] ICR 583; *Yasut v Aberplace Ltd (t/a GM Plastics)* (1984) EAT 197/83, [1984] ICR 850, EAT.
13   [1981] IRLR 224, CA; see too *Meek v City of Birmingham District Council* [1987] IRLR 250, CA.

based upon any such analysis. This, to my mind is to misuse the purpose for which reasons are given'.

Yet the discretion of employment tribunals under s 98(4) whilst extremely wide is not unbounded. An appeal may still be allowed from an employment tribunal decision on either of two grounds: misdirection on the applicable law or perversity.[14]

The traditional definition of perversity as a basis of appeal where an employment tribunal is engaged in making a finding of fact is that a tribunal can only be successfully overturned if the evidence for its decision is obviously so inadequate that 'no reasonable tribunal properly directing itself could, upon the facts before it, have come to the conclusion which it did'.[15]

In *Hereford and Worcester County Council v Neale*,[16] May LJ suggested that the test should be whether the appellate court could say 'My goodness, that was certainly wrong'. This was given explicit support by the Court of Appeal in *British Telecommunications plc v Sheridan*.[17] However, the Court of Appeal favoured the narrower formula in *Piggott Bros & Co Ltd v Jackson*,[18] that a decision of an employment tribunal can only be characterised as perverse if it was not a permissible option for the tribunal to take and this will almost always require the EAT to identify a finding of fact which was unsupported by any evidence. In *East Berkshire Health Authority v Matadeen*[19] the EAT urged that the test of perversity should be a free-standing ground in law based on a test closer to May LJ's test in *Neale* viz that the members of the EAT were satisfied in the light of their own experience and of sound industrial practice that the decision was not a permissible option or offended reason, or was clearly wrong or one which no reasonable tribunal could have reached.

14   See *British Telecommunications plc v Sheridan* [1990] IRLR 27, CA.
15   See eg *Global Plant Ltd v Secretary of State for Health and Social Security* [1972] 1 QB 139, [1971] 3 All ER 385. The standard has sometimes been described as 'where there was no evidence upon which a reasonable tribunal could have reached its conclusion of fact' (*Palmer v Vauxhall Motors* [1977] ICR 24, EAT), or where the evidence was 'wholly contradictory to that conclusion' (*Watling v William Bird & Son Construction Ltd* (1976) 11 ITR 70). See also *Retarded Children's Aid Society Ltd v Day* [1978] ICR 437, [1978] IRLR 128, CA.
16   [1986] IRLR 168, CA.
17   [1990] IRLR 27, CA.
18   [1991] IRLR 309, CA.
19   *East Berkshire Health Authority v Matadeen* [1992] IRLR 336, EAT.

The net effect of these decisions is to leave the EAT in a position to choose between these versions of perversity until the issue is settled by higher authority.

In one case, *Williams v Compair Maxam Ltd*,[20] a case concerning unfair redundancy, Browne-Wilkinson J suggested that there may be a feature of appeals on grounds of perversity that is unique to employment law. As he put it,

'In considering whether the decision of an [Employment] Tribunal is perverse in a legal sense, there is one feature which does not occur in other jurisdictions where there is a right of appeal only on a point of law. The [Employment] Tribunal is an industrial jury which brings to its task a knowledge of industrial relations both from the view point of the employer and the employee. Matters of good industrial relations practice are not proved before an [Employment] Tribunal as they would be proved before an ordinary court; the lay members are taken to know them. The lay members of the [Employment] Tribunal bring to their task their expertise in a field where conventions and practices are of the greatest importance. Therefore in considering whether the decision of an [Employment] Tribunal is perverse, it is not safe to rely solely on the common sense and knowledge of those who have no experience in the field of Industrial Relations. A course of conduct which to those who have no practical experience with industrial relations might appear unfair or unreasonable, to those with specialist knowledge and experience might appear both fair and reasonable: and vice versa'.

The EAT has applied this approach to perversity in the determination of the s 98(4) issue in non-redundancy dismissals.[1]

The second ground on which an appeal may be allowed from a decision of an employment tribunal under s 98(4) is that the tribunal has failed to direct itself properly upon the law.[2] It is quite true that the Court of Appeal

20   [1982] ICR 156 at 160–161, [1982] IRLR 83 at 86, EAT.
1   See eg *Payne v Spook Erection Ltd* [1984] IRLR 219, EAT.
2   See *Dobie v Burns International Security Services (UK) Ltd* [1984] IRLR 329, CA, which held that where a tribunal misdirects itself, … 'the next question to be asked is not whether the conclusion of the tribunal is plainly wrong, but whether it is plainly and unarguably right notwithstanding that misdirection. It is only if it is plainly and unarguably right notwithstanding the misdirection that the decision can stand. If the conclusion was wrong or *might* have been wrong, then it is for an appellate tribunal to remit the case to the only tribunal which is charged with making findings of fact'. See too *Morgan v Electrolux Ltd* [1991] IRLR 89, CA; *Wilson v Post Office* [2000] IRLR 834, CA.

and latterly the EAT have made it clear that the decisions of the EAT or even the Court of Appeal itself should not be taken to establish binding rules or presumptions for the tribunal to follow or take into account in applying s 98(4). Instead, tribunals have been urged to concentrate upon and take as their starting point the words of the statute itself.[3]

Nevertheless, as has also been made quite plain by the House of Lords, the Court of Appeal and the EAT, employment tribunals do not have complete *carte blanche* in interpreting s 98(4). It is clearly not the case that 'all the [Employment] Tribunal has to do is to recite the words of the statutes and ask itself was the dismissal fair or unfair and arrive at an unappealable decision'. Nor is it the case that in answering that question it is not required to apply any standard other than its own collective wisdom.[4]

For even the pure language of s 98(4) places certain limits upon the exercise of tribunal discretion. Thus, as has been clearly indicated by the House of Lords in *W Devis & Sons Ltd v Atkins*[5] the statutory test of fairness in s 98(4) directs the tribunal to focus its attention upon the conduct of the employers not on whether the employee in fact suffered any injustice. This means that, even where an employment tribunal concentrates solely upon the language of the statute, it is subject to certain constraints upon the way it must go about determining the reasonableness of the employer's decision to dismiss.

Hence in judging the reasonableness of an employer's action an employment tribunal must normally take into account only those circumstances actually known to the employer at the time of dismissal or circumstances of which he could and should have known at the moment of dismissal.[6] As Viscount Dilhorne put it in *W Devis & Sons Ltd v Atkins*:[7]

"'It' (s 98(4)) must refer to the reason shown by the employer and to the reason for which the employee was dismissed. Without doing very great violence to the language I cannot construe this paragraph as enabling the tribunal to have regard to matters of which the

---

3   See eg *Bailey v BP Oil (Kent Refinery) Ltd* [1980] ICR 642, [1980] IRLR 287, CA; *Rolls Royce Ltd v Walpole* [1980] IRLR 343, EAT; *Iceland Frozen Foods Ltd v Jones* [1983] ICR 17, EAT; *Anandarajah v Lord Chancellor's Department* [1984] IRLR 131, EAT.

4   *W Devis & Sons Ltd v Atkins* [1977] AC 931, [1977] ICR 662, HL.

5   Ibid.

6   *Earl v Slater & Wheeler (Airlyne) Ltd* [1973] 1 All ER 145, [1972] IRLR 115, NIRC; *St Anne's Board Mill Co Ltd v Brien* [1973] ICR 444, [1973] IRLR 309, NIRC; *Chrystie v Rolls Royce (1971) Ltd* [1976] IRLR 336, EAT.

7   [1977] AC 931, [1977] ICR 662.

employer was unaware at the time of dismissal and which therefore cannot form part of his reason or reasons for dismissing an employee'.

Thus clearly any event that occurs subsequent to the decision to dismiss, even though it may bear upon the correctness or incorrectness of the dismissal, will not normally be admissible in evidence either to support or to deny the reasonableness of the employer's decision to dismiss. For example, in misconduct cases where an employee is dismissed for an alleged criminal offence, although the fact that the police had arrested and charged the employee *before* the dismissal may be both relevant and important,[8] any development that occurs *after* the dismissal, whether a conviction, an acquittal or even a refusal of the police to take action, would not be a relevant circumstance in the determination of the reasonableness of the employer's decision to dismiss.[9] Moreover, in cases of redundancy, if an employer dismisses employees and at a later date the business recovers and new men are taken on, these events subsequent to the dismissal are only 'indirectly relevant if relevant at all'.[10]

Further, any information that becomes available to the employer after the dismissal is normally not admissible on the question of the reasonableness of his decision to dismiss, even if the information consists of evidence of misconduct by the employee or injustice to an employee[11] which occurred prior to the dismissal. For example, where, as in *Devis'* case, an employee is dismissed for a failure to comply with directions and is subsequently discovered to have been dishonest, the evidence of dishonesty may not normally be allowed on the question of the reasonableness of the employer's decision to dismiss. The test for the tribunal was the reasonableness of the employer's behaviour at and leading up to the time of dismissal.[12]

8   *Carr v Alexander Russell* [1979] ICR 469n, [1976] IRLR 220, Ct of Sess.
9   *Bates Farms and Dairy v Scott* [1976] IRLR 214, EAT. See also *West Midlands Co-operative Society Ltd v Tipton* [1985] IRLR 116, CA. At the same time, it would be relevant to the question of the employee's entitlement to compensation (see Chapter 16).
10 *O'Connell and Wood v Hiltop Steel Structures Ltd* (1976) EAT 27/76.
11 *W Devis & Sons Ltd v Atkins*, above.
12 [1977] AC 931, [1977] IRLR 314. *Devis'* case was decided under TULRA. Several law lords expressed reservations about their willingness to extend it to that Act as amended by EPA because of the entitlement of the employee to a basic award. At common law, the opposite rule applies for cases of wrongful dismissal. See eg *Boston Deep Sea Fishing and Ice Co v Ansell* (1888) 39 Ch D 339, 59 LT 345, CA; *Cyril Leonard & Co v Simo Securities Trust* [1971] 3 All ER 1318, [1972] 1 WLR 80, CA.

This constraint however does not operate to preclude evidence of which the employer ought to have known from being held against the employer even if he did not actually know of it. This point was first acknowledged by the NIRC in *St Anne's Board Mill Co Ltd v Brien*[13] when Sir Hugh Griffiths pointed out that the reasonableness of an employer's decision to dismiss was to be decided not only in the light of the circumstances known to the employer at the moment of dismissal, but also in the light of circumstances 'of which he ought reasonably to have known at the moment of dismissal'. It was later supported by the House of Lords in *W Devis & Sons Ltd v Atkins*,[14] in which Viscount Dilhorne stated:

> 'it cannot, in my opinion, be said that the employer acted reasonably in treating (the reason shown as sufficient) if he only did so in consequence of ignoring matters he ought reasonably to have known and which would have shown that the reason was insufficient'.

In *Weddel & Co Ltd v Tepper*[15] however, the Court of Appeal per Stephenson LJ added the cautionary note that

> 'Reading that passage as a whole I understand that last sentence to mean "what reasonably (the employers) ought to have known if it was a proper case to carry out a further investigation and if they had carried out that investigation".'

Furthermore, since the decision of the EAT in *National Heart and Chest Hospitals Board of Governors v Nambiar*[16] there may be an exception in a case where an employer provides an internal appeals procedure. Apart from this the constraint in *W Devis & Sons Ltd v Atkins* applies pervasively to tribunals applying s 98(4). It does not apply however, to exclude evidence on the later question of the amount of compensation to which an employee is entitled.[17]

The second constraint upon tribunal discretion in applying s 98(4) is that it must not impose upon an employer its view of what is a more reasonable decision. It must restrict itself to looking at what the employer has decided and ask itself whether the employer has acted reasonably in

---

13　[1973] ICR 444, [1973] IRLR 309, NIRC.
14　[1977] AC 931, [1977] ICR 662, HL.
15　[1980] ICR 286, [1980] IRLR 96, CA.
16　[1981] IRLR 196, EAT; see too *Drage v Governors of Greenford High School* [2000] IRLR 314, CA; *West Midlands Co-operative Society Ltd v Tipton* [1986] IRLR 112, HL. Cf *Cooke v Ministry of Defence* (1984) Times, 14 May, CA. See now *Greenall Whitley plc v Carr* [1985] ICR 451, EAT.
17　See discussion Chapter 17.

the circumstances in taking his decision to dismiss. The duty of the tribunal is to hear the evidence, putting itself in the position, as it were, of the employer. Having heard the evidence it must not fall into the error of asking itself the question 'if we had been the employer would we have done it this way?' Instead, the tribunal has to judge by the objective standard of whether the employer has acted as a reasonable employer in those circumstances would act in taking a decision to dismiss the employee. These propositions have been emphatically supported by the Court of Appeal. Thus as Lord Justice Donaldson put it in *Union of Construction, Allied Trades and Technicians v Brain*[18]

'this approach of Tribunals putting themselves in the position of the employer, informing themselves of what the employer knew at the moment, imagining themselves in that position and then asking the question, "Would a reasonable employer in those circumstances dismiss", seems to be a very sensible approach – subject to one qualification alone, that they must not fall into the error of asking themselves the question "Would we dismiss", because you sometimes have a situation in which one reasonable employer would and one would not. In those circumstances, the employer is entitled to say to the Tribunal, "Well you should be satisfied that a reasonable employer would regard these circumstances as a sufficient reason for dismissing because the statute does not require the employer to satisfy the tribunal of the rather more difficult considerations that *all* reasonable employers would dismiss in those circumstances".'

And as Lord Denning MR suggested in *British Leyland (UK) Ltd v Swift*:[19]

'The correct test is this: Was it reasonable for the employers to dismiss him? If no reasonable employer would have dismissed him, then the dismissal was unfair. But if a reasonable employer might reasonably have dismissed him, then the dismissal was fair. It must be remembered in all these cases there is a band of reasonableness, within which one employer might reasonably take one view; another quite reasonably take a different view'.

This second constraint is also pervasive. It operates to limit the way employment tribunals may satisfy themselves of the reasonableness of an

18   [1981] ICR 542, [1981] IRLR 224, CA.
19   [1981] IRLR 91 at 93, CA.

employer's decision under s 98(4) in respect of elements of that decision: viz, the employer's conclusions of fact; the choice of procedure and decision to dismiss on the overall merits of the case.

In the first place an employment tribunal must ascertain whether an employer acted reasonably in forming his view of the facts, for example in concluding that an employer in a misconduct case had committed an act of misconduct, or that an employee in a capability case was actually incompetent or too ill to warrant continued employment, etc. Employers do not necessarily have to provide the truth of their facts to the satisfaction of the tribunal. The tribunal is required only to satisfy itself that the employers had reasonable grounds for forming their factual conclusions and that they carried out as much investigation as was reasonable in the circumstances.[20]

Secondly, an employment tribunal must ascertain whether employers acted reasonably in the circumstances in the sense that they adopted a reasonable procedure in the course of taking their decision to dismiss.[1] The requirement is that of a reasonable procedure. Whilst a proper procedure is an important factor to be taken into account in assessing the reasonableness of the employer's decision to dismiss[2] and may itself justify a finding of unfair dismissal,[3] a procedural omission will not, as a matter of law, always result in a finding of unfair dismissal.[4] After all, s 98(4) specifically states that employment tribunals, in determining the reasonableness of the employer, must have regard to the substantial merits of the case.

Hence, in certain limited circumstances an employment tribunal may justifiably decide that a dismissal is not unfair despite a procedural omission where the procedural step if taken would have been futile or utterly useless in the light of the evidence available at the time of the dismissal.

In the case of certain types of dismissal, however, it may alternatively be legitimate for an employment tribunal to decide that a dismissal is unfair solely or predominantly because of a procedural unfairness.[5] In such a case the amount of the compensatory award can be adjusted to take into account the fact that the error by the employer was essentially or entirely

---

20   *British Home Stores Ltd v Burchell* [1980] ICR 303n, [1978] IRLR 379, EAT.

1   *Polkey v A E Dayton Services Ltd* [1987] IRLR 503, HL.

2   *W Devis & Sons Ltd v Atkins* [1977] AC 931, [1977] IRLR 314, HL.

3   See too *Polkey* n 1 above.

4   Ibid.

5   Ibid; see too *W Devis & Sons Ltd v Atkins* [1977] AC 931, [1977] ICR 662, HL; see also *Siggs & Chapman (Contractors) v Knight* [1984] IRLR 83, EAT.

procedural.[6] This issue appears to be subject to a wide discretion on the tribunal's part.[7]

Finally, a tribunal will examine the reasonableness of the employer's assessment of the overall merits of the case, that is to say whether dismissal is a penalty which a reasonable employer would impose in the circumstances. Assuming that employers have reasonable grounds for their factual conclusions, and assuming that their procedure was reasonable, an employment tribunal must still satisfy itself that it was reasonable of the employer in the circumstances to decide to dismiss. Here, too, as the Court of Appeal has warned, the tribunal must not substitute its view for that of the employer; it must allow a certain amount of discretion as long as the employer's decision is that of a 'reasonable employer'.

As the EAT put it in *Rolls Royce Ltd v Walpole*:

'In a given set of circumstances it is possible for two perfectly reasonable employers to take different courses of action in relation to an employee. Frequently there is a range of responses to the conduct or capacity on the part of an employer, from and including summary dismissal downwards to a mere informal warning, which can be said to be reasonable. It is precisely because this range of possible reasonable responses does exist in many cases, that it has been laid down, that it is neither for us on an appeal nor for an [employment] tribunal on the original hearing to substitute its views for those of the employer concerned'.[8]

Hence, where an employment tribunal substitutes its views for those of the employer concerned and fails to ask the question whether in the particular circumstances of the case, did the decision to dismiss the employee fall within the band of reasonable responses which a reasonable employer might have adopted, it could well be reversed on the grounds that it had applied the wrong test.[9]

In *Iceland Frozen Foods Ltd v Jones*[10] the EAT summarised the correct approach for employment tribunals to adopt in applying s 98(4) as follows:

6   See eg *British United Shoe Machinery Co Ltd v Clarke* [1978] ICR 70, [1977] IRLR 297, EAT.
7   See Chapter 17.
8   *Rolls Royce Ltd v Walpole* [1980] IRLR 343, EAT.
9   See eg *British Leyland (UK) Ltd v Swift* [1981] IRLR 91, CA; *Iceland Frozen Foods Ltd v Jones* [1983] ICR 17, [1982] IRLR 439, EAT; *Foley v Post Office* [2000] IRLR 827, CA.
10   [1983] ICR 17, [1982] IRLR 439, EAT.

(1) the starting point should always be the words of s 98(4) themselves;
(2) in applying the section an employment tribunal must consider the reasonableness of the employer's conduct, not simply whether they (the members of the employment tribunal) consider the dismissal to be fair;
(3) in judging the reasonableness of the employer's conduct an employment tribunal must not substitute its decision as to what was the right course to adopt for that of the employer;
(4) in many (though not all) cases there is a band of reasonable responses to the employee's conduct within which one employer might reasonably take one view, another quite reasonably take another;
(5) the function of the employment tribunal, as an employment jury, is to determine whether in the particular circumstances of each case the decision to dismiss the employee fell within the band of reasonable responses which a reasonable employer might have adopted. If the dismissal falls within the band the dismissal is fair: if the dismissal falls outside the band it is unfair.

At one point, Morrison J in *Haddon v Van den Bergh Foods Ltd*[11] argued that the range of reasonable employers was wrong because it reduced the decision of the tribunal to one of finding unfair only perverse decisions of employers and this was given some support in other EAT decisions,[12] but the Court of Appeal in *Foley v Post Office* rejected Morrison's attempted assault on the band of reasonableness and reaffirmed *Iceland Frozen Foods*.[13]

In asking itself whether an employer acted as a reasonable employer in the circumstances in deciding to dismiss, an employment tribunal often asks two questions. The first is whether the employee's conduct or performance by itself was sufficient to warrant dismissal. The second step, is whether the employer took adequate account of any relevant circumstances; the account that should be taken by a 'reasonable employer'. The conduct or performance of the employee cannot be looked at in isolation. In taking a decision to dismiss, an employer may not take an unduly narrow view of the circumstances that should affect his decision. As the Court of Appeal suggested in *Vokes Ltd v Bear*[14] the net must be cast fairly wide.

---

11   [1999] IRLR 672, EAT.
12   See eg *Wilson v Ethicon Ltd* [2000] IRLR 4, EAT.
13   [2000] IRLR 827, CA.
14   [1974] ICR 1, [1973] IRLR 363, NIRC.

'The circumstances embrace all relevant matters that should weigh with a good employer when deciding at a given moment in time whether he should dismiss an employee'.

Any important circumstance that mitigates the fault of the employee or otherwise calls into question the wisdom of dismissal should be taken into account in any reasonable decision to dismiss; for example, an employee's past record of good service, an explanation or excuse, provocation or inadvertence, a lowering of standards induced by the employment setting or the extent to which management by its own action or inaction was itself partly to blame for the employee's alleged deficiencies.

At the same time, however, the phrase 'in the circumstances' can be a two-edged sword. As s 98(4) makes explicit, the circumstances that must be taken into account include the size and administrative resources of the firm.[15] Particularly in cases of dismissals for reasons other than misconduct, such as ill health, redundancy, or some other substantial reason, an employer may argue that these factors may be important to take into account. As the EAT has stated, the general rule in the test under s 98(4) is that the dismissal must be fair in the circumstances – fair to the employee and fair to the business.[16]

To understand the precise way in which each of these tests must be applied in accordance with the legal constraints, it is necessary to look more closely at each of the three tests in some detail. Yet the pattern also varies depending upon the nature of the dismissal and this too requires close examination.

The scheme of this part of the book, therefore, will be to attempt first to provide an understanding generally of the three elements of the test of the reasonableness of the employer's decision in s 98(4), using a discussion of three tests as applied to conduct and occasionally, where useful, capability, to illustrate certain general propositions. The remainder of this chapter will thus serve both as a general discussion of the three tests and as a specific discussion of their application to dismissals for misconduct. All subsequent chapters will consider the test of fairness as it applies to one specific type of dismissal, but the treatment will presuppose that the reader has read this chapter as an introduction.

---

15   See eg *Henderson v Granville Tours Ltd* [1982] IRLR 494, EAT; *Bevan Harris Ltd (t/a the Clyde Leather Co) v Gair* [1981] IRLR 520, EAT; *Meikle v McPhail (Charleston Arms)* [1983] IRLR 351, EAT; *Royal Naval School v Hughes* [1979] IRLR 383, EAT.

16   See eg *Retarded Children's Aid Society Ltd v Day* [1978] ICR 437, [1976] IRLR 128, CA.

In the remainder of this chapter the three basic tests of reasonableness and misconduct will be considered under the following heads:

(2) Did the employer act reasonably in forming his or her view of the facts?
(3) Did the employer adopt a reasonable procedure?
(4) Did the employer act reasonably in concluding that dismissal was warranted in the circumstances?

2. DID THE EMPLOYER ACT REASONABLY IN FORMING HIS OR HER VIEW OF THE FACTS?

As we have seen, the first stage of the test of reasonableness, under s 98(1) and (2) requires employers merely to identify their reason for dismissal. It places upon employers only an onus of showing their real motive for dismissal. The second stage, under s 98(4), requires employers to take the process one step further and establish that they acted reasonably in forming their view of the facts.

This does not require the employer to prove to the satisfaction of the tribunal that the employee was actually guilty of the alleged misconduct or was in fact incapable. Instead, it has been interpreted to require of employers only that they acted reasonably in the sense of having reasonable grounds for their belief that an employee had actually committed an act of misconduct or was incapable as alleged. As the EAT put it in *British Home Stores Ltd v Burchell*,[17] in determining whether a dismissal is unfair, what an employment tribunal has to decide is, broadly expressed, whether the employer who discharged the employee on the ground of the misconduct in question entertained a reasonable suspicion amounting to a belief in the guilt of the employee of that misconduct at that time.[18] 'That is really stating shortly and somewhat compendiously ... more than one element. First of all, there must be established by the employer the fact of that belief; that the employer did believe it'. Secondly, it must be shown 'that the employer had in his mind reasonable grounds upon which to sustain that belief'. The third requirement is that employers at the stage at which they formed their belief on those grounds must have 'carried out as much investigation into the matter as was reasonable in all the circumstances'.

These guidelines were endorsed by the Court of Appeal in *W Weddel & Co Ltd v Tepper* as the preferred legal test.[19] Yet they were endorsed

---

17   [1980] ICR 303n, [1978] IRLR 379, EAT.
18   Cf *Distillers Co (Bottling Services) Ltd v Gardner* [1982] IRLR 47, EAT.
19   [1980] ICR 286, [1980] IRLR 96, CA.

only as valuable guidelines and not inflexible rules of law. Hence they are not automatically binding where an employer suspects more than one employee but in the circumstances, his suspicion cannot harden into belief in the guilt of either.[20]

Furthermore it is not entirely clear whether any priority must be given those guidelines inter se. For example, according to one view, it is a legitimate exercise of discretion for a tribunal to find a dismissal unfair because the employer has engaged in an inadequate investigation even where the employer had strong prima facie grounds for his decision.[1] A second view is that tribunals also have the discretion to excuse an employer from the requirement of further investigation where he has already reasonable evidence for his belief ie a prima facie case and where further investigation was not likely to produce a different result.[2]

Yet insofar as the evidence of the likelihood that the employee had committed the offence increases, the procedural standard of further enquiry lessens and at a certain point a tribunal insisting upon such a step could be regarded as coming to an unreasonable decision.[3] Nor should the guidelines in *Burchell*'s case generally, and the third guideline in particular, apply where an employee has admitted dishonest conduct and there is no question of suspicion or belief.[4] In such a case, rather than apply the guidelines in *Burchell*'s case slavishly, tribunals have been adjured to appraise all the circumstances of the case in the round under s 98(4).[5]

i) A reasonable investigation

Employers are required by s 98(4) to show that they made a reasonably diligent investigation. This is not an absolute obligation. It is an obligation to make reasonable efforts to find any relevant fact which was available of

---

20   *Monie v Coral Racing Ltd* [1981] ICR 109, [1980] IRLR 464, CA; *McPhie and McDermott v Wimpey Waste Management Ltd* [1981] IRLR 316, EAT; see also *Lintafoam (Manchester) Ltd v Fletcher* (1984) Times, 12 March.

1   *W Weddel & Co Ltd v Tepper* [1980] ICR 286, [1980] IRLR 96, CA.

2   See eg *Sillifant v Powell Duffryn Timber Ltd* [1983] IRLR 91, EAT.

3   See *ILEA v Gravett* [1988] IRLR 497, EAT; *Royal Society for the Protection of Birds v Croucher* [1984] IRLR 425, EAT; *Lintafoam (Manchester) Ltd v Fletcher* (1984) Times, 12 March.

4   See eg *Scottish Daily Record & Sunday Mail (1986) Ltd v Laird* [1996] IRLR 665, Ct of Sess.

5   Ibid.

which the employer ought reasonably to have known. As Viscount Dilhorne expressed it:

> 'it cannot be said that the employer acted reasonably in treating (the reason shown as a sufficient reason) if he only did so in consequence of ignoring matters which he ought reasonably to have known and which would have shown that the reason was insufficient'.[6]

In practice, therefore, to show that an inquiry was not reasonable an employee must establish two points. First, that the employer's method of investigation was inadequate in some respect, and second, that the inadequate method of investigation resulted in a failure to find out information which could have affected the result. An error of investigative method will not be enough; the error must be of some consequence.[7]

(a) An unreasonable method of investigation[8]

Clearly, where an employer has made practically no effort to investigate an alleged offence his decision to dismiss could be found to be unfair on that ground alone.[9] As Stephenson LJ stated, 'Employers suspecting an employee of misconduct justifying dismissal cannot justify their dismissal by simply stating an honest belief in their guilt'.[10]

Clearly, too, where an employer in the course of his investigation of the facts encounters a situation revealing the need for a supplementary investigation and does not follow up the lead, this may well cause doubt on the reasonableness of this grounds for belief. For example, in *Chrystie v Rolls Royce (1971) Ltd*[11] two employees were dismissed, for fighting, on a Friday and told to report for a hearing on the following Monday. Chrystie failed to attend. His non-attendance was due to illness but this was not known to the senior staff who, on Tuesday, wrote to him terminating his employment. On the same day, but after they had posted their letter of dismissal, they received a note from him explaining that he

6   *W Devis & Sons Ltd v Atkins* [1977] AC 931, [1977] ICR 662, HL.
7   *Boys and Girls Welfare Society v McDonald* [1996] IRLR 129, EAT.
8   See eg *John Lewis plc v Coyne* [2001] IRLR 139, EAT; *Read v Phoenix Preservations Ltd* [1985] IRLR 93, EAT.
9   See eg *Scottish Special Housing Association v Cooke* [1979] IRLR 264, EAT; *Hughes v Messrs Christie & Co (Insurance) Ltd* (1977) EAT 921/77.
10 *W Weddel & Co Ltd v Tepper* [1980] ICR 286, [1980] IRLR 96, CA.
11 [1976] IRLR 336, EAT; see also *Williamson v Alcan (UK) Ltd* [1978] ICR 104, [1977] IRLR 303, EAT.

was ill. They chose to disregard this letter. The EAT held that an employment tribunal could properly conclude that the dismissal was unfair.

'The employer ought reasonably to have reviewed their decision once they received the appellant's letter. It should immediately have been apparent to them that it had crossed their dismissal letter in the post and that the dismissal letter had been written when they were not in full possession of the facts.[12]

Further, if an employer completely omits an obvious step in an investigation, such as a hearing, this will cast doubt on the reasonableness of his belief. For example, in *Francis v Ford Motor Co*[13] employees found in a car park during working hours were dismissed without their explanation being sufficiently carefully investigated. The rejection of the employees' explanation without an inquiry made the dismissal unfair.

Yet the duty to hold a hearing, as indeed the duty to investigate the evidence, while often an integral part of a reasonable procedural approach,[14] is not an absolute obligation. As the EAT remarked in *Gray Dunn & Co Ltd v Edwards*, 'it is now well settled that common sense places limits upon the degree of investigation required of an employer who is seized of information which points strongly towards the commission of a disciplinary offence which merits dismissal'.[15] Thus, in a case where an employee is charged by the police with theft and has been caught with the employer's property and makes no protestations of innocence this may entitle the employer to dismiss without further investigation.[16] Moreover, where an employee charged with a criminal offence connected with work refuses to say anything until the trial in the criminal proceedings, a reasonable employer is entitled to consider whether the material he has is sufficiently indicative of guilt to justify dismissal without waiting.[17]

---

12 Ibid.
13 [1975] IRLR 25, IT.
14 *ILEA v Gravett* [1988] IRLR 497, EAT.
15 [1980] IRLR 23, EAT. See also *AEI Cables Ltd v McLay* [1980] IRLR 84, Ct of Sess, 'certainly is not the test for whether the employer has sufficient grounds for a reasonable belief in an employee's dishonesty'.
16 *Scottish Special Housing Association v Linnen* [1979] IRLR 265, EAT; cf *Carr v Alexander Russell Ltd* [1979] ICR 469n, [1976] IRLR 220, Ct of Sess.
17 *Harris and Shepherd v Courage (Eastern) Ltd* [1982] ICR 530, [1982] IRLR 509, CA. See also *Ahearn v National Coal Board* [1974] IRLR 372 (employee neglected to provide information for employer's records); *Ugoala v Godfrey Davis (Car Hire) Ltd* (7 June 1973, unreported) NIRC (employee refused to answer allegations, insisting on written notice beforehand).

(b) The effect of the faulty method

It is not enough for an employee to show that the employer's enquiry was inadequate in a formalistic sense. He or she must be able to show that the inadequacy of the employer's investigation was such that it precluded the employer from finding out information which a reasonable employer should have known and which might reasonably have been expected to affect the result. In other words an employee must be able to show, not only that there was a failure to pursue a careful inquiry, but also that there was a reasonable possibility, looked at from the time of dismissal, that the omission would have affected the result.[18]

For example, in *East Lindsey District Council v Daubney*[19] an employing organisation dismissed an employee for ill health on the strength of a medical report by its own medical advisor, without consulting the employee and exploring with him the possibility of a solution that would allow him to continue in employment. In the course of its judgment the EAT remarked:

'This seems to us to be precisely the kind of case where sensitive consultation and discussion *might* – nobody can say that it would – have resulted in some solution being found to his position consistent with continued employment by the District Council'.

The standard adopted in *Daubney*'s case, namely that the information revealed by a proper enquiry *might* have made a difference, has the virtue of being consistent with the principle in *W Devis & Sons Ltd v Atkins*.[20] The EAT could not have insisted that the test for an omission of a proper investigation was that it must be shown that it *would* in fact have produced a different result, since that would have made the error of using information obtained subsequent to the moment of dismissal to determine the reasonableness of the employer's decision. The advantage of the standard adopted in *Daubney*'s case is that the lack of investigative diligence of the employer affects the reasonableness of his decision if the omission, looked at from the time that the decision was taken, created a real possibility that the result would be unreasonable.

In *Henderson v Granville Tours Ltd*[1] the EAT Scottish Division asserted

---

18   See eg *British Labour Pump Co Ltd v Byrne* [1979] ICR 347, [1979] IRLR 94, EAT.
19   [1977] ICR 566, [1977] IRLR 181.
20   [1977] AC 931, [1977] ICR 662, HL.
1   [1982] IRLR 494, EAT.

'It is an error of law for an [Employment] Tribunal to hold that had an employer carried out further investigation into allegations against an employee, that investigation would have supported the complaint and the result would have been the same. Such an approach is appropriate only in cases involving defects in procedure. In considering whether there has been an adequate investigation, the Tribunal is concerned with the employer's state of mind at the moment of dismissal and the sufficiency of information to justify that state of mind that is not simply a procedural question; it goes to the heart of the fairness of the dismissal and to whether or not the test of fairness has been fulfilled. If a man is dismissed for dishonesty of suspicion, it is no answer for an employer to say that he was convicted of the offence months later on properly prepared evidence'.

Moreover, in *W Weddel & Co Ltd v Tepper*[2] the Court of Appeal agreed with the EAT that an employment tribunal had the discretion to decide that a failure by the employer to engage in *further* investigation could by itself make a dismissal unfair even where the employer already had evidence amounting to a strong prima facie case of a breach of regulations and indeed, a strong prima facie case that it was done dishonestly.

The court suggested however, that the limit to the tribunal's discretion to require further investigation was what 'ought to have been reasonably known to the employer in the circumstance'. That is to say that the employer had carried out as much investigation as was reasonable in all the circumstances of the case.

Later cases have elaborated this limit to tribunal discretion. Thus, in *Dick v Glasgow University*[3] the Court of Session stated that an employment tribunal is not entitled to use evidence discovered during the tribunal hearing as a basis for a finding that the employer's investigation had not been reasonable. The tribunal's role in determining whether the employers had carried out a reasonable investigation was to consider the nature of the material before the employer when the decision to dismiss was taken. Nor could an employment tribunal legitimately require an employer to carry out a quasi-judicial investigation where the employer chooses a more informal method. The test is the reasonableness of the employer's chosen method.[4]

---

2   [1980] ICR 286, [1980] IRLR 96, CA.
3   [1993] IRLR 581, Ct of Sess.
4   *Ulsterbus Ltd v Henderson* [1989] IRLR 251, NICA.

Finally, where allegations concerning an employee's conduct are made by an informant, a reasonable balance must be struck between the desirability to protect informants who are genuinely in fear and providing a fair hearing of issues for employees who are accused of misconduct.[5]

ii) Reasonable factual grounds

Assuming that the employer has made as careful an inquiry as was reasonable in the circumstances, the next question is, did the inquiry disclose adequate evidence – adequate enough to justify a reasonable employer taking the decision even if not adequate enough to convince the particular employment tribunal that the employer's decision was correct?[6]

In *British Home Stores Ltd v Burchell*[7] this test was stated to be: did the employer entertain a reasonable suspicion amounting to a belief in the guilt of the employee of that misconduct at that time? This test has been subsequently endorsed by the Court of Appeal[8] and applied quite widely to cases of misconduct.[9]

Under the *British Homes Stores* test the particular burden of proof placed upon the employer by the language of s 98(4) is not a heavy one. An employer does not have to prove that the offence was committed on the balance of probabilities, that is to say, to satisfy the tribunal of the likelihood that the offence was actually committed. A fortiori, it rejects the notion of a heavier burden of proof, such as that the employer must prove beyond a reasonable doubt that the offence was actually committed. Instead, a tribunal may only require that an employer show enough evidence to convince it that 'he acted reasonably' in drawing his conclusions of fact, ie that he had reasonable grounds for believing in the guilt of the employee. Indeed, in cases where more than one employee has been suspected of misconduct, it may not even be required of employers that their suspicion harden into belief.[10]

One implication of the *British Homes Stores* test is that where an employer is subsequently proved to have been mistaken in his judgment

---

5   See obiter in *Linford Cash & Carry Ltd v Thomson* [1989] IRLR 235, EAT.

6   See eg *Scottish Midland Co-operative Society Ltd v Cullion* [1991] IRLR 261, Ct of Sess.

7   [1980] ICR 303n, [1978] IRLR 379, EAT.

8   *W Weddel & Co Ltd v Tepper* [1980] ICR 286, [1980] IRLR 96, CA; *Foley v Post Office* [2000] IRLR 827, CA.

9   See eg *Distillers Co (Bottling Services) Ltd v Gardner* [1982] IRLR 47, EAT.

10 *Monie v Coral Racing Ltd* [1981] ICR 109, [1980] IRLR 464, CA.

of the facts, he may nevertheless be found to have acted fairly in dismissing an employee. Yet this implication is inherent in the language of s 98(4) and is not unique to this particular burden of proof. As long as the employer's decision must be judged only on the information available to him at the moment of dismissal, and any evidence discovered subsequent to the decision to dismiss is irrelevant, there will always be the possibility that a dismissal can be based on a mistake of fact and still be held to be fair. This point was made quite forcibly in *Ferodo Ltd v Barnes*[11] when Mr Justice Kilner Brown drew attention to the implications of *W Devis & Sons Ltd v Atkins*:

'It seems to have been thought by certain [employment] tribunals that, if it subsequently came to light that an offence had been committed or, in the converse position, if it subsequently came to light the offence had not been committed, that subsequent knowledge or proof would, of course, go to the providing one way or the other of whether there was in fact an event which gave rise to the act of dismissal ... this begs the real question, because the question which had to be decided by the [employment] tribunal is what was the state of evidence and information at the time of the notice of dismissal?'

Of course there are limits to the type of mistake an employer may make. In the *British Home Stores* case it was stressed that the test involved the requirement that the employer based his belief on reasonable grounds and that he had carried out as much investigation into the matter as was reasonable in the circumstances. In *W Weddel & Co Ltd v Tepper*, Lord Stephenson made it plain that an employer cannot justify a dismissal simply by stating an honest belief in his guilt. Hence there is a minimum objective element to the test industrial tribunals have to apply at this stage.[12]

Nevertheless the standard laid down in *British Home Stores* does mean that certain limits have been placed upon the extent to which an employment tribunal may properly re-hear a case and look at particular evidence to determine for itself whether it considers that the employer's factual basis was sufficient. This was implied by the EAT in *Ferodo* when it criticised the tribunal for attempting to satisfy itself that the employee committed the offence.

In *Trust House Forte Leisure Ltd v Aquilar*[13] the EAT was more explicit. It indicated that it was not open to the tribunal to decide an issue of fact by

11 [1976] IRLR 302 at 303.
12 See eg *Glaxo Operations (UK) Ltd v Carter* (1984) EAT 727/83.
13 [1976] IRLR 251, EAT.

judging for itself the demeanour evidence of witnesses. In that case an employee was accused of defrauding customers in the sale of drinks. The employer conducted an investigation which included a hearing monitored by a trade union representative, and an identification parade at which the customer made a positive identification of the employee. After hearing the employee, the tribunal indicated that it was in real doubt whether the employee was guilty[14] and found the dismissal unfair. The EAT held that

> 'it was impossible for the tribunal, in those circumstances, to say that the management, in reaching a decision which was hostile to the employee, had acted in a way which made the dismissal unfair: there was plenty of evidence and material upon which, if the matter was properly investigated, the management could reasonably dismiss Mr Aquilar. The error of the tribunal was that it paid too much attention to the fact that it, itself was not satisfied that Mr Aquilar was guilty of the misconduct alleged'.[15]

Similarly in *Morgan v Electrolux Ltd*[16] a tribunal was found to have erred in law when it found that an employee dismissed for overbooking her work assembling microwave ovens was unfairly dismissed because it thought that the employer's assessment of the evidence of another employee was unreasonable. The tribunal's error according to the Court of Appeal was that it substituted its own evaluation of the witness for that of the employer.

This inhibition upon tribunal fact-finding applies to the extent to which the employment tribunal can insist upon reviewing the evidence to determine whether the employer has a reasonable basis for belief, where the employer had already made a careful inquiry. In *Alidair Ltd v Taylor*[17] for example an appeal was allowed from an employment tribunal which had placed too much emphasis on considering the reasonableness of the procedure of a board of inquiry appointed and relied upon by the employer and insufficient weight to the question it was supposed to ask which was whether the employer's decision was honest and reasonable.[18] Similarly

---

14   Ibid at 253.
15   See also *Paterson v Barratt Developments (Aberdeen) Ltd* [1977] IRLR 214; *St Anne's Board Mill Co Ltd v Brien* [1973] ICR 444, [1973] IRLR 309, NIRC.
16   [1991] ICR 369, [1991] IRLR 89, CA; see too *Linfood Cash and Carry Ltd v Thomson* [1989] ICR 518, [1989] IRLR 235, EAT.
17   [1978] ICR 445, [1978] IRLR 82, CA.
18   Lord Eveleigh suggested that such a factor might be relevant where the genuineness of the employer's belief was in question.

in *Post Office v Mughal*[19] an employment tribunal was held to have erred in law by finding that an employer had failed to establish that the employee was, in fact, inefficient, because the employer had not provided any evidence that the employee's shortcomings resulted in complaints from customers or from members of staff, and because of the inadequacy of the samples of inefficient work provided by the employer. The EAT reversed the tribunal saying:

'It is in our view quite wrong to expect such evidence when the question is whether the employer has fairly and reasonably decided that a probationer is not up to the employer's standards. The superior officers have to arrange for supervision and make known to the employee the standard of performance that is set. The employer discharges the onus that the Act imposes upon him if he satisfies the [employment] tribunal that the supervising staff took proper trouble to assess conduct and capacity and warned of shortcomings when appropriate: and that the officer responsible for dismissal took proper steps to review the capacity and conduct of the probationer over a period before dismissal by examining written reports and, if necessary, discussing the history with the individual supervising officer or officers before deciding whether the probationer was someone whom the employer should take on the established staff. It would place an impossible burden on an employer to require him to call as witness dissatisfied members of the public or aggrieved members of the technical staff in order to satisfy a tribunal that an assessment of capability or efficiency was made fairly and reasonably'.

The EAT went on to say:

'The question for the tribunal is: has the employer shown that he took reasonable steps to maintain appraisal of the probationer throughout the period of probation, giving guidance by advice or warning when such is likely to be useful or fair; and that an appropriate officer made an honest effort to determine whether the probationer came up to the required standard, having informed himself of the appraisals made by the supervising officers and any other facts recorded about the probationer?

If this procedure is followed, it is only if the officer responsible for deciding upon selection of probationers then arrives *at a decision*

19   [1977] ICR 763, [1977] IRLR 178, EAT.

which no reasonable assessment could dictate, that an industrial tribunal should hold the dismissal to be unfair.'

These cases do not stand for the proposition that an employment tribunal can never re-hear a case to decide for itself what was wrong, and must always accept the facts as found by the employer. But they do assert that provided that an employer has made a careful inquiry and *provided there is enough evidence to show* that the decision was reasonable there is no entitlement to insist on hearing all the evidence. It also serves as a reminder that the test of sufficiency suggested by the EAT for the factual basis of the employer's decision in cases where the employer has made a careful inquiry is that the employer's grounds for belief must be unreasonable – so unreasonable that no reasonable employer who has made a careful inquiry would rely on such grounds. Thus only if an employee can show that there was insufficient evidence before the employer to justify the latter's supposition of fact,[20] or that the evidence was wholly contradictory, or that the evidence the employer relied on was intrinsically unsound,[1] will the employee have a potential basis for attacking the reasonableness of employers' grounds for their conclusions of fact.

If the employer's conclusions of fact cannot be shown to be unreasonable in this sense, and the employer's inquiry was careful, then the employment tribunal must move on to consider whether the employer's decision in the circumstances was reasonable on the basis of the facts as reasonably believed by the employer.[2]

3. DID THE EMPLOYER ADOPT A REASONABLE PROCEDURE?

Once employers have clarified and defined their reasons for dismissal, and presented sufficient evidence to show that they acted reasonably in forming their views of the facts, and that they had reasonable grounds for their suspicion or belief that the employee had committed the act or acts of

---

20   See *Hughes v Messrs Christie & Co (Insurance) Ltd* (1977) EAT 921/77; see also *Lees v The Orchard* [1978] IRLR 20, EAT.

1   See eg *Dexine Rubber Co Ltd v Alker* [1977] ICR 434, EAT.

2   As the EAT put it in *Refunds Rentals v McDermott* [1977] IRLR 59 at 61: 'The true questions ... were (1) did the respondents have reasonable ground on the facts of the case for believing that the applicant had deliberately failed to account for the money? ... and (2) if it was the real reason for dismissing, were the respondents reasonable in treating that belief as a ground for dismissal at the time when they dismissed him?'

misconduct, the next step for the tribunal is to determine whether their decision to treat these grounds as a sufficient basis for dismissal was reasonable in the circumstances. As the House of Lords held in *Polkey v A E Dayton Services Ltd*[3] this issue has been interpreted to include a test of whether the employer adopted a reasonable procedure.

In cases of dismissals for misconduct, the introduction of the requirement of an appropriate procedure as part of the test of s 98(4) has been influenced by the Code of Practice and its relationship to the Act.[4] The Code of Practice's recommendations that employers adopt certain procedural safeguards do not themselves have the force of law.

Nevertheless, any of its provisions which appear to a tribunal or court to be relevant to a question arising in the proceedings must be taken into account by the tribunal in determining that question. And indeed, the NIRC, the EAT and the House of Lords have all on occasion indicated that an employment tribunal may decide that a procedural omission could make a dismissal unfair notwithstanding that, had the proper procedure been followed, the dismissal would have been fair on its merits.[5] In such cases, the compensatory award would be adjusted to take into account the essentially procedural nature of the employer's unfairness.[6]

As we have seen the effect of the decision of the House of Lords in *Polkey v A E Dayton Services Ltd* was to attach considerable importance to the procedural failures of employers. The judgment reinstated the earlier decisions of the NIRC to the extent that a dismissal may be unfair for procedural reasons even if the employer had some substantive basis for its decision. It was still open to employers to argue that if a procedural step was pointless or futile or utterly useless judged from the time of dismissal, it was not necessarily unfair to omit it. However, it was no longer open to the employer to argue following *British Labour Pump Co Ltd v Byrne* that even if the employer omitted an important procedural step, the dismissal could be fair if the employer could prove on the balance of probabilities that if he had included the omitted procedural steps the employee *would have been* fairly dismissed. That line of defence was

---

3   [1987] IRLR 503, HL; see too *Whitbread plc v Hall* [2001] EWCA Civ 268, [2001] IRLR 275.

4   Originally the Industrial Relations Code of Practice, now the Code of Practice on Disciplinary and Grievance Procedures.

5   See *Earl v Slater & Wheeler (Airlyne) Ltd* [1973] 1 All ER 145, [1972] IRLR 115, NIRC; *British United Shoe Machinery Co Ltd v Clarke* [1977] IRLR 297, EAT; *W Devis & Sons Ltd v Atkins* [1977] AC 971, [1977] ICR 662, HL. *Polkey v A E Dayton Services Ltd* [1987] IRLR 503, HL.

6   *Devis'* case; see discussion in Chapter 17.

precluded by the *Polkey* decision on the grounds inter alia that it was inconsistent with the rule in *W Devis & Sons v Atkins*. Thus, under s 98(4), the standards of reasonable procedure set out in the Code of Practice's recommendations in respect of warnings, hearing and appeals have been accepted as a standard of reasonable behaviour against which tribunals may measure an employer's actions.

These procedural standards, however, are not absolute requirements. As Viscount Dilhorne stated in *W Devis & Sons Ltd v Atkins*,[7] 'it does not follow that non-compliance with the Code necessarily renders a dismissal unfair'.

In *Lewis Shops Group v Wiggins*,[8] the NIRC had stated 'it does not follow that a dismissal must as a matter of law be deemed unfair because an employer does not follow the procedures recommended in the Code. The Code is, of course, always one important factor to be taken into account in the case but its significance will vary according to the particular circumstances of each individual case.'

In *Lowndes v Specialist Heavy Engineering Ltd*,[9] the EAT endorsed this view but added

'as a general rule a failure to follow a fair procedure whether by warnings or by giving an opportunity to be heard before dismissal will result in the ensuing dismissal being found to be unfair'.

In *Hollister v National Farmers' Union*[10] the Court of Appeal explicitly disapproved of the EAT's interpretation of s 98(4) in *Lowndes*' case as a presumption or binding rule for tribunals to follow when exercising their discretion under s 98(4). Yet in *Hollister*'s case the Court of Appeal's concern with an excessively high general procedural standard was a compound containing two separate elements. First of all it reflected a concern that employment tribunals in applying s 98(4) should not follow guidelines which might lead them to elevate procedure over substance, that is to say to allow a minor procedural omission to be the basis for the finding of an unfair dismissal where the employer had a strong case on the merits.

Secondly, however, the Court of Appeal was also concerned more generally that judge-made interpretations of s 98(4) might be treated as rules of law binding upon employment tribunals. One consequence of this

7   [1977] AC 931, [1977] ICR 662, HL.
8   [1973] ICR 335, [1973] IRLR 205.
9   [1977] ICR 1, [1976] IRLR 246, EAT.
10   [1979] ICR 542, [1979] IRLR 238, CA.

was that even where the EAT and the Court of Appeal provided cautionary rules about the risks of elevating procedure over substance, those rules themselves might have the status only of 'guidelines' to employment tribunals rather than rules of law which provide a basis for appeal against a tribunal decision whenever they are not followed.

To understand the evolution of guidelines for the procedural test under s 98(4) it is useful to start with the case of *Earl v Slater & Wheeler (Airlyne) Ltd.*[11] That case established two propositions.

First, that an employment tribunal could decide that a dismissal which was fair in substance could be found to be unfair because of its unfair procedure. Secondly that where an employer omitted a procedural step, the guideline concerning the degree of proof required to justify such an omission was that there was no *possibility* that if the procedure had been followed it would have made a difference. As the NIRC put it in *Earl's* case 'The only exception to the need for a hearing is where there can be no explanation which could cause the employers to refrain from dismissing the employee'. The House of Lords in *W Devis & Sons Ltd v Atkins* clearly supported the first proposition. As Viscount Radcliffe put it 'I agree with the view expressed by Donaldson J in *Earl v Slater & Wheeler* that a failure to follow a procedure prescribed in the code may lead to the conclusion that a dismissal was unfair which if that procedure had been followed would have been held to be fair'. Yet nothing was said directly about the second proposition concerning the degree of proof required to justify a procedural omission.

After *Earl's* case there was a tendency for tribunals to apply quite high standards of procedural propriety under s 98(4). It was not long before there was a reaction to these developments. In *Carr v Alexander Russell Ltd* Lord McDonald indicated that he had reservations about an interpretation of *Earl's* case which always entitles an accused employee to a hearing. He thought that such a proposition was too universal and

> 'should certainly be applied with caution to any situation where an employee has been charged with the theft of his employer's property and is not due to stand trial for several months'.[12]

And in *Lowndes v Specialist Heavy Engineering Ltd* the EAT reminded that the NIRC in *Earl's* case had decided only that a tribunal could not say that a failure to observe a proper procedure was always fair; it did not

11   [1973] 1 All ER 145, [1972] IRLR 115, NIRC.
12   [1976] IRLR 220, Ct of Sess.

establish the opposite conclusion that a failure to observe a proper procedure would always make a dismissal unfair.

In *British Labour Pump Co Ltd v Byrne*[13] the EAT modified the general guidelines to the correct approach for an employment tribunal where an employer has not followed a proper procedure in the form of two questions. First, have the employers shown on the balance of probabilities that they would have taken the same course had they held an inquiry and had they received the same information which the inquiry would have produced? Secondly, have the employers shown that in the light of their information which they would have had, had they gone through the proper procedure, they would have been behaving reasonably in still deciding to dismiss?

The Court of Appeal in *W and J Wass Ltd v Binns*[14] endorsed the two rules of *British Labour Pump* as providing useful guidelines in the majority of cases where fairness required that an opportunity to explain be given. Yet it added a note of reservation to the effect that when an employment tribunal was faced with a dismissal that was clearly reasonable on the merits, it *retained the discretion* to decide that the dismissal was not unfair even if the employer had omitted a procedural step. The most graphic illustration of this position was that provided at an early stage by Lord Lawton in *Bailey v BP Oil (Kent Refinery) Ltd*:[15]

> 'In most unfair dismissal cases [Employment] Tribunals are likely to be critical and justly so of an employer who has dismissed a man without giving him an opportunity of explaining why he did what he did; but cases can occur where instant dismissal without any opportunity for explanation being given would be fair, as for example, when on the shop floor a worker was seen by the works manager and others to stab another man in the back with a knife. The dismissal in such a case would not be any the less fair because the employers did not follow a disciplinary procedure agreement'.

Included within this class of cases was a special category of cases where the dismissed employee was the subject of a criminal proceeding and the evidence already available to the employer was strongly indicative of the employee's guilt but the employer gave the employee no opportunity to explain his position.[16] The mere fact that the employee had been charged

---

13   [1979] ICR 347, [1979] IRLR 94, EAT.
14   [1982] ICR 486, [1982] IRLR 283, CA.
15   [1980] ICR 642, [1980] IRLR 287, CA.
16   See eg *Lovie Ltd v Anderson* [1999] IRLR 164, EAT; *Scottish Special Housing Association v Linnen* [1979] IRLR 265, EAT; *Carr v Alexander Russell Ltd* [1979]

with a criminal offence may not be enough;[17] there must be strong evidence of guilt.[18] In such cases, appeal courts have long been concerned to ensure that employment tribunals were entitled to excuse the procedural omission because of the strength of the merits of the employer's case at the time of the dismissal.[19]

Moreover from the earliest days of unfair dismissal legislation the appellate courts have asserted more generally that there was a category of cases in which the merits of the employer's case were so clear that employment tribunals should be allowed to find a dismissal fair despite the employer's failure of procedure. These were cases where a particular procedural step viewed from the point in time of the dismissal was clearly unnecessary or pointless. Thus in *James v Waltham Holy Cross UDC*,[20] the NIRC indicated that a hearing might not be necessary where an employee has already indicated his position in the course of his conduct. Furthermore, in cases of alleged incapability, the omission of a formal warning has not precluded a finding that the dismissal was fair where the employee was constitutionally incapable of getting on with other employees[1] or had a personality defect[2] or where an employee's inadequacy was so extreme that there was an irredeemable incapability,[3] or where an employee by his conduct showed that he was determined to go his own way.[4] Similarly, where other action by the employer provides an effective substitute for a procedural step that may be sufficient to make a dismissal fair despite a procedural omission. For example, a probationary period may be viewed as effectively constituting a warning.[5] In such cases,

ICR 469n, [1976] IRLR 220, Ct of Sess; *Harris and Shepherd v Courage (Eastern) Ltd* [1982] IRLR 509, CA; *Parker v Clifford Dunn Ltd* [1979] ICR 463, [1979] IRLR 56, EAT.

17   *Securicor Guarding Ltd v R* [1994] IRLR 633, EAT; *Lovie Ltd v Anderson* [1999] IRLR 164, EAT.

18   See too *P v Nottinghamshire County Council* [1992] IRLR 362, CA (where the employee had pleaded guilty or was found guilty of a criminal offence an employer could reasonably believe that the employee had committed the offence). See too cases note 16.

19   See cases note 16.

20   [1973] ICR 398, [1973] IRLR 202, NIRC.

1   *A J Dunning & Sons (Shop Fitters) Ltd v Jacomb* [1973] ICR 448, [1973] IRLR 206, NIRC.

2   *O'Hagan v Firestone Tyre and Rubber Co Ltd* [1974] IRLR 226, IT.

3   *James v Waltham Holy Cross UDC* [1973] ICR 398, [1973] IRLR 202, NIRC.

4   *Retarded Children's Aid Society Ltd v Day* [1978] 1 WLR 763, [1978] IRLR 128, CA.

5   *Judge International Ltd v Moss* [1973] IRLR 208, NIRC.

the fact that the procedural step was obviously superfluous *at the time that the decision to dismiss was taken* would allow an employment tribunal to find that it was not unreasonable for an employer to omit what would otherwise have been a pointless gesture.

These cases have on occasion been rationalised as being an endorsement of the proposition that procedural safeguards, whether recommendations of the Code of Practice or matters of common fairness, are to be treated not 'as matters of procedure but rather as matters of substance, that is to say as matters going to the basic sufficiency of the decision to dismiss'.

This approach, which was first articulated by the NIRC in *A J Dunning & Sons (Shopfitters) Ltd v Jacomb*,[6] but later endorsed by the EAT and the Court of Appeal,[7] implies that a procedural step is only required for the purposes of s 98(4) if it could be said that its implementation would have affected the substantive question of whether the employer had reasonable grounds for dismissal. For example, in respect of a hearing it was said in *Dunning*:

'It is a matter of substance, whether or not the reasons, no opportunity for explanation having been given, are adequate to justify dismissal'.

Similarly in respect of a warning, the question is whether the employee *might* or *would* be able to improve his performance. Again in *Dunning* it was said:

'In this case the question which the tribunal had to ask itself was whether Mr Jacomb's incapacity as it existed at the time of dismissal was of such a nature and quality as to justify a dismissal, or whether it was of such a nature and quality that, were Mr Jacomb to receive a warning, he might or would be able to improve his performance. If the latter, then the mere fact that his performance had not been up to standard in the past would not, or might not, justify his dismissal'.

At all events these lines of exceptional cases in which tribunals were held to have the discretion to decide that procedural omissions could be excused because of the obviousness of the merits of the employer's case had been long accepted as a legitimate area of tribunal discretion and were so endorsed by the *Polkey* decision in which Lord Mackay and Lord Bridge

6   [1973] ICR 448, [1973] IRLR 206, NIRC.
7   See eg *Scottish Special Housing Association v Linnen* [1979] IRLR 265, EAT; see too n 4 above.

expressed the view that where a procedural step normally appropriate would have been futile or utterly useless, when looked at at the time of dismissal, the employer may well not act reasonably even if the provisions of the Code had not been fully observed.

After *Polkey*, apart from the exceptions mentioned, a purely procedural unfairness may be the basis of a finding of unfair dismissal.[7a] Individual tribunals in applying s 98(4) are free to give adequate weight to the need to have regard to 'equity as well as the substantial merits of the case'.

As Stephenson LJ remarked in *W Weddel & Co Ltd v Tepper*, employers

'do not have regard to equity in particular if they do not give [an employee suspected of misconduct justifying a dismissal] a fair opportunity of explaining before dismissing him'.

The standards of equity and natural justice place greater importance upon the need for manifest justice. As was said in *Whyte v Burmah Oil Trading Ltd*,[8] 'Equity requires that not only must justice be done, it must be seen to be done'. Yet the issue of 'manifest justice' does not trump the *Polkey* rule that a futile or utterly useless procedural step may not be required under s 98(4).

After *Polkey*, and apart from the exceptions mentioned, it seems clear that tribunals retain a discretion to decide that a failure by the employer to follow a fair procedure as recommended by the Code of Practice by itself or in conjunction with other circumstances, makes a dismissal unreasonable under s 98(4). Moreover it would appear that employers continue to be faced with the onus of coming forward with evidence if indeed not proving the justification for any procedural omission. Thus in *Dunn v Pochin (Contractors) Ltd*[9] an employment tribunal was held to have erred in finding a dismissal to be fair despite the omission of a hearing because neither side had adduced any evidence as to what the position would have been had the employee been heard. Let us look more closely at the question of tribunal discretion and the standards applied for each of the most important procedural steps, viz:

(i)   warnings of dismissal,

(ii) adequate hearings,

(iii) appeals.

7a   See eg *Whitbread plc v Hall* [2001] EWCA Civ 268, [2001] IRLR 275.

8   [1976] IRLR 86, IT.

9   [1982] IRLR 449, EAT; see also *Charles Letts & Co Ltd v Howard* [1976] IRLR 248, 11 ITR 164, EAT.

i) Warnings of dismissal

Whether or not it is unfair for an employer to dismiss an employee without adequate warning is largely a question of fact for an employment tribunal to decide. As long as the tribunal does not make the mistake of deciding whether or not *it* would have given a further warning and direct itself that the question to be answered is whether the dismissal without a warning or further warning was within the band of reasonable responses of reasonable employers, its decision on the importance of a hearing can only be overturned if it is shown to be perverse.[10]

One guide to the standards of reasonable practice is the ACAS Code of Practice on Disciplinary and Grievance Procedures which provides that except in the case of gross misconduct a warning procedure should be followed consisting of an oral warning followed by a written warning and a final written warning which specifies that the recurrence of the offence might lead to dismissal.[11]

However as the Court of Appeal made clear in *Retarded Children's Aid Society Ltd v Day*[12] the recommendation in the Code of Practice relating to warnings is not a rule which has to be applied as a matter of law in every case. For example, where it is clear at the time that a warning would clearly not be effective because the employee is determined to go his own way[13] or disagree with the employee's methods[14] or has an irredeemable inadequacy[15] then since the question whether an employee was given a warning is ultimately one of substance,[16] a warning will not be necessary. Nor does the form of warning prescribed by the Code of Practice have any magic attached to it – a verbal warning can be just as effective as a written warning.[17]

Finally, even the sequence recommended in the Code of Practice is not necessary for the employer to follow. There may come a point where a combination of different infractions each having resulted in different

10   See eg *Grant v Ampex (GB) Ltd* [1980] IRLR 461, EAT.
11   Paragraph 15. In the latest version of the Code the exception for gross misconduct has been unaccountably omitted from para 15.
12   [1978] 1 WLR 763, [1978] IRLR 128, CA.
13   *Retarded Children's Aid Society Ltd v Day* [1978] 1 WLR 763, [1978] IRLR 128, EAT.
14   *Littlewoods Organisation Ltd v Egenti* [1976] ICR 516, [1976] IRLR 334, EAT.
15   See eg *Grant v Ampex (GB) Ltd* [1980] IRLR 461, EAT.
16   *Polkey v A E Dayton Services Ltd* [1987] IRLR 503, HL.
17   *McCall v Castleton Crafts* [1979] IRLR 218, EAT.

warnings, justifies an employer in issuing one final warning on the basis of the overall pattern of conduct.[18]

On the other hand, although the omission of a warning will not as a matter of law make a dismissal unfair,[19] where a warning if duly given could be seen at the time of dismissal as likely to influence the result, or even if there is a real possibility that it might influence the result its omission may convince a tribunal that the dismissal is unfair.[20]

To understand the situations in which employment tribunals may consider that it is within the range of responses of a reasonable employer to provide a warning, it is useful to remind oneself of the purposes of the warning from the viewpoint of a reasonable employer. The EAT in *Plasticers Ltd v Harold Amos*[1] once observed that the word 'warning':

'is only shorthand for steps which ought to be taken by the management and could otherwise be described in a case like this, as efforts to try to make the employee change, and (an indication) to him of the consequences if these efforts are unsuccessful'.

This emphasises that a reasonable employer will attempt to ascertain the possibilities of correcting an employee's behaviour before dismissing him or her for misconduct. This element of correction may be less important in the case of dismissals for ill-health[2] or redundancy,[3] where consultation provides the necessary information to employers. Moreover, it may apply only in a modified sense in cases of dismissal for incapability.[4] In case of misconduct, however, the emphasis on investigating the possibility of correction has been regarded as sufficiently important to prompt employment tribunals to ask two questions: First, did the employer make a reasonable effort to communicate to the employee that his actions were placing his job in danger?[5] Second, did the employer give the employee a reasonable opportunity to correct his behaviour to meet the standard set by the employer?

---

18   See *Auguste Noel Ltd v Curtis* [1990] IRLR 326, EAT.
19   *Polkey v A E Dayton Services Ltd* [1987] IRLR 503, HL.
20   Ibid.
1   *McCall v Castleton Crafts* [1979] IRLR 218, EAT.
2   See Chapter 6.
3   See Chapter 8.
4   See Chapter 7.
5   See eg *Bevan Ashford v Malin* [1995] IRLR 360, EAT.

(a) Was the warning that the job was at risk clearly communicated?

Since the purpose of a warning is to make the employee appreciate that his behaviour has placed his job in danger, an employment tribunal could ask in cases of warnings or misconduct[6] whether the warning included a clear and specific indication of the consequences of a failure to respond to the warning, that is to say that it specified that a further infringement would lead to the sanction of a dismissal.

In addition an employment tribunal may consider that reasonable employers would make reasonable efforts to ensure that the warning is effectively communicated; that is to say, that the warning is actually known and appreciated by the employee and the employee understands the precise start and end of the period of the warning.[7] Where an employer's disciplinary practice has created certain expectations, this may be taken into account by an employment tribunal in deciding on the reasonableness of the employer's decision to dismiss without a warning of the change of approach always presupposing that the tribunal appreciates that it must apply the test of whether the employer's response fell within the range of reasonable responses.[8] It is open to tribunals, for example, to find that a previous condonation of a disciplinary infraction such as a refusal to comply with instructions does not count against an employer where the decision to dismiss was otherwise reasonable in the circumstances.[9] Thus, in *Martin v Solus Schall*[10] it was held that past condonations by the employer of an employee's refusal to work overtime did not make it unfair to dismiss him for a later refusal to comply with his contractual obligation. The fact that the employers had been willing on previous occasions to suit his convenience where possible, should not count against them in deciding the reasonableness of their conduct at the time of dismissal.

On the other hand, where the employer has previously tended to interpret a disciplinary rule rather lightly, a sudden decision to dismiss employees for breaking the rule without a warning of the change in approach may be regarded as unfair by an employment tribunal. Thus in *Bendall v Paine*

---

6   See eg *Hewitson v Anderton Springs* [1972] IRLR 56, NIRC. In *Littlewoods Organisation Ltd v Egenti* [1976] ICR 516, [1976] IRLR 334, the EAT indicated that the question of sanction was not so important for purposes of warnings of lack of capability. But it added 'sanction, no doubt may very well be important in a case of discipline'. See also Code of Practice, para 12.

7   See *Bevan Ashford v Malin* [1995] IRLR 360, EAT.

8   See eg *Post Office v Fennell* [1981] IRLR 221, CA.

9   See eg *Hadjioannou v Coral Casinos Ltd* [1981] IRLR 352, EAT.

10   [1979] IRLR 7, EAT.

and Betteridge,[11] where the rule that smoking was strictly prohibited had been enforced in the past only by a request to put out cigarettes, and the employee was summarily dismissed for smoking on the premises, the tribunal held the dismissal unfair because the employer had 'lulled the employees into a false sense of security'.[12]

However, as the EAT put it in *Hadjioannou v Coral Casinos Ltd*,[13] an argument by a dismissed employee that the treatment he received was not on a par with that meted out in other cases is relevant in reviewing the fairness of the dismissal '… if there is evidence that employees have been led by an employer to believe that certain categories of conduct will be either overlooked, or at least will not be dealt with by the sanction of dismissal'. Yet this exercise of tribunal discretion too is subject to the constraint that it take into account the range of reasonable responses principle.[14]

Another extension of the concept of a warning in dismissal cases that might be applied by employment tribunals is offered by *Wallace v E J Guy Ltd*.[15] In this case the employee, a semi-skilled sheet metal worker, was dismissed when he refused an order to do pipe bending work without extra pay. He thought that the work was outside the contract. The tribunal disagreed and found that it was covered by the contract and that consequently he was fairly dismissed when he refused to obey the order without an increase in pay. The NIRC reversed the tribunal,[16] stating:

'Of course management is not bound to agree to the employee's demand. But at least management should tell the employee that the rate demanded is not acceptable and explain to the employee that the employee is faced with the option of accepting management's rate for the job or being served with notice of dismissal. The employee must be clearly given to understand what the choice is and must be given a reasonable opportunity to consider his position and decide what to do. This was not done in Mr Wallace's case. The position was rendered even less satisfactory because, according to his evidence, Mr Wallace thought that pipe bending was outside the

11   [1973] IRLR 44.
12   Cf *Paul v East Surrey District Health Authority* [1995] IRLR 305, CA.
13   [1981] IRLR 352, EAT.
14   Cf *Post Office v Fennell* [1981] IRLR 221, CA. See too *Paul*, n 12 above.
15   [1973] ICR 117, [1973] IRLR 175, NIRC.
16   [1973] ICR 117, [1973] IRLR 175, NIRC.

contractual scope of his employment and management knew that he laboured under that error'.[17]

Finally, where the warning procedure provides an opportunity to appeal, the existence of the appeal and the state of the appeal must be taken into account by the employer.[18]

(b) An opportunity to improve

In keeping with the philosophy expressed in the Code of Practice that a warning is a serious corrective measure, a tribunal could decide that reasonable employers would ensure that a warning is followed by a reasonable opportunity to improve.[19]

On the other hand, tribunals must assess the results during the warning period on the basis of the employee's record as a whole, taking into account whether the decision of the employer fell within the range of reasonable responses. Thus in *Newalls Insulation Co Ltd v Blakeman*[20] an employee was dismissed after being absent twice during a period of 14 days following a final written warning for absenteeism.

The tribunal held that the decision to dismiss was unfair on the basis of two days' absence during the period after the warning. The tribunal said:

'We have not so to speak wiped the slate clean for the earlier attendance record but we think that the correct way of taking account of that in law is to say, this is a man with a bad attendance record, admitted to be so. Would it be reasonable to sack such a man after two further days of absence following on to a warning? That question we give the answer "No".'

The EAT, however, reversed the tribunal's decision, commenting:

17   Of course, a warning cannot impose responsibilities upon an employee in addition to his contractual obligations. See eg *Canter, Smith and Gardener v Bowater Containers Ltd* [1975] IRLR 323, IT.

18   See eg *Tower Hamlets Health Authority v Anthony* [1989] IRLR 394, CA; *Louies v Coventry Hood & Seating Co Ltd* [1990] IRLR 324, EAT.

19   Cf *Mansfield Hosiery Mills Ltd v Bromley* [1977] IRLR 301, EAT; *Bell Fruit (UK) Ltd v Woolcombe* (1977) EAT 98/77 (need for warning to be updated).

20   [1976] ICR 543, [1976] IRLR 303, EAT. See *Yates v Post Office Telephones* [1976] IRLR 55, IT where a slight improvement during the warning period did not make an employer's decision to dismiss unfair, based on the whole record.

'In reaching its decision the [employment] tribunal should have looked at all the circumstances of the case and not simply at whether it was reasonable to dismiss for two further days absence after the warning was given. They should have considered critical issues such as what had happened before the final warning was given? What happened after the warning? How many absences were there? What sort of absences were there after the warning? How did these particular absences, in the light of the employee's own record, fit in as part of the general picture?'[1]

ii) Adequate hearings

Whether an employer has provided an adequate hearing is a question of fact for employment tribunals to decide as long as they ask themselves whether the employer's behaviour had gone outside the band of reasonable responses open to a reasonable employer. Alternatively they may ask whether it was fair to say that the employer had behaved as no reasonable employer would have behaved.[2] In exercising its discretion the tribunal is bound to take into account the recommendations of the Code of Practice where relevant. In cases of alleged misconduct, the Code of Practice recommends both that employers should establish a disciplinary procedure which provides a right for individuals to be informed of the complaints against them and to be given an opportunity to state their case before decisions are reached.[3] The purposes of a hearing are two-fold: first to have the employees input on the facts of the case; and secondly to allow representations on the case for a penalty other than dismissal. The Code of Practice endorses the idea of a hearing, even in cases of gross misconduct:

'In certain circumstances ... consideration should be given to a brief period of suspension with pay whilst an unhindered investigation is conducted (para 13). Before a decision is reached or any disciplinary action taken there should be a disciplinary hearing at which workers have the opportunity to state their case ... the worker should be

1   See eg *Metropole Group of Casinos v Macromelli* (1984) EAT 557/83. If the record shows an offence sufficiently far in the past, it may be unreasonable to include it as a major element in the decision to dismiss.

2   See eg *Metropole Group of Casinos v Macromelli* (1984) EAT 557/83.

3   A possibility of using a grievance procedure is not an adequate substitute. *Clarke v Trimoco Group Ltd* [1993] IRLR 148, EAT.

advised of any rights under the disciplinary procedure, including the statutory right to be accompanied'. (para 14)

Nevertheless under s 98(4) a statutory hearing is not required as a matter of law[4] and indeed it would be a mistake of law for a tribunal to decide that the omission of a hearing makes a dismissal automatically unfair.

In the proper exercise of its discretion under s 98(4) a tribunal is required to regard the omission of a hearing as only one of the factors to be looked at in the circumstances as a whole. Despite the rules of natural justice not being fulfilled, employers may be able to justify an omission of a hearing in a limited category of cases if they can meet the onus of proving that on the evidence available at the time of dismissal a hearing would have been futile or utterly useless. This may also be true even if the hearing was provided as a contractual right since the test is a statutory test not a contractual test.[5] As has been mentioned, when the misconduct consists of a criminal offence and charges have been made against the employee, the omission of a hearing may be justified.[6] Moreover, in cases where it is obvious at the time of dismissal that the employee's statement can provide no further information that will affect the result or is otherwise 'futile' then a failure to provide a hearing can be excused.[7]

Employment tribunals retain a discretion to decide that a dismissal is unfair because the employee was not given a proper hearing.[8] As long as they avoid the mistake of law of believing that a hearing is an essential formality without which the dismissal is automatically unfair.[9] In assessing both the need for a hearing and the adequacy of the hearing provided, employment tribunals have been influenced by their views of the functions of a hearing.

Tribunals have quite regularly considered that an important function of the hearing is to ensure that the employer is appraised of the employee's side of the case in respect of the charges that have been made against him. This of course presupposes that the employer has been made aware of the

4   *Bailey v BP Oil (Kent Refinery) Ltd* [1980] ICR 642, [1980] IRLR 287, CA; *Parker v Clifford Dunn Ltd* [1979] ICR 463, [1979] IRLR 56, EAT.

5   *Westminster City Council v Cabaj* [1996] IRLR 399, CA; cf *Stocker v Lancashire County Council* [1992] IRLR 75, CA.

6   See eg *Carr v Alexander Russell Ltd.* See also *Scottish Special Housing Association v Linnen* [1979] IRLR 265, EAT.

7   *Polkey v A E Dayton Services Ltd* [1987] IRLR 503, HL; *Slater v Leicestershire Health Authority* [1989] IRLR 16, CA. *Martin v Solus Schall* [1979] IRLR 7, EAT.

8   See eg *McLaren v National Coal Board* [1988] IRLR 215, CA.

9   See eg *Polkey v A E Dayton Services Ltd* [1987] IRLR 503, HL.

specific charges against him or her.[10] Similarly, in all but the most obvious cases, tribunals will look to see whether the employer has obtained the employee's reply to allegations of misconduct or incompetence *before* a decision was taken to dismiss the employee. For example, in *W Weddel & Co Ltd v Tepper*[11] an employee was not given a proper opportunity to respond to the employer's reasons for gross misconduct and then asked whether he had anything to say. The Court of Appeal upheld the tribunal's decision that the decision was unfair because of the complete failure of the employer to give the employee a proper opportunity to respond to the employer's reasons for dismissal.[12] Similarly in *Earl v Slater & Wheeler (Airlyne) Ltd*[13] an employee was presented at a meeting with a letter informing him that he was dismissed and that a replacement had already been appointed to his position. Although he might have attempted to give an explanation to his employers at this meeting, the NIRC held that he had no reasonable opportunity to state his case because the decision had already been taken.

Moreover, on occasion tribunals have also held that this function of a hearing cannot be fulfilled where the employer does not give the employee an adequate indication of the reasons for the intended dismissal.[14] For example, in *Bentley Engineering Co Ltd v Mistry*[15] two employees involved in a fight were interviewed separately and written statements were taken from witnesses. Mr Mistry was dismissed without seeing the written statements or having an account of their views or that of the other employee involved in the fight. The EAT, upholding the employment tribunal's decision that the dismissal was unfair partly because the dismissed employee was insufficiently informed of the nature and detail of the allegation to give him an opportunity to reply,

'The [Employment] Tribunal were entitled to find the respondent employee's dismissal for fighting unfair on grounds that as part of

10   *Spink v Express Foods Group Ltd* [1990] IRLR 320, EAT; *Louies v Coventry Hood & Seating Co Ltd* [1990] IRLR 324, EAT; the awareness requirement can be satisfied when the charges are obvious: *Fuller v Lloyds Bank plc* [1991] IRLR 336, EAT.
11   [1980] ICR 286, [1980] IRLR 96, CA.
12   See also *Sutton & Gates (Luton) Ltd v Boxall* [1979] ICR 67, [1978] IRLR 486, EAT.
13   [1973] 1 All ER 145, [19872] IRLR 115, NIRC.
14   See now *Birds Eye Walls Ltd v Harrison* [1985] IRLR 47, EAT; *Henry v ITT Industries* (1983) EAT 817/82.
15   [1979] ICR 47, [1978] IRLR 437, EAT (employee dismissed while away on holiday).

his disciplinary hearing he had not been given the written statements of the witnesses or of the other employee involved in the fight, nor did he have the opportunity to cross-examine. Although there was no question that the respondent had been involved in a fight, the procedure adopted by the employers meant that he did not have the opportunity of knowing in sufficient detail what was being said against him as to who or what had provoked the fight.

Natural justice, in a case such as the present one, requires not merely that a man shall have a chance to state his own case in detail; he must know sufficiently what is being said against him so that he can properly put forward his own case. In order to adequately satisfy the requirements of natural justice, it may be, according to the facts, that what is said against the employee can be communicated to him in a written statement, or it may be sufficient if he hears what the other protagonist is saying, or it may be adequate in an appropriate case for matters which have been said by others to be put orally in sufficient detail. There is no particular form of procedure that has to be followed in any and every case. It is all a question of degree.

In the present case, the [Employment] Tribunal's conclusion that the employers' failure in this respect, coupled with the less significant reason that the company had departed from the terms of its own disciplinary procedure, led to the dismissal being unfair could not be held to be a conclusion to which no reasonable Tribunal could come.'[16]

Furthermore in *W Weddel & Co Ltd v Tepper*[17] the employment tribunal's decision that a dismissal was unfair was due in part to the failure of the employer to give the employee a clear account of the reasons for dismissal.[18]

Employment tribunals have also held that a real opportunity to give an explanation in response to charges presupposes that the employee has an adequate time to respond, given the nature of the charges. For example, in *BG Electrical Co Ltd v Dyke*[19] a service engineer was dismissed for not completing calls to service television sets and failing to inform the employers that he had not completed the calls. The employer had

---

16   [1978] IRLR 437, EAT, see also *Khanum v Mid-Glamorgan Area Health Authority* [1979] ICR 40, [1978] IRLR 215, EAT; *Metropole Group of Casinos v Macromelli* (1984) EAT 557/83.

17   [1980] ICR 286, [1980] IRLR 96, CA.

18   See also *Bell v Devon and Cornwall Police Authority* [1978] IRLR 283, IT.

19   (1977) EAT 614/76.

interviewed the employee for a few minutes prior to the dismissal. The EAT upheld the tribunal's finding that the employee had not been given an opportunity to explain. As the EAT put it:

'It is recorded that the interview was very short ... if all that was in issue was whether reasonably Mr Dyke could have completed all the calls ... in the time available it is quite obvious that it would require a fairly clear, a fairly detailed, not a short ... explanation. What we think the [employment] tribunal are saying ... is not that he was not given an opportunity to explain, but that he was not given a proper opportunity, meaning by that one which was sufficient for the purpose'.

Yet these views are not rules of law which must always be applied by employment tribunals. For example in *Roberts and Ellison v Short Bros & Harland Ltd*,[20] the EAT upheld a tribunal which had found a dismissal fair in spite of the fact that the employer had not inter alia[1] given the employees a clear statement of the case which they had to meet. The EAT's view was:

'The answer is that this was not a situation nor were these complaints of a kind which require much elaboration. The complaint was, as they knew perfectly well, that in gross dereliction of duty as security patrolmen they were asleep on duty. That was the case they had to meet. It was for the alleged failure that they had been suspended. They knew perfectly well what they had to deal with'.

Further, employment tribunals have also on occasion been concerned that a hearing should be held in conditions where the employee is in a fit state to be interviewed. Thus in *Tesco Group of Companies (Holdings) Ltd v Hill*[2] an employee was held to be unfairly dismissed because the employee when interviewed was clearly suffering from shock and in no fit state to take part in an interview.

Finally, an excessive delay between the date of the alleged acts of misconduct and the date of the hearing may be legitimately regarded by an

---

20 (1976) EAT 318/76. See too *Fuller v Lloyds Bank plc* [1991] IRLR 336, EAT.
1   In the same case the EAT also rejected allegations that notice of the hearing was too short, that there was no opportunity to confront witnesses, that there was no opportunity for representation and that the hearing was too short. See also *Ayanlowo v IRC* [1975] IRLR 253, CA where an employee was not unfairly denied an oral hearing, the Court of Appeal stating that there was no requirement that hearings be oral and that written representations were enough.
2   [1977] IRLR 63, EAT. See also *Read v Phoenix Preservations Ltd* [1985] IRLR 93, EAT (police officer present without prior warning).

employment tribunal as the basis for a finding of an unfair dismissal because the delay makes it impossible for the employee to identify the incidents and to offer an explanation. Thus in *Marley Homecare Ltd v Dutton*[3] an employee accused of not complying with a company's cash handling procedure was informed seven days after the incident and asked for an explanation, at which time all she could say was that she couldn't remember the incident. The EAT upheld an employment tribunal's finding that the dismissal was unfair.

Under s 98(4) tribunals have also viewed a hearing as something more than simply an opportunity for the employee to be informed of and reply to allegations of fact and specific accusations. On occasion employment tribunals have decided that a reasonable employer would use a hearing for a second purpose, to provide an accused employee with an opportunity to raise any mitigating circumstances that ought to be taken into account. This view has been upheld by the EAT. As the EAT put it in *Harris (Ipswich) Ltd v Harrison*[4] the interview should cover both a discussion of the alleged offence and a discussion of the action the employer is proposing to take. And the EAT suggested that in *Budgen & Co Ltd v Thomas*,[5] there was a distinction to be drawn between the process of ascertaining the facts and the process of deciding whether dismissal was an appropriate penalty. Where both functions are performed by the same level of management, the two elements can be contained within the same hearing, although presumably it would be open to an employee to argue that such a hearing would be incomplete if it did not contain both elements. Where the two elements of the decision are vested in different levels of management, a failure to give the employee an opportunity to be heard at the second level at which the decision to dismiss is taken could also make a dismissal unfair. For example, in *Budgen*, a shop assistant was dismissed following an investigation by a security officer of an alleged till offence. The dismissal was decided at head office on the basis of the security officer's report which included a written statement by Mrs Thomas admitting the offence. The EAT agreed with the tribunal's conclusion that by separating the two processes of ascertaining the facts and deciding

---

3   [1981] IRLR 380, EAT; see also *Wm Low & Co Ltd v MacCuish* [1979] IRLR 458, EAT.
4   [1978] ICR 1256, [1978] IRLR 382, EAT.
5   [1976] ICR 344, [1976] IRLR 174, EAT; see also *Ladbroke Hotels Ltd v Woodcock* (1983) EAT 432/83.

the appropriate penalty the employer had unfairly precluded the employee from an opportunity to state her case on the second question.[6] Yet whilst it may be open to tribunals in the exercise of their discretion to apply the prescription of the EAT in the *Budgen* case, such a prescription is not of a status to allow an appeal against an employment tribunal which decides that a dismissal is not unfair despite a failure to provide a hearing by the employer to the employee.

The hearing by the employer is not required to have the formality of a court proceeding, or many of the safeguards required of a court hearing. Thus there is no automatic right to be present throughout a disciplinary hearing provided that the employees are safeguarded by their representatives.[7] Nor is an employee automatically entitled to a copy of all witness statements if the essence has been communicated to the employee and there is some good ground for withholding them.[8] Further, there is no automatic entitlement to cross question all persons providing evidence in the form of witness statement or even witnesses.[9]

The rules of natural justice cannot be slavishly applied.[10] This is particularly true in the cases where the independence of the employer's representative holding the hearing is called into question. Thus merely because a person conducted a preliminary inquiry did not preclude him from conducting the hearing.[11] Moreover, the involvement of managers in the appeal stage who had been active at an earlier stage has been held to be a procedural defect which can be cured by a rehearing.[12] However if the individual manager serving at more than one level is so involved in the employee's case that objectivity is lost, that would be viewed by a reasonable employer as disentitling the manager from conducting a fair hearing.[13] In general, to succeed, the argument of the employee must be not merely that the *form* of the hearing is technically lacking but that the

6 See also *O'Brien v Boots Pure Drug Co* [1973] IRLR 261, but cf *Okereke v Post Office* [1974] IRLR 170, IT. Furthermore, the 'second question' of mitigation may sometimes require an opportunity to allow an employee to make an apology. See *Charles Letts & Co Ltd v Howard* [1976] IRLR 248, EAT.

7 *Gray Dunn & Co Ltd v Edwards* [1980] IRLR 23, EAT.

8 *Hussain v Elonex plc* [1999] IRLR 420, CA.

9 See *Linfood Cash and Carry Ltd v Thomson* [1989] IRLR 235, EAT (setting out guidelines to balance the rights of fearful witnesses with the rights of the complainant); see too *Khanum v Mid-Glamorgan Area Health Authority* [1978] IRLR 215, EAT.

10 *Slater v Leicestershire Health Authority* [1989] IRLR 16, CA.

11 Ibid. But see *R v Chief Constable of Merseyside Police* [2000] IRLR 821, HC.

12 *Sartor v P&O European Ferries (Felixstowe) Ltd* [1992] IRLR 271, CA.

13 *Byrne v BOC Ltd* [1992] IRLR 505, EAT.

substance of the employee's rights to be informed of the main props of the employer's case and an opportunity to refute them as well as to make representations about the decision have been infringed.[14]

The status of such a statement is essentially that of an authority useful to attempt to persuade an employment tribunal to decide whether or not a dismissal was unfair. Just as a complete failure to provide a hearing may, in certain circumstances be viewed as being unreasonable, so too can a hearing which is incomplete in some respect recommended by the Code of Practice be condoned under certain conditions. For example, the Code recommends that a fair hearing includes a right to be accompanied by a representative of the employee's choice.[15] Yet a failure to allow representation may not always be fatal. Thus, in *Dacres v Walls Meat Co Ltd*[16] Mr Justice Phillips, sitting in the Queen's Bench Division, upheld an employment tribunal that had decided that an employer who dismissed an employee following a fight with another employee, after giving him an interview but no opportunity to be represented by his shop steward or other representative, was not unfair.

Mr Justice Phillips held that although the employer was at fault in not seeing that, in accordance with the domestic procedure and the Code of Practice, the appellant was accompanied by his union representative, in the circumstances this did not amount to such a defect in procedure as to render the dismissal unfair. The appellant had a good opportunity of saying that he was not fighting but his employer did not believe him. 'So the only question upon which the union representative could have assisted was the simple question of "fighting or not fighting".' That the appellant was not represented, therefore, 'really could have made no difference'.

And in *Bailey v BP Oil (Kent Refinery) Ltd*[17] an employee summarily dismissed because he had told the employer he was sick and instead went to Majorca for a holiday, was not allowed to be represented by a full-time official despite the provision in a collectively agreed disciplinary procedure that stipulated that a full-time official would be notified if dismissal was contemplated. The employer had attempted to contact the official and, when finding that he was unavailable, had provided a hearing for Mr Bailey

---

14   *Hussain v Elonex plc* [1999] IRLR 420, CA.
15   See Code of Practice. In some cases the representative can attend in place of the employee, see eg *Pirelli General Cable Works Ltd v Murray* [1979] IRLR 190, EAT. See also *Gray Dunn & Co Ltd v Edwards* [1980] IRLR 23, EAT.
16   [1976] ICR 44, [1976] IRLR 20, EAT.
17   [1980] ICR 642, [1980] IRLR 287, CA.

accompanied by two workshop union representatives. The Court of Appeal upheld an employment tribunal's exercise of discretion that the dismissal was not unfair despite the breach of the procedure by the employer and overruled at EAT decision that the dismissal was unfair.

On the other hand if a tribunal exercises its discretion to decide that an omission to allow adequate representation has been substantial in its effect it will be difficult to overturn that decision upon appeal.[18] Moreover, today tribunal attitudes toward representation in disciplinary cases may well be influenced by the new requirement in ERA 1999 ss 10–13 that employees should have a right to be accompanied by a representative at a disciplinary hearing. It is true that there is a separate remedy of compensation of up to two weeks' pay for a failure to give an employee such a right but the fact that the right is now required by statute and dismissal is the most important of all disciplinary sanctions may incline employment tribunals more often to the view that such an omission is outside the range of reasonable employer responses.

iii) Appeals

The Code of Practice endorses an opportunity to appeal against a disciplinary decision as essential to natural justice.[19] In *West Midlands Co-operative Society Ltd v Tipton*[20] the House of Lords confirmed that a dismissal may be unfair when the employer has refused to entertain an appeal to which the employee is contractually entitled and thereby denied to him the opportunity of showing that in all the circumstances the employer's reason for dismissing him could not reasonably be treated as sufficient. Hence, in a firm of the appropriate size and resources the absence of an appeal, or a defective appeal procedure can reinforce a complaint of unfair dismissal, particularly where it is likely, when viewed from the time of dismissal, to have some effect on the decision to dismiss and therefore cannot be dismissed as utterly useless or futile.[1]

---

18   See eg *Rank Xerox (UK) Ltd v Goodchild* [1979] IRLR 185; see also remarks in *Ladbroke Racing Ltd v Arnott* [1979] IRLR 192, EAT; affd [1983] IRLR 154, Ct of Sess.

19   Para 27; *Gray Dunn & Co Ltd v Edwards* [1980] IRLR 23, EAT.

20   [1986] IRLR 112, HL.

1   See eg *Polkey v A E Dayton Services Ltd* [1987] IRLR 503, HL; *Francis v Ford Motor Co* [1975] IRLR 25, IT; *Davison v Kent Meters Ltd* [1975] IRLR 145, IT;

Hence an appeal is not always required as a matter of law. The absence of an appeal or review procedure is just one of many factors to be considered in determining fairness even where there is a contractual right of appeal.[2] In particular in small firms it may not be regarded as essential.[3] Yet after *Polkey* there are definite limits to the jurisdiction of employment tribunals to condone the omission of an appeal.[4]

If a hearing is given, certain types of defects in procedure may be condoned where they are found not to result in an unreasonable decision.[5] For example, in *Palmer v Vauxhall Motors Ltd*[6] the EAT accepted that the failure to give an employee an opportunity to be present at the appeal did not make the dismissal unfair. As the EAT put it:

'Although it appears to have been in accordance with practice, and to the satisfaction of the union representative, it seems wrong that the employee was not afforded an opportunity to be present. However, it does not appear that any harm was done by her absence, or that the outcome could have been any different had she been present'.

A distinction ought to be drawn between a review and an appeal. In the former, an occasion may be had for the decision-taker to reconsider his decision in the light of the arguments of the employee.[7] Indeed, a serious procedural defect in the hearing can sometimes be cured by a thorough review of the original decision in the form of a rehearing.[8] In the latter, however, the individual(s) hearing the appeal should be of a different level

---

cf *Shannon v Michelin (Belfast) Ltd* [1981] IRLR 505, NICA. A failure to give the employee an appeal reinforced a case of unfair dismissal when it occurred in conjunction with another procedural omission, see *Scottish Co-operative Wholesale Society Ltd v Lloyd* [1973] ICR 137, [1973] IRLR 93, NIRC. *Rank Xerox (UK) Ltd v Goodchild* [1979] IRLR 185, EAT.

2   *Post Office v Marney* [1990] IRLR 170, EAT; *Westminster City Council v Cabaj* [1996] IRLR 399, CA.

3   See eg *Tiptools Ltd v Curtis* [1973] IRLR 276, NIRC. See also *Ayanlowo v IRC* [1975] IRLR 253, CA, where a probationary employee was not entitled to an appeal.

4   See eg *Stocker v Lancashire County Council* [1992] IRLR 75, CA.

5   Cf *Liverpool Area Health Authority (Teaching) Central and Southern District v Edwards* [1977] IRLR 471, EAT.

6   [1977] ICR 24. See also *Stevenson v Golden Wonder Ltd* [1977] IRLR 474, EAT; *Gray Dunn & Co Ltd v Edwards* [1980] IRLR 23, EAT; *Pirelli General Cable Works Ltd v Murray* [1979] IRLR 190, EAT.

7   But see *Byrne v BOC Ltd* [1992] IRLR 505, EAT.

8   *Sartor v P&O European Ferries (Felixstowe) Ltd* [1992] IRLR 271, CA.

of management particularly in the case of larger employers.[9] In several cases the EAT has suggested that it would be unwise as a matter of industrial practice for those managers who made the original decision to dismiss to sit on the appeal panel[10] and this would certainly make it extremely difficult if not impossible to cure procedural omissions at the original hearing.[11] However, it will not necessarily be an error of law for an employment tribunal to decide that a dismissal is not unfair despite an employer's failure to keep the two stages entirely disconnected. As the EAT pointed out in *Rowe v Radio Rentals Ltd*[12]

'in the case of internal appeal procedures run by commercial companies it was often inevitable that those involved in the original decision to dismiss were in daily contact with their superiors who were responsible for deciding the appeal and the initial dismisser is very often required to give information as to the facts to the person hearing the appeal. In the majority of cases rules about total *separation* of functions and lack of contact between those hearing the appeal and those involved in the original decision cannot be applied. If the person hearing the appeal in fact takes the decision and has given the employee a hearing and an opportunity to deal with the case against him, it would be difficult to show that the rules of natural justice had been infringed'.

In the *Radio Rentals*[13] case the employer had allowed the manager who originally dismissed the employee not only to outline the facts of the case to the manager hearing the appeal but also to remain in the room for the entire hearing. Moreover the manager hearing the appeal had been informed about his dismissal before the decision had been taken. The evidence before the tribunal indicated however that the manager hearing the appeal had taken no active part in the original decision and the manager taking the original decision had taken no active part in the decision to reject the appeal despite being in the room. Under these circumstances the EAT held that the tribunal was justified in deciding that the appearance of

---

9   See eg *Sartor v P&O European Ferries (Felixstowe) Ltd* [1992] IRLR 271, CA; *Byrne v BOC Ltd* [1992] IRLR 505, EAT; *Francis v Ford Motor Co* [1975] IRLR 25, IT; cf *Ladbroke Hotels Ltd v Woodcock* (1983) EAT 432/83.

10   See eg *Qualcast (Wolverhampton) Ltd v Ross* [1979] ICR 386, [1979] IRLR 98, EAT. See now *British Sugar Corpn v Russo* (1984) EAT 727/83.

11   *Byrne v BOC Ltd* [1992] IRLR 505, EAT.

12   [1982] IRLR 177, EAT.

13   [1982] IRLR 177, EAT.

intermingling of roles like the appeals procedure did not make the dismissal unfair in substance.[14]

One major issue raised by procedures for appeal from a dismissal is the relevance under s 98(4) of evidence obtained in the course of the appeal procedure. In *W Devis & Sons Ltd v Atkins*, the House of Lords held that any such evidence obtained after a dismissal was irrelevant to the determination of the reasonableness of the employer's decision to dismiss. For that reason the provision of an appeal after dismissal could not justify the failure of an employer to omit giving the employee an opportunity to explain before dismissal, although an appeal held before the decision to dismiss is finally taken could correct a procedural fault at the disciplinary hearing stage.[15] Nor could a failure by the employee to exercise an appeal be admissible evidence of his acquiescence to the dismissal.[16]

A further complicating factor in the application of the rule in *Devis* occurs however when the employer has provided an internal appeal procedure and new evidence supporting the employer's position emerges in the course of the appeal.[17] In *Devis* the employer had provided no internal appeal and he sought to rely on conduct of which he was unaware until after his final decision to dismiss.

In *Monie v Coral Racing Ltd*,[18] a case involving an internal appeal procedure the Court of Appeal made it clear that information that emerged after the decision to dismiss but before the decision was confirmed in the appeal was inadmissible following the rule in *Devis*. Yet the particular appeal procedure in *Monie* made no provision for keeping the employee on until the final confirmation of the dismissal.

In *National Heart and Chest Hospitals Board of Governors v Nambiar*,[19] the EAT held that in a case where the employer provided an internal appeal procedure with the employee suspended on full pay pending the results of an appeal, the employer could rely on the new information discovered in the course of the appeal particularly where it confirmed the decision to dismiss for the original reason. The decision that the time of dismissal was the date the dismissal was finally confirmed rather than the date it was originally decided, appeared to turn on the issue that technically

14   See too *R v Chief Constable of South Wales, ex p Thornhill* [1987] IRLR 313, CA.

15   See eg *Qualcast (Wolverhampton) Ltd v Ross* [1979] ICR 386, [1979] IRLR 98, EAT.

16   See *Metropole Group of Casinos v Macromelli* (1984) EAT 557/83.

17   *Chrystie v Rolls Royce (1971) Ltd* [1976] IRLR 336, EAT.

18   [1980] IRLR 464, CA.

19   [1981] ICR 441, [1981] IRLR 196, EAT.

the contract of employment as a whole had continued during the course of the appeal. Nevertheless, as the House of Lords held in *Tipton*'s case,[20] a dismissal can be unfair if the employer unreasonably treats his reason as a sufficient reason to dismiss the employee, either when he makes his original decision to dismiss or when he maintains that decision at the conclusion of an internal appeal.

4. DID THE EMPLOYER ACT REASONABLY IN CONCLUDING THAT DISMISSAL WAS WARRANTED IN THE CIRCUMSTANCES?

Assuming that employers have met the first two tests, that is to say, they have acted reasonably in forming their conclusions of fact and the procedure they adopted was reasonable in the circumstances, to what extent may an employment tribunal question the exercise of management discretion in taking the decision to dismiss? On its face, s 98(4) appears to provide that employment tribunals have an obligation to satisfy themselves that the employer acted reasonably in the circumstances in concluding that a response of dismissal was warranted on the merits of the case. It states that the tribunal must determine whether employers acted reasonably or unreasonably in treating their reason as *sufficient* for dismissal. This implies that a tribunal should be satisfied that in all the circumstances a management response as drastic as dismissal was a reasonable response.

Yet tribunals have been sharply reminded that in deciding this issue too they must not ask themselves what they would have done had they been the management, rather they must look at what the employer has decided and ask whether the employer's decision in the circumstances was reasonable.[1] Moreover, they must judge the reasonableness of the employer's decision remembering that in these cases 'there is a band of reasonableness within which one employer might reasonably take one view; another quite reasonably take a different view. And as long as it was quite reasonable to dismiss him then the dismissal must be upheld as fair even though some other employers may not have dismissed him'.[2]

Insofar as these points are established by the authorities as principles of law, an employment tribunal which fails to apply them will be regarded as having erred in law and be susceptible to an appeal on that ground.

20 See now *West Midlands Co-operative Society Ltd v Tipton* [1986] IRLR 112, HL.
1   *Union of Construction, Allied Trades and Technicians v Brain* [1981] ICR 542, [1981] IRLR 224, CA.
2   *British Leyland (UK) Ltd v Swift* [1981] IRLR 91, CA.

Thus in *Iceland Frozen Foods Ltd v Jones*[3] an employment tribunal was held to have misdirected itself when it stated expressly that it was not deciding the case on whether or not the decision to dismiss fell within the band of reasonable conduct which a reasonable employer would adopt. Moreover, in *British Leyland (UK) Ltd v Swift*[3a] an industrial tribunal was found to have misdirected itself when it concluded that '… a reasonable employer would in our opinion have considered that a lesser penalty was appropriate.'

As Lord Denning put it 'I do not think that this is the right test. The correct test is Was it reasonable to dismiss him? If no reasonable employer would have dismissed him, then the dismissal was unfair.'

Yet the view that there is an area of discretion within which reasonable employers might disagree, and that is when an employer's decision falls within that area it must be found to be fair by an industrial tribunal, raises a rather important further question. How is the legitimate area of discretion for the 'reasonable employer' to be determined? (The EAT at one stage suggested a rather subjective test to be applied by tribunals.) In *Vickers Ltd v Smith*[3b] the EAT, per Mr Justice Cummings Bruce, stated:

'the test to be applied by an industrial tribunal under s 98(4)] was not simply whether the tribunal thought that the employer's decision was wrong, but rather whether it was wrong that "no reasonable management could have arrived at the decision at which the management arrived …".'

The case itself concerned a question of reasonable selection for redundancy but the interpretation given to s 98(4) was not necessarily confined solely to that type of dismissal.

In subsequent cases, however, the EAT has made it quite clear that it is more concerned to ensure that tribunals do not substitute their view for that of the employer[3c] than to create a test of subjectivity as that in *Vickers Ltd v Smith* for all alleged unfair dismissals.[3d] The standard suggested in

3   [1982] IRLR 439 at 442, EAT.
3a   [1981] IRLR 91 at 93, CA.
3b   [1977] IRLR 11.
3c   *Trust House Forte Leisure Ltd v Aquilar* [1976] IRLR 251.
3d   Cf *Grundy (Teddington) Ltd v Willis* [1976] ICR 323, [1976] IRLR 118, in which Phillips J, sitting in the High Court, Queen's Bench Division, had earlier suggested a similar approach for tribunals to take in selection for redundancy cases. However, he had appeared to limit its application to cases where 'the candidates for selection were almost indistinguishably even matched'. In such instances, provided the employers 'have applied their minds to the problem, have acted from genuine

Vickers Ltd v Smith was first explicitly limited by the EAT to cases of selection for redundancy[3e] and later called into question as an appropriate standard in such cases by the EAT's assertion that in redundancy situations the fairness or unfairness of a dismissal is to be decided 'by the objective standard of the way in which a reasonable employer in the circumstances in that line of business would have behaved'.[4] This standard has been given explicit support by the Court of Appeal[5] even after a spirited attack on its low standards by Morrison P in *Haddon v Van den Bergh Foods Ltd*.[6]

However, as long as the tribunal does not indicated that it is imposing its own view of what the employer should have done and acknowledges the band of reasonableness principle as its guiding direction, the precise words used to describe the tribunal's conclusion of fact are not to be subject of a fine toothcomb by the EAT.

For example, in *Potterton International Ltd v Lewin*[7] an employment tribunal concluded that 'a reasonable employer giving due weight to those considerations would not have dismissed Mr Lewin but would have suspended him and issued a general warning that dismissal would be considered if anything of the kind happened in the future'. The employer argued that following *British Leyland (UK) Ltd v Swift* this was an error of law because the tribunal had asked whether a reasonable employer would have taken a different course instead of asking 'is this a case in which no reasonable employer would have dismissed (the employee)'. The EAT rejected the employer's argument suggesting that the distinction was 'too fine' particularly since the tribunal had directed itself that 'we have to take care not to decide this question in terms of what we would have done if we had been in management's place. We have to ask ourselves what a reasonable employer would have done and to remember that these are cases in which some reasonable employers might act differently from others'.

The EAT's reluctance to adopt the test of *Vickers Ltd v Smith* more widely has been understandable. Such a test would have far too obviously required employment tribunals to discover an extreme of unreasonableness by the employer which fell below the lower reaches of standards prevailing

---

motives and with proper notice', they could not be said to have acted unreasonably in choosing one employee for redundancy in preference to another.

3e   *Mitchell v Old Hall Exchange and Palatine Club Ltd* [1978] IRLR 160, EAT.

4   *N C Watling & Co Ltd v Richardson* [1978] ICR 1049, [1978] IRLR 225.

5   *British Leyland (UK) Ltd v Swift* [1981] IRLR 91, CA; *Union of Construction, Allied Trades and Technicians v Brain* [1981] ICR 542, [1981] IRLR 224, CA.

6   *Foley v Post Office* [2000] IRLR 827, CA.

7   (1984) EAT 370/83.

in industry. Moreover, quite importantly, it could have created a basis for frequent appeals against tribunals' decisions.

At the same time, the standard suggested in *British Leyland (UK) Ltd v Swift* also places quite severe limits on the discretion of employment tribunals under s 98(4) to establish their own norm of fairness and to impose it upon employers. The requirement that an employment tribunal should determine whether 'the employer acted as no reasonable employer would' still requires the standards of existing managerial practice to be the yardstick for the tribunal's decision. Its adoption still unduly lowers the standards of the basic test of fairness. Instead of requiring employers to satisfy employment tribunals that they have met a norm of fairness established by a tribunal with expertise in general industrial standards, it suggests to the tribunal that they must not apply a more stringent test than asking whether the employer meets the lowest acceptable standards of reasonable managerial practice. Yet, the tribunals are also required to apply a test that restricts managerial decisions to a standard of *reasonable* practice. If the tribunal decision condones too many failings of management it can be regarded as perverse by the EAT.[8]

In cases of dismissal for misconduct, the application by tribunals of the test of whether the employer acted as a 'reasonable employer' would in deciding to dismiss commonly includes two elements. First, a tribunal may look solely at the conduct of the employee and ask itself, was it reasonable to dismiss an employee for that conduct? The employee may have been dismissed for gross misconduct, for a single breach of discipline, or for misconduct constituting a series of acts and following a series of warnings, but in principle the first element of the test is the same. Would a reasonable employer have decided that the employee's conduct, taken on its own, was sufficiently serious to warrant the penalty of dismissal?

Secondly, even where the conduct of the employee taken by itself may have been sufficient to justify dismissal, a tribunal may nevertheless find a dismissal unfair because the employer gave inadequate consideration to one or more important extenuating factors. Let us consider each in turn.

i)   The sufficiency of the employee's conduct taken by itself

Where an employment tribunal considers that an employee's conduct taken by itself was insufficiently serious to warrant dismissal, it may decide that

---

8   The facts in the decision of the employment tribunal on the *Haddon v Van den Burgh Foods* [1999] IRLR 672, EAT for example would probably have supported an EAT reversal on grounds of perversity.

a dismissal is unfair on this ground alone as long as it observed the principle of a band of reasonable responses. As Donaldson LJ (as he then was) put it in *Union of Construction, Allied Trades and Technicians v Brain*[9] the third stage consists of the tribunal asking 'Has the employer … acted reasonably in treating this conduct as a sufficient reason for dismissing the employee'? In cases of dismissals for misconduct, there are two separate types of test of sufficiency depending on whether, on the one hand, the dismissal was for a single offence or for gross misconduct, or, on the other hand, the dismissal was for a series of acts of ordinary misconduct and constituted the final step of a disciplinary procedure under which previous warnings had been given.

(a) Gross misconduct and the sufficiency test

One major exception to the standard that a reasonable employer should not dismiss an employee for a first offence without previous warning is where the employer alleges that the employee has committed an act of gross misconduct. The Code of Practice gives some examples of gross misconduct (para 7) and describes acts which constitute gross misconduct as those resulting in a serious breach of contractual terms which may warrant summary dismissal. But what is gross misconduct has been held to be purely a question of fact in the sense that it is a question for employment tribunals to decide on the basis of the evidence subject only to the limits of misdirection[10] and perversity.[11]

Yet in cases of dismissal for gross misconduct the tribunal must not make the mistake of assessing the reasonableness of the choice of sanction of dismissal by whether it considers that a lesser penalty would have been appropriate[12] or by whether *a* reasonable employer might have considered a lesser penalty appropriate.[13] Instead it must ask whether it was within the range of reasonable responses for the employer to dismiss the employee summarily in the circumstances.[14] In *Swift's* case, once an employment tribunal found that an employer had reasonably characterised the employee's conduct as gross misconduct, it was not open to them to decide

9   [1981] IRLR 224 at 227, CA.

10   See eg *Booker v Heather Foods Ltd (t/a Holland & Barrett)* (1983) EAT 452/83.

11   This could be true even if the employee is dismissed with notice see eg *Springbank Sand and Gravel Co Ltd v Craig* [1974] ICR 7, [1973] IRLR 278, NIRC.

12   *British Leyland (UK) Ltd v Swift* [1981] IRLR 91, CA; see also *Taylor v British Sisalkdraft Ltd* (1980) EAT 80/80.

13   *Kelly v Bankers Automated Cleaning Services Ltd* (1984) EAT 550/83.

14   *British Leyland (UK) Ltd v Swift* [1981] IRLR 91, CA.

that the dismissal was unfair because in the circumstances dismissal was too severe a penalty unless they could say that that dismissal fell outside the range of reasonable responses.

On the other hand, where an employment tribunal considers that a dismissal is so severe that it falls outside the range of reasonable responses of reasonable employers, it has the discretion to find a dismissal unfair on that ground alone.[15] Indeed, where its evidence discloses that the penalty is 'extremely harsh' it may be a perverse judgment to find a dismissal fair.[16]

Even though the statutory concept of gross misconduct[17] is purely a question of fact it has its origins in the common law notion of repudiatory conduct by the employee entitling the employer to dismiss without notice. Moreover, it continues to be influenced by the more recent development of the concept of trust and confidence as an inherent feature of the employment relationship.[18] At common law, an employee's conduct is considered repudiatory where it is both wilful and a breach of an important contractual obligation. As Lord Evershed MR stated in *Laws v London Chronicle (Indicator Newspapers) Ltd*:[19]

> 'an act of disobedience can justify dismissal only if it is of a nature which goes to show in effect that the servant is repudiating the contract or one of its essential conditions. The disobedience must have the quality that it is wilful; (in other words) a deliberate flouting of the essential contractual conditions'.[1]

The continuing influence of the common law notion of repudiation upon the statutory test can be seen first of all in the requirement of the latter that gross misconduct generally presupposes intentional and deliberate misconduct.[2] This must now be taken with the caveat that under the modern view of employment contracts, even a deliberate breach of an important

---

15   *Booker v Health Foods Ltd t/a Holland & Barrett* (1983) EAT 452/83.
16   Cf *East Berkshire Health Authority v Matadeen* [1992] IRLR 336, EAT; see too *Kelly v Bankers Automated Cleaning Services Ltd* (1984) EAT 550/83. Cf the facts in *Haddon* n 8 above
17   Cf the statement by Sir Hugh Griffiths in *Dalton v Burton's Gold Medal Biscuits Co Ltd* [1974] IRLR 45: 'it is not possible to provide a legal definition of gross misconduct which will fit the circumstances of every case. It would in each case be a matter of fact to consider whether it was gross misconduct or not.'
18   *Neary v Dean of Westminster* [1999] IRLR 288 (special commissioner).
19   [1959] 2 All ER 285, [1959] 1 WLR 698, CA.
1   See also *Wilson v Racher* [1974] ICR 428, [1974] IRLR 114, CA.
2   See eg *Miller v Ferguson Foster Ltd* (1976) IT 37844/76. See also *London v James Laidlaw & Sons* [1974] IRLR 136, IT; *Jones v London Co-operative Society Ltd* [1975] IRLR 110, IT.

express contractual obligation may not be a repudiation if the employer has broken the *implied* term of mutual trust and confidence in enforcing an express contractual obligation.[3]

Nevertheless, the common law influence helps to explain the fact that, under statute law, there are certain well recognised categories of gross misconduct, eg theft, violence, gross negligence, wilful refusal to obey a legitimate order, and working in competition. These categories, together with the requirement of intentional misconduct, are sometimes used as a basis to judge the reasonableness of an employer's categorisation of particular offences as gross misconduct in disciplinary rules.[4] They are also used as a standard to justify dismissals for some offences even where the employer has failed to communicate any disciplinary rules to the employee, on the grounds that certain acts of serious misconduct are known and understood to be such by employees.[5] This core of recognised categories of gross misconduct derives from the duties of employers implied by the common law in contracts of employment, viz, the duty of honesty, the duty of obedience to lawful orders, the duty of faithful service, the duty of care, etc.[6] A wilful breach of any one of these implied terms may be viewed as a breach of an essential contractual condition.

Yet the statutory test of misconduct under s 98(4) applies its own rule of reasonableness to the employer's decision which both overrides the purely contractual position and places a greater emphasis on the need for the employer to make sure that employees are aware of those offences which are viewed as gross misconduct. Under the ERA 1996 the employer is required to give the employee a written statement including 'any disciplinary rules which apply'. Moreover, the Code of Practice recommends that:

'Workers should be made aware of the likely consequences of breaking disciplinary rules ... In particular they should be given a

---

3   See eg *United Bank Ltd v Akhtar* [1989] IRLR 507, EAT.
4   See eg *Clarkson v Brown, Muff & Co Ltd* [1974] IRLR 66; *Jones v London Co-operative Society Ltd* [1975] IRLR 110, EAT.
5   See eg *Fowler v Cammell Laird (Shipbuilders) Ltd* [1973] IRLR 72, NIRC; *C A Parsons & Co Ltd v McLoughlin* [1978] IRLR 65, EAT; *Bailey v BP Oil (Kent Refinery) Ltd* [1980] ICR 642, [1980] IRLR 287, CA. Cf *Distillers Co (Bottling Services) Ltd v Gardner* [1982] IRLR 47, EAT.
6   See the discussion by Hepple and O'Higgins, *Employment Law* (4th edn, Sweet and Maxwell, 1980); Freedland, *The Contract of Employment* (OUP, 1976); Smith & Wood *Industrial Law* (7th edn, Butterworths, 2000); Deakin & Morris *Labour Law* (2nd edn, Butterworths); Anderman *Labour Law* (4th edn, Butterworths, 2000).

clear indication of the type of conduct often referred to as gross misconduct which may warrant summary dismissal'.

Hence, where employers fail to meet these obligations, because they provide an insufficiently specific disciplinary rule or otherwise failed to ensure that the employee knew that such conduct merited dismissal[7] it will be open to an employment tribunal to decide that a dismissal is unfair because of a lack of forewarning to the employee of the seriousness with which the employer regards the breach.[8] Moreover, even where, as in *Gray Dunn & Co Ltd v Edwards,*[9] employers have negotiated a detailed disciplinary agreement with a recognised trade union, there may be limits to the extent to which they may reasonably assume that all employees who are members of the trade union know of and are bound by its provisions.[10]

The test is one of reasonableness. Consequently, where an act of serious misconduct is either well known and understood to constitute gross misconduct, or ought to be, then there is no need for a disciplinary rule to spell it out.[11]

Of course, if the employer has failed to make it clear that the sanction of dismissal will be applied, it may be regarded as unreasonable to dismiss without giving a clear enough indication that the particular offence was regarded as leading to instant dismissal.[12] Yet it is not necessary for the employer to state explicitly in the disciplinary rules that the dismissal will be the inevitable consequence of a breach of the rule. At one stage it appeared that the EAT was suggesting that the disciplinary sanction of dismissal had to be explicitly indicated.

Thus, in *Meridian Ltd v Gomersall*[13] the employer had a disciplinary rule stating that 'it is a serious breach of factory regulations to clock cards

---

7   See eg *W Brooks & Son v Skinner* [1984] IRLR 379, EAT.
8   *Trusthouse Forte (Catering) Ltd v Adonis* [1984] IRLR 382, EAT. *Dairy Produce Packers Ltd v Beverstock* [1981] IRLR 265, EAT; cf *Distillers Co (Bottling Services) Ltd v Gardner* [1982] IRLR 47, EAT; *Meyer Dunmore International Ltd v Rogers* [1978] IRLR 167, EAT. See eg *Singh v London Country Bus Services* [1976] IRLR 176, EAT.
9   [1980] IRLR 23, EAT.
10   *W Brooks & Son v Skinner* [1984] IRLR 379, EAT.
11   *Ulsterbus Ltd v Henderson* [1989] IRLR 251, NICA. See eg *C A Parsons & Co Ltd v McLoughlin* [1978] IRLR 65, EAT (fighting); *Bailey v BP Oil (Kent Refinery) Ltd* [1980] ICR 642, [1980] IRLR 287, CA (act of violence); cf *Distillers Co (Bottling Services) Ltd v Gardner* [1982] IRLR 47, EAT (gross neglect of duty).
12   Ibid.
13   [1977] ICR 597, [1977] IRLR 425, EAT.

other than their own'. However, the same rule defined the sanctions for such a serious breach in the following terms:

'Anyone found clocking cards on behalf of other personnel will render themselves liable to instant dismissal'.

The EAT commented

'It seems to us that when the words "liable to instant dismissal" are used an employee might well reasonably take the view that to be caught out once (even if suspected of doing it previously) does not necessarily lead to an instant dismissal. The employer, on whom lies the burden of proving that he acted reasonably, ought to recognise that an employee might in some circumstances not appreciate that one fall would be a final fall'.[14]

In *Elliott Bros (London) Ltd v Colverd*,[15] however, the EAT reversed an employment tribunal which held unfair a dismissal for a breach of a disciplinary rule which said 'you must not clock or sign in for someone else. If you do you are liable to instant dismissal' because the rule was not explicit enough that dismissal would inevitably follow. The EAT stated that:

'what the law requires is for an [Employment] Tribunal to concentrate on the wording of [s 98(4)] ... There is no rule of law to be imported into that (section) that a warning in circumstances such as these must indicate inevitable dismissal'.[16]

---

14   See also *Pringle v Lucas Industrial Equipment Ltd* [1975] IRLR 266 in which an employee was dismissed for having violated a works rule which provided that 'no employee may leave the works during normal working hours without permission ...'. The employer had not specified that breach of such a rule would incur instant dismissal (as another rule in the disciplinary code had specifically provided), he had simply provided that 'employees guilty of misconduct or breach of these rules will render themselves liable to suspension or instant dismissal and/ or prosecution'. As this did not clearly involve a penalty of instant dismissal, the employment tribunal held that the dismissal was unfair; see also *Lindsay v Fife Forge Co Ltd* [1976] IRLR 47 ('may lead to instant dismissal'). But compare *Dalton v Burton's Gold Medal Biscuits Co Ltd* [1974] IRLR 45, NIRC where rules gave a clear indication that clocking irregularities 'will result in instant dismissal'.

15   [1979] IRLR 92, EAT.

16   See also *Stewart v Western SMT Co Ltd* [1978] IRLR 553, EAT; *Laws Stores Ltd v Oliphant* [1978] IRLR 251, EAT.

Moreover, in *Procter v British Gypsum Ltd*,[17] the EAT reminded that the use of the word 'may' or 'liable' in disciplinary rules cannot be relied on to indicate that there is a general practice that dismissal would not be a likely sanction.

Yet even where an employer has reasonably communicated to the employee that certain misconduct constitutes gross misconduct warranting instant dismissal, and indeed has made such a disciplinary rule a contractual term, s 98(4) still superimposes a statutory test upon the employer's disciplinary rules to test whether the employer's assessment of the actual offence of the employee as gross misconduct was or was not reasonable. For example, in *Ladbroke Racing Ltd v Arnott*,[18] three employees were dismissed for breach of a company rule which stated that employees were not permitted to place bets, or allow other staff to do so, and that breach of the rule would result in immediate dismissal. Yet the bets had been placed with the knowledge of the office manager and the only minor infringements of the rule had involved no personal advantage to the employees. In these circumstances the Court of Session upheld the EAT's decision, which stated that, notwithstanding the mandatory terms of the disciplinary rule, the employers had not acted reasonably within the meaning of the statute in dismissing the employees for breach of the rule.

As the Court of Session put it,

'While the appropriate rule in each case specifically stated that a breach of the rule would result in dismissal that cannot in itself necessarily meet the requirements of (s 98(4)) which calls for the employer satisfying the Tribunal that in the circumstances (having regard to equity and the substantial merits of the case) he acted reasonably in treating it as sufficient reason for dismissal. This seems to me to predicate that there may be different degrees of gravity in the admitted or proved offence, and, as each case has to be considered on its own facts, consideration has to be given inter alia to the degree of culpability involved'.[19]

Similarly, in *Jones v London Co-operative Society Ltd*[20] an employee was dismissed for incorrectly ringing up a purchase even though this was

---

17 [1992] IRLR 7, EAT.
18 [1983] IRLR 154, Ct of Sess; *Trusthouse Forte (Catering) Ltd v Adonis* [1984] IRLR 382, EAT.
19 See also *Taylor v Parsons Peebles NEI Bruce Peebles Ltd* [1981] IRLR 119, EAT.
20 [1975] IRLR 110, IT.

found to be an honest mistake. The employer had relied upon a disciplinary rule which was a term of the employee's contract of employment, and which stated that an incorrect till reading was a serious offence meriting summary dismissal 'unless the employee could be proved to be justified in such reading'. The tribunal found the dismissal unfair despite the evidence of the rule as a term of employment. The employee's act had been a truly honest mistake, and the rule was unreasonable in failing to make an exception for an honest mistake and not drawing a distinction between that and an intentional act 'or a persistent failure to maintain cash control standards'.[1]

The test of reasonableness will also apply to the employer's classification of particular offences within the accepted categories of gross misconduct. A tribunal can find the employee's conduct must be sufficiently serious in the circumstances to warrant inclusion within the category of gross misconduct.

For example, in *Clarkson v Brown, Muff & Co Ltd*[2] an employee was dismissed for dishonesty because she failed to report her absence form work. The employers had indicated in the employee's conditions of employment that instant dismissal would be the normal penalty for cases of gross misconduct and had specified certain offences as amounting to gross misconduct, viz dishonesty, arson, violence, obscenity, neglect of safety standards, gross insubordination. The tribunal compared the action of the employee with the conduct specified in the employee's conditions of service and concluded that her dishonesty was not of the type intended to be covered in a list of that type. They considered that it would require an act of dishonesty which was more serious, such as theft of goods or money.

Similarly where an employer insists that an employee attend work and the employee fails to attend, depending on the circumstances the employee's conduct may be viewed as the lesser offence of absenteeism or bad timekeeping rather than a wilful refusal to obey an instruction or insubordination both of which can constitute gross misconduct.[3]

---

1   As to the reasonableness of the rule, see *Schmidt v Austicks Bookshops Ltd* [1978] ICR 85, [1977] IRLR 360, EAT; *Silentnight v Pitfield and Pitfield* (1983) EAT 106/82.

2   [1974] IRLR 66, IT; see also *Trusthouse Forte (Catering) Ltd v Adonis* [1984] IRLR 382, EAT.

3   See eg *Thornton v Champion Associated Weavers Ltd* (1977) IT 2112/77; but see *Bailey v BP Oil (Kent Refinery) Ltd* [1980] ICR 642, [1980] IRLR 287, CA.

The employer is not only required to make a reasonable judgment as to whether the employee's conduct was a type that may reasonably be classified as gross. Even where an employee's act of misconduct may take the form of a traditional or accepted category of gross misconduct, a tribunal may also decide that *in the circumstances* the decision to dismiss summarily for that one act of misconduct was not reasonable.

Thus, under the law of unfair dismissal, as at common law, a refusal to obey a legitimate instruction is a major category of gross misconduct.[4] To justify a decision to dismiss an employee for a refusal to obey an order under s 98(4), however, an employer must meet requirements which go beyond the purely contractual test provided by common law. The minimum requirements under s 98(4), as at common law, are that the order itself must be within the employer's contractual authority and not otherwise unlawful[5] or unsafe.[6] As far as 'safety dismissals' are concerned the ground rules have been extensively rewritten by new statutory provisions under ERA 1996, s 100.[7] Moreover, an employee's refusal to obey must be wilful or deliberate and made in the knowledge that his behaviour could result in dismissal.[8] Yet even if these requirements are fulfilled, it may be unfair to dismiss in circumstances in which it was unreasonable of the employer to issue the order in the first place and to insist on obedience to the point of dismissal.[9] Thus even where an employer has contractual authority to order an employee to do a particular kind of work, at a particular place or at a

---

4   See eg *Union of Construction Allied Trades and Technicians v Brain* [1980] ICR 779, [1980] IRLR 357; affd [1981] ICR 542, [1981] IRLR 224, CA. *Martin v Solus Schall* [1979] IRLR 7, EAT.

5   *London v James Laidlaw & Sons* [1974] IRLR 136, IT; *Dormer v Mollins Ltd* (1977) EAT 550/76; *Overseas School of English v Hartley* (1977) EAT 86/77; *W M Wright (Holdings) Ltd v Hendry* (1976) EAT 239/76.

6   *Associated Tunnelling Co Ltd v Wasilewski* [1973] IRLR 346, 8 ITR 651, NIRC (refusal to work at a site where flying pickets were expected).

7   See *Shillito v Van Leer (UK) Ltd* [1997] IRLR 495, EAT (victimisation); see too *Goodwin v Cabletel UK Ltd* [1997] IRLR 665, EAT; but see *Masiak v City Restaurants (UK) Ltd* [1999] IRLR 780, EAT; see too *Farrant v Woodroffe School* [1998] IRLR 176, EAT.

8   *Miller v Ferguson Foster Ltd* (1976) IT 37844/76; see also *Wallace v E J Guy Ltd* [1973] ICR 117, [1973] IRLR 175 (where employer was required to make reasonable effort to ensure that employee understood that the order he was refusing to obey was contractual).

9   One example could be where employer's conduct consisted of facts which can be viewed as a breach of the implied term of mutual trust and confidence; see too 'the long hair' cases; *Talbot v Hugh M Fulton Ltd* [1975] IRLR 52; *Greenslade v Hoveringham Gravels Ltd* [1975] IRLR 114.

particular time, an employer's decision to dismiss may be unreasonable in the circumstances. For example, in *Richards v Kier Ltd*[10] an employment tribunal decided that although an employer had contractual authority to order an employee from Setch to Great Lumley, it was unreasonable to dismiss the employee for refusing to obey in circumstances where his wife was ill. Moreover the exercise of express contractual authority over mobility and flexibility is now regulated by the implied term of mutual trust and confidence and this may be used as an argument against the employer's categorisation of an employee's conduct as gross misconduct.

Similarly fighting or violence is well established as a category of misconduct for which a single offence can justify instant dismissal.[11] Indeed, whilst normally a reasonable employer would be expected to indicate in his disciplinary rules that fighting or physical violence are serious misconduct punishable by summary dismissal,[12] a failure to provide such a disciplinary rule will not necessarily make the dismissal unfair.[13] Yet an employment tribunal has the discretion to determine whether a particular incident of fighting or violence by the employee could reasonably be regarded as gross misconduct; taking into account the employment context,[14] as well as such circumstances as the element of provocation,[15] the claim of self defence,[16] the extent of the violence[17] and any other mitigating circumstances.[18]

10   (1976) IT 38097/76.

11   See eg *Dacres v Walls Meat Co Ltd* [1976] ICR 44, [1976] IRLR 20, EAT.

12   See eg *Taylor Woodrow Construction Ltd v Veale* (1977) EAT 544/76.

13   See eg *C A Parsons & Co Ltd v McLoughlin* [1978] IRLR 65, EAT.

14   See eg *Greenwood v H J Heinz & Co Ltd* (1977) EAT 199/77 (fighting near dangerous machinery); *Dacres v Walls Meat Co Ltd* (above) (fighting in a slaughterhouse).

15   See eg *British Mail Order Corpn v Walley* (1983) EAT 415/83; *Kelly v Bankers Automated Clearings Services Ltd* (1984) EAT 550/83; *Richards v Bulpitt & Sons Ltd* [1975] IRLR 134, IT.

16   See eg *Forgings and Presswork Ltd v McDougall* [1974] ICR 532, [1974] IRLR 243, NIRC.

17   See eg *Meyer Dunmore International Ltd v Rogers* [1978] IRLR 167, EAT; *Mundle v Taylor Woodrow Construction (Midlands) Ltd* (1976) IT 40859/76 (technical assault not enough). See also IRLIB no 93 (1977).

18   *Taylor v Parsons Peebles NEI Bruce Peebles Ltd* [1981] IRLR 119, EAT. *Sherrier v Ford Motor Co Ltd* [1976] IRLR 141 (past record); *Bowie v British Leyland (UK) Ltd* [1976] IRLR 48 (inconsistent penalties); *Forgings and Presswork Ltd v McDougall* [1974] ICR 532, [1974] IRLR 243, NIRC; *Donnelly v London Brick Co Ltd* [1974] IRLR 331.

Acts of theft, dishonesty, fraud[19] or other criminal acts in the course of employment may also justify instant dismissal,[20] even if no specific reference to theft is contained within the disciplinary rules.[1] Unauthorised use of computers has been compared with dishonesty and where serious can amount to gross misconduct prima facie attracting summary dismissal.[2] The sufficiency test appears to apply more to a showing of deliberate dishonesty[3] rather than to the amounts involved.[4] It can be a dismissible offence wilfully to conceal a previous conviction when applying for a job.[5] If the conviction is 'spent' as defined under the Rehabilitation of Offenders Act 1974, a dismissal can be unfair.[6] Mitigating circumstances are almost always relevant[7] although not necessarily compelling.[8]

Where the employee has been caught red-handed by the police and makes no protestations of innocence to the employer it can be reasonable for the employer to treat the employee's conduct as a basis for immediate dismissal.[9]

Where however the employee has been charged with theft by the police or is otherwise under suspicion, this may not be enough to justify dismissal without further investigation or sufficient information to entitle the employer reasonably to assume that there was guilt on the part of the employee.[10]

Suspension pending further investigation is recommended in the Code of Practice and whether it is with or without pay will depend upon the

19 *United Distillers v Conlin* [1992] IRLR 503, EAT.
20 *AEI Cables Ltd v McLay* [1980] IRLR 84, Ct of Sess; *Rank Xerox (UK) Ltd v Goodchild* [1979] IRLR 185, EAT. See eg *Trust Houses Forte Hotels Ltd v Murphy* [1977] IRLR 186, EAT; *Docherty v Reddy* [1977] ICR 365, EAT; *Refund Rentals Ltd v McDermott* [1977] IRLR 59, EAT.
1   See eg *Distillers Co (Bottling Services) Ltd v Gardner* [1982] IRLR 47, EAT; *Fowler v Cammell Laird (Shipbuilders) Ltd* [1973] IRLR 72, NIRC.
2   See *Denco Ltd v Joinson* [1991] IRLR 63, EAT.
3   See eg *Trust Houses Forte Hotels Ltd v Murphy* [1977] IRLR 186, EAT (deficiency worth £2); *Refund Rentals Ltd v McDermott* [1977] IRLR 59, EAT (£3.50 not accounted for).
4   Ibid.
5   *Torr v British Railways Board* [1977] IRLR 184, EAT.
6   *Property Guards Ltd v Taylor* [1982] IRLR 175, EAT.
7   See eg *Budgen & Co v Thomas* [1976] ICR 344, [1976] IRLR 174, EAT; *Tesco Group of Companies (Holdings) Ltd v Hill* [1977] IRLR 63, EAT.
8   *Trust Houses Forte Hotels Ltd v Murphy* [1977] IRLR 186, EAT; *Conway v Matthew Wright & Nephew Ltd* [1977] IRLR 89, EAT.
9   *Carr v Alexander Russell Ltd* [1976] IRLR 220, Ct of Sess; *Scottish Special Housing Association v Linnen* [1979] IRLR 265, EAT.
10 *Scottish Special Housing Association v Cooke* [1979] IRLR 264, EAT.

employee's contractual authority. In principle employers may decide to dismiss on the basis of their own investigations and provided that it fits within the band of reasonableness, it may be fair even if the employee is dismissed well before the criminal proceedings occur.[11]

Where the act of misconduct by the employee consists of a criminal act committed *outside* the scope of employment, however, this may also be a sufficient ground to warrant dismissal, as long as the act has been shown to affect the business in some way.[12] The Code of Practice suggests the following:

'26 *Criminal charges or convictions outside employment.* These should not be treated as automatic reasons for dismissal. The main consideration should be whether the offence is one that makes workers unsuitable for their type of work. In all cases employers, having considered the facts, will need to consider whether the conduct is sufficiently serious to warrant instituting the disciplinary procedure. For instance, workers should not be dismissed solely because a charge against them is pending or because they are absent as a result of being remanded in custody'.

Thus the mere fact that an employee has been charged with a criminal offence unconnected with work will not justify the employer in dismissing the employee as opposed to suspending the employee or transferring the employee to a less sensitive position until the matter is resolved.[13] This will be particularly true in the case of larger employers.[14]

Where however the criminal act impinges in some way on the employment, either making the employee unsuitable for the job the

---

11   See eg *British Railways Board v Jackson* [1994] IRLR 235, CA; *Conway v Matthew Wright & Nephew Ltd* [1997] IRLR 89, EAT.

12   See eg *Moore v C and A Modes* [1981] IRLR 71, EAT; *Singh v London Country Bus Services Ltd* [1976] IRLR 176, 11 ITR 131, EAT. Even where the criminal act was not 'conduct in the course of employment', however, it might be viewed as some other substantial reason. See eg *Creffield v BBC* [1975] IRLR 23 (a case of a film cameraman convicted of assaulting a 13-year old girl).

13   *Securicor Guarding Ltd v R* [1994] IRLR 633, EAT; see *Jones v R M Douglas Construction Ltd* [1975] IRLR 175 (employee convicted of dishonestly handling a stolen engine was held unfairly dismissed because his act had no connection with his place of work).

14   *P v Nottinghamshire County Council* [1992] IRLR 362, CA.

employee held[15] or by affecting the reputation of the business[16] or the employee during the course of his work,[17] or where the employee has a position of special trust,[18] criminal acts committed outside the scope of employment may be sufficient grounds to justify dismissal.

Where an employee seeks to obtain other employment or to set up in competition, and thereby breaks the mutual confidence and trust between him and his employers, this could be sufficient to justify dismissal.[19] But this will not always be the case; there is a sufficiency test for this type of misconduct. For example, in *Harris and Russell Ltd v Slingsby*[20] an employee was dismissed for seeking to obtain employment with another employer during a period in which he had given notice of termination. A tribunal found this insufficient grounds for dismissal and hence unfair because there were no grounds for supposing that the employee's actions involved a breach of confidence.[1]

Moreover, in *Laughton and Hawley v Bapp Industrial Supplies Ltd,*[2] the EAT pointed out that even where an employee intends to leave and set up in business on his own account in competition with his former employer, there is no dismissible breach of contract unless there is either a specific term in the contract which so provides or he is intending to use the employer's confidential information or trade secrets. On the other hand, computer misuse can be a basis for dismissal even in the absence of a prior disciplinary rule.

---

15 *Mathewson v R B Wilson Dental Laboratory* [1988] IRLR 512, EAT; *Nottinghamshire County Council v Bowly* [1978] IRLR 252, EAT; *Norfolk County Council v Bernard* [1979] IRLR 220, EAT.

16 *Robb v Mersey Insulation Co Ltd* [1972] IRLR 18.

17 *Singh v London Country Bus Service Ltd* [1976] IRLR 176, 11 ITR 131, EAT ('it could be thought to be likely to affect the employee when he is doing his work'); *Gardiner v Newport Borough Council* [1974] IRLR 262; *Stevens v Associated Dairies* (1977) IT 548/77.

18 *Richardson v City of Bradford Metropolitan Council* [1975] IRLR 296. But see *Jones v R M Douglas Construction Ltd* [1975] IRLR 175.

19 See *Marshall v Industrial Systems & Control Ltd* [1992] IRLR 294, EAT; *Davidson and Maillou v Comparisons* [1980] IRLR 360, EAT; *McCall v Castleton Crafts* [1979] IRLR 218, EAT: *Mansard Precision Engineering Co Ltd v Taylor* [1978] ICR 44, EAT: *Richardson v Brady & Sons Ltd* (1981) EAT 363/80.

20 [1973] 3 All ER 31, [1973] IRLR 221, NIRC.

1 See also *Blacks of Greenock Ltd v Hamer* (1978) EAT 565/72; *Coleman v Skyrail Oceanic Ltd (t/a Goodmos Tours)* [1981] IRLR 398, CA; *Ladbroke Racing Ltd v Mason* [1978] ICR 49, EAT (need for warning procedure); *Hughes v Messrs Christie & Co (Insurance) Ltd* (1977) EAT 21/77.

2 [1986] IRLR 245, EAT.

Of course, if the employee had tendered for the future business of the employer's customers in competition with the employer that would be both a breach of the implied contractual duty to give faithful service and could be basis of dismissal for gross misconduct.[3]

Moreover, where employees work for another employer in their spare time it cannot automatically be assumed that the implied term of loyal service is breached. That will always be a question of fact and depend on the actual harm to the employer.[4]

Another type of misconduct that may justify instant dismissal is the use of offensive language. However, even at common law the use of grossly improper language must meet the test of being sufficiently extreme to justify instant dismissal. In *Wilson v Racher*[5] (a case of wrongful dismissal) the Court of Appeal considered that even where an employee committed the gross impropriety of using obscene and deplorable language to his employer, it did not amount to a contractual repudiation in a situation where the employer had been unduly provocative and had made unjust accusations. Similarly, in the test of unfair dismissal, something more than an isolated incident in which an employee gets caught in the 'heat of the moment' is called for.[6]

However, the use of offensive language does not always amount to gross misconduct. For example, in *W F Shortland Ltd v Chantrill*[7] an apprentice who was instantly dismissed when he told his managing director 'you couldn't have done any fucking better' in front of two other apprentices was found to be unfairly dismissed. The EAT approved the tribunal decision because it considered that one isolated incident of imprudence did not merit the very grave step of determining an apprenticeship that only had 10 months to run. In *Ismond v Nelson Coin Automatics Ltd*[8] it was found unreasonable to dismiss an employee for referring to a manager as a 'bastard' to another employee but not directly to the manager in question. And in *Anderson v British Uralite Ltd*[9] acts of tactlessness and discourtesy did not amount to gross misconduct.

3   See eg *Adamson v B & L Cleaning Services Ltd* [1995] IRLR 193, EAT.
4   See *Nova Plastics Ltd v Froggatt* [1982] IRLR 146, EAT.
5   [1974] ICR 428, [1974] IRLR 114, CA.
6   See eg *Walters v Top Crust Foods Ltd* [1972] IRLR 108, IT.
7   [1975] IRLR 208, IT.
8   [1975] IRLR 173, IT.
9   [1973] IRLR 292, IT.

Gross negligence can also amount to gross misconduct. For example, in *Comerford v Swel Foods Ltd*[10] a factory supervisor who allowed production to continue knowing that a pump was malfunctioning and wasted the output of a whole shift was found fairly dismissed.[11] However, the negligent act must itself be gross rather than simply producing substantial loss. For example, in *Day v Diemer and Reynolds Ltd*[12] an employee bound a book in the wrong order causing substantial loss to the employer but the tribunal held that a single mistake did not merit instant dismissal. Of course it also helped the employee that he had long service and no previous errors.

Finally, participation in industrial action may be regarded as repudiatory conduct by the employee.[13] Nevertheless, if the case falls under s 98(4) as opposed to ss 237 and 238, the employment tribunal must consider whether in the circumstances it was reasonable for the employer to dismiss the employee for that conduct.[14]

(b) Dismissal for ordinary misconduct

Where dismissal is for ordinary misconduct, such as swearing,[15] bad timekeeping,[16] absenteeism,[17] drinking[18] or negligence,[19] and consists of

10   [1972] IRLR 17, IT.
11   See also *Alidair Ltd v Taylor* [1978] ICR 445, [1978] IRLR 82, CA; *Turner v Pleasurama Casinos Ltd* [1976] IRLR 151; *Hedges v Phillips and Drew* [1975] IRLR 15; *Potter v W J Rich & Sons* [1975] IRLR 338; *Barber v Makro Self Service Wholesalers Ltd* [1975] IRLR 361. Cf *Distiller Co (Bottling Services) Ltd v Gardner* [1982] IRLR 47, EAT (gross neglect of duty).
12   [1975] IRLR 298.
13   See eg *Simmons v Hoover Ltd* [1977] QB 284, [1976] IRLR 266, EAT; *Heath v J F Longman (Meat Salesmen) Ltd* [1973] ICR 407, [1973] IRLR 214, NIRC; see Chapter 11.
14   See eg *Seed v Crowther (Dyers) Ltd* [1973] IRLR 199, 8 ITR 340; *Dobson, Bryant, Heather and Freeman v K P Morritt Ltd* [1972] IRLR 99, IT; *P J Mirrors Ltd v Speck* (1977) EAT 378/76. See discussion in Chapter 11.
15   See eg *W F Shortland Ltd v Chantrill* [1975] IRLR 208, IT; *Ismond v Nelson Coin Automatics Ltd* [1975] IRLR 173, IT.
16   See eg *Schembri v Scot Bowyers Ltd* [1973] IRLR 110, IT.
17   *Clapton v Ketton Foundry Co Ltd* [1972] IRLR 48, IT; *Williams v Lloyds Retailers Ltd* [1973] IRLR 262, IT.
18   See eg *Morrow v Scottish Special Housing Association* [1973] IRLR 40, IT; IRLIB No 108 (1978).
19   *Day v Diemer and Reynolds Ltd* [1975] IRLR 298, IT; *Ramroop v H Goldman Ltd* [1974] IRLR 313, IT.

a series of offences or course of conduct, an employment tribunal must still determine whether the course of conduct in the aggregate is sufficient to warrant dismissal by a reasonable employer. Employment tribunals have a discretion to determine whether or not the employer's decision to dismiss was reasonable in the circumstances, but that discretion is limited by the requirement that they must judge the reasonableness of the employer's decision taking into account the range of reasonable responses by employers. The particular act of misconduct which precipitates the dismissal does not have to be sufficiently serious in its own right to justify dismissal as long as it confirms a pattern by, for example, occurring after a final warning. The test for employment tribunals in such cases is whether the precipitating incident of misconduct, taken together with the employee's aggregate record of misconduct, was serious enough to justify dismissal by a reasonable employer.[20] At the same time the final act of misconduct should not be so trivial or minor that reasonable employers would not regard it as the 'last straw' in a series of acts of misconduct. For example, in *Silverstone v ECI (Midlands) Ltd*[1] an electrician's failure to turn up at a site when the foreman had cancelled unofficial transport arrangements was found by an employment tribunal to be an unreasonable final incident in an accumulation of complaints. And where the final incident is so unrelated to previous acts of misconduct as to negate the principles of a 'reasonable' warning procedure, an employment tribunal might find a decision to dismiss to be unreasonable.[2]

Moreover, in cases of ordinary misconduct, where the procedure itself provides for a series of steps to be taken before an employee can be dismissed, and these are not followed, an industrial tribunal might find it unfair to dismiss because a decision to dismiss in that situation might have been outside the range of reasonable employer responses,[3] although such a finding would not be inevitable.[4]

Furthermore, where the conduct complained of by the employer consists of conduct outside the scope of the employee's work, this may be an

---

20 See eg *Auguste Noel Ltd v Curtis* [1990] IRLR 326, EAT; *Newalls Insulation Co Ltd v Blakeman* [1976] ICR 543, [1976] IRLR 303, EAT.

1 [1976] IRLR 7, IT.

2 See eg *Canter Smith and Gardener v Bowater Containers Ltd* [1975] IRLR 323.

3 See *Maxwell v Grimwood Heating Elements Ltd* [1972] IRLR 81, where the fact that a final warning had lapsed in accordance with the procedure was ignored; see too *Wells v E & A West Ltd* [1975] IRLR 269, where the employer had agreed a procedure that provided for a warning and then a suspension but omitted that letter step in the progression of penalties leading to dismissal.

4 Cf *Bailey v BP Oil (Kent Refinery) Ltd*, above.

unreasonable basis for dismissal. In *Cassidy v H C Goodman Ltd*,[5] for example, an employer dismissed an employee because of his refusal to discontinue his relationship with a former female employee, after she had left. An employment tribunal found this was an insufficient ground for dismissal as the private conduct was neither of 'exceptional gravity' nor 'damaging to the employer's business'.[6] Of course, where the outside conduct impinges on the employment, as for example in *Treganowan v Robert Knee & Co Ltd*[7] where a woman's boasting of an association with a boy half her age created a tense atmosphere in the office, a different standard may apply.[8]

ii) The surrounding circumstances

Even where an employer has correctly classified the misconduct of the employee as sufficiently serious by itself to warrant dismissal, there is a further step in the analysis. An employment tribunal must determine whether it was reasonable of the employer to dismiss the employee in all the relevant surrounding circumstances. Any important circumstances that mitigate the fault of the employee or call into question the wisdom of dismissal should be taken into account in any reasonable decision to dismiss; for example, an employee's past record of good service, an explanation or excuse, provocation or inadvertence, a lowering of standards induced by the employment setting, or the extent to which management's own actions or omissions call into question the reasonableness of the decision to dismiss.

As mentioned, the 'surrounding circumstances' can be a two-edged sword. Where the size or other circumstances of the firm or the employment would lead a reasonable management to be less tolerant of an employee's actions this could provide support for an employer's decision to dismiss in the circumstances.

5   [1975] IRLR 86, IT.
6   See eg *Whitlow v Alkanet Construction Ltd* [1975] IRLR 321.
7   [1975] ICR 405, [1975] IRLR 247.
8   See also *Newman v Alarmco Ltd* [1976] IRLR 45, IT, where the employee was a general manager living with his secretary and 'showed affection' during office hours; *Spiller v F J Wallis Ltd* [1975] IRLR 362 where a shelf fitter's relationship with a senior employee which did not have an adverse effect on trade but violated a company rule, caused talk amongst employees when they should have been working, and was thought to jeopardise his marriage status, hence creating the possibility of angry scenes at work.

If the employer has actually taken all relevant circumstances into account and, the employee's complaint is that his assessment of their relative importance was unreasonable, the employee will have to convince an employment tribunal that the decision was outside the range of responses of 'reasonable employers'. Where, however, an employer has altogether omitted to take into account one or more important relevant circumstances, this will provide the employee with a readier basis for challenging the reasonableness of his decision. Let us consider each in turn.

(a) Was a relevant circumstance ignored by the employer?

Under s 98(4) the line of attack to which an employer's substantive decision to dismiss is most vulnerable is that he omitted entirely to take into account one or more factors that should have affected the decision.

Thus where an employer has a disciplinary rule and applies it too rigidly without taking into account mitigating or extenuating circumstances, this could take the employer's decision outside the range of reasonable responses. For example, in *Taylor v Parsons Peebles NEI Bruce Peebles Ltd*[9] an employment tribunal held a dismissal fair because it was in accordance with the employer's policy to dismiss any employee who deliberately struck another. Yet the employee who had 20 years' service and no record of serious disciplinary offences had been dismissed in a dispute with another employee which came to blows. The EAT reversed holding that the dismissal was unfair.

> 'The proper test is not what the policy of the respondents as employers was but what the reaction of a reasonable employer would have been in the circumstances. That reaction would have taken into account the long period of service and good conduct which the appellant was in a position to claim. It is not to the point that the employer's code of disciplinary conduct may or may not contain a provision to the effect that anyone striking a blow would be instantly dismissed. Such a provision, no matter how positively expressed, must always be considered in the light of how it would be applied by a reasonable employer having regard to circumstances of equity and the substantial merits of the case.'

9   [1981] IRLR 119, EAT.

Moreover, in *Richards v Bulpitt & Sons Ltd*[10] the company had a rigid policy that any employee striking another at the workplace would be dismissed. When an employee hit a chargehand he was dismissed in spite of his allegations of provocation because the employer considered dismissal to be automatic. The tribunal found the dismissal unfair, reminding the employer that whatever the virtues of an automatic disciplinary rule in respect of fighting 'management cannot refuse to consider the circumstances', and still claim to be reasonable. In particular, the surrounding circumstances, including the 13 years' service of the employee, made dismissal not warranted in the circumstances.

As well, in *Unkles v Milanda Bread Co Ltd*,[11] a foreman violated a company rule prohibiting smoking in certain areas and was dismissed by management in spite of his explanation of inadvertence, because management considered that they had no discretion in applying the disciplinary rule. The tribunal found the dismissal unfair because, taking into account all the circumstances including the 11 years' service of the employee and the facts that smoking occurred in a part of the premises not being used for food processes and that the employee was only technically still on duty, the penalty of dismissal was too severe.

A variation on the automatic dismissal is offered by the employer who shows himself to be clearly disinterested in any mitigating explanation proffered by the employee. For example, in *Wilson v IDR Construction Ltd*[12] an employee who was a bricklayer and subject to a mobility clause in his contract was dismissed for refusing to transfer on one occasion to a particular site. When threatened with dismissal he offered an explanation for his refusal to his supervisor. The supervisor's response was simply 'I am not interested in that. I am only interested in whether you are going to Lartington', and he dismissed the employee. The tribunal found the dismissal unfair because the employee had only refused to go for a day or two, his grounds for refusing were genuine and he had never previously refused to travel. The unfairness consisted of the failure to take such factors into account which should reasonably have affected the decision.[13]

---

10   [1975] IRLR 134, IT. See also *Stanton & Stavely Ltd v Ellis* (1984) EAT 48/84.
11   [1973] IRLR 76, IT.
12   [1975] IRLR 260, IT.
13   This type of case may be compared with cases displaying a procedural failure to give a hearing, in which the failure consists at the very least in failing to obtain information that could have affected the decision.

(b) Did the employers make a reasonable assessment of the circumstances?

Even where an employer has taken into account all the relevant circumstances, it may still be possible to argue that his assessment of their importance was unreasonable. In order for this line of challenge to succeed, however, an employment tribunal must be satisfied that the employer's assessment fell outside the range of responses of 'reasonable employers'. In other words, an employee must convince an employment tribunal that the employer's decision was so unreasonable in not giving adequate weight to an important mitigating circumstance that no reasonable employer could have acted in that way. This in practice will be extremely difficult to show but the following are examples of the factors that can be relevant under this head.

[I] THE EMPLOYEE'S LENGTH OF SERVICE AND PAST RECORD.
One factor that should be taken into account by a reasonable employer in a decision to dismiss is the past record of employees, that is to say their length of service and the quality of their past service. Long service together with a good record should normally operate as an extenuating circumstance when considering the appropriate penalty.

In conduct cases (and in general and gross misconduct cases in particular), a good past record and long service have been used as a successful basis to claim that dismissal was too severe a penalty for the individual in question even if the action might have justified dismissal. In *King v Motorway Tyres and Accessories Ltd*[14] an employee's six years' long service with a satisfactory record including a promotion was successfully used to make a dismissal too severe a penalty for an employee who had used improper and abusive language to another manager – the tribunal held that a severe reprimand and a final warning were the only reasonable penalty in the circumstances.[15]

14 [1975] IRLR 51, IT.
15 For similar cases see *Taylor v Parsons Peebles NEI Bruce Peebles Ltd* [1981] IRLR 119, EAT; *Day v Diemer and Reynolds Ltd* [1975] IRLR 298 (expensive error but nine years' service without a blemish); *Jones v R M Douglas Construction Ltd* [1975] IRLR 175 (criminal offence outside work); *Forgings and Presswork Ltd v McDougall* [1974] ICR 532, [1974] IRLR 243, NIRC (9 years of excellent service made dismissal for fighting unreasonable); *Richards v Bulpitt & Sons Ltd* [1975] IRLR 134 ('Dismissal after 13 years' service is not warranted in the circumstances (fighting) and we consider a period of suspension would have met the case').

Also, where two employees have committed similar offences and the employer considers that different penalties are warranted, differences in the employees' past records can be used to justify the decision to apply different penalties. For example, in *Sherrier v Ford Motor Co Ltd*[16] two employees had fought with each other; one had 15 years' service and no previous misconduct, the other had two years' service and six prior warnings. The company suspended the former and dismissed the latter. The tribunal found the dismissal fair, commenting:

> 'Thus having regard to the seriousness of the offence and the previous record of the applicant, the employers acted reasonably in treating the fight as a sufficient reason for dismissing him even though the other employee got off with suspension'.

Further, in *O'Brien v Boots Pure Drug Co*[17] an employee was dismissed when found by a security officer to be in possession of eight items, two of which were unrecorded as staff sales, which she had originally claimed were both paid for and duly recorded. She stated that she had simply forgotten about the two items. A tribunal found the dismissal unfair in large measure because the manager with the power to dismiss had insufficient personal knowledge of the employee to judge the truth of her claims. In particular the tribunal stated:

> 'In our view, the question of whether the employee is seeking to defraud the company, or has quite simply made a stupid and dangerous mistake, is one which cannot be fairly considered without knowledge of the particular employee, that is to say, we take the view that an employee of long standing and good conduct can and ought, to be better believed than one of short service and poor conduct'.

Moreover, in *Francis v Ford Motor Co*[18] an employment tribunal were presented with the argument that the long service of the employees meant that they should have known better. The tribunal rejected this argument, preferring instead to take into account the long service and completely clear records as one of the reasons for finding the dismissals unfair.

16   [1976] IRLR 141, IT.
17   [1973] IRLR 261, IT.
18   [1975] IRLR 25, IT.

However, whilst long service is frequently used as the basis of mitigation, it is not always regarded as sufficient counterweight to prevent dismissal.[19]

A second extenuating factor consists of an explanation of circumstances which might diminish the fault of the employee. This would include mistake, inadvertence or any other reasonable excuse. For example, in fighting cases, provocation[20] or self defence[1] may be considered by tribunals to be an important circumstance making a dismissal unfair, particularly in conjunction with other mitigating circumstances. In cases of alleged dishonesty or breach of a company rule, mistake or inadvertence has also been considered a relevant circumstance.[2] The ill health of a dependant or other personal relation may justify a refusal to obey an order or a refusal to attend work, but of course this will not always be the case.[3] Further, the employment setting may in part be an explanation for lower standards in the case of language. In *Rosenthal v Louis Butler Ltd*[4] the employee's use of disrespectful language towards her manager was looked on in the context that this was a 'small friendly factory in the East End of London, where we all know language can be somewhat robust at times'.[5]

[II]   MANAGEMENT'S OWN ACTIONS OR OMISSIONS.

A further circumstance that may convince a tribunal that a dismissal was not reasonable is where management's own action calls into question the appropriateness of taking the decision to dismiss. A failure adequately to communicate the disciplinary rules related to the job as well[6] as a failure to apply disciplinary rules with a reasonable degree of consistency should make a 'reasonable employer' hesitant to dismiss. The inconsistency could occur where two employees involved in the same incident are given different

19   See eg *Dalton v Burton's Gold Medal Biscuits Co Ltd* [1974] IRLR 45, NIRC.
20   *Richards v Bulpitt & Sons Ltd* [1975] IRLR 134, IT; *Munif v Cole and Kirby Ltd* [1973] ICR 486, NIRC.
1   *Forgings and Presswork Ltd v McDougall* [1974] ICR 532, [1974] IRLR 243.
2   *Jones v London Co-operative Society Ltd* [1975] IRLR 110, EAT.
3   *Richards v Kier Ltd* (1976) IT 38097/76; *Thornton v Champion Associated Weavers Ltd* (1977) IT 2112/77.
4   [1972] IRLR 39, IT.
5   Cf *Futty v D & D Brekkes Ltd* [1974] IRLR 130, where the tribunal in a case of alleged constructive dismissal stated that the words used by the foreman had to be interpreted not in isolation but against the background of a fish dock.
6   See eg *Trusthouse Forte (Catering) Ltd v Adonis* [1984] IRLR 382, EAT (inconsistent rules over penalties for smoking).

penalties.[7] It could also involve an employer acting in a particular case in a way inconsistent with previous cases.[8]

Of course, the differences in treatment must be shown to be genuine inconsistencies and not differences justified in the particular circumstance of the case.

As the Court of Appeal commented in *Post Office v Fennell*[9]

'The word "equity" in the phrase "having regard to equity and the substantial merits of the case" is s [98(4)] comprehends the concept that employees who behave in much the same way should have meted out to them much the same punishment. An [employment] tribunal is entitled to say that where that is not done and one man is penalised much more heavily than others who have committed similar offences in the past, the employee has not acted reasonably in treating whatever the offence is as a sufficient reason for dismissal'.

In *Fennell*'s case an employment tribunal found that an employer's decision to dismiss an employee summarily after assaulting another employee in the works canteen was unfair in part because the offence itself was not sufficiently serious but also because the employers had not acted consistently with their action in respect of similar cases in the past. Both the EAT and the Court of Appeal accepted that it was within the limits of the tribunal's discretion to find the dismissal unfair given the evidence in the case and that the tribunal had clearly appreciated that 'there must be considerable latitude in the way in which an individual employer deals with particular cases'.

Yet this is not a general rule that tribunals are bound to follow. In *Hadjioannou v Coral Casinos Ltd* for example, in the course of upholding a tribunal decision that a dismissal was fair despite the fact that in the past other employees who had broken the same rule were not dismissed, the EAT suggested that the argument of disparity of treatment would be relevant under s [98(4)] in only three situations.[10]

7   See eg *Cain v Leeds & Western Health Authority* [1990] IRLR 168, EAT; *Conlin v United Distillers* [1994] IRLR 169; *Kelly v Bankers Automated Clearings Services Ltd* (1984) EAT 550/83; *Bowie v British Leyland (UK) Ltd* [1976] IRLR 48 (one suspended, one dismissed; disparity made dismissal of employee unfair).

8   *Rennie v Eric Bembrose Ltd* [1974] IRLR 334 (unauthorised absence was not sufficient for gross misconduct where in previous cases no disciplinary action had been taken); *Bendall v Paine and Betteridge* [1973] IRLR 44; *Wilcox v Humphreys and Glasgow Ltd* [1975] ICR 333, [1975] IRLR 211.

9   [1981] IRLR 221, CA.

10   [1981] IRLR 352, EAT.

'Firstly, it may be relevant if there is evidence that employees have been led by an employer to believe that certain categories of conduct will be overlooked, or at least will not be dealt with by the same sanction of dismissal. Secondly, there may be cases in which evidence about decisions made in relation to other cases supports an inference that the purported reason stated by the employer is not the real or genuine reason for a dismissal. Thirdly, evidence as to decisions made by an employer in truly parallel circumstances may be sufficient to support an argument, in a particular case, that it was not reasonable on the part of the employer to visit the particular employee's conduct with the penalty of dismissal and that some lesser penalty would have been appropriate in the circumstances.

[Employment] tribunals would be wise to scrutinise arguments based upon disparity with particular care. It is only in the limited circumstances that we have indicated that the argument is likely to be relevant and there will not be many cases in which the evidence supports the proposition that there are other cases which are truly similar, or sufficiently similar, to afford an adequate basis for the argument. The danger of the argument is that a tribunal may be led away form a proper consideration of the issues raised by s [98(4)] ... The emphasis in that section is upon the particular circumstances of the individual employee's case. It would be most regrettable if tribunals or employers were to be encouraged to adopt rules of thumb, or codes, for dealing with industrial problems and, in particular, issues arising when dismissal is being considered. It is of the highest importance that flexibility should be retained, and we hope that nothing that we say in the course of our judgment will encourage employers or tribunals to think that a tariff approach to industrial misconduct is appropriate. One has only to consider for a moment the dangers of the tariff approach in other spheres of the law to realise how inappropriate it would be to import it into this particular legislation.'

Moreover, in *Paul v East Surrey District Health Authority*,[11] the Court of Appeal reiterated that in cases where disparity of treatment is an issue, tribunals should scrutinise the employer's decision with particular care. Ultimately the question for the employer is whether in the particular case, dismissal is a reasonable response to the misconduct proved taking into

11   [1995] IRLR 305, CA; see too *Proctor v British Gypsum Ltd* [1992] IRLR 7, EAT.

account the nature of the conduct, the surrounding facts and many mitigating circumstances affecting the employee concerned.

In *G S Packaging Ltd v Sealy*[12] an employment tribunal found that a dismissal of an employee for gross misconduct for leaving a machine unattended whilst in operation was unfair because another employee, an assistant, was not dismissed. The EAT allowed an appeal stating that the proper approach was to consider the dismissal in two stages. First, was the dismissal a reasonable response to Mr Sealy's conduct by itself? Secondly, if it did fall within the range of reasonable responses, was the inconsistent treatment justified? Similarly in *Securicor Ltd v Smith*,[13] the Court of Appeal stated that where two employees have been dismissed for the same offence but one is successful on appeal and the other is not, in determining the fairness of the latter's dismissal, the question for the tribunal is whether the appeal panel's decision was so irrational that no employer could reasonably have accepted it. Nevertheless subject to the range of reasonableness requirement, there is room for tribunals to take into account the inconsistency of the employer in evaluating the reasonableness of the dismissal.[14]

Where the employer has condoned an act of misconduct by the same employee in the past this does not necessarily mean that a dismissal for a later infraction will make a dismissal unfair. For example in *Martin v Solus Schall*[15] an employer dismissed an employee for refusing to comply with a contractual obligation to work overtime despite condoning such refusals in the past. The EAT upheld the tribunal's decision that the dismissal was fair, pointing out that the fact that the employers were prepared to deal as reasonably as they could with the employee on previous occasions and to suit his convenience if at all possible should not be allowed to count against them in deciding the reasonableness of their conduct at the time of dismissal.

Yet there may be circumstances where it would be outside the range of reasonable responses for an employer to ignore the fact that a manager or supervisor had condoned an employee's infringement of the rule.[16]

---

12   (1983) EAT 396/82.
13   *Securicor Ltd v Smith* [1989] IRLR 356, CA; see too *Harrow London Borough v Cunningham* [1996] IRLR 256, EAT.
14   *Post Office v Fennel*, n 9 above; *Hadjiouannou*, n 10 above; *Paul*, n 11 above.
15   [1979] IRLR 7, EAT.
16   See eg *Ladbroke Racing Ltd v Arnott* [1983] IRLR 154, Ct of Sess; *Rank Xerox (UK) Ltd v Goodchild* [1979] IRLR 185, EAT; *Bendall v Paine and Betteridge* [1973] IRLR 44, NIRC.

In *Wilcox v Humphreys and Glasgow Ltd*[17] an employee had argued that his failure to carry out a safety test was a practice which had been condoned by management in the past. The employment tribunal found that there had been neglect of safety precautions by management, but not any condonation of, or acquiescence in, the practice of omitting safety tests. In the course of remitting the tribunal's decision on another ground, Phillips J indicated the need for employers to take into account the previous pattern of enforcement of disciplinary rules in management's disciplinary decisions. He commented that if the safety test

'had been ignored for ages to everybody's knowledge it would not be right, without some kind of warning, to dismiss the first person to break it after the employers took it into their heads to enforce it'.[18]

Finally, where there is a breakdown in the working relationship between two employees, employers must take reasonable steps to try and improve the relation and establish whether or not the breakdown is irremediable before deciding whether to dismiss.[19]

Somewhat different is the notion that the employer may have condoned a practice by a delay in acting upon the disciplinary offence. Thus, in cases of gross misconduct, where an employer keeps an employee in a post for a significant period after the offence[20] or offers the job back to the employee[1] a tribunal may conclude that the employer's own treatment of the employee suggests that the misconduct fell short of that degree of gravity which warranted dismissal. This will not inevitably follow; it depends upon the circumstances of the case.[2]

If the statutory test of reasonableness in the circumstances has thus placed certain constraints on managerial discretion, it has not altogether

---

17   [1975] ICR 333, [1975] IRLR 211, EAT.

18   See also *Hackwood v Seal (Marine) Ltd* [1973] IRLR 17, IT.

19   *Turner v Vestric Ltd* [1981] IRLR 23, EAT.

20   *Morrow v Scottish Special Housing Association* [1973] IRLR 40, IT; *Abercrombie v Alexander Thompson & Co (London) Ltd* [1973] IRLR 326, IT; *Blanchard v DRE Holdings (1971) Ltd* [1974] IRLR 266, IT; *Donson and Frudd v Conoco Ltd* [1973] IRLR 258, IT.

1   *Gordons (Bottom) Ltd v Greaves* (1983) EAT 509/873. *Refund Rentals Ltd v McDermott* [1977] IRLR 59, EAT.

2   Ibid. See *W and J Wass Ltd v Binns* [1982] ICR 486, [1982] IRLR 283, CA; *Martin v Solus Schall* [1979] IRLR 7, EAT; Cf *Hamilton v Argyll & Clyde Health Board* [1993] IRLR 99, EAT (willingness to offer reemployment is not inconsistent with a conclusion that an employee has been guilty of gross misconduct in the first place).

eroded the contractual right of employers to dismiss without notice for serious offences, itself an important legal basis for managerial authority. Summary dismissal is still considered to be a justified disciplinary action for gross misconduct unless one of the above requirements of reasonableness is found not to have been met.

Finally, whatever the constraints on managerial discretion created by the statutory test of reasonableness, there is still the issue of how seriously these standards will be taken. An important factor influencing the seriousness with which legal standards are taken is the remedy available should the standards not be followed. Before looking more closely at the statutory remedies, however, we must first examine more precisely how the test of fairness is applied to dismissals for other reasons than misconduct.

Chapter 6.
Capability or qualifications: ill health

Where the reason for dismissal is related to the capability[1] or qualifications[2] of the employee for performing work of the kind which he was employed by the employer to do, the most common types of dismissal cases fall into two categories: dismissals for ill health and dismissals for unsatisfactory work performance.[3]

The test of whether an employer's decision to dismiss an employee for ill health was reasonable in the circumstances will vary, depending upon the size and nature of the firm as well as the circumstances of the individual.

For the tribunal the question must be whether it was reasonable of *the employer* in all the circumstances to decide to dismiss. The tribunal must not decide what it would have done had it been the employer but whether it was satisfied that the employer's decision was that of a reasonable employer in the sense that it fell within the range of reasonable responses which employers could have taken having regard to equity and the substantial merit of the case.[4] In determining whether the employer's

---

1 'Capability' is defined in s 98(3)(a) as 'capabilities assessed by reference to skill, aptitude, health or any other physical or mental quality'.

2 'Qualifications' are defined in s 98(3)(b) as 'any degree, diploma or other academic, technical or professional qualification relevant to the position which the employee held'.

3 See Chapter 7. There are few cases where the employee has been dismissed solely for inadequate qualifications. See *Blackman v Post Office* [1974] ICR 151, [1974] IRLR 46 and *Litster v M Thom & Sons Ltd* [1975] IRLR 47.

4 *Spencer v Paragon Wallpapers Ltd* [1976] IRLR 373, EAT; *Rolls Royce Ltd v Walpole* [1980] IRLR 343, EAT.

decision was reasonable in the circumstances, an employment tribunal will have regard to the conduct of the employer in reaching the decision including the procedure adopted by the employer[5] as well as the reasonableness of the employer's decision on the merits of the case.

I. PROCEDURAL REQUIREMENTS OF INVESTIGATION AND CONSULTATION

The specific standards of reasonableness, particularly in terms of the procedural requirements of investigation and consultation, will also vary depending upon whether the employee's absence is due to prolonged and continuing ill health or consists of persistent but intermittent absence for illness.

i) Prolonged ill health

In cases of prolonged ill health, as Phillips J put it in *Spencer v Paragon Wallpapers Ltd*[6]

'In cases of ill health the basic question that has to be determined in every case is whether in all the circumstances the employer can be expected to wait any longer and if so, how much longer. The nature of the illness, the likely length of the continuing absence, the need of the employers to have done the work which the employee was engaged to do – a need that presumably will vary with the size of the employing organisation – are some of the circumstances that must be taken in to account. In some cases, 4 to 6 weeks may justify dismissal, in others 6 months may not. What is reasonable will depend on the circumstances'.

In addition, tribunals are likely to take three other factors into account:
(i)   Did the employer make reasonable efforts to establish the true medical position and consult the employee?
(ii) Did the employer make a reasonable effort to look for alternative employment?
(iii) Was the decision reasonable on the merits of the case?

5   *Polkey v A E Dayton Services Ltd* [1987] IRLR 503, HL.
6   [1977] ICR 301, [1976] IRLR 373, EAT; *Tan v Berry Bros and Rudd Ltd* [1974] ICR 586, [1974] IRLR 244, NIRC.

(a)   Reasonable effort to establish the true medical position

The basic obligation of the employer in the long term ill health cases is to make a reasonable effort to inform himself of the true position of the employee's health. As the EAT put it in *Patterson v Messrs Bracketts*:[7]

> 'What is required in a particular case as far the employer informing himself about the ... employee's health is concerned will depend on the circumstances of the case. But the principle is twofold: First there should be the consultation or discussion with the employee; and secondly such other steps as are necessary should be taken to enable the employer to form a balanced view about the employee's health. In some cases that will require consultation with the doctors; in other cases it will not'.

[I]   CONSULTATION WITH A PHYSICIAN.
Consultation with a physician is generally regarded as appropriate in a reasonable effort to ascertain the true medical position of the employee who is about to be dismissed. Certainly, in any doubtful case an employer who dismisses an employee without obtaining medical opinion runs the risk of having the dismissal found to be unfair for that reason. In *David Sherratt Ltd v Williams*[8] an employee fell ill with Meniere's disease and was transferred to outside work. Over a three-year period he was absent for varying periods as a result of his illness. The employer decided to dismiss him because of the difficulties of finding work for him. There was some evidence that the employers had had some discussion with him previously, but the letter of termination 'came quite out of the blue'. It had not been preceded by consultation or warning. Nor had a medical report been obtained prior to the decision to dismiss. The EAT upheld the tribunal, stating:

> 'where appropriate – and in most cases it will be appropriate in one way or another – the employer ought to seek, with the assistance of the employee and his co-operation where necessary, to find out what is the true medical position. It may be that the employee knows because he has consulted his doctor and he can tell the employers; or he may give permission to the employer to consult his General Practitioner and so on'.[9]

7   [1977] IRLR 137.
8   (1976) EAT 573/76.
9   See also *Allan v F W Farnsworth Ltd* [1974] IRLR 370, IT.

Yet the requirement is only that the employer make a reasonable effort to consult in the circumstances to establish the true medical position. Where the employee fails to co-operate or refuses to consent to a medical examination or to an employer's request to consult the employee's own GP this factor will be taken into account in determining the reasonableness of the employer's efforts.[10]

Moreover, in certain cases where the nature of the injury is obvious, the pattern of consultation with the employee may be considered sufficient to establish adequate evidence of the medical position even without a medical report.[11]

Furthermore, where the employers have obtained reasonable medical evidence, they cannot be required to take elaborate steps to attempt to assess the relative worth of the medical evidence or resort to an independent verification of the medical evidence. As the EAT commented in *Daubney*'s case

'It is not the function of employers any more than it is [Employment] Tribunals to turn themselves into some sort of medical appeal tribunal to review the opinion and advice received from their medical advisor'.[12]

Thus, in *Liverpool Area Health Authority (Teaching) Central and Southern District v Edwards*[13] the EAT reversed an employment tribunal which had held that a dismissal was unfair because the employer had relied on a medical report that was 'woolly and indeterminate' and had failed to carry out further investigation into the nature and extent of the employee's disability. The EAT indicated that further medical investigation or independent verification of medical advice received is not necessary 'unless the medical evidence is plainly erroneous as to the facts in some way or plainly contains an indication that no proper examination of any sort had taken place'.

Similarly, where the employer makes a reasonable effort to determine the state of the employee's health by using a qualified medical practitioner of his own, he is entitled to rely on that advice even if it conflicts with the

---

10   See eg *Post Office v Jones* [1977] IRLR 422, EAT; *Cadbury Ltd v Doddington* [1977] ICR 982, EAT; *O'Brien v River Gardens Amenity Ltd* (1979) EAT 555/79.
11   See eg *Hall v Ross-shire Abattoir Ltd* (1977) EAT 580/77.
12   [1977] IRLR 181 at 18, EAT. But see *Ford Motor Co Ltd v Nawaz* [1987] IRLR 163, EAT.
13   [1977] IRLR 471, EAT.

employee's own doctor. For example, in *Jeffries v BP Tanker Co Ltd*[14] the employee, a radio officer, was dismissed after suffering a heart attack after the employers received advice from their own doctor, a qualified practitioner of occupational medicine, 'that the employee was permanently unfit for sea-going duties'. Even though the employee had consulted another doctor and there was some conflict in medical opinion, the employer was held to have acted reasonably in refusing to take the risks arising from a significant possibility of recurrence of coronary thrombosis, that they were advised could follow if they employed the employee.[15]

Furthermore, where the medical position is uncertain, the employer is obliged only to act as a reasonable employer in the circumstances. For example, in *Marder v ITT Distributors Ltd*[16] an employee was away ill for five weeks and unable to give evidence of when her return to work was likely because the doctor could not diagnose her illness. She was dismissed for ill health because of the employer's pressing need for a replacement, even though he didn't know exactly when she would come back. In this case, the tribunal found the dismissal unfair because the employer had failed to give the employee a date by which he must know when she could give him information about a return to work. However, it also suggested that had the employer said to the employee that they could make temporary arrangements for another week, but if by the end of that week there was no change in the situation a permanent appointment would have to be made, that would have made the employer's decision to dismiss a reasonable one.

[II] OTHER STEPS AS ARE REASONABLY NECESSARY.

Nevertheless, the obligation to conduct a reasonable process of investigation in ascertaining the true medical position could in certain circumstances be interpreted by employment tribunals to extend to seeing persons other than the employee or a physician. Thus, in *Ross Foods v Lamb*[17] the EAT upheld an employment tribunal's findings of unfairness where an employer dismissed a disabled employee without consulting the relevant Welfare Officer when such a step was the only reasonable course to take. Equally importantly, the duty of reasonable diligence extends more generally to the way the employer conducted the entire investigation. Thus it could be risky for an employer to make assumptions about facts of the

14   [1974] IRLR 260, IT.
15   See also *Singh-Deu v Chloride Metals Ltd* [1976] IRLR 56, EAT.
16   [1976] IRLR 105, EAT.
17   (1977) EAT 83/77.

employee's medical position such as the strength and nature of the illness and the duration of the illness or any other facts which can be ascertained by reference either to a physician[18] or to an employee.[19]

Moreover where the investigation clearly indicates a need for further investigation, an employment tribunal might find it unreasonable for an employer to fail to follow up that lead. For example, in *Edward's* case[20] the employee had obtained her own medical report and presented it to the tribunal, although the employer had refused her an opportunity to present one before the dismissal. The EAT remitted the case to the tribunal to consider whether the employer would have reached the same decision had a proper counter-report been obtained before the dismissal. And, in *Crampton v Dacorum Motors Ltd*[1] the employee, a service manager, fell ill and the GP initially diagnosed *Angina Pectoris*, advising a period of rest for four weeks. The employer, discovering informally from a doctor friend that *Angina Pectoris* was both incurable and a progressive disease, decided to terminate the employment. When, however, he informed the employer that he wished to meet him and discuss the position the employee told him that he had arranged a further meeting with his doctor on the next day and asked to postpone the meeting until after the results of that investigation. The employer refused to postpone saying that 'his decision was not contingent on what the doctor said', and dismissed the employee. The next day the employee's GP changed his diagnosis from *Angina Pectoris* to hypertension.

The tribunal found the dismissal unfair both because of the haste of the decision and because of the employer's reliance on the unconfirmed diagnosis of the GP and his informal advice.[2]

Indeed in *Williamson v Alcan (UK) Ltd*[3] where an employee let the employer know that he was consulting a specialist even though the appointment was after the date that notice of dismissal was given, that report was admissible in evidence on the issue of the reasonableness of the dismissal.

---

18   See eg *Allan v F W Farnsworth Ltd* [1974] IRLR 370, IT.
19   See eg *Tyringham Foundation v Frost* (1976) EAT 276/76 (no attempt to ascertain date of return to work). See also *Mackay v Robert Morton Temple Bakery* [1975] IRLR 57 (an unwarranted assumption that the employee had resigned).
20   [1977] IRLR 471, EAT.
1   [1975] IRLR 168, EAT.
2   See also *Cadbury Ltd v Doddington* [1977] ICR 982, EAT (where a further and final discussion was unreasonably omitted).
3   [1978] ICR 104, [1977] IRLR 303, EAT.

(b)   Communications and consultation with the employee

In ill health cases, a reasonable effort to ascertain the medical position of the employee may also be regarded as requiring some form of communication and consultation between employer and employee. As the EAT commented in *Spencer v Paragon Wallpapers Ltd*:[4]

> 'An employee ought not to be dismissed on the grounds of absence due to ill health without some communication being established between the employer and employee before he is dismissed. What is required will vary very much indeed according to the circumstances of the case. Usually what is needed is a discussion of the position between the employer and the employee. Obviously what must be avoided is a dismissal out of hand. There should be a discussion so that the situation can be weighed up, bearing in mind the employer's need for the work to be done and the employee's need for time in which to recover his health'.

In *Spencer*'s case the Employment Appeal Tribunal drew attention to the point that communication and consultation with the employee is part of the fact-finding exercise that should be engaged in by a reasonable employer. Moreover, in *A Links & Co Ltd v Rose*,[5] the Court of Session reinforced the point that in deciding whether an employer acted fairly in dismissing an employee on grounds of ill health, an employment tribunal must determine as a matter of fact and judgment what consultation if any was necessary or desirable in the known circumstances of the particular case; what consultation, if any in fact took place; and whether or not that consultation process was adequate in all the circumstances.

It is not a rule of law however that once an employer has obtained convincing medical advice he must present the information to the employee and offer him an opportunity to state his case. Rather it is a question of fact for employment tribunals to determine in the circumstances. In *East Lindsey District Council v Daubney*[6] an employment tribunal found a dismissal unfair where the employer had dismissed an employee on the basis of a medical opinion which had been obtained without any indication to the employee of its contents or existence. The EAT upheld the tribunal's decision stating:

4   [1977] ICR 301, [1976] IRLR 373, EAT.
5   [1991] IRLR 353, Ct of Sess.
6   [1977] ICR 566, [1977] IRLR 181, EAT; see also *Williamson v Alcan (UK) Ltd* [1978] ICR 104, [1977] IRLR 303, EAT.

'Unless there are wholly exceptional circumstances, before an employee is dismissed on the grounds of ill health it is necessary that he should be consulted and the matter discussed with him and that in one way or another steps should be taken by the employer to discover the true medical position ...

Discussions and consultations will often bring to light facts and circumstances of which the employers were unaware, and which will throw new light on the problem. Or the employee may wish to seek medical advice on his own account, which, brought to the notice of the employer's medical advisers, will cause them to change their opinion. There are many possibilities; only one thing is certain and that is if the employee is not consulted, and given an opportunity to state his case, an injustice may be done'.

Moreover, in *Williamson v Alcan (UK) Ltd*[7] the EAT indicated that the purpose of discussion and consultation with the employee was only partly to enable the true medical position to be discovered: 'It was also necessary because it is reasonably fair and good practice that a man who is going to be dismissed should have a say in the matter'.

Yet consultation or *further* consultation with the employee will not always be required. As the EAT in Scotland has pointed out in *Taylorplan Catering (Scotland) Ltd v McInally*[8] 'the extent to which consultation is required and the steps which an employer must take in order to act reasonably must always be considered in light of the facts and circumstances of the particular case'. In particular, where an employment tribunal finds that the circumstances were such that consultation would and could have made no difference to the result it will not be required. In *McInally*'s case the employer had dismissed the employee without *further* consultation once it was established that he was medically unfit to do his job. The tribunal's decision that the dismissal was unfair because of the failure of *further* consultation was reversed by the EAT because it was quite clear that the employee was medically unfit to do his job and would remain so and that the tribunal had found as a fact that further consultation would not have made a difference. As the EAT explained it:

'There is no doubt that in the normal case a measure of consultation is expected of an employer before he decides to dismiss an employee for ill-health ... the reason for this is to secure that the situation can be weighed up, balancing the employer's need for the work to be

7   [1978] ICR 104, [1977] IRLR 303, EAT.
8   [1980] IRLR 53, EAT.

done on the one hand, against the employee's need for time to recover his health on the other ...

If it is clear that purpose cannot be achieved, the need for consultation which on any view be pointless diminishes if indeed it does not disappear'.

Strictly speaking, the case was decided on the basis that the medical position of the complainant was so clear that this was a case of inevitability providing an exception to the general rule of a need for consultation.[9] However, in appropriate cases, it is open to tribunals in cases short of the limits of perversity to find that a dismissal for ill health is unfair because the employer was unreasonable in his investigation of the facts and consultation with the employee.[10]

ii) Persistent but intermittent absence for ill health

Where an employee is dismissed for persistent but intermittent absence for ill health then guidelines for a reasonable procedure may be different from those that have been evolved for prolonged absence owing to long-term illness.

In the former type of cases the use of formal medical investigation and inquiries into the genuineness of the illness are not as useful a procedure for the employer as one which helps the employer determine whether in the circumstances of the employment the employee's record of absence constitutes sufficient grounds for dismissal.[11] For even if the absence is due to genuine medical reasons it may still be regarded as sufficiently incompatible with the needs of the organisation. As the EAT suggested in *International Sports Co Ltd v Thomson*[12] in cases of persistent but intermittent absence a more appropriate procedure might be the following:

'... firstly, that there should be a fair review by the employer of the attendance record, and the reasons for it, and secondly appropriate warnings, after the employee has been given an opportunity to make representations. If then there is not adequate improvement in the attendance record, it is likely that in most cases the employer will be

---

9   See too *O'Brien v Prudential Assurance Co Ltd* [1979] IRLR 140, EAT.
10   Cf *Townson v Northgate Group Ltd* [1981] IRLR 382, EAT.
11   See eg *International Sports Co Ltd v Thomson* [1980] IRLR 340, EAT; *Rolls Royce Ltd v Walpole* [1980] IRLR 343, EAT.
12   [1980] IRLR 340, EAT.

justified in treating the persistent absences as a sufficient reason for dismissing the employee'.

In *Lynock v Cereal Packaging Ltd*,[13] the EAT reminded that a disciplinary approach involving warnings is not appropriate in cases of intermittent sickness absence but there should be some sort of cautioning of the employee that the stage has been reached when it becomes impossible to continue the relationship. In that case, the EAT also suggested that a sympathetic approach was appropriate where an employee has a poor record of sickness absence. The employer should take into account factors such as the nature of the illness; the likelihood of its recurrence; the timing of the absences; the need of the employer, the impact on other employees and the consultation with the employee.

Nevertheless, cases involving persistent but intermittent absence for ill health, whether or not mixed with absence for other reasons are not always to be regulated by the procedure set out in *East Lindsey District Council v Daubney.*[14] Thus in *Leonard v Fergus and Haynes Civil Engineering Ltd*[15] the Court of Session indicated that where it was an essential requirement of the employment, as expressly indicated in the employment contract, that the employee was in constant attendance shift after shift, an employment tribunal could find that it was not unreasonable of the employer to dismiss without following the procedural guidelines in *Daubney*'s case. And in *Taylorplan Catering (Scotland) Ltd v McInally*[16] the EAT could hold that the tribunal was wrong to insist that the employer must follow a procedure of consultation where it was clear that the result would have been the same in the sense that the employer could have reasonably dismissed the employee. Moreover a tribunal may decide that, in cases involving intermittent periods of absence from work, an employer has no obligation to consult a physician or make extensive medical inquiries before deciding to dismiss.[17]

Ultimately, however, in cases of persistent absenteeism whether the employer's procedure was reasonable is a question of fact for the tribunal – subject to the limits of the test of perversity. Thus as was acknowledged by the EAT in *Townson v Northgate Group Ltd*[18] it was open to a tribunal

13   [1988] IRLR 510, EAT.
14   [1977] ICR 566, [1977] IRLR 181, EAT.
15   [1979] IRLR 235, Ct of Sess.
16   [1980] IRLR 53, EAT.
17   *Lynock v Cereal Packaging Ltd* [1988] IRLR 510, EAT; *Post Office v Jones* [1977] IRLR 422, EAT.
18   [1981] IRLR 382.

to find that an employer has acted unreasonably in dismissing an employee for his record of absences for ill health because of a failure to carry out a more extensive review of the appellant's record and consult with him about the future.

2. ALTERNATIVE WORK

A similar rule of reasonableness applies to the good industrial relations practice that an employer has a duty to look for alternative employment for an employee whom the employer is considering dismissing for incapacity. In *Merseyside and North Wales Electricity Board v Taylor*[19] the High Court (QBD) allowed an appeal against an employment tribunal which had found that the Board had unfairly dismissed an employee with a heart condition. The tribunal had considered that the employee could have been found alternative employment of a semi-sedentary nature. The court stated:

'It cannot be right that in such circumstances an employer can be called upon by the law to create a special job for the employee no matter how long serving he may have been. On the other hand each case must depend upon its given facts. The circumstances may well be such that the employer may have available light work of the kind which is within the capacity of the employee to do, and the circumstances may make it fair to at least encourage him or to offer him the chance of doing that work even if it be at a reduced rate of pay'.

On the other hand, although employers cannot be expected to go to unreasonable lengths in seeking to accommodate an employee who is not able to carry out a job to the full extent, it is open to tribunals to find as a matter of fact that there was a job available which could be slightly modified to accommodate the employee.[20] For whether there is a suitable job in existence which could reasonably be offered to the employee is essentially a question of fact for tribunals to decide taking into account the circumstances of each case.[1] In *Shook v London Borough of Ealing*[2] the

---

19   [1975 ICR 185, [1975] IRLR 60; see too *Taylorplan Catering (Scotland) Ltd v McInally* [1980] IRLR 53, EAT.
20   See eg *Garricks (Caterers) Ltd v Nolan* [1980] IRLR 259, EAT.
1   Ibid, see also *Todd v North Eastern Electricity Board* [1975] IRLR 130, IT; *Spencer v Paragon Wallpapers Ltd* [1977] ICR 301, [1976] IRLR 373, EAT; cf *Brush Electrical Machines v Guest* (1976) EAT 382/76.
2   [1986] IRLR 46, EAT.

EAT held that the presence of a mobility clause in an employee's contract of employment did not carry with it a reciprocal obligation on the part of the employers to provide work elsewhere in the organisation in the case of employees' incapacity to perform their current job.

3. WAS THE DECISION REASONABLE ON THE MERITS?

Assuming that the employer made a reasonable effort to ascertain the true medical position and a reasonable effort to discover whether any suitable alternative work was available, the next question is whether the employer's assessment of the merits of the case was reasonable in the circumstances. In the case of ill health the issue may be phrased as 'has the time arrived when the employer can no longer reasonably be expected to keep the absent employee's post open for him?'[3]

Yet in asking this question the function of the tribunal is not to decide what it would do if it were management, but only to decide whether the decision taken by management was reasonable in the meaning of s 98(4).[4] Moreover, in deciding that question the employment tribunal should take into account if the management's decision could fall within a broad range of responses which reasonable employers could have taken having regard to equity and the substantial merits of the case.[5]

---

3   This type of question is similar to, but not identical with, the question that must be asked when an employment tribunal is considering whether the ill health of an employee has resulted in the termination of his contract through the operation of the doctrine of frustration. See *Egg Stores (Stamford Hill) Ltd v Leibovici* [1977] ICR 260, [1976] IRLR 376, EAT. Certain specific criteria used in the two tests are similar, viz length of previous employment, expected length of employment (cf *Terry v East Sussex County Council* [1977] 1 All ER 567, [1976] ICR 536, EAT), the nature, length and effect of the illness or disabling event and the need of an employer for the work to be done and the need for a replacement to do it. See *Hart v A R Marshall & Sons (Bulwell) Ltd* [1978] 2 All ER 413, [1977] ICR 539, EAT; *Marshall v Harland and Wolff Ltd* [1972] 2 All ER 715, [1972] ICR 101. Yet the issue of frustration is concerned, not with the question whether the employee has been fairly dismissed, but rather with the question of whether or not the employee has been dismissed in the first place. Consequently the criteria are not to be applied as if the tests were the same; cf *Tan v Berry Bros and Rudd Ltd* [1974] ICR 586, [1974] IRLR 244, NIRC.

4   See eg *Spencer v Paragon Wallpapers Ltd* [1977] ICR 301, [1976] IRLR 373, EAT.

5   See eg *Rolls Royce Ltd v Walpole* [1980] IRLR 343, EAT.

What factors figure prominently in the test? In *Spencer v Paragon Wallpapers Ltd*[6] the EAT suggested:

'The nature of the illness; the likely length of the continuing absence, the need of the employers to have done the work which the employee was engaged to do'.

Clearly the greater the need for a replacement, the more that the employee's absence is dislocating or unduly burdensome to the business the easier it will be to establish a reasonable basis for a decision to dismiss. Thus in *Leonard v Fergus and Haynes Civil Engineering Ltd*[7] the need of the employer for continuous shift coverage made it reasonable to dismiss for a relatively small amount of absence. And, in *Tan v Berry Bros and Rudd Ltd*[8] an employee who had a long and worsening record of frequent absence, culminating in a need for an operation, was given 14 days' notice by the employer. The tribunal found the dismissal fair, commenting that the employer's being faced with the Christmas rush and employing only a small labour force made the employee's absence 'a matter of some significance'.[9]

Where the nature of the illness indicates that continued employment will be risky to the health and welfare of other employees, or the employee himself, that may be a reasonable basis for a decision to dismiss. For example, where an employee is an epileptic,[10] a drug addict,[11] mentally ill,[12] suffers from deteriorating eyesight,[13] or depressive illness[14] and to return to employment might create a risk of harm to the employee himself or other employees, a decision to dismiss may be found to be reasonable.

---

6   [1977] ICR 301, [1976] IRLR 373.
7   [1979] IRLR 235, Ct of Sess.
8   [1974] ICR 586, [1974] IRLR 244; see also *McPhee v George H Wright Ltd* [1975] IRLR 132.
9   See also *Hall v Ross-shire Abattoir Ltd* (1977) EAT 580/77.
10 *Harper v National Coal Board* [1980] IRLR 260, EAT.
11 *Walton v TAC Construction Materials Ltd* [1981] IRLR 357, EAT: see too *Liverpool Area Health Authority (Teaching) Central and Southern District v Edwards* [1977] IRLR 471, EAT.
12 *O'Brien v Prudential Assurance Co Ltd* [1979] IRLR 140, EAT; *Burdekin v Dolan Corrugated Containers Ltd* [1972] IRLR 9, NIRC; *IRC v Green* (1977) EAT 550/77.
13 *Finch v Betabake (Anglia) Ltd* [1977] IRLR 470, EAT.
14 *Taylorplan Catering (Scotland) Ltd v McInally* [1980] IRLR 53, EAT.

Indeed, health and safety considerations may even in certain cases justify an automatic exclusion from work in such cases.[15] Where the employee is disabled similar considerations can apply. In *Pascoe v Hallen and Medway*[16] an employee who suffered from several asthma attacks was dismissed fairly because 'the consequences of her ill health were having a disrupting effect on the factory'. In that case the fact that the employee was a registered disabled person (a 'green card' holder) did not protect her from dismissal. The disability of the employee and the interests of the business could lead an employer reasonably to say: 'I cannot carry this green card holder any longer'. However, a tribunal can in its discretion find as a matter of fact that where the employee was disabled when hired, a reasonable employer would give consideration to providing the employee with work in which occasional and necessary chances can be absorbed by the company.[17] Finally, a disability-related dismissal which is not justified under the Disability Discrimination Act is not automatically unfair in terms of s 98(4) of the ERA 1996. Section 98(4) requires its own consideration of such dismissals.[18]

The needs of the business can also be a factor that, apparently, may allow an employer to dismiss an employee for ill health even before the sick pay entitlement of the employee under a sick pay scheme has been exhausted. In *Coulson v Felixstowe Dock and Rly Co*[19] the employee was dismissed because his extensive absence caused inconvenience as labour shortage at times made replacements difficult to arrange. Even though his conditions of service included an entitlement to sick pay of full pay for six months and half pay for six months and these were not exhausted, the dismissal was found to be reasonable. The sick pay scheme was held to be a financial arrangement only, and not to indicate the amount of absence to which an employee is entitled if he is sick.

Finally, the needs of the business may justify a firm dismissing an employee who is absent for a sustained period even where the illness or injury was caused by the employment.

15 [1975] IRLR 116, EAT; see also *Seymour v British Airways Board* [1983] IRLR 55, EAT.
16 [1975] IRLR 116, EAT; see also *Seymour v British Airways Board* [1983] IRLR 55, EAT; *Shook v London Borough of Ealing* [1986] IRLR 46, EAT.
17 See eg *Kerr v Atkinson Vehicles (Scotland) Ltd* [1974] IRLR 36, EAT; *Bareham v Suffolk Area Health Authority* (1978) EAT 303/78.
18 *HJ Heinz Co Ltd v Kenrick* [2000] IRLR 144, EAT.
19 [1975] IRLR 11, EAT. See too *Smiths Industries Aerospace & Defence Systems Ltd v Brookes* [1986] IRLR 434, EAT (limited effect of a contractual term providing for termination by minimum notice).

In *Davies v Odeco (UK) Inc*[20] a case of an employee injured whilst working on an oil rig, the EAT stated that 'the onus which rests upon an employer under s 98(4) is simply to satisfy the Tribunal that they have acted reasonably. The manner in which the ill health has come about may or may not be a matter which falls to be taken into account. It is not, however, a matter which can increase the burden of proof.' In *McPhee v George H Wright Ltd*[1] an employee of seven years' standing suffered from an 'anxiety state', caused by his work. The tribunal found dismissal fair, commenting:

'The more true it is that illness was occasioned by incidents or attitudes at his place of work, the more reasonable it becomes for the company to reach a decision that they can no longer employ him ... his work had to be done by somebody. ... It has to be borne in mind that this Act ... is designed to provide compensation for certain specific matters and cannot be used, nor was it intended, to provide an additional source of compensation for any illness'.

However where the illness is caused by physical working conditions a failure to take reasonable steps to remove the cause of the health problem may render the dismissal unfair.

In *Jagdeo v Smith Industries Ltd*[2] the employee after ten years of service was transferred to a job which involved soldering. She proved to be allergic to soldering fumes and wearing a mask did not resolve the problem. The company dismissed the employee on the ground that she was medically unsuitable to do the work and no suitable alternative work could be found.[3]

An officer of the Health and Safety Executive, testified before the employment tribunal that the respondents had dealt with the problem in another factory by installing extractor fans. Nevertheless, the tribunal found the dismissal to be fair. The EAT reversed and remitted the case to the tribunal to consider.

'what steps the company did take prior to dismissal to consider and utilise Mr Kemball's suggestion that extractor fans of some kind could be employed. In the light of this evidence, the Tribunal will have before it the evidence necessary to decide whether, before dismissing Mrs Jagdeo from the position to which the employers had transferred

20   (1980) EAT 702/79.
1   [1975] IRLR 132.
2   [1982] ICR 47, EAT.
3   On the issue of alternative employment see *Carricks (Caterers) Ltd v Nolan* [1980] IRLR 259, EAT; *Merseyside & North Wales Electricity Board v Taylor* [1975] IRLR 60.

her, the company had taken reasonable steps to ensure that she could not continue to hold that job'.

An employment tribunal can also take into account the risk of future illness in assessing whether or not the employer was reasonable in dismissing the employee, where these risks are substantiated by medical opinion.[4] Indeed in exceptional cases this may be a legitimate factor for the employer even where the employee has fully recovered.[5] Yet where a decision is taken on inadequate medical advice this may well be unreasonable.[6]

4   See eg *Harper v National Coal Board* [1980] IRLR 260, EAT.
5   See eg *Nicholl v Sir William Reardon Smith & Sons Ltd* (1982) EAT 463/81.
6   See eg *Converform (Darwen) Ltd v Bell* [1981] IRLR 195, EAT.

Chapter 7.
Capability or qualifications: unsatisfactory work performance

Where the reason for dismissal is the unsatisfactory work performance of the employee, that can also be a reason related to the capability of the employee for performing work of a kind which he was employed by the employer to do. In such a case, the test of s 98(4) is whether a 'reasonable employer' would have been justified in all the circumstances including the size and administrative resources of the employer in dismissing an employee for that incapacity or poor performance. For convenience this test can be broken down into three elements. First, the tribunal must be satisfied that the employer had reasonable ground for concluding, 'that the employee's incapacity as it existed at the time of dismissal was of such a nature and quality as to justify dismissal'.[1]

Secondly, the test of s 98(4) often, but not always, will include a test whether as a matter of fact the employer made reasonable efforts to warn the employee and ascertain whether he or she was capable of improvement.[2]

Thirdly, the tribunal must be satisfied that the employer acted reasonably in deciding that employee's incapacity justified dismissal in all the relevant circumstances; for example, that it was not caused by a failure on the part of management to meet its responsibilities or that extenuating circumstances on the part of the employee were given sufficient weight.

1 *A J Dunning & Sons (Shopfitters) Ltd v Jacomb* [1973] ICR 448, [1973] IRLR 206, NIRC.
2 See *Polkey v A E Dayton Services Ltd* [1987] IRLR 503, HL.

1. DID THE EMPLOYER ACT REASONABLY IN CONCLUDING THAT THE EMPLOYEE WAS, IN FACT, INCAPABLE?

In *Alidair Ltd v Taylor*,[3] Sir Geoffrey Lane LJ stated that under s 98(4) the question is

'whether the employer honestly and reasonably held the belief that the employee was not competent and whether there was a reasonable ground for that belief'.[4]

Strictly speaking, the test set out in *Taylor* is not purely subjective.[5] It requires an employer reasonably to hold his belief in the employee's incompetence and to have reasonable evidential grounds for that belief.[6] Lord Justice Stephenson's remarks in *W Weddel & Co Ltd v Tepper*[7] that 'an employer cannot justify a dismissal simply by stating an honest belief in his guilt', are probably just as apposite to cases of incapacity.

Yet it does not go so far as to require the employer to prove to the satisfaction of the tribunal that the employee was in fact incompetent.

For example in *MacKellar v Bolton*[8] the EAT allowed an appeal against an employment tribunal for misdirection where it had held that dismissal was unfair because the employee had failed to prove a connection between a doctor's receptionist's behaviour and the loss of patients. The correct question for the employment tribunal, according to the EAT, was not whether patients left the practice due to the employee's behaviour but whether the employer reasonably believed that was why they left and was he reasonable in dismissing her?

As long as the tribunal avoids misdirecting itself, it can find that an employer's belief was not genuine or that their assessment was so contrary to the weight of the evidence as to be unreasonable.

For example, in *Dexine Rubber Co Ltd v Alker*[9] the employee, a factory manager, was dismissed for incompetence and the employer submitted two types of evidence to support his contention. The first consisted of

3   [1978] ICR 445, [1978] IRLR 82, CA; see also *Inner London Education Authority v Lloyd* [1981] IRLR 394, CA.
4   [1978] IRLR 82 at 85.
5   But see Lord Denning MR's remarks, [1978] IRLR 82 at 84.
6   *Lees v The Orchard* [1978] IRLR 20, EAT.
7   [1980] ICR 286, [1980] IRLR 96, CA.
8   [1979] IRLR 59, EAT.
9   [1977] ICR 434, EAT; see also *Home Charm Retail Ltd v Smith* (1982) EAT 137/82 where there was no evidence of 'gross incompetence'; *Woods v Olympic Aluminium Co Ltd* [1975] IRLR 356, IT.

production figures over a 12-month period beginning before and continuing after the employee's dismissal. The second was a set of complaints from customers during the same period. The tribunal rejected the first submission as evidence of incompetence because there were no comparable figures for the preceding year. It rejected the second because no documents were supplied showing what complaints had been made in the comparable period in the previous year. The EAT held that it was open to the tribunal to take that view of the evidence.

Yet, as the EAT has also indicated on more than one occasion, the proper function of the tribunal is not simply to measure the employer's judgment against results.[10] For in the application of the test of reasonable grounds, the opinions and views of management in monitoring the performance of the employee have been held under certain conditions to constitute positive evidence of incompetence.

Thus, in *Cook v Thomas Linnell & Sons Ltd*[11] the EAT stated:

'When responsible employers have genuinely come to the conclusion over a reasonable period of time that a manager is incompetent we think that it is some evidence that he is incompetent. When one is dealing with routine operations which may be more precisely assessed there is no real problem. It is more difficult when one is dealing with such imponderables as the quality of management, which in the last resort can only be judged by those competent in the field. In such cases as this it can be demonstrated, perhaps by reason of some calamitous performance, that the manager is incompetent. The other extreme is the case where no more can be said than that in the opinion of the employer the manager is incompetent, that opinion being expressed for the first time shortly before his dismissal. In between will be cases such as the present where it can be established that throughout the period of employment concerned the employers had progressively growing doubts about the ability of the manager to perform his task satisfactorily. If that can be shown it is in our judgment some evidence of his incapacity. It will then be necessary to look to see whether there is any other supporting evidence'.

Moreover, the probative value of the genuine opinion of 'responsible employers' could offset a lack of clear and positive proof of a relationship

10 See eg *Miller v Grahams Executors* [1978] IRLR 309, EAT.
11 [1977] ICR 770, [1977] IRLR 132, EAT. See also *Okereke v Post Office* [1974] IRLR 170, IT.

between poor performance and a fall-off in trade. As the EAT put it in *Cook*'s case:

'While it could not be positively established that the fall-off was directly attributable to Mr Cook's incapacity, it seems to us that it must be reasonable for employers who have no confidence in their manager, where the fall-off in trade is of genuine concern and continuing, to come to the conclusion that he shares some responsibility for it. After all, a manager is in a position where he can expect to get the credit for success and the blame for failure. We do not think that this was a case in which the employer's view of the capability of Mr Cook was formed merely by the fall-off in trade at the Norwich depot. It was a view formed initially from the monitoring of his performance, independently of the fall-off in trade, but confirmed by the fall-off'.

Yet, the employer's evidence should be internally consistent. Thus, if an employer dismisses an employee for incapacity he may have difficulties in convincing a tribunal of the fact of poor performance if he has recently sent a glowing reference or a laudatory letter.[12]

2. DID THE EMPLOYER MAKE REASONABLE EFFORTS TO WARN THE EMPLOYEE AND TO ASCERTAIN WHETHER HE COULD IMPROVE?

The test of s 98(4) is not merely whether the employer was reasonable in concluding that the employee was incapable of performing his job at the time of dismissal, it is whether in all the circumstances an employer is justified in dismissing him for incapability.[13]

In *James v Waltham Holy Cross UDC*[14] the NIRC stated that:

'An employer should be very show to dismiss upon the grounds that the employee is incapable of performing the work which he is employed to do, without first telling the employee of the respects in which he is failing to do his job adequately, warning him of the possibilities or likelihood of dismissal on this ground and giving him an opportunity of improving his performance'.

---

12   *Scottish Co-operative Wholesale Society Ltd v Lloyd* [1973] IRLR 93, NIRC (employee received a letter at Christmas of a complimentary nature).

13   *Inner London Education Authority v Lloyd* [1981] IRLR 394, CA.

14   Cf *Turner v Vestric Ltd* [1980] ICR 528, [1981] IRLR 23, EAT.

Moreover, in *Sutton & Gates (Luton) Ltd v Boxall*[15] a finding by an employment tribunal that a dismissal for incapability was unfair because the employer hadn't given the employee an adequate opportunity to offer an explanation for his poor performance was held by the EAT to be within the tribunal's discretion since this was not a case where it is clear that the employee would have been dismissed even if he had been given an opportunity to explain.

In cases of dismissal for incapability, as in cases of dismissal for misconduct, these procedural steps are not required as a matter of law.[16] Essentially, the reasonableness of their omission is a question of fact for tribunals to decide taking into account the size and administrative resources of the employer.[17] Indeed, perhaps even more than in cases of conduct, the need for certain procedural steps has been viewed 'as a matter of substance', going to the basic sufficiency of the reasons which moved the employer to dismiss, in the sense that the procedural steps are regarded as overlapping with the need of a reasonable employer to make an effort to determine whether or not the poor performance of the employee was 'redeemable'. In *James'* case it was suggested that an employer may reasonably omit to give a prior warning or an opportunity to improve performance, in the exceptional case where 'the inadequacy of performance is so extreme that there must be an irredeemable incapability'.[18] As the NIRC put it:

'In such circumstances, exceptional as they no doubt are, a warning and an opportunity for improvement are of no benefit to the employee and may constitute an unfair burden on the business'.[19]

For example, in the *Dunning* case the employee, a contracts manager, was found to be unco-operative and unbending when performing his duties and this had caused acute and serious difficulties for his employers with

15 [1979] ICR 67, [1978] IRLR 486, EAT.
16 *A J Dunning & Sons (Shopfitters) Ltd v Jacomb* [1973] ICR 448, [1973] IRLR 206, NIRC. See also *Taylor v Alidair Ltd* [1978] ICR 445, [1978] IRLR 82, CA; *Grant v Ampex (GB) Ltd* [1980] IRLR 461, EAT; *Brown v Hall Advertising Ltd* [1978] IRLR 246, EAT.
17 *Royal Naval School v Hughes* [1979] IRLR 383, EAT.
18 A second exception – those employed in senior management – has been rejected by the EAT. See *McPhail v Gibson* [1977] ICR 42, [1976] IRLR 254, EAT; *Cook v Thomas Linnell & Sons Ltd* [1977] ICR 770, [1977] IRLR 132, EAT. However, the senior status of an employee may affect his compensation by a higher measure of contributory fault; see *McPhail v Gibson* [1977] ICR 42 at 46, [1976] IRLR 254 at 256.
19 [1973] ICR 398, [1973] IRLR 202.

large and regular clients. The employer had dismissed the employee without a warning and this led the tribunal to find the dismissal unfair. The Industrial Court reversed the tribunal on the ground that the 'constitutional inability' of the employee to change his attitude to clients, a fact which was recognised by the tribunal, made the purely procedural step of a warning unnecessary.

In addition to cases of constitutional incapability, there are also cases where an employee may have received an effective substitute for a warning, eg a probationary period,[20] or an adverse performance appraisal.[1]

Those types of exception were approved by the EAT and indeed were extended to questions of whether an employee dismissed for incapacity is entitled to a hearing.[2] In *Lowndes v Specialist Heavy Engineering Ltd*[3] the employee was dismissed for persistent negligence without being given a final written warning or an opportunity to answer complaints, yet the tribunal considered the dismissal not unfair in spite of these procedural omissions because there was no reasonable possibility that the result would have been any different if the procedures had been observed. The employee's repeated negligence had made him incapable of doing his work properly. In *Lowndes'* case the decision and reasoning of the employment tribunal were upheld by the EAT.

Since the decision of the House of Lords in *Polkey v A E Dayton Services Ltd*,[4] however, the test has been stiffened to one of whether the omitted procedural step would have been futile or utterly useless judged from the time the employer took the decision to dismiss. It is no longer permissible for tribunals to excuse procedural omissions on the basis of a 'likelihood' that the omitted procedural step would have been unnecessary.[5]

---

20   See eg *Kendrick v Concrete Pumping Ltd* [1975] IRLR 83 (a probationary period).
1   *Littlewoods Organisation Ltd v Egenti* [1976] ICR 516, [1976] IRLR 334.
2   In an earlier case, *Okereke v Post Office* [1974] IRLR 170, the NIRC had cast some doubt on the functional importance of a hearing in incapability cases; 'There is no reason why an employee whose capability is complained of should be given an opportunity to explain away what is being held against him. The proper test of fairness in capability cases is whether the employee was made aware of his failings and given a last opportunity over a reasonable period to show that he could do the job'. See also *Cook v Thomas Linnell & Sons Ltd* [1977] ICR 770, [1977] IRLR 132, EAT; but see *Tobin v Sika Contracts Ltd* [1973] IRLR 12 (employee should be asked why he is not performing well).
3   [1977] ICR 1, [1976] IRLR 246.
4   [1987] IRLR 503, HL.
5   Ibid.

Thus, whilst breaches of procedure in cases of incapability may not always be regarded as of the same order of importance as breaches of disciplinary procedure,[6] they may nevertheless be the basis for a finding of unfair dismissal. In such cases an employer who omits an important procedural step bears the onus of justifying this omission.[7] And the wide discretion retained by tribunals to decide whether to treat the procedural omission as a ground for a finding of unfair dismissal ensures that the steps suggested in *James'* case retain their importance as a guide to reasonable procedure in capability cases. Thus tribunals may decide that a dismissal is unfair because employers have not met the standard of all 'reasonable employers' in respect of communicating their dissatisfaction to the employee, with an adequate indication of the employee's shortcomings[8] as well as providing an adequate indication that his job has been placed in jeopardy by these shortcomings.[9] Moreover, tribunals remain entitled to find a dismissal unfair where the employer fails to provide the employee with a reasonable opportunity to demonstrate an improvement.[10]

3. WAS THE DISMISSAL FOR INCAPABILITY REASONABLE IN ALL THE CIRCUMSTANCES?

Assuming that employers succeed in proving that they acted reasonably in concluding that the employee was not capable of performing the work he was employed to do, and that the employer made a reasonable effort to see whether the employee could improve, there is a further question, whether the employer was reasonable in deciding to dismiss the employee for that incapability in all the circumstances.

In deciding this question, tribunals must not make the mistake of deciding what they would have done had they been the employer. They must ask whether the employer's decisions fell within the range of options open to a reasonable employer.[11]

6   *Cook v Thomas Linnell & Sons Ltd* [1977] ICR 770, [1977] IRLR 132, EAT; *Littlewoods Organisation Ltd v Egenti* [1976] ICR 516, [1976] IRLR 334.
7   Cf *Charles Letts & Co Ltd v Howard* [1976] IRLR 248, EAT.
8   *A W Goodhew & Son Ltd v Webber* (1977) EAT 104/77.
9   *Mansfield Hosiery Mills Ltd v Bromley* [1977] IRLR 301; but cf *Littlewoods Organisation Ltd v Egenti* [1976] ICR 516, [1976] IRLR 334.
10 *A W Goodhew & Sons Ltd v Webber* (1977) EAT 104/77; *Reeves Burgess Ltd v Wilkinson* (1983) EAT 700/82; *Winterhalter Gastronom Ltd v Webb* [1973] ICR 245, [1973] IRLR 120, NIRC.
11 See eg *Gair v Bevan Harris Ltd* [1983] IRLR 368, Ct of Sess; cf *British Leyland (UK) Ltd v Swift* [1981] IRLR 91, CA.

Yet given this constraint tribunals may determine whether employers acted reasonably in terms of; (a) meeting their responsibilities, and (b) giving adequate weight to the past record of the employee.

(a) Management responsibilities

Where an employer has omitted to discharge one of his responsibilities towards the employee, it may be regarded by employment tribunals as a circumstance which makes it unreasonable to dismiss the employee for incapability. For example, where management can be shown to have failed to meet its general responsibility under the Code of Practice to organise work effectively by giving an adequate definition to the job to be done and providing adequate supervision, training,[12] or support,[13] a tribunal may conclude 'that the (employee) was not wholly to blame for his deficiencies and shortcomings and the responsibility for them must be substantially with the (employers) themselves'.[14]

A confirmation of the scope of the employment tribunal's discretion in these matters was provided by the Court of Appeal in *Inner London Education Authority v Lloyd*.[15] In that case a probationary teacher was found to be unfairly dismissed because, although incompetent, he did not receive the support, advice and guidance appropriate for probationary teachers. The employer had failed to realise that he was in fact a probationary teacher until more than halfway through his probationary period. Both the EAT and the Court of Appeal held that in such circumstances the tribunal was entitled to find the dismissal unfair. The Court of Appeal found that it was not a perverse decision of the tribunal to take the view that given the failure of the employer to provide adequate support, advice and guidance to the probationary employee, it was unreasonable to treat the employee's incompetence as a sufficient reason for dismissal.

---

12 See *Fox v Findus Ltd* [1973] IRLR 8; *Welsh v Associated Steels and Tools Co Ltd* [1973] IRLR 111 and *Bradley v Opperman Gears Ltd* [1975] IRLR 13, IT.

13 See *Cockroft v Trendsetter Furniture Ltd* [1973] IRLR 6; *Woodward v Beeston Boiler Co Ltd* [1973] IRLR 7 and *Green v Moyses Stevens Ltd* [1974] IRLR 274.

14 See *Burrows v Ace Caravan Co (Hull) Ltd* [1972] IRLR 4, IT; *Mansfield Hosiery Mills Ltd v Bromley* [1977] IRLR 301, EAT; *Davison v Kent Meters Ltd* [1975] IRLR 145, IT.

15 [1981] IRLR 394, CA.

Finally, before an employer decides to dismiss an employee for incapability, he has some responsibility to look to see whether there is any suitable alternative employment available for the employee. There is no duty in all cases to offer employment. Each case must turn on the circumstances of the case.

In *Bevan Harris Ltd v Gair*,[16] the EAT allowed an appeal against an employment tribunal that had found a dismissal unfair because a 'reasonable employer would have demoted rather than dismissed the employee'. Instead the EAT substituted a finding that the employee had not been unfairly dismissed, commenting:

> 'In any event we do not consider that there is necessarily an obligation upon every employer who dismisses an employee on the grounds of capability to offer him employment in a subsidiary or another position. Every case must depend upon its own circumstances. Different considerations may apply to dismissals for other reasons. For instance where an employee is dismissed because he is redundant there may be in certain situations an obligation upon his employer to do his best to attempt to fit him in in some other capacity within his own enterprise (*Vokes Ltd v Bear* [1974] ICR 1, [1973] IRLR 363; *Thomas & Betts Manufacturing Co Ltd v Hardin* [1978] IRLR 213). Where however the reason for dismissal is shown to be capability and where it is shown that the employee received adequate warning as to his shortcomings and adequate opportunity to improve and has failed to do so we do not think that there is the same obligation upon an employer to attempt to fit him in a subordinate capacity. Even if there is this must to a very great extent be influenced by the size and administrative resources of his undertaking. These words were incorporated into [s 98(4)] ... and they are of particular relevance in our view to the present case. The small scale of the appellants' business and the circumstances of the respondent's proposed demotion were such as would, in our opinion, entitle a reasonable employer to conclude that even if he had a job to offer it would not be to the advantage of his business that the employee should continue in it'.[17]

---

16 [1981] IRLR 520, EAT.

17 [1981] IRLR 520 at 521, see also *Tyndall v Burmah Oil Trading Ltd* (1984) EAT 655/83.

(b) The employee's record

Where an employee has had a long record of good service in the past, this is a factor that may be taken into account by tribunals in judging the reasonableness of management's decision to dismiss.[18] Furthermore, where an employee's past record has been such as to result in promotion, as we have seen, this may be viewed by tribunals as increasing the degree of responsibility to be borne by management.[19]

Conversely, where the employee has a probationary appointment, the test of reasonableness is adjusted to take into account a duty on the part of the employee to establish himself, as well as the employer's duty to give him a reasonable opportunity to do this. In *Hamblin v London Borough of Ealing*[20] a tribunal remarked 'we think that the test of reasonableness in the case of probationary appointments is not quite the same as in the case of other employees'.[1] Yet whilst there may be no need for a warning, there is a need to communicate clearly and unambiguously any dissatisfaction.[2]

---

18   See eg *Tobin v Sika Contracts Ltd* [1973] IRLR 12, IT.
19   See eg *Kendrick v Concrete Pumping Ltd* [1975] IRLR 83, IT.
20   [1975] IRLR 354, IT.
1   See also *Ayanlowo v IRC* [1975] IRLR 253, CA; *Flude v Post Office* [1975] IRLR 330, IT.
2   See eg *Post Office v Mughal* [1977] ICR 763, [1977] IRLR 178, EAT.

Chapter 8.
Unfair redundancy

I. INTRODUCTION

An employee's claim that a dismissal for redundancy is unfair is only one tier of a three-tiered set of legal rights that attempts to regulate managerial decisions about redundancy. The unfair dismissal claim is poised between the law of redundancy payments[1] and the law of consultation with trade unions over the handling of redundancies.[2]

In theory these other two tiers of legal regulation apply quite separately from the unfair dismissal claim. Thus whether an employee qualifies for a redundancy payment under s 139(1) is entirely dependent upon whether he or she fits into the definition of redundancy contained within that statutory provision. Moreover the requirement that an employer must consult with a recognised trade union over redundancies in accordance with s 188 of TULRCA 1992, appears to be self-contained in terms of its remedy. Section 188(8) states quite explicitly that a failure to adhere to the standards of that section shall not give rise to any other legal remedy than a protective award set out in ss 189–192.

Nevertheless both tiers of legal regulation in fact overlap with, and influence the claim of unfair dismissal for redundancy. Thus, in order for an employee to claim that he or she was unfairly dismissed for redundancy it is necessary that he or she has, in fact, been dismissed for redundancy

---

1   ERA 1996, s 139(1).
2   TULRCA, ss 188–192. This legal structure is also affected by the various provisions of the Transfer of Undertakings Regulations, see Chapter 14.

as defined in s 139(1).[3] Moreover, whether an employer had consulted with a recognised trade union broadly in accordance with s 188 of TULRCA 1992 is one of the factors in the test of the reasonableness of the employer's decision to dismiss an employee for redundancy under s 98(4) of ERA 1996.[4]

Since 1971, an employee dismissed for redundancy as defined in ERA 1996, s 139(1), can also claim that the dismissal was an unfair dismissal for redundancy under ERA 1996, s 98(2)(c) and 98(4), whether or not he or she had already received a redundancy payment, or claims for both concurrently,[5] or even if he or she was excluded[6] or disqualified[7] from a redundancy payment. And of course where employees are successful in a complaint of unfair dismissal they may obtain a remedy of compensation and or even reinstatement or re-engagement as well as the equivalent of a redundancy payment in the form of a basic award where appropriate.

Nevertheless, cases have often appeared in which employers have attempted to show that their reason for dismissal was redundancy as a response to the employee's claim for unfair dismissal. For employers to show that their reason for dismissal was redundancy and that it was a fair dismissal for that reason, can often have the result of limiting their liability to a redundancy payment.

In such cases, however, employers receive no assistance from the presumption contained in ERA 1996, s 163(2).[8] Moreover, under ERA 1996, s 98(2)(c), employers have the onus of proving that their reason fits within the definition of redundancy under ERA 1996, s 139(1).[9]

---

3   See eg *Murphy v Epsom College* [1985] ICR 80, [1984] IRLR 271, CA; *O'Hare and Rutherford v Rotaprint Ltd* [1980] ICR 94, [1980] IRLR 47, EAT; *Robinson v British Island Airways Ltd* [1978] ICR 304, [1977] IRLR 477, EAT; *Gorman v London Computer Training Centre Ltd* [1978] ICR 394, [1978] IRLR 22, EAT.

4   See eg *Williams v Compair Maxam Ltd* [1982] ICR 156, [1982] IRLR 83, EAT; *Rowell v Hubbard Group Services Ltd* [1995] IRLR 195, 197 EAT.

5   Indeed, even if both claims are not entered in the originating application they will be considered by an employment tribunal if they are justified by the facts see *Coates v C J Crispin Ltd* [1973] ICR 413, [1973] IRLR 211, NIRC.

6   Owing to inadequate length of continuous service.

7   If the employee was disqualified for a redundancy payment then these could be questions raised under s 98(4) as well as on the issue of mitigation of loss.

8   *Sutton v Revlon Overseas Corpn Ltd* [1973] IRLR 173, NIRC. Where an employer disputes a claim for redundancy payment as well as unfair dismissal, the employee will enjoy the presumption of redundancy under ERA 1996, s 163(2) (see *Runnals v Richards and Osborne Ltd* [1973] ICR 225, [1973] IRLR 124; *Midland Foot Comfort Centre Ltd v Moppett* [1973] 2 All ER 294, [1973] ICR 219, NIRC.

9   *Nelson v BBC* [1977] ICR 649, [1977] IRLR 148, CA; see discussion in Chapter 4.

Where an employer has successfully shown that an employee has been dismissed for redundancy an employee may also be entitled to complain that the redundancy was an unfair dismissal under either of two heads. In the first place, the redundancy may be an automatically unfair selection under ERA 1996, s 105. Secondly, the redundancy may have been 'unreasonable' under ERA 1996, s 98(4).

2. 'AUTOMATICALLY UNFAIR SELECTION'

Where an employer has established that the reason for dismissal was redundancy an employee can claim that the dismissal constituted an automatically unfair selection under s 105 of ERA 1996. In such a case, the employee must establish *two facts*: that 'the circumstances constituting the redundancy applied equally to one or more other employees in the same undertaking who held positions similar to those held by them and who have not been dismissed by the employer'. In addition the employee must show that the selection was for a reason related to trade union membership or activities, or that it was for an 'inadmissible reason', that is a prohibited reason such as pregnancy or childbirth, making a health and safety complaint, asserting a statutory right, being a protected shop worker, acting as an employee representative or pension fund trustee or exercising rights to the national minimum wage or under the Working Time Regulation or for whistleblowing.[10] The purpose of this protection is to prevent the employer from using selection for redundancy as a backdoor device to avoid dismissing employees more overtly for what are now designated as automatically unfair reasons.

i) Did the redundancy apply equally to one or more employees in the 'same undertaking' in a 'similar' position who were not dismissed?

Under s 105(1)(b) the 'unit of selection', that is, the unit within which comparisons must be made, is determined by two factors: the organisational unit with which similar positions must be considered, and the jobs which must be grouped together as 'similar positions'.

---

10   S 153 of TULRCA. See discussion in Chapter 10. For all other prohibited reasons, see Chapter 4.

(a) 'The same undertaking'

The unit of organisation within which similar positions must be considered is the undertaking. An 'undertaking' would appear to be a wider unit than an 'establishment', which is a particular production unit at a particular place.[11] For example, in *Oxley v Tarmac Roadstone Holdings Ltd*,[12] where two plants shared the same works manager and were situated a quarter of a mile apart, an employment tribunal held that the unit of selection was the two plants and that the employer could not regard each plant on a separate basis despite different hours of working, different canteens, etc. The tribunal commented that:

> 'of course in a larger company there must be a common management at some level, but when it is as low down the scale as Works Manager we consider it is a strong indication that the two plants should not be regarded as separate entities'.[13]

Further, because the statutory test applies to the 'same undertaking' it is not normally appropriate to confine comparison between employees in similar positions to a unit smaller than the undertaking such as the department or section. For example, in *Heathcote v North Western Electricity Board*[14] a driver's mate who was a labourer could not be compared only with the other workers in the Transport Section. He had to be compared with labourers in all sections of the factory, since labourers were treated as a common pool. As the tribunal commented:

> 'We think it would be quite wrong if any undertaking when faced with redundancy could treat its entirety as divided into small sections, so that the selection of redundancy should be made entirely within an individual section'.

(b) 'Similar positions'

Although the organisational unit of comparison must be the undertaking or production unit, the actual comparisons of seniority within the

---

11   See *Kapur v Shields* [1976] 1 All ER 873, [1976] ICR 26, QBD.
12   [1975] IRLR 100, IT.
13   The tribunal's comment, with respect, appears not to give full weight to the presence of the words 'in the same undertaking' in s 105(1)(b).
14   [1974] IRLR 34, IT.

undertaking are required only to be made between employees in 'similar positions'. In practice, therefore, the unit of selection may be circumscribed by the level of skill as well as the kind of work and thereby be restricted to a department or section.

For example, in *Powers and Villers v A Clarke & Co (Smethwick) Ltd*[15] the EAT found an employment tribunal not to have erred in law in holding that a redundancy applied solely to Class 1 drivers as opposed to across Class 1 and Class 3 drivers was not unfair where the interchangeability between classes did not work both ways. Whilst the Class 1 drivers could drive four wheel vehicles as well as articulated vehicles, the Class 3 drivers could not drive articulated vehicles. As the EAT put it, that distinction made it impossible to hold that Class 3 drivers were in similar positions to the Class 1 drivers.

The EAT drew a distinction between the facts of the present case and those in *Heathcote v North Western Electricity Board*[16] and *Thomas & Betts Manufacturing Co Ltd v Harding*[17] which were both concerned with employment of an unskilled nature where a high degree of flexibility could be expected.

Moreover, tribunals have looked closely at the actual work being done and its interchangeability with other work, rather than relying purely on formal job titles or job grading schemes. For example, in *Simpson v Roneo Ltd*[18] an inspector in one department was found not to be interchangeable with 'inspectors' in other departments. And in *Gargrave v Hotel and Catering Industry Training Board*[19] the grade 10 category was found to be too wide to group employees together for the purpose of comparing employees in similar positions. In both cases, the net result of the finding of a dissimilarity of position was to reduce the unit of selection to the department.[20]

15 [1981] IRLR 483, EAT.
16 [1974] IRLR 34, IT.The tribunal did also comment in *Heathcote*'s case: 'If there are specialists in one department they could no doubt form a group of persons from whom the selection should be made without recourse to other departments or sections'.
17 [1978] IRLR 213, EAT.
18 [1972] IRLR 5.
19 [1974] IRLR 85, NIRC.
20 Cf *Wailes Dove Bitumastic Ltd v Woolcocks* [1977] ICR 817, EAT.

3. AN 'UNREASONABLE' DISMISSAL FOR REDUNDANCY UNDER s 98(4)

In addition to s 105, an employee may claim under s 98(4) that a dismissal for redundancy was unfair, ie unreasonable in the circumstances having regard to equity and the substantial merits of the case.

In *Polkey v A E Dayton Services Ltd*[1] a case of redundancy dismissal, Lord Bridge set out a general guideline that in cases of redundancy, the employer will not normally act reasonably unless he warns and consults any employees affected or their representative, adopts a fair basis on which to select for redundancy and takes such steps as may be reasonable to avoid or minimise redundancy by redeployment within his own organisation.

In exercising their discretion under s 98(4), employment tribunals have been urged to act as 'industrial juries', taking everything into account subject only to an appeal on a matter of law.

As Roskill LJ commented in *Bessenden Properties Ltd v Corness*:

'It may be hard on employers in the embarrassing situation in which (the employer) found himself in this case to have the matter so largely removed out of their control and left to the discretion of this so-called industrial jury. But once the case falls within (s 98(4)) then the Tribunal is entitled to take everything into account'.[2]

Moreover, at an early stage, the NIRC in *Vokes Ltd v Bear*[3] indicated that the circumstances which an employment tribunal should take into account should not be limited in scope, but should 'embrace all relevant matters that should weigh with a good employer when deciding at a given moment in time whether or not he should dismiss his employee'.

Yet in exercising their discretion to apply s 98(4) tribunals have been placed under two types of related constraints. First, they have been told that they must not judge the employer's decision on the basis of what they would have done had they been the employer. Rather they must apply the standard of the reasonable employer, ... that is to say, they must judge by 'the objective standard of the way in which a reasonable employer in those circumstances in that line of business would have behaved',[4] and they must judge the reasonableness of employers' decisions on the basis

1   [1987] IRLR 503, HL.
2   [1974] IRLR 338, CA.
3   [1973] IRLR 363, NIRC.
4   *BL Cars Ltd v Lewis* [1983] IRLR 58, EAT: *NC Watling & Co Ltd v Richardson* [1978] ICR 1049, [1978] IRLR 255, EAT.

of whether their action fell within the range of reasonable responses of employers generally. A failure to follow *either* direction could be the basis of an appeal from the tribunal on a point of law.[5]

On the other hand they have also been urged that in the field of redundancy dismissals, they must be satisfied that it was reasonable to dismiss *each* of the applicants on the grounds of redundancy. It is not enough to show simply that it was reasonable to dismiss *an* employee; it must be shown that the employer acted reasonably in treating redundancy 'as a sufficient reason for dismissing *the* particular employee' complaining of dismissal.[6] Therefore, if the circumstances of the employer make it inevitable that some employee must be dismissed, it is still necessary to consider the means whereby the applicant was selected to be the employee to be dismissed and the reasonableness of the steps taken by the employer to choose the applicant, rather than some other employee, for dismissal.

Under the residual test of s 98(4), tribunals and appellate courts have developed three main heads under which dismissals for redundancy could be regarded as unreasonable.

(i)   where the employer's method of selection as between comparable employees was unreasonable;
(ii) where the employer failed to adopt a proper procedure of warnings and consultation;
(iii) where the employer failed to make reasonable efforts to look for alternative employment before declaring the employee redundant.

These three heads are so well established that where an employee complains of unfair dismissal by reason of redundancy it is incumbent on employment tribunals to consider each of these three heads in the same way as the *Burchell* test is considered in conduct cases.[7]

In rare cases tribunals have been prepared to include a fourth head:

(iv) the reasonableness of the employer's decision to dismiss for redundancy to determine whether the decision was necessary at that particular time and in those particular circumstances.

Thus in rare cases some redundancies have been held to be unreasonably premature under s 98(4)[8] whereas others have been held to be unwarranted by the prevailing economic conditions.[9]

---

5   *Watling v Richardson* [1978] IRLR 255, EAT: *BL Cars v Lewis* (above).
6   *Williams v Compair Maxam Ltd* [1982] ICR 156, [1982] IRLR 83, EAT.
7   *Langston v Cranfield University* [1998] IRLR 172, EAT.
8   See eg *Costello v United Asphalt Co Ltd* [1975] IRLR 194; *Tomson v Fraser Pearce Ltd* [1975] IRLR 54; *Hammond-Scott v Elizabeth Arden Ltd* [1976] IRLR 166.
9   See eg *Allwood v William Hill (North East)* [1974] IRLR 258.

However, in *Moon v Homeworthy Furniture (Northern) Ltd*[10] the EAT called this line of decisions in question. In *Moon*'s case, the employer had decided to shut down the factory following a series of disputes. The applicant complained that the redundancies were unfair under s 98(4) because the employer's decision to close the factory was unfair. The tribunal was reluctant to apply s 98(4) to challenge the creation of a redundancy. The EAT agreed with this view adding that whilst the employment tribunal can investigate the operating of a redundancy situation including questions such as unfair selection and lack of notice, it has no power under s 98(4) to investigate the reasons for creating redundancy or to challenge the creation of a redundancy on its merits because tribunals might otherwise be used as platforms for the ventilation of industrial disputes.

Whilst the particular facts of the case were those of a factory shutdown in the face of an industrial dispute, the case nevertheless provides a strong indication of the reluctance of the EAT under the rubric of unfair dismissal to explore the possibilities of questioning the exercise of management discretion in deciding the need of the business for redundancy.

If the courts have been reluctant to allow tribunals to question the employer's assessment of the need of the business to declare redundancies, they have accepted that a reasonableness test can be applied to the employer's method of selection, both to the criteria for selection and to the way they have been applied.

i) Unreasonable methods of selection

The question of how a tribunal should decide whether an employer has acted reasonably or unreasonably in selecting one employee rather than another under s 98(4) has seemed to be a particularly troublesome one for the EAT. On the one hand the EAT has accepted that an individual tribunal would not be exercising its function under s 98(4), to act as an industrial jury if it defers entirely to an employer's discretion.[11] Thus on occasions, the EAT has suggested that tribunals should ensure that the criteria used by the employer are reasonable criteria for selection. As the EAT stated in *Compair Maxam*, even

---

10   [1977] ICR 117, [1976] IRLR 298.
11   *Kelly v Upholstery and Cabinet Works (Amesbury) Ltd* [1977] IRLR 91, EAT.

'if the circumstances of the employer make it inevitable that some employee must be dismissed, it is still necessary to consider the means whereby the applicant was selected to be the employee to be dismissed and the reasonableness of the steps taken by the employer to choose the applicant, rather than some other employee, for dismissal.'[12]

And as the Court of Appeal in *British Aerospace plc v Green* concluded:

'The [employment] tribunal must, in short, be satisfied that redundancy selection has been achieved by adopting a fair and reasonable system and applying it fairly and reasonably as between one employee and another; and must judge that question objectively by asking whether the system and its application fall within the range of fairness and reason (regardless of whether they would have chosen to adopt such a system or apply it in that way themselves).'[13]

On the other hand the EAT has long been concerned that the residual test in s 98(4) should not be used by tribunals to apply too strict a test to an employer's decision to select employees for redundancy once the hurdle of s 105 has been successfully overcome. As Lord Justice Waile expressed it in *British Aerospace*:

'Employment law recognises, pragmatically, that an over-minute investigation of the selection process by the tribunal members may run the risk of defeating the purpose which the tribunals were called into being to discharge – namely a swift, informal disposal of disputes arising from redundancy in the workplace. So in general the employer who sets up a system of selection which can reasonably be described as fair and applies it without any overt sign of conduct which mars its fairness will have done all that the law requires of him.'[14]

Indeed, in Scotland the EAT has on more than one occasion suggested that 'where the reason for dismissal is redundancy and that dismissal has survived the tests prescribed in (s 105) it will in most cases be extremely difficult for any tribunal to hold that in dismissing the particular individual, his employers acted unreasonably in the sense prescribed by (s 98(4))'.[15]

---

12   *Williams v Compair Maxam Ltd* [1982] ICR 156, [1982] IRLR 83, EAT.
13   [1995] IRLR 433.
14   Ibid. See too *Buchanan v Tilcon Ltd* [1983] IRLR 417, Ct of Sess.
15   *Atkinson v George Lindsay & Co* [1980] IRLR 196, Ct of Sess; *Jackson v General Accident Fire and Life Assurance Co Ltd* [1976] IRLR 338, EAT. See also *Valor Newhome Ltd v Hampson* [1982] ICR 407, EAT.

Underlying this view in part is the fact that where the parties have selected employees for dismissal in accordance with an agreed procedure, unless the procedure itself is unfair, it is reasonable for the employer to follow that procedure and it would be unreasonable for a tribunal to interpose other procedures than those which were agreed between management and unions.[16]

Furthermore, the judiciary have indicated their awareness in redundancy selection cases that an employee has already received a redundancy payment.[17]

Thus it was not entirely surprising that cases of redundancy selection produced the first formulation of the more general guideline limiting tribunal discretion to intervene in the management decision process. For example, in *Grundy (Teddington) Ltd v Willis*,[18] the idea was first expressed that the tribunal should not decide for itself what management should have done.

Judicial concern that tribunals should not intervene too closely in the selection process was given its most forceful expression in *Vickers Ltd v Smith*[19] where a tribunal considered that it was unreasonable of an employer to insist on choosing one employee to be made redundant when another employee had volunteered for redundancy. In this case the EAT rather over-reacted, expostulating that the tribunal had erred in law for

'failing to appreciate that not only was it necessary to arrive at the conclusion that the decision of the management was wrong, but that it was necessary to go a stage further, if they thought that the management decision was wrong, and to ask themselves the question whether it was so wrong that no sensible or reasonable management could have arrived at the decision at which the management arrived in deciding who should be selected ... for redundancy'.

This standard was borrowed from administrative law and appeared to place upon tribunals a standard of review of managerial decisions to dismiss employees which was identical to the standards placed on the judicial review of administrative decisions.

---

16   *Forman Construction Ltd v Kelly* [1977] IRLR 468, EAT.
17   See eg *O'Hare and Rutherford v Rotaprint Ltd* [1980] ICR 94, [1980] IRLR 47; *British United Shoe Machinery Co Ltd v Clarke* [1978] ICR 70, [1977] IRLR 297, EAT.
18   [1976] ICR 323, [1976] IRLR 118, QBD.
19   [1977] IRLR 11, EAT.

Subsequent cases acknowledged that *Vickers Ltd v Smith* had perhaps gone too far both as a general standard for s 98(4) and as a specific standard for selection for redundancy. It was not long before the standard was adjusted to one more apparently consistent with the private law standard of s 98(4) but one which nevertheless places considerable inhibition upon tribunal discretion.

As the EAT put it in *N C Watling & Co Ltd v Richardson*[20] what the authorities, including *Vickers Ltd v Smith* have decided is that ... the employment tribunal, while using its own collective wisdom, is to apply the standard of the reasonable employer, that is to say the fairness or unfairness of the dismissal is to be judged not by the hunch of the particular [Employment] Tribunal, which (though rarely) may be whimsical or eccentric, but by the objective standard of the way in which a reasonable employer in those circumstances, in that line of work would have behaved'. It has to be recognised that there are circumstances where more than one course of action may be reasonable.

'In the case of redundancy, ... where selection of one or two employees to be dismissed for redundancy from a large number is in issue, there may well be and often are, cases where equally reasonable fair and sensible employers would take different courses one choosing 'A' another 'B' and another 'C'. In those circumstances for an [Employment] Tribunal to say that it was unfair to select 'A' for dismissal rather than 'B' or 'C' merely because they had been the employers, that is what they would have done, and not the test of what a reasonable employer would have done. In such cases where more than one course of action can be considered reasonable, if an [employment] tribunal equates its view of what itself would have done with what a reasonable employer would have done, it may mean that an employer will be found to have dismissed an employee unfairly although in the circumstances many perfectly good and fair employers would have done as that employer did.'

In setting this standard the EAT was aware that there were limits to which the tribunal's discretion could be curtailed. At a later point in the opinion it added:

'The moral is that none of the phrases used in the authorities, such as did the employer act in a way in which no reasonable employer

20   [1978] ICR 1049, [1978] IRLR 255, EAT.

would have acted? is to be substituted as the test to be applied. The test is and always is, that provided by (s 98(4)). The authorities do no more than try, according to the circumstances to indicate the *standard* to be used by the [Employment] Tribunal in applying (s 98(4)). But every time the starting point for the [Employment] Tribunal is the language of (that provision)'.

Yet the authorities provide more than merely guidelines to tribunal discretion, certain authorities provide constraints which make it an error of law to ignore. Thus, even where an employment tribunal directs itself by the more 'objective' standard of *Watling v Richardson*[1] it can still commit an error of law if it judges an employer's decision on the basis of what it would have done had it been the employer.

In *BL Cars Ltd v Lewis*[2] for example, an employment tribunal was found to have erred in law when it decided that an employee's selection for redundancy was unfair because the employer had given insufficient weight to the employee's length of service. The criteria applied by the employer had consisted of a combination of service, occupation, and skill on apparatus all on equal bases. By insisting on greater points for the criteria of service, the tribunal had in effect asked itself whether it would have made that selection rather than the proper question 'was the selection one which a reasonable employer would have made?'.

The constraints placed on tribunals by the band of reasonable responses test of *Watling v Richardson* and its counterpart limitation in *BL Cars v Lewis* have the effect of requiring the employee to prove that the employer has acted manifestly unreasonably in his or her decision to dismiss the employee for redundancy. For unless it can be shown to a tribunal that the employer's decision has fallen below the lowest acceptable standard of management practice, it is incorrect in law for a tribunal to find an unfair dismissal under s 98(4).

This rather limited test nevertheless appears to leave open two lines of attack for employees. First it still requires that employers show what their criteria for selection were and how they were applied in practice. Secondly, it allows an employment tribunal to determine whether the employer's criteria or their application were manifestly unreasonable.

---

1   [1978] ICR 1049, [1978] IRLR 255, EAT.
2   [1983] IRLR 58, EAT.

(a) Showing the selection criteria

Tribunals are entitled to require that employers clearly show their criteria for selection and who within management took the decision to dismiss. Thus in *Bristol Channel Ship Repairers Ltd v O'Keefe*[3] the EAT stated that a tribunal would expect to be satisfied by an employer's evidence how the employee came to be dismissed, and who and what body, and in what circumstances, took the decision to dismiss him. And in *Cox v Wildt Mellor Bromley Ltd*[4] the EAT reiterated that an employer should be prepared to deal in sufficient detail with the matters summarised in *Bristol Channel* and in outline at least with any general points which a reasonable employer would consider to be important in the circumstance of the case, such as efforts to find him other employment or to assist him. Clearly where an employer fails to come forward with evidence on the basis of selection and an indication of how the criteria were applied in practice, an employment tribunal would be entitled to conclude that he acted unreasonably.[5]

Moreover, where an employer does come forward with some evidence of his criteria for selection and how they were applied, tribunals have on occasion asked management to indicate the factual basis for the criteria they applied. Thus in *Paine and Moore v Grundy (Teddington) Ltd*[6] a case involving attendance records as a criteria, the EAT said:

'In general terms, if employers are going to rely upon what we will describe briefly as an "attendance record criterion" in redundancy cases, we think that it is desirable that they should seek to ascertain the reasons for the absences which made up the attendance record of the particular employees concerned and, for instance, if an employee happens still to be absent at the time that the redundancies have to be put into effect, that they should try to find out when that employee is likely to return to work. We think that this is merely a particular application of the much more general principle of industrial relations that employers should do all that is reasonable to ensure that they have in their possession as full information as is reasonable about their employees and the relevant situation before coming to any decision, for instance, to dismiss on the grounds of redundancy'.

3   [1977] 2 All ER 258, [1978] ICR 691.
4   [1978] ICR 736, [1978] IRLR 157, EAT.
5   These principles also received strong support in *John Brown Engineering Ltd v Brown* [1997] IRLR 90, EAT; and *FDR Ltd v Holloway* [1995] IRLR 400, EAT.
6   [1981] IRLR 267, EAT. See too cases n 16.

On the other hand, tribunals have also been told that they must not impose too high a standard of proof upon employers to show that their criteria have been met. Thus in *Buchanan v Tilcon Ltd*[7] an employment tribunal insisted that the employers prove the accuracy of the information upon which they acted by providing direct evidence of the employee's relatively high absence rate. The Court of Session reversed this decision pointing out that the employee's only complaint was that of unfair selection for redundancy.

Moreover, in *British Aerospace plc v Green*,[8] a large-scale redundancy of 530 employees selected from 7,000 workers, the Court of Appeal was unwilling to allow discovery of documents relating to retained employees for the purpose of determining whether there were any faults in selection. The Court found that the EAT had erred in ordering discovery because the applicants had failed to specify any fault or formulate an issue upon which to base the discovery. The Court was influenced by the sheer size of the 'mass redundancy'. On the other hand, in *FDR Ltd v Holloway*,[9] the EAT was prepared to allow a discovery order of information of the eight employees not selected for redundancy, where there was an issue raised about the fairness of the selection because of the shorter service and poor record of one of the retained employees. Moreover, in *John Brown Engineering Ltd v Brown*[10] the EAT indicated that a fair redundancy selection process requires that individual employees have the opportunity to contest selection, either by themselves or through their trade union, and an employer's decision to withhold all markings may result in an unfair selection for redundancy. In *King v Eaton Ltd (No 2)*[11] the Court of Session acknowledged in obiter that in an appropriate case an employment tribunal can enquire into the markings and assessment of those selected for redundancy, whether at the stage of enquiry into merits or at the stage of remedy and *Polkey* reduction.

Lord Emslie, the Lord President stated:

'In the event the appellant, apart from throwing out the suggestion that he might have been victimised because of dislike, merely expressed his concern that others, with even less seniority than he and employed in the same work (labouring) had been kept on. In this

7   [1983] IRLR 417, Ct of Sess.
8   [1995] IRLR 433, CA.
9   [1995] IRLR 400, EAT. (In *King v Eaton Ltd* (below) the Court of Session doubted the correctness of this decision.)
10   [1997] IRLR 90, EAT.
11   [1998] IRLR 686, Ct of Sess.

situation where no other complaints were made by the appellant all that the respondents had to do was to prove that their method of selection was fair in general terms and that it had been applied reasonably in the case of the appellant by the senior official responsible for taking the decision. As was pointed out by Phillips J in *Cox v Wildt Mellor Bromley Ltd* [1978] IRLR 157 it is quite sufficient for an employer in a case such as this to call witnesses of reasonable seniority to explain the circumstances in which the dismissal of an employee came about and it was not necessary to dot every "i" and to cross every "t" or to anticipate every possible complaint which might be made.'[12]

(b)   Unreasonable criteria

Where the employer's criteria are manifestly unreasonable, tribunals have a discretion to find a dismissal for redundancy unfair on that ground alone. For they can justify their decision on the basis that the employer's criteria were outside the range of criteria adopted by reasonable employers. For example, in *N C Watling & Co Ltd v Richardson*[13] the employer, an electrical contractor, had a largely unrestricted freedom of who among the electricians to retain and who to let go when contracts expired. Nevertheless where the employer chose an employee of only a half day's work over another employee of more than 10 months' service claiming that the former was more suitable for deployment, the tribunal was entitled to decide that the employer's basis for selection was unreasonable. And in *Greig v Sir Alfred McAlpine & Son (Northern) Ltd* an employment tribunal found a dismissal unfair because of a failure by the company to show that it used an objective system of assessment in selection. The method of selection including service, performance, and attendance was not made on the basis of company productivity records and the chargehand who applied the criteria testified that he had relied solely on management's skill and judgment.[14]

This principle was endorsed in *Williams v Compair Maxam Ltd*[15] in which an employment tribunal had found it reasonable for the employer to select on the basis of one manager's view of which employees it would be

12   Ibid at 418. See too *Clyde Pipeworks Ltd v Foster* [1978] IRLR 313, EAT.
13   [1978] ICR 1049, [1978] IRLR 255, EAT.
14   [1979] IRLR 372, IT.
15   [1982] ICR 156, [1982] IRLR 83, EAT.

best to retain in the interests of the company in the long run. The EAT overturned the tribunal's decision stating:

'The so-called criteria in this case lack any real objective element; the retention of those who, in the opinion of the managers concerned, would be able to keep the company viable. Such a criterion is entirely subjective and, as Mr Hennessy in his evidence accepted, was applied subjectively. The purpose of having, so far as possible, objective criteria is to ensure that redundancy is not used as a pretext for getting rid of employees who some manager wishes to get rid of for quite other reasons, eg for union activities or by reason of personal dislike ... The danger of purely subjective selection is illustrated in this very case. It was common ground that the relations between Mr Hennessy and one of the applicants, Mr H. Williams, were not good. Mr Hennessy accepted in evidence that he did not care for Mr H. Williams and thought him a bit belligerent. They did not "pass the time of day". Except in cases where the criteria can be applied automatically (eg last in, first out), in any selection for redundancy elements of personal judgment are bound to be required thereby involving the risk of judgment being clouded by personal animosity. Unless some objective criteria are included, it is impossible to demonstrate to an employee like Mr H. Williams who is not on good terms with the person making the selection that the choice was not determined by personal likes and dislikes alone: we would also have thought it was extremely difficult for an [Employment] Tribunal to be satisfied on the point.

The majority of the [Employment] Tribunal expressed surprise at the lack of established criteria for selection, but said that it was "a considerable factor" in their decision that even if criteria had been laid down the same result *might* have applied. This passage is the one which gives rise to doubt whether the majority did not misdirect itself in law. The [Employment] Tribunal had to be satisfied that the applicants before them had been fairly selected: mere speculation as to whether they would have been selected had consultation taken place and criteria been agreed cannot constitute grounds sufficient to "satisfy" the [Employment] Tribunal as required by s 98(4)'.

The EAT then recommended as a matter of good industrial relations practice that whether or not an agreement as to the criteria to be adopted has been negotiated with the union, the employer will seek to establish criteria for selection which so far as possible do not depend solely upon the opinion of the person making the selection but can be objectively checked against such things as attendance record, efficiency at the job, experience, or length of service. It also recommended that the employer should seek to ensure that the selection is made fairly in accordance with these criteria and consider any representations the union has to make as to such selection.

Of course, the recommendations of *Compair Maxam*[16] are themselves only guidelines to tribunal discretion. The evaluation of criteria for selection will be left to the discretion of the tribunal .The extent to which they apply in a given case will depend upon the circumstances. For example in a case where management simply follow criteria established in an agreed redundancy procedure, the *Compair Maxam* guideline may not be appropriate.[17]

Further it is clearly the case that purely objective criteria such as 'last in, first out' are not always required.[18] In the exercise of their discretion under s 98(4), tribunals have on occasion approved criteria of a subjective kind or a mixed system with objective and subjective factors.[19]

Nevertheless, the tribunals do have discretion should they choose to exercise it, to apply a reasonable employer test to the criteria for selection and their application. This discretion has been exercised inter alia in cases concerning the scope of the unit of selection chosen by the employer.[20] In *Thomas & Betts Manufacturing Co Ltd v Harding*,[1] the EAT rejected the employer's argument that where a redundancy situation occurs in one section of a business, the employer when making his selection ought to consider only that section in which redundancies have been established and ought not to look to see whether a place can be found for the redundant employee in some other section of the business. There was no *rule of law*, said the EAT, which limits the area where an industrial tribunal may look or says where a reasonable employer ought reasonably to have looked. This

---

16   [1982] ICR 156, [1982] IRLR 83, EAT.
17   See eg *Mehmi v Sterling Metals Ltd* PA/501/83.
18   See eg *Corning Ltd v Stubbs* (1981) EAT 569/80 'we do not think that the decision in *Bessenden Properties Ltd v Corness* establishes the proposition that in all circumstances without exception, length of service must be one of the criteria by which the selection for redundancy is judged'. See too *Rolls-Royce Motors Ltd v Dewhurst* [1985] IRLR 184, EAT.
19   See eg *Cruickshank v Hobbs* [1977] ICR 725, EAT.
20   See eg *Thomas & Betts Manufacturing Co Ltd v Harding* [1980] IRLR 255, CA; *Calvert v Allisons (Gravel Pits) Ltd* [1975] IRLR 71.
1   [1978] IRLR 213, EAT. But see *Barratt Construction Ltd v Dalrymple* [1984] IRLR 385, EAT; *Babar Indian Restaurant v Rawat* [1985] IRLR 57, EAT.

was approved by the Court of Appeal, which said that s 105 does not operate to limit s 98(4), so that it could not be said that selection must be limited to employees doing the same kind of work or in positions similar to that of the employee claiming compensation.[2]

ii) Reasonable procedure and unfair redundancy: warnings and consultation

In addition to asking whether management acted reasonably in selecting an employee for redundancy, an employment tribunal will also ascertain whether the procedure used by the employer was that of a reasonable employer in the circumstances. The importance of procedural steps in redundancy cases was emphasised in the House of Lords in *Polkey v A E Dayton Services Ltd*.[3] Lord Bridge stated that 'in cases of redundancy the employer will not normally act reasonably unless he warns and consults any employees affected or their representative'.

The Code of Practice quite specifically mentions warnings and consultation as measures that management should take if redundancy becomes necessary.

Moreover, the EAT has stressed the importance of warning and consultation to explore the possibilities of avoiding the redundancy decision in the case of the individual employee. As the EAT put it in *Grundy (Teddington) Ltd v Plummer*:[4]

'In the particular sphere of redundancy, good industrial practice in the ordinary case requires consultation with the redundant employee so that the employer may find out whether the needs of the business can be met in some other way than by dismissal and, if not, what other step the employer can take to ameliorate the blow to the employee'.

Further, in *Williams v Compair Maxam Ltd*[5] the EAT indicated that where the employer recognises an independent union there are certain

---

2   [1980] IRLR 255, CA; but see *Green v A & I Fraser (Wholesale Fish Merchants) Ltd* [1985] IRLR 55, EAT; *Powers and Villiers v A Clarke & Co (Smethwick) Ltd* [1981] IRLR 483, EAT.
3   [1987] IRLR 503, HL.
4   [1983] ICR 367, [1983] IRLR 98, EAT.
5   [1982] ICR 156, [1982] IRLR 83, EAT.

principles of good industrial practice which reasonable employers will follow, eg:

'1. The employer will seek to give as much warning as possible of impending redundancies so as to enable the union and employees who may be affected to take early steps to inform themselves of the relevant facts, consider possible alternative solutions and, if necessary, find alternative employment in the undertaking or elsewhere.

2. The employer will consult the union as to the best means by which the desired management result can be achieved fairly and with as little hardship to the employees as possible. In particular, the employer will seek to agree with the union the criteria to be applied in selecting the employees to be made redundant. When a selection has been made, the employer will consider with the union whether the selection has been made in accordance with those criteria ...'.

This principle must now be extended to apply to other employee representatives elected for the purpose of consultation under s 188 of TULRCA 1992. In *Compair Maxam* these principles were put forward to clarify the basis upon which an employment tribunal could be found to be making a legally perverse decision.[6] As such, they were meant to apply only to 'exceptional cases' where dismissals are carried out in blatant contravention of the standards of fair treatment.[7]

Both the recommendations of the Code of Practice and the guidelines of the EAT are clearly not rules of law in the sense that a failure by an employer to meet such procedural standards will invariably lead to a finding of unfair dismissal. Nevertheless the Code of Practice *must* be taken into account where relevant. And the guidelines of the EAT *may* be applied by tribunals as long as they take into account all the relevant circumstances of the case.[8] More importantly, since 1987, the employment tribunals must have regard to the stricter tests proposed by Lord Bridge and Lord Mackay in *Polkey*.[9] Lord Mackay stated that a failure to consult or warn could be reasonable only in the exceptional case where 'the procedural steps normally appropriate would have been futile, could not have altered the

---

6   Ibid.
7   See also *Freud v Bentalls Ltd* [1982] IRLR 443, EAT; *Petter v George Glenton Ltd* (1983) EAT 276/83.
8   *Grundy (Teddington) Ltd v Plummer and Salt* [1983] ICR 367, [1983] IRLR 98, EAT.
9   [1987] IRLR 503, HL.

decision to dismiss and therefore could be dispensed with.' Or, as Lord Bridge put it, 'If the employer would reasonably have concluded in the light of the circumstances known to him at the time of dismissal that consultation or warning would be utterly useless.'[10]

Hence, the principles in the *Compair Maxam* case continue to provide 'guidelines' to tribunal discretion by suggesting to tribunals what the reasonable employer will seek to do if circumstances permit. The extent to which any one of them applies in a given case depends upon the circumstances of that case. An employment tribunal may take them into account as long as it also looks at the circumstances of the case in the round and doesn't assume that an employer's failure to adopt one or more of the recommended practices necessarily makes a dismissal unfair.[11] Thus where a small firm is involved and there is no recognised trade union, it has been held not to be appropriate to apply the five principles of *Compair Maxam*.[12]

Consequently, it is now well established that an employment tribunal can in certain circumstances make a finding of unfair dismissal even where the employer's unreasonableness consists mainly or even entirely of a failure of procedure.[13]

One important reason for this interpretation of s 98(4) is that it is accepted that there is a point when a failure of procedure can amount to a failure of substance. For example, as the EAT put it in *Grundy (Teddington) Ltd v Plummer*,[14]

'if as a result of proper consultation different criteria would have been adopted or had been applied differently, a different employee might have been selected. Therefore, although in one sense proper consultation is a "procedural" matter, it has a direct bearing on the substantive decision to select that particular employee. It is not necessarily enough for an employer to say "I adopted reasonable criteria" if, after consulting as a reasonable employer would have done, different criteria leading to a different result might have been adopted. Similarly, the failure to look for alternative employment has

10   See too *Duffy v Yeomans & Partners* [1994] IRLR 642, CA.
11   *Grundy (Teddington) Ltd v Plummer and Salt* [1983] ICR 367, [1983] IRLR 98, EAT; *Robinson v Carrickfergus Borough Council* [1983] IRLR 122, NICA.
12   See eg *A Simpson & Son (Motors) v Reid and Findlater* [1983] IRLR 401, EAT: *Meikle v McPhail (Charleston Arms)* [1983] IRLR 351, EAT; *Gray v Shetland Norse Preserving Co Ltd* [1985] IRLR 53, EAT.
13   Ibid, see too *W Devis & Sons Ltd v Atkins* [1977] AC 931, [1977] ICR 662, HL.
14   [1983] ICR 367, [1983] IRLR 98, EAT.

a direct bearing on the reasonableness of the decision to dismiss: if alternative employment had been found for the complainant, he would not have been dismissed'.

Indeed, in an extreme case, it might be legally perverse for an employment tribunal to find a dismissal fair where the employer has failed to follow all the canons of good industrial practice. Thus in *Williams v Compair Maxam Ltd*[15] itself the EAT reversed an employment tribunal which had found a dismissal not unfair despite the employer's failure to consult the union on the criteria for selection of employees for redundancy and to look for alternative employment for the employees made redundant. And in *Freud v Bentalls Ltd*[16] the EAT decided that an employment tribunal's decision was legally perverse where it found a dismissal for redundancy fair and the employers had intentionally omitted to consult the employee and failed to give any good reason justifying this omission. The company simply indicated that it was company policy not to consult employees at managerial level over redundancy.

Yet since *Polkey*[17] the test is not whether a procedural omission is in fact substantially unreasonable. Tribunals are guided by the rather stricter test suggested by Lord Bridge and Lord Mackay to the effect that it will normally be viewed as unreasonable to omit a warning or consultation unless it could be shown that such an omission was futile or utterly useless at the time of dismissal.[18]

iii) Consultation with trade unions

A further effect of *Compair Maxam* as reinforced by *Grundy (Teddington) Ltd* and later cases has been to make it plain that not only consultation with the individual employee but also consultation with recognised trade unions could and should be regarded by tribunals as part of the responsibilities of 'reasonable employers'.

The Code of Practice specifically recommends that the employer should consult with employees and their representatives and recommends that employers should ensure that no announcement has been made before the employees and their representatives and trade unions have been

---

15 [1982] ICR 156, [1982] IRLR 83, EAT.
16 [1982] IRLR 443, EAT, see also *Pepper v George Glenton Ltd* (1983) EAT 276/83.
17 [1987] IRLR 503, HL.
18 See too *Duffy v Yeomans & Partners* [1994] IRLR 642, CA.

informed. *Compair Maxam* established as a 'guideline' to good industrial practice that consultation with trade unions is an integral part of the procedural duty of employers in redundancy cases where employees are represented by a recognised independent trade union and this obligation will today extend to elected employee representatives.[19] The extent to which the guidelines in *Compair Maxam* apply in any given case must of course depend upon the circumstances.[20]

Thus in *Mugford v Midland Bank plc*[1] the EAT, with Clark J as Chairman, stated that having regard to the authorities,

(1) where no consultation about redundancy has taken place with either the trade union or the employee the dismissal will normally be unfair, unless the employment tribunal finds that a reasonable employer would have concluded that consultation would be an utterly futile exercise in the particular circumstances of the case ...

(2) it will be a question of fact and degree for the employment tribunal to consider whether consultation with the individual and/or his union was so inadequate as to render the dismissal unfair.

Other cases have made it clear that it can be unreasonable not to consult the individual employee and consultation with the representative alone may not be enough.[2]

In considering the adequacy of the employer's consultation, in *King v Eaton Ltd*[3] the Court of Session indicated that such consultations whether with individuals or representatives must be fair or proper consistent with the definition set out in *R v British Coal Corpn, ex p Price*.

In that case it was stated that

'fair consultation means
(a) consultation when the proposals are at a formative stage;
(b) adequate information on which to respond;
(c) adequate time in which to respond; and
(d) conscientious consideration by an authority of a response to consultation.'

19   This is in addition to TULRCA 1992, s 188 which also applies on its own terms.
20   *Grundy (Teddington) Ltd v Plummer and Salt* [1983] ICR 367, [1983] IRLR 98, EAT; *Robinson v Carrickfergus Borough Council* [1983] IRLR 122, NICA.
1   [1997] IRLR 208, EAT.
2   *Rolls Royce Motor Cars Ltd v Price* [1993] IRLR 203, EAT; cf *Walls Meat Co Ltd v Selby* [1989] ICR 601, CA. *Huddersfield Parcells v Sykes* [1981] IRLR 115, EAT; *Dyke v Hereford and Worcester County Council* [1989] ICR 800, EAT.
3   [1996] IRLR 199, Ct of Sess; see too *Rolls Royce Motor Cars Ltd v Price* [1993] IRLR 203, EAT (on 'full' consultation).

iv) A reasonable investigation of alternative employment

Closely related to this line of case has been a group of cases that have indicated that as a matter of good industrial practice[4] management should make *reasonable* efforts to look for alternative employment for employees before making them redundant. At an early stage the NIRC in *Vokes Ltd v Bear*[5] had found that a redundancy was unfair on the grounds that the employer had failed to investigate whether there were job vacancies within the group which might have been offered to the employee as an alternative to being made redundant. As the NIRC put it:

'The employer had not yet done that which in all fairness and reason he should do, namely to make the obvious attempt to see if Mr Bear could be placed somewhere else in this large group'.

In *Modern Injection Moulds Ltd v Price*[6] the EAT, per Mr Justice Phillips, adopted the statement of the law in *Vokes Ltd v Bear*, adding to it the following:

'In our judgment it can be said that in as much as there is this obligation on the part of the employers to try to find suitable alternative employment within the firm, it must follow that if they are in a position pursuant to their obligation to make an offer to the employee of suitable alternative employment they must give him sufficient information on the basis of which the employee can make a realistic decision whether to take the new job'.

Quite clearly neither *Vokes Ltd v Bear* nor *Modern Injection Moulds* stood for the proposition that there was a duty to find alternative employment.[7] The employer's duty under s 98(4) was to *try to find* alternative employment.

Thus, if the employer makes no effort at all to ascertain the possibility of alternative employment, that ground alone could be the basis for a tribunal decision that he acted unfairly in dismissing that employee for redundancy.[8] Assuming, however, that employers have made some effort,

---

4   See eg *Williams v Compair Maxam Ltd* [1982] ICR 156, [1982] IRLR 83, EAT.
5   [1974] ICR 1, [1973] IRLR 363, NIRC.
6   [1976] ICR 370, [1976] IRLR 172, EAT.
7   *Brush Electrical Machines Ltd v Guest* (1976) EAT 382/76.
8   Cf *Thomas & Betts Manufacturing Co Ltd v Harding* [1980] IRLR 255, CA. This, of course, is subject to some consideration of whether the procedural defect affected the eventual outcome.

by what standard should their efforts be measured? In *Vokes Ltd v Bear* the suggested standard was 'to take all reasonable steps'. In *Modern Injection Moulds* it was 'to do their best to find him suitable alternative employment'.

The EAT initially was so concerned to establish that tribunals should not substitute their judgment for that of the employer in looking at the employer's efforts to seek alternative employment, that they formulated rather restrictive criteria for assessing the employers efforts under this head.[9] However, in *British United Shoe Machinery Co Ltd v Clarke*[10] they adopted a criterion quite close to that set out in *Vokes Ltd v Bear*: 'employers when dismissing an employee for redundancy ought to make reasonable efforts to find him other employment'. Yet the EAT in *British United Shoe* signalled that there would be two types of qualification to tribunal discretion. The first was a warning that, as the EAT put it,

> 'It is perhaps worth stressing that in determining whether the employer has discharged the obligation the standard to be applied is that of the reasonable employer and that [employment] tribunals ought to avoid demanding some unreal or Elysian standard'.

In *Barratt Construction Ltd v Dalrymple*,[11] the EAT emphasised this point by overturning an employment tribunal decision that a dismissal was unfair because the employer had only investigated the possibilities of similar alternative employment in the company and not considered the possibility of offering employment in a subordinate post to the employee. The EAT considered that it was not open to an employment tribunal to speculate as to what *further* steps the employer ought to take and to draw an inference adverse to the employer because he had failed to take them. Similarly, in *MDH Ltd v Sussex*[12] the EAT held that a tribunal had erred in law when it found a redundancy dismissal unfair because the employer had failed to look for alternative job opportunities beyond his own company in other companies in the same corporate group.

These cases are a reminder of the way the range of reasonable responses test places limits on the scope of the tribunals determination of reasonableness. Nevertheless, a complete failure of investigation of the

---

9   See eg *Quinton Hazell Ltd v Earl* [1976] IRLR 296, EAT; *George M Whiley Ltd v Anderson* [1977] ICR 167, [1976] IRLR 293, EAT.
10   [1978] ICR 70, [1977] IRLR 297, EAT.
11   [1984] IRLR 385, EAT.
12   [1986] IRLR 123, EAT.

possibilities of alternative employment will be difficult to justify as reasonable without meeting the 'futility' test of *Polkey*.[13] Similarly, there may be a higher standard required of the reasonable employer to offer *long standing* employees an opportunity of alternative employment which arises, even during the notice period.[14] In *Thomas & Betts Manufacturing Co Ltd v Harding*[15] the Court of Appeal endorsed the wide discretion of tribunals by rejecting the argument that the tribunal's investigation of possibilities for alternative employment must be limited to the 'section of the business' in which the individual was employed. The Court also indicated that tribunals should have the discretion to take into account the possibility that it might be reasonable for the employer to 'bump', ie dismiss, another employee to provide alternative employment for the redundant employee. Yet the Court's statements on the latter issue was made in a case where the employer had made no effort to justify his failure to offer alternative employment.

Where the employer has some justification for the decision not to displace another employee, an employment tribunal might not be allowed the discretion to find the dismissal for redundancy unfair on the ground that the effort was insufficient.[16] And in *Avonmouth Construction Co Ltd v Shipway*[17] the EAT stated that implicit in the duty to look for alternative employment in a redundancy situation is the responsibility on the employer to give careful consideration to the possibility of offering the employee another job, including a possible demotion. Yet this was a case where another, subordinate, job was actually available and the employer's reasons for not offering it to the employee were not accepted as reasonable by the tribunal.[18]

13 [1987] IRLR 503, HL.
14 *Stacy v Babcock Power Ltd (Construction Division)* [1986] IRLR 3, EAT.
15 [1980] IRLR 255, CA. But see *Green v A & I Fraser (Wholesale Fish Merchants) Ltd* [1985] IRLR 55, EAT.
16 See eg *Huddersfield Parcels Ltd v Sykes* [1981] IRLR 115, EAT, which drew attention to the difficulties to the employer of adopting the bumping practice. See also *Tocher v General Motors Scotland Ltd* [1981] IRLR 55, EAT; *Bowater Containers Ltd v McCormack* [1980] IRLR 50, EAT, which indicated that an employer could not be expected to offer alternative work where it would contravene an agreement with the union.
17 [1979] IRLR 14, EAT.
18 See *Gwent County Council v Lane* [1978] ICR 357, [1977] IRLR 337, EAT, on the lesser obligations of the employer in a case of an employee on a temporary short term contract. However, an employee may now be able to invoke the new Directive on Fixed Term Work 1999/70 with its basic principle of non-discrimination against fixed-term workers.

In *Barratt Construction Ltd v Dalrymple*[19] the EAT stressed the two-sided nature of the reasonableness test. After stating that a reasonable employer will not make an employee redundant if he can employ him elsewhere even in another capacity, it added in obiter:

> 'Without laying down any hard and fast rule we are inclined to think that where an employee at senior management level who is being made redundant is prepared to accept a subordinate position he ought, in fairness, to make this clear at an early stage so as to give his employer an opportunity to see if this is a feasible solution'.[20]

19   [1984] IRLR 385, EAT.
20   Ibid at 386.

Chapter 9.
Some other substantial reason

Where the employer claims that his reason for dismissal is 'some other substantial reason' of a kind such as to justify the dismissal of an employee holding the position which the employee held, there are in principle two separate tests under ERA 1996, s 98(1)(b). First, the employer must show that the reason is potentially valid – that is a reason that can justify a dismissal.[1] Second, if employers succeed in meeting this test they then have to go on and show that their decision to dismiss for that reason was reasonable in the circumstances in accordance with s 98(4). In principle under s 98(1)(b), the preliminary test of showing a potentially valid reason has an added degree of difficulty; employers must show that their reason falls within a category which employment tribunals view as 'substantial'.[2]

Yet, this category of 'some other substantial reason' is also meant to be a general residual category of reasons for dismissal and not one restricted to the class of reasons otherwise listed in s 98(4).[3] At an early stage the NIRC indicated that there were 'not only legal but also practical objections to a narrow construction of "some other reason"'.[4]

1 See *Mercia Rubber Mouldings Ltd v Lingwood* [1974] ICR 256, [1974] IRLR 82, NIRC.
2 See eg the following cases where it was held not to be 'some other substantial reason'; *Haspell v Rostron & Johnson Ltd* [1976] IRLR 50 (where an employee gave advance warning of intention to resign); *Siburn v Modern Telephones Ltd* [1976] IRLR 81 (a non-economic salesman); *Blackman v Post Office* [1974] ICR 151, [1974] IRLR 46 (a failure to pass an aptitude test).
3 *RS Components Ltd v Irwin* [1973] ICR 535, [1974] 1 All ER 41, NIRC.
4 Ibid.

'Parliament may well have intended to set out in [s 98(4)] the common reasons for a dismissal, but can hardly have hoped to produce an exhaustive catalogue of all the circumstances in which an employer would be justified in terminating the services of an employee'.[5]

The NIRC also added however that

'It ought not as a matter of good industrial relations and common fairness to be considered too widely against any employee'.

In subsequent cases, this latter injunction has not always been heeded. Instead s 98(1)(b) has been used by employment tribunals, the EAT and the Court of Appeal to carve out new categories of justifiable dismissal, inter alia in the following situations:

(1) where the employee refuses to agree to a repudiatory change in terms and conditions or a new contract on different terms after a reorganisation of the business;

(2) where the employer has failed to meet the requirements of one of the other statutory reasons for dismissal but is regarded as entitled to qualify under s 82(1)(b);

(3) where the employer has felt compelled to dismiss the employee despite a lack of fault;

(4) conduct which causes conflict between employees at the work place;

(5) the termination of temporary and short term employments;[6]

(6) the personal characteristics[7] of employees.

This loosening of the potential categories of some other substantial reason has not been accompanied by a corresponding tightening of the standard of reasonableness under s 98(4). In the event, employment tribunals, the EAT and the Court of Appeal have created a method of undermining the original concept of the statutory right to complain of unfair dismissal.

I. A REFUSAL TO ACCEPT A CHANGE IN CONTRACTUAL TERMS OR A NEW CONTRACT WITH CHANGED TERMS FOLLOWING UPON A REORGANISATION

One of the most significant developments under s 98(1)(b) has been the inclusion of cases where an employer unilaterally insists on a change in an

5   Ibid.
6   This category is discussed in Chapter 14 dealing with fixed-term contracts.
7   *Saunders v Scottish National Camps Association* [1980] IRLR 174, EAT.

employee's existing contractual terms and conditions following upon a reorganisation of the business. In such a case, as we have seen, the employer would be regarded as repudiating the contract and the employee would have a remedy for wrongful dismissal at common law[8] as well as a case of constructive dismissal.[9] Nevertheless, such cases have been regarded as potentially valid dismissals under s 98(1)(b), to be tested under s 98(4) as dismissals for some other substantial reason.[10]

In a similar but related development, cases where an employer has reorganised a business using the technique of dismissing employees with proper notice and offering contracts on new terms have also been swept into s 98(1)(b) where such dismissals fall short of redundancy under s 98(2)(c). In such cases the changes may involve changes in hours or wages but since there is no reduction in the employer's need for a number of employees or changes in the kind of work in the meaning of ERA, s 139(1),[11] the dismissal does not qualify as a redundancy. Nevertheless since *Gorman v London Computer Training Centre Ltd*[12] the EAT has been prepared to countenance such dismissals under s 98(1)(b). This section was first used as a receptacle category for reorganisations when the NIRC in *RS Components Ltd v Irwin*[13] accepted the possibility that a dismissal for a refusal to accept a unilateral variation in a contractual condition which restricted an employee from acting in competition could count as 'some other substantial reason'. In that case the NIRC said:

'it is not difficult to imagine a case where it would be essential for a company embarking eg on a new technical process, to invite existing employees to agree to some reasonable restriction on their use of the knowledge they acquire of the new technique; and where it would

---

8   See eg *Gunton v Richmond-upon-Thames London Borough Council* [1981] Ch 448, [1980] ICR 755, CA.
9   See Chapter 3.
10   See eg *Ellis v Brighton Co-operative Society* [1976] IRLR 419, EAT; *Greenaway Harrison Ltd v Wiles* [1994] IRLR 380, EAT.
11   See eg *Robinson v British Island Airways Ltd* [1978] ICR 304, [1977] IRLR 477; *Wilson v Underhill House School Ltd* [1977] IRLR 475, EAT.
12   [1978] ICR 394, [1978] IRLR 22, EAT.
13   [1974] 1 All ER 41, [1973] ICR 535. For other 'working in competition' cases classified as 'some other substantial reason', see *Foot v Eastern Counties Timber Co Ltd* [1972] IRLR 83; *McCullough v Industrial Cleaners Ltd* (1972) IT 12933/ 72; but see also *Harris & Russell Ltd v Slingsby* [1973] 3 All ER 31, [1973] ICR 454; *Cox Denholm Ltd v Stevenson* (1980) EAT 1243/80.

be essential for the company to terminate, by due notice, the services of an employee who was unwilling to accept such a restriction'.

In subsequent cases the NIRC was prepared to allow tribunals to extend the category to cases of reorganisation involving changes in hours of work, changes in wages, residence, job content and fringe benefits, though during the same period some industrial tribunals had doubts about the reasonableness of repudiating existing contracts.

The EAT first gave its unreserved support to the notion that an employer's repudiatory insistence upon a change in contractual terms could under certain circumstances qualify as 'some other substantial reason' for dismissal under s 98(1)(b) in its decision in *Ellis v Brighton Co-operative Society Ltd.*[14] In that case a reorganisation of the dairy business which had been agreed with the trade union involved a longer working week for Mr Ellis, a foreman. Instead of a basic work week of 48 hours he was required to work an average of 58 hours as well as to assume more onerous duties. Contractually he had no obligation to go along with the new duties because, as a non-member of the trade union, he was not bound by the change. Nevertheless, the EAT considered that his refusal amounted to grounds for dismissal for 'some other substantial reason' and that the employers had acted reasonably in accepting the view that no exception could be made.

Although in *Ellis* the EAT endorsed the proposition that a refusal to agree to a contractually repudiatory change may amount to a good reason for dismissal, it somewhat misleadingly appeared to suggest there might be certain finite limits to the extent to which an employer could impose a change in contractual terms as a result of a reorganisation.

Thus, in *Ellis*, the tribunal found that the reorganisation was prompted by business necessity. Indeed as the EAT remarked, the reorganisation if not done 'would bring the whole business to a standstill'. This seemed to imply that business necessity would be a strict requirement for a dismissal in the course of a reorganisation to be reasonable. Secondly, in *Ellis* the reorganisation was negotiated. The EAT also talked about 'a properly consulted upon reorganisation'. Again this could have been interpreted to be a condition so that a reorganisation unilaterally imposed without negotiation or proper consultation could be regarded as unreasonable in most circumstances. Thirdly, in *Ellis*, the EAT found that the employer had acted reasonably in deciding that the employee could not be an exception to the reorganisation. Was this substantive test of

14   [1976] IRLR 419, EAT.

reasonableness also to be regarded as a more general requirement when the s 98(4) test was applied to s 98(1)(b) cases?[15]

In *Hollister v National Farmers' Union*[16] however the Court of Appeal made it quite clear that the test of some other substantial reason under s 98(4) could not be interpreted quite so schematically. The court established that the test of s 98(1)(b) was to be essentially a test of fact applied by employment tribunals using the language of s 98(4) as a broad guide, rather than being encumbered by presumptions or rules in the form of appellate tribunals' interpretations of that provision. The facts of *Hollister*'s case were somewhat unusual in that the reorganisation of the employee's remuneration arrangements was actually undertaken in response to a request from employees, in this case a group of insurance agents, including Mr Hollister, for a change. The resulting rearrangement of compensation whilst more favourable to Mr Hollister in certain respects was less favourable in terms of the pension scheme. Mr Hollister refused to accept the new terms and was dismissed. The employment tribunal's decision that the dismissal was for some other substantial reason and was fair was reversed by the EAT on the basis that consultation with the employee had been inadequate. The tribunal had considered that consultation was unnecessary because there was no recognised trade union representative. The Court of Appeal found that the EAT's insistence upon consultation 'nearly always before a person was dismissed' was as Lord Denning put it,

> 'going too far and is putting a gloss on the statute. It does not say anything about consultation or negotiation in the statute. It seems to me that consultation is only one of the factors. Negotiation is only one of the factors which has to be taken into account when considering whether a dismissal is fair or unfair. It was putting the case far too high to suggest that as a general rule a failure to follow a fair procedure whether by warnings or by giving an opportunity to be heard before dismissal will result in the ensuing dismissal being found to be unfair'.[17]

---

15 See eg *Singh v British Castors Ltd* (1977) EAT 518/77 the EAT upheld the decision of a Birmingham tribunal that a refusal to join a compulsory pension scheme was not sufficient reason for dismissal where the employer had inadvertently neglected to require membership in the scheme as a condition of employment when the employee was engaged, and where the consequences of the refusal had very little adverse effect on the employer's position.

16 [1979] ICR 542, [1979] IRLR 238, CA.

17 [1979] ICR 542, [1979] IRLR 238, CA.

As mentioned, in *Hollister*'s case the Court of Appeal were concerned to establish that the test of some other substantial reason under s 98(4) was to be a test of fact applied by employment tribunals unencumbered by presumption and rules.

Moreover they were also concerned to establish that employment tribunals should enjoy a wide discretion and that the decisions should not be easily overturned by the appeal tribunal.

Consequently where as in *Hollister*'s case an employment tribunal could satisfy itself that consultation was not 'essential to the decision' it was not open to an appellate tribunal to reverse the employment tribunal.

i) Procedure and reorganisation

However since *Hollister*'s case, the principle of the House of Lords' decision in *Polkey v A E Dayton Services Ltd*[18] reinstates proper procedures such as consultation as a prerequisite for a reasonable dismissal subject to the 'futility' test. For example, where employers imposed a unilateral variation of their employee's contract using an improper procedure, this could in certain circumstances provide the basis for a tribunal to decide within its discretion that they did not act reasonably under s 98(4). Thus a tribunal could decide that it was unreasonable for an employer to stop short at collective consultations with employee representatives without dealing directly with the employee as an individual,[19] or that it was unreasonable for an employer in the course of consultation to omit to make an attempt to demonstrate to the employee the need for the reorganisation and answer the employee's representations, or that it was unreasonable for an employer not to use consultation to investigate whether or not it is possible to make an exception for the employee rather than forcing him into a collective change without any such investigation.[20] Moreover, before excusing a procedural impropriety, an employment tribunal would now have to ask whether it would have been futile to have used a proper procedure[1] rather than simply asking itself whether any particular procedural step if taken would have been likely to make a difference to the result.[2]

---

18   [1987] IRLR 503, [1988] ICR 142, HL.
19   See eg *Martin v Automobile Proprietary Ltd* [1979] IRLR 64, EAT.
20   Ibid.
1   *Polkey v A E Dayton Services Ltd* n 16a above.
2   *Chubb Fire Security Ltd v Harper* [1983] IRLR 311, EAT.

ii) The business need for the reorganisation

At the same time, in *Hollister*'s case the Court of Appeal indicated that in looking at the reasonableness of the decision to dismiss for a refusal to accept a change in contractual terms, the issue posed in the employment tribunal was not so much one of whether the employer's reason for the reorganisation was substantial. Rather, it was more one of asking whether given the employer's reason for the reorganisation it was reasonable for the employer to dismiss the employee for refusing to accept the variation in the contract or to dismiss the employee and offer a contract on changed terms.

Thus, in *Hollister*'s case the Court of Appeal made it clear that the standard implied by *Ellis* that the reorganisation if not done would 'bring the business to a standstill' was not a fixed and immutable requirement. It was enough for the tribunal to find that there was a sound, good business reason for the reorganisation.[3] And indeed, in subsequent cases, the EAT formulated this test of substantiality in increasingly less stringent terms. In *Bowater Containers v McCormack* for example it was enough that the 'reorganisation was beneficial to the running of the company'.[4] In *Banerjee v City and East London Area Health Authority*, moreover, it was sufficient to show that there were 'discernible advantages to the organisation'.[5] Furthermore in *Catamaran Cruisers Ltd v Williams*[6] a reorganisation of terms and conditions was negotiated with trade union representatives by the new owner of a firm taken over after being in financial difficulties. This reorganisation introduced new terms which were less favourable than existing employer federation rates. The tribunal was overturned by the EAT for insisting that the employer could only be acting fairly in introducing less favourable terms if the existence of the business depended upon it. The EAT stressed that there had to be a balancing test in which the potential benefit to the employer was considered as well. In these cases, the Court of Appeal and the Appeal Tribunal appeared to be moving towards a formulation that posited an extremely limited role for employment tribunals to examine the employer's *motivation* for the reorganisation under s 98(4).

This attempt to insist on a limited role for tribunals on the issue has now been reconciled with the wide discretion they have over the question

3   [1979] IRLR 238 at 280.
4   [1980] IRLR 50, EAT.
5   [1979] IRLR 147, EAT.
6   [1994] IRLR 386, EAT.

of reasonableness generally under s 98(4), ie by the application of the range of reasonable employer decisions principle to this type of dismissal. Thus, whilst an employment tribunal cannot say that a dismissal was unfair because the employer's reason for reorganisation was inadequate in the tribunal's view, it has the discretion to decide that a dismissal in the course of certain types of reorganisation may be unreasonable because it was beyond the pale of reasonable employer decisions.[7]

The types of actions in the course of reorganisation that employment tribunals in the exercise of their discretion might find so unreasonable that they fall outside the range of reasonable responses of employers could extend, as mentioned, to procedural mistakes by the employer in particular in the case of a failure to consult. The House of Lords decision in *Polkey v A E Dayton Services Ltd*[8] would suggest that tribunals may impose standards of reasonable procedure even when limited by a 'range of reasonable responses' test on substance. They could also extend to a test of employer's factual basis for their decision to reorganise and to their judgment on the merits of deciding to dismiss employees for the refusal to go along with the reorganisation.

For example, even under s 98(1)(b), in cases where an employer has asserted that dismissal was due to a reorganisation short of redundancy there has been some need to show that there was some factual basis to the assertion. A belief however genuine will not be adequate if it is unaccompanied by some evidence of the grounds for that belief. For example, in *Humphreys and Glasgow Ltd v Brook and Holt*,[9] the EAT upheld an employment tribunal which found that an employer who increased working hours from 37 to 40 a week without an increase in pay and without compensation, arguing that there was a need to cut overheads had failed to show any evidence of the need. There was no indication of pressure from the parent company to reduce costs or improve losses; nor was there any other evidence of pressing financial need.[10] Moreover in *Ladbroke Courage Holidays Ltd v Asten*[11] the EAT indicated that an

---

7   *Richmond Precision Engineering Ltd v Pearce* [1985] IRLR 179, EAT.

8   [1987] IRLR 503, [1988] ICR 142, HL.

9   [1989] IRLIB 369, EAT. See too *Grootcon (UK) Ltd v Keld* [1984] IRLR 302, EAT.

10   If external pressure for change from insurers, creditors or customers, can be shown, there is still a need to show that the employer's response was reasonable. See eg *Dobie v Burns International Security Services UK Ltd* [1984] IRLR 329, CA.

11   [1981] IRLR 59, EAT; see also *Robinson v British Island Airways Ltd* [1978] ICR 304, [1977] IRLR 477 which talked of 'a genuine reorganisation' as a condition to s 98(1)(b).

employer relying on business reorganisation as a reason for dismissal had to produce some evidence of the reorganisation as well as the need for economies. And in *Orr v Vaughan*[12] the EAT was willing to uphold a tribunal that found that an employer had not made reasonable inquiry to ascertain the financial position.

Moreover it has been acknowledged that under s 98(4) a tribunal must have before it sufficient evidence of how the decision to reorganise was made[13] to allow it to draw the conclusion that the decision to reorganise was that of a reasonable employer. Thus where employers make no attempt to bring forward such evidence to justify their position but simply claim that they acted on the recommendation of a body appointed to advise them it could be an error of law for a tribunal to find such a decision reasonable.

Furthermore under s 98(4), it is now also clear that it is necessary for a tribunal to understand the factual basis of the employer's reasons for reorganisation in order to ask the further question: was the change in contractual terms imposed upon the employee reasonable in the sense of being reasonably related to the reasons for the reorganisation? This had been hinted at by Lord Denning in *Hollister*'s case when he suggested that 'it must depend in all the circumstances whether the reorganisation was such that the *only sensible thing to do* was to terminate the existing contracts unless (the employee) would agree to a new arrangement'.[14] Lord Denning also drew attention to the point that once the commercially necessary rearrangements were made 'it was *absolutely essential* for new contracts to be made with existing group secretaries and the *only way to deal with* it was to terminate the agreements and offer them reasonable new ones'.[15] Whilst these remarks were made in his discussion of the s 98(1)(b) issue they could be taken to suggest that similar circumstances could be taken into account by tribunals under s 98(4).

In *Evans v Elemeta Holdings Ltd*[16] the EAT had occasion to deal more directly with this element of the reasonableness test under s 98(4). In *Evans'* case an employer had sought to change the provisions of his employee's contracts from voluntary overtime paid after the first five hours to a position where all overtime was to be unpaid and unlimited in extent except on Saturdays, and the additional argument for overtime was withdrawn.

12   [1981] IRLR 63, EAT.
13   *Banerjee v City and East London Area Health Authority* [1979] IRLR 147, EAT.
14   [1979] ICR 542 at 551, CA.
15   [1979] ICR 542 at 551, CA.
16   [1982] IRLR 143, EAT.

Mr Evans refused to accept the new terms because the obligation to work compulsory unpaid overtime was so open-ended. The EAT overturned the tribunal's finding of fair dismissal indicating that the tribunal had to address itself more carefully to the question of the reasonableness of the change in terms introduced by the employer, especially the need for the employer to present some evidence of the need for the particular type of change in the contractual provisions.

As the EAT put it

'If it had been shown in this case that there was some immediate need for the employer to increase the overtime work or to require mandatory overtime as opposed to voluntary overtime, that might have fundamentally altered the position'.

At one point in *Evans'* case the EAT appeared to suggest that the test of reasonableness could be posed in terms of the reasonableness of the change from the employee's point of view. It stated

'the question under s 98(4) is whether the employee's conduct was reasonable. But, as the [employment] tribunal recognised that question necessarily required the [employment] tribunal to find whether it was reasonable for Mr Evans to decline the new terms of the contract. If it was reasonable for him to decline these terms, then obviously it would have been unreasonable for the employers to dismiss him for such refusal'.[17]

In *Chubb Fire Security Ltd v Harper*[18] however, the EAT, Mr Justice Balcombe presiding, reminded that the test under s 98(4) was essentially whether the *employer* acted reasonably in dismissing the employee for refusing to enter into the new contract and could not be examined solely from the employee's point of view.

As the EAT put it:

'It may be perfectly reasonable for an employee to decline to work extra overtime, having regard to his family commitments. Yet from the employer's point of view, having regard to his business commitments, it might be perfectly reasonable to require an employee to work overtime'.[19]

17   [1982] IRLR 143 at 145, EAT.
18   [1983] IRLR 311, EAT.
19   Ibid at 313.

In *Chubb Fire Security Ltd v Harper*, the EAT also pointed out that some sort of balancing of advantages might be appropriate under s 98(4). Thus,

> 'in answering that question, the [employment] tribunal should have considered whether the employer was acting reasonably in deciding that the advantages to them of implementing the proposed reorganisation outweighed any disadvantages which they should have contemplated Mr Harper might suffer'.[20]

In *Richmond Precision Engineering Ltd v Pearce*,[1] however, the EAT held that the task of weighing the advantages to the employer against the disadvantages to the employee is only one factor which the Tribunal have to take into account under s 98(4). The test is whether the terms offered are, from the employee's point of view, ones which a reasonable employer would offer in the circumstances. To find an offer unreasonable, however, a tribunal must be able to say that the offer was not within the range of offers that was reasonable in all the circumstances.

In *St John of God (Care Services) Ltd v Brooks*[2] the EAT pointed out that the reasonableness of the terms and conditions offered by the employer was only one element in the test of whether the dismissal of an employee for refusal to accept substantial changes in terms and conditions is reasonable. The employer's offer could not be looked at in isolation from the employee's response to the offer and particularly the response of other employees to the offer. In that case an NHS hospital dealt with a reduction in funding by offering employees new and less favourable terms including lower rates of pay and a cancellation of overtime premia for weekend and holiday work. An employment tribunal found the dismissals of recalcitrant employees unfair but was overturned on appeal by the EAT which held that it was wrong to look at the employer's offer in isolation because this would give undue importance to the reasonableness of the employee's decision in refusing the offer.

In *Catamaran Cruisers Ltd v Williams*,[3] the EAT stated that the balance between disadvantage to employees and benefit to employers should be considered. It went on to remind however that there was no principle of law that if the new terms are much less favourable to an employee than the

20   [1983] IRLR 311 at 313. But see now *Richmond Precision Engineering Ltd v Pearce* [1985] IRLR 179, EAT.
1   [1985] IRLR 179, EAT.
2   [1992] IRLR 546, EAT.
3   [1994] IRLR 386, EAT.

old terms, dismissal of the employee for refusing to accept them will be unfair unless the reasons are so pressing that it is vital to the survival of the employer's business that the new business terms be accepted.

Subject to the important constraint of the range of reasonable employer responses test, the area of discretion accorded to employment tribunals over the question of fact under s 98(4) extends to the weight to be given particular factors that make up the reasonableness of the employer's decision to vary their employee's contracts or to end existing contracts and offer new contracts on different terms. In *Kent County Council v Gilham*[4] it was also made clear that this discretion could extend to the issue of the nature of the breach of contract by the employer.

In *Gilham's* case, an employment tribunal considered it extremely important in weighing the reasonableness of an employer's decision to dismiss an employee that the employer, a local authority, had broken a term of a collective agreement incorporated into the employee's contract of employment. Consequently even though the tribunal accepted the substantial reason for economies to be introduced, they were convinced that the decision to dismiss employees on the basis of abrogated agreements was unreasonable. As they put it

'We do not propose to put forward our solution (that is to say what the County Council could otherwise have done). We do not have one, but we do feel that reasonable Councils could not act in this way. There is the matter of their word to an agreement and there are far greater implications as we have seen. We regret that they have approached matters by this means'.

On appeal it was argued that the tribunal had treated the issue of the natural agreement as a 'sacred cow', taking the position that any breach of the natural agreement was automatically unfair and rendered the dismissal in the circumstances unreasonable. The EAT however accepted that the tribunal had acted within its jurisdiction balancing a number of factors in reaching its decision and not treating any one point as by itself decisive. In the event, the EAT held that the tribunal had neither misdirected itself nor come to a perverse decision.

This case reminds us of the fundamental point that in other cases where an employer in the course of a reorganisation chooses to abrogate existing contracts and collective agreements, the EAT, supported by the Court of Appeal, has allowed the reasonableness test to be applied so as to

4   [1983] IRLR 353, EAT.

undermine the sanctity of such agreements. It is the case that technically the reasonableness test as a statutory test can override contractual obligations. This is true of the application of the reasonableness test to employers' disciplinary rules. Yet if a statute has been enacted to provide an enhancement of employee rights it would have been perfectly proper to treat the contract and collective agreement as establishing *minimum* rights for employees which could be improved upon by statute, rather than using the statutory test of fairness to undermine contractual rights. The interpretation of s 98(1)(b) in respect of the rights of employees in the course of reorganisation operates to undermine the protective purpose of the legislation and creates a judicially inspired insecurity for employees in respect of their job rights generally.

The underlying motivation for this expansion of the statute has long been plain. Thus, in *RS Components Ltd v Irwin*, the NIRC made it clear that they were concerned about the possibility that technical progress might be inhibited by employees' exercise of their legal rights. As they put it

'It would be unfortunate for the development of industry if an employer was unable to meet such a situation without infringing or risking infringement of rights conferred by unfair dismissal provisions'.[5]

And in *Robinson v British Island Airways Ltd* the EAT said

'where there is a genuine reorganisation which has dislodged an employee who cannot be fitted in to the reorganisation, it must be open to the employer to dismiss him and in such circumstances the dismissal will be for some other substantial reason'.[6]

Yet judicial obeisance before the twin gods of reorganisation and efficiency has led the EAT and the Court of Appeal to go rather far in their use of some other substantial reason as a device to ensure that contractual commitments do not inhibit changes in industry.

Ironically, the one limitation upon judicial enthusiasm for managerially defined efficiency may be the wide discretion enjoyed by employment tribunals over questions of fact as a result of another major judicial concern with limiting the scope for appeal from employment tribunal decisions strictly to questions of law.

---

5   [1974] 1 All ER 41, [1973] ICR 535, NIRC.
6   [1978] ICR 304, [1977] IRLR 477, EAT.

2. EXTENDING THE DESIGNATED REASONS FOR DISMISSAL

Section 98(1)(b) has been used quite consistently to act as a residual category to allow dismissals which do not fit within the other gateways of s 98 to slip through the sluice of 'some other substantial reason'.

In all such cases there is an important distinction that should be drawn. On the one hand cases which should be allowed to fall into the residual category of s 98(1)(b) because they are in fact analogous *substantial* reasons which whilst not mentioned explicitly in the statute nevertheless merit inclusion. On the other hand, these are cases which are so contrary to the requirements of specific express statutory reasons that by allowing s 98(1)(b) to be used as an alternative gateway, a backdoor method is created which undermines the standards of the express statutory reason for dismissal. There appears to be little evidence that tribunals or indeed the EAT have consciously sought to maintain this distinction in their acceptance of s 98(1)(b) cases. As mentioned, there have been cases under s 98(1)(b) which have allowed dismissals to be classified as for a substantial reason where they did not fit within the definition of redundancy under s 98(2)(c).[7] There has also been the case of *Bouchaala v Trusthouse Forte Hotels Ltd*[8] where s 98(1)(b) was extended to a dismissal required by a statutory enactment. The employee could not qualify under the gateway of s 98(2)(b) because he was mistaken in his belief about the application of the statute. He was allowed through s 98(1)(b), however, because his belief though mistake was genuine.

Another use made of some other substantial reason has been to provide a device which allows cases beyond the boundaries of capability and 'conduct'[9] related dismissals as defined in s 98(2)(b). For example insofar as conduct has been defined to consist of behaviour by the employee *at work* the category of some other substantial reason has been extended to conduct outside the scope of employment,[10] and misleading the employer about a material fact when applying for the job.[11]

---

7   See discussion Chapter 4.
8   [1980] ICR 721, [1980] IRLR 382, EAT.
9   See eg *Kingston v British Railways Board* [1982] ICR 392, [1982] IRLR 274, EAT; *Blackman v Post Office* [1974] ICR 151, [1974] IRLR 46, NIRC; *Megennis v Stephen Austin & Sons Ltd* [1974] IRLR 357, IT.
10   See eg *Singh v London Country Bus Services Ltd* [1976] IRLR 176, EAT (criminal conduct outside the scope of employment); *Creffield v BBC* [1975] IRLR 23, IT; *Bell v Devon and Cornwall Police Authority* [1978] IRLR 283, IT.
11   See eg *O'Brien v Prudential Assurance Co Ltd* [1979] IRLR 140, EAT; *Johnson v Tesco Stores Ltd* [1976] IRLR 103, IT; cf *Saunders v Scottish National Camps Association Ltd* [1980] IRLR 174, EAT.

3. WHERE THE EMPLOYER HAS DECIDED TO DISMISS THE EMPLOYEE DESPITE THE LACK OF FAULT BY THE EMPLOYEE

In a number of cases employees have been dismissed without any element of fault attached directly to them.

In some cases this has been caused by external pressure placed on the employer to dismiss the employee. Thus in *Scott Packing and Warehousing Co Ltd v Paterson*,[12] the EAT held that a dismissal in response to customer pressure could be fair dismissal for some other reason. Similarly in *Moody v Telefusion Ltd*[13] it was held that a dismissal could be fair for some other substantial reason where the employee was unable to obtain a fidelity bond.

Furthermore in *Pillinger v Manchester Area Health Authority*[14] an employer claimed that the withdrawal of funds by an outside body required the employee's dismissal. Yet in that case the point was made that in all such cases there must be a separate consideration of the reasonableness of the dismissal. External considerations will not per se justify a dismissal. And in *Dobie v Burns International Security Services*[15] the Court of Appeal confirmed that the determination of the reasonableness of such a dismissal must take into account the injustice suffered by the employee as well as the effect of the pressure upon the employer. For the former category the Court of Appeal included the employee's length of service, his service record and the difficulties the employee must face in obtaining other employment.

On occasion 'some other substantial reason' has functioned as a residual category of dismissal where the employer claims that there *may be* external pressure from customers. For example in *Saunders v Scottish National Camps Association*[16] a homosexual employee dismissed from his position as attendant in a boys' camp was found to be fairly dismissed for 'some other substantial reason' because most employers would have decided not to have homosexual employees in such a position by implication because of effect on the camp's customers.

---

12   [1978] IRLR 166, EAT. See too *Dobie v Burns International Security Services (UK) Ltd* [1984] IRLR 329, CA; *Grootcon (UK) Ltd v Keld* [1984] IRLR 302, EAT; *Cross v British Bakeries Ltd* (1983) EAT 188/83.
13   [1978] IRLR 311, EAT.
14   [1979] IRLR 430, EAT.
15   [1984] IRLR 329, CA.
16   [1980] IRLR 174, EAT; see too *Boychuk v H J Symons Holdings* [1977] IRLR 395, EAT (clerk dismissed for insisting on wearing badge saying 'Lesbians ignite'). See discussion by Watt 'HIV Discrimination, Unfair Dismissal and Pressure to Dismiss' [1992] 1 LJ 280.

A second category of such cases are those cases where a husband and wife are hired as a team and one of the spouses is dismissed for some reason and the employer dismissed the other. For example in *Kelman v Oram*[17] husband and wife were employed at a public house. After the employer dismissed the husband for stock deficiencies, he then dismissed the wife. A tribunal found that Mr Kelman's dismissal was unfair under but that Mrs Kelman's dismissal was fair under s 98(1)(b) and s 98(4). The EAT upheld the tribunal concluding that the test of some other substantial reason, eg whether it was practicable to continue to employ the wife after the husband was dismissed, had to be applied independently of the fairness of the husband's dismissal.

4. CONFLICTS BETWEEN EMPLOYEES

A further category of dismissals for 'some other substantial reason' consists of behaviour by employees causing conflict at the workplace. For example, in *Treganowan v Robert Knee & Co Ltd*[18] a personality clash between an employee and other employees, caused by her insistence upon openly bragging about her sexual exploits, had created a tense atmosphere in the office and was affecting business. This was 'some other substantial reason' for dismissal under s 98(1)(b) and justified under s 98(3) because she was completely insensitive to the effect she was having.

Yet in *Turner v Vestric Ltd*[19] the EAT allowed an appeal against a tribunal decision that a secretary who had worked successfully under two managers but had a personality conflict with a third manager, could be fairly dismissed for a s 98(1)(b) reason because one employee had to go and it would have been unreasonable for it to be the manager .The EAT pointed out that before an employment tribunal could find that an employer acted reasonably in such a situation it would have to find that before dismissing an employee whose work is perfectly satisfactory the employer made some sensible, practical and genuine efforts to see whether an improvement could be effected.

17 [1983] IRLR 432, EAT; but see *Hendry v Scottish Liberal Club* [1977] IRLR 5; cf *Coleman v Skyrail Oceanic Ltd (t/a Goodmos Tours)* [1981] IRLR 398, CA.
18 [1975] ICR 405, [1975] IRLR 247, QBD. See also *Bennett v Morgan Brushes Ltd* (1977) EAT 386/77.
19 [1980] ICR 528, [1981] IRLR 23, EAT.

CONCLUSIONS

The case law under the head of 'some other substantial reason' has become too friendly to managerial prerogative in a statute explicitly proclaiming itself to provide a 'right' to protection against unfair dismissal. Too many of the cases have the effect of undermining elements of what one might have thought was a fundamental statutory right. Judicial and tribunal interpretation have read into reasonableness an overly generous view of managerial prerogative.

As a result of the House of Lords decision in *Polkey* the test of reasonable procedure will be treated with greater rigour. The consultation principle will also be reinforced by any new national legislation implementing the new European Directive on Information and Consultation with Employee Representatives. Nevertheless, the test of reasonableness under s 98(4) should also include the application of a *proportionality* test to the means chosen by employers in pursuit of their reorganisational aims.

Chapter 10.
Dismissals for trade union membership and activity and for non-membership[1]

1. INTRODUCTION

Dismissals on grounds of trade union membership and activity and non-membership fall into one of two different categories. First they may be dismissals which arise out of employees' exercise of their rights of association, that is to say the right to join a trade union and take part in its activities. Secondly, they may be dismissals which arise out of an employee's exercise of his right of disassociation, his right not to belong to a trade union. The right to non-membership parallels the right of membership. Thus, as TULRCA 1992, s 152(1) now states, if an employee is dismissed for trade union membership or activity, or *non-membership*, then the dismissal will be automatically unfair.[2]

2. DISMISSAL FOR S 152 REASONS: GENERALLY

Under s 152(1) if the reason (or the principal reason) for dismissal was that the employee:

1   The judgment in *Young, James and Webster v United Kingdom* [1981] IRLR 408 (European Court of Human Rights) indicated that 'the negative aspect of a person's freedom of association' does not fall completely outside the ambit of Article 11 of the European Convention for the Protection of Human Rights and Fundamental Freedoms. To explore this question, it would be necessary for an individual first to petition the European Commission of Human Rights and then be referred to the European Court of Human Rights.

2   Trade Union and Labour Relations (Consolidation) Act 1992.

(a)   was, or proposed to become, a member of an independent trade union;
(b)   had taken part, or proposed to take part at any appropriate time in the activities of an independent trade union; or
(c)   was not a member of any trade union, or of a particular trade union or of one of a number of particular trade unions or had refused, or proposed to refuse, to become or remain a member;[3]

then the dismissal shall be regarded as having been automatically unfair.

Section 153 makes it also automatically unfair to dismiss an employee for redundancy where an employee is selected for redundancy for a s 152(1) reason and the circumstances constituting the redundancy applied equally to one or more other employees in similar positions in the same undertaking who were not dismissed.

Dismissals for s 152(1) reasons have certain unique characteristics in terms of their (i) qualifications, (ii) remedies and (iii) onus of proof.

Firstly, in the case of all such dismissals there is no qualifying period of service or upper age limit.[4] Secondly, in the case of all dismissals for a s 152(1) reason there are special rules relating to compensation. Thus, there is a minimum basic award of £3,100, instead of the usual basic award.[5] Moreover, while the *special award* was abolished by the Employment Relations Act 1999, it has been replaced by an *additional award* up to a maximum of £11,960 where an employer fails to comply with an order of reinstatement or reengagement.[6] Thirdly, in the case of all such dismissals an employee may be entitled to a remedy of interim relief, that is an order providing for the continuation of the contract pending the tribunal hearing, in addition to the other remedies of re-employment and compensation.[7] Finally, in a case where the employer has been induced to dismiss an employee for non-membership by the pressure of industrial action, it may be possible to join those persons or trade unions organising the industrial action in the unfair dismissal proceedings.[8]

Furthermore where an employee claims that the reason for the dismissal was trade union membership or participation in trade union activities, there is, according to the case law, a difference in the onus of proof depending on whether or not the employee is qualified to bring a claim of unfair dismissal. In the ordinary case, where the question of the tribunal's jurisdiction does not arise, employers have the onus of proof under s 152(1)

3   TULRCA 1992, s 152(1)(c).
4   TULRCA 1992, s 154.
5   TULRCA 1992, s 156; see discussion in Chapter 17.
6   ERA 1996, s 117; see discussion in Chapter 17.
7   TULRCA 1992, ss 161–166. See Chapter 18.
8   TULRCA 1992, s 160.

to show their reason or principal reason for dismissal (if there were more than one) and that the reason was within one of the categories which the statute specified as potentially valid. If the employer fails to meet this onus then the dismissal will be unfair.

Where the employee challenges the employer's reason and alleges that the employer's real reason was that of trade union membership and activity, the employee must at least come forward with sufficient evidence to show that there was an issue to warrant investigation. In other words, as the Court of Appeal in *Maund v Penwith District Council*[9] put it, he must produce evidence that establishes on the balance of probabilities the existence of the issue. Once the employee has met this onus, however, the onus of showing which of the two competing reasons, or more if there have been more, is the principal reason, remains on the shoulders of the employer. Thus in *Maund*'s case, where the employer had shown that there was a redundancy situation but the employee had established by his evidence that there was at least an issue that the redundancy was a pretext for dismissing that particular employee for trade union membership and activity, it was held to be an error of law for the industrial tribunal to direct itself that the employee has the further onus of convincing the tribunal that on the balance of probabilities the real or principal reason for dismissal was the trade union activities of the employee.[10] This as has been pointed out in the similar case of *Shannon v Michelin (Belfast) Ltd*[11] would be to confuse the position with a case where an employee's length of service was inadequate and an employee would be entitled to claim unfair dismissal only if he could show that trade union activities were the employer's real motivation for the dismissal. Where the question of jurisdiction does not arise there is no onus upon the employee to prove the employer's reason on the balance of probabilities and it would be an error of law for an industrial tribunal to insist otherwise.

On the other hand where an employee's length of service or retiring age might otherwise disqualify him from a claim of unfair dismissal, then the burden of proof of showing the employer's reason rests on the employee where he alleges that the employer's reason fell under s 152(1). Thus in *Smith v Hayle Town Council*,[12] Eveleigh LJ drew attention to the difference

---

9   [1984] ICR 143, [1984] IRLR 24, CA. See too *CGB Publishing v Killey* [1993] IRLR 520, EAT (dismissing a 'but for' test in the context of s 152(1)).

10   Ibid. Cf *Timex Corpn v Thomson* [1981] IRLR 522, EAT.

11   [1981] IRLR 505, NICA.

12   [1978] ICR 996, [1978] IRLR 413, CA; see also *Goodwin Ltd v Fitzmaurice* [1977] IRLR 393, EAT; *Gardner v Peeks Retail Ltd* [1975] IRLR 244, IT.

between [s 152(1)] which requires 'the employer to show' and [s 153] which says instead 'if it be shown' and suggested that since [s 153] is an exception, 'it is for the person relying on the exception to bring himself within it'. Sir David Cairns put it this way:

> 'It appears to me that the language of [s 152] clearly on the face of it places the burden of showing that the reason was an inadmissible reason upon the person who asserts it. The appropriate language, if the burden was put the other way, would be in such form as "unless it is shown that the reason or the principal reason was not an inadmissible reason"'.

Yet neither of the two judges directly addressed themselves to the issue raised by Lord Denning in dissent which was that in interpreting the onus of proof to rest with the employee to show the employer's reason, the court was not giving full weight to the view that

> 'in considering the amount of evidence necessary to shift the burden of proof the Court has regard to the opportunities of knowledge with respect to the fact to be proved which may be possessed by the parties respective'.

This point may be reinforced by the argument that the test of s 152(1) on its face has a neutral burden of proof. In other words, one is not compelled by this statutory language to place the burden of proof entirely on the employee.

3. THE SCOPE OF TRADE UNION MEMBERSHIP AND ACTIVITY UNDER s 152(1)

The right not to be dismissed for trade union membership or activity are component parts of an array of individual employment protection rights which taken together provide the basis of a positive legal right to associate under British law. Their scope has been quite carefully circumscribed by statutory design and judicial interpretation in several important respects.

First, the rights of trade union membership and activity under s 152(1) are restricted to those of an 'independent' trade union, that is, one that is:

> '(a) not under the domination or control of an employer or group of employers or of one or more employer associations, and (b) is not liable to interference by an employer or any such group or association

(arising out of the provision of financial or material support or by any other means whatsoever) tending towards such control.'[13]

Secondly, the precise scope of the right of trade union *membership* has not been clearly defined in the case law. On the one hand the House of Lords in *Wilson and Palmer*,[14] a s 146 case, has stated that the statutory protection of 'trade union membership' is intended to protect only trade union membership *as such*. On the other hand in *Discount Tobacco v Armitage*[15] and *Specialty Care plc v Pachela*,[16] both dismissal cases, the EAT was prepared to give a reading to trade union membership which included 'invoking the assistance of the union in relation to his employment'. The House of Lords in *Wilson and Palmer* also indicated that they could accept the *Discount Tobacco* decision on its facts. Since, for the purposes of s 152, dismissal on grounds of trade union activity is protected as well as dismissal on grounds of trade union membership, it will only be necessary to rely on trade union membership as a ground where the grounds for dismissal fall outside the scope of trade union activity.

Thirdly, dismissal for trade union activities has been restrictively defined by the case law. Thus, on the one hand the activities cannot be too 'collective'. As the Court of Appeal put it in *Therm-A-Stor Ltd v Atkins*[17]

'[s 152] is not concerned with an employer's reactions to a trade union's activities, but with his reaction to an individual employee's activities in a trade union context. Hence where an employer dismisses a group of employees in response to a demand for trade union recognition, the Court could exclude the dismissal from [s 152] on the ground that the "section is concerned solely with the dismissal

---

13   A trade union may be independent if it meets those criteria even without a certificate of independence but in cases of dispute, a certificate is conclusive evidence of independence: TULRCA 1992, s 5. The Certification Officer has defined s 5(a) in several cases: see eg *Blue Circle Staff Association v Certification Officer* [1977] IRLR 20, EAT; *HSD (Hatfield) Employees Association v Certification Officer* [1977] IRLR 261, EAT. For s 5(b) see eg *Squibb UK Staff Association v Certification Officer* [1979] IRLR 75, CA; *A Monk & Co Staff Association v Certification Officer* [1980] IRLR 431, EAT; *Government Communications Staff Federation v Certification Officer* [1993] IRLR 260, EAT.

14   *Associated Newspapers Ltd v Wilson; Associated British Ports v Palmer* [1995] IRLR 258, HL.

15   *Discount Tobacco Confectionery Ltd v Armitage* [1990] IRLR 15, EAT.

16   [1996] IRLR 248, EAT; cf *Harrison v Kent County Council* [1995] ICR 434, EAT.

17   [1983] IRLR 78, CA.

of an employee and provides that it shall be regarded as unfair if the reason was that the (ie that) employee had done or proposed to do one or more specified thing"'.

On the other hand, it has been said that the activities cannot be purely personal grievances. The activities for which an employee is dismissed must be the activities of the trade union itself whether the national, branch or section organisation.[18] It is not enough for the issues to be 'matters which people associate with trade union activities but which are basically individual grievances treated as such by the individual concerned'.[19]

Whilst the question must be judged objectively[20] and is essentially one of fact for employment tribunals to decide, there has been a tendency to require the activity to be connected with the more institutional aspects of trade union organisational activity, such as taking part in trade union meetings or discussion of matters with which trade unions are concerned;[1] attempts to recruit a fellow employee[2] consulting a shop steward or full-time trade union representative[3] or attempting to form a workplace union group.[4] This category has also included the activities of an unaccredited shop steward,[5] where the union was a recognised union.

Yet in *Chant v Aquaboats Ltd*[6] an employee who was not a shop steward acted as an informal spokesman for a group of employees raising a grievance with management and organising a petition. Even though he had the petition vetted by the union office, his activities were held not to be the activities of a trade union. In the circumstances, the fact that he was a spokesman who happened to be a trade unionist was not enough.

Fourthly, the right not to be dismissed for participation in trade union activities is circumscribed by the requirement that the activities must occur at an 'appropriate time' as defined by s 152(2), that is, they must be either

---

18   TULRCA 1992, s 6.
19   See eg *Drew v St Edmundsbury Borough Council* [1980] ICR 513, [1980] IRLR 459, EAT; *Gardner v Peeks Retail Ltd* [1975] IRLR 244, IT.
20   See *Port of London Authority v Payne* [1992] IRLR 447, EAT; *Miller v STH Rafique* [1975] IRLR 70, IT.
1   *British Airways Engine Overhaul Ltd v Francis* [1981] ICR 278, [1981] IRLR 9, EAT.
2   *Brennan and Ging v Ellward (Lancs) Ltd* [1976] IRLR 378, EAT.
3   *Lyon and Scherk v St James Press Ltd* [1976] ICR 413, [1976] IRLR 215, EAT.
4   *Dixon and Shaw v West Ella Developments Ltd* [1978] ICR 856, [1978] IRLR 151, EAT.
5   *Marley Tile Co Ltd v Shaw* [1980] ICR 72, [1980] IRLR 25, CA; revsg [1978] ICR 828, [1978] IRLR 238, EAT.
6   [1978] 3 All ER 102, [1978] ICR 643, EAT.

outside working hours or not at a time when the employee is contractually required to be at work. This would include lunch hours, dining breaks, or just before starting work and just after quitting time.[7] Alternatively, if the activities occur during working hours, they must occur with the agreement or consent of the employer. For example a sudden stoppage of work during working hours without consent even for the purpose of consulting a trade union official might not be trade union activity at the appropriate time.[8]

An employer's consent may be implied as well as expressed.[9] For example, in *Zucker v Astrid Jewels Ltd*[10] the EAT upheld a tribunal's decision that an employee had the implied consent of the employer to talk to other employees about trade union issues during working hours where the work process was not disrupted by chat between employees or during paid meal breaks.

Yet in *Marley Tile Co Ltd v Shaw*[11] the Court of Appeal was unwilling to allow industrial tribunals to infer consent from the silence of a manager when he said nothing in response to an announcement of an unaccredited shop steward that he would be calling a meeting during working hours.

Once an employer has given his consent, however, he may not be completely free to withdraw it. For example, in the case of a meeting with no fixed duration an employer's order to return to work may not automatically be regarded as a 'revocation' of consent within the meaning of s 152(1)(b), even though the employer may be entitled after a time to say 'Well, enough's enough – we want you to go back to work'.[12] An employer's consent to an employee's entitlement to time off to attend regular trade union meetings may become a term of the employee's contract of employment. Additionally, an employer's consent for a shop steward to use a company organised course as a forum for union recruitment could not be taken to imply a condition that he should say nothing to criticise or undermine the company.[12a]

Moreover, it has been held that trade union activity protected by the statute applies only to activity during current employment so that activity before employment commences may not count as trade union activity for

---

7   See *Post Office v Union of Post Office Workers* [1974] 1 All ER 229, [1974] ICR 378, HL.
8   See *Brennan and Ging v Ellward (Lancs) Ltd* [1976] IRLR 378, EAT.
9   See *Marley Tile Co Ltd v Shaw* [1980] ICR 72, [1980] IRLR 25, CA.
10   [1978] ICR 1088, [1978] IRLR 385, EAT.
11   [1980] ICR 72, [1980] IRLR 25, CA.
12   See eg *P J Mirrors Ltd v Speck* (1977) EAT 378/76.
12a   *Bass Taverns Ltd v Burgess* [1995] IRLR 596, CA.

the purposes of s 152(1)(b). In *Birmingham City District Council v Beyer*[13] a noted trade union activist was dismissed by the corporation for gross deceit, once the corporation discovered that he had given the corporation a false name and a bogus reference. An employment tribunal held that he had been dismissed for trade union activities and ordered reinstatement. The EAT reversed the tribunal on the ground that the statutory protection did not apply to activities before employment commenced. On the other hand in *Fitzpatrick v British Railways Board*[14] it was made clear that employers can be in breach of s 152(1)(b) if they dismiss an employee because of trade union activities in former employment and the only rational basis for that decision was the fear that the trade union activities would be repeated in the present employment. The *Beyer* decision did not mean that activities in previous employments had no relevance to a s 152(1)(b) question. They can be probative evidence on the point that the dismissal was because the employer feared that the employee was intending to take part in trade union activities.

Furthermore, a stoppage of work during working hours may not be trade union activities at the appropriate time. A strike or other form of industrial action may not be protected under s 152(1) despite being in layman's terms the very essence of trade union activities. The EAT stated obiter in *Drew v St Edmundsbury Borough Council*[15] that taking part in industrial action does not constitute taking part in the activities of an independent trade union within the meaning of s 152(1). Such dismissals are governed by the special statutory rules that apply to employees dismissed for taking part in industrial action.[16] On the other hand dismissal for participation in the planning and organisation of industrial action can amount to taking part in trade union activities in the meaning of s 152.[17]

Where an employee is dismissed for taking part in the activities of one trade union at a particular working place even though another trade union is recognised, he may still be protected under s 152(1).[18]

13   [1978] 1 All ER 910, [1977] IRLR 211, EAT.
14   [1991] IRLR 376, CA.
15   [1980] ICR 513, [1980] IRLR 459, EAT; see also *Rasool v Hepworth Pipe Co Ltd* [1980] ICR 494, [1980] IRLR 88, EAT.
16   See TULRCA 1992, ss 237–238A discussed in Chapter 11.
17   *Britool Ltd v Roberts* [1993] IRLR 481, EAT.
18   See *Post Office v Union of Post Office Workers* [1974] 1 All ER 229, [1974] ICR 378, HL.

4. THE RIGHT TO DISASSOCIATE

As a result of the amendments introduced by the Employment Act 1988 the provisions on unfair dismissal contained in the ERA 1996 give recognition to a right not to be dismissed for non-membership in a trade union whether or not there is a closed shop. Thus even in the absence of a closed shop, s 152(1)(c) provides that if the reason or the principal reason for the dismissal of an employee was that he was not a member of any trade union, a particular trade union, or one of a number of particular trade unions or had refused or proposed to refuse to become or remain a member, then that dismissal shall be automatically unfair.[19]

Moreover, s 152(3) provides that a dismissal of a non-member who refuses to make payments in lieu of membership (normally to a charity) or objects to a deduction for similar purposes is to be treated as a dismissal because of his non-membership.

Finally, under s 153 it is also an automatically unfair dismissal to select an employee for redundancy because of non-membership in a trade union if other employees holding similar positions in the same undertaking have not been dismissed by that employer.

Consequently, while the institution of the closed shop is not prohibited *per se*, the current legislation gives no legal support for it and ss 152 and 153 make it automatically illegal to dismiss an employee who refuses to join or resigns or is expelled or excluded from a trade union. In such circumstances, a post-entry closed shop would be difficult to enforce. Section 137 of TULRCA makes it illegal for an employer to refuse to offer employment on the ground of non-membership in a trade union thus making it difficult for employers and trade unions to operate a pre-entry closed shop.

5. DISMISSALS AND INDUSTRIAL PRESSURES TO DISMISS

Where an employee is dismissed owing to the industrial pressure or threat of industrial action exerted on an employer by a trade union or a work group, this may result in a finding of unfair dismissal, because the tribunal is precluded from taking such pressure into account in considering the employer's reason for dismissal under ERA 1996, s 107. The employer will have failed to show a reason for dismissal under s 98(1) and (2), and the

---

19   *Crosville Motors Services Ltd v Ashfield* [1986] IRLR 475, EAT.

dismissal will be automatically unfair. Thus, in *Hazels Offsets Ltd v Luckett*[1] a studio manager, after an unhappy start, was dismissed owing to the pressure caused by trade union representatives indicating that they would no longer co-operate with him. The industrial tribunal's decision that the dismissal was unfair was upheld by the EAT on the grounds that the employer had failed to show a reason for dismissal, his real reason having been barred from being taken into account by s 107.

> 'Maybe it is a fiction, maybe it is an unhappy situation, but in our view ... [s 107] does in the circumstances override all the other reasons contemplated in [s 98]. And so, if he cannot take into account the real reason, the unfortunate employer is left with the situation that, if there be no reason upon which he is allowed to rely, then he has no reason and it must be unfair dismissal. It does not sound fair, it does not sound right, but that is what Parliament has decided should be the position and apparently so decided even in the days of the National Industrial Relations Court'.

Moreover, in *Ford Motor Co Ltd v Hudson*[2] the EAT indicated that for a case to fall under s 107 it was not necessary that those exerting pressure on the employer explicitly sought the dismissal of the employee, the test that tribunals should apply is: Was the pressure exerted on the employers such that it could be foreseen that it would be likely to result in the dismissal of those employees in respect of whom the pressure was being brought?

---

1   [1977] IRLR 430, EAT; see also *McColm v Agnew and Lithgow Ltd* [1976] IRLR 14, IT.
2   [1978] 3 All ER 23, [1978] ICR 482, EAT. See also *British United Trawlers (Grimsby) Ltd v Carr* [1977] ICR 622, EAT.

Chapter 11.
Dismissal in connection with industrial action

INTRODUCTION

At common law, virtually all forms of industrial action are treated alike, as a breach of employment contracts by employees. A strike is regarded as a serious breach, or repudiation, of the contract because the employee has disregarded an essential condition of the contract of service – the performance of work.[1] Industrial action short of a strike is also a breach.[2] though its seriousness will vary with the tactic used.

This legal view of strikes is at odds with the reality that in most cases both parties normally accept that employment will continue once the industrial action is ended, but a doctrine of the strike as a suspension of the employment contract has not evolved at common law. In *Morgan v Fry*[3] Lord Denning was prepared to recognise that in the modern law of trade disputes a right could be implied into contracts that 'upon due strike notice, the contract is suspended during the strike and revives again when the strike is over'. In *Simmons v Hoover Ltd*,[4] however, Phillips J rejected this reason, stating that it would require legislation to establish a principle of suspension in English law. In *Boxfoldia Ltd v NGA*,[5] moreover, it was made clear that a notice of industrial action was not enough to avert a

1   *Simmons v Hoover Ltd* [1977] QB 284, [1977] ICR 61, EAT.
2   See eg *Wiluszynski v London Borough of Tower Hamlets* [1988] IRLR 154.
3   [1968] 2 QB 710, [1968] 3 All ER 452, CA.
4   [1977] QB 284, [1977] ICR 61, EAT.
5   [1988] ICR 752, [1988] IRLR 383.

breach. To do that, it was necessary for employees to give notice of termination of contract. Today, s 180 of TULRCA 1992 places limits upon the incorporation of the peace obligation in the collective agreement into the contract of employment, but this simply removes an alternative basis for repudiation. There has been no legislative provision to the effect that a strike is no more than a suspension of the contract, such as is found in the law of many European countries.[6]

In *Simmons v Hoover Ltd*[7] one reason given by Phillips J for rejecting an implied right of suspension was that the statutory employment protections such as unfair dismissal, redundancy payments and continuity of service operate on the assumption that participation in strikes is repudiatory conduct and then graft on special rules to apply.

Thus, statute law makes provision to ensure that where an employee is away form work because he or she is taking part in a strike, or has been locked out, the week during which the employee is away from work will not destroy the continuing of service even if it does not count towards total service.[8] However, whilst this may protect continuity for the purposes of notice of termination, redundancy payment or unfair dismissal as well as other employment protections, it goes no further.

Since 1999, the Employment Relations Act has created a new legal framework for dismissals for industrial action as well as dismissals in the course of a lockout.

The main thrust of the changes is to remove the employer's former immunity from a claim of unfair dismissal for industrial action in cases where the industrial action is 'official', ie authorised by the trade union and is action which is lawful under the TULRCA 1992. The aim of the new provisions is to align the protections against dismissals for employees who take part in official and lawful industrial action with the immunities conferred upon the leaders and organisers of 'protected' industrial action ie the trade union officials and the trade union organisations themselves. Hence, if industrial action is official and lawful under TULRCA 1992, s 219 (tort immunities) and s 226(1) (secret ballots), then employees who are dismissed for participating in such action will be treated as automatically dismissed if certain other conditions are met. In a sense, the new provisions of the 1999 Act attempt to encourage a form of de facto suspension of the contract of employment during a 'reasonable' period of industrial action, ie the first

---

6   See Wedderburn 'The Right to Strike' in *Employment Rights in Britain and Europe* (1991) Lawrence and Wishart.

7   [1977] QB 284, [1977] ICR 61, EAT.

8   ERA 1996, s 216.

eight weeks of a strike, and a resumption of employment when the industrial action ends. It is not a direct statutory suspension; rather it takes the form of a deterrent to employers to use participation in protected industrial action as a basis for dismissing employees. Yet its effects can be similar to a suspension in view of the provisions of ERA 1996, s 216.

Since 1999, the law of unfair dismissals in relation to industrial action has to be divided into three categories: official and lawfully organised ('protected') industrial action, unofficial industrial action and official ('unprotected') industrial action.

i) Dismissals for taking 'protected' industrial action[9]

Under s 238A of TULRCA 1992, where an employee takes 'protected industrial action' and is dismissed for that reason the dismissal will be *automatically unfair*[10] provided one of three conditions is met.

(a)   the dismissal must take place within eight weeks of the day on which the employee began to take protected industrial action; or

(b)   the dismissal took place *after* the end of that eight week period but the employee had stopped taking the protected industrial action *before* the end of that period; or

(c)   the dismissal took place after the eight week period and the employee was still taking industrial action but the employer had failed to take 'reasonable' steps to resolve the dispute relating to the protected industrial action.

While this protection has been limited normally to protected industrial action which ends before the end of the eighth week, even if the protected industrial action continues after that period, employees may be protected if the employer is at fault for not taking reasonable procedural steps.

Section 238A(6) states that employment tribunals must have regard to the following factors when deciding whether or not the employer took reasonable steps:

(a)   whether the employer or a union had complied with procedures established by an applicable collective agreement;

---

9   Under TULRCA, s 238A(1) industrial action is 'protected' if the employee has committed an act or series of acts which have been induced by an act which is not actionable in tort by virtue of TULRCA, s 219.

10   Neither the qualifying period of continuous service (ERA 1996, s 108) nor the upper age limit (ERA 1996, s 109) shall apply: TULRCA, s 239(1).

(b)   whether either employer or union had offered or agreed to resume or commence negotiations after the start of the protected industrial action;

(c)   whether either party unreasonably refused a request for conciliation or mediation services to be used – the latter to help adopt a procedure to resolve the dispute.

For the purpose of this tribunal decision, the tribunal is not to take into account the underlying merits of the dispute.

ii) Dismissals for taking unofficial industrial action

Since 1990 s 237 of TULRCA has provided that an employee will have no right to complain of unfair dismissal, 'if at the time of dismissal he was taking part in an unofficial strike or other unofficial industrial action'[11] as long as some or all of the striking employees are union members. This withdrawal of the right to complain of unfair dismissal will clearly help to deter unofficial strikes by allowing employers to respond to such action by dismissing either unofficial leaders or participants selectively, though its stated motive was to preclude the possibility that organisers of unofficial action could be successful in an unfair dismissal case.[12] Moreover, if an employer dismisses one or more employees under this section, any industrial action taken in response to such a dismissal or in the belief that such a dismissal has occurred will lose its statutory immunity even if otherwise lawful (TULRCA, s 223).

Section 237 defines industrial action as 'unofficial' in respect of an employee unless the employee is:

(a)   a member of a trade union which 'authorised' or 'endorsed' the action in accordance with s 20(2) of TULRCA;

(b)   not a union member but others participating in the action are members of a union which has authorised or endorsed the action; or

(c)   none of the participants in the industrial action are union members.

The question of when industrial action is unofficial is explicitly made a question of fact for the tribunal to decide by reference to the facts at the time of the dismissal (s 237(4)). However, the issue of whether a trade union has authorised or endorsed the industrial action will be determined by reference to rules of trade union responsibility for industrial action set out

11   The removal of the right to complain is not the same as removal of tribunal jurisdiction. Unofficial strikers may still be relevant employees for the purpose of s 238. See Simpson, B 'The Employment Act 1990 in Context' [1991] MLR 418 at 436.

12   'Unofficial Action and the Law' Cm 821 London HMSO 1989 para 3.7.

in s 20(2) of TULRCA.[13] If a trade union decides to repudiate industrial action in accordance with that section, the Act provides a breathing space of at least one full working day for unofficial strikers to reconsider their position (s 237(4)) before they will be vulnerable to selective dismissal. In such a situation the trade union also has at least one full working day within which it may decide to make the strike official by holding a ballot and obtaining protection under s 219.

The one limit to s 237, as well as s 238, is that the employer cannot use industrial action as a pretext for dismissing employees for prohibited reasons, such as selection for redundancy for family reasons including time off under s 57A of the 1996 Act, health and safety, working time, employee representation and where the employee has made a protected disclosure under the 'whistleblowing' section of ERA 1996.[14] In such cases the dismissals will be automatically unfair.

Otherwise in cases of dismissals of employees for participating in unofficial action employers are given the freedom to select the leaders and dismiss them without facing any claim on their part for unfair dismissal.

iii) Dismissals for taking part in 'unprotected' industrial action or a lockout

Where employees are dismissed in connection with unprotected industrial action or a lockout, they may find that an employment tribunal is deprived of jurisdiction to consider the fairness of the dismissal.

TULRCA 1992, s 238 specifically provides that an employment tribunal *shall not* determine whether a dismissal is fair or unfair where at the date of dismissal
(a) the employer was conducting or instituting a lockout or
(b) the employee was taking part in a strike or other industrial action.

To qualify for what is in effect an 'immunity' from complaints of unfair dismissal under this provision, an employer must show first of all that there was in fact a strike or industrial action or lockout as defined by the Act and that, at the date of dismissal,[15] the dismissed employee was participating in industrial action or was dismissed in the course of a lockout.

---

13   See Anderman, *Labour Law* (4th edn, Butterworths, 2000); Smith and Woods *Industrial Law* (7th edn, Butterworths, 2000); Deakin and Morris *Labour Law* (3rd edn, Butterworths, 2001).

14   TULRCA, s 237(1A) and s 238(2A) added by ERA 1999.

15   As to the time when a dismissal becomes effective when a letter is sent, see *Hindle Gears Ltd v McGinty* [1984] IRLR 477, EAT.

Secondly, the employer must establish that the dismissals were non-selective within the meaning of s 238(2) or as the statute puts it: 'that one or more relevant employees of the employer have not been dismissed'. In the case of industrial action all employees at the establishment of the employer taking part in the industrial action at the complainant's date of dismissal are 'relevant employees' and therefore must have been dismissed.[16] In the case of a lockout, all employees directly interested in the dispute leading to the lockout are relevant employees and therefore must have been dismissed.[17]

Thirdly, s 238 further provides that the tribunal will retain jurisdiction over the dismissal if it can be shown that one or more 'relevant employees' of the same employer has been offered re-engagement during the three months after the complainant's date of dismissal, and the complainant has not been offered re-engagement.[18]

Finally, the tribunal also retains jurisdiction if it can be shown that the reason for the dismissal or the reason for selecting the employee in a redundancy case was a prohibited reason specified in or under ERA 1996, ss 99, 100, 101A(d) or 103, ie dismissal for pregnancy and other family reasons, health and safety, working time and employee representative cases, and s 104 in its application to time off under s 57A of the Act.

If any of the pre-conditions of s 238 are not met and the employment tribunal retains jurisdiction to entertain an unfair dismissal complaint, this will be dealt with under s 98(4)[19] or any other relevant provision, though in the former case there will be limits to the extent to which the tribunal will go into the merits of the underlying dispute.[20]

---

16   S 238(3)(b).

17   S 238(3)(a).

18   S 238(2)(b). See eg *Highland Fabricators Ltd v McLaughlin* [1984] IRLR 482, EAT.

19   See eg *Hindle Gears Ltd v McGinty* [1984] IRLR 477, EAT; *Laffin & Callaghan v Fashion Industries Hartlepool Ltd* [1978] IRLR 448, EAT: *Edwards v Cardiff City Council* [1979] IRLR 303, EAT.

20   See *Crosville Wales Ltd v Tracey (No 2)* [1997] IRLR 691, HL (dictum Lord Nolan).

I. DISMISSALS AND STRIKES OR OTHER INDUSTRIAL ACTION

i) Was there a strike or other industrial action?

The first fact that must be established to deprive a tribunal of jurisdiction over dismissal under s 238(2) is that the industrial action that the employee is alleged to have taken part in was 'a strike or other industrial action' or that he or she was dismissed in the course of a lockout.

In deciding this question the tribunal is 'engaged in deciding an issue of fact'.[1] The test is essentially an objective one, to determine whether the action of the employee fits within the words of the statute.[2] Yet tribunals have to contend with the difficulty that neither 'other industrial action' nor 'lockout' are defined specifically for the purposes of s 238.

(a) A 'strike'

Whilst there is no definition of strike in s 238 of TULRCA, s 246 defines it as 'any concerted stoppage of work'.

Moreover, in *Tramp Shipping Corpn v Greenwich Marine Inc*[3] Lord Denning suggested the following definition …

> 'a strike is a concerted stoppage of work by men done with a view to improving their wages or conditions, or giving vent to a grievance or making a protest about something or other, or supporting or sympathising with other workmen in such endeavour'.

(b) 'Other industrial action'

In contrast there is no definition of 'other industrial action' in s 238 or any other part of the Act. There is little doubt that 'other industrial action' consists of a partial stoppage of work or withdrawal of labour rather than a strike which is a complete cessation of work. Thus, 'other industrial action'

---

1   *Bolton Roadways Ltd v Edwards* [1987] IRLR 392, EAT. See eg *Midland Plastics v Till* [1983] ICR 118, [1983] IRLR 9, EAT; *Naylor v Orton & Smith Ltd* [1983] ICR 665, [1983] IRLR 233, EAT.

2   *Coates v Modern Methods and Materials Ltd* [1983] QB 192, [1982] ICR 763, CA; *Manifold Industries v Sims* [1991] IRLR 242, EAT.

3   [1975] ICR 261 at 266, CA.

has been held to consist of a slow down or work to rule, an overtime ban or a picket line around a machine.

Yet the Court of Appeal has emphatically rejected the requirement that 'other industrial action' must also be in breach of contract. Thus in *Power Packing Casemakers Ltd v Faust*,[4] an employment tribunal held that those employees who had refused to work voluntary overtime were unfairly dismissed because since their contracts contained no requirement to work reasonable overtime, there was no misconduct on their parts in refusing to work overtime. On appeal to the EAT the employers for the first time argued that s 238 applied since the employees were taking part in industrial action at the time of the dismissal. The EAT allowed the appeal on the ground that since the refusal to work overtime was for the purpose of a wage dispute it was 'other industrial action' in the meaning of s 238, notwithstanding that there was no contractual obligation on the employees to work overtime when requested. The Court of Appeal upheld the EAT stating that other industrial action applies to a refusal to do overtime used as a bargaining weapon whether or not it was a breach of contract.

(c) Industrial action as collective action

What both a strike and other industrial action also have in common under s 238 is that they are essentially collective rather than individual activities. Thus an employer who dismisses an individual employee for refusing to perform contractual work will not be able to claim that s 238 applies to that dismissal. This is ensured by the definition of strike as 'any *concerted* stoppage of work'. For example in *Bowater Containers Ltd v Blake*[5] an employee refused an instruction to help in another section unless his query about a bonus was sorted out. His dismissal for refusing to obey the instruction was found unfair. On appeal, the EAT rejected the company's argument that s 238 applied on the grounds that 'in our view the ordinary meaning of the words "industrial action" does not include action by one person alone'. Moreover the tribunal suggested that, 'the words "taking part in" suggest some participation with other people or some concerted action and the provisions of s 238(2) indicate that the action ... is action by at least two persons'.[6]

4   [1983] QB 471, [1983] ICR 292, CA.
5   (1982) EAT S52/S1.
6   Ibid.

In *Lewis and Britton v E Mason & Sons*[7] however, the EAT upheld the finding of an employment tribunal that a lorry driver refusing to drive a lorry with no overnight heater in mid-December unless he was given an extra payment for overnight accommodation was dismissed for taking part in industrial action because the conduct was designed to coerce the employer to improve terms and conditions. The EAT was concerned to underline the point that the issue was one of fact and the tribunal's decision was not perverse. It seems unlikely that this decision will survive the subsequent enactment of s 246 of TULRCA 1992 with its emphasis on 'concerted stoppage of work' in its definition of strike.

On the other hand not all concerted action is necessarily industrial action under s 238. Schedule 23 states that the cessation of work must be done 'as a means of compelling the employer or any person or body of persons employed or to aid other employees in compelling their employers or any person or body of persons employed to accept or not to accept terms and conditions of employment'. Lord Denning in *Tramp Shipping Corpn*[8] emphasised that a strike is done

> 'with a view to improving ... wages or conditions or giving vent to a grievance or making a protest about something or other, or supporting or sympathising with other workmen in such endeavour. It is distinct from a stoppage which is brought about by an external event such as a bomb scare or by apprehension of danger'.[9]

And Lord Stephenson in the same case added:

> 'What kind of concerted stoppages are properly called strikes today? It must be a stoppage [sic] intended to achieve something or call attention to something; as Lord Denning has said: a rise in wages, improvement of conditions, support for other workers or for political changes; an expression of sympathy or protest'.[10]

Furthermore in *Power Packing Casemakers Ltd v Faust*,[11] Lord Justice Stephenson distinguished between employees who refused to work because of a personal preference for a football match or a private commitment to visit a sick person and those who are taking industrial action. Where an employee refuses to work 'because he and others who refused

7   [1994] IRLR 4, EAT; see note by Dolding (1994) 1 LJ 243.
8   [1975] ICR 261, CA.
9   Ibid at 246.
10   [1975] ICR 261 at 266, CA.
11   [1983] IRLR 117 at 119, CA.

with him hope to extract an increase in wages out of his employer because then business will be disrupted if they do not grant it, that constrained application of pressure is industrial action in the common sense of the words'.

Subject to the possibility of misdirection, what is or is not a strike or other industrial action is essentially a question of fact for employment tribunals.[12] In exercising their discretion as finders of fact, tribunals have drawn certain fine distinctions between industrial action and trade union activity and between industrial action and precursors to industrial action. Thus where there is a disruption of production for the purpose of preparing a wage claim, it is open to an employment tribunal to decide as a matter of fact that this is 'trade union activity' under ERA 1996, s 152(1)(b) rather than industrial action as defined by s 238. For example in *Rasool v Hepworth Pipe Co Ltd*[13] employees were dismissed for stopping work to attend a meeting without authorisation during working hours to consider impending wage negotiations. The tribunal held that attendance of the meeting did not necessarily constitute industrial action even though it disrupted the manufacturing process. It could more properly be regarded as 'trade union activity'. The EAT upheld the tribunal's decision though it expressed reservations about its attempt to limit industrial action to concerted action undertaken 'with the intention of putting pressure on an employer to do something which he otherwise would not do'. The EAT thought that it was 'probably incorrect to attempt to interpret the expression narrowly in terms of specific intention'.

Further it is possible for tribunals in the exercise of their discretion to draw a distinction between 'industrial action' as defined by s 238 and the 'preparations for industrial action'. For example in *Midland Plastics v Till*[14] a member of the works committee wrote a letter to the employer indicating that unless the committee's demands were not met 'it is our intention to take industrial action' by a deadline. In response the employer interviewed employees and four who indicated that they would take industrial action were dismissed before the deadline. The tribunal and the EAT agreed they were not taking part in industrial action at the time because the threat of industrial action could not itself amount to taking industrial action for the purpose of s 238.

Moreover it has been possible for a meeting called to discuss industrial action to be held not itself to be industrial action. Thus in *Naylor v Orton*

12   *Naylor v Orton & Smith Ltd* [1983] ICR 665, [1983] IRLR 233, EAT.
13   [1980] ICR 494, [1980] IRLR 137, EAT.
14   [1983] ICR 118, [1983] IRLR 9, EAT.

& *Smith Ltd*,[15] a number of employees held a meeting at which they decided to impose an immediate overtime ban to support a pay claim. Later all employees at the meeting, apart from three, refused to sign a form to the effect that they would work normally. Those who refused to sign were dismissed. The employers sought to argue that the three non-signing employees' attendance at the meeting at which an immediate overtime ban was imposed meant that they took part in industrial action even though the actual refusals to work overtime occurred at a later date. The tribunal however held that the decision to impose the ban was not industrial action and the EAT upheld the decision as a reasonable conclusion on the facts as found.

In contrast, in *Winnet v Seamarks Bros Ltd*[16] it was held that an employee was dismissed for taking part in industrial action when he indicated at an interview during off duty hours that he would not be working the next day and intended to join in the picketing. This was true even though the dismissal occurred during the interview and before his work was due to start.

As the issue is one of fact for employment tribunals, it is now quite possible, as the EAT has acknowledged, for tribunals to reach different conclusions and still not be in error as long as the particular conclusion is itself reasonable on the facts as found. As the EAT put it in *Naylor*'s case

'... on the primary facts as found by the [Employment] Tribunal in this case, another [Employment] Tribunal could reasonably have found that the imposition of the immediate ban on overtime itself constituted industrial action and that those who voted for it took part in it'.

The EAT also drew attention to the unpredictability of the consequences of dismissing employees in this kind of situation.

'If both views (ie that the imposition of the ban did or did not constitute industrial action) can properly be held, an employer confronted with an overtime ban who asks for advice can only be advised to dismiss everyone who could conceivably have taken part in the industrial action. If he follows that advice, the consequence to the employees who might be considered not to be taking part is that they lose their jobs. Whether such employees have a claim for

15   [1983] ICR 665, [1983] IRLR 233, EAT. See also *South East Kent Health Authority v Gillis* (1984) EAT 927/83.
16   [1978] ICR 1240, [1978] IRLR 387, EAT.

unfair dismissal will depend on whether or not the [Employment] Tribunal they chance to come before takes the view that they were taking part in industrial action'.

ii) Taking part in industrial action

The issue of whether the employee was taking part in industrial action at the time of dismissal is also a question of fact for tribunals to decide.[17] It is often raised where industrial action has been found as a matter of fact and the question left to be answered under s 238(2)(b) is whether the individual bringing the complaint himself was at the date of dismissal 'taking part'. Yet the issue also applies under s 238(2) in which a 'relevant employee' is defined in s 238(4)(b) 'in relation to a strike or other industrial action', as 'employees who took part in it'.[18]

In both types of cases, tribunals have found it necessary to inquire into the employees' motivation for refraining from coming into work. Where an employee has been absent owing to sickness, it will require exceptional circumstances to convince a tribunal that he has been taking part in industrial action.[19] However, in *Bolton Roadways Ltd v Edwards*,[20] the EAT held that employees lawfully absent during a strike could still be regarded as 'taking part' if they associated themselves with the strike, attended a picket line etc. Taking part in a strike did not require a breach of the contract of employment.

A refusal to cross a picket line however is more controversial. The Court of Appeal first pronounced upon this issue in *McCormick v Horsepower Ltd*.[1] In *McCormick*'s case the alleged relevant employee, a fitter's mate returned from holiday to find a picket line of boiler makers at the employer's premises. He refused to cross it and went each week to the employer's office with the striking boiler makers to obtain the income tax rebates to which he was entitled. He returned to work two weeks before the strike ended and was dismissed for redundancy two weeks later.

---

17   *Hindle Gears Ltd v McGinty* [1984] IRLR 477, EAT.
18   See *P&O European Ferries (Dover) Ltd v Byrne* [1989] IRLR 254, CA (on the time for showing when other employees who took part in a strike were dismissed).
19   *Hindle Gears Ltd v McGinty* [1984] IRLR 477, EAT; cf *Williams v Western Mail and Echo Ltd* [1980] ICR 366, [1980] IRLR 222, EAT.
20   [1987] IRLR 392, EAT.
1   [1981] 2 All ER 746, [1981] ICR 535, [1981] IRLR 217, CA.

The Employment Appeal Tribunal found, however, that since Mr Brazier had not been motivated by fear, his actions in not crossing the picket line could only be explained in terms that he withdrew his labour to aid the strikers. It concluded, therefore, that contrary to the finding of the employment tribunal Mr Brazier had taken part in the strike and was, in consequence a 'relevant employee' within the meaning of s 238(4)(b).

The Court of Appeal disagreed with the EAT on this issue. Though their remarks were, strictly speaking, obiter because of the nature of the case, they made it plain that to establish that an employer was taking part in industrial action it was not enough to show simply that the employee had voluntarily decided not to work and had not been dissuaded from working through fear of a picket line.

It was necessary, as Lord Lawton put it, to find some commonality of purpose between the individual employee and others taking part in the strike.

> 'The statutory words "who took part in it" (that is, the strike) mean giving help by acting in concert with each other and in withdrawing their labour for a common purpose or pursuant to a dispute which they or a majority of them or their union have with their employers and staying away from work as long as the strike lasts. Some held by standing on picket lines or by doing organising work in committee rooms. Evidence of Mr Brazier's refusal to cross the boilermakers' picket lines even though, as the [Employment] Tribunal found, his refusal was not brought about by fear, was not in my judgment enough to prove that he was taking part in the boilermakers' strike. He was not shown to have had a common purpose with them or any interest in their dispute with their employers. He was not acting in concert with them as was shown by the fact that he returned to work on 13 November 1978 whilst they were still on strike. In my judgment there was evidence upon which the [Employment] Tribunal could find, as it did, that he was not taking part in the strike and in consequence was not a relevant employee'.[2]

In the later case of *Coates v Modern Methods and Materials Ltd*,[3] however, a majority of the Court of Appeal suggested that motive or purpose was not relevant in judging whether an employee was taking part in a strike within the meaning of s 238. What was relevant was the employee's actions.

2   See too remarks by Lord Justice Templeman stressing the absence of an agreement or obligation to participate in the strike.
3   [1983] QB 192, [1982] ICR 763, CA.

The facts in *Coates'* case were that the employees were dismissed for taking part in a strike. The tribunal held that s 238 did not deprive it of jurisdiction because another employee, Mrs Leston, who had not been dismissed had also taken part in a strike. Mrs Leston had stayed away from work during the strike partly because she was frightened of the abuse that must follow if she went into work and partly because she was sick during the period. She had attended strike meetings but she did not draw strike pay because of the view that she 'was sick and was not on strike'. The EAT allowed the appeal from the tribunal decision because it thought that the only conclusion that the tribunal could properly have reached was that Mrs Leston was not taking part in a strike. The Court of Appeal overruled the EAT on the grounds that there was adequate evidence before the tribunal to allow it to reach its conclusion and that was the only question to be asked on appeal.

Yet in the course of allowing the appeal the judges offered differing views on whether there should be an objective or subjective test of participation. The majority of the court, Lord Justice Stephenson and Lord Justice Kerr favoured an objective approach. Lord Stephenson said

> '... participation in a strike must be judged by what the employee does and not by what he thinks or why he does it. If he stops work when his workmates come out on strike and does not say or do anything to make plain his disagreement, or which could amount to a refusal to join them, he takes part in their strike. The line between unwilling participation and not taking part may be difficult to draw, but those who stay away from work with the strikers without protest for whatever reason are to be regarded as having crossed that line to take part in the strike. In the field of industrial action those who are not openly against it are presumably for it'.

Lord Justice Kerr took an even firmer line in rejecting a subjective approach. As he put it, whether a person was taking part in a strike could 'in practice only be answered on the basis of his or her action by either staying out or going in. Of course if the employee does not go to work for reasons which have nothing to do with the strike such as illness or being on holiday then the position would be different. But when the employee's absence from work is due to the existence of the strike in some respect, because he or she chooses not to go to work during the strike, then I think that the employee should be regarded as taking part in the strike'. Reasons or motives were irrelevant, 'nor would it be relevant to consider whether their utterances or actions or silence or inaction, showed support, opposition or indifference in relation to the strike'.[4] Only Eveleigh LJ in a dissenting judgment agreed that the fact that a worker stayed away from work because of her fear was evidence that she was not acting in concert with the other strikers.[5]

Clearly in both *McCormick* and in *Coates* however the Court of Appeal was more concerned to ensure that the EAT should not interfere with an employment tribunal decision unless misdirection or perversity could be shown than to lay down rules of law. This was clearly acknowledged by the EAT in *Naylor*'s case.[6] To some extent this has been made more explicit in *Power Packing Casemakers Ltd v Faust*.[7]

iii) Was the employee taking part in industrial action at the date of dismissal?

Whether an employee was taking part in a strike or industrial action or dismissed in the course of a lockout at the date of the dismissal are also questions of fact for tribunals to determine.[8] The issue is doubly important since s 238 was amended, because even if an employee had taken part at a date prior to the date the employee is dismissed he is not a relevant employee if he is not taking part at the date of the dismissal.[9]

In the first place, the date of dismissal is affected by the time the employee effectively communicates the dismissal, so that employees returning to work before receiving a letter of dismissal may not be dismissed for 'taking part' in industrial action.[10] Secondly where an employee is dismissed after he indicates that he intends to return to work, even if the dismissal occurs on a date during which he has been on strike, as long as the strike has ceased and the employer knows that he will be returning to work an employment tribunal will not lose its jurisdiction over that dismissal under s 238. In that sense, the date of the dismissal in s 238 has been interpreted to mean the *time* of dismissal. Thus in *Heath and Hammersley*

---

4   [1981] 2 All ER 746, [1981] ICR 535, CA.
5   [1983] QB 192, [1982] ICR 763, CA.
6   [1983] ICR 665, [1983] IRLR 233, EAT.
7   [1981] ICR 484, [1981] IRLR 120, EAT.
8   *Naylor v Orton & Smith Ltd* [1983] ICR 665, [1983] IRLR 233, EAT.
9   S 238(3).
10 *Hindle Gears Ltd v McGinty* [1984] IRLR 477, EAT; *Brown v Southall and Knight* [1980] ICR 617, [1980] IRLR 130, EAT.

v J F Longman (Meat Salesman) Ltd,[11] a striking employee rang the employer and told him that all the striking employees wished to return to work. The employer dismissed them later that day. The NIRC held that once the employer knew that he would be having his workforce back, he could no longer dismiss and be entitled to the immunity of s 238.

As the court put it the word 'date' in (s 238) should be construed as 'at the time', so that if on a given date an employer has been told that the strike is over, he is not free during the rest of that calendar day to dismiss the men who took part in it without running the risk that an employment tribunal will hold that he acted unfairly.

Similarly, in *Williams v Western Mail and Echo Ltd*[12] an employee who took part in a one day strike but also stayed away the next day owing to illness was held to be taking part in industrial action on that day despite being away through illness. The tribunal held that he had not stopped supporting the industrial action and hence he was still taking part. The EAT upheld the tribunal stating that 'once men have stated that they will apply sanctions and do so, they may be regarded as applying the sanctions either until they are discontinued or until they indicate or state an intention of stopping them'.[13]

When an individual has begun to take part in industrial action is also a question of fact. This is made plain by comparing *Winnett v Seamarks Bros Ltd* with *Naylor v Orton & Smith Ltd*, on the issue of whether taking part in industrial action occurs only when the employee actually stops work as opposed to announcing that he will stop work when he is due to work. In *Winnett* the EAT said the following:

'If, for example in a particular case all the employees of a company which is engaged on a three-shift system of work meet and decide that as from the time of their meeting they will all stop work, we do not consider that the only ones who are taking part in strike action or other industrial action are those whose shift is due to work at the moment of the decision. It seems to us that those employees who are due to work on the next two following shifts are taking part in strike action or other industrial action when they intimate that their labour will be withdrawn at a time when the current shift actually stops work. They do not only begin to take part in strike action or other industrial action when the time of the shift comes and they do not actually work'.

11   [1973] 2 All ER 1228, [1973] ICR 407, NIRC; see also *Gallagher v Wragg* [1977] ICR 174, EAT.
12   [1980] ICR 366, [1980] IRLR 222, EAT.
13   See discussion at pp 253–254.

Yet in *Naylor* the EAT upheld a tribunal which decided that attendance at a meeting at which an immediate overtime ban was imposed was not participation in industrial action.

Where an employee is dismissed while taking part in a strike or other industrial action the *reason* for the dismissal is not relevant; it is sufficient that at the date of dismissal the employee was taking part in it. As Lord Stephenson reminded in *Power Packing Casemakers Ltd v Faust*[14]

'Once an [Employment] Tribunal ... decides that an employee was, at the date of his dismissal, taking part in industrial action ... the Tribunal must refuse to entertain the complaint or to go into the questions of the employers' motive or reasons for dismissing'.

Hence even where it is alleged that the employer engineered or provoked the strike[15] and purposely dismissed the employees for trade union membership and activities,[16] this apparently would not prevent s 238 from conferring an immunity against a claim for unfair dismissal.[17]

2. DISMISSALS AND LOCKOUTS

i) Was there a 'lockout'?

An employment tribunal may under certain conditions lose its jurisdiction to consider the reasonableness of a dismissal where at the date of the complainant's dismissal 'the employer was conducting or instituting a lock-out'. Again, even though s 238 provides no definition of a lock-out, the courts held that it is a question of fact for tribunals to decide.[18] ERA 1996, s 235 gives a definition in the context of calculating a period of employment. Under s 235 a lockout 'means the closing of a place of employment, or the suspension of work, or the refusal by an employer to continue to employ any number of persons employed by him in consequence of a dispute, done with a view to compelling those persons, or to aid another employer in compelling persons employed by him to accept terms or conditions

---

14   [1981] ICR 484, [1981] IRLR 120, EAT; affd [1983] QB 471, [1983] ICR 292, CA.
15   See eg *Marsden v Fairey Stainless Ltd* [1979] IRLR 103.
16   See eg *Drew v St Edmundsbury Borough Council* [1980] ICR 513, [1980] IRLR 459, EAT; *Rasool v Hepworth Pipe Co Ltd* [1980] ICR 494, [1980] IRLR 88, EAT.
17   See now Mr Justice Waite's remarks in *Hindle Gears Ltd v McGinty* [1984] IRLR 477, EAT.
18   See eg *Express and Star Ltd v Bunday* [1987] IRLR 422, CA.

affecting employment'. In *Fisher v York Trailer Co Ltd*[19] the EAT upheld an employment tribunal that adopted this statutory definition of a lockout but there seems to be no obligation on tribunals to adopt all elements of that definition.[20]

ii) A 'relevant employee' in respect of a dismissal in the course of a lockout

In the case of a lockout 'relevant employees' are defined as 'employees who were *directly interested* in the dispute in contemplation or furtherance of which the lock-out occurred'.[1]

Employees can be said to be directly interested in a dispute when their terms of employment are likely to be immediately and automatically affected by the outcome of the dispute.[2] This category is quite wide ranging. It is restricted neither to employees of the same employer nor to employees who remain locked out until the date of the complainants dismissal.

In *Fisher v York Trailer Co Ltd*[3] the employer wrote to each of the 34 employees taking part in a 'go slow' saying that unless they signed an undertaking to work at a normal incentive pace they would be suspended from the start of their next shift. The following day, a number of men met in the factory to discuss the matter and within two days, 27 of the 34 had given the required undertaking. Those who did not sign even after another warning and were dismissed, claimed that the dismissal was unfair and that they were not barred by s 238 on the basis that other 'relevant' employees had not been dismissed. The EAT upheld the tribunal's decision that a lockout occurred when the men were suspended and that it continued throughout the dispute, while they refused to sign the undertaking. The EAT however, disagreed with the tribunal's conclusion that only the seven dismissed employees were directly interested in the dispute. It held that all 34 employees were directly interested. To decide which employees were directly interested required a finding of 'when the lock-out occurred and what was the ... dispute in contemplation of furtherance of which the lockout was put in effect'.

---

19   [1979] ICR 834, [1979] IRLR 385, EAT.
20   See eg *Express and Star Ltd v Bunday* [1987] IRLR 422, CA.
1   TULRCA 1992, s 238(3)(a).
2   Ibid.
3   [1979] ICR 834, [1979] IRLR 385, EAT.

The dispute, the EAT decided, was over the obligation to sign the undertaking. When the lockout occurred on 8 February, none of the 34 employees had agreed to sign and there was then a dispute between all of them and the company. All 34 were therefore 'directly interested' in the dispute at some time and the tribunal had jurisdiction to hear the claims of the dismissed employees. The EAT stated it was 'clear that there are no express words which limit the employees who are to be treated as directly interested to those who remain right through to the end'. The EAT also indicated that it thought that employees who were not locked out at all could nevertheless have a direct interest in the dispute.

Thus an employer cannot claim the protection of s 238 by simply dismissing all those employees who are locked out at any particular time. The test under s 238 is whether the employer has dismissed all those who were locked out at any stage of the dispute as well as any other employees who might have been directly interested in the underlying dispute.

3. DISCRIMINATORY RE-ENGAGEMENT

Even if employers have not dismissed employees discriminatorily they can still act discriminatorily in their decisions to re-engage employees. Section 238(2)(b) allows a tribunal to retain jurisdiction if the employee can show that the employer had offered re-engagement to any relevant employee within three months after the date of the dismissal and had not offered re-engagement to the complainant.[4] The offer of re-engagement must be actually known to be an offer of re-engagement in the meaning of s 238.[5] However, it need not be made directly in writing as long as the employee knows of it.[6] A general advertising campaign indicating that there were job vacancies however, would not amount to a job offer.[7] Moreover, the employer can attach certain conditions to the offer to certain employees such as that the returning employee be regarded as having received a warning for the purposes of a disciplinary procedure even if other employees are not similarly treated.[8] This is because the offer of

4   *Highland Fabricators Ltd v McLaughlin* [1984] IRLR 482, EAT.
5   *Bigham and Keogh v GKN Kwikform Ltd* [1992] IRLR 4, EAT.
6   See eg *Marsden v Fairey Stainless Ltd* [1979] IRLR 103, EAT (misaddressed letter); cf *Bolton Roadways Ltd v Edwards* [1987] IRLR 392, EAT (offer held open).
7   *Crosville Wales Ltd v Tracey* [1996] IRLR 91, CA.
8   *Williams v National Theatre Board Ltd* [1982] ICR 715, [1982] IRLR 377, CA.

re-engagement must be only of a 'job' and ERA 1996, s 235(1) defines a job in terms of 'the nature of the work which the employee is employed to do in accordance with his contract and the capacity and place in which he is so employed'. As to defined, there is no requirement that the re-engagement be on the identical terms of the previous employment.[9] The Court of Appeal so held in *Williams v National Theatre Board Ltd*,[10] with Lord Denning MR adding that the differences must be 'reasonable in all the circumstances of the case'.

Fox LJ also suggested that the 'capacity' in which a man was employed could not be considered entirely apart from the terms of employment which attach to it.

> 'The job which a dismissed employee is offered may have the same name and involve the same duties in the same place of work as previously but have conditions attached to it which are so disadvantageous as compared with the position before he was dismissed that it cannot realistically, in the context of this legislation, be said that he is being offered re-employment in the same capacity as before. An example, mentioned in argument, is a large reduction in pay'.

The legislation as it was formulated from 1982 to 1999 offered a wide discretion to employers to dismiss employees in response to strikes or other forms of industrial action. It was legally possible for employers to dismiss an entire workforce for taking part in industrial action which was provoked by the employer in the first instance, and replace them with permanent replacements. This was quite rare in the case of firms with large workforces, although it was not unheard of. The Murdoch company News International's move to Wapping was a notable example.[11] However, where the numbers of employees out on strike were small, such a step was more conceivable for employers, particularly as part of a campaign to resist trade union recognition and as a deterrent to employees.

With the changes in the law introduced by the 1999 Act it will be more difficult for employers to use dismissals for participation in industrial action as a device to resist trade union membership or organisation or recognition. The new protection against unfair dismissals of employees who participate in lawful official action introduced by the Employment Relations Act restore a more appropriate balance to the legal framework.

9   Ibid.
10   Ibid.
11   See Ewing and B Napier 'The Wapping Dispute and Labour Law' (1986) Camb LJ 285.

Chapter 12.
Dismissal for contravention of a statutory enactment

Under ERA 1996, s 98(2)(d), employers may show that their dismissal of the employee was for the reason that 'the employee could not continue to work in the position which he held without contravention (either on his part or that of his employer) of a duty or restriction imposed by or under any enactment'. For example, where an employee's duties consist exclusively or normally of driving a motor vehicle and he is disqualified from driving, this would fall within the provision. The test under s 98(2)(d) is objective.[1] It is whether the employee is unable either to do a significant part of his job[2] or to meet an essential requirement of his job.[3] If the employer dismisses the employee on mistaken advice, that will not meet the requirements of s 98(2)(d).[4] Moreover, if the employee's work which is prohibited by statutory enactment constitutes a lesser part of his overall duties this may not be an adequate reason for dismissal under s 98(2)(d).[5] Alternatively, if the nature of the employee's contractual duties has been modified to enable him to work without contravening a statutory enactment, that might make a dismissal unfair.[6]

1   See eg *Bouchaala v Trust House Forte Hotels Ltd* [1980] ICR 721, [1980] IRLR 382, EAT.
2   See eg *Fearn v Tayford Motor Co Ltd* [1975] IRLR 336, IT (40% of employee's time spent driving and testing cars).
3   See eg *Appleyard v F M Smith (Hull) Ltd* [1972] IRLR 19, IT.
4   *Bouchaala*'s case above.
5   See eg *Williams v Michelin Tyre Co Ltd* (1976) IT 29803/76 (driving duties on public roads of disqualified employee constituted only about 25% of his time).
6   See eg *Mathieson v W J Noble & Son Ltd* [1972] IRLR 76 (employee made arrangements for a chauffeur to drive him).

Even where an employer may meet the standards of showing a potentially valid reason under s 98(2)(d) he must also show that he acted reasonably in dismissing him under s 98(4).[7] This may involve an obligation to give warnings where appropriate, and look for any suitable alternative employment available.[8] It may also require the employer to act reasonably in the timing of the dismissal, particularly where the possibilities exist to extend the period of employment without contravening a statutory enactment.[9]

---

7   See eg *Sandhu v (1) Department of Education and Science, (2) London Borough of Hillingdon* [1978] IRLR 208, EAT.
8   See eg *Williams v Michelin Tyre Co Ltd* (1976) IT 29803/76; see also *O'Connor v Lothian Health Board* (1977) IT 51008/77.
9   See eg *Sutcliffe & Eaton Ltd v Pinney* [1977] IRLR 349, EAT.

Chapter 13.
Dismissal on the grounds of pregnancy, childbirth or family reasons

1. DISMISSALS CONNECTED WITH PREGNANCY OR OTHER FAMILY REASONS

Under s 99 of the Employment Rights Act 1996 and reg 20 of the Maternity and Parental Leave etc Regulations 1999 all employees have a right from the start of employment not to be dismissed on the grounds of pregnancy, childbirth or specified family reasons, in addition to the right to take time off for ante natal care[1] and the right to maternity leave with pay[2] and parental leave.[3]

Under that Act and the Regulations, a woman will be regarded as automatically unfairly dismissed where the dismissal *is connected with* any of the following:

(a) her pregnancy;

(b) childbirth;

(c) her suspension from work on maternity grounds;

(d) the fact that she took, or sought to take or availed herself of the benefits of ordinary maternity leave, additional maternity leave, parental leave or time off to take care of dependants;

(e) the fact that she refused to sign a workforce agreement in relation to parental leave;

---

1   Employment Rights Act 1996, s 55.
2   Employment Rights Act 1996, s 71(4) and (5).
3   Maternity and Parental Leave etc Regulations 1999, reg 14(1).

(f)   the performance of her functions as an employee representative for the purpose of the provisions on parental leave.[4]

In addition, under the Act and the Regulations, dismissals for redundancy during the employee's ordinary or additional maternity leave[5] can be automatically unfair where it can be shown that the employee was selected for redundancy among comparable employees for a reason connected to any of the above reasons specified in reg 20(3).[6]

The wide definition of reasons *connected with* pregnancy as well as the provisions on pregnancy related redundancy dismissals show that the drafters of the Regulations were aware of the need to remove loopholes which had been revealed in the case law, particularly that of the House of Lords, surrounding the previous legislation.[7] Even without the added legislative provisions it had already been established that a dismissal of a woman intending to take maternity leave for whom the employer failed to find a temporary replacement was for a reason connected with pregnancy.[8] Moreover, where a woman becomes ill with post-natal depression during a period of maternity leave and that illness is a direct cause of dismissal at a later stage even after the maternity leave had expired, it is for a reason connected with her pregnancy and the dismissal can be automatically unfair.[9]

On the other hand the employee must be able to show that the employers knew or believed that the woman was pregnant or that they were dismissing her for a reason connected to her pregnancy.[10] If they did not know of the pregnancy or did not believe it existed, or if the dismissal was for pregnancy and a related reason, the employee has to show the facts grounding the alleged related reason and that the employer knew that those facts were connected with the woman's pregnancy.[11]

---

4   MPL etc Regulations, reg 20(3).
5   MPL etc Regulations, reg 20(4).
6   MPL etc Regulations, reg 20(2).
7   *Brown v Stockton-on-Tees Borough Council* [1988] IRLR 263, HL.
8   *Clayton v Vigers* [1990] IRLR 177, EAT; see too *George v Beecham Group Ltd* [1977] IRLR 43, IT (absence connected with miscarriage).
9   *Caledonia Bureau Investment & Property v Caffrey* [1998] IRLR 110, EAT.
10   *Del Monte Foods Ltd v Mundon* [1980] ICR 694, [1980] IRLR 224, EAT.
11   Ibid.

2. EXCLUSIONS FROM THE PROTECTIONS

There are two major exclusions from these protections against dismissal for pregnancy. The first, the small firm exclusion, is where the employer, together with any associated employer, employs five or fewer people immediately before the dismissal or the end of the employee's additional maternity leave and it was not reasonably practicable for the employer (or the employer's successor) to permit the employee to return to a job which which is both suitable for her and appropriate for her to do in the circumstances or for an associated employer to offer her a job of that kind.[12]

The second, which applies to employers of any size, is where it is not reasonably practicable for a reason other than redundancy for the employer, or its successor, to permit her to return to a job which is both suitable for her and appropriate for her to do in the circumstances and an associated employer offers her a job *of that kind* and she accepts or unreasonably refuses that offer.[13]

3. OFFERS OF SUITABLE AVAILABLE VACANCIES

Finally, under reg 10, where there is a redundancy situation during the employee's ordinary or additional maternity leave which makes it impracticable for the employer to continue to employ her under her original employment the employee is entitled to be offered suitable employment. A 'suitable' vacancy is one which is suitable in relation to the employee and appropriate for her to do in the circumstances. The terms and conditions of the new contract, including the provisions as to capacity and place in which she is to be employed, must not be substantially less favourable than corresponding provisions of her previous employment.[14]

Moreover, the offer to re-engage the employee must be made before the end of her existing contract and the new contract of employment offered must take effect immediately on the ending of the previous contract.[15]

The test of suitability and appropriateness are to be applied taking into account the 'circumstances of the employee'. Presumably this would include not only the fact of pregnancy but also, where it is the case, that the offer of alternative employment is not meant to be a permanent change

---

12   MPL etc Regulations, reg 20(6).
13   Ibid, reg 20(7).
14   MPL etc Regulations, reg 10.
15   See eg *Martin v BSC Footwear (Supplies) Ltd* [1978] IRLR 95, IT.

of employment. This is reflected in the test of the terms of alternative employment. Unlike the test under the redundancy provisions of ERA 1996 which concerns a more permanent change of employment, the test for the terms of suitable alternative employment for a pregnant employee is whether they are not *substantially* less favourable. This test presupposes the possibility of some decline in basic terms and conditions such as status or pay.

The potentially wider field of suitable alternative employment for pregnant employees is a two-edged sword. It increases the possibility that the employer may find alternative work but at the same time it increases the possible number of jobs of which it may later be said that a suitable alternative vacancy existed in the firm. Whether a vacancy is available is a question of fact.[16] The Regulations place on the employer the onus of proving that it was not reasonably practical to permit her to return to her earlier job or a suitable alternative as well as to prove that an offer of alternative employment complied with the requirements listed above. In addition, in the event of no offer the employer must prove that there was no suitable vacancy for the employee.[17] Moreover, if there is no suitable alternative vacancy with the employee's employer or associated employer, the employee will not be regarded as unfairly dismissed.

---

16   See eg *Community Task Force v Rimmer* [1986] ICR 491, EAT.

17   MPL etc Regulations, reg 20(8). This rather unusually places a burden on the employer of proving a negative. In practice it might well come down to a requirement that the employer show the steps he took to investigate the possibilities of suitable alternative vacancies in the firm.

Chapter 14.
Dismissals in connection with a transfer of the undertaking

Under the Transfer of Undertakings (Protection of Employment) Regulations 1981 (TUPE) where there is a 'relevant transfer' of the business or 'undertaking', the contracts of employment of the transferor's employees, which would otherwise have been terminated by the sale of the business at common law, instead undergo a statutory novation and automatically transfer into the same contracts of employment with the new employer, unless the employee disagrees.[1]

The intention of the Regulations, as well as the Directive which it implements (Acquired Rights Directive EEC Council Directive No 77/187 EEC No 77/187), is to provide the safeguard to the employees of the transferor firm that they may enter into their relationship with the transferee employer with all or almost all their individual and collective rights, powers, duties and obligations vis-à-vis their former employer, in place and not lose them as a result of the transfer.[2]

In pursuit of this objective, the TUPE Regulations also provide that where as a result of a transfer an employee is dismissed, whether before or after the transfer, the dismissal may be treated as unfair in one of two ways. First, such a dismissal could be automatically unfair under regulation 8(1) if the transfer or a reason connected with it is the sole reason or principal reason for the dismissal. Secondly, regulation 8(2) provides employers with the defence that if the reason for the dismissal is a reorganisation of the

1   See *Katsikas v Konstantinidis*: C-132/91 [1993] IRLR 179, ECJ.
2   See eg *Wendelboe v LJ Music ApS*: 19/83 [1985] ECR 457, [19865] 1 CMLR 476, ECJ.

business for economic, technical or organisational reasons by either the transferor or transferee employer and entails changes in the workforce either before or after the relevant transfer, then the dismissal is not automatically unfair but must be treated as for a substantial reason and be tested under ERA, s 98(4) for reasonableness.

1. RELEVANT TRANSFER

For the transfer of Undertakings Regulations to apply in the first place there must be a 'relevant transfer'. Regulation 3 defines such a transfer as a transfer[3] from one person to another of an undertaking situated immediately before the transfer in the UK, or part of one which is so situated. It thus excludes takeovers of businesses by the purchase of shares – a common type of takeover in the United Kingdom[4] – because no change of 'employer' is involved, and applies solely to changes of the proprietorship of the undertaking to another employer.[5] Nevertheless, the regulations apply to a wide variety of transfers including those between non-commercial ventures[6] and those involving the initial or 'first generation' contracting out of services or part of an operation from one employer (public or private) to another,[7] as well as 'second generation' contracting out or

---

3   The transfer can be a sale, another disposition, such as a gift or can be by operation of law eg through succession. See eg *Cook v Kingston-upon-Hull City Council* (1984) EAT 660/83. Under regulation 3(4) a transfer of an undertaking may be 'effected by a series of two or more transactions'. See eg *P Bork International A/S v Foreningen af Arbejds ledere i Danmark* [1989] IRLR 41, ECJ; *Daddy's Dance Hall* [1988] IRLR 315, ECJ; *Longden v Ferrari Ltd* [1994] IRLR 157, EAT.

4   *Brookes v Borough Care Services* [1998] IRLR 636, EAT.

5   If the transfer is effected by a receiver or liquidator special 'hiring down' provisions apply. Under regulation 4, the transfer will be deemed not to have been effected until the transferee company ceases to be a wholly owned subsidiary of the transferor company or the relevant undertaking is transferred by the transferee company to another person. As a consequence employer roles are transferred to an outside employer and will be regarded to have been reasonably employed by the receiver. Employees who are dismissed by the receiver will be affected by regulation 8. See Davies and Freedland, 'The effects of receivership upon employees of companies' (1980) ILJ 95; Pollard 'Insolvent companies and TUPE' [1996] ILJ 191; McMullen *Business Transfer and Employee Rights* (2nd edn, 1992, Butterworths).

6   See eg *Dr Sophie Redmond Stichting v Bartol* [1992] IRLR 366, ECJ.

7   *Rask and Christensen v ISS Kantineservice AS*: C-209/91 [1993] IRLR 133, ECJ; see too *Sánchez Hidalgo*: C-173/96 [1999] IRLR 136, ECJ.

contracting back in [8] as long as the business has retained its identity as an economic 'entity' and the operation is continued from the first employer to the second.[9]

The ECJ has taken a wide view of 'undertaking', one more concerned with economic substance than legal forms of ownership. The Directive can apply to a business lease.[10] Nor does it matter that the transferor retains ownership, or a degree of control,[11] of the assets used, or that the service is performed exclusively for the transferor, or that the service is performed for a fixed fee and hence the contractor's risk of loss is nil, as long as the original undertaking retains its identity as an 'economic entity'.[12] A transfer between two members of the same group can be a relevant transfer of an undertaking.[13]

i) Has an 'undertaking' been transferred?

Since an 'undertaking' is defined in regulation 2(i) as including any trade or business, it is likely to exclude a simple transfer of assets which falls short of a complete transfer of the wider business operation.[14] The test of whether a transfer is one of the business or solely of its physical assets is essentially a question of fact for employment tribunals as long as they correctly direct themselves on the law.[15]

The ECJ has regularly held that under the Directive an 'undertaking' must have the characteristics of a 'stable economic entity'.[16] In *Süzen*[17] the Court stated that the concept of an 'entity' refers to an organised

8   Ibid. See eg *Süzen v Zehnacker*: C-13/95 [1997] IRLR 255, ECJ.

9   Ibid.

10   See eg *P Bork International* and *Daddy's Dance Hall* n 3 above.

11   See eg *Rask* and *Sánchez Hidalgo* n 7 above.

12   See eg *Rask* and *Sánchez Hidalgo* n 7 above.

13   See *Allen v Amalgamated Construction Ltd* [2000] IRLR 119, ECJ.

14   See eg *Woodhouse v Peter Brotherhood Ltd* [1972] 2 QB 520, [1972] ICR 186, CA; *Melon v Hector Powe Ltd* [1981] 1 All ER 313, [1981] ICR 43, HL.

15   See eg *Melon v Hector Powe Ltd* [1981] 1 All ER 313, [1981] ICR 43, HL; *SI (Systems and Instruments) Ltd v Grist and Riley* [1983] ICR 788, [1983] IRLR 391, EAT; *Modiwear Ltd v Wallis Fashion Group* (1980) EAT 535/80; *Kenmir Ltd v Frizzell* [1968] 1 All ER 414, 3 KIR 240; *Woodhouse v Peter Brotherhood Ltd* [1972] 2 QB 520, [1972] ICR 186, CA.

16   *Schmidt v Spar- und Leihkasse der früheren Amter Bordesholm, Kiel under Cronshagen*: C-392/92 [1994] IRLR 302, ECJ.

17   *Süzen v Zehnacker Gebäudereinigung GmbH Krankenhausservice*: C-13/95 [1997] IRLR 255, ECJ; see *Davies* (1997) ILJ 190.

grouping of persons and assets facilitating the exercise of an economic activity. In *Sanchez Hidalgo*[18] the Court added that its management must be 'sufficiently structured and *autonomous*' from other undertakings.[19] Thus, if an activity is integrated into a larger organisation it may not pass the test. If it is sufficiently structured and autonomous it can.

In *Spijkers*[20] the ECJ suggested that a multi-factor test was required to determine whether an 'undertaking' was transferred: (i) the type of undertaking or business concerned; (ii) whether assets tangible or intangible are transferred; (iii) whether employees are taken over; (iv) whether customers are transferred; and (v) the degree of similarity of activities before and after the transfer.

The *Spijkers* test emphasises the need for continuity and thus moves beyond a mere test of whether the business as a going concern versus the physical assets. Yet the difficulty with it is that it offers no guidance as to the weighting of its various factors. It leaves that task to employment tribunals. In *Schmidt*[1] a case concerning the contracting out of a cleaning contract for an office, the ECJ held that if a specific activity of the transferor performed by a specific employee is taken over by another employer that is sufficient to constitute a transfer of an undertaking. A transfer of assets is not a necessary condition of a transfer of an undertaking; in such cases of service contracts, the identity of the undertaking rests with its employees and if the transferee employer takes on the same employee(s) there could be a transfer of an undertaking.

In *Süzen*[2] a transfer of a cleaning contract from one contractor to another, however, the Court appeared to change tack by offering a tighter definition of undertaking in relation to service contracts. It held that, assuming no significant transfer of assets, whether tangible or intangible, even if the transferee employer engaged in a similar activity and employed the same employees to do similar work, there was no transfer of the undertaking unless the transferee employer took over a *major part of the workforce*.

Before *Oy Liikerne Ab* the UK courts had become concerned with the issue of whether the employer's motive of avoiding the Regulation in refusing to take on the transferor's employees was a relevant circumstance.

---

18 See note 7 above.
19 In *ECM (Vehicle Delivery Service) Ltd v Wilcox* [1999] IRLR 559, the Court of Appeal used the term 'discrete'.
20 For the full list see eg *Spijkers v Gebroeders Benedik Abbatoir CV*: 24/85 [1986] ECR 1119, ECJ.
1 [1994] IRLR 302, ECJ.
2 [1997] IRLR 255, ECJ.

In *ECM (Vehicle Delivery Service) Ltd v Cox*[3] an undertaking with an identifiable operation consisting of 19 dedicated drivers and a few administrative staff lost its contract to a second delivery service company who deliberately refrained from hiring any of the former employees of the transferor employer because they wished to avoid the effects of the Regulation. The Court of Appeal upheld the EAT on the point that the reason why the employees were not appointed by ECM was a relevant circumstance.

In the later case of *Oy Liikerne Ab*,[4] the Court of Justice added a further condition to the *Süzen* test. If the activities of the transferor are based on significant tangible assets as well as employees, if there is no transfer of assets, there is no transfer. *Oy Liikerne Ab* involved the transfer of a franchise to run bus lines in Helsinki from one bus operating company to another where the transferee employer took on 33 of the 45 dismissed drivers of the transferor offering them less favourable terms (although terms that were above the minima established by collective agreement). The Court took the view that it was only where the activities of the transferor were 'based essentially on manpower' that 'a group of workers engaged in a joint activity on a permanent basis may constitute an economic entity'.

Where however, 'tangible assets' contribute significantly to the performance of the 'activity' (as in the case of a bus operating company) the absence of a transfer of such assets to a significant extent from the old to the new contractor must lead to the conclusion that the entity does not retain its identity.[5]

Following *Oy Liikerne Ab* there would appear to be three possible types of factual situations which need to be distinguished. First, if there are no tangible assets of any significance in the activity, the transferee employer's decision not to hire any of the transferor's employees to avoid the effects of the Transfer Regulations will be a relevant circumstance. Secondly, this will also be true where there are significant tangible assets used in the activity but they are owned and provided by the main contractor who will continue to provide them to the transferee employer. Thirdly, where the activity itself consists of tangible assets provided by the transferor employer and the transferee employer refuses to take on employees with the proven motive of avoiding the effect of the transfer, it will now be able

---

3   [1999] IRLR 559, CA.
4   *Oy Liikerne Ab v Pekka Liskjarvi and Pentti Juntunen* [2001] IRLR 171, ECJ. See Davies (2001) ILJ 231.
5   Ibid at para 38.

to argue that, following *Oy Liikerne Ab*, its motive is irrelevant since in any case there could be no transfer.

2. WHAT IS THE EFFECT OF A TRANSFER?

Under TUPE regulation 5(1)

> 'A relevant transfer shall not operate so as to terminate the contract of employment of any person employed by the transferor ... but any such contract ... shall have effect after the transfer as if originally made between the person so employed and the transferee.'

Regulation 5(1) incorporates the principle of the automatic transfer of employment contracts. The transfer occurs whether or not the employer complies with the formalities.[6]

At the individual level, regulation 5(2)(a) ensures that 'all the transferor's rights, powers, duties and liabilities *under or in connection with any such contract* shall be transferred ... to the transferee'. This means that, assuming a relevant transfer of the business, the transferee employer is required to take on all contractual obligations,[7] apart from those rights under an occupational pension scheme (regulation 7).[8] Moreover, where statutory obligations arise in connection with the contract, such as unfair dismissal, redundancy, national insurance, and liabilities for negligence, these too are transferred under regulation 5(2).[9]

---

6   See *Rotsart de Hertaing v J Benoidt SA* [1997] IRLR 127, ECJ.

7   A profit-related pay scheme can transfer: *Unicorn Consultancy Services Ltd v Westbrook* [2000] IRLR 80, EAT.

8   Regulation 7 has been amended by TURERA 1993, s 33 of which narrows the pensions exception so that it applies only to those provisions of occupational schemes which relate only to old age, invalidity and survivor's benefits (regulation 87(1) and (2)). See *Adams v Lancashire County Council and BET Catering Services Ltd* [1997] IRLR 436, CA (transferee employers are not obliged to provide comparable occupation schemes to employees who transfer but must protect accrued pension rights in respect of periods of service occurring prior to the transfer).

9   Certain liabilities, such as criminal liabilities (rule 5(4)), vicarious liability to third parties and liability for a failure to consult with trade unions over redundancies, are cut off by the transfer. Tort liabilities in connection with accidents at work prior to the transfer do transfer, as does insurance cover. See *Bernadone v Pall Mall Services Group* [2000] IRLR 487, CA. Liability for a protective award transfers. See, eg, *Kerry Foods Ltd v Creber* [2000] IRLR 10, EAT.

At the collective level, regulation 6 of the Transfer Regulations provide that the collective agreement made by the transferring employer in respect of any employer whose contract has been preserved by regulation 5 shall continue to have effect as between the trade union and the transferred employee. Regulation 9 provides that recognition of the trade union is transferred from the transferor to the transferee.[10] Finally, regulations 10 and 11 place certain obligations upon the transferring employer to inform and consult with recognised trade union representatives in respect of the transfer. Under regulation 10 the obligation to consult has been amended by TURERA to extend to a duty to consult with a view to reaching agreement. This at the very least requires the employer to go beyond the mere disclosure of information and may require some evidence of attempting to reach a consensus or compromise. Regulation 11 has been changed to provide slightly stiffer penalties.[11] The maximum penalty for non-compliance has been increased from two weeks' to four weeks' pay for each employee and there are no deductions permitted for any compensation paid to employees for a failure to consult on redundancies.[12]

Furthermore, regulation 6 provides specifically for the transfer of the collective rights of employees where there is in existence a collective agreement. Since collective agreements are not normally legally enforceable in the UK, however, the only rights under collective agreements that will be preserved are those which can be incorporated in individual contracts and transferred under regulation 5(2). If the term of a collective agreement is incorporated into the contract of employment then it can continue as an obligation of the transferee employer even if he or she derecognises the union and withdraws from the collective agreement.[13]

3. DISMISSALS, REORGANISATIONS AND TUPE

i) Automatically unfair dismissals

Under regulation 5 of TUPE a transfer of the undertaking that is a relevant transfer will not operate as such to terminate the contract of employment

---

10 This is not now legally binding but could be so because of the statutory recognition procedure provided in the Employment Relations Act 1999.
11 See amendment introduced by s 33 of TURERA.
12 Ibid.
13 See *Whent v T Cartlidge Ltd* [1997] IRLR 153, EAT.

of any employees employed immediately before the transfer[14] as long as the transferee employer provides them with the same job without any substantial change in their working conditions to their detriment. In this way the regulation overrides the common law rule that a contract of employment, because of its personal nature would be terminated by such a change of employer.[15] The effect of regulation 5 is that the individual's contract of employment does not cease but is transferred to the transferee employer as if it had originally been made with that employer.

Consequently, where an employee is dismissed[16] and the transfer or a reason connected with it is the reason or principal reason for the dismissal, regulation 8(1) provides that such a dismissal will be automatically unfair.

In order for regulation 8(1) to apply there must be a causal link shown between the transfer and the dismissal. The timing itself is not decisive. Thus the transfer can occur in the course of a transfer or be caused by the prospect of a transfer as long as a link is shown.[17] Where an employee is dismissed with notice by the transferor employer but the notice expires after the transfer, it is the transferor's reason for the dismissal notice which is the relevant reason even though liability may be transferred.[18]

Where employees are dismissed prior to a transfer for a reason connected with the transfer they are deemed to be employed in the undertaking immediately before the transfer and the employment statutorily continues with the employer. Where however the transferee employer does not take on the transferor's employees either because they have already been dismissed by the transferor or by the transferee, the remedies available to such employees are those of re-engagement or compensation for unfair dismissal (or wrongful dismissal). They have no remedy of nullification of the employer's decision to dismiss and a confirmation of employment with the new employer.[19]

14 See eg *Apex Leisure Hire v Barratt* [1984] ICR 452, [1984] IRLR 224, EAT.
15 See eg *Nokes v Doncaster Amalgamated Collieries Ltd* [1940] AC 1014, [1940] 3 All ER 549, HL.
16 Under regulation 5(5) employees can treat themselves as constructively dismissed if there is a detrimental change in their working conditions: *Delabole Slate Ltd v Berriman* [1985] IRLR 305, CA; *Rossiter v Pendragon* [2001] IRLR 256, EAT; *University of Oxford v Humphreys* [2000] IRLR 183, CA.
17 See eg *Morris v John Grose Group* [1998] IRLR 499, EAT disagreeing with the view in *Ibex Trading Co Ltd* [1994] IRLR 564, EAT that dismissals prior to the transfer are ipso facto not by reason of the transfer. See too *Harrison v Bowden* [1994] ICR 186, EAT.
18 See *BSG Property Services v Tuck* [1996] IRLR 134, EAT.
19 See *Wilson v St Helens Borough Council; British Fuels Ltd v Baxendale* [1998] IRLR 706, HL; *Kerry Foods Ltd v Creber* [2000] IRLR 10, EAT.

Where, however, an employer dismisses an employee for a reason *not linked* to the transfer, such as a dismissal for capacity or conduct, or for a reason falling under regulation 8(2), it can escape the *automatic unfairness* rule of regulation 8(1). Regulation 8(2) specifically provides that where an employee is dismissed, whether *before* or *after* the transfer, for an 'economic, technical or organisational' reason entailing changes in the workforce there is no automatic unfairness. Instead, the employer can justify a dismissal as having been for a substantial reason for dismissing that employee from the position which that employee held. In order for the dismissal to fall within regulation 8(2), however, the employer must be able to show that the reason for the dismissal fits within the definition of an economic, technical or organisational reason, eg redundancy or reorganisation.[20] If the reason is an economic one, it must, on the balance of authority, be related to the future viability of the entity regardless of the transfer and not merely relate to a desire to achieve a sale and make the business more attractive to a buyer or to raise its price. Yet that distinction is difficult to draw.

Thus in *Wilson v St Helens Borough Council; British Fuels Ltd v Baxendale*,[1] where the transferor employer agreed to a reduction in force of employees of a Community Home from 162 to 72 in order to ensure that the Community Home would not run at a loss, the House of Lords accepted that since those changes would have had to be made anyway, the dismissals were not for a transfer related reason. And, in *Whitehouse v Charles Blatchford & Sons*[2] a technician was dismissed when the preferred bidder for a contract with the hospital to supply appliances was told that as a condition of obtaining the contract they must reduce their staffing costs by cutting their technicians from 13 to 12. The employment tribunal found that the reason was an 'economic' one and not a reason connected with the transfer since it was connected with the future conduct of the business as a going concern. The Court of Appeal, as well as the EAT, dismissed the appeal. The Court reasoned that it was open to the tribunal to conclude that the transfer was not the reason for dismissal. The Court could not accept that there was no difference between a dismissal to secure a sale and one to obtain a contract. The current position was not analogous to a

---

20   See eg *Gorictree Ltd v Jenkinson* [1985] ICR 51, [1984] IRLR 391, EAT; *Anderson v Dalkeith Engineering Ltd* [1985] ICR 66, [1984] IRLR 429, EAT.

1   Cf *Wilson v St Helens Borough Council; British Fuels Ltd v Baxendale* [1998] IRLR 706, HL.

2   [1999] IRLR 492, CA; see too *Longden and Paisley v Ferrari Ltd and Kennedy Intl Ltd* [1994] IRLR 157, EAT.

situation where a vendor sets out to achieve a better sale price by dismissing employees. The Court went on to state that regulation 8(1) did not apply at all to the situation, a surprising conclusion in view of previous case law.[3] Hence, the issue of the employer's reason for dismissal is a question of fact for tribunals and where the initiative for a reduction in force prior to the transfer is taken by the transferee a tribunal may find that it is for an economic reason *if it relates to the future viability of the firm* and would have occurred in any case.[4] The Court endorsed the tribunal's holding that while the transfer might have been the reason for the dismissal, it was not the cause.[5]

Yet the distinction between regulation 8(1) and 8(2) has been held to turn merely on the fact that the transferee employer takes the initiative in requiring the dismissals. An 'economic' reason for the dismissals must relate to the conduct of the business by analogy with 'technical' and organisational reasons and not merely its attractiveness as a purchase. Otherwise, as the EAT pointed out in *Wheeler v Patel and J Goulding Group*,[6] all dismissals by the transferor employer at the insistence of the transferee employer would be for economic reasons.

Moreover, to provide an effective defence to regulation 8(1), regulation 8(2) requires a showing not only that the employer's reason for dismissal was for an economic, organisational or technical reason relating to the transfer, but that the action taken by the employer involved *a change in the workforce.* Thus in *Berriman v Delabole Slate Ltd*[7] the company gave the employee an ultimatum to accept a reduced rate of pay because it wished to standardise rates of pay between new and existing employees. The Court of Appeal held that Mr Berriman's resignation in response to the ultimatum was a constructive dismissal and automatically unfair under regulation 8(1). The employer's argument that the dismissal was a regulation 8(2) reason could not be accepted because a change in rates of pay by itself was not a change in the workforce. To be a reason entailing a change in the workforce, the Court stated there must be a change either in the 'overall numbers or the functions of the employees looked at as a whole ...'. The

3   See eg *Warner v Adnet Ltd* [1998] IRLR 394, CA.

4   See *Wilson and British Fuels* n 1 above.

5   See too *Wheeler v Patel and J Goulding Group* [1987] IRLR 211, EAT; *May & Mossell (West) Ltd v Jensen* (1983) EAT 526/83.

6   [1987] IRLR 211, EAT not following *Anderson and McAlonie v Dalkeith Engineering* [1984] IRLR 429, EAT in Scotland. *Wheeler* later preferred by Scottish EAT in *Gateway Hotels Ltd v Stewart* [1988] IRLR 287, EAT.

7   [1985] ICR 546, [1985] IRLR 305, CA.

Court's view was that the word 'workforce' denotes the whole body of employees as an entity – its 'strength' or 'establishment'. So that if one employee is dismissed and another is engaged in his place, there is no change in the workforce.

The dismissal therefore fell within the automatically unfair rule of regulation 8(1).

On the other hand, if there is a change in the functions of the employees, that is to say in the jobs that they do, that could be a 'change in the workforce' even if there is no change in the identity or total number of the workforce. For example in *Crawford v Swinton Insurance Brokers Ltd*[8] a clerk-typist was ordered by the transferee employer to change to a job as an insurance salesman. This was a change in the workforce in the meaning of regulation 8(2) because there was one less clerk-typist and one more insurance salesman.

Where a dismissal falls within the formula of regulation 8(2), it could provide the basis for a claim of a redundancy payment as well as unfair dismissal.

In *Gorictree Ltd v Jenkinson*,[9] the EAT sitting in England held that the fact that a dismissal was for 'economic, technical or organisational reasons' does not prevent it from constituting dismissal by reason of redundancy.

Finally, once the employer has shown that the dismissal falls within regulation 8(2) it is neither automatically *unfair* nor automatically *fair*. Instead, it is deemed to be for 'some other substantial reason' under s 98(1) and the employer must show that the dismissal was 'reasonable' under ERA, s 98(4).[10] In the case of redundancy dismissals under regulation 8(2) the test will include a test of unfair selection for redundancy.[11] In the case of reorganisation the ordinary principles of 'some other substantial reason' would apply as adapted.

In all such cases, as the EAT pointed out in *Kerry Foods Ltd v Creber*[12] if the reason for a dismissal by a *transferor* employer is an economic,

---

8 [1990] IRLR 42, EAT; see too *Porter and Nanayakkara v Queens Medical Centre* [1993] IRLR 486, HL (change of method of providing services can amount to a change in the workforce).

9 [1984] IRLR 391, EAT. See too *Anderson and McAlonie v Dalkeith Engineering* [1984] IRLR 429, EAT rejecting *Canning v Niaz and McLoughlin* [1983] IRLR 431, EAT and preferring *Gorictree*.

10 *McGrath v Rank Leisure Ltd* [1985] IRLR 323, EAT; *Gorictree Ltd v Jenkinson* [1984] IRLR 391, EAT.

11 See eg *Warner v Adnet Ltd* [1998] IRLR 394, CA.

12 [2000] IRLR 10, EAT.

technical or organisational reason and the dismissal is nevertheless unfair, the employer may recover only from the transferor employer. The *Litser* principle applies only to a regulation 8(1) dismissal.

Chapter 15.
Fixed-term contracts

1. INTRODUCTION

Under ERA 1996, s 95(2)(b), where an employee is employed under a fixed-term contract and that term expired without being renewed under the same contract, the employee is regarded as being dismissed.[1] This provision has been included to attempt to ensure that where a contract terminates by the 'mere effluxion of time' and nothing is said by the employer, an employee nonetheless may claim that the non-renewal is unfair within the meaning of s 98(4). Section 95(2)(b) can also extend to a case where an employer renews a fixed-term contract on terms which are substantially different. Thus in *Ioannou v BBC*,[2] the NIRC indicated that whereas Ioannou's original three-year contract was renewed by a two-year contract, thus making a five-year fixed-term contract, the important changes introduced into a further one-year contract, meant that it could not be regarded as the 'same contract' as before.[3]

Moreover if an employee is dismissed in the sense of s 95(2)(b) an employer may nevertheless be able to show that such a 'dismissal' was for some other substantial reason under s 95(1)(b) and was reasonable under s 98(4).

---

1   See eg *Thames Television Ltd v Wallis* [1979] IRLR 136, EAT.
2   [1974] ICR 414, [1974] IRLR 77, NIRC.
3   *Dixon v BBC* [1979] QB 546, [1979] ICR 281, CA.

2. WHAT IS A FIXED-TERM CONTRACT?

Of course all three legal consequences presuppose that the contract is in fact a fixed-term contract in the first place, and not some other form of employment contract. To be a contract for a fixed term, a contract must clearly be a contract for a specifically stated period. What happens however when a contract not only stipulates that it will expire after a term of years but also provides that either party has a right to terminate the contract upon notice? Initially in *BBC v Ioannou* the Court of Appeal suggested that a contract was not 'fixed-term' if it contained a provision for termination by notice. As Lord Denning MR put it:

> 'In my opinion, a "fixed term" is one which cannot be unfixed by notice. To be a fixed term the parties must be bound for the term stated in the agreement: and unable to determine it by notice on either side. If it were only determinable for misconduct, it would, I think, be a "fixed term" because that is imported by the common law anyway. But determination by notice is destructive of any "fixed term"'.

In *Dixon v BBC*[4] the Court of Appeal agreed with the EAT that a contract is for a 'fixed term' for the purposes of the definition of dismissal under s 95(1)(b) even though the contract contains a provision that it may be terminated by notice on either side before the term expires. The court reasoned that to allow the insertion of a notice clause to a fixed-term contract would provide the employer with too ready a means of evading the legislation.[5] It also went on to state obiter that the same rule should apply to the definition of a fixed-term contract for the purpose of a waiver because different rules for the two situations would be unacceptable. Today whilst the employer may ask the employee to agree to insert a waiver into a fixed-term contract of two years or more for the purposes of a redundancy claim,[6] the power to insert a waiver for the purpose of an unfair dismissal claim in fixed-term contracts of one year or more has been repealed by the Employment Relations Act 1999.

The Court of Appeal has also held in *Wiltshire County Council v National Association of Teachers in Further and Higher Education*[7] that

---

4   [1979] QB 546, [1979] ICR 281, [1979] IRLR 114, CA.
5   Ibid.
6   ERA 1996, s 197(3)–(5); *Kingston-upon-Hull City Council v Mountain* [1999] ICR 715, EAT.
7   [1980] ICR 455, [1980] IRLR 198, CA. See too *Ironmonger v Morefield Ltd* [1988] IRLR 461, EAT.

a contract to perform a specific task will not be regarded as a contract for a fixed term where it is indeterminate in terms of the time required to perform that task. The court reasoned that a contract is for a particular purpose which is discharged by performance and hence there is no dismissal.[8] Similarly in *Brown v Knowsley Borough Council*[9] an employment contract which was expressly subject to the confirmation of external funding was held to terminate automatically when the funding dried up. This would allow employers to avoid an end to a contract of employment fitting into one of the existing statutory definitions of dismissal by shaping the form of the contract. In due course, when the Fixed Term Worker Directive 1999/70/ EC is implemented, this 'loophole' should be closed since the Directive defines a protectable dismissal as 'where the end of the employment contract or relationship is determined by objective conditions such as reading a specific date, completing a specific task or the occurrence of a specific event'.

Finally, in *Weston v University College Swansea*[10] a tribunal chose to regard a three-year appointment as not counting as a fixed-term contract where the terms of the appointment contained a salary scale which extended considerably beyond the three-year period of initial appointment.

3. FIXED-TERM CONTRACTS AND 'SOME OTHER SUBSTANTIAL REASON'

In *Terry v East Sussex County Council*[11] the EAT stated that the non-renewal of fixed-term contracts could be regarded as 'some other substantial reason' under s 98(1)(b):

'We think it would be useful to add some observations about the considerations proper to be taken into account in a case such as the present when considering the applicability of [s 98(1)(b)] and whether "some other substantial reason" has been shown. What an [employment] tribunal must do is to ensure that the case is a genuine

---

8   See also *Ryan v Shipboard Maintenance Ltd* [1980] ICR 88, [1980] IRLR 16, EAT.
9   [1986] IRLR 102, EAT.
10 [1975] IRLR 102, IT.
11 [1977] 1 All ER 567, [1976] ICR 536, EAT; approved in *North Yorkshire County Council v Fay* [1985] IRLR 247, CA; *DHSS v Hughes, DHSS v Coy, DE v Jarnell* [1985] IRLR 263, HL; *Harrison v Norwest Holst Group Administration Ltd* [1985] IRLR 240, CA.

one where an employee has to his own knowledge been employed for a particular period, or a particular job, on a temporary basis. We accept counsel for the local authority's suggestion that there may be a wide scale in what can ordinarily be described as "temporary" jobs. At one end is the plain case where a person (for example a school teacher) is employed to fill a gap where somebody is absent, and it is made plain at the moment of engagement that he is only being employed during the period of the absence of the person he is temporarily replacing. At the other end is the case of the employee who is engaged on a short fixed-term contract, perhaps described as "temporary", in an employment where as a general rule the employees are engaged on a weekly basis and where there is no particular end served by the employment being arranged in the manner in which it has been. In between, there will be every possible variety of case. We would not wish the actual words which we have used in this judgment, for the purpose of indicating the matters which we have in mind, to be taken in other cases as a touchstone, as though they were to be found in an Act of Parliament laying down the test. They are merely indications of the sort of points which an [employment] tribunal should have in mind'.

The EAT went on to emphasise that the case should be a genuine one where an employee has to his own knowledge been employed for a particular period or a particular job on a temporary basis. It suggested that tribunals would have to strike a balance. On the one hand, they would have to recognise the need of employers for protection against having to pay unfair dismissal compensation for genuine fixed-term employment which can be seen from the outset not to be ongoing, such as teachers and lecturers engaged for a term or shorter period, or construction workers retained for particular jobs. On the other hand, employees need to be protected against being deprived of their rights through ordinary employments being dressed up in the form of temporary fixed-term contracts. Thus, it set aside the tribunal's decision on the ground that although the non-renewal of Mr Terry's one-year contract could rightly be regarded as 'some other substantial reason' under s 98(1)(b), it was necessary to give explicit consideration to the reasonableness of that non-renewal under s 98(4) and this the tribunal had failed to do.

In *Cohen v London Borough of Barking*[12] the EAT further emphasised the need to draw a balance under s 98(4) in cases of non-renewal of fixed-

12   [1976] IRLR 416, EAT.

term contracts, and possibly enlarged the basis upon which the unreasonableness of the employer's decision could be contested from those suggested in *Terry*'s case. In *Cohen*'s case, the EAT stated that the fact that the employee's contract was from the start not assured of continuation beyond a fixed term was a material factor to be considered in assessing the reasonableness of the decision not to renew. However, it also indicated that it would be wrong to consider that it was a conclusive justification for dismissal. Thus in *Cohen*'s case, where the employee's contract was from the start for 'one year only' as a trainee educational psychologist, the fact that she was unable to complete her qualifications to become a fully trained psychologist (which was the type of employee the local authority had the need of) was a good ground for the tribunal to conclude that the decision not to renew the temporary contract was unreasonable. In the event, the test of reasonableness is not restricted to the question whether the contract was a genuine fixed-term contract or to the point that the employee knew the temporary nature from the start – the true criteria of reasonableness suggested by *Terry*'s case. It could also include a more comprehensive look at the decision by management not to renew in all the surrounding circumstances. Thus in *Beard v Governors of St Josephs School*,[13] the EAT advised tribunals not to omit a 'full consideration of the circumstances surrounding a decision to dismiss at the end of a temporary fixed-term contract', including whether the employer gave the employee an opportunity to be considered if a full-time position became available.

---

13   [1978] ICR 1234, [1979] IRLR 144, EAT.

Chapter 16.
Reinstatement and re-engagement

Once an employment tribunal finds that an employee has been unfairly dismissed, it must consider the appropriate remedy. Under ERA 1996, for most types of unfair dismissals there are three possible forms of relief; an order of reinstatement, an order of re-engagement, or an award of compensation. In cases of dismissals for trade union membership and activity, or non-membership, health and safety reasons, pension trustees, elected employee representations, working time complaints and whistle-blowers, there is in addition a special procedure available to complainants which offers 'interim relief' to attempt to maintain the contract subsisting until the case actually reaches the hearing stage.[1]

Although, in practice, the most common remedy is an award of compensation[2] the Act expressly provides that reinstatement and re-engagement are the primary remedies. Thus, s 112 states that where a complaint of unfair dismissal is well founded an employment tribunal must first explain that an order for reinstatement or reengagement may be made and then ask whether the complainant wishes the tribunal to make such an order. The requirements of s 112 of the Act are mandatory and require that in every case where a dismissal is found to be unfair, the employment tribunal must explain the orders of reinstatement and re-engagement and ask if the complainant wants either type of order. If he says he does, then it must go on to consider whether or not to make either order in the light of the provisions of s 116 and give both complainant and employer the

1   See Chapter 17.
2   See Chapter 17.

opportunity to be heard, before exercising its discretion to make such an order or not. This procedure must be followed even in a case where the complainant is professionally represented. If not followed, the order of the EAT may be set aside.[3]

An 'order of reinstatement' is defined as an order that the employer restores the employee to his former position treating him in all respects as if he had never been dismissed.[4] In addition to specifying the date for compliance, the industrial tribunal must specify any benefits the employee might '*reasonably be expected to have had*' but for the dismissal, including arrears of pay and any rights and privileges including seniority and pension rights, which must be restored. The tribunal must also require the employee to be treated as if he had benefited from any improvement in terms and conditions of employment, such as a wage increase, if the employee *would have benefited* from an improvement had he not been dismissed.[5]

An order of re-engagement is a more flexible remedy. It can include an order that the employee be engaged by the same employer, his successor or an 'associated employer'.[6] It can also include an order that the employee be engaged in work comparable to that from which he was dismissed or some other suitable employment. Further, the tribunal must specify the main terms on which re-engagement is to take place: that is, the identity of the employer, the nature of the employment, any amount to be paid for 'reasonably expected benefits' lost owing to the dismissal, any rights and privileges which might be restored, and the date for compliance.[7] In cases where the employee caused or contributed to his own dismissal, a tribunal

---

3   *Pirelli General Cable Works Ltd v Murray* [1979] IRLR 190, EAT;*Cowley v Manson Timber Ltd* [1995] IRLR 153, CA.

4   See eg *Artisan Press v Strawley and Parker* [1986] IRLR 126, EAT.

5   ERA 1996, s 114. However, in the case of an order of reinstatement as well as an order of re-engagement, the sums awarded to an employee must be reduced by the industrial tribunal to take into account any sums received by the employee for pay in lieu of notice, ex gratia payments or pay or other remuneration from another employer as well as 'such other benefits as the tribunal thinks appropriate', ERA, s 114(4).

6   See definition in ERA 1996, s 115.

7   See eg *O'Laoire v Jackal International Ltd* [1991] IRLR 170, CA; [1990] IRLR 70, CA; *Electronic Data Processing Ltd v Wright* [1986] IRLR 8, EAT; *Lilley Construction v Dunn* [1984] IRLR 483, EAT; *Rank Xerox (UK) Ltd v Stryczek* [1995] IRLR 568, EAT. See also ERA 1996, s 115(3).

has some discretion in determining these terms.[8] In all other cases, the tribunal must order re-engagement on terms which are as far as reasonably practicable, as favourable as would apply under an order for reinstatement.[9]

In the case of both reinstatement, and re-engagement, the employee's continuous service is preserved and the period between the dismissal and re-employment counts as a period of employment.[10]

1. DETERMINING THE APPROPRIATENESS OF REINSTATEMENT AND RE-EMPLOYMENT

Under ERA, s 112 an employment tribunal's consideration of the remedy of either reinstatement or re-engagement must take place in two separate stages. In the first stage the tribunal must determine whether either reinstatement or re-engagement is appropriate and, if re-engagement is appropriate, under what terms. In the second stage, if an order has not been complied with, the tribunal must determine the penalty for non-compliance. Although the remedy of reinstatement or re-engagement may take the form of an order, the penalties for non-compliance, as we shall see, are exclusively financial.[11]

When determining whether to make an order for either reinstatement or re-engagement following ERA, s 116 a tribunal must take into account three main factors:
(i)   the wishes of the employee,
(ii) the practicability of compliance by the employer,
(iii) whether the employee caused or contributed to some extent to the dismissal.[12]

---

8   ERA 1996, s 116(4). For excellent discussions of the actual effects of tribunals application of this remedy see: Dickens, Hart, Jones and Weekes, 'Re-employment of Unfairly Dismissed Workers – The Lost Remedy' (1981) 1 LJ 160; P Lewis, 'An Analysis of Why Legislation has failed to Provide Protection for Unfairly Dismissed Workers (1981) BJIR 316; Dickens, Jones, Weekes and Hart, *Dismissal* (Blackwells, 1985).
9   ERA 1996, s 116(4).
10 Employment Protection (Continuity of Employment) Regulations 1996, SI 1996/3147.
11 Cf *Lilley Construction Ltd v Dunn* [1984] IRLR 483, EAT.
12 ERA, s 116(1)(c).

i) The wishes of the employee

Once an employment tribunal finds an employee to be unfairly dismissed, it must give the individual an explanation of the possible orders of reinstatement or re-engagement that may be made and ask if the employee wishes such an order to be made. Only if the employee expresses a wish for the tribunal to make a particular order is the tribunal empowered to exercise a discretion to do so.[13] Once the employee indicates that he or she wishes reinstatement or re-engagement, the employment tribunal must follow a procedure set out in s 116. The tribunal must first decide whether to make an order for reinstatement and only if it decides not to do so, should it consider whether or not to order re-engagement and on what terms. Even if the employee desires to be re-employed, however, the tribunal must go on to consider (i) the practicability that the employer could comply with the order and (ii) the contributory fault, if any, of the employee.

ii) Practicability of compliance by the employer

In deciding whether or not reinstatement or re-engagement is 'practicable' for the purposes of s 116(1)(b) and 116(3)(b), the tribunal must consider whether objectively it is feasible that such an order could be complied with. As the Court of Appeal put it in *Coleman v Magnet Joinery Ltd*,[14] 'practicable' is not to be equated with 'possible'.

The burden of proving impracticability lies with the employer. The test for the tribunal is objective impracticability not that it would not be 'expedient' for the employer or the firm.[15]

Impracticability is a question of fact in each case; the tribunal must exercise a discretion in evaluating the likely consequences of its order. If the industrial relations situation points overwhelmingly to the conclusion that the consequence of any attempt to re-engage the employee will be serious industrial strife, then an order may not be practicable.[16] But even

13   ERA 1996, s 112(3).
14   [1975] ICR 46, [1974] IRLR 343, CA. See also *Bateman v British Leyland (UK) Ltd* [1974] ICR 403, [1974] IRLR 101, NIRC.
15   *Qualcast (Wolverhampton) Ltd v Ross* [1979] IRLR 98, EAT. Cf *Clancy v Cannock Chase Technical College* [2001] IRLR 331, EAT.
16   See eg *Coleman v Magnet Joinery* [1974] IRLR 343, CA; *Bateman v British Leyland (UK) Ltd* [1974] ICR 403, [1974] IRLR 101, NIRC. See too *Port of London Authority v Payne* [1994] IRLR 9, CA; *Sarvent v Central Electricity Generating Board* [1976] IRLR 66, IT.

in such circumstances, an order of reinstatement may be made where a tribunal finds that 'there is not likely to be any difficulty in the parties agreeing the terms of that reinstatement'.[17]

The likelihood of friction between supervisors or other employees and a reinstated or re-engaged employee or a breakdown in trust and confidence between employer and employee can be taken into account even where there is no prospect of collective action.[18] Moreover, the size and scale of the organisation may be a relevant factor. Reinstatement or re-engagement may be less practicable in smaller firms.[19]

A further basis for a tribunal finding of non-practicability of reinstatement or re-engagement might be, in the case of an order of reinstatement to a particular job, where the employee was not fit to do the job either because of incompetence[20] or ill health[1] but the manner of the dismissal was found to be unfair. This however, would not preclude a tribunal from investigating the possibilities of re-engagement in other comparable employment[2] or, in certain circumstances, even from reconsidering re-engagement at a future point in time when the individual's incapacitating illness had been cured.[3]

Moreover, there is clearly no basis for an order of reinstatement where the job itself has disappeared, owing to redundancy, at least where the workplace has closed down. The inability to take the employee back without dismissing another employee may be a factor.[4] Where the dismissal from redundancy is a case of unfair selection, the tribunal may exercise discretion.[5]

A tribunal will have the discretion under s 115 to order re-engagement even where there is no existing vacancy if it considers that one is likely to

---

17   See *Goodbody v British Railways Board* [1977] IRLR 84, IT.
18   See eg *Wood Group Heavy Turbines Industrial Turbines Ltd v Crossan* [1998] IRLR 680, EAT; *Nothman v London Borough of Barnet (No 2)* [1980] IRLR 65, CA; *Thornton v S J Kitchin Ltd* [1972] IRLR 46; *Butler v J Wendon & Son* [1972] IRLR 15, IT; *Schembri v Scot Bowyers Ltd* [1973] IRLR 110, IT.
19   See eg dicta in *Enessy Co SA (t/a Tulchan Estate) v Minoprio* [1978] IRLR 489, EAT.
20   *Oliso-Emosingoit v Inner London Education Services* (1977) EAT 139/77.
1   *Parrott v Yorkshire Electricity Board* [1972] IRLR 75, IT.
2   See eg *Todd v North Eastern Electricity Board* [1975] IRLR 130, IT.
3   See eg *Newlands v J Howard & Co Ltd* [1973] IRLR 9, IT.
4   *Freemans plc v Flynn* [1984] IRLR 486, EAT; see too *Cold Drawn Tubes Ltd v Middleton* [1992] IRLR 160, EAT.
5   See eg *Calvert v Allisons (Gravel Pits) Ltd* [1975] IRLR 71, IT; *Dorrell and Ardis v Engineering Developments (Farnborough) Ltd* [1975] IRLR 234, IT.

arise in the near future. As the EAT pointed out in *Timex Corpn v Thomson*,[6] s 116 does not require the tribunal to be completely satisfied that an order is practicable before it is made – it only obliges them to take this into account.

The one issue upon which an employment tribunal's discretion is specifically curtailed, however, is the issue of when a replacement makes reinstatement impracticable.

Under ERA 1996, s 116(5), where an employer seeks to establish that, or an employment tribunal to determine whether, his engagement of a permanent replacement makes reinstatement impracticable, the tribunal may not take into account the fact that the vacancy was filled in determining the practicability of reinstatement or re-engagement unless the employer shows one of two things. Either the employer must show that it was not practicable for him to arrange for the dismissed employee's work to be done without engaging a permanent replacement, say by having a temporary replacement. Or, he must show that he only engaged the replacement after the lapse of a reasonable period without having heard from the dismissed employee that he wished to be reinstated or re-engaged. Even if the employer can show this latter proposition to be true, he must go on to show that when the replacement was engaged it was no longer reasonable for him to arrange for the dismissed employee's work to be done except by a permanent replacement.[7]

iii) Contributory fault and reinstatement and re-engagement

Where an employment tribunal finds that an employee has caused or contributed to some extent to the dismissal,[8] it must also consider this factor in determining whether it would be just to order reinstatement or re-engagement. In cases of a high rate of contributory fault, a tribunal can decide not to make an order of re-engagement on that ground.[9] In the case of an order for reinstatement, the tribunal may only take into account the employee's degree of 'fault' when considering whether or not to order reinstatement; it has no discretion to take into account that factor in deciding the terms of reinstatement. In the case of re-engagement, however, the employment tribunal may take into account contributory fault in setting

---

6   [1981] IRLR 522, EAT; *Electronic Data Processing Ltd v Wright* (1983) EAT 292/83.
7   ERA 1996, s 116(5).
8   Cf *Boots Co plc v Lees-Collier* [1986] IRLR 485, EAT.
9   *Nairne v Highland and Islands Fire Brigade* [1989] IRLR 366, Ct of Sess.

the terms on which it makes the order. But in all other cases it must provide terms which are 'so far as reasonably practicable as favourable as an order of reinstatement'.[10]

2. PENALTIES FOR NON-COMPLIANCE

Although the remedies of reinstatement and re-engagement take the form of orders, the penalty for non-compliance is exclusively financial. In a case where an employer has reinstated or re-engaged an employee in response to an order but the compliance is only partial in any respect, a tribunal must make an award of compensation which it considers to be fit having regard to the loss sustained by the employee as a consequence of the employer's failure fully to comply with the terms of the order.[11]

Where the employer's non-compliance extends to a failure to reinstate or re-engage on any terms, the tribunal may make an additional award of compensation of an amount not less than 26 weeks' nor more than 52 weeks' pay[12] over and above the basic and compensatory awards.[13] The amount of the award within the scale is likely to be influenced by the fact that the award is a form of exemplary damages, designed to allow tribunals to mark their disapproval of the employer's decision to refuse to comply in the particular circumstances of the case rather than simply to compensate for the additional loss attributable to the refusal.[14]

Where a tribunal has made an order of reinstatement or re-engagement and the employer does not comply, it nevertheless has the discretion not to make an additional award of compensation if the employer satisfies it

---

10 ERA, s 116(4), see eg *McCarthy v Fried (t/a Charleton Garage)* (1976) IT 32231/ 76.

11 ERA 1996, s 117(2). See *Selfridges Ltd v Malik* [1997] IRLR 577, EAT; *Artisan Press v Strawley and Parker* [1986] IRLR 126, EAT.

12 A week's pay is calculated the same way and is subject to the same maximum as the basic award. Since February 2000 the maximum weekly pay is £230. Hence the maximum additional award is £11,960.

13 ERA, s 117(3). These are calculated in accordance with ERA 1996, ss 118– 127A; see discussion Chapter 17.

14 See eg *George v Beecham Group Ltd* [1977] IRLR 43; *Morganite Electrical Carbon Ltd v Donne* [1987] IRLR 363, EAT; if the tribunal finds that the employee has unreasonably prevented an order under s 113 from being complied with, such conduct may be taken into account as a failure to mitigate loss in making an award of compensation: ERA, s 117(8). But see *Mabirizi v National Hospital for Nervous Diseases* [1990] IRLR 133, EAT. See Chapter 17.

that it was not reasonably 'practicable' to comply with the order.[15] As the EAT pointed out in *Freemans plc v Flynn*[16] there is a second stage test of practicability created by s 117(4) where the employer fails to comply with an order of re-engagement and this test unlike the first stage test of s 116(1)(b) and (3)(b), places the burden of proof on an employer if he is to escape the consequences of non-compliance, to satisfy the tribunal that it was not practicable to make the order. Otherwise, in the second stage test, the test is essentially the same. The first stage test can be more 'provisional' leaving it to the employer to prove impracticability at the second stage.[17] The test at the second stage is impracticability not impossibility.[18] At the earlier stage practicability of compliance is only a consideration, which among others, tribunals have to take into account.[19] Where the employer's claim of impracticability under s 117(4), however, is based upon his engagement of a permanent replacement, the tribunal must ignore the claim unless the employer can show that it was not practicable for him to have the employee's work done without engaging a permanent replacement, say by a temporary replacement.[20]

---

15   ERA 1996, s 117(4).
16   [1984] ICR 874, [1984] IRLR 486, EAT; see too *Boots Co plc v Lees-Collier* [1986] IRLR 485, EAT.
17   *Port of London Authority v Payne* [1994] IRLR 9, CA.
18   Ibid.
19   Ibid, see also *Timex Corpn v Thomson* [1981] IRLR 522, EAT.
20   ERA 1996, s 117(7).

Chapter 17.
Compensation

Although reinstatement and re-engagement are regarded as the primary remedies of the Act, in practice the effective remedy for the overwhelming majority of unfair dismissals is some form of compensation. If an employment tribunal finds that a dismissal is unfair and makes no order of reinstatement or re-engagement, in most cases it must make an award of compensation under two separate heads: (i) a basic award (calculated in accordance with ERA 1996, ss 119–122 and 126) and (ii) a compensatory award (calculated in accordance with ERA 1996, s 123, 124, 126 and 127A). In cases of dismissals found to be unfair under ss 100, 101, 102, 103 and 105, there are special rules governing the basic award and the compensatory award.[1]

Moreover, as mentioned, where an order of reinstatement or re-engagement has been made by an employment tribunal and the employer refuses to re-employ the employee on any terms a tribunal must also make an 'award of additional compensation' of between 26 and 52 weeks' pay.[2] If the employer re-employs the employee but not fully in accordance with an order, then a separate rule of compensation applies.[3]

---

1   See ERA 1996, ss 120 and 124(1A).
2   See ERA 1996, ss 117(3) and 124(4). The current maximum for a week's pay is £230, the same as that for the basic award. This additional compensation is not simply compensation for loss; it is meant to deter and it can include a punitive element.
3   See ERA 19916, ss 117(1), (2) and 124.

1. THE BASIC AWARD

The basic award is designed to provide an element of compensation for the value of the accrued service or seniority lost by the employee owing to the unfair dismissal. Before deductions are made, it is calculated as a full equivalent to the employee's entitlement to a statutory redundancy payment.

The amount of the award is related to the employee's age, the number of years of continuous service[4] as at the effective date of termination[5] and the gross weekly earnings[6] of the employee, subject to a maximum of £230 per week.[7]

Under ERA 1996, s 119,[8] the award is calculated by first counting the number of years of continuous employment starting with the effective date of termination and reckoning backwards to the time of hiring subject to a maximum of 20 years.[9] That number is then multiplied by

(a) 1½ weeks' pay for each year of employment in which the employee was not below the age of 41;[10]

(b) 1 week's pay for each year of employment not for 11 days in which the employee was not below the age of 22;

(c) half a week's pay for each year of employment not falling within (a) and (b) (NB even if the employee's age is under 18).

Where a year straddles the employee's 22nd or 41st birthday, then that year clearly counts but it would appear to count at the lower rate since it was a year in which the employee was below the relevant age.

Since 1980, there has been no general irreducible minimum basic award of 2 weeks' pay. However, for dismissals for trade union membership or activities or non-membership, health and safety reasons, pension trustees, elected employee representatives or complaints under the working time provisions, ERA, s 120 provides a minimum basic award of £3,100. Moreover, in the case of certain redundancy dismissals, ERA, s 121 provides that the basic award *shall* be two weeks' pay. Apart form these

---

4   See Chapter 1.
5   See Chapter 2.
6   A week's pay is determined in accordance with the provision of Part XIV, Chapter II of ERA 1996.
7   This figure is renewed each year.
8   ERA, ss 119–122 and 126.
9   ERA, s 119(1).
10   From age 64 for men and 59 for women the basic award is reduced by 1/12th for each whole month worked. ERA, s 119(2) and (4).

exceptions, it is quite clear that the basic award can be reduced, even to a nil award by four types of deductions:

(a) reduction of the award by a proportion which an industrial tribunal considers just and equitable having regard to any conduct of the complainant before dismissal (or if notice of dismissal was given, before that notice was given).[11] This would of course include conduct which was not known to the employer before the dismissal but was subsequently discovered,[12]

(b) by the amount of any redundancy payment paid to the employee by the employer either under Part XI of ERA 1996 or otherwise,[13]

(c) any other sum paid by the employer and accepted by the employee expressly or implicitly referable to the basic award,[14]

(d) failure by the employee to mitigate his loss by unreasonably refusing an offer by the employer which if accepted would have the effect of reinstating the employee in all respects as if he had not been dismissed. In the event the basic award may be reduced by an amount which the tribunal considered just and equitable.[15]

2. THE COMPENSATORY AWARD

The basic principle governing the compensatory award is that unfairly dismissed employees are to be compensated for the entire financial loss caused by their employer's decision to dismiss them,[16] subject to a maximum limit of £50,000. As the ERA 1996, s 123(1) puts it:

'the amount of the compensatory award shall be such amount as the tribunal considers just and equitable in all the circumstances having regard to the loss sustained by the complainant in consequence of

---

11 ERA, s 122(2). Note that this proportion may or may not be the same as the proportion reducing the compensation award not least because s 123(6) does not allow conduct coming to light after the dismissal to be taken into account. See *Les Ambassadeurs Club v Bainda* [1982] IRLR 5, EAT, but see *G McFall & Co Ltd v Curran* [1981] IRLR 455, NICA.

12 See eg *W Devis & Sons Ltd v Atkins* [1977] AC 931, [1977] ICR 662, HL.

13 ERA, 122(4). Indeed, any excess paid by the employer over the basic award can be deducted from the compensatory award; see s 123(7).

14 See eg *Chelsea Football Club and Athletic Co Ltd v Heath* [1981] ICR 323, [1981] IRLR 73, EAT.

15 ERA, s 122(1). See *Muirhead & Maxwell Ltd v Chambers* (1982) EAT 16/82.

16 ERA 1996, s 126.

the dismissal in so far as that loss is attributable to action taken by the employer'.

This statutory language is meant to be applied by employment tribunals using their discretion to assess what is just and equitable having made a careful assessment of the entire financial loss actually caused by the dismissal. Tribunals are not to modify the statutory test by introducing common law concepts of foreseeability or remoteness.[17]

Under the statutory test, the loss consists of 'loss of any benefit which the dismissed employee might reasonably be expected to have had but for the dismissal and any expenses reasonably incurred as a result of the dismissal'[18] as well as any entitlement to a redundancy payment which would have exceeded the basic award.[19]

The onus of proving loss under each head of damages will lie with the complainant, even though the information is more often in the hands of the employer.[20] Yet the employment tribunals have been told to be realistic in the standards of proof they apply in view of the difficulties of obtaining certain types of evidence.[1] They have a duty to inquire into all relevant heads of loss which are to be assessed as part of the compensation award and to take responsibility for resolving quantification difficulties without hiding behind the burden of proof.[2]

This principle of compensation for loss caused by the employer is modified in four important respects. First, an award of compensation must be reduced by an amount an employee either has earned or would have earned if he had met his obligation to make reasonable efforts to mitigate the loss caused by the unfair dismissal.[3] Secondly, where the employment tribunal finds that the dismissal has to any extent been caused or contributed to by any action of the complainant, the amount of compensation must be reduced by a proportion which the tribunal finding considers just and equitable having regard to that action.[4] The first type

---

17   *Leonard v Strathclyde Buses Ltd* [1998] IRLR 693, Ct of Sess, disapproving *Simrad Ltd v Scott* [1997] IRLR 147, EAT.

18   ERA 1996, s 123(2).

19   ERA 1996, s 123(3).

20   *Britool Ltd v Roberts* [1993] IRLR 481, EAT: *Copson v Eversure Accessories Ltd* [1974] ICR 636, [1974] IRLR 247, NIRC.

1   *Barley v Amey Roadstone Corpn Ltd* [1977] ICR 546, [1977] IRLR 299, EAT.

2   *Tidman v Aveling Marshall Ltd* [1977] ICR 506, [1977] IRLR 218, EAT; see section ii below.

3   ERA 1996, s 123(4).

4   ERA 1996, s 123(6); see eg *Courtaulds Northern Spinning Ltd v Moosa* [1984] ICR 218, [1984] IRLR 43, EAT; *Iggesund Converters Ltd v Lewis* [1984] ICR 544, [1984] IRLR 431, EAT.

of reduction operates to reduce only the compensatory award. It may be regarded as part of the process of calculating the amount of financial loss thought to have been sustained. The second type of reduction is a separate step: it proportionally reduces not only the compensatory award but also the basic award.[5] Thirdly, in determining how far any loss sustained by the dismissed employee was attributable to action taken by the employer no account may be taken of any pressure exercised on the employer by industrial action to dismiss the employee. The question of loss caused by the employer in such cases must be determined as if no such pressure had been exercised.[6] Fourthly, the compensatory award must be reduced where the employer has paid to the employee a redundancy payment (whether under the statutory provisions of ERA 1996 or not) which exceeds the amount of the employee's statutory redundancy payment entitlement. In the event the full amount by which the redundancy payment exceeds the statutory redundancy entitlement is deducted from the compensatory award before the statutory maximum is applied.[7]

i) What types of loss are compensated?

Although employment tribunals have a wide discretion under s 123(1) to determine the amount of the compensatory award, the loss to which the compensatory award is designed to apply is essentially financial loss to the employee insofar as that loss is caused by employer.[8] This clearly includes expenses incurred and loss of financial benefits caused by the dismissal, particularly loss of income. However, it excludes compensation for non-pecuniary loss such as unpleasantness and inconvenience,[9] injured feelings, or loss of face, unless these are capable of being translated into calculable financial loss.[10]

For example, where emotional upset caused by the dismissal affects the length of time that elapses before the ex-employee obtains suitable

5   ERA 1996, s 122(2). Except in certain cases of redundancy.
6   ERA 19965, s 123(5); see eg *Courtaulds Northern Spinning Ltd v Moosa* [1984] ICR 218, [1984] IRLR 43, EAT.
7   ERA 1996, s 123(3).
8   *Norton Tool Co v Tewson* [1972] IRLR 86, NIRC.
9   *Fougère v Phoenix Motor Co Ltd* [1976] ICR 495, [1976] IRLR 259, EAT.
10 *Norton Tool Co Ltd v Tewson* [1973] 1 All ER 183, [1972] ICR 501, NIRC; see also *Lifeguard Assurance Ltd v Zadrozny* [1977] IRLR 56 (claims of loss should not be speculative); *Malik v BCCI* [1997] IRLR 462, HL. But see now *Johnson v Unisys Ltd* [2001] UKHL 13, [2001] IRLR 279, para 55, noted (2001) ILJ 305.

employment,[11] or where an unsatisfactory reference in addition to creating injury to feelings injures an employee's job prospects, that could be taken into account.[12] More recently, in *Malik v BCCI*[13] the House of Lords held that an employee may be compensated for loss of reputation caused by the employer's breach of the implied term of mutual trust and confidence where the employer's conduct has prejudicially affected the employee's future prospects so as to give rise to continuing financial losses. However, emotional suffering by itself has not been regarded as compensatable.[14]

Nor has there been any element of exemplary or punitive damages contained within the calculation of the compensatory award.[15] The principle that the purpose of compensation is only to compensate for financial loss and not to express disapproval of a company's industrial relations has until recently been widely followed, at least in the ground rules governing the compensatory award.[16]

Yet the statutory discretion given to employment tribunals to assess whether compensation is just and equitable can also operate to lower the compensatory award below the estimated financial loss.[17] Indeed the compensatory award could be reduced to nil under certain circumstances.

In *W Devis & Sons Ltd v Atkins*[18] the House of Lords, per Viscount Dilhorne, agreed that an award of nil compensation was appropriate under s 123(1) where the evidence satisfied an industrial tribunal that the employee had not suffered any injustice.

'[s 123(1)] does not ... provide that regard should be had only to the loss resulting from the dismissal being unfair. Regard must be had to that, but the award must be just and equitable in all circumstances and it cannot be just and equitable that a sum should be awarded in

---

11   Ibid: see also *Johnson v Unisys Ltd* n 10 above; *John Millar & Sons v Quinn* [1974] IRLR 107, NIRC.
12   *Canter v Bowater Containers Ltd* [1975] IRLR 323, IT. But see *Gallear v J F Watson & Son Ltd* [1979] IRLR 306, EAT.
13   [1997] IRLR 462, HL. See too *Johnson v Unisys Ltd* n 10 above.
14   See eg *Vaughan v Weighpack Ltd* [1974] IRLR 105, NIRC. Cf the position at common law for wrongful dismissal; *Cox v Philips Industries Ltd* [1976] 3 All ER 161, [1976] ICR 138, QB.
15   *Babcock FATA Ltd v Addison* [1987] IRLR 173, CA; *Lifeguard Assurance Ltd v Zadrozny* [1977] IRLR 56, EAT.
16   *Clarkson International Tools Ltd v Short* [1973] ICR 191, [1973] IRLR 90, NIRC; see also *Cadbury Ltd v Doddington* [1977] ICR 982, EAT.
17   See eg *Townson v Northgate Group Ltd* [1981] IRLR 382, EAT.
18   See *W Devis & Son Ltd v Atkins* [1977] AC 931, [1977] ICR 662, HL.

compensation when in fact the employee has suffered no injustice by being dismissed'.

In that case, the employee was found to be unfairly dismissed because the employers had no valid reason for dismissal, but compensation was addressed at nil because evidence of misconduct coming to light after the dismissal indicated that the employee had been behaving fraudulently towards his employer during his employment.

Moreover, where there has been a procedural omission by the employer which has resulted in a finding of unfair dismissal, under s 123(1) the employment tribunal must make an assessment of what would have been the likely outcome had the procedural omission not occurred.

As the House of Lords pointed out in *Polkey v A E Dayton Services Ltd*[19] if the employment tribunal thinks that there is reason to doubt whether the employee would have been dismissed had the employer followed the correct procedure, it should make a percentage estimate of the likelihood that the employee would still have lost his employment and reduce the compensatory award accordingly. The calculation of this so called 'Polkey reduction' requires the employment tribunal to investigate the hypothetical question, what would have happened had the employer adopted a fair procedure? The tribunal must conduct its own investigation and reach its own conclusions.[20] It should not use post dismissal conduct[1] but limit itself to what is likely viewed from the time of the dismissal.[2]

Where an employment tribunal finds that a procedural mistake on the part of an employer, such as a failure to warn of misconduct or capability or to consult over redundancy, or to communicate in respect of ill health, would not in fact have affected the eventual outcome and hence would not have resulted in financial loss, it may award nil compensation.

In *Earl v Slater & Wheeler (Airlyne) Ltd*[3] for example, where an employee was dismissed without an opportunity to be heard in his own defence, but it emerged at the tribunal hearing that he would have had no valid explanation to offer for his behaviour had he been given a hearing as he would have been dismissed in any event. Moreover, in cases of dismissal on grounds of ill health, the compensatory award may be reduced drastically

19   [1987] IRLR 503, HL.
20   *Fisher v California Cake and Cookie Ltd* [1997] IRLR 212, EAT.
1   *Soros and Soros v Davison and Davison* [1994] IRLR 264, EAT.
2   *Fisher v California Cake and Cookie Ltd* [1997] IRLR 212, EAT.
3   [1973] 1 All ER 145, [1972] ICR 508, NIRC; see also *Clarkson International Tools Ltd v Short* [1973] ICR 191, [1973] IRLR 90, NIRC.

where the dismissal was unfair on procedural grounds but medical evidence made it clear that the employee was incapable of performing the functions of the job at the time of the dismissal.[4]

Where, however a tribunal is uncertain that the procedural omission would have resulted in no loss, it must address the question as a matter of probability to be assessed in percentage terms.[5] For example where a redundancy dismissal is unfair because of the employer's failure to follow a fair procedure, following *Polkey*, an employment tribunal is required to ask two questions: if the proper procedure had been followed, would it have resulted in an offer of employment; if so, what would that employment have been and what wage would have been paid?[6]

The loss flowing from the employer's procedural omission can be reduced by a tribunal's assessment of the probable effects of the employers having met their procedural obligation. For example, in the case of a failure to give an adequate warning the loss may be limited to earnings for the period of time of an appropriate warning period where a tribunal considers it likely that the warning would not have produced an improvement in performance.[7] On the other hand if the tribunal considers that the likelihood is that the warning will take effect, then the loss may be substantial. The relevant principles for cases of dismissals for incapability were spelt out at an early stage by the NIRC in *Winterhalter Gastronom Ltd v Webb*.[8] To take into account the uncertainty whether the warning, if given, would have had its intended effect of correcting the employee's behaviour, the NIRC suggested the following method of assessing compensation under the forerunner of s 123(1):

'The tribunal should have approached the assessment by deciding what in all the circumstances they thought would have been a fair period to give the employee to improve his performance after a warning and then evaluating the chance that he would have been able to improve his sales performance after a warning and then evaluating the chance that he would have been able to improve his sales performance to a satisfactory level within that period and so retain his position as sales director. Adopting this approach this

4   *Slaughter v C Brewer & Sons Ltd* [1990] IRLR 426, EAT.
5   *Fisher v California Cake and Cookie Ltd* [1997] IRLR 212, EAT.
6   *Red Bank Manufacturing Co Ltd v Meadows* [1992] IRLR 209, EAT.
7   *Tidman v Aveling Marshall Ltd* [1977] ICR 506, [1977] IRLR 218, EAT.
8   [1973] ICR 245, [1973] IRLR 120, NIRC.

Court considers that in the particular circumstances of this case 3 months would have been a fair period to give the employee to prove himself capable of carrying out his duties efficiently. He was not given this period and so is entitled to 3 months at his net monthly salary of £194, ie £582.

Then how does one value the chance that he would have been able to continue in this employment at the end of the warning period? If one concludes that there was a high degree of probability that he would have been able to continue as sales director, then the loss that flows from the dismissal is substantial and, on the figures in this case, would approach the statutory maximum permitted under the Industrial Relations Act 1971. If, at the other end of the spectrum, one concludes that he would not have been able to hold down the job even after a warning period, the loss is nil'.

Similarly, in cases of dismissal for redundancy, where there has been a failure by the employer to consult or otherwise adopt an appropriate procedure, and an employment tribunal finds that even had proper consultation taken place the probability was that the redundancies would not have been prevented but only delayed, it could properly limit the employee's compensatory award to pay for the period during which consultations would have taken place.[9] Of course, where the tribunal finds that consultation might have changed the result because of an alternative job being found then it must award compensation which reflects that probability.[10]

The EAT has reminded that *Polkey* percentage reductions are only appropriate in cases of procedural omission. Consequently where the employer's failure is not one of procedure but rather one of substance, such as the improper application of a rule in a disciplinary code to a case of alleged misconduct or a mistaken application of criteria for selection for

---

9   See eg *Barley v Amey Roadstone Corpn Ltd* [1977] ICR 546, [1977] IRLR 299, EAT in which the EAT approved an industrial tribunal decision to limit compensation to a 28 day period. See also *Abbotts and Standley v Wesson-Glynwed Steels Ltd* [1982] IRLR 51, EAT, where compensation was limited to two weeks' pay because proper consideration would only have postponed the date of dismissal by that period of time.

10 See eg *Airscrew Howden Ltd v Jacobs* (1983) EAT 773/82; *Vokes Ltd v Bear* [1974] ICR 1, [1973] IRLR 363, NIRC.

redundancy, a *Polkey* percentage reduction is not appropriate.[11] Nor will it be appropriate in cases, such as *Boulton & Paul Ltd v Arnold*[12] where the employer acts unfairly by taking positive steps which ought not to have been taken.

Further, although s 123(1) appears to qualify the loss sustained by the employee as a consequence of the dismissal by the phrase 'in so far as that loss is attributable to action taken by the employer', this does not mean that the employer can claim that the personal characteristics of the employee, age, disability, health, etc were responsible for the loss of income resulting from the unfair dismissal. The employer must take the employee as he finds him, and the loss under s 123(1) consists of the financial loss estimated as likely to be suffered by him during the period which he could be expected to be unemployed. Thus, where an employer unfairly dismisses an elderly employee or one in poor health then the loss occurring from prolonged unemployment has been held to be attributable to the dismissal, that is 'action taken by the employer'.[13]

ii) The calculation of specific heads of loss

The compensatory award will generally be calculated under the following seven heads:

(a)   loss of earnings and benefits prior to the hearing (immediate loss)
(b)   loss of future earnings and benefits (future loss)
(c)   loss of benefits
(d)   loss of pension rights
(e)   loss arising from the manner of dismissal[14]

---

11   *King v Eaton (No 2)* [1998] IRLR 686, Ct of Sess; see too *Steel Stockholders (Birmingham) Ltd v Kirkwood* [1993] IRLR 515, EAT criticised in *O'Dea v ISC Chemicals Ltd* [1995] IRLR 599, CA but supported in *King v Eaton (No 2)*, above.

12   [1994] IRLR 532, EAT.

13   *Fougère v Phoenix Motor Co Ltd* [1976] ICR 495, [1976] IRLR 259, EAT.

14   The compensatory award is based upon financial loss so that an amount may be granted under this head if the manner of dismissal affected the employee's future employment prospects. See eg *Norton Tool Co Ltd v Tewson* [1973] 1 All ER 183, [1972] ICR 501, NIRC; *Colin Johnson (t/a Richard Andrews Ladies Hairdressers) v Baxter* [1984] ICR 675, [1985] IRLR 96, EAT; *John Millar & Sons v Quinn* [1974] IRLR 107, NIRC; but see *Vaughan v Weighpack Ltd* [1974] ICR 261, [1974] IRLR 105, NIRC; *Brittains Arborfield Ltd v Van Uden* [1977] ICR 211, EAT.

(f)   loss of accrued statutory rights[15]

(g)   expenses.[16]

(a) Loss of earnings and benefits prior to the hearing

Under the first head of compensation, the employee is entitled to loss of earnings or benefits from the date of dismissal to the date of assessment ie the hearing or the date of the decision.

The starting point for the calculation will be the employee's take home pay multiplied by the number of weeks in the period. If there is a dispute over the amount of take home pay to which the employee is entitled, the tribunal must investigate the issue and determine the appropriate figure.[17] Take home pay will be net of tax and national insurance deductions but, unlike the basic awards will include bonuses, overtime pay,[18] accrued holiday pay[19] and other types of fluctuating payments.[20] To this base figure will be added any other financial benefits to which the employee may be

---

15   The loss of accrued statutory rights to notice is often compensated by a *Muffet* award of £100, see *S H Muffet Ltd v Head* [1986] IRLR 488, EAT, rather than the formula of half the wages for the statutory minimum entitlement which was suggested in *Daley v A E Dorsett (Almar Dolls) Ltd* [1982] ICR 1, [1981] IRLR 385 (loss of accrued right to statutory periods of notice); *Hilti (GB) Ltd v Windridge* [1974] IRLR 53, NIRC. For loss of accrued extra redundancy rights see *Lee v IPC Business Press Ltd* [1984] ICR 306, EAT.

16   ERA 1996, s 123(2) includes any expenses reasonably incurred as a result of the dismissal such as the expenses of seeking other employment but does not extend to the costs of preparing the unfair dismissal action itself. See eg *Leech v Berger, Jensen & Nicholson Ltd* [1972] IRLR 58, IT; *Scottish Co-operative Wholesale Society v Lloyd* [1973] ICR 137, [1973] IRLR 93, NIRC; *Co-operative Wholesale Society Ltd v Squirrell* [1974] 9 ITR 191, NIRC (expenses involved in securing new job); see also *Gardiner-Hill v Roland Berger Technics Ltd* [1982] IRLR 498 (expenses in setting up as self-employed); *Sparkes v E T Barwick Mills Ltd* [1977] COIT 611/68. Costs are treated separately. See eg *Davidson v (1) John Calder (Publishers) Ltd and (2) Calder Educational Trust Ltd* [1985] IRLR 97, EAT; *Colin Johnson (t/a Richard Andrew Ladies Hairdressers) v Baxter* [1984] ICR 675, [1985] IRLR 96, EAT; *Lothian Health Board v Johnstone* [1981] IRLR 321, EAT.

17   See eg *Kinzley v Minories Finance Ltd* [1987] IRLR 490, EAT; *Mullet v Brush Electrical Machines Ltd* [1977] ICR 829, EAT.

18   See eg *Brownson v Hire Service Shops Ltd* [1978] ICR 517, [1978] IRLR 73.

19   See eg *Tradewinds Airways Ltd v Fletcher* [1981] IRLR 272, EAT.

20   See eg *Palmanor Ltd v Cedron* [1978] ICR 1008, [1978] IRLR 303, EAT.

entitled such as the use of a company car,[1] telephone payments,[2] etc. Furthermore where the employee is able to show that the dismissal resulted in a loss of a tax rebate because the employer terminated without following the correct procedure, that too may be included as an element in loss of wages attributable to the action of the employer.[3]

Where employees have been dismissed without proper notice or without pay in lieu of notice, they are entitled to be awarded full net pay for the period of notice to which they were entitled normally without a duty to mitigate.[4] If the employee is dismissed without proper notice and receives a sum which is less than his net pay for the full notice period to which he is entitled he is entitled to an award of compensation for the balance of the proper period of notice, again normally not subject to a duty to mitigate. If however the ex-employee earns a large sum in relation to the notice money due there will be a deduction for any remuneration received from other employment during this period.[5]

After the notice period, the amount of the employee's loss of net pay and benefits must be reduced by any income received from other sources during the period. For example, if the employee received a sum from his employer which exceeded his entitlement to pay for the due period of notice, the excess must be deducted from compensation during this period.[6] Similarly ex gratia severance payments must be deducted[7] and retirement pension payments must be taken into account,[8] before the statutory maximum is applied.[9] Where however the employee receives a tax rebate and the amounts are not large it will be correct for tribunals to ignore this

---

1   *TBA Industrial Products Ltd v Locke* [1984] ICR 228, [1984] IRLR 48, EAT.
2   Ibid. This will not include tax free allowances to recompense for expenses. See *Tradewinds Airways Ltd v Fletcher* [1981] IRLR 272, EAT.
3   *Lucas v Lawrence Scott and Electromotors Ltd* [1983] ICR 309, [1983] IRLR 61, EAT. See discussion in Section c, below.
4   *Babcock FATA Ltd v Addison* [1987] IRLR 173, CA; *Vaughan v Weighpack Ltd* [1974] IRLR 105, NIRC; *Hilti (GB) Ltd v Windridge* [1974] IRLR 53, NIRC.
5   See eg *Isleworth Studio Ltd v Rickard* [1988] IRLR 137, EAT.
6   See *Babcock FATA Ltd v Addison* [1987] IRLR 173, CA (if employer has paid wages in lieu of notice the employee cannot have a compensatory award for loss of wages during the notice period).
7   *Digital Equipment Co Ltd v Clements (No 2)* [1998] IRLR 134, CA; *Horizon Holidays Ltd v Grassi* [1987] IRLR 371, EAT; but see contra *Roadchef Ltd v Hastings* [1988] IRLR 142, EAT (where ex gratia payment was due anyway even if dismissal was not unfair); *Leonard v Strathclyde Buses Ltd* [1998] IRLR 693, Ct of Sess; *Darr v LRC Products Ltd* [1993] IRLR 257, EAT.
8   *MBS Ltd v Calo* [1983] ICR 459, [1983] IRLR 189, EAT.
9   *McCarthy v British Insulated Callenders Cables plc* [1985] IRLR 94, EAT.

sum received in assessing the compensatory award.[10] Further, retirement pension payments could be taken into account.[11] Tribunals must specify such amounts in their award as the 'prescribed element' thereby placing the Department of Trade and Industry in the position of serving a recoupment notice upon the employer for that amount.[12]

Since 1977, no deductions are made from the compensatory award for any unemployment benefit[13] in the form of job seeker's allowance or income support received by the employee during the period from the date of dismissal to the date when the tribunal hearing is concluded.

Where there is no provision in the contract of employment for an employee to receive full wages in addition to sickness benefit, there should be a reduction in the compensatory award by the amount of any sickness benefit received by the employee during the period covered by the award.[14] Similarly, invalidity benefit received by the employee following dismissal should also be deducted from the compensatory award.[15]

Moreover, where an employee has obtained fresh employment during this period, the net pay received from the new employment will be deducted from the net pay he was entitled to under his previous job in order to calculate the compensation for loss of income for those weeks in which he received pay for the fresh employment.[16]

Where the dismissed employee obtains fresh employment and then is dismissed again before the date of assessment the tribunal may not award loss of pay for the period of unemployment following the second job. In *Courtaulds Northern Spinning Ltd v Moosa*[17] the EAT held that the loss following the end of the second job could not be regarded as loss attributable to action taken by the first employer under s 123(1).

---

10 *MBS Ltd v Calo* [1983] IRLR 189, EAT; *Adda International Ltd v Curcio* [1976] 3 All ER 620, [1976] ICR 407, EAT.

11 *Wood v Louis C Edwards & Sons (Manchester) Ltd* [1972] IRLR 18.

12 Job Seeker's Allowance and Income Support Regulations 1996, SI 1996/2349. The current regulations do not provide for recoupment of benefits where a claim is settled through agreement since the regulations only apply to tribunal awards.

13 *Mullet v Brush Electrical Machines Ltd* [1977] ICR 829, EAT.

14 *Puglia v C James & Sons* [1996] IRLR 70, EAT.

15 Ibid. Disapproving *Hilton International Hotels (UK) Ltd v Faraji* [1994] IRLR 267, EAT.

16 *TBA Industrial Products Ltd v Locke* (above); *Scottish Co-operative Wholesale Society Ltd v Lloyd* [1973] ICR 137, [1973] IRLR 93.

17 [1984] ICR 218, [1984] IRLR 43, EAT, but see *Townson v Northgate Group Ltd* [1981] IRLR 382 at 385, EAT; *Morgan Edwards Wholesale Ltd/Gee Bee Discount Ltd v Hough* (1978) EAT 398/78.

Even where employees have not obtained other employment, there may be a deduction made if they have failed to mitigate their loss by accepting other employment or failed to make reasonable efforts to find other employment. The employee, though unfairly dismissed has a duty to make reasonable efforts to avoid unnecessary loss.[18] Section 123(4) of the ERA 1996 states that:

'In ascertaining (the compensatory award) the tribunal shall apply the same rule concerning the duty of a person to mitigate his loss as applies to damages recoverable under the common law of England and Wales or of Scotland, as the case may be'.

As the EAT put it in *Gallear v J F Watson & Son Ltd*[19] the duty on an employee to mitigate his loss requires him to act reasonably. Whilst it is not his duty to take any job that might be offered, he has to be reasonable about an offer of employment and take employment that is reasonably offered to him.[20]

This question is one of fact for employment tribunals and an appeal can only be had to the EAT on grounds of misconduct or perversity.[1] Moreover, the onus of proof lies upon the employer.[2]

If the employer can show that the employee has refused a job which is roughly comparable in content even if it involves less pay, then an employment tribunal can decide that pay he would have received at that job, had he taken it, should be deducted from the award of compensation. In *A G Bracey Ltd v Iles*[3] Sir John Donaldson (as he then was) gave the following illustration:

'A man who is dismissed from a £40 a week job may act unreasonably if he does not accept a job bringing in say £35 a week. If he does not do so, a tribunal is fully entitled to say, "we are going to take no account of any loss which one could have avoided by taking the £35 a week job"'.

18　See now *Westwood v Secretary of State for Employment* (above).

19　[1979] IRLR 306, EAT.

20　Ibid.

1　See eg *Bessenden Properties Ltd v Corness* [1974] IRLR 338, CA. See also *Penthouse Publications Ltd v Radnor* (1978) 13 ITR 528, EAT.

2　*Bessenden Properties Ltd v Corness* [1974] IRLR 338, CA; see too *Fyfe v Scientific Furnishings Ltd* [1989] IRLR 331, [1989] ICR 648, EAT disapproving *Scottish and Newcastle Breweries plc v Halliday* [1986] ICR 577, [1986] IRLR 291, EAT.

3　[1973] IRLR 210, NIRC.

The appropriate method for the tribunal to use is to estimate when the employee would on a balance of probabilities have gained employment and then apply the amount he or she would have received to extinguish or reduce the loss flowing from the dismissal.[4]

At the same time, if an employee accepts employment at an unreasonably low level it may be open to the employer to argue that the mere fact that the employee obtained that employment at that particular wage did not mean that he had taken reasonable steps to avoid unnecessary loss. As Sir John Donaldson commented in *Archbold Freightage Ltd v Wilson:*[5]

'it is the duty of the employee who has been dismissed to act reasonably and to act as a reasonable man would do if he had no hope of seeking compensation from his previous employer'.

The test is whether that particular individual, given his skills, training, age, health[6] and intellect in his particular job market could reasonably have found other work. Evidence of the state of the local labour market will be relevant, but of course evidence of an unreasonable refusal to accept suitable alternative employment will be more conclusive.

Where the former employer offers re-engagement to the employee after the dismissal the employee's refusal of re-engagement may be regarded by tribunals as a failure by the employee reasonably to mitigate the loss caused by the dismissal. In *Kendrick v Aerduct Productions*[7] an employee was unfairly dismissed and offered the same job by the employer. He refused to accept re-engagement with his former employer and instead took a lower paid job with another employer on the Monday following the tribunal hearing when the offer was made. The tribunal awarded compensation to the employee only for loss of wages up to the Monday on the grounds that any later loss had not been caused by the dismissal but had been voluntarily incurred. The idea that the employee is not entitled to refuse re-engagement with the employer simply because he is a former employer and one with whom he does not wish to re-commence

---

4   *Gardner-Hill v Roland Berger Technics Ltd* [1982] IRLR 498, EAT (a percentage reduction in the total sum is not appropriate).
5   [1974] IRLR 10, NIRC. But see *Daley v A E Dorsett (Almar Dolls) Ltd* [1982] ICR 1, [1981] IRLR 385, EAT.
6   See eg *Brittains Arborfield Ltd v Van Uden* [1977] ICR 211, EAT; *Fougère v Phoenix Motor Co Ltd* [1976] ICR 495, [1976] IRLR 259, EAT.
7   [1974] IRLR 322, IT; see also *Martin v Yeoman Aggregates Ltd* [1983] ICR 314, [1983] IRLR 49, EAT.

employment might apply even where the offer or re-engagement is made prior to a hearing.[8]

However, an employee does not always have to accept such an offer. Certain circumstances may make a refusal reasonable.[9] For example, in *Crampton v Dacorum Motors Ltd*[10] an unfairly dismissed employee was offered his old job back after he had already obtained alternative employment, albeit at a lower salary. His refusal was not a failure to mitigate in spite of the difference in salaries, because he didn't want to change jobs again and, having once been dismissed by the employer, he felt no security against the possibility of being dismissed again.[11] Moreover, where the job offered to the employee is substantially less favourable in certain respects, the employee could reasonably refuse the offer and still not be held to have failed to mitigate his loss.[12] Furthermore, a decision to become self-employed could have consequences for the duty to mitigate.[13]

In *How v Tesco Stores Ltd*[14] an employee dismissed for an inaccurate till reading and reported to the police by the employer was offered re-engagement by the employer at a time when their security officer was still trying to ascertain whether the police were proposing to take criminal proceedings. The tribunal considered the employee's refusal reasonable in the circumstances and not a breach of her duty to mitigate.

Where an employer has repudiated the contract by insisting that the employee accept a change in his contract, and offers of re-engagement on the new terms, would a refusal by the employee be regarded as a failure to mitigate? One difficulty caused by a decision that the employee's refusal of an offer of re-engagement constitutes a failure to mitigate is that it allows the employer to achieve indirectly what he has set out to achieve directly – a non-consensual change in terms. Technically according to the EAT in

---

8   See eg *Sweetlove v Redbridge and Waltham Forest Area Health Authority* [1979] ICR 477, [1979] IRLR 195, EAT; *Hoover v Forde* [1980] ICR 239, EAT. But see *Seligman & Latz Ltd v McHugh* [1979] IRLR 130, EAT.

9   *Fyfe v Scientific Furnishings Ltd* [1989] IRLR 331, EAT.

10   [1975] IRLR 168, EAT of *Courtaulds Northern Spinning Ltd v Moosa* [1984] ICR 218, [1984] IRLR 43, EAT.

11   See eg *Devitt v Greenham Plant Hire Ltd* (1976) EAT 174/76.

12   See eg *Ramsay v W B Anderson & Sons Ltd* [1974] IRLR 164, IT; *Tiptools Ltd v Curtis* [1973] IRLR 276, NIRC.

13   See eg *Lee v IPC Ltd* (1983) EAT 105/83; *Gardiner-Hill v Rowland Berger Technics Ltd* [1982] IRLR 498, EAT.

14   [1974] IRLR 194, NIRC. *William Muir (Bonds) Ltd v Lamb* [1985] IRLR 95, EAT; but see *Hoover Ltd v Forde* [1980] ICR 239, EAT. See too *Lock v Connell Estate Agents* [1994] IRLR 444, EAT.

Savoia v Chiltern Herb Farms a refusal of an offer *before dismissal* cannot amount to a failure to mitigate.[15] Yet, a refusal by the employee might be regarded as a basis for a finding of contributory fault.[16]

Further, a decision by an employee not to follow an internal appeals procedure before making an application to an employment tribunal is not necessarily a failure to mitigate loss under ERA 1996, s 123(4)[17] but it can result in a reduction in compensation under ERA 1996, s 127A(1).

Finally, if an employee, through no fault of his own, loses a job he obtained subsequent to dismissal, this will not necessarily be regarded as a failure to mitigate. In *Barrel Plating and Phosphating Co Ltd v Danks*[18] an employee, having found a job after being dismissed, was dismissed from the second company when it became clear that she did not have the experience to perform that particular type of work. The EAT upheld the employment tribunal's decision not to reduce compensation by the pay she would have received from the second company had she not been dismissed.

> 'It was not the case that she had obtained permanent employment and had lost it for reasons for which she was culpable. She could not have obtained longer employment with the new employer than she actually did by any action she could have taken'.[19]

Finally if the employee has received unemployment benefit in the form of a job seeker's allowance, the tribunal does not deduct the amount representing the job seeker's allowance or income support paid during the period prior to the date of the hearing. Instead, it will instruct the employer not to pay over the entire 'prescribed element' of the compensation, ie the loss of income suffered by the complainant, and the DTI will serve a recoupment notice upon the employer requiring the employer to pay back that part of the prescribed element which represents the amount of the job seeker's allowance or income support paid to the employee.[20]

---

15 Cf [1981] IRLR 65, EAT; affd [1982] IRLR 166, CA. See also *Trimble v Supertravel Ltd* [1982] ICR 440, [1982] IRLR 451, EAT. Cf *Seligman & Latz Ltd v McHugh* [1979] IRLR 130, EAT, in which it was held that a failure to use a grievance procedure was not a failure to mitigate.
16 *Singh v British Castors Ltd* (1977) EAT 518/77.
17 *Lock v Connell Estate Agents* [1994] IRLR 444, EAT.
18 [1976] 3 All ER 652, [1976] ICR 503, EAT.
19 Ibid.
20 See Employment Protection (Recoupment of Jobseeker's Allowance and Income Support) Regulations 1996, SI 1996/2349; cf *Mason v Wimpey Waste Management* [1982] IRLR 454, EAT.

(b) Loss of earnings after the hearing; future loss

The second stage of the calculation of the compensatory award consists of an estimate of the loss of expected earnings during the period after the hearing. The calculation of future earnings inevitably involves an employment tribunal in a forecast of several different types of probabilities. Normally, if an industrial tribunal's forecast proves to be inaccurate in any respect it cannot be overturned. Only if there is a fundamental change in the basis of the tribunal's calculations of the amount, and this arises very shortly after its original decision, is a tribunal required to review its original decision.[1]

If the tribunal finds that there is a likelihood that the employee would anyway have been dismissed from his job after a period owing to redundancy[2] or other causes[3] that factor limits the extent of the period for calculating future loss. Otherwise the tribunal must engage in an estimate that varies depending upon whether (a) the employee has found employment or (b) is still unemployed at the time of the hearing.

Where the employee has already obtained a job by the date of the hearing the main task for the tribunal is to determine the difference between the take home pay of the old and new jobs and project this difference into the future, taking into account possible changes in earnings levels in the two jobs and the possibility that the employee may have left the original job at some stage either voluntarily or because of a fair dismissal.[4] Where an employee has a considerable period of years of actual service in the former job, a tribunal may consider a five-year period a fair period to compensate the employee for the loss caused by the difference in salaries.[5]

In considering the difference in pay between old and new jobs, the tribunal is not restricted to a static view of either figure. Thus where a salary increase was a likely development, it could be taken into account even if it

---

1   *Yorkshire Engineering and Welding Co Ltd v Burnham* [1973] 3 All ER 1176, [1974] ICR 77; *Studio Press (Birmingham) Ltd v Davies* (1976) EAT 396/76; *Help the Aged Housing Association (Scotland) Ltd v Vidler* [1977] IRLR 104, EAT.

2   *Young's of Gosport Ltd v Kendell* [1977] ICR 907, [1977] IRLR 433, EAT.

3   See discussion on pp 292–293.

4   This period may not be the 'actual estimated' period as the award will be received in a lump sum so justifying a lesser period.

5   *Scottish Co-operative Wholesale Society Ltd v Lloyd* [1973] ICR 137, [1973] IRLR 93, NIRC; cf *Beams v Nesbitt Thomson & Co Ltd* (1972) 12901/72, in which a 59-year-old employee had four years of loss calculated.

wasn't a certainty.[6] At the same time if there was a likelihood that the employee might have lost income in the old job, say owing to his background of ill health and the absence of a sick pay scheme, that may call for a deduction.[7]

Further, where an apprentice is dismissed, the difference in earnings will consist of the difference between what the employee would have earned had he completed his contract and the earnings he received from his second job.[8] On the other hand, if the job obtained does not reflect the true earning abilities of the employee, this will be taken into account.[9] As well, if the new job is less secure than the old, a sum may be added to compensate for possible future losses of rights in respect of statutory benefits.[10] And where the new job involves increased travelling expenses or increased rents and rates, this may result in higher compensation.[11] The tribunal may include a discount factor to take account of the fact that there was an accelerated receipt of earnings.[12]

Where employees have not yet found a job a the time of the tribunal hearing, and the tribunal does not consider that they have failed in their duty to mitigate the loss, it must make an assessment of at least two elements: the length of time the employee is likely to remain unemployed expressed as a 'multiplier' in weeks, months or years during which the period of unemployment might continue;[13] and the level of pay the employee is likely to receive at the next job. For example, in *Winterhalter Gastronom Ltd v Webb*,[14] the tribunal fixed a sum of compensation on the basis that Mr Webb was likely to be out of work for six months and that when he found a job it would be at a level of roughly two-thirds of his present net salary.

Employment tribunals have considerable discretion to assess, in the light of local conditions and the personal characteristics of complainants,

---

6   *York Trailer Co Ltd v Sparkes* [1973] ICR 518, [1973] IRLR 348, NIRC.
7   See *Curtis v James Paterson (Darlington) Ltd* [1973] ICR 496, [1974] IRLR 88.
8   *F C Shepherd & Co Ltd v Jerrom* [1985] IRLR 275, EAT; *W F Shortland Ltd v Chantrill* [1975] IRLR 208, IT; *Paviour v Whitton's Transport (Cullompton) Ltd* [1975] IRLR 258, IT.
9   *Donnelly v Feniger & Blackburn Ltd* [1973] ICR 68, [1973] IRLR 26, NIRC.
10 See *Norton Tool Co Ltd v Tewson* [1973] 1 All ER 183, [1972] ICR 501, NIRC.
11 *Scottish Co-operative Wholesale Society Ltd v Lloyd* [1973] ICR 137, [1973] IRLR 93, NIRC.
12 *Brown's Cycles Ltd v Brindley* [1978] ICR 467, EAT.
13 *Cartiers Superfoods Ltd v Laws* [1978] IRLR 315, EAT.
14 [1973] ICR 245, [1973] IRLR 120, NIRC.

the period they are likely to be employed.[15] For example, in *Coleman v Tolemans Delivery Service Ltd*[16] the tribunal commented:

> 'from our knowledge of the local employment position we consider that up to a year may elapse before the applicant can obtain employment with a level of earnings comparable with that which he enjoyed in his last employment. He may be successful in obtaining employment much earlier but at a much reduced level of earnings and we therefore think it proper to assess his loss over a period of 1 year ... and to compensate him accordingly'.[17]

Moreover, the tribunals must take into account the personal characteristics of the complainant rather than simply making an assessment on the basis of an average employee's prospects of finding a new job. Hence where the employee is an older employee or in a poor state of health,[18] had poor eyesight[19] or low intelligence,[20] these all have to be taken into account by the employment tribunal. Furthermore, that an employee is nearing retirement age may be a factor that allows an employment tribunal to allow loss of earnings up to the retirement date[1] and even beyond if it was likely that the employee would be retained in employment after retirement.[2]

In calculating loss of future earnings, potential unemployment benefits in the form of jobseeker's allowance or income support are not deducted, since employees are no longer entitled to obtain such benefits in respect of future wages loss awarded by tribunals.[3]

The onus of proof of future loss is placed upon the employee. As the EAT remarked in *Adda International Ltd v Curcio*,[4]

---

15   *Morganite Crucible Carbon Ltd v Donne* [1987] IRLR 363, EAT (an award based on 82 weeks was not excessive). *Moncur v International Paint Co Ltd* [1978] IRLR 223, EAT.

16   [1973] IRLR 67.

17   See also *Perks v Geest Industries Ltd* [1974] IRLR 228, NIRC.

18   *Fougère v Phoenix Motor Co Ltd* [1976] ICR 495, [1976] IRLR 259, EAT.

19   *Brittains Arborfield Ltd v Van Uden* [1977] ICR 211, EAT.

20   See eg *Green v J Waterhouse & Sons Ltd* [1977] ICR 759, EAT.

1   See eg *Isle of Wight Tourist Board v Coombes* [1976] IRLR 413, EAT; *Penprase v Mander Bros Ltd* [1973] IRLR 167, NIRC.

2   *Barrel Plating and Phosphating Co Ltd v Dank* [1976] 3 All ER 652, [1976] ICR 503, EAT.

3   Employment Protection (Recoupment of Jobseeker's Allowance and Income Support) Regulations 1996, SI 1996/2349.

4   [1976] 3 All ER 620, [1976] ICR 407, EAT.

'there must be some evidence of future loss and the scale of future loss to enable the tribunal to make any award under that head. The tribunal must have something to bite on and if an applicant produces nothing for it to bite on he will have only himself to blame if he gets no compensation for loss of future earnings'.[5]

(c) Loss of contractual benefits

The purpose of compensation for unfair dismissal is to restore the employee to the financial position he would have been in had the dismissal not occurred. Consequently any contractual benefits other than basic pay which the employee loses as a result of the ending of his employment and the acquisition of a new job may be taken into account in calculating both the loss prior to the hearing and future loss.

A prominent claim of loss of fringe benefits has been the loss of use of a company car.[6] The principle of compensation may extend to use of a car for personal purposes,[7] as well as for transport specifically connected with work.[8]

The method of calculating this loss has varied from tribunal to tribunal from a fair sum chosen by the tribunal on the basis of its knowledge and experience in these matters to the use of Inland Revenue scales,[9] AA estimates[10] and even awarding the difference between purchase price and resale value. Where the employer contributes to an employee's HP payments, that too may be a loss for which compensation is obtained.[11]

In addition, compensation may be obtained for the loss of special travel allowances connected with the employment,[12] car allowances and hotel

---

5 Cf *Barley v Amey Roadstone Corpn Ltd* [1977] ICR 546, [1977] IRLR 299, EAT; *UBAF Bank Ltd v Davis* [1978] IRLR 442, EAT.
6 *TBA Industrial Products Ltd v Locke* [1984] ICR 228, [1984] IRLR 48, EAT.
7 *Moore v Rowland Winn (Batley) Ltd* [1975] IRLR 162 (£10 per week added to award). *Texter Ltd v Greenhough* (1982) EAT 410/82.
8 *Crampton v Dacorum Motors Ltd* [1975] IRLR 168 (£8 per week); *Blair Moore v Girling's Ferro-Concrete Co Ltd* [1974] IRLR 294 (£5 per week); *Yorkshire Engineering and Welding Co Ltd v Burnham* [1973] 3 All ER 1176, [1974] ICR 77 (£10 per week); *Morgan Edwards Wholesale Ltd v Francis* (1978) EAT 205/78.
9 But see *Shove v Downs Surgical plc* [1984] 1 All ER 7, [1984] IRLR 17.
10 Cf *Shove v Downs Surgical plc* (above).
11 *S and U Stores Ltd v Worm Leighton* (1977) EAT 477/77.
12 *De Cruz v Airways Aero Association Ltd* (1972) IT 6066/72.

expenses,[13] coal allowances,[14] and loss of income from shares under an employer's option scheme.[15] The loss of luncheon vouchers, private medical insurance,[16] free food in canteens, rent free accommodation, subsidised housing[17] or subsidised housing loans[18] would be compensatable. Loss of potential gratuities may be difficult to obtain because of the uncertainties,[19] but loss of 'tronc' money is compensatable as long as the tax element is subtracted from the gross amount.[20] Tax free allowances for the purpose of reimbursing expenses will not be compensatable where there is no 'profit element'.[1]

Finally where employees enjoy a contractual entitlement to a redundancy payment in excess of the statutory entitlement, they may claim compensation for the loss of the enhancement of the redundancy payment entitlement owing to the unfair dismissal. The measure of compensation would have to include some estimate of the probability of the employee ever being made redundant.[2]

(d) Loss of pension rights

Assessment of loss of pension rights is difficult and complicated. There is no one right way of assessing this type of loss to the exclusion of any others.[3] There is a set of guidelines prepared by a committee of employment tribunal chairmen in consultation with the Actuary's Department[4] but this is not binding upon employment tribunals in assessing compensation for loss of pension rights.[5]

---

13   *Leech v Berger, Jensen & Nicholson Ltd* [1972] IRLR 58, IT.
14   *Dono v National Coal Board* (1972) IT 12004/72.
15   *Bradshaw v Rugby Portland Cement Co Ltd* [1972] IRLR 46.
16   *Ross v Vewlands Engineering Co Ltd* IT 17321/83/LN.
17   *Scottish Co-operative Wholesale Society v Lloyd* [1973] ICR 137, [1973] IRLR 93, NIRC.
18   *UBAF Bank Ltd v Davis* [1978] IRLR 442, EAT.
19   *Ismond v Nelson Coin Automatics Ltd* [1975] IRLR 173, IT.
20   *Palmanor Ltd v Cedron* [1978] ICR 1008, [1978] IRLR 303, EAT.
1   *Tradewinds Airways Ltd v Fletcher* [1981] IRLR 272, EAT.
2   *Lee v IPC Business Press Ltd* [1984] ICR 306, EAT.
3   *Copson v Eversure Accessories Ltd* [1974] ICR 636, [1974] IRLR 247, NIRC.
4   *Industrial Tribunals: Compensation for Loss of Pension Rights* (1991, HMSO) (Guidelines) see Appendix IV. This supersedes the former government Actuary's Department Guideline recommendations.
5   *Bingham v Hobourn Engineering Ltd* [1992] IRLR 298, EAT.

The estimate of loss must take into account first of all whether employees have had to take, or have chosen to take, deferred pensions from their existing employments and whether the employees have the opportunity to build up a pension entitlement in their new employment.[6] It has long been recognised that there 'are two distinct types of loss to which dismissal from pensionable employment can give rise'.[7] The first is the loss of the pension position which has been earned, eg 15 years' service towards a pension of £x in 40 years' time at the age of 65. The Guidelines expand this to include the loss of pension rights from the date of the dismissal to the date of the hearing (para 8). The second is the loss of future pension opportunity, ie opportunity of improving this position until the time at which the pension becomes payable. The Guidelines refer to this in part as the loss of benefits which employees would have gained if they remained in employment beyond the date of the hearing (para 9). They add a third head, loss of enhancement of already accrued pension rights (para 10). They differ in important respects and have to be evaluated separately.[8]

[i]   LOSS OF PRESENT PENSION POSITION.
One way of assessing loss under this head is to calculate it in terms of the loss of contributions. As the NIRC put it in *Copson*'s case:

'Properly funded pensions are built up by the payment of periodical contributions by employers and usually also by employees. These contributions are invested under favourable taxation provisions and built up to a capital sum which at retirement age will buy an annuity equal to the amount of the pension. Thus, a rough assessment of the accrued value of a worker's pension position at any point in time can be achieved by taking the sum of the contribution already paid

6   Employees should not be penalised if they chose not to take a deferred pension: *Sturdy Finance Ltd v Bardsley* [1979] IRLR 65, [1979] ICR 249, EAT.
7   Ibid, see also *Manpower Ltd v Hearne* [1983] ICR 567, [1983] IRLR 281, EAT. Both types of loss will be affected by the new earnings-related state pensions scheme; see Social Security Pensions Act 1975. The burden of proving the loss of pension rights and its extent lies upon the claimant notwithstanding that there may be difficulties in obtaining the evidence from the employer; *Cawthorne and Sinclair Ltd v Hedger* [1974] ICR 146, [1974] IRLR 49, NIRC; *Hilti (GB) Ltd v Windridge* [1974] ICR 352, [1974] IRLR 53, NIRC; *Scottish Co-operative Wholesale Society Ltd v Lloyd* [1973] ICR 137, [1973] IRLR 93. In cases where a claimant is not represented, however, a tribunal has a duty to raise the question and investigate the amount of the loss; see eg *Smith, Kline and French Laboratories Ltd v Coates* [1977] IRLR 220, EAT.
8   *Copson v Eversure Accessories Ltd* [1974] ICR 636, [1974] IRLR 247, NIRC.

increased by compound interest from the date of payment. The calculation of compound interest is not easy without tables, but an increase in the rate of simple interest applied to the capital sum will achieve rough and ready justice'.[9]

Under this method an employee will normally be entitled to the value of the employer's contributions[10] as well as his own[11] up to the date of dismissal and from the date of dismissal until the date of the hearing. To this is added a sum equal to the interest accrued on a compound basis, to take into account the return that has already accrued to the pension contribution.

From the accrued value of the employee's pension position based on contributions, certain discounts must be made. Where the employer has repaid the employee's contributions credit must be given for this amount.[12] Where the employee on dismissal becomes entitled to a paid up pension payable on retirement[13] or has the right to transfer his pension,[14] the loss under this head may be nil. If there is a real chance that the employee might otherwise have failed to qualify for a pension eg because of a resignation or withdrawal this may result in a discount.[15]

The mere return of an employee's pension contribution will rarely compensate for the full loss of present pension position.[16] And indeed in the case of the longer service employee,[17] the method of calculating loss of present position solely in terms of contribution by employer and employee may underestimate the full loss, particularly in the case of final salary schemes.[18]

Where the employee is close to retiring age and already has a long period of contributions, the tribunal may decide to take the capital sum that would

---

9   *Copson v Eversure Accessories Ltd* [1974] ICR 636, [1974] IRLR 247, NIRC; see too *Clancy v Cannock Chase Technical College* [2001] IRLR 331, EAT.

10   *Smith, Kline and French Laboratories Ltd v Coates* [1975] IRLR 220, EAT; *Sturdy Finance Ltd v Bardsley* [1979] ICR 249, [1979] IRLR 65, EAT.

11   Ibid; *Hill v Sabco Houseware (UK) Ltd* [1977] ICR 888, AT; *Willment Bros Ltd v Oliver* [1979] ICR 378, [1979] IRLR 393, EAT.

12   *Copson v Eversure Accessories Ltd* [1974] ICR 636, [1974] IRLR 247, NIRC.

13   See eg *Yeats v Fairey Winches Ltd* [1974] IRLR 362, IT; *Page v East Midlands Electricity Board* [1975] IRLR 21.

14   *Freemans plc v Flynn* [1984] ICR 874, [1984] IRLR 486, EAT.

15   See *Manpower Ltd v Hearne* [1983] ICR 567, [1983] IRLR 281, EAT; *Linver Ltd v Hammersley* (1983) EAT 226/83.

16   *Willment Bros Ltd v Oliver* [1979] ICR 378, [1978] IRLR 393, EAT.

17   Ibid.

18   Ibid.

have been provided at retirement to purchase an annuity had he not been dismissed and discount this by such factors as the acceleration of the payment and the chance that the employee might not have continued in employment until retirement.[19]

For the longer service employee therefore a method based on the actuarial assessment of the benefits earned at the date of dismissal will be more accurate. There are three major methods of calculating loss of pension position based on benefits. The cost of annuity method; in which the measure of the loss is calculated as the difference between the cost of an annuity equal to the pension that the employee would have received had he stayed in the job and whatever deferred pension the employee has received. From this figure would be discounted the value of the accelerated payment of the award and the possibility that the employee may not continue to work until retirement.[20] Resort to this method still leaves unresolved the issue of whether the calculation should be based on the employee's salary at the date of dismissal or at the anticipated date of retirement.[1] Secondly an employment tribunal can adopt a method that attempts to make some allowance for the fact that inflation and the chances of real increases in the value of the pension made a figure based on the employee's final salary at the date of dismissal too pessimistic, whilst acknowledging that the employee's final salary at retirement is too speculative. Thirdly, a variation on the cost of annuity method is the cost of buying an equivalent pension. This method attempts to assess the difference in value between the pension under the new position and that which would have been payable under the old, by estimating what it would cost to buy into an equivalent scheme in the old pension.[2]

[II]   LOSS OF FUTURE PENSION OPPORTUNITIES.

If the unfairly dismissed employees had continued in their previous employment they could have gone on improving their pension position. If they can do the same in their new employment at the same rate of benefit, at no greater cost to themselves and with no interim loss owing to the

---

19   Ibid; *Powrmatic Ltd v Bull* [1977] ICR 469, [1977] IRLR 144, EAT; *Tesco Stores Ltd v Heap* (1978) 13 ITR 17, EAT; *Scottish Co-operative Wholesale Society Ltd v Lloyd* [1973] ICR 137, [1973] IRLR 93, NIRC.

20   See eg *Smith, Kline and French Laboratories Ltd v Coates* (above); *John Millar & Sons v Quinn* (above).

1   See *Smith, Kline and French Laboratories Ltd v Coates* (above); *John Millar & Sons v Quinn* (above); *Willment Bros Ltd v Oliver* (above).

2   See eg *Willment Bros Ltd v Oliver* [1979] ICR 378, [1979] IRLR 393, EAT.

change in pension arrangements, then there is no loss under this head.[3] But this is rarely the case. Far more often a dismissal will result in a real loss of the future opportunity to build on the pension earned at the time of dismissal, ie loss of the opportunity to enhance accrued pension rights (Guidelines, para 10).

Let us consider the position first under the assumption that the employee has found new employment with a pension entitlement, then we can consider the position where the employee obtains a new job without any pension entitlement.

[III] NEW EMPLOYMENT WITH A PENSION ENTITLEMENT.

Even where the employee finds new employment with a pension entitlement there is still an entitlement to compensation for the period of unemployment. This could be by a contributions method (Guidelines, paras 7 and 8(1)). Moreover, as the EAT indicated in *Hill v Sabco Houseware (UK) Ltd*,[4] compensation for the interim loss that occurs owing to a change from one employer to another should also include, where relevant, compensation for the loss caused by the qualifying period for pension entitlement in the new job.[5]

Where the pension scheme in the old employment has a lower rate benefit than that in the old, there is a basis for compensation for loss of expected benefit. This would take the form of a loss of benefit period which considers the difference between the benefits offered by the two schemes and discounts this difference by the possibility that the employee might not live to enjoy them. The discounting process may result in a relatively short loss of benefit period. For example, in *Powrmatic Ltd v Bull*[6] an employment tribunal assessed the difference between the scheme in the former job (Powrmatic) and that in the new job (Mysons) on the assumption that the employee would continue to work until he was 65 and live 8 years later, to the average span of a healthy man of 73 years. The tribunal postulated a salary at retirement of £18,000 pa and concluded that under

3   See eg *Sturdy Finance Ltd v Bardsley* [1979] ICR 249, [1979] IRLR 65, EAT (self-employed); *Sweetlove v Redbridge and Waltham Forest Area Health Authority* [1979] ICR 477, [1979] IRLR 195, EAT (tribunal ordered reinstatement).
4   [1977] ICR 888, EAT.
5   See also *Smith, Kline and French Laboratories v Coates* [1977] IRLR 220, EAT; *Page v East Midlands Electricity Board* [1975] IRLR 21. Cf *Freemans plc v Flynn* [1984] ICR 874, [1984] IRLR 486, EAT. See too Guidelines, paras 9.2 and 9.3.
6   [1977] ICR 469, [1977] IRLR 144, EAT.

the Powrmatic scheme he would enjoy a pension of £12,000 pa. As far as the discounting process was concerned, the tribunal said:

'it would not be possible to say that the applicant's loss would be that amount. There could be many intervening factors such as the death of the applicant, a change of job and the like, but even taking such matters into account we consider that the applicant's loss of pension far outstrips the maximum compensation we can award which is £5,200'.

The EAT's view was that:

'it cannot be right to consider the loss of benefit period simply on the basis that he will after serving 33 years in business then live to the average life span of a healthy male, that is to say 73. Just as he may never reach 65 at all, and you may discount your award for that, so also having reached 65 he may well not be a normal healthy male, or, as it does many people, retirement may kill him even if he is a normal healthy male. We think that 3 to 5 years is the appropriate order of multiplier for the loss of benefit period'.

If the employee is unfairly dismissed from a job with a non-contributory scheme and moves to a job with a contributory scheme, there is a further basis for compensating for the additional cost of the new scheme. The amount will be based upon the annual cost of contribution times a multiplier applicable to the individual.[7]

In all cases where compensation is awarded in the form of a capital sum, allowance must be made for the fact that the payment of the lump sum constitutes an acceleration of the payments that would have been received under the pension scheme, and hence must be discounted. As the EAT put it in *Powrmatic*:

'In the hands of the person compensated it can earn interest over those periods, and so, in order that he does not receive more by way of compensation than the loss he has truly suffered, you must discount the award so that taking into account interest as well as capital you arrive at the appropriate amount. The principle here is the same as in awards of compensation for serious injury'.

---

7   See eg *Powrmatic Ltd v Bull* [1977] ICR 469, [1977] IRLR 144, EAT, in which a multiplier of 15 years was allowed. See also *Pringle v Lucas Industrial Equipment Ltd* [1975] IRLR 266, EAT, where allowance was made for the reverse situation.

[IV] NEW EMPLOYMENT WITHOUT A PENSION ENTITLEMENT.

Where the new job has no pension entitlement, the employee is entitled to compensation for the loss of employer's contributions for a period in the future depending upon the tribunal's assessment of the employee's chance of finding a job with an equivalent pension scheme. Alternatively, an actuarial method can be adopted. In any case some allowance should be made for the employer's contribution to the State Earnings Related Pension Scheme (SERPS) to reduce the employer's contribution rate (Guidelines, para 9G).

3. CONTRIBUTION

Under ERA 1996, s 123(6) where a tribunal finds that the dismissal was to any extent caused or contributed to by any action of the complainant, it must reduce the amount of the compensatory award by such proportion as it considers just and equitable having regard to that finding. Under s 122(2) a proportionate reduction for contributory fault must be applied to the basic award.[8]

As was the case with its statutory forerunners, under s 123(6) the amount of the deduction from compensation is a discretionary matter for an employment tribunal hearing the evidence.[9]

In calculating the extent of an employee's contributory fault, employment tribunals are to be allowed to take a wide view of the relevant circumstances. The view of the NIRC is *Maris v Rotherham Corpn*,[10] although an interpretation of the predecessor provision, applies with equal force to s 123(6):

'(The provision is) of wide import ... (it) brings into consideration all the circumstances surrounding the dismissal, requiring the tribunal to take a broad common sense view of the situation and to decide what if any part of the applicant's own conduct played in contributing

---

8   There is no requirement that the same proportionate reduction for contributory fault must be applied to the basic award as is applied to the compensatory award. See eg *Charles Robertson (Developments) Ltd v White* [1995] ICR 349, EAT; see too *Optikinetics Ltd v Whooley* [1999] ICR 984, EAT; but see *contra G McFall & Co Ltd v Curran* [1981] IRLR 455, NICA.

9   See eg *Iggesund Converters Ltd v Lewis* [1984] ICR 544, [1984] IRLR 431, EAT.

10   [1974] 2 All ER 776, [1974] ICR 435, NIRC; see too *Morrison v Amalgamated Transport and General Workers Union* [1989] IRLR 361, NICA.

to his dismissal and then in the light of that finding decide what, if any, reduction should be made in the assessment of this loss'.

Moreover as the Court of Appeal held in *Hollier v Plysu Ltd*,[11] the EAT was not entitled to interfere with a tribunal's conclusion on the question of contribution unless the tribunal had gone wrong in law or their conclusion was one which no reasonable tribunal could have reached on the evidence. As Lord Justice Stephenson put it,

'In a question which is so obviously a matter of impression, opinion and discretion as in this question of appointment of responsibility, there must be either a plain error of law or something like perversity to entitle an appellate tribunal to interfere with the decision of the industrial tribunal which is entrusted by Parliament with the difficult task of making the decision'.

In that case the Court of Appeal reversed a decision by the EAT to alter the decision of the employment tribunal from 75% to 25% and restored the original decision.

Yet of course industrial tribunals must correctly direct themselves.[12] Thus in *Nelson v BBC (No 2)*[13] the Court of Appeal suggested that tribunals must make three findings under this section.

First, there must be a finding that there was conduct on the part of the employee in connection with his unfair dismissal which was culpable or blameworthy.

Secondly, there must be a finding that this conduct actually caused or contributed to the unfair dismissal. Thirdly, there must be a finding that it is just and equitable to reduce the assessment of the complainant's loss to a specific extent.

In *Nelson*'s case the Court of Appeal described the concept of culpability or blameworthiness in wide terms. It

'does not necessarily involve only conduct amounting to a breach of contract or a tort. It ... also includes conduct which while not amounting to a breach of contract or a tort is nevertheless perverse or foolish or bloody minded. It may also include action which though

---

11   [1983] IRLR 260, CA. See too *Warrilow v Robert Walker Ltd* [1984] IRLR 304, EAT.

12   See eg *Portsea Island Mutual Co-operative Society Ltd v Rees* [1980] ICR 260, EAT.

13   [1980] ICR 110, [1979] IRLR 346, CA; cf *Morrison v Amalgamated Transport & General Workers Union* [1989] IRLR 361, NICA.

not meriting any of those more pejorative epithets, is nevertheless unacceptable in the circumstances. But all unreasonable conduct is not necessarily culpable or blameworthy; it must depend upon the degree of blameworthiness involved'.

Yet where the employee has shown that what he did was not unlawful this has provided a basis for arguing that his conduct was not culpable or blameworthy under s 123(6). For example in *Property Guards Ltd v Taylor and Kershaw*,[14] a failure by two individuals to disclose previous convictions for dishonesty when applying for a position as security guards was held not to be a basis for a reduction of their compensation for unfair dismissal under s 123(6) because there was no obligation to disclose the spent convictions owing to the Rehabilitation of Offenders Act 1974.

And in *Morrish v Henlys (Folkestone) Garage Ltd*[15] the NIRC held that the employee's compensation could not be reduced where he refused to obey an order from the employer which itself was outside the scope of the contract, and possibly illegal. The employee's action could not be held to have contributed to his dismissal since he had been justified in refusing to comply with an unreasonable order and was entirely free of fault in taking this stand. Since the assessment may only be reduced to the extent that it is just and equitable, it would have been inequitable to reduce an award if a man had been quite blameless.[16] Yet in *Hollier v Plysu Ltd* the Court of Appeal accepted that an employment tribunal was entitled to deduct 75% for contributory fault for an employee's behaviour with the police.

Moreover, although under s 123(6) the employment tribunal is entitled to cast its net widely and consider aspects of the employee's conduct, looking at the realities of the situation rather than being limited to the stated reasons for dismissal,[17] it is nevertheless the case that the conduct of the unfairly dismissed employee relied on by the employment tribunal must be causally linked to the dismissal.

Thus the tribunal must confine itself to taking into account the conduct of the complainant alone. It must not confuse it with the conduct of another employee involved in the incident[18] or mix in the employer's conduct.[19]

---

14   [1982] IRLR 175, EAT.
15   [1973] 2 All ER 137, [1973] ICR 482, NIRC.
16   Conduct by the employee could include the acts of his agents such as his solicitors, see eg *Allen v Hammett* [1982] IRLR 89, EAT.
17   See eg *Robert Whiting Ltd v Lamb* [1978] ICR 89, EAT; *Jameson v Aberdeen County Council* [1975] IRLR 348, Ct of Sess; *Maris v Rotherham Corpn* (above).
18   *Parker Foundry Ltd v Slack* [1992] IRLR 11, CA.
19   *Allders International Ltd v Parkins* [1981] IRLR 68, EAT.

Moreover, it is not enough for an employment tribunal to find that an employee had engaged in bad behaviour. There must be a further finding that his bad behaviour actually caused the dismissal. For example in *Hutchinson v Enfield Rolling Mills Ltd*[20] an employment tribunal found that an employee who was dismissed for taking part in a union demonstration whilst away from work on a sickness certificate was unfairly dismissed for this reason. Yet the tribunal decided to reduce his compensation by 100% because of his generally unfavourable work record. The EAT allowed an appeal because there was no finding that the misconduct described by the employment tribunal had any part in inducing the dismissal.

Where the ground for dismissal was misconduct and the grounds for unfair dismissal are procedural omission, evidence of misconduct by the employee may be used to support a finding by the employment tribunal of a percentage reduction for contribution.[1] In cases of incapacity the question of contribution is less clear cut. Unless the incapacity is in the control of the employee a reduction for contributory fault will be rare.[2] Similarly, in cases of unfair dismissal on grounds of ill health, there will only rarely be reductions for contributory fault unless the employee blatantly and persistently refuses to obtain appropriate medical reports or attend for medical examination.[3]

Furthermore, however wide the discretion enjoyed by employment tribunals in assessing the extent to which the employee's conduct played any part in the history of events leading to dismissal, they cannot under s 123(6) take into account conduct occurring[4] or discovered *after* the dismissal. In *W Devis & Sons Ltd v Atkins*[5] the House of Lords indicated

---

20 [1981] IRLR 318, EAT; see too *Polentarutti v Autokraft Ltd* [1991] IRLR 457, EAT (it does not require that the action of the complainant was the sole or principal or operative cause).

1 *Moyes v Hylton Castle Working Men's Social Club & Institute Ltd* [1986] IRLR 482, EAT.

2 *Moncur v International Paint Co Ltd* [1978] IRLR 223, EAT: *Kraft Foods Ltd v Fox* [1977] IRLR 431, EAT; *Finnie v Top Hat Frozen Foods* [1985] IRLR 365, EAT (overruled on other grounds by *Babcock FATA Ltd v Addison* [1987] IRLR 173, CA); see too *Brown's Cycles Ltd v Brindley* [1978] ICR 467, EAT: *Sutton & Gates (Luton) Ltd v Boxall* [1978] IRLR 486, EAT.

3 *Slaughter v C Brewer & Sons Ltd* [1990] IRLR 426, EAT.

4 Eg where the employee fails to make use of his right of appeal in an internal appeals procedure: *Hoover Ltd v Forde* [1980] ICR 239, EAT.

5 [1977] AC 931, [1977] ICR 662, HL. Such loss may be taken into account in calculating the basic award where the causation requirement is dropped: ERA 1996, s 122(2).

that subsequently discovered misconduct could not be taken into account because it did not cause or contribute to the dismissal and the tribunal is restricted to assessing the effects of the employee's action on the dismissal. In *Jamieson v Aberdeen County Council*[6] the Scottish Court of Session indicated that it thought that it would be improper to include in the contributory action aspect matters established at the tribunal but not known or taken into account by the employer when deciding to dismiss. And in *Trend v Chiltern Hunt Ltd*[7] the EAT stated:

'... we doubt whether a case such as *W Devis & Sons Ltd v Atkins* where a subsequently discovered dishonesty would have justified a dismissal had it been known, can be properly dealt with under [s 123(6)] by a 100% apportionment. However widely "the matters to which the complaint relates" are construed, it is difficult to see how they can extend to facts which were unknown to all concerned at the date of dismissal'.

It went on to suggest that even if such a case should plainly result in a nil award it should do so under s 123(1) and if this cannot be achieved under s 123(1) it would seem that it cannot be achieved at all.

Nevertheless, in *Ladup Ltd v Barnes Ltd*[8] where the applicant dismissed for an alleged criminal offence was subsequently found guilty of that offence in a Crown Court, the EAT was prepared to allow a review of an industrial tribunal's decision not to reduce compensation on grounds of contributory fault. Certainly, in cases where an employee was unfairly dismissed owing to a procedural impropriety on the part of the employer the entire record of the employee's conduct can be taken into account.[9] Moreover, in cases of constructive dismissal it is possible for employment tribunals to find that the employee has contributed to the dismissal.[10]

Furthermore, whilst s 123(5) specifically provides that no account may be taken of industrial pressure on the employer to dismiss the employee,

6   [1975] IRLR 348, Ct of Sess; see too *Tele-Trading Ltd v Jenkins* [1990] IRLR 430, CA.
7   [1977] ICR 612, [1977] IRLR 66, EAT.
8   [1982] IRLR 7, EAT.
9   See eg *Jamieson v Aberdeen County Council* [1975] IRLR 348, Ct of Sess.
10   See eg *Allders International Ltd v Parkins* [1981] IRLR 68, EAT; *Garner v Grange Furnishings Ltd* [1972] IRLR 206, EAT; *Savoia v Chiltern Herb Farms Ltd* [1982] IRLR 166, CA; *Trimble v Supertravel Ltd* [1982] ICR 440, [1982] IRLR 451, EAT; *Morrison v ATGWU* [1989] IRLR 361, NICA; *Polentarutti v Autokraft Ltd* [1991] IRLR 457, EAT. But see *Holroyd v Gravure Cylinders Ltd* [1984] IRLR 259, EAT; *Renie v Northsound Radio Ltd* (1984) EAT/490.

where the employee has engaged in conduct which resulted in fellow employees putting pressure upon the employer to dismiss him, that could be taken into account under s 123(6).[11]

To what extent is it just and equitable to reduce the assessment of the complainant's loss?

According to *Nelson*'s[12] case the final finding that the tribunal must make having regard to the first and second findings is the extent to which it is just and equitable to reduce the assessment of the complainant's loss. As the Court of Appeal expressed it in *Nelson*'s case[13] assuming that it would be right for there to be some reduction of compensation under s 123(6), the assessment of the amount of compensation is in principle for the industrial tribunal to decide.

And in *Hollier v Plysu Ltd*[14] the Court of Appeal made it clear that only in the most extreme cases ie misconduct or perversity may appellate tribunals interfere with industrial tribunals' decisions even if they consider that they would have found a different judgment to the degree of fault attributable to the employer.

Finally, the House of Lords decision in *W Devis & Sons Ltd v Atkins* stated that there was no inconsistency between finding a dismissal unfair and reducing the compensation award by 100% to a nil award under s 123(6) since 'a man may bring about his dismissal wholly by his own misconduct and the dismissal may be unfair through a failure to warn him that his employment was in jeopardy'.

In the event, cases such as *Maris v Rotherham Corpn*[15] remain good law. In *Maris*' case an employee was held to be 100% to blame for his dismissal and his compensation reduced to nil under s 123(6). The facts were rather unusual in that the employee had in fact been convicted of making fraudulent expense claims but the cause of the dismissal was the pressure by the workforce on the employer to reconsider a decision to reinstate him. As the EAT has more recently pointed out however in *Gibson*

---

11 See eg *Colwyn Borough Council v Dutton* [1980] IRLR 420, EAT; *Sulemanji v Toughened Glass Ltd* [1979] ICR 799, EAT.
12 [1980] ICR 110, [1979] IRLR 346, CA.
13 [1980] ICR 110, [1979] IRLR 346, CA.
14 [1983] IRLR 260, CA. See also *Acorn Shipyard Ltd v Warren* (1981) EAT 20/81.
15 [1974] 2 All ER 776, [1974] ICR 435, NIRC.

v British Transport Docks Board[16] a 100% reduction presupposes that the employee is completely at fault for the dismissal and cannot be awarded by an employment tribunal which has found that the employer was to some extent at fault.

4. THE ORDER OF DEDUCTIONS

In many cases, there may be more than one deduction to be made from the compensatory award including deductions for contributory fault, 'Polkey deductions' and mitigation. Recent case law has established a particular order for tribunals to follow in such cases.

First, any amounts in mitigation of loss received either from the ex-employer or a new employer or viewed by the tribunal as likely to be received from a new employer. This amount should not include a redundancy payment in excess of the statutory payment,[17] but it does include payments made in lieu of notice.[18]

Secondly any *Polkey* percentage deduction should be applied.[19]

Thirdly, any percentage for contributory fault should be made.[20]

Fourthly, there should be a reduction for any redundancy payment in excess of the statutory payment.[1]

Finally, the statutory maximum limit should be applied.[2]

16 [1982] IRLR 228, EAT.
17 *Digital Equipment Co Ltd v Clements (No 2)* [1998] IRLR 134, CA; *Babcock FATA Ltd v Addison* [1987] IRLR 173, CA.
18 *Heggie v Uniroyal Englebert Tyres Ltd* [1999] IRLR 802, Ct of Sess.
19 Ibid; *Cox v London Borough of Camden* [1996] IRLR 389, EAT.
20 Ibid.
1   *Leonard v Strathclyde Buses Ltd* [1998] IRLR 693, CS; *Darr v LRC Products Ltd* [1993] IRLR 257, EAT; *McCarthy v British Insulated Callenders Cables plc* [1995] IRLR 94, EAT.
2   *Walter Braund (London) Ltd v Murray* [1991] IRLR 100, EAT.

Chapter 18.
Interim relief for dismissals for trade union membership and activity and other prohibited reasons

A special interim remedy is provided by TULRCA 1992, s 161 for employees who claim that they have been dismissed and that the dismissal is unfair by virtue of s 152 of TULRCA 1992 ie for reasons of trade union membership or activity or non-membership of a trade union. A parallel remedy of interim relief is provided by ERA 1996, s 128 for dismissals for the following reasons:
(a) health and safety cases (ERA, s 100(1));
(b) workforce representatives;
(c) for working time issues (ERA, s 101A(d));
(d) trustees of occupational pension schemes (ERA, s 102(1));
(e) employee representatives (ERA, s 103);
(f) whistleblowers (ERA, s 103A).

In such cases the Act provides that an employment tribunal may order either the revival of the employee's contract if it has been terminated or its continuation if it is still in force until the hearing or the settlement of the dismissal complaint. In practice, this may mean that the tribunal orders either the reinstatement of an employee, or, if mutually agreed, a re-engagement of the employee. If the employer refuses either order an employment tribunal may make an order to continue the employee's contract of employment in force until a final determination of the complaint.[1] The order would not require the employer specifically to perform the contract by retaining the employee at work; it would however revive or continue the contract for the purpose of ensuring that employers continue to meet their obligations under the contract in respect of pay, seniority, pension

1   TULRCA 1992, s 164; ERA 1996, s 130.

rights and continuous employment.[2] It thus may at the very least provide in statutory form the equivalent of a precautionary suspension with pay, pending the hearing or settlement of the complaint.

Moreover, if this remedy is successful in convincing the employer to take the employee back pending determination of the complaint it will have the same effect as a 'status quo' clause in a procedure agreement.[3] In its order, an employment tribunal must specify the amount payable by the employer and this may be reduced by any payment by the employer in the form of wages or a lump sum payment which is paid at least in part in lieu of notice. The employee, however, is under no duty to mitigate the loss.[4]

To qualify for an interim relief order an employee must present an application within seven days immediately following the effective date of termination. During the same period, solely in cases of dismissal for trade union membership and activity, the employee must also produce where appropriate a written certificate from an authorised official of the relevant independent trade union stating that there appears to be reasonable grounds for supposing that the employee's complaint was valid.[5]

After receiving an application an employment tribunal is required to hold a hearing as soon as practicable,[6] giving the employer at least seven days' notice of the hearing and a copy of the complaint and the certificate.[7] For the purposes of hearing an application for interim relief, a tribunal may consist solely of a chairman without the two 'wingmen'.

At this hearing the tribunal must determine whether it is likely that the employee will succeed in his or her complaint at the final hearing.[8]

In *Taplin v C Shippam Ltd*,[9] the EAT suggested that in making this determination under s 161, the correct approach of the tribunal is to ask itself whether the employee has established that he has a 'pretty good' chance of succeeding in the final application to the tribunal. In order to obtain an order under s 163, the employee must achieve a higher degree of certainty in the mind of the tribunal than that of showing that he had just a 'reasonable' prospect of success.

---

2   TULRCA 1992, s 164(3); ERA 1996, s 130(3).
3   See Anderman, 'Status Quo Provisions in Industrial Disputes Procedures: Some implications for Labour Law' (1975) 4 ILJ 131.
4   TULRCA 1992, s 164(2); ERA 1996, s 130(2).
5   TULRCA 1992, s 161(3); see eg *Bradley v Edward Ryde & Sons* [1979] ICR 488, EAT; *Farmeary v Veterinary Drug Co Ltd* [1976] IRLR 322, IT.
6   TULRCA 1992, s 162; ERA 1996, s 128(5)
7   TULRCA 1992, s 162; ERA 1996, s 128(4).
8   TULRCA 1992, s 163(1). See eg *Farmeary* (above).
9   [1978] ICR 1068, [1978] IRLR 450, EAT.

If it appears at the hearing that the likely result will be a finding that the employee has been unfairly dismissed on s 152 grounds of trade union membership and activity[10] or non-membership or on any of the grounds specified in ERA 1996, s 128,[11] the tribunal must ask the employer whether he is willing to reinstate the employee, or re-engage him in another job on not less favourable terms. If the employer is willing to reinstate the employee then the tribunal shall make an order to that effect. If the employer states that he is willing to re-engage the employee in another job and specifies its terms and conditions, the tribunal will ask the employee if he or she is willing to accept re-engagement on those terms. If so the tribunal shall make an order to that effect. If the employee is unwilling to accept such an offer, the tribunal shall determine the reasonableness of the refusal and if it is found to be reasonable, the tribunal shall make an order for the continuation of the contract. Otherwise, the tribunal shall make no order.[12] Where the employer fails to attend the hearing or is unwilling either to reinstate or re-engage the employee, the tribunal must make an order for revival or continuation of the employee's contract of employment.[13]

Once made, an order can be varied or revoked on the grounds of a relevant change of circumstances.[14] Such an application can be made to a different tribunal.[15] However, where after the hearing the employer has not complied with an order, on application by the employee, the tribunal is empowered to award compensation in respect of the loss such as loss of pay suffered by the employee in consequence of the non-compliance.[16]

If the complaint is determined along with the hearing of the complaint of unfair dismissal and there is a finding of unfair dismissal, the compensation for such loss is to be awarded 'separately from' any other sum awarded to the employee.[17]

If the loss suffered by the employee as a consequence of the employer's non-compliance consists of loss other than loss of pay, the amount of compensation shall be such as the tribunal considers just and equitable.[18]

---

10 For a definition of trade union membership and activity see Chapter 10.
11 ERA 1996, s 129(1).
12 TULRCA 1992, s 165(2)–(6); ERA 1996, s 129(3)–(8).
13 TULRCA 1992, s 163(6); ERA 1996, s 129(9).
14 ERA 1996, s 165(1).
15 *British Coal Corpn v McGinty* [1988] IRLR 7, EAT.
16 TULRCA 1992, s 166; ERA 1996, s 132.
17 TULRCA 1992, s 166(4); ERA 1996, s 132(5).
18 TULRCA 1992, s 166(5); ERA 1996, s 132(6).

Conclusions

The current unfair dismissals legislation was designed with at least two aims in view. One was to provide a general protection for individual employees against the arbitrary termination of employment by employers. The second, a more complex motive, was to create a further element in the legal framework provided for collective labour relations.

UNFAIR DISMISSALS IN ITS COLLECTIVE SETTING

From the outset the legislation was never conceived of simply as an individual worker's right designed solely to create legislative protection for the weaker party to the contractual relationship. It was consciously designed to influence collective activity at work whether through managerial practice or collective bargaining.

To some extent the full collective implications of individual employment law were only imperfectly understood at the time the statute was drafted. Thus, the elaborate concern with the provision for approved voluntary procedures to qualify for exclusion from the legislation is now seen to have been misplaced. Only one sector has actually succeeded in contracting out of the statutory procedure.[1] Few others have bothered to try. Nevertheless the statute has undoubtedly resulted in a widespread change in managerial practice and the formalisation of disciplinary procedures in

---

1   Anderman: Unfair Dismissals and Redundancy in R Lewis, *Labour Law in Britain* (Blackwell, 1986).

industry. Interestingly the introduction of more formalised disciplinary procedures has not only offered protection to employees from their immediate supervision and middle management. It has also operated to give management more confidence to dismiss when the procedure has been used properly.

There was some suggestion that the creation of a statutory procedure might itself serve to provide an alternative to collective action.[2] Yet the attempt to make use of the tribunal procedure directly to institutionalise industrial conflict by providing individual adjudication as a substitute for collective action was only a thin thread of aspiration running through the preparation of the legislation. Procedural reform in industry was given a higher priority.

While these collective labour relations issues provide a context for the adoption of unfair dismissals legislation, it was undoubtedly true that the statute was conceived of and took the form of a fundamental right for individual employees against arbitrary termination of employment, whether or not such employees were trade union members.

I. INDIVIDUAL EMPLOYMENT PROTECTION

The introduction of the statutory protection against unfair dismissal originally constituted legislative recognition that a job a man or woman does is sufficiently important to the individual, as well as to his or her family, that a decision to end that job should not be left entirely to the discretion of an employing organisation or individual employer. The statutory enactment represented a rejection, albeit somewhat belatedly, of certain nineteenth-century common law values,[3] in particular, the application of the commercial concept of freedom of contract to employment which gave employers an excessive freedom of termination of employment contracts. For most employees the statutory protections, certainly at the outset, improved considerably upon the position at common law.

An employee, having the choice of the two actions,[4] often found that the statutory right was more advantageous to pursue both in terms of the

---

2   See eg Conservative Governments Consultative Document to the Industrial Relations Act 1971.

3   Of course, the statute continues to reflect certain other common law values. See eg Chapters 3 and 5.

4   The right to complain of unfair dismissal under the statutory procedure applies to a large group of dismissed employees who have no claim of wrongful dismissal

remedies it offered[5] and in terms of the greater comprehensiveness of the test of 'reasonableness in the circumstances' under s 98(4) by comparison with the more restrictive contractual test of 'wrongful dismissal'. Yet this is no longer invariably the case, in part because of advances in the common law remedies for breach of employment contracts,[6] which can now include injunctive relief in certain cases. Moreover, the increased scope of the implied obligation of mutual trust and confidence has expanded the scope of the substantive test of wrongful dismissal.[7] Nevertheless, the increase in the maximum compensation for unfair dismissal to £50,000 and the new categories of automatically unfair dismissal indicate that the statutory claim will continue to be a favourable route of redress.

Yet it is not appropriate to judge the effect of unfair dismissal legislation by comparing it with the position at common law. It is also important to look at certain positive principles underlying the legislation, and ask to what extent these principles have been implemented. Following the ILO Convention No 119 there are three positive principles underlying the statutory employment right. The first is that a dismissed employee shall have a right to require his or her employer to satisfy an independent third party[8] of the fairness, as defined by the Act, of the decision to dismiss. The second principle is that this right should be enjoyed by *all* employees.

---

at common law, notably employees who have been dismissed with proper contractual notice or individuals employed under a fixed-term contract which expires without being renewed.

5   In particular the increase in the maximum compensation of £50,000. A major exception occurs in the case of highly paid employees on fixed-term contracts whose damages for breach of contract can exceed the maximum limits for compensation for unfair dismissal. As well, 'office holders' may enjoy superior equitable remedies at common law. See eg *McClelland v Northern Ireland General Health Services Board* [1957] All ER 129, [1957] 1 WLR 594. See also Napier, B, 'Office and Office Holder in British Labour Law, in *In Memoriam Sir Otto Kahn Freund* (Munich 1980). Further, employees who are unqualified under or excluded by the statutory procedure are left with their common law action as their sole legal protection against arbitrary dismissal.

6   See generally Smith and Wood *Industrial Law* (7th edn, Butterworths, 2000) ch 7; Deakin and Morris *Labour Law* (3rd edn, Butterworths, 2001) ch 5; Anderman *Labour Law* (4th edn, Butterworths, 2000) ch 6. Recent case law suggests that the law of breach of employment contracts, as well as wrongful dismissal, has considerably expanded.

7   See eg Brodie 'Beyond Exchange – The New Contract of Employment' (1998) 27 ILJ 79.

8   This could be either an employment tribunal or a suitably constituted body of an approved voluntary procedure. It could also be an arbitrator appointed under the provisions of the Employment Rights (Dispute Resolution Act) 1988.

The third principle is that the remedies provided should be adequate to redress the wrong.

The original statute, enacted in 1971, contained provisions which fell short of the aspirations contained within these principles. Amendments, in the TULRA 1974 and the Employment Protection Act 1975, improved the position in all three respects. From 1980–96, however, the Conservative Government considerably reduced the scope of the Act in pursuit of its policy of deregulation and its opposition to trade unions and collective bargaining.[9] In the Employment Relations Act 1999 the Labour Government introduced a number of amendments which strengthened the protections in all three respects. As we have seen in this book, however, the characteristics of the unfair dismissals legislation are not entirely the result of legislative design; they are also a consequence of the particular interpretation given by the judiciary to the existing statutory provisions. These developments can best be looked at under three heads:

(i)   the scope and coverage of the legislation;
(ii) the remedies for unfair dismissal, and
(iii) the test of fairness.

i) The scope and coverage of unfair dismissals legislation

One of the most noteworthy changes introduced by the Employment Relations Act 1999 has been the increase in the coverage of unfair dismissals legislation. The decrease in the qualifying period from two years to one year, the ending of the exceptions for employees of small firms and the possibilities of a waiver of statutory rights within a fixed term contract of one year or more have all been introduced with particular policy objectives. Yet despite these changes a two-tier labour market has continued to develop consisting of a group of workers provided with statutory protection against unfair job termination surrounded by a significant proportion of workers without such protection.[10]

The decision of the House of Lords in *Carmichael v National Power plc*[11] has made it clear that there are groups of casual workers who will continue to be excluded from the protections of the statute.

In the Employment Relations Act 1999, the Labour Government has redefined the statutory test to limit the unpredictability of the judicial

9   See eg B Hepple 'A Right to Work?' (1981) ILJ 65.
10   See eg B Hepple 'A Right to Work?' (1981) ILJ 65.
11   [2000] IRLR 43, HL.

treatment of employee status. Section 12(6) states that, 'a reference to "employee" in Chapter II of Part X of the 1996 Act is to be taken as a reference to a "worker"'. Section 13(1) then defines 'worker', for the purpose of sections 10–12 (ie for the purposes of representation rights at grievance or disciplinary hearings), to include inter alia 'homeworkers' and 'agency' workers as well as the more traditional category of worker under section 230(3) of the Employment Rights Act 1996.[12] This method offers a useful way forward to deal with the problems of ensuring that statutory protection against unfair dismissals can apply to other types of atypical workers such as regular casuals or others on short term contracts.

The time has come for the Government to make greater use of its powers to deem particular categories of individuals covered by an expanded definition of 'employee'.[13] Such a move would be more closely in step with EU directives[14] and will produce a less arbitrary and discriminatory pattern of coverage of the unfair dismissal protection.

ii) Remedies for unfair dismissal

The experience of the application of the remedies of reinstatement and re-engagement for unfairly dismissed employees reflects judicial and tribunal conservatism in effectuating a legislative policy. Thus the provisions of the Act were amended specifically to prompt tribunals to consider reinstatement as the primary remedy. Yet, the statistics and the case law reflect a reluctance to provide this remedy in practice. Reinstatement and re-engagement have been ordered in less than 5% of successful cases at employment tribunals and the proportion of re-employments secured at the conciliation stage is almost the same. In those rather limited cases when such orders have actually been made they have tended to be effective in the sense that employees continue in employment for a considerable period.[15]

---

12 See too, ERA 1996, s 143K as amended by the Public Interest Disclosure Act 1998, s 1, which now provides a widened definition of worker for the purposes of the whistle-blower protections. Cf Sex Discrimination Act 1975, s 9 (contract workers); s 3 (duties to persons other than employees) and Health and Safety at Work Act 1974, s 51A (police).

13 See ERA 1999, s 23; see too, Fairness at Work, Cm 3968, para 3.18.

14 See eg discussion by McColgan (2000) ILJ 125 at 143.

15 See Williams and Lewis above, Chapter 2.

Whilst the rarity of re-employment measures is largely due to the reluctance of tribunals to make such orders, it is also true that employees do not always take advantage of the option when it is offered to them.[16] One factor that undoubtedly influences the great majority of non-unionised complainants of unfair dismissal is that they may be isolated and vulnerable where there is no organisation at workplace level that could help them face up to the day to day pressures of being back at work after a reinstatement or re-engagement order.

At all events, the statistics puncture the myth that the statute offers a form of job security by providing an effective remedy against an employer who is unwilling to abide by an order of reinstatement with the statute in practice providing so few reinstatements, it is inaccurate to characterise it as providing security of employment. Rather at most it provides a form of compensation for loss of employment.

Though in practice compensation is the most prevalent remedy, the awards prior to 1999 were made at levels which barely met the ILO standards of 'adequacy'. Moreover, there has been a discernible tendency for employers to be wary about hiring an employee who has made an unfair dismissal complaint to an employment tribunal.

Since 1999 the maximum level of the compensation award has been raised to £50,000 which should result in an increase in the average level of awards and more adequate compensation. Yet it is too soon to see precisely what the levels will be. At all events there should also be an increase in the number of higher paid employees who make use of their right to complain of unfair dismissal.

iii) The test of reasonableness

When the test of reasonableness was reformulated in 1974, Parliament not only reaffirmed the position that employment tribunals were meant to act as industrial juries deciding the essentially factual question of the reasonableness of the employer's decision in the round, it also attempted to ensure that the burden of proof was placed squarely upon the employer to satisfy the employment tribunal of the reasonableness of his actions.

Yet it was not long before the interpretation of s 98(4) by the EAT, the Court of Appeal and on occasion the House of Lords established certain constraints on the discretion of employment tribunals to determine the

---

16   See sources in note 7, above.

justification for the dismissal. These constraints were articulated at all three levels of the reasonableness decision, ie the 'factual' test, the 'procedural' test and the test 'on the merits'.

Thus, as has been extensively analysed in the text, the cases from *Ferodo Ltd v Barnes* to *British Home Stores Ltd v Burchell* and *Monie v Coral Racing Ltd* established quite clearly that the courts were concerned to interpret the statute not to require the employer to meet the more objective test of establishing on the balance of probabilities that the employee had in fact committed the act(s) or omission(s) complained of, but rather to interpret the statutory language to establish a relatively subjective test, with only a minimum residual standard of objectivity ie that the employer had reasonable grounds for his or her belief and had carried out as much investigation into the matter as was reasonable in the circumstances. This, in effect, is to select from the range of possible interpretations one which is the most favourable from the employer's point of view. It suggests that in striking a balance between the respective claims of employer and employee, the courts have been willing to sacrifice the 'protective' function of the statute because of their concerns that the statute should not place too great a limitation upon managerial authority.

A similar point can be made about the 'range of reasonableness test' endorsed by the Court of Appeal in *British Leyland (UK) Ltd v Swift* and by the EAT in *Iceland Frozen Foods v Jones*. This test offers further evidence that the courts have been determined to limit the extent to which tribunals may use the test of reasonableness to interfere with management discretion. In effect the judiciary has read into the Act a self-denying ordinance which establishes a standard reflecting the lowest common denominator of acceptable managerial practice,[17] rather than imposing upon employers an objective notion of fairness in the interpretation of the statutory standard.

To this picture of a general lowering of standards may be added the specific development of some other substantial reason category of fairness which tends to undermine employee contractual rights in the context of employer reorganisations.

The judicial reluctance to place tribunals in a position to second-guess the substance of management decisions may be caused by a genuine, if exaggerated, respect for managerial expertise which requires training or experience beyond the ken of the judiciary, in much the same way as judges

---

17 See remarks by Elias 'Fairness in Unfair Dismissal Trends and Tensions' (1981) ILJ 201.

have regarded questions of the reasonable standard of care of doctors in negligence actions. Equally, it may stem from a practical concern to avoid courts or tribunals getting involved in over-lengthy reviews of managerial judgments. Finally, there is a possibility that the judges feel that too interventionist a standard would itself place a burden on management efficiency.

Whatever the judicial motivation, one effect of the range of reasonable responses test as currently being applied by tribunals is to produce occasional cases where harsh employer decisions are being viewed as reasonable by some tribunals who give too wide a reading to the range of reasonable responses test. In such cases, and the decision of the employment tribunal in *Haddon v Van der Bergh Foods Ltd* offers a good example, the only limit to an excessively wide reading of the range of reasonable responses test is the limited test of perversity on appeal.

Yet, *Iceland Frozen Foods* never intended such a result. The formula used for the interpretation of what is now ERA 1996, s 98(4) in *Iceland* was that the test should be one of a range of reasonable responses of a *reasonable employer*, a test which contains within it a minimum objective standard of reasonableness.

It is true that the width of the issue of fact in ERA 1996, s 98(4), combined with the limited scope of the perversity test, leaves considerable room for employment tribunals to apply the positive standards of the Code of Practice and a high standard of reasonableness so long as they recite the mantra that they are applying the range of reasonable responses test and thereby avoid misdirection.

Nevertheless, despite all the guidance of the Code, the 'guideline' precedents of the EAT and the courts, and the industrial experience of the wing persons, the problem of inadequate minimum standards persists. The answer must lie with a change in the way the range of reasonable responses test itself is interpreted.

The most recent attempt to address the issue of too low a minimum objective standard within the range of reasonable employer responses test was that of Morrison P in *Haddon v Van der Bergh Foods Ltd*. He argued that the range of reasonable responses test was a gloss in the statute and resulted in decisions which allow tribunals to test the fairness of dismissals by reference to the extremes of employer behaviour. He proposed that the test of ERA 1996, s 98(4) should consist of the application of the pure words of the statute. The EAT decision in *Haddon* was overruled by the Court of Appeal in *Post Office v Foley*. The Court insisted that employment tribunals continue to follow the *Iceland Frozen Foods* approach in general and the range of reasonable employer responses test in particular. Mummery LJ, speaking for the Court, stated that the range of reasonable responses test was not as low as a perversity test and hinted that there was an objective minimum standard to the range of reasonable employer responses test.

Nevertheless, the underlying problem raised by Morrison P in *Haddon* remains unaddressed because as interpreted today, the test is not always clearly perceived as containing a floor with certain minimum standards. Morrison's own proposed solution in *Haddon* was not entirely satisfactory not only because it upset well established precedent but also because the pure language of ERA 1996, s 98(4) itself clearly implies a version of the range of reasonable responses test albeit a narrower one than the present test. If the test is one of reasonableness in the circumstances there must logically be a number of factual circumstances in which it can be reasonable of management to dismiss and reasonable of management not to dismiss and instead transfer, demote or warn. The problem is that some tribunals are refraining from reading a minimum objective standard of the *reasonable* employer into the range of reasonable employers test. In such cases, that problem is exacerbated by the fact that the only safeguard against too low a standard of reasonableness is the perversity test.

One answer to the problem is for employment tribunal chairpersons to be more forcibly reminded by the EAT or Court of Appeal to direct their wing persons that the *Iceland Frozen Foods* case limits the range of reasonable employer responses test to those which a *reasonable employer* would have adopted. This can be reinforced by emphasising that a minimum is established more by focusing on what is unreasonable rather than on what is reasonable. Thus, if employment tribunals have established as a matter of fact that an employer has behaved unreasonably in any particular in the course of taking a decision to dismiss, say by acting inconsistently through two different managers, as in *Haddon*, or providing a penalty which is harsh in relation to the conduct of the employer, then the tribunal should not excuse the fact of unreasonableness merely by a general reference to its obligation to apply the range of reasonable employer test. Tribunals should be required to see the test as a two-stage process in which the second stage consists of findings of further facts which excuse or justify the employer's unreasonable act or omission and thereby make the overall decision reasonable despite that unreasonable element.

A good example of this technique is offered by the decision in the House of Lords in *Polkey v A E Dayton Services Ltd*. After the *Polkey* decision, if an employer omits an important step in a fair procedure, the test that must be applied by employment tribunals is whether at the time of dismissal, the employer could have reasonably concluded that such a step would have been *useless* or *futile*.

On closer analysis, the *Polkey* test can be seen to consist of two discrete stages with a complex second stage. First there must be a finding of a procedural failure by the employer. The second stage then requires both that the employer must provide a justification for the procedural omission and meet the minimum standard for that justification, ie that judging from the time the employer made the decision to dismiss, it would have been *futile* or *useless* to have gone through the omitted procedural step. The *Polkey* test thus ensures a minimum objective standard for employer procedural reasonableness which is consistent with the range of reasonable responses test.

What is needed in cases of discipline, ill health, capability and reorganisation is a variation of the two stages in the *Polkey* test. First, has the tribunal identified a breach of the standard of reasonableness by the employer? If so, secondly, the tribunal must ask were there any other factors which justified the employer dismissing the employee in spite of its own unreasonable act or omission? The second stage test should at the very least require the employment tribunal to point to the features of the employer's behaviour which compensate for and justify the employer in proceeding to dismiss in spite of these mistakes.

In some cases, it can be the limited size and administrative resources of the employer, in others the conduct of the employee. In yet other cases, it can be the needs of the business. In all such cases the tribunal, at the very least, should be held responsible for identifying the specific element which excuses or justifies the employer's initial unreasonable act.

Once employment tribunals adopt such an approach, the next step is to ask whether it is possible to articulate a general test for minimum standards of justification for the reasonable employer in such situations. It has been suggested that a proportionality test might be usefully applied to the employer's justification.[18] This would require employers first to show that their aims were legitimate and secondly to show that the means used were necessary and proportionate to those objectives. This offers a promising approach, particularly in reorganisation cases.

Another way of shoring up the minimum standards in ERA 1996, s 98(4) is to make more active use of the concept of 'modern employment practice' established by the Code, judicial guidelines and industrial experience.[19] This concept can be used both to establish a standard from which a deviation is prima facie unreasonable and a standard to measure the

18   See H Collins. Note (2000) ILJ 288 at 293.
19   This point was suggested to me by my colleague Bob Watt who also reminded me about the reasonable employer point and the use that can be made of the 'size and administrative resources' as an employer justification.

reasonableness of the employer's justification for falling below that standard in any particular and nevertheless dismissing the employee.

The more immediate task, however, is to ensure that employment tribunals are required to make *specific* findings of fact to justify employer's decisions to dismiss despite their own unreasonable conduct, rather than relying on a *general* recitation of the mantra of the range of reasonable responses test. This would make a good start in the direction of ensuring that the range of reasonable responses test is applied with respect for its minimum standard of a 'reasonable employer'.

It is worth recalling that one further effect of the development of a minimalist standard of fairness has been to contribute to the decline in the rate of success of complaints of unfair dismissal before employment tribunals. The decline has been precipitous; from a figure of 37.6% in 1976 to 30.7% in 1982 and 29% in 1998/9.[20] Clearly other developments have also contributed to the lower success rates of complaints of unfair dismissal before tribunals. For example, the growth of disciplinary procedures, the tendency for employees to face legally represented employers without themselves having the benefit of legal representation,[1] and the increase in redundancy cases as a proportion of all cases have all been important factors. Furthermore certain legislative developments may have contributed to the difficulties of presenting cases. This is true for example of the change in the burden of proof in 1980 and the requirement in s 98(4) that employment tribunals must have regard to the size and administrative resources of the employer's undertaking, though the latter had already been read into the statute to some extent. Nevertheless it is difficult to deny that the judicial guidelines to the interpretation of ERA 1996, s 98(4) which tend to require tribunals to accept wide areas of managerial discretion, have contributed to the lowering of the success rate for complainants.

One of the unresolved questions presented by this study of the interpretation of the legislation is the relationship between the discretion of employment tribunals to make a finding of 'reasonableness' as a question of fact and the accretion of judicial 'guidelines' to the exercise of the discretion in the case law of the EAT and Court of Appeal.

In 1984 the President of the EAT, following the lead of the Court of Appeal[2] emphasised that tribunals must have a wide discretion 'to be their own guide on issues of reasonableness'.[3]

---

20 See Employment Gazettes. The one year low was 23% in 1981. The one year high was 40% in 1997/8.
1 See Kevin Williams 'Unfair Dismissal Myths and Statistics' (1983) ILJ 157.
2 *Bailey v BP Oil (Kent Refinery) Ltd* [198-0] IRLR 287, CA.
3 *Anandarajah v Lord Chancellor's Department* [1984] IRLR 131, EAT.

In the earliest phase of the EAT, following the practice of the NIRC, judicial guidelines were offered for most categories of dismissal in an attempt to achieve consistency in tribunal decisions. Moreover, good industrial practice was also commonly taken as the standard against which the actions of the employer were to be measured. A tribunal's failure to apply such a standard could result in a reversal by the EAT on grounds of perversity.

During the early 1980s the Court of Appeal strongly reacted to the way judicial guidelines were being treated as binding precedent and the way this legalism resulted in excessive appeals. It preferred to view the issue of reasonableness as essentially an issue of fact.

In *Bailey v BP Oil (Kent Refinery) Ltd*[4] Lord Justice Lawton articulated this view as follows:

'Each case must depend upon its own facts. In our judgment it is unwise for the Court or the Employment Appeal Tribunal to set out guidelines, and wrong to make rules and establish presumptions for Industrial Tribunals to follow or to take into account when applying [ERA s 98(4)].'

This seems to overstate the overall position of the Court because certain judicial guidelines were approved by the Court of Appeal during the period. Moreover, it ignored the adverse consequences of the approach it advocated.

One consequence of the judicial narrowing of issues of 'law' and increased scope of issues of 'fact' in the test of reasonableness was the increased unpredictability of results at tribunal level. One cost of this unpredictability was the loss of normative guidelines to industrial organisations who depended on clear legal norms to operate disciplinary procedures as well as to prepare for and settle potential tribunal cases.

Moreover, as Mr Justice Browne-Wilkinson, the former President of the EAT pointed out, there was an unfairness in the inconsistency of results:[5]

'Although it is not possible to be dogmatic on the point, I think there are signs that because of the more restricted role which the Appeal Tribunal has had to adopt [Employment] Tribunals are beginning to demonstrate a lack of uniformity in their approach to what constitutes fair industrial practice. To my mind this is an undesirable tendency.

4   [1980] IRLR 287 at 289; [1980] ICR 642 at 648, CA.
5   Hon Mr Justice Browne-Wilkinson 'The Role of the EAT in the 1980s' (1982) ILJ 69.

Although each case must, in the end, depend on its own facts, it is not right that the principles by which the "fairness" of conduct is judged should differ according to the region in which the case is heard. If the approach enforced by the Court of Appeal is taken to its logical conclusion, we will be left with a large number of industrial "palm trees", under which [Employment] Tribunals give effect to their own individual ideas of fair industrial practice. ...'

In *Williams v Compair Maxam Ltd*,[6] Browne-Wilkinson attempted to reconcile these views by not only defining the principles of good industrial practice in unfair redundancy cases but also elevating them into an enhanced perversity test. Mr Justice Browne-Wilkinson's views were not accepted by his immediate successors. Both Waite P and Popperwell P were more inclined to follow the lead of the Court of Appeal using the explicit language of the statute[7] and by avoiding citing of authority as much as possible.[8]

The tide began to turn in the 1990s however, with the presidency of Sir John Wood. Then in succession, Mummery P and Morrison P, until *Haddon*, supported the use of guideline authority.

In the event, the position today seems to be that certain judicial guidelines to the interpretation of ERA, s 98(4) such as *British Home Stores* and *Iceland Frozen Foods* are regarded as binding. Other types of guidelines, in particular guidelines to good (or modern) industrial practice have a less certain legal effect. While an employment tribunal which relies on these guidelines will be better placed if there is an appeal, a failure to take into account certain guidelines or good practice will not necessarily be viewed as an error in law.

In principle however a failure by an employment tribunal to take into account *relevant* guidelines should be treated more seriously by the Appeal Tribunal. There is a case for saying that such a failure of instruction should be tested on appeal not merely by whether it has led to a perverse outcome; rather, it should be viewed as a possible error of law in the form of misdirection.

The employment tribunals should be required to instruct themselves on the relevant judicial guidelines (as indeed on the code of practice as well as the canons of modern industrial practice). However the instruction

6   [1982] IRLR 83, EAT.
7   *Anandarajah v Lord Chancellor's Department* [1984] IRLR 131, EAT.
8   Popperwell, 'Random Thoughts From the President's Chair' (1982) ILJ 209. See excellent discussion in Smith and Wood's *Industrial Law* (7th edn, Butterworths, 2000) pp 407–415.

should be to the effect that these are guidelines to the standards of good industrial practice against which the employer's decision should be measured rather than rules of law. Since the overall test of ERA, s 98(4) is reasonableness in the circumstances, the judicial guidelines (as well as the code and modern industrial practice) should be viewed only as establishing a prima facie standard of reasonableness, not a *conclusive presumption* of reasonableness. As I have argued earlier, the tribunal then has the task of deciding whether the deviation from the standard can be justified in the circumstances by other factors.

It is difficult to gainsay that guidance to a prima facie standard of reasonableness, in the form of judicial guidelines and canons of modern industrial practice is essential to maintain minimum standards of consistency as well as minimum standards of reasonableness in employment tribunal decisions.

Finally, the big increase in the categories of automatically unfair dismissals can be seen as a reflection of the absence of a commitment to an objective minimum test of reasonableness in the range of reasonable responses in the test of unfair dismissals. Lacking any assurance that the general test of unfairness will protect against certain types of dismissals, legislators have opted to take discretion away from the tribunals in increasing categories of dismissal. The characteristic feature of the automatically unfair dismissal is that the employment tribunal has little discretion to weigh competing interests: that balance has been predetermined by the definition of the prohibited reason. The employment tribunal is directed simply to determine as a matter of fact whether the employer's real reason for a dismissal fits into the prohibited category and then to apply the relevant remedies. If the tribunals had been allowed or encouraged to provide a minimum standard, not all existing categories of prohibited reasons would have been necessary.

A prime candidate for improved protection under the general test of unfairness is the version of some other substantial reason that applies to reorganisations. There are economic dismissals which fall through the net of redundancies or transfers of undertaking. They are often dismissals without fault by the employee yet can be found fair without a particularly strict test of the employer's need for reorganisation. Compensation in such cases is called for by the notions of modern managerial practice and partnership.

In this edition, I have refrained from speculating about the possible changes to unfair dismissals law which will be caused by the Human Rights Act. The case law needs to be monitored to obtain a full picture.

Appendix I.
Statutory materials

TRADE UNION AND LABOUR RELATIONS
(CONSOLIDATION) ACT 1992

237   Dismissal of those taking part in unofficial industrial action

(1)   An employee has no right to complain of unfair dismissal if at the time of dismissal he was taking part in an unofficial strike or other unofficial industrial action.

(1A)   Subsection (1) does not apply to the dismissal of the employee if it is shown that the reason (or, if more than one, the principal reason) for the dismissal or, in a redundancy case, for selecting the employee for dismissal was one of those specified in or under—
  (a)   section 99, 100, 101A(d), 103 or 103A of the Employment Rights Act 1996 (dismissal in family, health and safety, working time, employee representative and protected disclosure cases),
  (b)   section 104 of that Act in its application in relation to time off under section 57A of that Act (dependants).

  In this subsection 'redundancy case' has the meaning given in section 105(9) of that Act; and a reference to a specified reason for dismissal includes a reference to specified circumstances of dismissal.

(2)   A strike or other industrial action is unofficial in relation to an employee unless—
  (a)   he is a member of a trade union and the action is authorised or endorsed by that union, or

(b) he is not a member of a trade union but there are among those taking part in the industrial action members of a trade union by which the action has been authorised or endorsed.

Provided that, a strike or other industrial action shall not be regarded as unofficial if none of those taking part in it are members of a trade union.

(3)   The provisions of section 20(2) apply for the purpose of determining whether industrial action is to be taken to have been authorised or endorsed by a trade union.

(4)   The question whether industrial action is to be so taken in any case shall be determined by reference to the facts as at the time of dismissal.

Provided that, where an act is repudiated as mentioned in section 21, industrial action shall not thereby be treated as unofficial before the end of the next working day after the day on which the repudiation takes place.

(5)   In this section the 'time of dismissal' means—
(a) where the employee's contract of employment is terminated by notice, when the notice is given,
(b) where the employee's contract of employment is terminated without notice, when the termination takes effect, and
(c) where the employee is employed under a contract for a fixed term which expires without being renewed under the same contract, when that term expires;

and a 'working day' means any day which is not a Saturday or Sunday, Christmas Day, Good Friday or a bank holiday under the Banking and Financial Dealings Act 1971.

(6)   For the purposes of this section membership of a trade union for purposes unconnected with the employment in question shall be disregarded; but an employee who was a member of a trade union when he began to take part in industrial action shall continue to be treated as a member for the purpose of determining whether that action is unofficial in relation to him or another notwithstanding that he may in fact have ceased to be a member.

238   Dismissals in connection with other industrial action

(1)   This section applies in relation to an employee who has a right to complain of unfair dismissal (the 'complainant') and who claims to have been unfairly dismissed, where at the date of the dismissal—
(a) the employer was conducting or instituting a lock-out, or
(b) the complainant was taking part in a strike or other industrial action.

(2)   In such a case an employment tribunal shall not determine whether the dismissal was fair or unfair unless it is shown—

    (a) that one or more relevant employees of the same employer have not been dismissed, or

    (b) that a relevant employee has before the expiry of the period of three months beginning with the date of his dismissal been offered re-engagement and that the complainant has not been offered re-engagement.

(2A)   Subsection (2) does not apply to the dismissal of the employee if it is shown that the reason (or, if more than one, the principal reason) for the dismissal or, in a redundancy case, for selecting the employee for dismissal was one of those specified in or under—

    (a) section 99, 100, 101A(d) or 103 of the Employment Rights Act 1996 (dismissal in family, health and safety, working time and employee representative cases),

    (b) section 104 of that Act in its application in relation to time off under section 57A of that Act (dependants).

In this subsection 'redundancy case' has the meaning given in section 105(9) of that Act; and a reference to a specified reason for dismissal includes a reference to specified circumstances of dismissal.

(2B)   Subsection (2) does not apply in relation to an employee who is regarded as unfairly dismissed by virtue of section 238A below.

(3)   For this purpose 'relevant employees' means—

    (a) in relation to a lock-out, employees who were directly interested in the dispute in contemplation or furtherance of which the lock-out occurred, and

    (b) in relation to a strike or other industrial action, those employees at the establishment of the employer at or from which the complainant works who at the date of his dismissal were taking part in the action.

Nothing in section 237 (dismissal of those taking part in unofficial industrial action) affects the question who are relevant employees for the purposes of this section.

(4)   An offer of re-engagement means an offer (made either by the original employer or by a successor of that employer or an associated employer) to re-engage an employee, either in the job which he held immediately before the date of dismissal or in a different job which would be reasonably suitable in his case.

(5)   In this section 'date of dismissal' means—

(a) where the employee's contract of employment was terminated by notice, the date on which the employer's notice was given, and

(b) in any other case, the effective date of termination.

238A   Participation in official industrial action

(1) For the purposes of this section an employee takes protected industrial action if he commits an act which, or a series of acts each of which, he is induced to commit by an act which by virtue of section 219 is not actionable in tort.

(2) An employee who is dismissed shall be regarded for the purposes of Part X of the Employment Rights Act 1996 (unfair dismissal) as unfairly dismissed if—

(a) the reason (or, if more than one, the principal reason) for the dismissal is that the employee took protected industrial action, and

(b) subsection (3), (4) or (5) applies to the dismissal.

(3) This subsection applies to a dismissal if it takes place within the period of eight weeks beginning with the day on which the employee started to take protected industrial action.

(4) This subsection applies to a dismissal if—

(a) it takes place after the end of that period, and

(b) the employee had stopped taking protected industrial action before the end of that period.

(5) This subsection applies to a dismissal if—

(a) it takes place after the end of that period,

(b) the employee had not stopped taking protected industrial action before the end of that period, and

(c) the employer had not taken such procedural steps as would have been reasonable for the purposes of resolving the dispute to which the protected industrial action relates.

(6) In determining whether an employer has taken those steps regard shall be had, in particular, to—

(a) whether the employer or a union had complied with procedures established by any applicable collective or other agreement;

(b) whether the employer or a union offered or agreed to commence or resume negotiations after the start of the protected industrial action;

(c) whether the employer or a union unreasonably refused, after the start of the protected industrial action, a request that conciliation services be used;

    (d) whether the employer or a union unreasonably refused, after the start of the protected industrial action, a request that mediation services be used in relation to procedures to be adopted for the purposes of resolving the dispute.

(7) In determining whether an employer has taken those steps no regard shall be had to the merits of the dispute.

(8) For the purposes of this section no account shall be taken of the repudiation of any act by a trade union as mentioned in section 21 in relation to anything which occurs before the end of the next working day (within the meaning of section 237) after the day on which the repudiation takes place.

239   Supplementary provisions relating to unfair dismissal

(1) Sections 237 to 238A (loss of unfair dismissal protection in connection with industrial action) shall be construed as one with Part X of the Employment Rights Act 1996 (unfair dismissal); but sections 108 and 109 of that Act (qualifying period and age limit) shall not apply in relation to section 238A of this Act.

(2) In relation to a complaint to which section 238 or 238A applies, section 111(2) of that Act (time limit for complaint) does not apply, but an employment tribunal shall not consider the complaint unless it is presented to the tribunal—
    (a) before the end of the period of six months beginning with the date of the complainant's dismissal (as defined by section 238(5)), or
    (b) where the tribunal is satisfied that it was not reasonably practicable for the complaint to be presented before the end of that period, within such further period as the tribunal considers reasonable.

(3) Where it is shown that the condition referred to in section 238(2)(b) is fulfilled (discriminatory re-engagement), the references in—
    (a) sections 98 to 106 of the Employment Rights Act 1996, and
    (b) sections 152 and 153 of this Act,

to the reason or principal reason for which the complainant was dismissed shall be read as references to the reason or principal reason he has not been offered re-engagement.

(4) In relation to a complaint under section 111 of the 1996 Act (unfair dismissal: complaint to employment tribunal) that a dismissal was unfair by virtue of section 238A of this Act—
    (a) no order shall be made under section 113 of the 1996 Act (reinstatement or re-engagement) until after the conclusion of

protected industrial action by any employee in relation to the relevant dispute,

  (b) regulations under section 7 of the Employment Tribunals Act 1996 may make provision about the adjournment and renewal of applications (including provision requiring adjournment in specified circumstances), and

  (c) regulations under section 9 of that Act may require a pre-hearing review to be carried out in specified circumstances.

EMPLOYMENT RIGHTS ACT 1996

152   Likelihood of full employment

(1)   An employee is not entitled to a redundancy payment in pursuance of a notice of intention to claim if—

  (a) on the date of service of the notice it was reasonably to be expected that the employee (if he continued to be employed by the same employer) would, not later than four weeks after that date, enter on a period of employment of not less than thirteen weeks during which he would not be laid off or kept on short-time for any week, and

  (b) the employer gives a counter-notice to the employee within seven days after the service of the notice of intention to claim.

(2)   Subsection (1) does not apply where the employee—

  (a) continues or has continued, during the next four weeks after the date of service of the notice of intention to claim, to be employed by the same employer, and

  (b) is or has been laid off or kept on short-time for each of those weeks.

Supplementary

153   The relevant date

For the purposes of the provisions of this Act relating to redundancy payments 'the relevant date' in relation to a notice of intention to claim or a right to a redundancy payment in pursuance of such a notice—

  (a) in a case falling within paragraph (a) of subsection (2) of section 148, means the date on which the last of the four or more consecutive weeks before the service of the notice came to an end, and

(b)   in a case falling within paragraph (b) of that subsection, means the
date on which the last of the series of six or more weeks before the
service of the notice came to an end.

154   Provisions supplementing sections 148 and 152

For the purposes of sections 148(2) and 152(2)—
(a)   it is immaterial whether a series of weeks consists wholly of weeks
for which the employee is laid off or wholly of weeks for which he
is kept on short-time or partly of the one and partly of the other,
and
(b)   no account shall be taken of any week for which an employee is
laid off or kept on short-time where the lay-off or short-time is
wholly or mainly attributable to a strike or a lock-out (whether or
not in the trade or industry in which the employee is employed and
whether in Great Britain or elsewhere).

Chapter IV
General Exclusions From Right

155   Qualifying period of employment

An employee does not have any right to a redundancy payment unless he
has been continuously employed for a period of not less than two years
ending with the relevant date.

156   Upper age limit

(1)   An employee does not have any right to a redundancy payment if
before the relevant date he has attained—
(a)   in a case where—
(i)   in the business for the purposes of which the employee was
employed there was a normal retiring age of less than sixty-
five for an employee holding the position held by the employee,
and
(ii)   the age was the same whether the employee holding that
position was a man or woman,
that normal retiring age, and
(b)   in any other case, the age of sixty-five.

(2)   . . .

157   Exemption orders

(1)   Where an order under this section is in force in respect of an agreement covered by this section, an employee who, immediately before the relevant date, is an employee to whom the agreement applies does not have any right to a redundancy payment.

(2)   An agreement is covered by this section if it is an agreement between—
    (a)   one or more employers or organisations of employers, and
    (b)   one or more trade unions representing employees,

under which employees to whom the agreement applies have a right in certain circumstances to payments on the termination of their contracts of employment.

(3)   Where, on the application of all the parties to an agreement covered by this section, the Secretary of State is satisfied, having regard to the provisions of the agreement, that the employees to whom the agreement applies should not have any right to a redundancy payment, he may make an order under this section in respect of the agreement.

(4)   The Secretary of State shall not make an order under this section in respect of an agreement unless the agreement indicates (in whatever terms) the willingness of the parties to it to submit to an employment tribunal any question arising under the agreement as to—
    (a)   the right of an employee to a payment on the termination of his employment, or
    (b)   the amount of such a payment.

(5)   An order revoking an earlier order under this section may be made in pursuance of an application by all or any of the parties to the agreement in question or in the absence of such an application.

(6)   . . .

158   Pension rights

(1)   The Secretary of State shall by regulations make provision for excluding the right to a redundancy payment, or reducing the amount of any redundancy payment, in such cases to which subsection (2) applies as are prescribed by the regulations.

(2)   This subsection applies to cases in which an employee has (whether by virtue of any statutory provision or otherwise) a right or claim (whether or not legally enforceable) to a periodical payment or lump sum by way of pension, gratuity or superannuation allowance which—

(a) is to be paid by reference to his employment by a particular employer, and

(b) is to be paid, or to begin to be paid, at the time when he leaves the employment or within such period after he leaves the employment as may be prescribed by the regulations.

(3)   The regulations shall secure that the right to a redundancy payment shall not be excluded, and that the amount of a redundancy payment shall not be reduced, by reason of any right or claim to a periodical payment or lump sum, in so far as the payment or lump sum—

(a) represents compensation for loss of employment or for loss or diminution of emoluments or of pension rights, and

(b) is payable under a statutory provision (whether passed or made before or after the passing of this Act).

(4)   In relation to any case where (in accordance with any provision of this Part) an employment tribunal determines that an employer is liable to pay part (but not the whole) of a redundancy payment the references in this section to a redundancy payment, or to the amount of a redundancy payment, are to the part of the redundancy payment, or to the amount of the part.

159   Public offices etc

A person does not have any right to a redundancy payment in respect of any employment which—

(a)   is employment in a public office within the meaning of section 39 of the Superannuation Act 1965, or

(b)   is for the purposes of pensions and other superannuation benefits treated (whether by virtue of that Act or otherwise) as service in the civil service of the State.

160   Overseas government employment

(1)   A person does not have any right to a redundancy payment in respect of employment in any capacity under the Government of an overseas territory.

(2)   The reference in subsection (1) to the Government of an overseas territory includes a reference to—

(a)   a Government constituted for two or more overseas territories, and

(b)   any authority established for the purpose of providing or administering services which are common to, or relate to matters of common interest to, two or more overseas territories.

(3)   In this section references to an overseas territory are to any territory or country outside the United Kingdom.

161   Domestic servants

(1)   A person does not have any right to a redundancy payment in respect of employment as a domestic servant in a private household where the employer is the parent (or step-parent), grandparent, child (or step-child), grandchild or brother or sister (or half-brother or half-sister) of the employee.

(2)   Subject to that, the provisions of this Part apply to an employee who is employed as a domestic servant in a private household as if—
- (a)   the household were a business, and
- (b)   the maintenance of the household were the carrying on of that business by the employer.

Chapter V
Other Provisions about Redundancy Payments

162   Amount of a redundancy payment

(1)   The amount of a redundancy payment shall be calculated by—
- (a)   determining the period, ending with the relevant date, during which the employee has been continuously employed,
- (b)   reckoning backwards from the end of that period the number of years of employment falling within that period, and
- (c)   allowing the appropriate amount for each of those years of employment.

(2)   In subsection (1)(c) 'the appropriate amount' means—
- (a)   one and a half weeks' pay for a year of employment in which the employee was not below the age of forty-one,
- (b)   one week's pay for a year of employment (not within paragraph (a)) in which he was not below the age of twenty-two, and
- (c)   half a week's pay for each year of employment not within paragraph (a) or (b).

(3)   Where twenty years of employment have been reckoned under subsection (1), no account shall be taken under that subsection of any year of employment earlier than those twenty years.

(4)   Where the relevant date is after the sixty-fourth anniversary of the day of the employee's birth, the amount arrived at under subsections (1) to (3) shall be reduced by the appropriate fraction.

(5)   In subsection (4) 'the appropriate fraction' means the fraction of which—

  (a) the numerator is the number of whole months reckoned from the sixty-fourth anniversary of the day of the employee's birth in the period beginning with that anniversary and ending with the relevant date, and

  (b) the denominator is twelve.

(6)   Subsections (1) to (5) apply for the purposes of any provision of this Part by virtue of which an employment tribunal may determine that an employer is liable to pay to an employee—

  (a) the whole of the redundancy payment to which the employee would have had a right apart from some other provision, or

  (b) such part of the redundancy payment to which the employee would have had a right apart from some other provision as the tribunal thinks fit,

as if any reference to the amount of a redundancy payment were to the amount of the redundancy payment to which the employee would have been entitled apart from that other provision.

(7)   ...

(8)   This section has effect subject to any regulations under section 158 by virtue of which the amount of a redundancy payment, or part of a redundancy payment, may be reduced.

163   References to employment tribunals

(1)   Any question arising under this Part as to—

  (a) the right of an employee to a redundancy payment, or

  (b) the amount of a redundancy payment,

shall be referred to and determined by an employment tribunal.

(2)   For the purposes of any such reference, an employee who has been dismissed by his employer shall, unless the contrary is proved, be presumed to have been so dismissed by reason of redundancy.

(3)   Any question whether an employee will become entitled to a redundancy payment if he is not dismissed by his employer and he terminates his contract of employment as mentioned in section 150(1) shall for the purposes of this Part be taken to be a question as to the right of the employee to a redundancy payment.

(4)   Where an order under section 157 is in force in respect of an

agreement, this section has effect in relation to any question arising under the agreement as to the right of an employee to a payment on the termination of his employment, or as to the amount of such a payment, as if the payment were a redundancy payment and the question arose under this Part.

164   Claims for redundancy payment

(1)   An employee does not have any right to a redundancy payment unless, before the end of the period of six months beginning with the relevant date—

    (a)   the payment has been agreed and paid,

    (b)   the employee has made a claim for the payment by notice in writing given to the employer,

    (c)   a question as to the employee's right to, or the amount of, the payment has been referred to an employment tribunal, or

    (d)   a complaint relating to his dismissal has been presented by the employee under section 111.

(2)   An employee is not deprived of his right to a redundancy payment by subsection (1) if, during the period of six months immediately following the period mentioned in that subsection, the employee—

    (a)   makes a claim for the payment by notice in writing given to the employer,

    (b)   refers to an employment tribunal a question as to his right to, or the amount of, the payment, or

    (c)   presents a complaint relating to his dismissal under section 111,

and it appears to the tribunal to be just and equitable that the employee should receive a redundancy payment.

(3)   In determining under subsection (2) whether it is just and equitable that an employee should receive a redundancy payment an employment tribunal shall have regard to—

    (a)   the reason shown by the employee for his failure to take any such step as is referred to in subsection (2) within the period mentioned in subsection (1), and

    (b)   all the other relevant circumstances.

165   Written particulars of redundancy payment

(1)   On making any redundancy payment, otherwise than in pursuance of a decision of a tribunal which specifies the amount of the payment to be

made, the employer shall give to the employee a written statement indicating how the amount of the payment has been calculated.

(2)   An employer who without reasonable excuse fails to comply with subsection (1) is guilty of an offence and liable on summary conviction to a fine not exceeding level 1 on the standard scale.

(3)   If an employer fails to comply with the requirements of subsection (1), the employee may by notice in writing to the employer require him to give to the employee a written statement complying with those requirements within such period (not being less than one week beginning with the day on which the notice is given) as may be specified in the notice.

(4)   An employer who without reasonable excuse fails to comply with a notice under subsection (3) is guilty of an offence and liable on summary conviction to a fine not exceeding level 3 on the standard scale.

Chapter VI
Payments by Secretary of State

166   Applications for payments

(1)   Where an employee claims that his employer is liable to pay to him an employer's payment and either—
  (a) that the employee has taken all reasonable steps, other than legal proceedings, to recover the payment from the employer and the employer has refused or failed to pay it, or has paid part of it and has refused or failed to pay the balance, or
  (b) that the employer is insolvent and the whole or part of the payment remains unpaid,

the employee may apply to the Secretary of State for a payment under this section.

(2)   In this Part 'employer's payment', in relation to an employee, means—
  (a) a redundancy payment which his employer is liable to pay to him under this Part,. . .
  (aa) a payment which his employer is liable to make to him under an agreement to refrain from instituting or continuing proceedings for a contravention or alleged contravention of section 135 which has effect by virtue of section 203(2)(e) or (f), or
  (b) a payment which his employer is, under an agreement in respect of which an order is in force under section 157, liable to make to him on the termination of his contract of employment.

(3)   In relation to any case where (in accordance with any provision of this Part) an employment tribunal determines that an employer is liable to pay part (but not the whole) of a redundancy payment the reference in subsection (2)(a) to a redundancy payment is to the part of the redundancy payment.

(4)   In subsection (1)(a) 'legal proceedings'—
   (a)   does not include any proceedings before an employment tribunal, but
   (b)   includes any proceedings to enforce a decision or award of an employment tribunal.

(5)   An employer is insolvent for the purposes of subsection (1)(b)—
   (a)   where the employer is an individual, if (but only if) subsection (6) is satisfied, . . .
   (b)   where the employer is a company, if (but only if) subsection (7) is satisfied, and
   (c)   where the employer is a limited liability partnership, if (but only if) subsection (8) is satisfied.

(6)   This subsection is satisfied in the case of an employer who is an individual—
   (a)   in England and Wales if—
       (i)he has been adjudged bankrupt or has made a composition or arrangement with his creditors, or
       (ii)he has died and his estate falls to be administered in accordance with an order under section 421 of the Insolvency Act 1986, and
   (b)   in Scotland if—
       (i)sequestration of his estate has been awarded or he has executed a trust deed for his creditors or has entered into a composition contract, or
       (ii)he has died and a judicial factor appointed under section 11A of the Judicial Factors (Scotland) Act 1889 is required by that section to divide his insolvent estate among his creditors.

(7)   This subsection is satisfied in the case of an employer which is a company—
   (a)   if a winding up order or an administration order has been made, or a resolution for voluntary winding up has been passed, with respect to the company,
   (b)   if a receiver or (in England and Wales only) a manager of the company's undertaking has been duly appointed, or (in England and Wales only) possession has been taken, by or on behalf of the holders of any debentures secured by a floating charge, of any property of the company comprised in or subject to the charge, or

(c) if a voluntary arrangement proposed in the case of the company for the purposes of Part I of the Insolvency Act 1986 has been approved under that Part of that Act.

(8)   This subsection is satisfied in the case of an employer which is a limited liability partnership—
  (a) if a winding-up order, an administration order or a determination for a voluntary winding-up has been made with respect to the limited liability partnership,
  (b) if a receiver or (in England and Wales only) a manager of the undertaking of the limited liability partnership has been duly appointed, or (in England and Wales only) possession has been taken, by or on behalf of the holders of any debentures secured by a floating charge, of any property of the limited liability partnership comprised in or subject to the charge, or
  (c) if a voluntary arrangement proposed in the case of the limited liability partnership for the purpose of Part I of the Insolvency Act 1986 has been approved under that Part of that Act.

167   Making of payments

(1)   Where, on an application under section 166 by an employee in relation to an employer's payment, the Secretary of State is satisfied that the requirements specified in subsection (2) are met, he shall pay to the employee out of the National Insurance Fund a sum calculated in accordance with section 168 but reduced by so much (if any) of the employer's payment as has already been paid.

(2)   The requirements referred to in subsection (1) are—
  (a) that the employee is entitled to the employer's payment, and
  (b) that one of the conditions specified in paragraphs (a) and (b) of subsection (1) of section 166 is fulfilled,

and, in a case where the employer's payment is a payment such as is mentioned in subsection (2)(b) of that section, that the employee's right to the payment arises by virtue of a period of continuous employment (computed in accordance with the provisions of the agreement in question) which is not less than two years.

(3)   Where under this section the Secretary of State pays a sum to an employee in respect of an employer's payment—
  (a) all rights and remedies of the employee with respect to the employer's payment, or (if the Secretary of State has paid only part of it) all the rights and remedies of the employee with respect to

that part of the employer's payment, are transferred to and vest in the Secretary of State, and

(b) any decision of an employment tribunal requiring the employer's payment to be paid to the employee has effect as if it required that payment, or that part of it which the Secretary of State has paid, to be paid to the Secretary of State.

(4) Any money recovered by the Secretary of State by virtue of subsection (3) shall be paid into the National Insurance Fund.

Appendix II.
ACAS Code of Practice 1
Disciplinary and Grievance Procedures

Preamble

This Code from pages 4 to 23 is issued under section 201 of the Trade Union and Labour Relations (Consolidation) Act 1992 and was laid before both Houses of Parliament on   . The Code comes into effect by order of the Secretary of State on   .

A failure on the part of any person to observe any provision of this Code of Practice does not of itself render that person liable to any proceedings. In any proceedings before an employment tribunal any Code of Practice issued under sections 199 and 201 of the Trade Union and Labour Relations (Consolidation) Act 1992 is admissible in evidence and any provision of the Code which appears to the tribunal to be relevant to any question arising in the proceedings is required to be taken into account in determining that question. (Trade Union and Labour Relations (Consolidation) Act 1992, section 207) This Code has also to be taken into account by the arbitrators appointed by ACAS to determine cases brought under the ACAS Arbitration Scheme (see Section 212A of the Trade Union and Labour Relations (Consolidation) Act 1992).

Some of the provisions referred to in this code only apply by statute to employees. But others, such as the right to be accompanied at disciplinary and grievance hearings, apply to all workers. This Code is about good employment practice. Therefore where workers are involved in grievance and disciplinary proceedings, it would be good practice to apply the standards set out in the guidelines in sections one and two to those proceedings.

For ease of reference, text in bold type in this code summarises statutory provisions, whilst practical guidance is set out in ordinary type. Whilst every effort has been made to ensure that the explanations included in the Code are accurate, only the Courts or Tribunals can give authoritative interpretations of the law.

Introduction

This code aims to help employers, workers and their representatives by giving practical guidance on how to deal with disciplinary and grievance issues in employment. It also provides guidance on the statutory right of a worker to be accompanied at a disciplinary or grievance hearing. In small establishments it may not be practicable to adopt all the detailed provisions relating to disciplinary and grievance procedures, but most of the essential features listed in paragraphs 9 and 38 to 41 could be adopted and incorporated into a simple procedure.

Disciplinary issues arise when problems of conduct or capability are identified by the employer and management seeks to address them through well recognised procedures. In contrast, grievances are raised by individuals bringing to management's attention concerns or complaints about their working environment, terms and conditions and work-place relationships.

The code is divided into three sections as follows

Section 1 – deals with disciplinary practice and procedures;

Section 2 – considers the handling of grievances

Section 3 – is concerned with the statutory right to be accompanied at disciplinary and grievance hearings.

SECTION I – DISCIPLINARY PRACTICE AND PROCEDURES IN EMPLOYMENT

Why have disciplinary rules and procedures?

1. Disciplinary rules and procedures are necessary for promoting orderly employment relations as well as fairness and consistency in the treatment of individuals. They enable organisations to influence the conduct of workers and deal with problems of poor performance and attendance thereby assisting organisations to operate effectively. Rules set standards of conduct and performance at work; procedures help ensure that the standards are adhered to and also provide a fair method of dealing with alleged failures to observe them.

2. It is important that workers know what standards of conduct and performance are expected of them. The Employment Rights Act 1996 requires employers to provide written information for their employees about certain aspects of their disciplinary rules and procedures.[1] Managers should also know and be able to apply the rules and the procedures they are required to follow.

3. The importance of having disciplinary rules and procedures and ensuring that they are followed has also been recognised by the law relating to dismissals, since the grounds for dismissal and the way in which the dismissal has been handled can be challenged before an employment tribunal or an ACAS-appointed arbitrator.[2] Where either of these is found by a tribunal or arbitrator to have been unfair, the employer may be ordered

---

1   Section 1 of the Employment Rights Act 1996 requires employers to provide employees with a written statement of particulars of employment. Such statements must also specify any disciplinary rules applicable to them and indicate the person to whom they should apply if they are dissatisfied with any disciplinary decision. The statement should explain any further steps which exist in any procedure for dealing with disciplinary decisions. The employer may satisfy certain of these requirements by referring the employees to a reasonably accessible document which provides the necessary information. The statutory requirements relating to disciplinary rules and procedures do not apply where on the day the employee's employment began the total number of employees employed by the employer and any associated employer was less than twenty.

2   Section 111 (2) of the Employment Rights Act 1996 specifies that a complaint of unfair dismissal has to be presented to an employment tribunal before the end of the three month period beginning with the effective date of termination.

to re-instate or re-engage the employees concerned where requested and may be liable to pay compensation to them. In coming to a decision about the fairness or otherwise of a dismissal, the tribunal, or arbitrator, will consider whether the employer acted reasonably in all the circumstances, having regard to the size and administrative resources of the undertaking.

Formulating policy

4. Management is responsible for maintaining discipline and setting standards of performance within the organisation and for ensuring that there are appropriate disciplinary rules and procedures covering issues of worker conduct and capability. If they are to be fully effective, however, the rules and procedures need to be accepted as reasonable both by those who are covered by them and those who operate them. Management should therefore aim to secure the involvement of workers and where appropriate their representatives and all levels of management when formulating new or revising existing rules and procedures. Where trade unions are recognised, trade union officials[3] may, or may not, wish to participate in the formulation of the rules but they should participate fully with management in agreeing the procedural arrangements which will apply and in seeing that these arrangements are used properly, fairly and consistently.

Rules

5. When drawing up disciplinary rules, the aim should be to specify clearly and concisely those that are necessary for the efficient and safe performance of work and for the maintenance of satisfactory relations within the workforce and between workers and management. It is unlikely that any set of disciplinary rules can cover all circumstances that may arise. However, it is usual that rules would cover issues such as misconduct, sub-standard performance (where not covered by a separate capability procedure), harassment or victimisation, misuse of company facilities including computer facilities (eg, e-mail and the Internet), poor timekeeping and unauthorised absences. The rules required will necessarily vary according to particular circumstances, such as the type of work, working

3   Throughout this code, trade union official has the meaning assigned to it by section 119 of the Trade Union and Labour Relations (Consolidation) Act 1992 and means, broadly, officers of the union, its branches and sections, and anyone else, including fellow employees, appointed or elected under the union's rules to represent members.

conditions and size and location of the workplace. Whatever set of rules are eventually drawn up they should not be so general as to be meaningless.

6. Rules should be set out clearly and concisely in writing and be readily available to all workers, for example in handbooks or on company Intranet sites. Management should make every effort to ensure that all workers know and understand the rules including those whose first language is not English or who have a disability or impairment (eg, the inability to read). This may best be achieved by giving every worker a copy of the rules and explaining them orally. In the case of new workers this might form part of any induction programme . It is also important that managers at all levels and worker representatives are fully conversant with the disciplinary rules and that the rules are regularly checked and updated where necessary.

7. Workers should be made aware of the likely consequences of breaking disciplinary rules or failing to meet performance standards. In particular, they should be given a clear indication of the type of conduct, often referred to as gross misconduct, which may warrant summary dismissal (ie, dismissal without notice). Summary is not necessarily synonymous with instant and incidents of gross misconduct will usually still need to be investigated as part of a formal procedure. Acts which constitute gross misconduct are those resulting in a serious breach of contractual terms and will be for organisations to decide in the light of their own particular circumstances. However, they might include the following:

i) theft, fraud and deliberate falsification of records;
ii) physical violence;
iii) serious bullying or harassment;
iv) deliberate damage to property;
v) serious insubordination;
vi) misuse of an organisation's property or name;
vii) bringing the employer into serious disrepute;
viii) serious incapability whilst on duty brought on by alcohol or illegal drugs;
ix) serious negligence which causes or might cause unacceptable loss, damage or injury;
x) serious infringement of health and safety rules;
xi) serious breach of confidence (subject to the Public Interest (Disclosure) Act 1998).

As indicated earlier this list is not intended to be exhaustive.

Essential features of disciplinary procedures

8. Disciplinary procedures should not be viewed primarily as a means of imposing sanctions. Rather they should be seen as a way of helping and encouraging improvement amongst workers whose conduct or standard of work is unsatisfactory. Some organisations may prefer to have separate procedures for dealing with issues of conduct and capability but it is important to remember that any hearing which might result in a formal warning or some other action will be covered by the provisions on accompaniment set out in the Employment Relations Act 1999 (see section three). Smaller organisations may wish to deal with issues of conduct and capability within one disciplinary procedure.

9. When drawing up and applying disciplinary procedures employers should have regard to the requirements of natural justice. This means workers should be informed in advance of any disciplinary hearing of the allegations that are being made against them together with the supporting evidence and be given the opportunity of challenging the allegations and evidence before decisions are reached. Workers should also be given the right of appeal against any decisions taken. Consequently good disciplinary procedures should:

i)   be in writing;
ii)   specify to whom they apply;
iii) be non-discriminatory;
iv)   provide for matters to be dealt with without undue delay;
v)   provide for proceedings, witness statements and records to be kept confidential;
vi)   indicate the disciplinary actions which may be taken;
vii) specify the levels of management which have the authority to take the various forms of disciplinary action;
viii) provide for workers to be informed of the complaints against them and where possible all relevant evidence before any hearing;
ix)   provide workers with an opportunity to state their case before decisions are reached;
x)   provide workers with the right to be accompanied (see also section three for information on the statutory right to be accompanied);
xi)   ensure that, except for gross misconduct, no worker is dismissed for a first breach of discipline;
xii) ensure that disciplinary action is not taken until the case has been carefully investigated;

xiii) ensure that workers are given an explanation for any penalty imposed;
xiv) provide a right of appeal – normally to a more senior manager – and specify the procedure to be followed.

10. It is important to ensure that all managers and, where appropriate, worker representatives understand the organisation's disciplinary procedure. Training in the use and operation of the procedure may also be appropriate. There can be benefits in undertaking such training on a joint basis.

The procedure in operation

11. When a disciplinary matter arises, the relevant supervisor or manager should first establish the facts promptly before recollections fade, and where appropriate obtain statements from any available witnesses. It is important to keep a record for later reference. Having investigated all the facts the manager or supervisor should decide whether to, drop the matter; arrange informal coaching or counselling; or arrange for the matter to be dealt with under the disciplinary procedure.

12. Minor cases of misconduct and most cases of poor performance may best be dealt with by informal advice, coaching and counselling rather than through the disciplinary procedure. Sometimes managers may issue informal oral warnings – but they need to ensure that problems are discussed with the objective of encouraging and helping workers to improve. It is important that workers understand what needs to be done, how performance or conduct will be reviewed and over what period. Workers should also be made aware of what action will be taken if they fail to improve either their performance or conduct. Informal warnings and/or counselling are not part of the formal disciplinary procedure and the worker should be informed of this.

13. In certain circumstances, for example in cases involving gross misconduct, where relationships have broken down or where it is considered there are risks to an employer's property or responsibilities to other parties, consideration should be given to a brief period of suspension with pay whilst an unhindered investigation is conducted. Such a suspension should only be imposed after careful consideration and should be reviewed to ensure it is not unnecessarily protracted. It should be made clear that the suspension is not considered as disciplinary action.

14. Before a decision is reached or any disciplinary action taken there should be a disciplinary hearing at which workers have the opportunity to state their case and to answer the allegations that have been made. Wherever possible the hearing should be arranged at a mutually convenient time and in advance of the hearing the worker should be advised of any rights under the disciplinary procedure including the statutory right to be accompanied (see section three). Prior to this stage, where matters remain informal, the statutory right of accompaniment does not arise.

15. Where the facts of a case appear to call for formal disciplinary action a formal procedure should be followed. The type of procedure will vary according to the circumstances of the organisation. Depending on the outcome of the procedure some form of disciplinary action may be taken as follows:–

First Warning:

Oral – In the case of minor infringements the worker should be given a formal oral warning. Workers should be advised of the reason for the warning, that it constitutes the first step of the disciplinary procedure and of their right of appeal. A note of the oral warning should be kept but should be disregarded for disciplinary purposes after a specified period (eg, six months).

Or

Written – If the infringement is regarded as more serious the worker should be given a formal written warning giving details of the complaint, the improvement or change in behaviour required, the timescale allowed for this and the right of appeal. The warning should also inform the worker that a final written warning may be considered if there is no sustained satisfactory improvement or change. A copy of the written warning should be kept on file but should be disregarded for disciplinary purposes after a specified period (eg, 12 months).

Final written warning – Where there is a failure to improve or change behaviour during the currency of a prior warning, or where the infringement is sufficiently serious, the worker should normally be given a final written warning. This should give details of the complaint, warn the worker that failure to improve or modify behaviour may lead to dismissal or to some other action short of dismissal and refer to the right of appeal. The final written warning should normally be disregarded for disciplinary purposes after a specified period (eg, 12 months).

Dismissal or other sanction – If the worker's conduct or performance still fails to improve the final step might be disciplinary transfer, disciplinary suspension without pay[4] , demotion, loss of seniority, loss of increment (provided these penalties are allowed for in the contract) or dismissal. The decision to dismiss should be taken only by the appropriate designated manager and the worker should be informed as soon as reasonably practicable of the reasons for the dismissal, the date on which the contract between the parties will terminate, the appropriate period of notice (or pay in lieu of notice) and information on the right of appeal including how to make the appeal and to whom. The decision to dismiss should be confirmed in writing. Employees with one year's continuous service or more have the right, on request, to have a 'written statement of particulars of reasons for dismissal[5] '.

16. When deciding whether a disciplinary penalty is appropriate and what form it should take it is important to bear in mind the need to act reasonably in all the circumstances. Factors which might be relevant include, the extent to which standards have been breached, precedent, the worker's general record, position, length of service and special circumstances which might make it appropriate to adjust the severity of the penalty.

17. When operating disciplinary procedures employers should be particularly careful not to discriminate on the grounds of race, gender or disability, eg, whilst it is not unlawful to take disciplinary action against a pregnant woman for some reason unconnected with her pregnancy it is unlawful sex discrimination and automatically unfair to dismiss a woman on the grounds of her pregnancy.

18. In the course of a disciplinary case a worker might sometimes raise a grievance about the behaviour of the manager handling the case. Where

---

4   Where a disciplinary suspension without pay is imposed it should not exceed any period allowed by the contract of employment.

5   The right to a written statement of reasons for dismissal applies automatically to employees dismissed while pregnant or during ordinary maternity leave without them having to request it.

this happens, and depending on the circumstances it may be appropriate to suspend the disciplinary procedure for a short period until the grievance can be considered. Consideration might also be given, where possible, to bringing in another manager to deal with the disciplinary case.

Dealing with absence

19. When dealing with absence a distinction should always be made between absences on grounds of medically certificated illness, both physical and mental, and those which may call for disciplinary action. All unexpected absences should be investigated promptly and the worker asked to give an explanation[6]. If, after investigation, it appears that there were no acceptable reasons for the absence the matter should be treated as a conduct issue and be dealt with under the disciplinary procedure. It is important that the worker is told what improvement in attendance is expected and warned of the likely consequences if this does not happen.

20. Where the absence is due to medically certificated illness the issue becomes one of capability and employers should take a sympathetic and considerate approach to these sort of absences. In deciding what action to take in these cases employers will need to take into account, the likelihood of an improvement in health and subsequent attendance (based where appropriate on professional medical advice), the availability of suitable alternative work, the effect of past and likely future absences on the organisation, how similar situations have been handled in the past and whether the illness is a result of a disability as defined in the Disability Discrimination Act 1995. Even though employers may have a separate procedure for dealing with illness any hearing which could result in a formal warning or some other action will attract the statutory right of accompaniment (see section three).

21. In cases of extended sick leave both statutory and contractual issues will need to be addressed and specialist advice may be necessary.

6   When considering the reasons for absence or sub-standard performance employers should bear in mind the provisions of the Disability Discrimination Act 1995. In particular employers should note the obligations placed on them by the Act to make reasonable adjustments when dealing with sickness related absences.

Dealing with poor performance

22. Individuals have a contractual responsibility to perform to a satisfactory level and should be given every help and encouragement to do so. Employers have a responsibility for setting realistic and measurable standards of performance and for explaining these standards carefully to employees.

23. Where workers are found to be failing to perform to the required standard the matter should be investigated before any action is taken[6]. Where the reason for the sub standard performance is found to be a lack of the required skills the worker should, wherever practicable, be assisted through training or coaching and given reasonable time to reach the required standard. Where the sub standard performance is due to negligence or lack of application on the part of the worker then some form of disciplinary action will normally be appropriate. Failures to perform to the required standard can either be dealt with through the normal disciplinary procedure or through a separate capability procedure.

24. A worker should not normally be dismissed because of a failure to perform to the required standard unless warnings and an opportunity to improve (with reasonable targets and timescales) have been given. However, where a worker commits a single error due to negligence and the actual or potential consequences of that error are, or could be, extremely serious, warnings may not be appropriate. The disciplinary or capability procedure should indicate that summary dismissal action may be taken in such circumstances.

25. Employers may need to have special arrangements for dealing with poor performance of workers on short-term contracts or new workers during their probationary period.

Dealing with special situations

26. Certain situations will require special consideration.

Workers to whom the full procedure is not immediately available. Special provisions may be necessary for the handling of disciplinary matters among nightshift workers, workers in isolated locations or depots or others who may pose particular problems.

Trade union officials. Disciplinary action against a trade union official can lead to a serious dispute if it is seen as an attack on the union's functions. Although normal disciplinary standards should apply to their conduct as workers, if disciplinary action is contemplated then the case should be discussed with a senior trade union representative or full-time official.

Criminal charges or convictions outside employment. These should not be treated as automatic reasons for dismissal. The main consideration should be whether the offence is one that makes workers unsuitable for their type of work. In all cases employers, having considered the facts, will need to consider whether the conduct is sufficiently serious to warrant instituting the disciplinary procedure. For instance, workers should not be dismissed solely because a charge against them is pending or because they are absent as a result of being remanded in custody.

Appeals

27. The opportunity to appeal against a disciplinary decision is essential to natural justice. Workers may choose to raise appeals on a number of grounds which could include the perceived unfairness of the judgement, the severity of the penalty, new evidence coming to light or procedural irregularities. These grounds need to be considered when deciding the extent of any new investigation or re-hearing in order to remedy previous defects in the disciplinary process.

28. Appeals should be dealt with as promptly as possible. A time limit should be set within which appeals should be lodged. This time limit may vary between organisations but five working days for lodging an appeal is usually appropriate. A time limit should also be set for hearing the appeal.

29. Wherever possible the appeal should be heard by an appropriate individual, usually a senior manager, not previously involved in the disciplinary procedure. In small organisations it may not be possible to find such an individual and in these circumstances the person dealing with the appeal should act as impartially as possible. Independent arbitration is sometimes an appropriate means of resolving disciplinary issues and where

the parties concerned agree it may constitute the appeals stage of procedure.

30. Individuals should be informed of the arrangements for appeal hearings and also of their statutory or other right to be accompanied at these hearings (see section three). Where new evidence arises during the appeal the worker, or their representative, should be given the opportunity to comment before any action is taken. It may be more appropriate to adjourn the appeal to investigate or consider such points.

31. The worker should be informed of the results of the appeal and the reasons for the decision as soon as possible and this should be confirmed in writing. If the decision constitutes the final stage of the organisation's appeals procedure this should be made clear to the worker.

Records

32. Records should be kept detailing the nature of any breach of disciplinary rules or unsatisfactory performance, the worker's defence or mitigation, the action taken and the reasons for it, whether an appeal was lodged, its outcome and any subsequent developments. These records should be kept confidential and retained in accordance with the disciplinary procedure and the Data Protection Act 1998 which requires the release of certain data to individuals on their request. Copies of any meeting records should be given to the individual concerned although in certain circumstances some information may be withheld, for example to protect a witness.

Further action

33. Rules and procedures should be reviewed periodically in the light of any developments in employment legislation or good employment practice and if necessary, revised in order to ensure their continuing relevance and effectiveness. Any amendments and additional rules imposing new obligations should be introduced only after reasonable notice has been given to all workers and, where appropriate, their representatives have been consulted. Except in very exceptional circumstances, where legal advice

should be sought, changes to individual contracts may only be made with agreement.

SECTION 2 – GRIEVANCE PROCEDURES

Why have a grievance procedure?

34. In any organisation workers may have problems or concerns about their work, working environment or working relationships that they wish to raise and have addressed. A grievance procedure provides a mechanism for these to be dealt with fairly and speedily, before they develop into major problems and potentially collective disputes.

35. Whilst employers are not required by statute to have a grievance procedure it is good employment relations practice to provide workers with a reasonable and prompt opportunity to obtain redress of any grievance. Employers are statutorily required in the written statement of terms and conditions of employment to specify, by description or otherwise, a person to whom the employee can apply if they have a grievance and they are also required by statute to allow a worker to be accompanied at certain grievance hearings (see section three).

36. In circumstances where a grievance may apply to more than one person and where a trade union is recognised it may be appropriate for the problem to be resolved through collective agreements between the trade union(s) and the employer.

Formulating procedures

37. It is in everyone's best interest to ensure that workers' grievances are dealt with quickly and fairly and at the lowest level possible within the organisation at which the matter can be resolved. Management is responsible for taking the initiative in developing grievance procedures which, if they are to be fully effective, need to be acceptable to both those they cover and those who have to operate them. It is important therefore that senior management aims to secure the involvement of workers and their representatives, including trade unions where they are recognised,

and all levels of management when formulating or revising grievance procedures.

Essential features of grievance procedures

38. Grievance procedures enable individuals to raise issues with management about their work, or about their employers', clients' or their fellow workers' actions that affect them. It is impossible to provide a comprehensive list of all the issues that might give rise to a grievance but some of the more common include: terms and conditions of employment; health and safety; relationships at work; new working practices; organisational change and equal opportunities.

39. Procedures should be simple, set down in writing and rapid in operation. They should also provide for grievance proceedings and records to be kept confidential.

40. It is good practice for individuals to be accompanied at grievance hearings (see also section three for information on the statutory right to be accompanied).

41. In order for grievance procedures to be effective it is important that all workers are made aware of them and understand them and if necessary that supervisors, managers and worker representatives are trained in their use. Wherever possible every worker should be either given a copy of the procedures or provided with access to it (eg, in the personnel handbook or on the company intranet site) and have the detail explained to them. For new employees this might best be done as part of any induction process. Special allowance should be made for individuals whose first language is not English or who have a visual impairment or some other disability.

The procedure in operation

42. Most routine complaints and grievances are best resolved informally in discussion with the worker's immediate line manager. Dealing with grievances in this way can often lead to speedy resolution of problems and can help maintain the authority of the immediate line manager who may well be able to resolve the matter directly. Both manager and worker may find it helpful to keep a note of such an informal meeting.

43.   Where the grievance cannot be resolved informally it should be dealt with under the formal grievance procedure. The number of stages contained in the procedure will depend on the size of organisation, its management structure and the resources it has available. In larger organisations the procedure might contain all the following stages, but for the smaller business the first and final stages might be sufficient :-

First Stage: Workers should put their grievance, preferably in writing, to their immediate line manager. Where the grievance is against the line manager the matter should be raised with a more senior manager. If the grievance is contested the manager should invite the worker to attend a hearing in order to discuss the grievance and should inform the worker of his or her statutory right to be accompanied depending on the nature of the grievance (see section three). The manager should respond in writing to the grievance within a specified time (eg, within five working days of the hearing or, where no hearing has taken place, within five working days of receiving written notice of the grievance). If it is not possible to respond within the specified time period the worker should be given an explanation for the delay and told when a response can be expected.

Second Stage: If the matter is not resolved at Stage 1 the worker should be permitted to raise the matter in writing with a more senior manager. The choice of this person will depend on the organisation but could be a departmental, divisional or works' manager. The manager should arrange to hear the grievance within a specified period (eg, five working days) and should inform the worker of the statutory right to be accompanied (see section three). Following the hearing the manager should, where possible, respond to the grievance in writing within a specified period (eg, ten working days). If it is not possible to respond within the specified time period the worker should be given an explanation for the delay and told when a response can be expected.

Final Stage: Where the matter cannot be resolved at Stage 2 the worker should be able to raise their grievance in writing with a higher level of manager than for Stage 2. The choice of this person will depend on the organisation but could include directors or in certain cases the chief executive or managing director. Workers should be permitted to present their case at a hearing and should be informed of their statutory right to be accompanied (see section three). The manager dealing with the grievance should give a decision on the grievance within a specified period (eg, ten working days). If it is not possible to respond within the specified time period the worker should be given an explanation and told when a response can be expected.

44. In most organisations it should be possible to have at least a two stage grievance procedure. However, where there is only one stage, for instance in very small firms where there is only a single owner/manager, it is especially important that the person dealing with the grievance acts impartially.

45. In certain circumstances it may, with mutual agreement, be helpful to seek external advice and assistance during the grievance procedure. For instance where relationships have broken down an external facilitator might be able to help resolve the problem. Where the grievance is against the chief executive or managing director an external stage using some form of alternative dispute resolution might be helpful.

Special considerations

46. Some organisations may wish to have specific procedures for handling grievances about unfair treatment eg, discrimination or bullying and harassment, as these subjects are often particularly sensitive.

47. Organisations may also wish to consider whether they need a whistleblowing procedure in the light of the Public Interest Disclosure Act 1998. This provides strong protection to workers who raise concerns about wrongdoing (including frauds, dangers and cover-ups). While the Act reassures workers that it is safe to raise such a concern internally, it also protects disclosures to key regulatory authorities and – provided they are reasonable and made with good cause – wider disclosures.

48. Sometimes a worker may raise a grievance about the behaviour of a manager during the course of a disciplinary case. Where this happens and depending on the circumstances, it may be appropriate to suspend the disciplinary procedure for a short period until the grievance can be considered. Consideration might also be given to bringing in another manager to deal with the disciplinary case.

Records

49. Records should be kept detailing the nature of the grievance raised, the employers response, any action taken and the reasons for it. These records should be kept confidential and retained in accordance with the Data Protection Act 1998 which requires the release of certain data to individuals on their request. Copies of any meeting records should be given to the individual concerned although in certain circumstances some information may be withheld, for example to protect a witness.

SECTION 3 – THE STATUTORY RIGHT TO BE ACCOMPANIED AT DISCIPLINARY AND GRIEVANCE HEARINGS

What is the right?

50. Workers have a statutory right to be accompanied by a fellow worker or trade union official[7] where they are required or invited by their employer to attend certain disciplinary or grievance hearings and when they make a reasonable request to be so accompanied. This right is additional to any contractual rights.

To whom does the right apply?

51. The statutory right to be accompanied applies to all workers, not just employees working under a contract of employment. 'Worker' is defined in the legislation and includes anyone who performs work personally for someone else, but is not genuinely self-employed, as well as agency workers and home workers, workers in Parliament and Crown employees other than members of the armed forces[8] . There are no exclusions for part-time or casual workers, those on short term contracts or for people who work overseas (subject to any jurisdictional rules).

---

7   See paragraph for more information on who can accompany a worker at a disciplinary or grievance hearing.
8   See Section 13 (1), (2) and (3) of the Employment Relations Act 1999 for definitions of 'worker' 'agency worker' and 'home worker'.

Application of the statutory right

52. The statutory right applies where a worker:–
i)   is required or invited to attend a disciplinary or grievance hearing, and
ii)   reasonably requests to be accompanied at the hearing.

What is a disciplinary hearing?

53. Whether a worker has a statutory right to be accompanied at a disciplinary hearing will depend on the nature of the hearing. Employers often choose to deal with disciplinary problems in the first instance by means of an informal interview or counselling session. So long as the informal interview or counselling session does not result in a formal warning or some other action it would not generally be good practice for the worker to be accompanied as matters at this informal stage are best resolved directly by the worker and manager concerned. Equally, employers should not allow an investigation into the facts surrounding a disciplinary case to extend into a disciplinary hearing. If it becomes clear during the course of the informal or investigative interview that formal disciplinary action may be needed then the interview should be terminated and a formal hearing convened at which the worker should be afforded the statutory right to be accompanied.

54. The statutory right to be accompanied applies specifically to hearings which could result in:
i)   the administration of a formal warning to a worker by his employer (ie, a warning, whether about conduct or capability, that will be placed on the worker's record);
ii)   the taking of some other action in respect of a worker by his employer (eg, suspension without pay, demotion or dismissal); or
iii) the confirmation of a warning issued or some other action taken.[9]

What is a grievance hearing?

55. The statutory right to accompaniment applies only to grievance hearings which concern the performance of a 'duty by an employer in

9   See section 13(4) of the Employment Relations Act 1999.

relation to a worker'[10]. This means a legal duty arising from statute or common law (eg, contractual commitments). Ultimately, only the courts can decide what sort of grievances fall within the statutory definition but the individual circumstances of each case will always be relevant. For instance:–

i) An individual's request for a pay rise is unlikely to fall within the definition unless specifically provided for in the contract. On the other hand a grievance about equal pay would be included as this is covered by a statutory duty imposed on employers.

ii) Grievances about the application of a grading or promotion exercise are likely to be included if they arise out of the contract but not grievances arising out of requests for new terms and conditions of employment, for instance a request for subsidised health care or travel loans where these are not already provided for in the contract.

iii) Equally an employer may be under no duty to provide car parking facilities and thus a grievance on the issue would not attract the right to be accompanied. However, if the worker was disabled and needed parking facilities in order to attend work the employer's duty of care becomes relevant and the worker is likely to have a statutory right to be accompanied.

iv) Grievance arising out of day to day friction between fellow workers may not involve the breach of a legal duty unless the friction develops into incidents of bullying or harassment which would be included as they arise out of the employer's duty of care.

What is a reasonable request?

56. In order for workers to exercise their statutory right to be accompanied they must make a reasonable request to their employer. It will be for the Courts to decide what is reasonable in all the circumstances. There is no test of reasonableness associated with the choice of companion and workers are therefore free to choose any one fellow worker or trade union official (within the limitations of paragraph 57). However, in making their choice workers should bear in mind that it would not be appropriate to insist on being accompanied by a colleague whose presence would prejudice the hearing or who might have a conflict of interest. Nor would it be sensible for a worker to request accompaniment by a colleague from

10   See section 13(5) of the Employment Relations Act 1999.

a geographically remote location when someone suitably qualified was available on site. The request to be accompanied need not be in writing.

The accompanying person

57. A worker has a statutory right to be accompanied at a disciplinary or grievance hearing by a single companion who is either a:
i)   Fellow worker, ie, another of the employer's workers;
ii)   A full-time official employed by a trade union[11]; or a lay trade union official, so long as they have been reasonably certified in writing by their union as having experience of, or as having received training in, acting as a worker's companion at disciplinary or grievance hearings. Such certification may take the form of a card or letter.

Workers may, however, have contractual rights to be accompanied by persons other than those listed above, for instance a partner, spouse or legal representative.

58. Workers are free to choose an official from any trade union to accompany them at a disciplinary or grievance hearing regardless of whether the union is recognised or not. However where a trade union is recognised in a workplace it is good practice for an official from that union to accompany the worker at a hearing.

59. There is no duty on a fellow worker or trade union official to accept a request to accompany a worker and no pressure should be brought to bear on a person if they do not wish to act as a companion.

60. Accompanying a worker at a disciplinary or grievance hearing is a serious responsibility and it is important therefore that trade unions ensure their officials are trained in the role. Even where a trade union official has experience of acting in the role there may still be a need for periodic refresher training.

61. A worker who has been requested to accompany a colleague employed by the same employer and has agreed to do so is entitled to take a reasonable amount of paid time off to fulfil this responsibility. The time off should not

---

11   As defined in sections 1 and 119 of the Trade Union and Labour Relations (Consolidation) Act 1992.

only cover the hearing but should also allow a reasonable amount of time off for the accompanying person to familiarise themselves with the case and confer with the worker before and after the hearing. A lay trade union official is permitted to take a reasonable amount of paid time off to accompany a worker at a hearing so long as the worker is employed by the same employer.[12]

The statutory right in operation

62. It is good practice for an employer to try to agree a mutually convenient date for the disciplinary or grievance hearing with the worker and their companion. This is to ensure that hearings do not have to be delayed or postponed at the last minute. Where the chosen companion cannot attend on the date proposed the worker can offer an alternative time and date so long as it is reasonable and falls before the end of the period of five working days[13] beginning with the first working day after the day proposed by the employer. In proposing an alternative date the worker should have regard to the availability of the relevant manager. For instance it would not normally be reasonable to ask for a new date for the hearing where it was known the manager was going be absent on business or on leave unless it was possible for someone else to act for the manager at the hearing. The location and timing of any alternative hearing should be convenient to both worker and employer.

63. Both the employer and worker should prepare carefully for the hearing. The employer should ensure that a suitable venue is available and that, where necessary, arrangements are made to cater for any disability the worker or their companion may have. Where English is not the worker's first language there may also be a need for translation facilities. The worker should think carefully about what is to be said at the hearing and should discuss with their chosen companion their respective roles at the meeting. Before the hearing the worker should inform the employer of the identity of their chosen companion. In certain circumstances, for instance where the chosen companion is an official of a non-recognised trade union, it

---

12 Time off for a lay official to accompany a worker at another employer is a matter for agreement by the parties concerned.

13 See section 13(6) of the Employment Relations Act 1999 for a definition of 'working day'.

might also be helpful for the employer and chosen companion to make contact with each other before the hearing.

64. The chosen companion has a statutory right to address the hearing but no statutory right to answer questions on the worker's behalf. Companions have an important role to play in supporting a worker and to this end should be allowed to ask questions and should, with the agreement of the employer, be allowed to participate as fully as possible in the hearing. The companion should also be permitted reasonable time to confer privately with the worker, either in the hearing room or outside.

What if the right to be accompanied is infringed?

65. If an employer fails to allow a worker to be accompanied at a disciplinary or grievance hearing or fails to re-arrange a hearing to a reasonable date proposed by the worker when a companion cannot attend on the date originally proposed, the worker may present a complaint to an employment tribunal. If the tribunal finds in favour of the worker the employer may be liable to pay compensation of up to two weeks pay as defined in statute[14]. Where the failure leads to a finding of unfair dismissal greater legal remedies might be involved.

66. Employers must be careful not to place any worker at a disadvantage for exercising or seeking to exercise their right to be accompanied as such detriment is unlawful and may lead to a claim to an employment tribunal. Equally employers must not place at a disadvantage those who act or seek to act as the accompanying person.

14   See Chapter II of Part XIV of the Employment Rights Act 1996.

Appendix III.
The exclusion of approved voluntary procedures

The requirements for the formal exclusion of voluntary procedures from the statutory machinery

To be excluded from the statutory machinery, a procedure must meet the requirements set out in ERA, s 110. The six criteria required by these provisions may be conveniently grouped into three categories:

(i)   the parties and type of procedure;
(ii) the scope and employee coverage of the procedure;
(iii) the specific safeguards required in excluded procedures.

I   The parties and type of procedure

As long as the voluntary procedure is based on collective agreement, the requirements as to the parties and the type of procedure are quite flexible. The employer's side can consist of a firm, an establishment or an organisation of employers. The conditions for the trade union side are no less flexible. It can consist of a trade union or group of trade unions. The one requirement the trade union side must meet is that of 'independence'. As ERA 1996, s 110(3)(a) puts it:

> 'that every trade union which is party to the dismissal procedure agreement is an independent organisation'.

One important implication of the flexible requirements as regards the parties to excluded voluntary procedures is that domestic or internal procedures will be eligible just as well as external procedures providing, of course, that they meet the other requirements for exclusion. Thus, it is open to employers and trade union officials to consider anew whether they wish to use the external disputes procedure in their industries as the appeals machinery for dismissal cases or whether they would prefer to add a final stage of arbitration to their domestic procedure and apply for exclusion at that level.

II The scope and employee coverage of the procedure

The second set of requirements for excluded voluntary procedures relate to their scope and employee coverage.

Section 110(3)(b) states:

'that the procedure agreement provides for procedures to be followed in cases where an employee claims that he has been, or is in the course of being unfairly dismissed'.

Yet s 110(3)(b) is subject to s 110(2) which allows the parties to exclude certain types of dismissals from the scope of the agreement. In such cases, employees will retain a right of access to employment tribunals.

Otherwise, s 110(3)(b) requires the voluntary procedure to be available for employees against all types of complaints of unfair dismissal that can be brought before the statutory tribunals. Voluntary procedures will therefore have to allow complaints against dismissal whether summary or with notice, and in the latter case, even after notice has expired. They must also be available for appeals against dismissal for all reasons that would fall under the rubric of 'unfair', as set out in s 98(4).

Section 110(3)(f) is more indirect. It requires:

'that the provisions of the procedure agreement are such that it can be determined with reasonable certainty whether a particular employee is one to whom the procedure agreement applies or not'.

This provision states directly only that the parties to the procedure must specify with reasonable certainty what groups of employees will be covered by the voluntary procedure. It intimates that the parties are free to choose whether to make their procedure domestic, company or industry wide in scope. What is left unsaid, however, is that the subsection presents the parties with an option: whether to include or exclude non-union employees within a given grade, enterprise, firm or industry.

This issue is more complex and contentious than might at first be apparent. At this stage it is sufficient simply to establish that under s 110(3)(f), it will be open to the parties to voluntary procedures to assert in their applications to the Secretary of State for Employment whether they wish non-union members to be covered by their excluded procedure and hence denied access to the statutory tribunals. The restrictions on the parties' exercise of this option would appear to be twofold. First, the trade union would probably have to show that it represented a substantial proportion of employees covered by the voluntary procedure.

The second important constraint on the parties' exercise of the option given them in s 110(3)(f) is the general requirement in s 110(3)(c) that the procedures are available without discrimination to all employees falling within any description to which the procedure agreement applies. The way in which this requirement will operate as a constraint can best be demonstrated in the context of the other specific safeguards required of excluded voluntary procedures.

III   The specific safeguards required in excluded voluntary procedures

The specific safeguards required of voluntary procedures to qualify for exclusion can be conveniently considered under three heads: (a) the final appeals body, (b) the rights of the individual employee in the collective procedure and (c) the remedies offered by the voluntary procedure.

(A)   THE FINAL APPEALS BODY

Under s 110(3)(e), voluntary procedures must 'include' a right to arbitration in cases where (by reason of an equality of votes or for any other reason) a decision cannot otherwise be reached on a right to submit to arbitration any question of law. The aim of this subsection is to ensure that the arbitrator acts as a long stop for the parties in case they fail to agree. Either party must be given the right unilaterally to invoke arbitration as the final stage of procedure to resolve a deadlock. Any formula which required consent by both sides to arbitration when both had failed to agree at the penultimate stage or only made a vague reference to the possibility of arbitration would probably not meet the requirement of s 110(3)(e).

There is a further aspect of s 110(3)(e) that remains to be clarified. What rights must the procedure give to the individual employee to appeal to the arbitrator under s 110(3)(e)? This can be best considered in the following section.

(B)   THE RIGHTS OF THE INDIVIDUAL UNDER THE COLLECTIVE PROCEDURE

Under the scheme of s 110(1) individual employees covered by excluded voluntary procedures will be denied access to the employment tribunals in respect of unfair dismissals complaints. Yet the parties to voluntary procedures are not, strictly speaking, required to give such employees protections against unfair dismissal which are directly comparable to those enjoyed by employees under the statutory scheme. The only entitlement to treatment 'on the whole as beneficial' as that provided by the statutory machinery is to be found in the case of the remedies given by the voluntary procedure. Instead, s 110 protects the individual employee by the provision of s 110(3)(e) which requires that the voluntary procedure must be available without discrimination to all employees falling within any description to which the procedure agreement applies.

The question of whether a procedure 'is available without discrimination' at first glance relates to the accessibility of the procedure to all employees, ie whether all employees, including non-unionists and members of other trade unions, are allowed to pursue their complaints through the initial stage of procedure. Yet the matter does not rest there. Should the parties agree to give formal access to all employees covered by this procedure, they will have to weigh two other considerations. First, to what extent does s 110(3)(c) require the trade unions party to the voluntary procedure to represent non-unionists or non-members in such procedures? Secondly, to what extent does the requirement that procedures must be made available without discrimination entail the right of employees to appeal through higher stages of procedure and to the independent body even where the trade union considers that the result has been satisfactory? Let us consider each of these issues in greater detail.

As mentioned, the requirements of s 110(3)(e) are quite straightforward on the question of access to the initial stage of voluntary procedures. If the parties have chosen to include non-unionists or non-members in their description of the coverage of their procedure under s 110(3)(f), they must arrange to give such employees formal access to the early stages of the procedure. The provision of access to non-unionists will present more of a problem to external procedures than internal procedures or certain procedures in the public sector, for the latter are already often available to 'employees', ie union members and non-unionists alike, although of course the non-member rarely enjoys the support and assistance of the trade union officials. The parties to external procedures will have to make the greatest adjustment, for most collective procedures today do not offer formal access to non-unionists. Yet there are procedures in both the public and private sectors which formally extend facilities to all employees, suggesting that the difficulties of adjusting external procedures are not insuperable.

Whether the duty under s 110(3)(c) to make procedures available without discrimination includes the provision of trade union representation to all employees covered by excluded voluntary procedures is a less easy issue to resolve.

The parties to a voluntary procedure allow employees a choice between trade union representation or an alternative form of representation. A procedure incorporating such a formula can escape the charge of being inherently discriminatory, as long as it is clear that the choice lies with the employee. But this does not preclude the possibility that a non-union employee may feel that such a procedure is being operated in a discriminatory manner, eg where a trade union official refuses to take a case for a non-unionist, or argues the case 'without enthusiasm'.

In such situations, the question of whether the procedure is discriminatory in the sense that it violates s 110(3)(c) will depend on whether, as is likely, the condition 'that procedures are available without discrimination' is interpreted to apply to the way the procedure is operated as well as to whether employees enjoy access to the procedure.

Closely related to this is the question of the rights of the non-unionist or non-member who disagrees with the union official's decision not to take his case to the final stage of the procedure. Does his right to have the procedure 'available without discrimination' under s 110(3)(c) extend to the point of an independent right to appeal to the final stage? Apparently, s 110(3)(e) does not require voluntary procedures to give employees the right to decide to take their appeal to the independent element in the procedure even where the trade union official agrees with the employer's decision.

Although a refusal by a trade union official to take the case of a non-unionist or non-member covered by the excluded procedure to the final stage will not necessarily be viewed as discriminatory and therefore a failure to fulfil the condition in s 110(3)(e), it will always raise the possibility of such a claim. It might be argued that such an employee enjoys the same rights and privileges as the union member under the procedure and hence its provisions have been made available without discrimination according to s 110(l)(c). However, there is a further point to consider. The trade union member who is dissatisfied with the decision of his official not to process his appeal is likely to have an alternative avenue of appeal against that decision. He may complain through the internal complaints procedure of his union organisation. The non-member will have no such avenue of appeal.

If, therefore, an employee feels rightly or wrongly, that the trade union official's decision not to take his case to the final stage of procedure was prompted by the fact that he was a non-unionist or non-member, he could complain to the Secretary of State that the procedure no longer fulfils the conditions required by s 110(3). In the event it would be open to the Secretary of State to apply to the EAT under s 110(4) to revoke the exclusion order on the grounds that the procedure has ceased to fulfil all the conditions specified in s 110. Further, if the trade union in question enjoyed sole bargaining rights, an employee might attempt to find a legal remedy based on an implied duty of the trade union to represent all employees in the employment unit affected by his status.[1]

Finally, he might attempt to bring an action to the ordinary courts on the point of law that the decision in the voluntary procedure deprives him unfairly of his right to work.[2] One way of avoiding these complications and ensuring equality of rights in voluntary procedures is to reform voluntary procedures to allow every employee covered by the procedure the right independently to appeal through all stages. This will not only avoid the possible allegation that the procedure is discriminatory — it will also preclude the possibility of parties going outside procedure to challenge decisions made under procedure. These considerations apply even though s 110(3)(e) probably does not require voluntary procedures to take such an approach. Section 110(3)(e) requires the voluntary procedures to provide a right to arbitration, but it fails to specify very precisely to whom that right must be given. Since the subsection provides that the right is to be exercised only in cases where the two collective parties disagree, the implication is quite clear that the right is to be limited only to the organisations who are party to the procedure. Although requiring such protection for all individuals covered by voluntary procedures might have been the fairest legislative solution, this has not been adopted. Under the scheme of s 110(3)(e) the parties appear not to be compelled to give all employees the formal right to take their case independently through all stages of procedure.

---

1   Such a duty has been implied in the US legislation by the courts and NLRB. See eg Wellington *Labor and the Legal Process* ch 4.
2   For a discussion of attempts to create a legal doctrine of the 'right to work' as a limitation on the arbitrary decisions of voluntary procedures or tribunals, see eg Hepple and O'Higgins *Employment Law* (4th edn, Sweet & Maxwell, 1981).

Appendix IV.
Compensation for loss of
pension rights[1]

I INTRODUCTION

1.1 Compensation for loss of pension rights following a finding of unfair
dismissal in an Industrial Tribunal is just a part of the whole issue of
compensation for loss of employment. The starting point is s 74 of the
Employment Protection (Consolidation) Act 1978 which provides:

> 'The amount of the compensatory award shall be such amount as
> the tribunal considers just and equitable in all the circumstances
> having regard to the loss sustained by the complainant in
> consequence of the dismissal in so far as that loss is attributable to
> action taken by the employer.'

1.2 The Tribunal is not obliged, as a court is, to seek to calculate as
precisely as possible the loss that the Applicant has suffered, but to order
a 'just and equitable' sum by way of compensation. This entitles the
Tribunal to use a rough and ready system if necessary, *Manpower Ltd v
Hearne* [1983] IRLR 281.

1.3 Industrial Tribunals were established to provide an economical and
expeditious means of resolving disputes. There is an upper limit on the
amount of compensation which they can award in the case of unfair
dismissal. Our task has been to set out guidelines for the assessment of

1 Guidelines prepared by a committee of chairmen of Industrial Tribunals in
consultation with the Government Actuary's Department (2nd edn, 1991).

compensation for loss of pension rights which are consistent with the constraints within which an Industrial Tribunal operates.

1.4   We believe that many people underestimate the value of an occupational pension. It can be a very significant financial asset, worth at least as much as the family home. This is illustrated in the examples in Appendix 5, part 1.

1.5   The Social Security Acts of 1985 and 1990 have improved the position of employees who leave prior to retirement. This applies to those who leave voluntarily as well as to those who are dismissed. An employee whose employment is terminated on or after 1 January 1991 has his or her pension entitlement indexed (up to retirement) to the Retail Price Index or 5% per annum whichever is the lower. This is considerable improvement since before 1 January 1985 an employee's pension entitlement was 'frozen' at the level which pertained when the employment was terminated, However, even for an employee whose pension entitlement is 'index-linked' in accordance with the 1990 Act, the loss on leaving employment can be considerable if he or she has a number of years before retirement age.

2   OUR APPROACH

2.1   As will appear from this paper, the whole subject of pensions and the losses which may arise on dismissal is a complex one. In our view it is vital that the method used to calculate loss of pension rights should be readily comprehensible and acceptable to ordinary litigants. Where there is a conflict between technical purity and comprehensibility we make no apology for choosing comprehensibility. This is not an actuarial paper and does not pretend to be. It has, however, received the approval of the Employment Appeals Tribunal in general terms in *Benson v Dairy Crest Ltd* (EAT/192/89).

2.2   Pension provision is but one of the financial advantages of employment. The benefit an employee derives, or the cost that the employer has to incur to fund that provision, may well vary according to a variety of factors. In times of high inflation the employee with a public sector index-linked inflation-proofed pension may well enjoy a coveted position which may not be matched by any privately funded scheme. In times when inflation is low and yet interest rate yields are high, or where equities have made substantial gains, an index-linked pension may not be as attractive as a privately funded scheme. Pension fund managers in the late 1970s were worried whether they could continue to fund any post retirement increases without enormous increases in the contributions made by the employers. By the mid 1980s certain pension funds were so well funded that employers were having pension contribution 'holidays' to prevent the fund becoming overfunded.

2.3   In these circumstances because there are so many variable factors it is impossible to foresee with any great precision exactly what the financial consequences may be for an employee who is unfairly dismissed and therefore loses certain entitlements to a pension. Our guidelines therefore have to be broadly based and we have consciously ignored certain factors in the interest of simplicity.

2.4   These recommendations are put forward to assist tribunals who find themselves without adequate evidence to reach a conclusion on loss of pension rights without applying some kind of formula. Nevertheless we are very much aware that the recommendations, particularly in respect of loss of enhancement of accrued pension rights, are based on assumptions which may not apply to the particular case in question. Accurate assessments in any particular case can only be reached with the assistance of actuarial evidence. It is always open to either or both parties to call actuarial evidence and it is hoped that the more general parts of this paper will assist Industrial Tribunals in assessing such evidence where it is called.

3   STATE PENSION PROVISION

3.1   The retirement pension payable by the State can be made up of the Basic Pension, a Graduated Pension and an Additional Pension payable pursuant to the State Earnings-Related Pension Scheme:—

The Basic Pension

This pension is much the same as the old flat rate National Insurance pension. Provided that certain contribution requirements have been completed the Basic Pension is payable to all persons over State pension age.

Graduated Pension

This pension is based on the amount of graduated National Insurance contributions paid by an employee in the period between April 1961 and April 1975. The amount of an individual's Graduated Pension varies according to the number of units of Graduated Pension contributions paid by him.

The State Earnings-Related Pension Scheme ('SERPS')

This pension is earnings related and varies according to an individual's earnings in respect of which he has paid full National Insurance contributions as an employee since April 1978. This is the so called 'Additional Pension'.

Contracting Out

3.2   Since its introduction it has been possible for employers to contract out of SERPS those employees who are members of a final salary scheme which satisfies certain criteria. National Insurance contributions payable in respect of employees who are members of an occupational pension scheme which is contracted out are paid at a lower rate than that payable for employees not in such a scheme. A final salary scheme which is contracted out must provide a Guaranteed Minimum Pension ('GMP') as a substitute for the Additional Pension which would otherwise be provided by the State. The GMP is broadly equivalent to the Additional Pension paid under SERPS and is the minimum amount of occupational pension which must be paid from a contracted out scheme. Often a contracted out scheme provides benefits which are higher than and additional to the GMP. An employee who has served all his pensionable service under a contracted out scheme will receive the Basic Pension paid by the State as well as a pension pursuant to the contracted out scheme. When the State pension is paid the Basic Pension and Additional Pension have an inflation protection element built into them. For an employee who is still employed the GMP increases with wage inflation. For the tax year 1988—89 and later years after retirement the GMP element of the retired employee's pension will be increased in line with price inflation subject to an upper limit of 3% per annum.

3.3   From April 1988 it has been possible for money purchase schemes to be contracted out of SERPS by employers. Since the 1st July 1988 employees have been able to make their own pension arrangements and opt out of SERPS or their employer's pension schemes. In this case both the employer and the employee pay the full rate National Insurance contributions and part of these (grossed up at the appropriate tax rate) is paid by the Department of Social Security into the employee's personal pension scheme. If an employee has not been in a contracted out pension scheme for the two calendar years before commencing his personal pension scheme, an additional 2% of relevant earnings is paid into the pension plan by the Department during the period to April 1993 as an incentive to the employee to set up the scheme.

3.4   In line with our general conclusions set out below we recommend that the assumption is made that there is no loss of pension rights in respect of a dismissed employee who is not in an occupational pension scheme.

4   OCCUPATIONAL PENSION SCHEMES

4.1   Occupational pension schemes come into two main categories: final salary and money purchase.

Final salary schemes

4.2   These are schemes where the amount of pension paid is based not on the contributions made by the employer or the employee, but on a proportion of the salary of the employee when he retires (eg 1/60th of his final salary for each year of service). This proportion depends on the number of years he has been in the company pension scheme.

Example I:—

A joined the company scheme in 1970. He retires in 1990 on a salary of £20,000 pa. The scheme is based on 1/60th of his final salary for each year. Therefore his annual pension will be 20/60ths of his final salary ie £6,667.

We have used males as examples throughout this paper but all examples apply equally to females.

4.3   In about 80% of cases the employee makes a contribution of a fixed percentage of his income into the fund throughout his employment. The employer usually agrees to make contributions to the fund at least matching those made by the employees as a whole. There is usually little difficulty in establishing the contributions currently made by the employer as a percentage of the total pay-roll but this may vary from year to year depending on how well the pension fund is keeping up with the demands that are likely to be made on it. Sometimes there will be contribution 'holidays'. Where there is a lack of accurate evidence or where the current contribution position is anomalous we are advised that on average the overall contribution for a good scheme is 15% of the pay-roll made up in a contributory scheme as to 10% from employers and 5% from employees. It is important to note that the employer's contribution is not ear-marked for the pension of any individual employee and that the pension an employee actually receives will not necessarily be proportional to his and the company's contributions.

4.4   On the face of it non-funded schemes (particularly publicly financed schemes like the civil service pension) might seem to be different from normal final salary schemes because, as there is no fund, there are no contributions as such. However, although the pension is paid out of the Consolidated Fund and not out of any specific ear-marked fund, the notional contributions are fixed by the scheme's actuary and should be easily obtainable. These non-funded schemes, therefore, can be treated in the same way as any other final salary scheme. Most publicly financed schemes, however, do have a special advantage, which is unusual in other schemes, in that they are index-linked to the cost of living index (though not to average increases in earnings) both from the date of leaving until retirement and after retirement and without any top limit.

4.5   Not all final salary schemes are the same. Not all schemes use the same fraction. Some schemes use the best of the employee's last few years as final salary; others may use the average of the last few years. However, the essence of a final salary scheme is that the employee's pension is based on his earnings and service and not directly on what he or his employers have contributed to the fund.

4.6   'Additional Voluntary Contributions' (AVCs) have existed for many years but the Social Security Act 1986 has now made it compulsory for employers to allow them to be made. Additional voluntary contributions usually operate on a money purchase basis, even where the main scheme is a final salary scheme. As such they should be treated in the same way as company money purchase schemes (see 4.8 below). However, some schemes (mainly public sector) allow employees to buy extra years. If this has been done the additional years already bought will be put into the equation as if the employee had actually worked those extra years.

4.7   AVC contributions are made by the employee alone. They, therefore, have no significant bearing when future loss of pension rights comes to be considered. Such 'AVCs' should be distinguished from the new 'free-standing additional voluntary contributions' introduced in October 1987 which are in effect separate money purchase plans and should be dealt with as personalised money purchase plans.

Money Purchase Schemes

4.8   **Company Money Purchase Schemes**:—
These are quite different from final salary schemes. The pension payable is directly related to the contributions made by the employer and the employee to the fund over the years. In the past they have made inadequate allowance for inflation and have become unpopular, but there is a move back to them, because they enable the employer as well as the employee to know exactly how much the scheme will cost them each year and to budget accordingly whereas a final salary scheme may be an open-ended commitment.

> Example 2:—
> A joined the company in 1970. He retires in 1990. Over the 20 years he and his employers have contributed £20,000 to the scheme, but let us say that contributions are now worth £50,000. For this, on current annuity rates, he gets a pension of about £6,667 per annum. The amount of the pension, of course, varies not only according to the success of the investment policy but also with the age and even the sex of the annuitant and the interest rates current at the date of his retirement.

4.9   **Personalised plans**, including personalised life insurance backed schemes: —
These are the plans introduced for employees by the Social Security Act 1985 and include the 'free standing additional voluntary contribution' plans.

They are similar to plans that have been available to self-employed persons since 1956. The idea, very simply, is that the employee and the employer or either of them make contributions to a private pension policy with an insurance company or other pensions provider of the employee's choice. On retirement the employee then receives an annuity based on the value of his personalised fund. The main difference between these plans and company money purchase schemes is that it is the employee and not the employer who decides where the money is to be invested. They can now also be used to contract out of SERPS.

4.10   Free standing additional voluntary contributions are a form of personalised plan designed as a private top up for employees in company pension schemes.

Life Assurance Cover

4.11   Many pension schemes provide, or have associated with them, schemes which provide life assurance benefits for their members. In appropriate cases it may be just and equitable to compensate former employees for the loss of the benefit of belonging to such schemes.

5   EARLY LEAVERS

5.1   Anyone who leaves pensionable employment before retirement is known as an 'early leaver'. A person who is unfairly dismissed is one example. The effect of leaving early will depend on whether the scheme is a final salary or a money purchase scheme.

5.2   Where the scheme is a money purchase scheme, whether company or personalised, the fund contributed to the date of leaving by employer and employee remains invested for the employee's benefit. Accordingly what the employee loses on dismissal is the prospective value of the further contributions that his employer would have made. As far as his own future contributions are concerned there is no loss since he can use the money to pay into a different scheme.

5.3   In addition a person dismissed who is a member of a money purchase scheme may be required to pay a penalty for leaving the scheme early.

This is also a loss directly attributable to the dismissal, but it is easily quantifiable. Apart from this he does not lose any part of the current value of contributions already made by his employer and himself.

5.4   In a final salary scheme the position is much more complicated. By being dismissed the employee loses the prospective right to a pension based on his final salary. In most cases that come before the Tribunal, however, he will be entitled to a deferred pension. It is the difference between this deferred pension (including any cost of living increases and other benefits) and the pension and other benefits that he would have received had he not been unfairly dismissed that constitutes his loss.

6   DEFERRED PENSION

6.1   When a person who is a member of a final salary scheme is dismissed or leaves for any other reason he is entitled to a pension payable at what would have been his retirement date as an annuity for the rest of his life. This is referred to in this paper as a 'deferred pension'.

6.2   In the most common form of this scheme an employee when he retires receives 1/60th of his final salary for each year he has worked for the employer. For the employee retiring at age 60 there is a maximum of 40/60ths. Frequently part of this pension is commuted to provide a lump sum.

6.3   The early leaver receives a deferred pension representing 1/60th of his final salary for each year he has worked for the employer (providing he has 2 years' service as nearly all applicants to the tribunal must have). The problem was that until the Social Security Act 1985 came into force the final salary which used to be used for calculating this figure was his salary at the date he left. This is likely to be much less than the final salary would have been had he remained with the company until retirement or indeed until the next pay rise.

Example 3 (Pre-1985):—
A worked for his employers for 15 years; he left on 1 December 1983 with a final salary of £10,000. His basic deferred pension is 15/60ths of £10,000 = £2,500 p.a.

Example 4:—
Instead of leaving he stays with the company for another 15 years

when he retires with a final salary of £25,000 (an increase of not much more than 5% a year). His pension is £12,500 a year, of which £6,250 is referable to his first 15 years service.

6.4   By leaving early he has lost £3,750 a year from retirement to his death. This is the case even on the assumption that he obtains fresh employment with identical salary and identical increases and with an identical pension scheme. There will be a corresponding reduction in any lump sum on retirement and any widow's or widower's benefit.

6.5   In order to alleviate this unfairness the Social Security Act 1990 provides that the deferred pension increases by 5% per annum up to retirement or by the annual price rises if lower than 5%.

> Example 5:—
> B left on 1 January 1991 after 15 years service at the age of 50 years with a final salary of £10,000 a year. His deferred pension is still £2,500, but it goes up by 5% each year until it vests (that is comes into payment) unless price inflation is less than 5%.

6.6   What he has lost, however, is not simply a question of finding the difference between example 4 and example 5, because he might well not have stayed with the company until retirement even if he had not left at 50 years of age. He might have left or been sacked or the company might have gone into liquidation. Equally he might have ended up as managing director with a salary of £100,000 a year and a pension of £50,000 a year. Alternatively he might move to a new job where his pension can be transferred in such a way as to preserve his years of service. Who knows? Nevertheless his real loss on leaving could be substantial.

6.7   A fresh element was introduced by s 2 of the Social Security Act 1985, which entitles a person to require his ex-employee to transfer the value of his accrued pension either to a similar scheme run by a new employer or personally to make other arrangements meeting the prescribed requirements (Para 13(2) of Sch 1A to the Social Security Pensions Act 1975 as amended by the 1985 Act).

6.8   The transfer value is calculated in accordance with the Occupational Pension Schemes (Transfer Values) Regulations 1985 SI 1985/1931 which came into force on 1 January 1986. These refer in turn to 'Retirement Benefit

Schemes — Transfer values (GN11) issued by the Institute of Actuaries and the Faculty of Actuaries and issued on 18 December 1985'. We have inspected this document. It gives the actuary a certain amount of discretion and, anyway, the pension fund trustees may, if they wish, be more generous to early leavers than the law requires eg they may allow them to participate in excess profits or (most importantly) may allow the whole of the accrued pension to increase in line with the cost of living and not just the post 1985 element. However, our understanding is that the transfer value is an actuarial figure which represents the present value of the deferred pension he can anticipate.

6.9   In theory, he should be no better or worse off by taking the transfer value and re-investing it than if he chooses to leave the deferred pension in the fund. However, it does create the additional possibility that the employee will find a better private pension fund to put his money into or that the transfer values will be assessed on a generous basis.

6.10   A common fallacy is the belief that an employee does not lose financially if his pension is transferred from his old employer's pension fund to his new employer's pension fund. In fact this transfer value will usually be assessed on the limited commitment in example 5 and will not take account of the additional benefits he might have received if he had stayed on as in example 4. The position is explained further in paragraph 10.11.

7   THE PROBLEMS

7.1   It is impossible to know what would have happened to the employee had he not been dismissed. It is the attempt to find a way of assessing what is 'just and equitable' compensation for the loss of that contingent interest which is the subject of this paper.

7.2   About half of all employees are in occupational pension schemes. The pension losses suffered by an employee who is unfairly dismissed come into three main categories:
(1)   Loss of pension rights which would have accrued during the period between dismissal and the hearing,
(2)   Loss of future pension rights which would have accrued between the date of hearing and the date of retirement and
(3)   Loss of enhancement of the pension rights which had already accrued at the date of his dismissal ('accrued pension rights').

7.3   Industrial Tribunals have to deal with cases which cover a wide range of employers who vary in their administrative and financial resources and the sophistication of their management. It is inevitable, therefore, that there should be a wide variety of pension provision resulting in variations in the losses suffered by employees on dismissal. We are only dealing with the mainstream schemes.

7.4   It is unlikely that in most cases the parties will come equipped with the necessary information to calculate loss of pension rights. The best course seems to be to assess in the first place the basic and the compensatory award without taking account of loss of pension rights. As is explained below it may also be possible, with only very limited information about the pension scheme, to calculate the loss of pension rights between the date of dismissal and the date of hearing and also future loss of pension rights.

7.5   Once these figures are calculated, it is necessary to consider next whether, for the various reasons set out below, there is no loss of accrued pension rights or even that it is not so important to consider this issue because the statutory limit for compensation has been reached.

7.6   If there is a loss which has to be assessed, the matter can, if necessary, be put back to a later date to enable a sum representing loss of accrued pension rights to be agreed or failing agreement to be determined at a further hearing. Even where the statutory limit has been reached it may be necessary to make some assessment of the full value of compensation in order to calculate the pro rata deduction under the Recoupment Regulations.

8   LOSS OF PENSION RIGHTS FROM THE DATE OF DISMISSAL TO THE DATE OF HEARING

8.1   This is dealt with first because it is the simplest and most precisely quantifiable of the different types of loss of pension rights. Had the applicant remained in employment between the date of his dismissal and the hearing he would have gained the right to additional pension benefits. Equally he would have made additional contributions to the pension fund and his employer may well have also made contributions to the pension fund because of his continued employment.

8.2   In the case of a money purchase scheme it is easy to calculate the money value of the additional benefits he would have received in respect of the employer's contributions. In a final salary scheme this is not possible. Had he remained in the scheme until the date of the hearing and then left he would have qualified for a slightly higher deferred pension, but had he still been in employment at the date of the hearing then he would simply have gained additional service to put into the calculation of his final pension.

8.3   We consider that the fairest method, though not technically correct, is to look not at the additional contingent benefits he would have gained, but at the contributions which his employer would have made to the pension fund. If this is done it is not necessary to consider refinements such as widow's benefits or inflation-proofing after retirement since the better the scheme the more money will have to go into it. This is the approach which was recommended in the 1980 Government Actuary's paper which is referred to in Section 10.

8.4   When calculating loss of earnings during this period it is necessary to work out the weekly loss and multiply it by the number of weeks between the applicant's dismissal and the hearing (allowing for any sums paid in lieu of notice). Our recommendation for calculating the loss of pension rights during this period is simply to include a sum to represent what the employer would have contributed notionally towards the applicant's pension had he still been employed. Of course in the case of a final salary scheme this is not strictly a correct method of assessing the applicant's loss since the benefit that would have accrued to the applicant by remaining in employment does not necessarily correspond to this figure, but it would, we believe, be regarded as fair by both applicants and respondents. It is not, in our view, inconsistent with *Dews v NCB* [1987] ICR 602 where the Plaintiff remained in the Defendants' employment and where he suffered no loss of pension rights as a result of the absence of contributions during his period off work.

8.5   In a typical final salary pension scheme the employer does not make a specific contribution to each person's pension, but makes a contribution to the general pension fund which is related to the total wage bill or to some part of the wages bill, such as basic wages excluding commission and/or overtime. The normal cost of the scheme to the employer is usually given as a percentage in the actuary's report. This percentage should be applied to the applicant's gross pensionable pay to produce a weekly figure for loss of pension rights. 'Pensionable pay' is that part of the applicant's pay which is used for calculating his pension. It may be all of his pay, or his basic pay or some other figure. In the absence of evidence from the employer it should be assumed against him that pensionable pay is the same as actual gross pay.

8.6   If the percentage contributed by the employer cannot be easily ascertained or is currently anomalous (eg because of a 'contributions holiday') apply the figure of 10% (or 15% for a non-contributory scheme) to his pensionable pay. Whether a scheme is contributory or not can usually be determined by inspection of a wages slip. Applying this percentage to the applicant's gross pensionable pay is, in our view, the fairest and simplest way of calculating his continuing loss of pension rights.

Example 6:—
A earns £150 a week gross, which is his pensionable pay. He contributes £7.50 a week to the pension fund. His employers contribute 10% of the gross wage bill to the pension fund. A's continuing loss of pension rights is £15 a week.

8.7   Although to this extent pension provision is being treated as part of the applicant's weekly loss, it is not part of his pay and the Recoupment Regulations do not apply to the pension element.

8.8   Where there is a company money purchase scheme or where the employer is contributing to a personalised plan or a money purchase top up then assessing the contribution that the employer would have made is both the simplest and the most accurate way of assessing the employee's loss. The same system, therefore, can be applied using the percentage contributed by the employer towards the pension on a weekly basis.

9   LOSS OF FUTURE PENSION RIGHTS

9.1   The Applicant's loss on dismissal may include the loss of benefits he would have gained under his employer's pension scheme if he had continued in the employment beyond the date of the hearing. As with Section 8, our recommendation is to treat these additional pension rights as being equivalent to the contributions that the employer would have made to the pension fund in respect of his employment. For the purpose of calculating compensation, this employer's contribution can then be treated as if it was additional earnings which the employee would have received but for the dismissal. If the employer's contributions are taken as the basis of assessment it is not necessary to go into the details of the precise benefits under the scheme (eg widow's pension, disability payments etc).

9.2   Sometimes the Applicant has not found other employment by the date of the hearing, in this situation the Tribunal is engaged in the highly speculative process of deciding when he is likely to find other employment and how much he is likely to earn if and when he does. Forecasting the likely pension, if any, in such employment is just one part of this highly speculative process which includes whether the Applicant would have left his job anyway and whether he would have been promoted if he had not been dismissed. If the Tribunal takes the view that the Applicant is likely to obtain fresh employment in, say, one year or two years and that his earnings in that new employment are likely to be comparable, it is reasonable to assume that the pension scheme will also be comparable.

9.3   It is unlikely today that there will be a substantial qualification period before an employee can benefit from a new employer's pension scheme. Therefore if the Tribunal's decision is that his new employment terms are likely to be comparable, then the calculation is simply the multiplicand, being his previous net earnings including the pension contributions, with a multiplier of the time during which it is determined that he is likely to be unemployed.

9.4   Even if there is a qualification period, benefits are often back-dated once the qualification period has been met. An assumption of five years before any benefits would accrue from a new pension scheme has been held to be far too long, *Freemans v Flynn* [1984] ICR 874. We consider that if the qualification period is two years or less and if, on the qualification period being met, the entitlement is back-dated to the beginning of employment there is no need to make any allowance for this period. After all, the usual assumption of any award for loss of future earnings where the applicant has got a new job, is that he is no more likely to lose that job than if he had stayed with the respondent.

9.5   If the Applicant has found other employment the Tribunal has to compare the remuneration from that employment against the remuneration from his previous employment. This comparison will include the respective pension provisions just as much as the pay and such fringe benefits as the use of a company car.

9.6   If the new employment has no pension scheme then any continuing loss of earnings will be increased by the value of his previous employer's pension contribution assessed as a weekly or other periodic sum. However, in this event the employee will be in the State Earnings Related Scheme (SERPS). Therefore the contribution made to SERPS by the new employer should be deducted. If the SERPS contribution is not known it can be assumed that the new employer is contributing 3% of the employee's gross pay to SERPS.

9.7   If the new employment does have a pension scheme then the Tribunal will have to weigh up this scheme against the old one. Again a good rule of thumb is to compare the employer's contribution under the new scheme with the employer's contribution under the old scheme. The difference can be regarded as the weekly loss of future pension rights under the new scheme and can be used as a multiplicand to which the Tribunal can apply an appropriate multiplier.

9.8   Where the scheme is a company money purchase scheme or where the employer is contributing to a personalised plan the same method can be used with greater certainty since the contributions which would have been made by the employer amount, in effect, to a payment by the employer into an investment fund for the employee's benefit.

10   LOSS OF ENHANCEMENT OF ACCRUED PENSIONS RIGHTS

10.1   Apart from the additional rights the Applicant would have been gaining had he still been employed, he may also have lost the benefit of further enhancement of the rights which have already accrued. In some cases he may forfeit his accrued rights.

10.2   Where the scheme is a money purchase scheme the sums accrued at the date of leaving continue to be invested just as they would have been had the employee remained with the company though sometimes employees have to pay a penalty on leaving money purchase schemes. Such penalties do not usually create great difficulties since the amount of compensation referable to the loss of accrued rights will simply be the amount of the penalty.

10.3   Where, however, the scheme is a final salary scheme it is obvious that even the post-1990 provision can involve loss representing the difference between the deferred pension he will receive and that part of the pension he would have received had he stayed with the company which is referable to his employment to date. There is a good chance that the applicant's salary would have increased at more than 5% or the annual price rise whichever is the lower and furthermore the employee might well anticipate promotion. On the other hand he may have lost his job before long anyway. He may find a fresh lease of life in new employment or self-employment. Assessing this loss is undoubtedly the most difficult aspect of compensation for loss of pension rights.

10.4   In 1980, long before there was any statutory dynamism in deferred pensions, the Government Actuary's Department produced a paper. This was intended to provide a simple system of calculating the difference between the value of the deferred pension to which the applicant was actually entitled and what he would have received in respect of service to date if he had not been dismissed (described in the 1980 paper as 'the accrued pension'). In most cases it recommended an actuarial method. As explained above this involved balancing a mass of uncertainties, such as anticipated wage rises and mobility of labour of employees at different ages. It sought to produce a 'rough and ready' formula. It also dealt with loss during the period of unemployment and with new employment without occupational pension rights.

10.5   Everyone, including the Government Actuary's Department, agrees that the 1980 Government Actuary's paper now requires revision. Firstly the assumptions for salary rises and mobility of labour are not necessarily the same now as they were when the paper was written. Secondly the problems of assessing the withdrawal rate accurately in any particular case are enormous and any alteration in the withdrawal rate applied can make a great difference to the sum assessed. We consider that this is a matter which should be assessed by the Tribunal on the facts of each individual case and therefore it is not appropriate to use generalised withdrawal rates. Thirdly it did not deal satisfactorily with the fact that some pensions are index-linked in payment, nor could it deal with the effect of the dynamism subsequently built into deferred pensions by the Social Security Acts *1985* and 1990. The Government Actuary's Department sought to deal with these points by adding notes to the tables (Table 1 Notes 3 and 4). However, the suggestion that compensation be reduced by half for each of these factors is undoubtedly a rough and ready approach.

10.6   We are also very much aware that Tribunals and parties have found the method difficult and rather daunting to operate, partly at least because the concepts it enshrines are not easy to understand. The reported cases have borne this out.

10.7   In trying to resolve this problem we have considered three possible approaches. We have concluded that none of these is appropriate to all circumstances but each can be of value in particular categories of case. Of course it is always open to an applicant to argue that a different approach should be adopted by the Tribunal in calculating the compensation to be awarded.

(a)   No compensation at all

10.8   We consider that in respect of certain categories of cases it would be just and equitable not to make any award of compensation in respect of loss of accrued pension rights.

10.9   These categories are:—
(1)   All public sector schemes;
(2)   Private sector schemes where the applicant is near retirement (eg has five years or less until retirement).

10.10   The reason for this recommendation is that the uncertainties are such that the best 'rough and ready' approach is to regard the cost of living increases as broadly in line with forecast improvements. This approach assumes the increases which the state regards as reasonable for persons who have left the company of their own accord, usually to better themselves, or for people who have already retired, are equally reasonable for a person who has been unfairly dismissed.

10.11   The problem with this approach is that in fact the evidence suggests that earnings rise faster than prices and therefore a cost of living inflation proofing does not correspond to anticipated increases in salary. Furthermore even cost of living inflation may well exceed 5% per annum.

10.12   We recommend that this approach should be used in cases where the applicant is fairly near to his anticipated retirement date eg within 5 years of retirement, because the difference between cost of living increases and anticipated increases in earnings has less cumulative effect over this shorter period.

10.13   We also recommend that there should be no compensation for loss of enhancement of accrued pension rights for all Applicants who are dismissed from the public service whose pensions are index-linked without the 5% limit. The justification for this approach is that their pensions are completely inflation-proofed albeit only against increases in the cost of living.

10.14   Where the Tribunal finds as a fact that the employment would have terminated in any event within a period of up to a year it would not be appropriate to order any compensation for loss of accrued pension rights.

(b)   The Government Actuary's New Table

10.15   Where the Applicant was in the private sector and had more than 5 years to retirement we recommend a different approach. Whilst preparing this paper we have had detailed consultations with Derek Renn of the Government Actuary's Department and he has put forward a simplified actuarial method set out in Appendix 3 and the table of multipliers in Appendix 4.

10.16   His approach is actually similar to that in the 1980 Paper. It takes as the starting point that deferred pension to which the applicant is entitled (without any allowance for anticipated cost of living increases or other benefits) and then applies a multiplier based on the applicant's age. The figure resulting from this calculation is the starting point for working out the award for loss of enhancement of accrued benefit rights.

10.17   To calculate this figure, therefore, all that is needed is the deferred annual pension (see Section 6), the applicant's age and the anticipated age at retirement. It is entirely an arithmetical calculation. The table assumes that the Applicant would not have left his employment before retirement for reasons other than death or disability.

10.18   The figure obtained by applying the multiplier should be reduced if appropriate by a percentage representing the likelihood that the applicant would have lost his job before retirement even if he had not been unfairly dismissed for other reasons such as a fair dismissal, redundancy, leaving voluntarily etc. The earlier paper set out a table of such deductions called the 'withdrawal factor', but we have come to the conclusion that any such figures are inappropriate and that it is best to leave this percentage to the discretion of the Tribunal.

10.19   The appropriate reduction is not the same as the percentage likelihood that the successful Applicant would have left his employment anyway before retirement. Even if he remained only for a few years more his accrued pension would still have been enhanced. However, we consider that a Tribunal can make a reasonable assessment of the appropriate reduction without guidance tables.

10.20   Appendix 2 Table 3 is a flow chart which should be of assistance in calculating the figure. Some examples of the general principles in assessing the withdrawal reduction are given in Appendix 5 part 2.

10.21   The rationale of this scheme is that the amount a person will lose over the years can be seen as a proportion of the value of his pension and can be related to his age. Generally the younger he is the greater the loss.

10.22   Because of the simplification on which we have insisted Appendix 4 makes various assumptions. It assumes that:—
(1)   There is a widow or widower's pension at 50% of the members' rate.
(2)   There will be no lump sum.
(3)   There is a 3% per annum increase in most of the pension after retirement.
(4)   It applies equally to men and women.

10.23   The effect of inflation and taxation, have been taken into account

in the assumptions used in the table in Appendix 4. The actuarial basis is
set out in Appendix 3.

10.24   Assumptions of this nature are the only way in which the kind of
simple table set out in Appendix 4 can be put into effect. However, both
the assumptions are liable to change fairly rapidly and we feel that the table
and the assumptions on which it is based should be considered every year.

10.25   We have come to the conclusion that despite these crude
assumptions it is the best system that can be devised in most
circumstances. We therefore recommend it for use. If either party considers
that it is inapplicable in any particular case he can put forward his arguments.
The point is that it provides a starting point which can be used in the
absence of more detailed evidence and modified as necessary.

(c)   The Contribution Rate Method

10.26   The other method suggested is the contributions method. This
involves adding up the contributions made by the employer and the
employee to the pension fund and thereby assessing the value of the
applicant's accrued pension. If what he has actually received is a deferred
pension it is then necessary to work out the cash value of that deferred
pension, by assessing its transfer value in accordance with the 1985 Act.

10.27   Despite its superficial attraction, however, this is an even more
difficult calculation than the actuarial method in the 1980 Government
Actuary's paper and is much more complex than the formula we recommend.
The amount contributed by the employer to the pension scheme will vary
from year to year and a complex calculation is needed to work out the
current value of a contribution of say £5 a week made 15 years ago.

10.28   We have tried to simplify this method by using the contribution
rate method which works on the basis of the current rate of contributions.
However, after consultation with interested bodies we have come to the
conclusion that it is less accurate than our formula and, furthermore, adds
a further and unnecessary complication to the task facing the Tribunal.
We do not, therefore, recommend that this method be used in unfair
dismissal cases. However, if evidence is adduced that the difference
between the contributions made and the transfer value is far greater than

the loss assessed in accordance with the tables the Tribunal may decide to take this into account in assessing a fair and equitable award.

10.29 None of the other methods suggested to us of calculating loss under this section provide, in our view, a simpler or fairer solution.

11 GENERAL CONCLUSIONS

11.1 It is important to note that where the compensation exceeds the statutory limit even without consideration of loss of pension rights, the importance of calculating the sum involved diminishes. However, it must be remembered that the Recoupment Regulations (r 5(2)) provide for a pro rata deduction from the sum repayable to the Department of Employment where the award of compensation would have exceeded the limit. Therefore, though the assessment is less important, it is still necessary to assess a figure where the Recoupment Regulations apply, to enable the Tribunal to assess how much to reduce the sum repayable to the Department of Employment.

11.2 These recommendations are only guidelines. They will become trip-wires if they are blindly applied without considering the facts of each case. Any party is free to canvass any method of assessment which he considers appropriate. We hope that this paper will be found useful as a starting point.

11.3 Appendices 1 and 2 set out respectively a practical guide and a flow chart for applying our recommendations. Appendix 3 is the Government Actuary's paper on which our conclusions as to loss of enhancement of accrued pension rights are based. Appendix 4 contains the table of multipliers and Appendix 5 gives examples showing in Part 1 the importance of assessing pension loss and in Part 2 problems connected with the likelihood of withdrawal.

Prepared by

Cohn Sara	Full-time chairman Bristol
David Pugsley	Full-time chairman Birmingham
Douglas Crump	Pan-time chairman Birmingham

APPENDIX I

I Loss of pension rights from date of dismissal to the hearing

Unless there are arguments to the contrary we consider that the following formula should apply:—

(a) Ascertain the employer's contribution as a percentage of the Applicant's pay. It may be necessary to adjust this figure if exceptional circumstances pertain; if for example the pension fund is over-funded and the employer is having a pension contribution holiday. If the pension is a non-contributory one which is not funded eg a civil service pension, then it may be necessary to impute a notional employer's contribution.

(b) If the figure for the employer's contribution is not readily forthcoming then assume that the employer's contribution is 10% (15% in the case of non-contributory schemes).

(c) Treat the employer's contribution as a weekly loss, in the same manner as a weekly loss of earnings.

2 Loss of future pension rights

Use the same rate of contributions as for 1 and the same multiplier as for assessment of future loss of earnings.

3 Loss of enhancement of accrued pension rights

Assume no loss of enhancement of accrued pension benefit unless the contrary is proved in:—

(a) Schemes in which pension benefits are referable to contributions made and not final salary (ie company money purchase schemes, personalised plans etc).

(b) Public sector schemes — funded and non-funded.

(c) Private sector final salary schemes where the applicant has less than 5 years until retirement.

Loss of enhancement of accrued benefit in final salary schemes (where condition 5 c(i) and c(ii) do not apply):

(1) Ascertain the deferred pension he will receive (ignoring any anticipated increases or additional benefits).
(2) Ascertain the applicant's present age and his anticipated age of retirement.
(3) Apply the appropriate multiplier as set out in the table in Appendix 4.
(4) Reduce the resulting figure by a reasonable percentage for the likelihood of withdrawal (ie that he would have left before retirement for reasons other than death or disability).

APPENDIX 2   TABLE I

Flow chart for calculation of loss of pension rights from date of dismissal to the hearing

1. Ascertain the employee's gross weekly pensionable pay	£
2. Ascertain the employer's normal contribution as a % of the pay-roll	
3. If the figure for the employer's contribution is not readily forthcoming then assume that the employer's contribution is 10% (15% for non-contributory schemes)	
Weekly continuing pension loss	£
4. Multiply by number of weeks between effective date of termination and date of hearing	X
AWARD	

NB This is not part of the prescribed element

APPENDIX 2   TABLE 2

Flow chart for calculation of loss of future pension rights

1.	Ascertain the employee's gross weekly pensionable pay	£
2.	Ascertain the employer's normal contribution as a % of the pay-roll	
3.	If the figure for the employer's contribution is not readily forthcoming then assume that the employer's contribution is 10% (15% for non-contributory schemes)	
	Weekly continuing pension loss	£
4.	Multiply by number of weeks allowed for future loss of earnings whether total or partial	X
	AWARD	

APPENDIX 2 TABLE 3

Flow chart for calculation of loss of enhancement of accrued pension rights

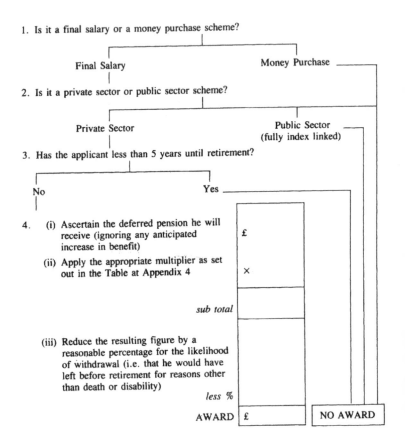

1. Is it a final salary or a money purchase scheme?

      Final Salary   Money Purchase

2. Is it a private sector or public sector scheme?

      Private Sector   Public Sector
                                   (fully index linked)

3. Has the applicant less than 5 years until retirement?

   No   Yes

4.   (i) Ascertain the deferred pension he will
        receive (ignoring any anticipated   £
        increase in benefit)

   (ii) Apply the appropriate multiplier as set
        out in the Table at Appendix 4   ×

                          sub total

  (iii) Reduce the resulting figure by a
        reasonable percentage for the likelihood
        of withdrawal (i.e. that he would have
        left before retirement for reasons other
        than death or disability)
                      less %

                 AWARD £   NO AWARD

APPENDIX 3

Assessing loss of occupational pension scheme rights following a finding of unfair dismissal by an industrial tribunal

The Government Actuary's 1980 paper under the above title was intended to provide chairmen of Industrial Tribunals with a simple system of assessing the loss in respect of service before dismissal by calculating the difference between the value of the deferred pension to which the applicant remained entitled and what he would have received had he not been dismissed. It is acknowledged that the formula is now less satisfactory because of the recent legislation aimed at preserving at least some of all pension entitlement, for which only very approximate adjustments were proposed in the notes issued in 1980 and 1987.

This paper puts forward a revised system to take account of the legislation, together with an approximate simple formula which may be useful to chairmen in the absence of expert evidence. The formula relates to a pension derived from final salary at exit, continuing (at one-half rate) to a dependant.

If a member of a final-salary pension scheme withdraws, he loses potential benefits in respect of his past service to the extent that the accrued benefits are not fully indexed in line with salaries (including an allowance for possible future promotion) until normal retirement age.

The value of each pension unit depends on many factors, in particular:—
*   sex, attained age, normal retirement age
*   estimates of future rates of salary progression and promotion, of inflation (prices and/or pensions) and of interest on investments
as well as of estimates of rates of withdrawal (dismissal, redundancy, resignation, transfer), death (in service and after retirement) retirement (age and ill-health) and for (dependants' benefits) age and death rates of dependants and the proportion of staff leaving an eligible dependant on their own death.

The 1980 tables were constructed on simplified assumptions, assuming that money could be invested to earn an average of 9 per cent per annum.

For continuing benefits (based on final salary with a half-rate pension continuing to a dependant wife (but not husband)), salary was assumed to increase at 7½ % per annum and pension at 3 % per annum.

Frozen (deferred) benefits were assumed to increase at 3 % per annum after dismissal. Mortality was assumed to be similar to that experienced by a large public sector scheme, and ill-health retirement benefits were assumed to be worth as much as those on normal retirement. No allowance was made for exits except by death; chairmen were expected to assess for themselves the reduction for the possibility of withdrawal (by resignation etc. but *not* unfair dismissal) before normal pension age.

The revised tables shown below in this paper assume that money can be invested to earn 8½ % per annum on average. Salaries are assumed to increase at 7% per annum and pensions to increase by 3% per annum. Mortality is assumed to be similar to that estimated to apply to current insured pensioners.

Transfer values of pension rights are calculated on different assumptions from those used in valuing benefits to continuing staff. A transfer value passes between pension schemes in cash form, so the sending scheme has to realize assets at current market rates, not the long-term average assessment. Further, there is a change in benefit expectations: the salary linkage is broken, and there are often differences in death and ill-health benefits between schemes (especially enhancement on early exit).

Consequently it can be inequitable to value benefit loss by deducting the transfer value from a standard table of continuing benefit values. It may be fairer to use a standard table representing the loss of benefit on dismissal allowing for standard deferred benefits, including the guaranteed minimum pension (GMP) required by legislation for contracted-out schemes. This GMP is assumed in the table to increase by 7% per annum to State Pension age but only to the extent of post March 1988 service wilt it increase (by 3% per annum) thereafter.

The maximum required by legislation is for 5% increases in frozen pensions up to normal pension age. A pensions increase of 3% per annum is also assumed to apply to any balance of pension over the GMP.

This requires each pension to be divided into 3 parts namely the continuing benefit value, pre and post 1988 GMP and any balance above GMP and a different factor applied to each part. Tables are given at the end of this Appendix.

To simplify procedures, a single factor has been found (varying with age) (Appendix 4) to apply to the accrued pension to estimate the loss of pension rights assuming:—
(i)   accrued pension for past service equals that preserved on dismissal;
(ii)   GMP represents two-thirds of the total pension and will be revalued at least to the same extent as any balance. (At present the post-1988 service need not be separated).

These fractions will change with time.

Appendix 4 may be compared with the difference between the columns of the 1980 paper. For men retiring at 65 the figures are:—

Age last birthday	Under 30	40	45	50	55	60	64
1980 values	4.3	4.2	3.9	3.4	2.7	1.6	0.2
1991 values	1.5	1.5	1.4	1.3	1.2	0.8	0.2

All estimates of loss need to be reduced by an individual assessment of the likelihood of withdrawal from the pension fund other than on account of unfair dismissal.

It has been suggested that the value of continuing benefits in a good (sixtieths) scheme can be estimated at 15 % or so of the product of pensionable salary and service. As the tables show, this factor is a reasonable one at certain ages only. The pension multiplier for men retiring at 65 is about 10.5 (corresponding to 17½ %) shortly before that age but only 5.5 (corresponding to 9%) at age 25. It must be emphasized that pensionable salary may not be the same as total salary.

Government Actuary's Department

July 1991

Table 1 to Appendix 3

Value of pension of 1 per annum

(1) Salary linked until vesting then 3% pension increase
(2) Salary linked until vesting then NO pension increase
(3) 5% increase until vesting then 3% pension increase

Females Normal Retirement Age 60

AGE LAST BIRTHDAY	(1)	(2)	(3)
Under 30	7.5	5.8	3.7
30 — 34	8.2	6.4	4.7
35 — 39	8.8	6.9	5.6
40	9.3	7.3	6.4
41	9.4	7.4	6.6
42	9.5	7.5	6.8
43	9.7	7.6	7.0
44	9.8	7.7	7.3
45	10.0	7.8	7.5
46	10.1	7.9	7.8
47	10.3	8.0	8.1
48	10.5	8.1	8.4
49	10.6	8.3	8.7
50	10.8	8.4	9.0
51	11.0	8.5	9.3
52	11.2	8.6	9.7
53	11.4	8.8	10.0
54	11.6	9.0	10.4
55	11.8	9.2	10.8
56	12.0	9.4	11.2
57	12.2	9.5	11.6
58	12.4	9.7	12.1
59	12.7	9.9	12.6

Table 2 to Appendix 3

Value of pension of I per annum

(1)   Salary linked until vesting then 3% pension increase
(2)   Salary linked until vesting then NO pension increase
(3)   5% increase until vesting then 3% pension increase

Females Normal Retirement Age 65

AGE LAST BIRTHDAY	(1)	(2)	(3)
Under 30	6.0	4.8	2.7
30 — 34	6.7	5.4	3.5
35 — 39	7.2	5.8	4.2
40	7.5	6.1	4.7
41	7.6	6.2	4.8
42	7.7	6.3	5.0
43	7.8	6.4	5.2
44	8.0	6.4	5.4
45	8.1	6.5	5.6
46	8.2	6.6	5.8
47	8.3	6.7	6.0
48	8.5	6.8	6.2
49	8.6	6.9	6.4
50	8.7	7.0	6.6
51	8.9	7.1	6.8
52	9.0	7.3	7.0
53	9.2	7.4	7.3
54	9.3	7.5	7.6
55	9.5	7.6	7.9
56	9.6	7.7	8.2
57	9.8	7.9	8.5
58	10.0	8.0	8.8
59	10.2	8.2	9.2
60	10.4	8.3	9.6
61	10.6	8.5	10.0
62	10.8	8.7	10.4
63	11.1	8.9	10.8
64	11.3	9.1	11.2

Table 3 to Appendix 3

Value of pension of I per annum

(1)   Salary linked until vesting then 3% pension increase
(2)   Salary linked until vesting then NO pension increase
(3)   5% increase until vesting then 3% pension increase

Males Normal Retirement Age 60

AGE LAST BIRTHDAY	(1)	(2)	(3)
Under 30	7.0	5.4	3.6
30 — 34	7.7	6.1	4.5
35 — 39	8.3	6.5	5.4
40	8.7	6.8	6.0
41	8.8	6.9	6.2
42	9.0	7.0	6.4
43	9.1	7.1	6.6
44	9.3	7.3	6.9
45	9.4	7.4	7.1
46	9.6	7.5	7.3
47	9.7	7.6	7.6
48	9.9	7.7	7.9
49	10.0	7.8	8.2
50	10.2	8.0	8.5
51	10.4	8.1	8.8
52	10.6	8.3	9.1
53	10.7	8.4	9.5
54	10.9	8.5	9.9
55	11.2	8.6	10.3
56	11.4	8.8	10.7
57	11.6	9.0	11.1
58	11.9	9.2	11.5
59	12.1	9.5	12.0

Table 4 to Appendix 3

Value of pension of 1 per annum

(1)   Salary linked until vesting then 3% pension increase
(2)   Salary linked until vesting then NO pension increase
(3)   5% increase until vesting then 3% pension increase

Males Normal Retirement Age 65

AGE LAST BIRTHDAY	(1)	(2)	(3)
Under 30	5.7	4.8	3.0
30—34	6.3	5.1	3.5
35 — 39	6.8	5.5	4.0
40	7.1	5.6	4.5
41	7.2	5.7	4.7
42	7.3	5.8	4.9
43	7.4	6.0	5.0
44	7.5	6.1	5.2
45	7.6	6.2	5.4
46	7.8	6.3	5.5
47	7.9	6.4	5.7
48	8.0	6.5	5.9
49	8.1	6.6	6.1
50	8.3	6.7	6.3
51	8.4	6.8	6.5
52	8.5	6.9	6.8
53	8.7	7.0	7.0
54	8.8	7.1	7.2
55	8.9	7.2	7.5
56	9.1	7.4	7.8
57	9.3	7.5	8.1
58	9.4	7.6	8.4
59	9.6	7.7	8.7
60	9.8	7.9	9.1
61	10.1	8.1	9.5
62	10.3	8.3	10.0
63	10.6	8.5	10.4
64	10.9	8.7	10.8

Appendix 4

1991 Edition

Tables of multipliers to be applied to the deferred annual pension to assess compensation for loss of enhancement of accrued pension rights.

Age last birthday at dismissal	Normal retirement age 60	Normal retirement age 65
Under 35	1.9	1.5
35—44	1.8	1.5
45—49	1.7	1.4
50	1.6	1.4
51	1.5	1.4
52	1.4	1.3
53	1.3	1.3
54	1.1	1.3
55	1.0	1.2
56	0.8	1.2
57	0.6	1.1
58	0.3	1.0
59	0.1	0.9
60	NIL	0.8
61		0.6
62		0.4
63		0.3
64		0.2

APPENDIX 5 — EXAMPLES

Part One — Illustrations of the value of an occupational pension

An occupational pension can be a very significant financial asset. This can be illustrated by comparing the position of twin sisters: Betty a civil servant and Beryl who has throughout worked as a music teacher on a self-employed basis. Both retire when they are 60, having worked for the same number of years and with the same final salary of £10,000 per annum.

Betty has an occupational pension which provides her with the maximum permitted pension; namely a lump sum of 1½ times her final salary and an index linked pension of half her final salary. She therefore receives £15,000 as a lump sum and a pension of £5,000 per year and is secure in the belief that her pension will rise with inflation. In addition she is entitled to the basic state pension.

Beryl being self-employed was not covered by an occupational scheme and had made no private pension provision. All she receives is the same basic state pension as her sister. To buy an annuity to provide her with a pension of £5,000 would, depending on interest rates which pertain at the time, cost her between £40,000 and £60,000. If she were to attempt to protect herself against her pension being eroded by inflation she would have to pay much more and even then she would be unlikely to be able to purchase an annuity which was completely inflation proofed rather than providing yearly increases at predetermined rates.

Assume Betty and Beryl have a rich aunt who is in the last stages of a terminal illness and is revising her will on the basis she wishes to see both her nieces equally well provided for in their old age. If she were to lay these facts before a professional adviser and ask how much it would cost to place Beryl in the same position as Betty the advice would be that given the incidence of inflation, the legacy to Beryl would probably need to be £75,000 to £100,000 more than to Betty to ensure that they were both placed in comparable positions.

Although actuaries can advise companies or particular individuals on the cost of providing pensions no actuary can define with precision the exact value that the recipient of a pension will derive from the pension scheme.

The fact that Beryl would need £75,000 to £100,000 to place her in a comparable position to her sister, Betty, does not mean that Betty is necessarily going to receive that sum from her pension fund. She may die next year in which case the cost to the pension scheme is minimal; she may live to be 100 in which case the total cost of her pension will be enormous.

Part Two — Likelihood of withdrawal

(1) A & B are planning to set up their own business. X their employer finds out about this and dismisses them forthwith. The Tribunal find that the dismissal is unfair since neither A nor B were in breach of any contractual obligation and neither had the opportunity of giving any explanation of their actions before they were dismissed. However it is accepted that they were intending to set up their own business and would have left X's employment in any event. By the time of the hearing their new business is trading. Since they would have left X's employment anyway there is no significant loss on enhancement of accrued pension rights arising from the dismissal.

(2) C has been unfairly dismissed. He had been a salesman with the respondent company for 3 years. He is 28 years of age. The Tribunal conclude that given his age and the general mobility of salesmen, which has been illustrated by his own career pattern, he would have left of his own accord within 12 months. The Tribunal follow the recommendation (made in paragraph 10.14) and award no compensation for the loss of enhancement of accrued pension rights.

(3) D had been employed for 15 years when he was dismissed. He is 52 years of age and had been earning £14,000 a year. The Tribunal accept his evidence that he had no intention of leaving the respondent company. However D admits that it was unlikely he would have continued to work to 65, the normal retirement age of that company's scheme. His wife (who is older than he is) is a doctor and earns much more than he does. D accepts that he would probably have resigned when his wife retired as they would have been financially secure and they intended to join their only child who lives in Australia. On the evidence before it, the Tribunal conclude that there would have been little prospect of D leaving his employment for five years but thereafter there was an increasing likelihood of his leaving so that there was a near certainty he would have left within 10 years. In assessing the prospects of withdrawal the Tribunal has to give weight to these two findings of fact.

(4) E has been with the company for twenty-five years. He is 53 years of age. The Tribunal accept his evidence that it was his intention to stay with the company for the rest of his working life. A Tribunal might well conclude that the percentage chance of his having left the company (other than by death or disability) before retirement was small. Consequently any reduction from the sum produced by the application of the formula should be modest.

Index